THE WARS FOR ASIA, 1911–1949

This book shows that the Western treatment of World War II, the Second Sino-Japanese War, and the Chinese Civil War as separate events misses their intertwined causes, connections, and consequences and, in so doing, misinterprets each. The long Chinese civil war precipitated a long regional war between China and Japan that became global in 1941 when the Chinese found themselves fighting a civil war within a regional war within an overarching global war. The global war that consumed Western attentions resulted from Japan's peripheral strategy to cut foreign aid to China by attacking Pearl Harbor and Western interests throughout the Pacific on 7–8 December 1941. S. C. M. Paine emphasizes the fears and ambitions of Japan, China, and Russia, and the pivotal decisions that set them on a collision course in the 1920s and 1930s. The cascading wars – the Chinese Civil War (1911–49), the Second Sino-Japanese War (1931–45), and World War II (1939–45) – together yielded a viscerally anti-Japanese and unified Communist China, the still-angry rising power of the early twenty-first century. Although these events are history in the West, they live on in Japan and especially in China.

S. C. M. Paine is Professor of Strategy and Policy at the U.S. Naval War College; the editor of *Nation Building, State Building, and Economic Development* (2010); and the author of *The Sino-Japanese War of 1894–1895* (Cambridge 2003) and *Imperial Rivals: China, Russia, and Their Disputed Frontier* (1996). Paine coauthored with Bruce A. Elleman *Modern China: Continuity and Change, 1644 to the Present* (2010) and coedited *Naval Power and Expeditionary Warfare* (2011), *Naval Coalition Warfare* (2008), and *Naval Blockades and Seapower* (2006).

THE WARS FOR ASIA, 1911–1949

S. C. M. PAINE
U.S. Naval War College

CAMBRIDGE
UNIVERSITY PRESS

32 Avenue of the Americas, New York NY 10013-2473, USA

Cambridge University Press is part of the University of Cambridge.

It furthers the University's mission by disseminating knowledge in the pursuit of education, learning and research at the highest international levels of excellence.

www.cambridge.org
Information on this title: www.cambridge.org/9781107697478

First published 2012
First paperback edition 2014

A catalogue record for this publication is available from the British Library

Library of Congress Cataloguing in Publication data
Paine, S. C. M., 1957–
The wars for Asia, 1911–1949 / S. C. M. Paine.
p. cm.
Includes bibliographical references and index.
ISBN 978-1-107-02069-6 (hardback)
1. China – History, Military – 1912–1949. 2. Japan – History, Military – 1868–1945. 3. Sino-Japanese War, 1937–1945. 4. World War, 1939–1945 – China. 5. World War, 1939–1945 – Japan. 6. China – History – Civil War, 1945–1949. I. Title.
DS775.4.P35 2012
355.00951–dc23 2012012496

ISBN 978-1-107-02069-6 Hardback
ISBN 978-1-107-69747-8 Paperback

To Anna and Steven Elleman, who have my deepest respect, admiration, and love

CONTENTS

MAPS

ACKNOWLEDGMENTS

As Robert Frost wrote, "Two roads diverged in a yellow wood and I – / I took the one less traveled by, / And that has made all the difference." My career has not followed the typical academic track. After a ten-year PhD in Russian and Chinese history from Columbia University, entailing five years of research and language study in China, Taiwan, Japan, and Russia, I went to work in the Strategy & Policy Department of the U.S. Naval War College, which offers an MA in National Security and Strategic Studies. Half of my colleagues and all of my students have chosen either military or government service careers. Teaching or studying at the Naval War College requires a steep learning curve because none of us can remain in our intellectual or career comfort zones. As my wonderful colleague David Kaiser has remarked, the Strategy & Policy Department requires you to "think big," to consider problems of vital national import, and to work out solutions in a world of incomplete information and insufficient time and resources.

Since the Vietnam War, history departments across the United States virtually without exception have marginalized the study of war. Yet the Vietnam War so influenced those called upon to serve in it that the Vietnam generation, which has dominated history departments ever since, has discouraged their students from studying war, diplomacy, and politics – subjects concerning the allocation and exercise of power. In 1938, Mao Zedong unapologetically wrote that "whoever has an army has power and that war decides everything."[1] As this book will show, ignorance of the strategic effects of military operations caused millions of deaths in the twentieth century. If Japanese prime ministers, generals, and admirals of the mid-twentieth century could be returned to life, they would be horrified to realize that three generations later, their decisions have left Japan despised by many of its neighbors and its foreign policy hamstrung by their failure to consider the political implications of violence. The inability to see the limitations of intervening in someone else's civil war had dire consequences, not only for Japan, but also for the United States and Russia, whose leaders all thought they knew what to do about China. The failure to study war does not make wars go away; rather it positions a country badly to survive war when it comes and to commit foreign policy blunders in wars fought by others.

I have attempted to incorporate the methodology taught in the Strategy & Policy Department. The name of the department embodies a key part of the methodology: governments have national policy objectives, and the more comprehensive their strategies, the more likely they are to attain their objectives. It is useful to analyze wars in terms of policy and strategy to see whether there is a match or a mismatch, and if so, why. Wars are not all of one type: insurgencies generally seek regime change within a single country – so the stakes are high for both sides. Because insurgencies require little equipment and few forces to wage, they are hard to eliminate and tend to protract. Victory in regional and global wars generally involves large conventional battles requiring quantities of military hardware. In regional wars, the stakes vary and the higher their value to both sides, the more likely the conflict will protract. Global wars contest the nature of the global order. Therefore, they are wars of extraordinarily high stakes, usually of long duration, and usually coalition wars. Wars protract not only because of the stakes and number of parties involved, but also when they threaten third parties, which intervene to shape the outcome. Good strategy works to prevent hostile third-party intervention.

I have disaggregated the warfare in China in the twentieth century to analyze the long Chinese civil war (1911–49), the Second Sino-Japanese War (1931–45), and World War II (1939–45). The first began as a mutiny and entailed a bitter insurgency, the second began as a regional war, and the third resulted from the escalation into a global war of two regional conflicts, one in Europe and the other in China. Each of the three wars was fought for different objectives and with different strategies. The stakes were high in all three, creating mayhem of incredible scale and duration. I have also introduced terminology useful for analyzing wars that I will explain as I go along: proximate and underlying causes, limited and unlimited objectives, positive versus negative objectives, center of gravity, military versus grand strategy, operational versus strategic effects, a prevent-defeat versus a deliver-victory strategy, a peripheral theater versus the main theater, conventional versus guerrilla war, land powers versus sea powers, people's war, sanctuary, jackal state, script-writing, death ground, sunk costs, the principle of continuity, a decisive battle, a disposal force, and the tactical, operational, and strategic levels of war.

I am grateful for generous grants from the Hoover Institution for two Title VIII fellowships to use Hoover's archives and Stanford's libraries; the International Exchange of Scholars for a Fulbright fellowship funding a year of research at the Defense Research Center Archives and the Foreign Ministry Diplomatic Records Office in Tokyo; the Slavic Research Center at Hokkaido University for a year of research using Japanese, Chinese, and Russian materials; and the National Library of Australia's Harold White Fellowship and the Chiang Ching-kuo Foundation for a year of writing in Canberra. I am also indebted to the extraordinarily helpful staffs of the Academia Sinica archives of the Institute of Modern History, the Australian National University libraries, the Defense Research Center Archives of Japan's Defense Agency, the Diplomatic Records Office of the Japanese Foreign Ministry, Harvard University libraries, Hokkaido University libraries, the Hoover Institution Archives, the National Library of Australia, the Naval War College library, Princeton University libraries, the Slavic Research Center library, and Stanford University libraries. I am also grateful to Alice K. Juda, David E. Kaiser, Robin A. Lima, and Yu Miin-ling for help on sources; to Yu Miin-ling and Arakawa Ken-ichi for proofreading the Chinese and Japanese sources in the Bibliography; and to a former student, Commander Patrick Hansen, who helped me better understand the military writings of Mao Zedong. At Cambridge University Press, editor Eric Crahan, his assistant Abigail Zorbaugh, and production manager Marielle Poss carefully guided the manuscript from review through production; Susan Thornton took charge of copy-editing; David Cox drew up the very complicated maps; David Levy designed the cover; and project manager Bhavani Ganesh assembled all the pieces.

In particular, I wish to thank my senior colleagues in the Strategy & Policy Department, both present and former – George W. Baer, William C. Fuller, Jr., Michael I. Handel, David E. Kaiser, Bradford A. Lee, John

H. Maurer, and Steven T. Ross – who, along with John P. LeDonne, have been my finest teachers. The analytical tools they shared combined with knowledge accumulated over eight years of research abroad form the basis for this book. Above all, I am grateful to Bruce A. Elleman, whose numerous publications I have relied on throughout.

Finally, as a government employee, I am required to make clear that the thoughts, opinions, and mistakes expressed in this volume are my own and are not necessarily those of the U.S. government, the U.S. Department of Defense, the U.S. Navy Department, or the U.S. Naval War College; nor do I represent any of these institutions.

TECHNICAL NOTE

For simplicity, the term "Russia" has been used to refer to the Soviet period. This obviates the need to introduce the designation Soviet Russia for the early period of Bolshevik rule. When I use the term "Soviet" or "Soviet Union," I do so to emphasize Russia under communist rule. Just as France has been called France whether under monarchical or republican rule, so should Russia be referred to as Russia. The Communists made a big to-do about their supposed break with history and requirement for a new name. It turns out that they were temporary, while Russia endures.

Unless otherwise specified, "Chinese" refers to the nationals of China, while "Taiwanese" refers to the nationals of Taiwan. "Han" refers to the predominant ethnic group of China. "Manchurian" refers to the residents of Manchuria with no implied ethnicity. I use the term "Nationalist Party" to refer to the Kuomintang (KMT) or Guomindang (GMD) to avoid confusing transliteration systems altogether. KMT is used only in the Chronology for considerations of space. Similarly, CCP for Chinese Communist Party appears there.

Chinese and Japanese names follow Asian conventions to list surname first. All Chinese names have been rendered in pinyin except for some very common exceptions: Chiang Kai-shek (not Jiang Jieshi), his son Chiang Ching-kuo (not Jiang Jingguo), his adopted son Chiang Wei-kuo (not Jiang Weiguo), his wife Soong Mayling (not Song Meiling), his sister-in-law Soong Chingling (not Song Qingling), Sun Yat-sen (not Sun Zhongshan), his son Sun Fo (not Sun Ke), Confucius (not Kongzi), Harbin (not Haerbin), Chahar (not Chahaer), Yangzi River (not Changjiang), and Manchukuo (not Manzhouguo or Manshūkoku).

Counting soldiers turns out to be a tricky business. Unit sizes vary by country and by era and not all units were always fully manned. During the Second Sino-Japanese War, a Nationalist division had 11,000 men compared to a Japanese division with 24,000 to 28,000 men.[1]

Dating is not straightforward either. The international dateline divides the Pacific Ocean so that correct dating in Asian sources differs from U.S. sources. For instance, the Japanese attack on Pearl Harbor took place on 7 December 1941 Washington time but on 8 December 1941 Tokyo time. This book is based on a combination of Japanese, Chinese, Russian, and U.S. sources, which sometimes date according to home-country time and sometimes according to battle-theater time. Likewise, battle and campaign dates are not straightforward. Do they begin when one side deploys or reaches a particular place or starts shooting? Do they end when troops reach a city center or when enemy main forces give up or when mopping up operations end? The sources do not agree. I have done my best to date events according to local time in the theater or the venue of the diplomacy.

The term "warlord" is problematic and all substitutes for it are also problematic. For thousands of years, Chinese history has been divided between periods of unified dynastic rule and periods of divided rule. In the past, such rulers were called kings and, in periods of unified rule, emperors. The first half of the twentieth century was a period of divided rule, but the pejorative term "warlord" came into general use to refer to the many aspiring leaders of China. Such people, while often generals, exercised both civil and military power, hence the agglomeration of "war" for the military side and "lord" for the civil side of their rule. Alternate terminology includes "militarist" (also pejorative and missing the civil side), "military ruler" (less pejorative but still missing the civil side), and "military executive" (pedantic and unclear). So I apologize in advance for the lack of imagination to think of a nonpejorative word to replace "warlord."

PART I

FEAR AND AMBITION JAPAN, CHINA, AND RUSSIA

飲鴆止渴

Drink poison to quench thirst.
(The remedy is worse than the disease.)

1

INTRODUCTION

The Asian Roots of World War II

天災人禍
Heaven-made disasters, manmade calamities.
(Natural disasters and wars.)

Wars produce sudden and irrevocable changes. Although they are fought for reasons, they can stampede passions, and mass passions give no quarter to reason, let alone to any individuals barring the way. Millions of lives lost mean millions of roads not taken, altering the roster of the born and unborn, and producing decisions informed by the road taken. The passions elicited by the killing, the dying, and the witnessing put a period on the way the world was. The combustion of reason and passion leaves transformative and often unintended outcomes, which in the long term may prove more important than the war's original purpose. Given the costs, unpredictability, and irretrievability, wars are important to understand.

We in the West treat World War II, the Second Sino-Japanese War, and the Chinese Civil War as distinct events, and in doing so we misunderstand each one. The conventional tale of World War II divides into two fronts, a European theater, opening in 1939, and a Pacific theater, opening in 1941, and the tale ends in 1945 with the fall of Berlin in May and with atomic bombs on Japan in August. Yet Japan's war began a decade prior in 1931, and that war precipitated its attack on Pearl Harbor, which drew the United States into World War II, and thus precluded a Japanese victory in China. The conventional tale does little to explain Japan's curious behavior. An attack on one's most important trading partner and source of the war matériel necessary to continue the fight in China would seem remarkably counterproductive.

The conventional tale of the Second Sino-Japanese War is equally illogical. The Japanese won every battle, including the 1944 Ichigō

Campaign, which was their last, biggest, and best, and then they suddenly collapsed. Although World War II explains this collapse, accounts of the Second Sino-Japanese War routinely gloss over the global war. More importantly, there is no explanation for the Dr. Jekyll–Mr. Hyde transformation of Japan from the model developing country of the nineteenth century to Japan at the forefront of germ warfare, prisoner abuse, civilian massacres, and the murder of its own wounded.

The conventional tale is no more illuminating for the Chinese Civil War, portrayed as an existential struggle between good and evil and between a longing for change and the weight of corruption. Yet the alleged master of military incompetence, Generalissimo Chiang Kai-shek, fought the Imperial Japanese Army to a stalemate by 1938 and fought it alone from 1937 to 1941. Japanese accounts emphasize their fight not against the Communists but against the Nationalists. During these years, the Imperial Japanese Army sent not its rejects but its best to China. Thereafter, Americans, despite their overwhelming industrial superiority, also found fighting the Japanese bitter indeed. Again, the facts on the ground do not square with the story told.

As it turns out, Japan attempted to settle its long war in China with a peripheral strategy targeting U.S. and British interests in Asia in order to compel them to cut off their aid to China. This was a peripheral strategy because the theaters were peripheral to the main theater, which for Japan was China, not the disease-infested jungles and isolated islands where the United States soon fought. Japan's prior alliance with Germany then sent the United States into the European theater when Germany interpreted the alliance broadly to declare war. In other words, a regional war in Asia made another regional war in Europe global when the Japanese and German declarations of war relegated U.S. isolationism to the trash heap of history.

China's war began even earlier with the demise of the Qing dynasty in 1911 and the escalating civil war to determine the nature of New China. Initially the civil war was multilateral. It did not fully settle into a bilateral Nationalist-Communist fight until 1945 and did not end until the Communist victory in 1949. As the fighting moved northward in the 1920s toward the Japanese sphere of influence and focus of investments in Manchuria, Japanese leaders became increasingly concerned. In the 1930s army leaders and many other Japanese concluded that only direct military intervention could protect their national security.

In other words, the long Chinese civil war precipitated a regional war between China and Japan so that by the time the conflict became global in 1941, the Chinese were fighting a civil war within a regional war within an overarching global war.

At different times, the intervening foreign powers – Japan, Russia, and the United States – focused on different layers of this complex war. The conventional tale focuses on the global war, which was the outermost and least fundamental layer. In fact, each layer grew out of the preceding layer, with the civil war at the core. Those who attempted to fight within one layer without consideration of the others courted disaster. Japan's operational focus on the regional war produced the opposite of intended outcomes in the civil and global wars. The U.S. attempt to focus exclusively on the global war left postwar U.S. China policy in shambles. Russia's comparatively astute Asia policy rested on an appreciation of all three layers of warfare: it brokered a truce in the civil war to promote a Sino-Japanese war to save itself from a two-front global war on the correct assumption that Japan would fight either China or Russia, but not both.

The conventional tale does not emphasize Russia's peculiar position among the Allies of World War II. Russia allied with Britain and the United States against Germany but maintained remarkably cordial relations with Japan until the last two weeks of the war, when it suddenly deployed 1.5 million men to Manchuria in its most ambitious campaign of the war.[1] Most histories of World War II omit the Eurasian connection between the European and Pacific theaters to tell separate tales. Russians, however, saw clear connections. German units advanced within eyesight of Moscow, the country's rail hub, the one the Bolsheviks had leveraged to win the Russian Civil War. In World War I, Russia had fallen to a one-front war against Germany and would probably not have survived a two-front war against both Germany and Japan. Russian leaders played a deft game of diplomacy to forestall this eventuality.[2]

Japan's war had other implications that did not reveal themselves by 1945, when the conventional tale ends, but only in 1949, when the Chinese Communists attained power. Paradoxically, the Communists greatly benefited from Japan's intervention in the long Chinese civil war because the Japanese focused on annihilating Nationalist conventional forces, fatally weakening them in eight years of high-tempo warfare.

Yet Japan lacked sufficient troops to garrison China's vast hinterland, where the Communists used the breathing space from Nationalist persecution to organize the peasantry. These two factors – Japanese weakening of the Nationalists and the Communist breathing space to organize – tipped the post–World War internal balance of power in favor of the Communists.

The ensuing decisive battles of the long Chinese civil war concentrated in Manchuria, which was the heart of overseas Japanese investments and the only theater with a dense railway grid and road system to move vast armies and the agricultural surplus to feed them. This theater also bordered on Russia, which has not received adequate credit for its role in the outcome of the long Chinese civil war. The Communists won this war in huge conventional battles. Yet they were a rural movement and agrarian China did not produce the weaponry to fight let alone to win huge conventional battles. Where did the weapons come from? The Communists did indeed capture many from defeated Nationalist units – but how did they acquire enough weapons to defeat the well-armed Nationalist units in the first place? Again the conventional tale is silent.

Americans often portray international events in terms of what the United States did or did not do. This outlook presumes enormous influence for themselves and discounts the ability of others to make choices. Such presumptions also obviate the need to understand the motivations and decisions of others. The conventional tale of World War II focuses on the heroism of American commanders and the brilliance of American leaders and, if generous, gives some credit to the civil and military leaders of Great Britain. It is amazing how many histories ignore the contribution of Russia, where until the end of the war Germany always deployed at least two-thirds and generally four-fifths of its army.[3] The contribution of China to the victory over Japan receives still less attention even though from 1942 until 1945 Japan deployed more forces against China than against the United States for every year except 1944.[4] American soldiers found their German and Japanese counterparts to be lethal foes, and yet Americans too often fail to credit those who fought the preponderance of these forces.

There is no shame in leaving the ground fighting to others; rather this is a hallmark of a sound maritime strategy. As Britain's great philosopher, scientist, lawyer, and statesman Sir Francis Bacon (1561–1626) observed, "[H]e that commands the sea is at great liberty, and may take as much and as little of the war as he will. Whereas those that be strongest by land are many times in great straits."[5] The United States has emulated the British maritime strategy of keeping the seas open to trade so that the home economy can produce uninterrupted by warfare, of relying on its oceanic moat to insulate itself from foreign threats, and of fighting wars far from home, at times and places of its choosing. Land powers possess no such strategic flexibility: fighting often occurs on home territory, which disrupts the economy, while a maritime enemy can cut off their overseas markets and an attacking neighbor can choose the time and place of hostilities.

Maritime powers, such as the United States, primarily influence the littoral – the places where they can most easily project military, diplomatic, and economic influence. Continental powers such as China and Russia influence events deep inland along their land borders. Curiously, although Japan was a maritime power by geography, its leaders conceived of their homeland as a continental power, with the Imperial Japanese Army the dominant military service. This misidentification entangled Japan in wars on the Asian mainland that it need never have fought.

The conventional tale also misses many of the key turning points. History is the study of choices, not of immutable fate. If Japan had halted its expansion with Manchuria, an area sufficiently large to grant it the comparative economic self-sufficiency its leaders craved, Japan could have awaited either U.S. entry into the brewing war in Europe or the Russian collapse from the Nazi onslaught. Either alternative would probably have left Japan in control of Manchuria. The Japanese decision to extend war to the rest of China was a point of no return that entailed expanded war aims, growing foreign support for the Nationalists, and escalating foreign embargoes on Japanese trade. The decision to escalate in 1937 was just one of many turning points.

The Japanese call these turning points "incidents," and the Chinese have adopted this nomenclature. They range from strikes to coup attempts, to assassinations, to regional wars. The word usage suggests a fork in the road and a choice that forever forecloses certain alternatives. Generally, such incidents are named by date or place, as if to absolve human beings of any responsibility for them. Incidents litter modern Japanese and Chinese history. The so-called China Incident of 1937 was no minor untoward event but a massive escalation of a regional war that resulted from decisions made by leaders on both sides: the decision of the Japanese to attack and the decision of the Chinese to resist. Often neither the Chinese nor the Japanese wanted to acknowledge their wars. So the Japanese downgraded their wars and battles in China to "incidents," while the Chinese refer to their civil wars as mere "rebellions."

Long ago Confucius admonished the educated to choose their words carefully lest they misidentify phenomena: "If the names are not rectified, then words are not appropriate. If words are not appropriate, then deeds are not accomplished."[6] Even a modest attempt at multiculturalism would reveal a surprisingly complicated nomenclature for World War II, the generic title for the conventional tale. Imperial Japanese leaders called the war against the United States, the British Commonwealth, and the Netherlands the War of Greater East Asia (大東亜戦争)[7] and defined all the prior sound and fury emanating from Manchuria and China as mere "incidents" – the 1931 Manchuria Incident and the 1937 China Incident, respectively. This reflected a practical consideration: before Pearl Harbor, a declaration of war on China would have triggered the U.S. Neutrality Act and embargoes of war matériel against both sides.[8]

Postwar Japanese historians divide into two groups: one highlights the Fifteen Year War (十五年戦争) from 1931 to 1945, and the other distinguishes a Japanese-Chinese War (日中戦争) from 1937 to 1945 from a Pacific Ocean War (太平洋戦争) from 1941 to 1945. Those who begin the war in China in 1937, not 1931, consider the invasion of Manchuria to have been an "incident" and focus on Japan's fight against the Nationalists, which did not begin until 1937. This version of events ignores the fact that the Nationalists never controlled much of North China, let alone Manchuria, and so discounts all the northern Chinese who fought Japan from 1931 to 1937. As it turns out, whatever the euphemism, Japan conducted uninterrupted conventional and counterinsurgent military operations on the internationally recognized territory of China from 1931 to 1945.

The Chinese and the Taiwanese focus on their War of Resistance against Japan (抗日戰爭) from 1937 to 1945 with minimal reference to the United States let alone, in the case of the Communists, to the Nationalist contribution to Japan's defeat. This tale emphasizes the heroic fight of the Communists or the Nationalists, opinions dividing along the Taiwan Strait. Communist dating follows their division of the long Chinese civil war into the First Revolutionary Civil War from 1924 to 1927 (the years of the First Nationalist-Communist United Front), the Second Revolutionary Civil War from 1927 to 1937 (the years of Nationalist encirclement campaigns against the Communists), and the Third Revolutionary Civil War from 1945 to 1949 (the showdown phase of the long civil war).

In fact from 1931 to 1934, the Communists could not fight the Japanese because repeated Nationalist encirclement campaigns sent them on a Long March to desolate Yan'an. Even after 1937, Nationalist, and not Communist, forces did virtually all of the conventional fighting by Chinese. In the end, the U.S. naval offensive homing in on Japan, the U.S. air campaign over Japan, and the Russian pincer from mainland Asia account for the Japanese capitulation. Yet the U.S. offensive on Japan could not have occurred without China's pinning the bulk of the Imperial Japanese Army far from the U.S. invasion route.

In other words, each country has its own conventional tale. Each discounts the contributions of others. The tale told in the United States omits many of the most interesting people, who failed to leave adequate records in Western European languages, an insurmountable problem for most Russians, Chinese, and Japanese. Their diverse places of origin gave rise to interests and priorities different from those of Americans or Britons. Often their choices do not seem "normal" and "rational" to many Americans because (surprise, surprise) their actions did not reflect American norms. An examination of why they made the portentous choices that they did is a fascinating story, well worth the telling.

The tale told here is one of nested wars set off by fears and ambitions against a backdrop of lethal national dilemmas. The choices made by national leaders reflected not only the ambitions for empire of Japan, China, and Russia, but also deep fears and dilemmas with no obvious solutions. After World War I shattered the international political order and the Great Depression then shattered the global economic order, the Western democracies bloodied themselves on the shards, discrediting liberal democracy and liberal economics in the process. In retrospect the belated post–World War II turn toward expansionist economic policies seems obvious, but it was not so at the time. Economic and political recovery required the massive stimulus of the war spending to get Americans back to work and the postwar Marshall Plan to restore Western Europe. Back in the 1930s, fascism and communism appeared to offer more promising solutions to the depression than did the worn-out paradigm offered by the stagnant Western democracies.

Both fascism and communism appealed to important segments of Chinese and Japanese society. The Nationalists attempted to create a hybrid out of communist political institutions and fascist economic institutions, while the Communists preferred the authentic dish of unadulterated communism. Fears and ambitions animated both the Communists and Nationalists, who dreamed of a reunified Qing empire and the restoration of China as the greatest power in Asia if not the world. Meanwhile, the Japanese feared the expansion of Soviet influence in Asia and the Western protectionist response to the Great Depression. Their fears and ambitions for empire met in Manchuria. Fears and ambitions also drove the Russians, who envisioned their country in the vanguard of a new international order replacing the discredited liberal democratic status quo. Yet everywhere the Chinese, the Japanese, and the Russians faced danger, hostile neighbors, and internal foes. Meanwhile, the Americans dreamed away the 1920s, ignoring the need to contain Germany and the many interconnections of the global economy. Desperation did not reach American shores until the stock market crash in 1929. Soon desperate decisions around the globe reflected the desperate times.

In the 1930s, China, Japan, Russia, and the United States all tried to go their separate ways. But the long Chinese civil war fed into a regional war that escalated into a global war, demonstrating the inescapable connections of living on a shared planet. Eventually, the separate ways converged into a global war, which determined the outcome of the regional war, and the outcome of the global and regional wars then strongly influenced that of the long Chinese civil war – a war whose ramifications preoccupy policy makers still.

The butchery of the fighting defies description. One guesstimate puts the number of Chinese dead during the two-generation long Chinese civil war at more than 20 million.[9] The sheer breadth of these wars has shaped the current Asian balance of power as well as national perspectives on the requirements for national security and the appropriate treatment of neighbors. At the beginning of the third millennium, the rubble left by a half-century of unrelenting warfare in China preoccupies the current generation of Asian leaders. Whereas World War II is history in the West, it remains embedded in current events in the East and an unsurmounted barrier between China and Japan.

Adding and connecting the missing links not included in the conventional tale shed light on the critical events that have helped make the Chinese and Japanese who they are today. The missing connections, which primarily concern non-Western protagonists, are necessary to understand current Asian relations, whose fulcrum is not bilateral U.S. relations with any one power, but remains the nexus of Chinese, Japanese, and Russian relations that the conventional tale skips. The tale told here begins with three protagonists: Japan, China, and Russia.

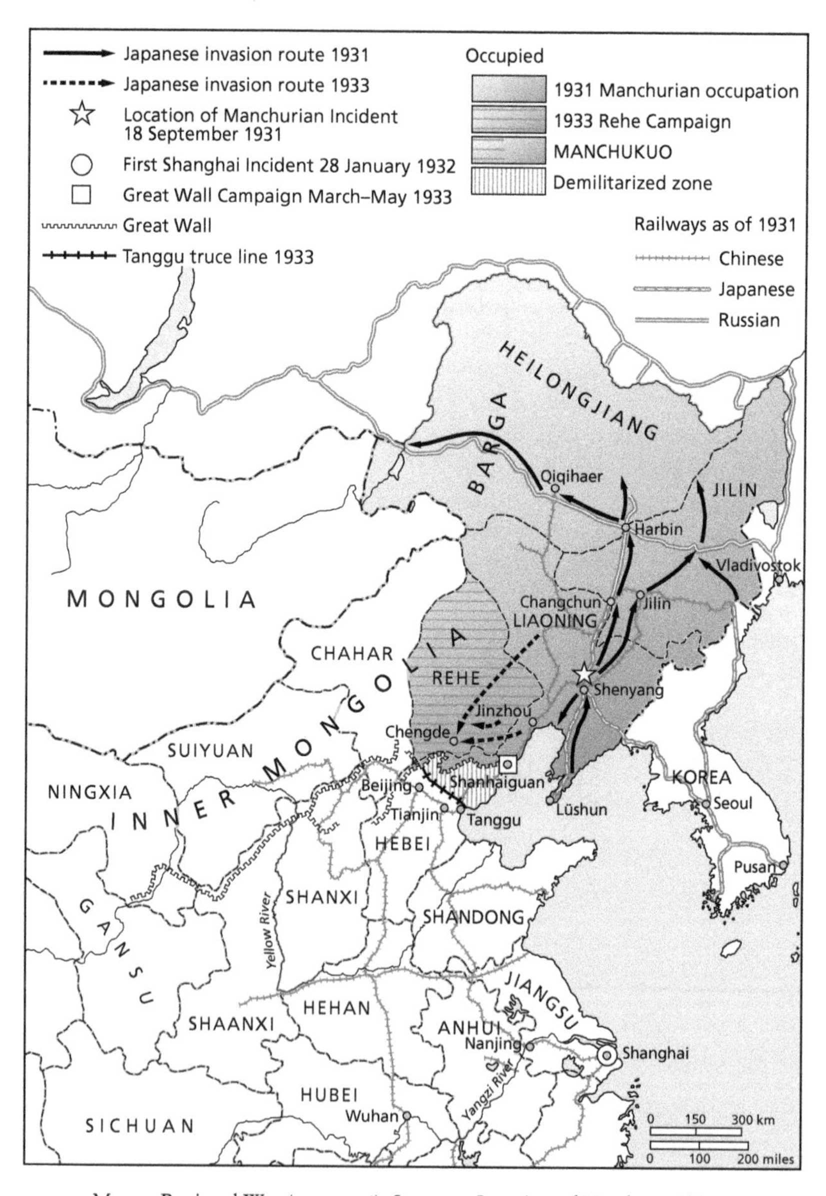
Japanese invasion route 1931
Japanese invasion route 1933
Location of Manchurian Incident 18 September 1931
First Shanghai Incident 28 January 1932
Great Wall Campaign March–May 1933
Great Wall
Tanggu truce line 1933
Occupied
1931 Manchurian occupation
1933 Rehe Campaign
MANCHUKUO
Demilitarized zone
Railways as of 1931
Chinese
Japanese
Russian
HEILONGJIANG
BARGA
Qiqihaer
JILIN
Harbin
Vladivostok
MONGOLIA
Changchun
Jilin
LIAONING
CHAHAR
REHE
Shenyang
Jinzhou
Chengde
INNER MONGOLIA
SUIYUAN
NINGXIA
Beijing
Shanhaiguan
KOREA
Seoul
Tianjin
Tanggu
Lüshun
HEBEI
Pusan
SHANXI
Yellow River
SHANDONG
GANSU
JIANGSU
HEHAN
SHAANXI
ANHUI
Nanjing
Shanghai
HUBEI
Yangzi River
SICHUAN
Wuhan
0 150 300 km
0 100 200 miles

Map 1 Regional War (1931–36): Japanese Invasion of Northern China.

2

JAPAN 1931–1936

The Containment of Russia and National Restoration

順水推舟
Push a boat with the current.
(Take advantage of circumstances.)

On 18 September 1931 Japan launched a full-scale invasion of Manchuria in response to an explosion near Shenyang, bending a few meters of its railway track, which it repaired by 6 a.m. the following day. Both the Chinese and Japanese call this event the Manchurian Incident. Although the Japanese government accused the Chinese of perpetrating the vandalism, before long its own internal investigation held members of the Japanese army responsible. And although the Manchurian warlord, Zhang Xueliang, ordered his troops to offer no resistance and Chiang Kai-shek declined to offer any assistance, the Japanese invasion continued apace.[1] On 19 September, Japanese forces took Shenyang, the provincial capital of Liaoning and the historical capital of Manchuria, known as Mukden. Liaoning together with Jilin and Heilongjiang Provinces constituted Manchuria. On 20 September, the Japanese took Changchun, the junction between the Japanese-owned and Russian-owned railway systems, and on 22 September they occupied the provincial capital of Jilin, unimaginatively called Jilin City. After the 8 October bombing of Jinzhou, Liaoning, the location of the government in exile of Zhang Xueliang, the international press excoriated Japan for conducting the first urban aerial bombings since World War I.[2] The city did not fall until 3 January 1932.

Although on 17 October 1931 (the so-called October Incident) the Japanese government arrested the key perpetrators of the railway sabotage and pretextmakers for the rapid military escalation, bitter fighting over Heilongjiang, Manchuria's northernmost province, consumed the second and third weeks of November, and on 19 November, the provincial capital of Qiqihaer fell. That same month, the Japanese army in Manchuria (known as the Kantō Army or the Kwantung Army, depending on one's sympathies) took advantage of unrest in Tianjin, the port city for Beijing, to spirit away to Manchuria the deposed Xuantong emperor, downgraded upon the fall of the Qing dynasty in 1911 to Henry Puyi, but soon to be retrofitted as the emperor of Manchukuo.[3] Puyi, a man of ambition but not ability, had taken his English name from Henry VIII and his consort's from Elizabeth I.[4] The change of venue for Puyi became known as the First Tianjin Incident, and the fighting later that month between Japanese and Chinese main units in Tianjin became known as the Second Tianjin Incident. On 5 February 1932, Japan took Harbin, the main railway hub and seat of Russian influence. By the end of the month, Japan had occupied all of Manchuria as well as northeastern Inner Mongolia and Barga (the easternmost portion of Mongolia or westernmost portion of Heilongjiang, depending on one's sympathies).[5] Expansion of the fighting to Shanghai became known as the Shanghai Incident.

Both the Japanese and Chinese view these events through the prism of incidents: the Manchurian Incident, the October Incident, the Tianjin Incidents, the Shanghai Incident, to name just the opening numbers. The Manchurian Incident was no trivial event but the beginning of a fifteen-year regional war. The proliferating incidents beg a question: What had possessed the Kantō Army to invade all of Manchuria over a small section of easily repaired track belonging to the South Manchurian Railway Company?

ECONOMIC DEPRESSION AND COMMUNIST EXPANSION

Japan concentrated its overseas investments in Manchuria and managed them through the South Manchurian Railway Company, an umbrella organization for the vertically integrated railway as well as for the many related industries such as coal, steel, telegraph, and electric power generation. The Kantō Army controlled the company. After the Russo-Japanese War (1904–5), when Japan had acquired the railway in lieu of a Russian indemnity, company investments increased more than fifty times between 1907 and 1930. Prior to Japan's invasion, it accounted for 72 percent of the region's foreign investments and Russia 24 percent. Great Britain, the next largest foreign investor, controlled just 1 percent.[6] Industrial development in the rest of China lagged far behind Manchuria, which accounted for 90 percent of China's oil, 70 percent of its iron, 55 percent of its gold, and 33 percent of its trade.[7] If Shanghai remained China's commercial center, by 1931 Manchuria had become its industrial center.

Japan's civil and military leaders had been watching the unfolding global economic depression and activist Soviet foreign policy in Asia with growing concern. Civil-military tensions arose not over the objective of stabilizing and dominating Manchuria, and eventually the rest of China as well, since neither believed Japan could prosper while China remained in chaos and the communists at large. Tensions arose over timing and strategy.[8] Many civil leaders recommended cooperation with the West to stabilize China gradually. When military leaders demanded ever increasing military appropriations at the expense of the civilian economy, Japanese economists recommended domestic over military spending in order to build the infrastructure and industrial base for national prosperity and for military modernization.

Instead, the arrest of those guilty of the railway sabotage led to a curtailment not of military operations, but of government authority. On 13 December 1931, the cabinet fell over its inability to compel the army to conform to the government's foreign policy emphasizing cooperation with the West, not the invasion of its neighbors. The retiring prime minister, Wakatsuki Rejirō, may have reflected on the fate of his immediate predecessor, Hamaguchi Osachi, who had lingered for many months at death's door before succumbing that August to a bullet fired the preceding November by an ultranationalist.[9]

There was a naval dimension to the assassination and to Japan's malaise. The 1922 Washington Naval Treaty fixed the capital ships of Great Britain, the United States, and Japan to a tonnage ratio of 5:5:3, respectively. While the limitations left the Imperial Japanese Navy dominant in Asian waters, they permitted Britain and the United States navies with a global reach. The treaty occurred after a series of events that Japanese saw as reducing their country to an inferior status: the U.S. failure to join the League of Nations, Japan's return to China of Germany's former concessions in Shandong in 1922, and U.S. renunciation of the 1917 Lansing-Ishii agreement recognizing Japan's special interests in China and the end of the Anglo-Japanese alliance, both in 1923.[10] Although the London Naval Conference of 1930 modified the tonnage ratio in Japan's favor to 10:10:7, this did not mollify the Imperial Japanese Navy.[11] Within the year, the responsible Japanese prime minister, Hamaguchi, had been assassinated from office.

Two days after the fall of the Japanese cabinet, the Chinese government also fell, when Chiang Kai-shek, the president of the national government, chairman of the Nationalist Party, and commander of its armed forces, resigned to allow the creation of a national unity government to deal with the Japanese invasion. In late 1931, Wang Jingwei's Guangzhou group, named for the city known to Westerners as Canton, had fomented riots in the capital, Nanjing, forcing Chiang Kai-shek from power on 15 December 1931.[12] Not until mid-January 1932, after virtually all of Manchuria had fallen to Japan, did the competing factions of Chinese high politics finally cobble together a government, with Chiang Kai-shek in command of the military and his bitter rival, Wang Jingwei, serving as its primary civil leader, the president of the Executive Yuan.[13]

Even with two governments down for the count, events did not move swiftly enough for the Japanese army faction outraged by the arrest of the railway saboteurs. After two failed assassination attempts against the new prime minister, Inukai Tsuyoshi, in February and March 1932, they got their quarry on 15 May (the May 15 Incident), precipitating the formation of yet another cabinet, this time under an admiral, Saitō Makoto. Inukai had been trying to negotiate with Chiang Kai-shek to arrange for a peaceful resolution, but the military was interested in retribution not peace.[14]

Meanwhile on 21 September 1931, three days after the railway sabotage, the Chinese government appealed to the League of Nations to live up to its charter and halt the Japanese aggression. Nine days later, the league passed its first resolution on Manchuria, a month later its second, and a month later it established a commission to investigate. The Lytton Commission, so named in honor of its elaborately initialed British chairman, Victor A. G. R. Bulwer-Lytton, second earl of Lytton, set off on 4 January 1932 for Asia, where events went from bad to worse.

In Shanghai, the Japanese military opened a secondary front, or peripheral operation, to divert Western attention away from the focus of Japanese investments and military operations (Manchuria) to the focus of Western investments (Shanghai), and to threaten the Nationalist financial center in order to force a settlement on Japanese terms. The Imperial Japanese Army hired agents provocateurs to leverage the growing Chinese popular outrage and provoke incidents against Japanese nationals to serve as pretexts for military operations. When a melee resulted in the deaths of two Japanese on 18 January 1932 and the Chinese refused to meet Japanese demands to punish those responsible, fighting broke out between main units on 28 January, and soon the Imperial Japanese Navy landed reinforcements.[15] Whereas the invasion of Manchuria was an army event, Shanghai allowed the navy to showcase its repertoire and in doing so justify its proportion of the defense budget, which in every year but three from 1926 to 1936 exceeded the army's share.[16] On 19 January, the Lytton Commission had arrived in Tokyo, while pitched battles continued for months in Shanghai.

On 29 February 1932, the Kantō Army held a meeting in Shenyang on the future of Manchuria. It unilaterally changed the name, long known as the Northeast or the Northeastern Three Provinces by the Chinese, to Manchuland, but better known internationally by the more plausible sounding transliteration of Manchukuo. The army upgraded Changchun, whose name meant "Long Springtime," with the upwardly mobile new name of Xinjing, or New Capital, to make it the capital of its freshly minted puppet state. Control over Manchukuo put the Kantō Army on a par with the many regional Chinese armies that also ran their own states.[17] In China the leaders of such army-states were called warlords and the term was highly pejorative but accurate in that it highlighted both the civil and military dimensions of warlord power.

The Japanese military hoped to trade its promise to withdraw from Shanghai for Chinese recognition of Manchurian independence.[18] Instead, its actions in Manchuria and Shanghai fueled the already seething anti-Japanese sentiments of the general Chinese population. When Chiang Kai-shek rejected the trade, Japan retaliated by having Manchukuo declare independence on 1 March and enthroning Puyi as its emperor on 9 March. The Kantō Army had taken Puyi from Tianjin on consignment, with a promise to determine within the year whether Manchuria would become republican or imperial. Puyi had impeccable credentials as the former Manchu emperor of the Qing empire, now reduced to a rump state comprising his ancestral homelands.[19]

The fighting in Shanghai became known as the January 28 Incident in Chinese and as the First Shanghai Incident in Japanese. The fighting did not end until a foreign-brokered cease-fire signed on 5 May. (From the Japanese point of view the Second Shanghai Incident refers to the Shanghai Campaign during the Japanese invasion of coastal China in 1937.) All told, military operations in Manchuria and Shanghai cost Japan 3,000 killed, 5,000 wounded, and 2,500 frostbitten, out of the 150,000 soldiers deployed.[20] Three-quarters of the Japanese casualties occurred in Shanghai, where the Chinese suffered 14,326 military casualties, 6,080 civilian deaths, 2,000 wounded, and 10,400 unaccounted for. Forty-five percent of the city's population suffered losses, totaling approximately 1.5 billion yuan. Half the businesses in the war zone (or about one-eighth of all the factories in the city) and one-quarter of the city's primary schools were destroyed, while the railway lines suffered extensive damage. Trade plummeted. Soon 80 percent of Shanghai workers lost their jobs.[21] The National Eastern Library and its irreplaceable collection of rare books burned to the ground.[22]

Japan took Manchuria (or more territory than France, Germany, and Austria combined) in just five months, dispersed the guerrilla resistance within a year and a half, and expanded the borders to incorporate an area greater than Italy by 1933.[23] No one knows how many Chinese died in Manchuria, where fighting peaked in the fall of 1932 and declined significantly by March of 1933. By early 1934 Japanese authorities bragged that they had the lingering guerrilla resistance largely under control.[24] Their later estimates of ten thousand festering insurgents in 1938 suggest a more difficult problem.[25]

When the Lytton Commission arrived, the Japanese government presented an extensive list of grievances concerning the various governments of China. Although the Nationalist Party of Chiang Kai-shek dominated the internationally recognized government, he had unified the country only three years earlier in a nationwide military campaign known as the Northern Expedition (1926–8). Since the fall of the Qing dynasty, China had lacked effective central institutions, but had rival governments in North and South China as well as a plague of other warlord governments in between. From 1912 to 1928 more than thirteen hundred Chinese had a personal army and a territorial base, meeting the minimum qualifications for a warlord.[26] Japan had negotiated its treaties either with the former internationally recognized government in Beijing or with the Manchurian warlord, Zhang Zuolin. Chiang inherited these treaties.

On 4 June 1928 a railway explosion, also arranged by the Kantō Army, had detonated under an unfortunate Zhang Zuolin's railway carriage with fatal results for both Zhang and the Japanese government, which fell as a result. The Kantō Army feared a growing Nationalist influence in Manchuria and erosion of Japanese privileges and so took preemptive action that paradoxically guaranteed the opposite of its intended outcome.[27] Zhang's death (the Zhang Bomb Assassination Incident) coincided with the final stages of the Northern Expedition, when Chiang Kai-shek overthrew the internationally recognized government in Beijing and soon cut a deal with Zhang's son, a youth besotted with opium but angry and fearful after his father's murder. The deal produced a very nominal reunification of China. On 7 November 1930 despite Japanese objections to moving "local" negotiations to Nanjing, the son, Zhang Xueliang agreed to subsume Manchurian foreign relations under the Nationalist Foreign Ministry and resume salt tax remittances to the central government but retained military control over the territory north of the Yellow River.[28] His agreement marked a northward expansion of Nationalist influence – a highly undesirable turn of events from the point of view of the Kantō Army. Back in Tokyo, Prime Minister Tanaka Giichi assumed responsibility for the murder of Zhang senior and the government fell, leading to a short-lived cabinet under a civilian, Hamaguchi Osachi, to be shot within the year for his naval transgressions.

In 1931 Chiang had numerous problems on his plate: keeping together his warlord coalition, defeating a growing Communist insurgency, surviving the Great Depression, and somehow building a prosperous China on the rubble of decades of civil war. Upholding warlord treaties with Japan could not have been high on his list of priorities.

On the eve of the Manchurian invasion, Japan had more than three hundred pending cases alleging Chinese violations of their mutual treaties. The accusations concerned defaults on loans, illegal tariffs and taxes, import-substitution schemes threatening Japanese exports, restrictions on the residence of and unwillingness to sell land to Japanese nationals, harassment of Japanese businesses, discrimination against Japan's Korean subjects farming in Manchuria, and anti-Japanese educational materials, including such texts as *The National Humiliation Readers.*

The Japanese particularly condemned the Chinese for the construction of railway lines potentially competing with Japanese-owned lines and their unwillingness to link up Chinese- and Japanese-owned railways to create a unified transportation grid.[29] This problem became acute between 1928 and 1930 when nearly 90 percent of the Chinese-built railway lines began operation.[30] Ominously, in the spring of 1931 Chiang Kai-shek made the nationalization of the Japanese railway concessions in Manchuria a principle of Nationalist foreign policy.[31]

The Japanese also feared other forms of Chinese economic competition. Since 1905 Japan's trade with Manchuria had exceeded China's, but the gap had narrowed so that in 1930, Chinese trade was poised to turn the tables.[32] On 7 December 1928, the Nationalists unilaterally announced tariff autonomy as of 1 February 1929, with the goal of increasing customs revenues. The changes in the tax law greatly increased the levies on bulk items (i.e., items shipped by rail), which were taxed by quantity – promising a major impact on Japanese businesses.[33] The United States agreed to the Nationalist demand that China, not outside powers, should set its tariffs. Other nations followed suit. Japan alone resisted until 1930.[34]

Then the 1929 stock market crash in New York followed by protectionism everywhere undermined international trade and forced the Great Depression into full flower. Between 1929 and 1931, Japanese exports halved.[35] To the outrage of the Japanese, the Nationalists responded in 1931 with a major upward revision to their tariffs, followed by another in 1933. Chinese customs revenues skyrocketed from 46 million yuan in 1927 to 385 million in 1931.[36]

To Japan's three hundred–plus legal cases, the Chinese responded that they could do what they liked in their own country. The associate director of the China Institute in America made an analogy, "After the burglar has beaten the owner of the house and occupied part of his home, could the burglar expect the owner to treat him courteously and scrupulously, as if he were a legitimage tenant?"[37] When the Japanese pointed to signed treaties, the Chinese refused to recognize the authority of the Chinese signatory – either a warlord or the former internationally recognized Beijing government.

Treaty enforcement would have been politically costly for Chiang because public sentiment was viscerally anti-Japanese given Japan's repeated military incursions into Chinese territory – the First

Sino-Japanese War of 1894–5 fought in Korea and Manchuria, the Russo-Japanese War of 1904–5 fought in Manchuria, and its periodic troop deployments to Shandong. Its Twenty-One Demands of 1915 for extensive economic rights in Shandong, Manchuria, and Inner Mongolia so galled the Chinese that the date entered the official calendar as a publicly recognized day of national humiliation.

Japanese grievances extended beyond treaty violations. The Chinese public devised a devastating counterstrategy to Japan's growing interference in their domestic affairs: They refused to buy Japanese goods, and in doing so they struck at vital Japanese economic interests. Between 1908 and 1931, they conducted eleven boycotts for periods of three to thirteen months, averaging one boycott per year between 1925 and 1931. Most centered in southern and central China, the seat of Nationalist influence, and safely outside the range of the Kantō Army, which apparently fumed at its inability to stop them. The Chinese retelling of these events in their history texts and their various "national humiliation days" and "national commemoration days" made the Japanese even angrier. However economically effective, the boycotts backfired to become a key Japanese justification for further aggression.[38]

If the preceding were the proximate causes for the invasion, what were the underlying causes?

Prior to the Great Depression, a crisis mood had already descended on Japan. Ninety-eight percent of men had remained disenfranchised until a 1925 law expanded the suffrage from property holders above a certain tax threshold to virtually all financially independent men aged-twenty-five or older. The 1928 elections put eight leftist members in the Diet.[39] The government responded with a nationwide dragnet putting 1,568 Communists, as well as leaders of labor and peasant organizers behind bars; the expulsion of left-wing faculty members from the imperial universities; and a law making attempts to change the "national polity" a capital offense.[40]

The Great Depression then hit hard. Japan had already endured one depression caused by the post–World War I economic recovery of the European powers, which recaptured, at Japanese expense, their market shares in Asia forfeited during the war. In 1927 thirty-five banks went under. This put Japan in a particularly weak position when the 1929 New York Stock Exchange crash reverberated across the globe. Agriculture was hit particularly hard.[41] In the best of times resource-poor Japan depended heavily on trade and particularly trade with China, but the Chinese inability to restore order after the fall of the Qing dynasty caused growing concern. Economic growth required stability, something conspicuously absent in China.

Western protectionism in response to the Great Depression made Japan's leaders fearful of economic disaster at home. It also discredited Japan's civil leaders, who had so consistently promoted cooperation with the West ever since Japan's Westernization of its civil and military institutions in the Meiji Restoration beginning in 1868. What had this cooperation gained Japan in its hour of need? Insurmountable tariff walls and ears deaf to its repeated warnings about the dangers of Chinese instability. When the Japanese observed the West with unemployment rates at historic highs, plummeting prices driving even well-managed firms into bankruptcy, businesses operating far below capacity despite a crying need for their goods, and governments unable to reverse this downward spiral, many concluded that the Western liberal economic and political model was too deeply flawed to save. Japan must look elsewhere. It is no coincidence that the Kantō Army invaded Manchuria a year after the Hawley-Smoot Tariff set U.S. tariffs at historic highs.[42]

On 2 June 1932, the former military adviser to Zhang Zuolin and now the commanding officer of the Kantō Army, General Honjō Shigeru[43] – so someone with firsthand knowledge and long-standing expertise about China – provided his assessment to the Lytton Commission.[44] He emphasized that the Kantō Army and the Japanese government had divergent foreign policies. (The admission glossed over the constitutionality of a military's, let alone a regional army's, having an independent foreign policy.) He emphasized Japan's vital military and economic interests in Manchuria, the impact of the worsening Great Depression, and the escalating international protectionism that put resource-poor, overpopulated, and trade-dependent Japan in a particularly vulnerable position.

Honjō believed that inaction would mean domestic catastrophe. He called Manchuria Japan's "absolute life line" a turn of phrase that the Lytton Commission might have considered to be hyperbole but that probably reflected his perceptions and was used by many of his countrymen to indicate Japan's economic links with Manchuria.[45] Marshal and eventually Prince Yamagata Aritomo had coined the term in his famous edict on Japanese foreign policy a generation earlier.[46] From 1926 to 1931, Manchuria absorbed 70 percent of Japanese foreign investments, which as a result of the Great Depression and the 1930 Chinese boycott produced high losses.[47] Honjō accused the Zhang family dominating Manchuria of incompetent governance and anti-Japanese sentiments and argued its warlord government constituted a state independent of China. He considered a Manchuria under Zhang rule to be highly vulnerable to invasion, which he had just proven, but he meant vulnerable to Russian invasion.

Honjō emphasized the Russian threat, pointing to its recent domination of Outer Mongolia and its massive rearmament program under its first two five-year plans. Russian expansion now focused on Asia and particularly China. He argued that not only was Japan's first line of defense the Amur River, separating Manchuria and Russia, but the containment of Russia and the spread of communism were matters of global security. If Japan withdrew, communism would spread across China. Therefore, the West should support Japan's frontline efforts to contain communism. Honjō pleaded for patience from the League of Nations as his army strove to restore order and prosperity to Manchuria. He concluded with a request that the Lytton Commission keep his remarks confidential, and it did.[48] Japan might have been better served if Honjō had made his comments public.

From the 1917 Bolshevik Revolution forward, the Russians made clear their intent to impose a new world order, called communism. In the 1920s, the Russians had focused on expanding their influence in Asia, where they had helped found Communist Parties all along their borders. In 1924, they had helped establish the Whampoa Military Academy near Guangzhou. This modern military training and Russian military aid tipped the internal balance of power to permit Chiang Kai-shek's victory in the Northern Expedition, in contrast to earlier but unsuccessful Nationalist attempts to reunify China militarily. Although Russian-Nationalist relations were often tense, Russians remained deeply involved in China through 1960, with the exception of the four-year hiatus during the Nazi invasion. Honjō correctly identified a spreading communist influence that would have serious and long-term ramifications.

Japanese foreign policy had long focused on the containment of Russian expansion. Japan had already fought two wars, the First

Sino-Japanese War, which expelled Russian influence from Korea, and the Russo-Japanese War, which reduced Russian influence in Manchuria to the northern half.[49] With the Manchurian Incident (more accurately the Manchurian War), Japan soon cleared out Russian influence from the rest of Manchuria. Unlike the previous two wars, however, when the Manchus of the Qing dynasty and the Russians of the Romanov dynasty had agreed to negotiated settlements on Japanese terms, the Nationalists refused to recognize Japan's seizure of Manchuria. Instead, they tirelessly petitioned, boycotted, and, in the end, fought to expel Japan from the Asian mainland.

Back in 1931, an Osaka newspaper railed against the double standard maintained by the West: "Why is the American annexation of the Philippines justified, while the Japanese seizure of Formosa is not? Why is it just for Great Britain to control India, but not for Japan to control Korea?"[50] Foreign Minister Shidehara Kijūrō compared Japanese interests in Manchuria to U.S. interests in the Panama Canal Zone, areas where neither power brooked treaty infringements. His logic went downhill when he tried to argue that the full-scale invasion of Manchuria was a "police function" not a military operation.[51]

He would have done better pointing out the numerous and ongoing multiyear U.S. occupations of Caribbean nations such as in Haiti (1915–34) and Nicaragua (1912–33). He could have amplified with a history lesson concerning prior U.S. interventions in Cuba (1892–1902, 1906–9), the Dominican Republic (1916–24), and, most obtrusively, in Colombia (1903), where the parallels with China were obvious. U.S. involvement made possible Panama's secession from Colombia in 1903, just before U.S. construction began on the Panama Canal. Thereafter the United States repeatedly sent troops to Panama (1908, 1912, and 1918) and did not return the Canal Zone to Panamanian sovereignty until 2000 by a treaty signed in 1977, long after most of the people discussed in this unconventional tale had died.[52] If the United States could carve off Panama from Colombia for a canal, why could Japan not carve off Manchuria from China for a railway?

In early 1932, Foreign Minister Shidehara's successor, Yoshizawa Kenkichi, reasoned with much justification that "the present development of Manchuria is entirely due to Japanese efforts," which have kept Manchuria "free of the constant turmoil of China Proper" and turned "Manchuria into a land of peace and prosperity," but his argument went downhill when he tried "to make it clear that Japan harbors no territorial designs in Manchuria."[53] The future lieutenant general, Ishiwara Kanji, who as a lieutenant colonel had been one of the key planners of the fateful railway sabotage of 1931, tried to demonstrate that "[i]n comparison to the Han race, the Manchu people are more closely related to the great Japanese race."[54] In addition to the specious genealogy, Japan's own 1940 census of Manchukuo counted 85 percent of the population as Han Chinese and only 6 percent Manchu, while Mongols made up 3 percent and Japanese 2 percent.[55]

In 1933 the League of Nations rejected Japan's argument that a unified China had ceased to exist since the death of the Chinese president, Yuan Shikai, in 1916 and so treating China as "a single organized state" constituted a "fiction," "a convenient formula" for the league, and a "generous aspiration of the Powers," which, unlike Japan, "have little interest in China" and "can afford to preserve the convenient fiction." Japan warned quite prophetically, "Communism has already invaded China, and the alarming extent and success of the invasion is far too seldom realized. A communized China would constitute a problem for Europe and America beside which other questions would pale into insignificance." Japan offered Manchukuo as a barrier against the spread of communism.[56] There were no takers.

STATE BUILDING AND ECONOMIC DEVELOPMENT IN MANCHUKUO

Economic development, political stability, and trade remain at the top of many countries' political agendas. Japan was remarkably successful in Manchuria in these areas, despite the unpromising environment of global economic depression and regional anarchy.[57] It is not coincidental that the focus of its colonial investments – Manchuria, Korea, and Taiwan – became the postwar economic miracles. Japan applied the economic model, which it had used to transform itself into a great power, to its frontier island of Hokkaido and then to its colonies.[58]

If the West would not trade, then Japan would turn to the alternate economic model of the time, autarky, or economic self-sufficiency. Since Japan lacked the resources to become self-sufficient, it needed an empire of adequate size to become so. In this way fear combined with ambition. Japan already possessed Taiwan and Korea, colonies since 1895 and 1910, respectively, and had considerable investments in Manchuria, but turmoil in China threatened their profitability.[59]

According to the Lytton Commission, the Zhang clan ruled Manchuria through corruption, nepotism, confiscatory taxes, monopolies, and a private army that consumed 80 percent of government revenues. This left little for the infrastructure development necessary to sustain economic growth. The Zhang clan used accusations of Japanese predations – often in the form of infrastructure investments – to deflect popular attention away from its own long list of sins.[60] Included in these sins was currency debasement caused by Zhang Zuolin's intense involvement, as leader of the Fengtian group, in the North China wars of the 1920s that put the currency printing presses in high gear. From 1920 to 1928 his primary currency fell to less than 2 percent of its previous value against the yen.[61] The Zhang clan also spearheaded the effort to build a competing Manchurian railway system so that the Chinese could boycott not only Japan's goods but also its railways. The Japanese cried foul at this treaty violation. The Chinese cried bandit go home: "bandit" was the name long used in China for the Japanese.

As indicated by the multiplicity of currencies, the Zhangs had not managed to assert full military control over Manchuria. While Zhang Xueliang commanded 170,000 troops on the eve of the Japanese invasion – he had deployed just 50,000 in Liaoning and the remaining 120,000 south of the Great Wall in the hopes of spreading his influence to Beijing and by extension over North China – the associated warlords Wan Fulin commanded 30,000 soldiers in Heilongjiang, Zhang Zuoxiang controlled 50,000 more in Jilin, and Tang Yulin had 15,000 others in Rehe (known as Jehol to the Manchus), creating a law-enforcement and businessman's nightmare.[62] When Japan occupied Manchuria, Zhang Xueliang's total forces alone outnumbered the Kantō Army fifteen or twenty to one.[63]

As Japanese policy makers contemplated the mess that China was in the 1920s – the Zhili-Anhui War (1920), the First and Second Zhili-Fengtian Wars (1922, 1924), the Fengtian-Zhejiang War (1925), the Fengtian-Feng Yuxiang War (1925–6), and the Northern Expedition (1926–8) – they moved increasingly to the opinion that incorporation of Manchuria into the Japanese empire would bring the latter up to the size of Western Europe and create a market adequate to practice autarky. Today it boggles the mind to contemplate taking Manchuria, an area four times the size of Japan and despoiled by decades of warlord mismanagement, and then rapidly transforming it into a productive part of the Japanese empire. Apparently the magnitude of the task did not faze Japanese commanders, who pushed ahead with great determination. It is hard to say whether fear or ambition served as the greater inspiration.

Incredibly, the Japanese economic development program proved remarkably successful.[64] Under Zhang senior, large-scale industry did not exist outside the foreign concession areas at Yingkou (Newchwang), Dalian (Dairen), Lüshun (Port Arthur), and Andong (Dandong). Zhang junior established a few large match, textile, and brick factories in the three years between his father's assassination and the Japanese invasion, but the result was a far cry from a modern economy.[65] Thereafter, as Japanese investments poured in and as employment rolls expanded, Japan's urban economy rapidly recovered, in contrast to the West, where unemployment rates remained high. This economic about-face in combination with deeply felt nationalism contributed to strong public support for the military.[66]

The Japanese government invested massively in Manchukuo, on the order of at least 100 million yen per annum and often a multiple of that, totaling more than 9 billion yen between 1932 and 1944. As a result, Manchukuo ran a huge trade deficit with Japan. Included in the service deficit were the costs incurred by the Kantō Army, which provided the dubious service of occupation. Japan footed the occupation bill until 1941, when it turned from resource development to resource extraction and left Manchukuo to bear these costs because of the war with the United States. This helps to explain the decline of the Manchukuo economy from the outbreak of the global war forward.[67]

Initially Japanese investments focused on infrastructure development. In 1933, Manchukuo (i.e., Japan) nationalized the Chinese-owned railways, transferring to the South Manchurian Railway about one-third of the Manchurian railway system. The 1935 purchase of the Chinese Eastern Railway from Russia, representing another third, put Japan in possession of all railways.[68] Meanwhile, between 1933 and 1945, Japan laid enough new lines nearly to double the preinvasion grid to a total of 11,004 kilometers.[69] Japanese made equally impressive investments in the road system, adding 14,482 kilometers between 1932 and 1939.[70]

Japan expropriated a fragmented railway system. The Russians had built their tracks to a wide gauge to integrate their lines into the Russian not Chinese system, while the formerly Chinese-owned railways were undercapitalized, possessing inadequate numbers of locomotives and rolling stock. Few links connected the three systems. Japanese investments solved these problems. On 18 June 1937, Japan finished standardizing the track to the Chinese gauge, creating a unified transportation grid just in time for its upcoming invasion of coastal China the following month.[71]

Next the Japanese turned to investments in resource development, particularly in the areas of heavy industry and mining in order to produce the war matériel essential for managing an expanded empire.[72] The Japanese coveted Manchuria's resources. They imported more than 90 percent of their iron and 75 percent of their lead, zinc, oil, dyes, and chemicals.[73] By 1930 they imported 64 percent of their coal and 46 percent of their cast iron from Manchuria. In addition, Manchuria accounted for 37 percent of China's forests, 41 percent of its railway lines, and one-third of its trade. These highly flattering statistics reflected the massive investments Japan had made since the Russo-Japanese War and the failure of the Chinese to make comparable investments – most Chinese government resources flowed to the military, not to economic development.[74]

Manchukuo promised to fill key gaps. Investments in mining grew by nearly seventy times between 1936 and 1943, the peak year for mineral extraction. Japan developed Manchuria's rich endowment of antimony, bauxite, chrome, coal, copper, dolomite, gold, graphite, iron, lead, limestone, magnesite, manganese, mercury, molybdenite, shale oil, silica, sulfur, talc, tungsten, and zinc.[75] In August of 1935 mineral extraction became a Manchukuo monopoly.[76] Large Japanese holding companies, known as zaibatsu, such as Mitsui and Mitsubishi, established extensive operations, building numerous factories to make bricks, construction materials, chemicals, processed food, machine tools, and textiles as well as to engage in metallurgy and publishing.[77]

Output rose rapidly. By 1943 Manchuria produced 49.5 percent of all Chinese coal, 78.2 percent of its electricity, 87.7 percent of its pig iron, 93.0 percent of its steel, 66 percent of its concrete, and 99 percent of its oil. Whereas industry had accounted for 29.4 percent of the Manchurian economy in 1931, it grew to 59 percent in 1943. Chemical and machine tool production quadrupled between 1937 and 1943.[78] Between 1931 and 1941, electric power generation increased more than 900 percent.[79]

By 1945 Manchuria had a per capita income 50 percent higher than that of China proper and had become the most industrialized part of Asia outside the Japanese home islands, out-producing even Shanghai and the Yangzi River valley, long the heart of China's modern economy.[80] Japan could not have prosecuted the long war against China, let alone the Pacific Ocean war against the United States without the resources of Manchuria.[81] Among Manchuria's most important contributions to the Pacific War were its export to Japan of pig iron, aluminum, magnesite, food, iron, steel, coal, metals, and synthetic fuel.[82]

Manchukuo's first Five Year Plan (1936–41) reflected Japanese priorities. Fifty-four percent of investments went to industry and manufacturing, 30 percent to transportation and communications, 11 percent to immigration, and a mere five percent to agriculture.[83] Yet 70 percent of the population found employment in agriculture, animal husbandry, or forestry.[84] Agricultural production corrected for inflation increased just 10 percent between 1937 and 1943. Consumer good output stagnated, so that the general standard of living did not necessarily improve.[85] Prior to the Japanese occupation, the Chinese had developed numerous small-scale food processing businesses producing soybean oil, flour, and distilled sorghum; they had also invested in the textile industry.[86] These consumer industries atrophied. Manchurians worked in the service of Japan.

On 15 March 1932, Japan reduced Manchuria's fifteen circulating currencies and 136 types of bank notes to two major currencies, one for domestic use and the other for trade. The latter, a gold-backed convertible note, was eliminated in 1935 after the domestic note became convertible into yen. Previously, three to six currencies had circulated in each city. By mid-1935 currency reform was completed, ending decades of financial anarchy.[87]

Currency reform went hand in hand with the expropriation of Chinese-owned banks and the creation of a central bank on 11 June 1932. The Central Bank of Manchukuo set monetary policy, created a stable credit system, and gave Japan control over much of the Manchukuo economy because general banking constituted only a fraction of the expropriated Chinese banks' business. Previously banks bought and sold, produced and invested in soybeans, as well as in brewing, cereals, flour milling, forestry, mining, petroleum products, power generation, shipping, sugar, and textiles. These banks handled more than half of the soybean crop, Manchuria's primary export. Their nationalization included all of their subsidiary enterprises, which were then separated from banking and put under Japanese administration.[88] Therefore, banking reform, like railway unification, constituted a massive transfer of Chinese assets to Japan.[89]

To administer Manchukuo, Japan created an elaborate government structure consisting of the imperial family and associates, organizations under the central administrative structures, and the government ministries (called departments). The government had four branches: the legislative, the administrative, the judicial, and the investigatory. These mirrored China's government minus the examination branch, mandated in the model devised by the founding father of the Republic of China, Sun Yat-sen. In 1937, Japan dispensed with the investigatory branch, as redundant with the Kantō Army's activities.[90] The reorganization of local administration in December 1934 entailed the establishment of governmental institutions at the provincial, county, village, and street levels.[91] The 1936 tax reform law reduced household and business taxes to one-quarter of their former rates, and early 1937 saw the introduction of new criminal, civil, and commercial laws based on Japanese models.[92] Together these reforms ended decades of governmental paralysis.

Ostensibly this government was under the authority of the local emperor, the bespectacled Henry Puyi, now outfitted in stunning imperial regalia and the immodest reign title of *Datong*, or utopia.[93] Upon his enthronement as emperor of Manchukuo in 1934, when the Kantō Army decided on imperial over republican institutions, his reign title changed to *Kangde,* or abundant virtue. In 1940 a Shinto ritual of rebirth made Puyi the junior half brother of the offshore emperor, Hirohito, and all Manchurians Japanese subjects. In reality Japan ruled, but not as it constitutionally should have, through the prime minister and his cabinet, but through the Kantō Army.[94] The latter financed its operations from customs revenues, the salt tax, and, more notoriously, from opium sales.[95] Manchukuo soon had more than half a million opium addicts.[96] Yet under article 35 of the 1908 army criminal law, the deployment of troops abroad without proper authorization was a capital crime. Throughout the long war in China, a proliferation of armies ignored article 35, beginning with the Kantō Army and followed closely by the Chōsen Army (Japan's army in Korea), which joined the invasion of Manchuria.[97]

Of course, Manchukuo was not supposed to be a colony, but a sovereign country under an independent monarch. In practice the chain of command went from the Kantō Army, to the Assembly of the Legislative Yuan to the Office of the Councilors and only then to the emperor of Manchukuo, who obligingly made any necessary public announcements. In fact, the Kangde emperor had trouble accomplishing the one task that the Japanese could not delegate away from him – the dynastic requirement to produce progeny, something he never did. So the Kantō Army lined up a suitable mate for his younger brother, Pujie, choosing a distant relative of the Meiji emperor's mother for his bride.[98] The emperor of Japan, literally the "emperor of the heavens" (天皇), like the emperor of Manchukuo, literally the "emperor of the emperors"(皇帝), both reigned but did not usually rule. They served as powerful symbols of national unity at least in Japan, and so the Japanese hoped in Manchukuo.

Japan tried to cobble together a nation out of Manchuria's diverse population of Han Chinese, Manchus, Mongols, Koreans, and Japanese but put them under different and supposedly culturally appropriate legal regimes, which separated rather than unified them.[99] In the early years, Manchurians of both Han and Manchu extraction headed the institutions associated with the imperial family, but in later years each chairman general had a Japanese vice-chairman.[100] Although Manchurians manned many parts of the government bureaucracy, police force, and army, Japanese nationals held virtually all of the senior positions.[101] The Manchukuo Army depended on numerous Japanese officers but still suffered constant desertion from the ranks.[102]

Japan subdued the general population through China's traditional method of local control through collective responsibility, backed up by the army and comprehensive fingerprinting. In January of 1934, the Japanese resurrected the *baojia* system. They divided the Han population into a pyramid of groups of ten: every ten household heads elected a leader, ten such leaders elected their leader, and so on, to create four layers that together produced a 10,000-family unit. If anything went wrong within the unit, potentially all paid. Law enforcement and militia organizations paralleled the *baojia* system.[103] The Japanese did not submit Manchurians of Mongolian, Korean, let alone Japanese nationality to this system as it was thought to be culturally inappropriate for them.[104]

In an attempt to instill concord, the Japanese founded Concordia Association offices throughout Manchuria. From 1934 to 1944, branches expanded from 900 to more than 5,000, and the membership grew from 300,000 to more than 4 million.[105] Yet the Japanese presented themselves as the "leading race" – a concept ill suited to cultivate the allegiance of others.[106] Likewise, wage policies reinforced rather than overcame divisions; Japanese earned the most followed by Koreans.[107] The Japanese soon became notorious for their ill treatment of the local population, whose rents and taxi fares they did not necessarily pay. They provided inferior educational facilities to others, demanded that the non-Japanese bow as they passed, and as the war went badly, denied them desirable food, while the Japanese ate comparatively well. They did not distinguish among the Han Chinese but treated all as third-class citizens, with many innocents caught in the cross fire of military operations.[108]

Even more alienating, they imposed a "strategic hamlet" program. In order to cut off insurgents from local support, they uprooted the rural population to live in fortified hamlets. By mid-1937, there were more than two thousand.[109] By then Japanese nationals controlled more than one-quarter of the cultivated land through long-term leases and Tokyo had a twenty-year plan to send 5 million settlers. The idea was to relieve rural poverty at home while strengthening Japanese local control in Manchuria and improving defenses against Russian expansion, but the changes were at the expense of the local population.[110] As Japanese rule became increasingly oppressive, with restrictions on movement along the borders and secrecy laws in 1936, the local population found even less in common with their overlords.[111]

Japan also financed a major building spree particularly in the new capital, but also in other cities, to create carefully organized boulevards, logical traffic patterns, spacious central parks, Shintō shrines, and a proliferation of large government buildings in the Asian totalitarian style.[112] In the more expensive of these buildings, optimistically upturned Chinese rooflines relieved the dour poured-concrete structures below. Cheaper buildings lacked the Chinese ornamentation and stuck with a basic shoebox design. These planned cities served as architectural symbols of authority and the new order.[113]

The Japanese published a vast array of economic and technical statistics to demonstrate to the population their enormous investments in economic development. They published dozens of professional journals in law, politics, education, economics, mining, transportation, agriculture, and medicine in order to drum up support and to spread best practices.[114] They could point to Manchukuo's rapid economic growth, stability compared to its recent past and to China's anguished present, and the expansion of education between 1933 and 1939 from 441,000 to 1,579,000 children in primary school and from 28,000 to 60,000 children in middle school.[115] The unkindness of Japanese teachers in these schools and favoritism of Japanese over Manchurian children undermined the potential positive effects on popular loyalties.[116]

Thus, while Japanese administrators excelled at the technical side of administration, they failed at the human side, creating bitter enemies of a potentially sympathetic population. Although the Nationalists and the Chinese Communists showed no more compunction than the Japanese when dealing with political foes or concern for collateral damage from their own military operations, they offered some categories of Chinese the hope to rise within the system, whereas Japan blocked all chances. Of the three, the Chinese Communists were the most attuned to popular perceptions.

Japan's occupation of Manchuria hurt China in numerous ways. Beyond all the lost natural resources and personal property, Manchukuo constituted 10 percent of Chinese territory, the primary internal market for Chinese goods, and a major source of customs revenues.[117] The proportion of Manchuria's trade with China dropped from 30 percent to 5 percent, while trade with Japan rose from 40 percent to 85 percent.[118] The Manchurian salt tax, formerly remitted to the Nationalist government, alone provided 10 percent of the Kantō Army income.[119]

The public outcry south of the Great Wall then hamstrung Chinese foreign policy when the most vocal elements of the Chinese public made the restoration of sovereignty over Manchuria their priority whatever the political and economic constraints facing their government. China, with its government down for the count, was not in a position to act, but the Chinese public responded with a comprehensive nationwide boycott of Japanese goods. Within three months Japan abandoned the gold standard, the value of the yen fell to about 40 percent of its previous gold value, and Japan's credit rating declined. In the first eight months after the invasion, the value of Japanese gold dollar bonds in New York fell by almost half.[120] Although Japan rapidly stabilized the

Manchurian economy and laid infrastructure that would benefit future generations, its trade with China imploded, anti-Japanese sentiments across China went viral, and these widely shared sentiments increasingly forced an anti-Japanese agenda on any Chinese government that hoped to retain or gain power.

JAPAN'S WARLORDS ABROAD AND AT HOME

By many quantifiable measures, the Japanese did well for themselves: They took Manchuria in one hundred days,[121] they turned chaos into order, their own economy recovered while those of others faltered, and their output rates for virtually all goods rapidly increased. A decade later when the war with the United States turned catastrophic, some Japanese leaders must have pondered: What if they had left well enough alone and stopped with Manchuria? How would events have turned out then?

In practice, the Japanese never did stop. There was no hiatus in military operations between 1931 and 1937. After the conquest of Manchuria, during the supposed period of peace after 1933, Japan occupied China north of the Yellow River, whose valley forms the cradle of Han civilization.[122] Although the Japanese rarely fought Nationalist forces in this period, they constantly fought Chinese. On 23 December 1932, the Kantō Army reached Shanhai Pass, known as Shanhaiguan, where the Great Wall meets the sea. The pass is the gateway to Rehe Province and forms the junction of the main transportation link between Manchuria and North China. On 1 January 1933, Japan took the town named for the pass from the forces of Zhang Xueliang.[123]

In 1933, the leaders of the Kantō Army considered all of Manchuria pacified, except for the southernmost province of Rehe, an exception that clearly grated.[124] Rehe was known in the West by its Manchu name, *Jehol*, because it was the historic center of Manchu power, the location of the most important Manchu imperial palace, and the site of the original imperial burial grounds. It was also an integral part of Inner Mongolia. Even with a bona fide Manchu emperor on duty, Manchukuo must have seemed bereft without the core lands of the Manchu imperium. On 17 February, Japan invaded with 20,000 men, and on 3 March the provincial capital of Chengde fell. Within a fortnight Japan had occupied a province whose area approximated the combined size of Virginia, West Virginia, and Maryland.[125]

None of this impressed the League of Nations, which on 24 February 1933, with Siam abstaining and twelve others absent, voted 42 to 1 (Japan was the 1) to denounce the occupation of Manchuria as a violation of Japan's many treaties with China and the West, not to mention the Charter of the League of Nations.[126] The Japanese withdrawal from the league on 27 March signaled their rejection of the global order and, in the stroke of a pen, transformed Japan into a diplomatically isolated nation.[127] The walkout made Japan's representative to the league and future foreign minister, Matsuoka Yōsuke, internationally famous. Japan had joined the league in 1920, serving as both one of the forty-two charter members and one of the four permanent members of League of Nations Council, and had been active in humanitarian, political, and judicial matters. Only Britain, Germany, and France paid more into the budget.[128] Japan's withdrawal marked the end to its long and constructive role in international affairs.

Matsuoka Yōsuke fulminated: "Humanity crucified Jesus of Nazareth two thousand years ago.... Japan stands ready to be crucified! But we do believe, and firmly believe, that, in a very few years, world opinion will be changed and that we also shall be understood by the world as Jesus of Nazareth was."[129] Jesus of Nazareth came out considerably better in the courthouse of history than did Japan, let alone Matsuoka, whose misreading of Russian, German, Chinese, and U.S. intentions contributed to an unworkable foreign policy once he became foreign minister in 1940.

Upon quitting the league, Japan's only potential friends were other diplomatically isolated countries such as Germany and Russia, whose own agendas for world domination were not necessarily compatible with those of Japan. When the league took no punitive action and no great power threatened to intervene, the Kantō Army kept on going, and this left Chiang Kai-shek with a difficult choice. He could resist and probably lose (his estimation), or he could sue for peace to focus on the civil war at home before he took on Japan and added a regional war to his list of problems.[130]

When Japan quit the league, its troops fought the Great Wall Campaign from 5 March until 30 May 1933, so that the Great Wall became its line of control. In early April it broke through the Great Wall to move into the core area of Han civilization, starting with Hebei.[131] Chiang Kai-shek sued for peace and on 31 May 1933 signed the Tanggu Truce, whereby Japanese troops withdrew north of the Great Wall, Chinese troops withdrew from eastern Hebei, and a neutral zone remained in between.[132] Tanggu lies at the mouth of the Yongding River connecting Tianjin and Beijing with the sea and with the Grand Canal, the great north-south internal waterway and former conduit of imperial tax revenues. Japan subsequently transformed Tanggu into North China's largest port.[133] The agreement constituted de facto Chinese recognition of Japanese dominance over Manchuria and Rehe. Chiang Kai-shek then spent the better part of 1933 fighting the Communists to flush them out of South China as well as the Christian warlord of North China, Feng Yuxiang, who rarely went along with Chiang's plans. General Feng acquired his sobriquet for his unique military training program combining instruction in drills, ethics, literacy, and Christianity, with baptism by water hose.[134] In the 1920s, his daughter had been living with Chiang's son in Moscow, where they were both studying.[135]

The Japanese kept reinterpreting the Tanggu peace agreement to permit continued southward conquests into the demilitarized zone and beyond.[136] As their operations expanded, so did their inventory of armies. The Kantō Army ran the show in Manchuria through 1937, when it had the sole Japanese military headquarters in the former Qing empire. After the 1937 escalation, the number of military headquarters proliferated to two in 1938, four in 1939, six in 1941, and a peak of ten in 1942.[137] The Kantō Army and the China Garrison Army based in Tianjin were the oldest expeditionary armies, but by the end of World War II, three armies under a China Expeditionary Army occupied China south of the Great Wall: The former China Garrison Army became the North China Area Army, activated in August 1937. On 30 October 1937 the Central China Expeditionary Army (originally called the Central China Area Army and then the China Expeditionary Army) was created to oversee the Shanghai Campaign. The third army was the South China Area Army.[138] Japan's armies, like China's warlord armies, competed with each other for control over territory and remained only nominally under the authority of a civilian government based in the capital. In fact, the commanders of these armies often struck out to make foreign policy on their own and so did not necessarily cooperate with each other.

In addition to conventional and counterinsurgent military operations, Japan's armies developed a two-pronged political and economic strategy. First they gradually set up a confusion of puppet governments under an evolving set of names and jurisdictions, all geared to cause maximum irritation to the Chinese. Little thought was given to garnering loyalties. Then the South Manchurian Railway administration established franchises with the authority to develop virtually all the resources in each army's area of occupation.

From 1935 to 1936 Japan's warlord armies worked to partition North China, beginning with Inner Mongolia.[139] In the first half of 1935, the commander of the China Garrison Army since 1934, Lieutenant General Umezu Yoshijirō, attempted to occupy Chahar in the Chahar Campaign but succeeded in taking only the eastern part.[140] Chahar, Suiyuan, and Rehe together constituted Inner Mongolia, or Mongolia south of the Gobi Desert, in juxtaposition to Outer Mongolia, north of the desert.[141] This area soon fell under the jurisdiction of the Kantō Army.

So Umezu turned his attention southward and used the pretext of the murders of two pro-Japanese newspaper owners in Tianjin to deliver an ultimatum, which the Japanese-educated General He Yingqin, who served as Chiang Kai-shek's minister of war from 1930 to 1944, rapidly accepted. In the Umezu Yoshijirō-He Yingqin Agreement of 10 June 1935, the Nationalist government agreed to withdraw all troops and party offices from the rest of Hebei. Although the agreement also promised that the Nationalists would squelch the anti-Japanese movement not only in the demilitarized zone, but throughout China, they lacked both the capacity and the desire to do so.

The Kantō Army also pressured Inner Mongolia, where the Nationalists backed down again, to sign the Doihara Kenji-Qin Dechun Agreement of 27 June 1935 over the arrest by Chahar authorities of several Japanese intelligence officers. Japan demanded punishment of the guilty, protection of Japanese in Chahar, and a withdrawal of hostile troops from the Manchukuo border. The Nationalists ordered General Song Zheyuan, the commander of the 29th Army, to remove his force, but his deputy commander, General Qin Dechun, replaced Song as governor. At the time both Chinese generals were serving in obscurity in Chahar but would soon became famous for the order in 1937 to the 29th Army to resist Japan at the Marco Polo Bridge outside Beijing. These later hostilites rapidly spiralled into a nationwide war. General Doihara's fame preceded him. He had been a key instigator of the invasion of Manchuria. The Doihara-Qin agreement expelled Nationalist troops from Chahar and marked the highpoint of the Nationalists' strategy of accommodation in order to buy time to win the civil war against the Communists before taking on Japan.[142] As with Germany, no accommodation ever appeased Japan and the strategy of appeasement soon acquired a bad name, with a British newspaper describing it as "a clever plan of selling off your friends in order to buy off your enemies."[143]

Inner Mongolians felt increasingly helpless, surrounded as they were by China, Russia, and Japan. In 1929 the Chinese had carved up Inner Mongolia into four "normal" Chinese provinces: Rehe, Chahar, Suiyuan, and Ningxia. Meanwhile Russia and Japan took away three-quarters of what had been Mongolia, the former by lopping off Outer Mongolia to form a puppet state in the early 1920s, and the latter by incorporating eastern Inner Mongolia into Manchukuo. When the Inner Mongolians tried to cut a deal for greater autonomy from the Nationalists, the latter responded in 1934 by kidnapping and fatally shooting Kokebagatur, the chief of staff of Demchugdongrob. Demchugdongrob, known to the Chinese as De Wang or King De, was the most important leader of Inner Mongolia, a thirty-first-generation lineal descendent of Ghengis Khan. He responded to the murder of his chief of staff by throwing in his hat with the Japanese, but this act fractured his Mongol following.[144]

Japan's China Garrison Army, in competition with the Kantō Army, which ran the mother puppet government, Manchukuo, seized the opportunity to establish not one, but eventually a covey of puppet states in North China.[145] In May 1935 with Japan's blessing and loose change, Demchugdongrob became the head of an Inner Mongolian government, formalized in February of 1936 as the Inner Mongolian Military Government. Fighting broke out in November 1935 between Demchugdongrob and defecting Mongols under the command of the Han Chinese governor of Suiyuan, Fu Zuoyi, a man of shifting alliances, who limited Demchugdongrob's territory to eastern Chahar – the territory taken by Umezu.[146] Much later Fu Zuoyi became famous (or infamous, depending on one's sympathies) for surrendering Beijing to the Communists in the final stages of the long Chinese civil war – his own Nationalist forces intact.

On 28 August 1936, more fine-tuning made Demchugdongrob the head of state for a Mongol homeland, Mengkukuo, a matching bookend for Manchukuo – a Mongolland for a Manchuland.[147] Japanese military advisers trained the Inner Mongolian army. In mid-November, the Manchukuo Army combined forces with Demchugdongrob in a campaign to annex Suiyuan, but Nationalist Chinese forces under Fu Zuoyi successfully counterattacked on 18 November 1936, the so-called Suiyuan Incident, and in December Demchugdongrob abandoned the campaign.[148]

South of Inner Mongolia lay the core lands of Han Chinese civilization, where partition justified by Manchu or Mongol ethnicity was a nonstarter. Nevertheless, on 14 May 1935, the Kantō and China Garrison Armies decided to detach the five North China provinces of Hebei, Shandong, Shanxi, Chahar, and Suiyuan. On 13 January 1936 the cabinet in Tokyo confirmed this decision.[149]

While the Kantō Army was attempting to clone a puppet state in Inner Mongolia, the China Garrison Army set to work in North China. Just fifteen miles outside Beijing in Tongzhou, located in the demilitarized zone established under the Umezu-He Agreement, Yin Rugen proclaimed the independence of the East Hebei Anti-Communist Autonomous Government in November 1935. In 1937 it would be amalgamated into a later-model puppet government, the Provisional Government of the Chinese Republic based in Beijing. The East Hebei puppet government put Beijing and Tianjin outside Nationalist control. Yin, who had been educated in and later in the employ of Japan, immediately cut Chinese tariffs by 75 percent. Yin's funding was via the Inner Mongolian Military Government.[150] With the invasion of North China, Japan levied increased taxes on foreign goods – meaning Chinese goods – and decreased taxes on local goods, while taking over North Chinese resources to funnel them into Manchukuo and Japan.[151]

The Japanese military believed the establishment of governments south of Manchukuo would undercut the anti-Manchukuo resistance movement on its frontiers and provide complementary resources. In 1933 and 1934, as soon as Rehe fell, the Japanese conducted extensive surveys of North China's resources, which they found too tempting to ignore. North China was East Asia's key producer of high-grade coal, high-grade iron, salt, and cotton, which did not do well in Manchukuo's colder climate. It had more coal and iron than did Manchukuo and accounted for 55 percent of China's coal, 40 percent of its iron reserves, and 50 percent of its railways – Hebei alone produced 25 percent of China's cotton. North China also had important deposits of bauxite (aluminum), gold, iron, mica, and quartz and was a major producer of leather and wool.[152] Before long, Japanese authorities were putting out three- and five-year plans for North China economic development. In other words, at a very early stage, Japanese military leaders in China had an unlimited objective: They did not want a mere chunk of Chinese territory but eventually China in its entirety, with no role for the incumbent government.

To erode North China's ties with China (a difficult task since North China was the cradle of Han civilization), the Imperial Japanese Army made smuggling to evade Nationalist tariffs an officially sanctioned and highly profitable form of commerce. The smuggling began with silver and moved into sugar, rayon, flour, cigarettes, textiles, gasoline, foodstuffs, toys, opium, and other illegal drugs. Since the Nationalists backed their currency with silver, the illegal silver trade undermined the currency.[153] With the creeping Japanese occupation of North China, the Nationalists lost at least 20 percent of their customs income, important because customs constituted more than half of Nationalist government revenues. The Japanese then used this customs windfall to fund the kaleidoscope of puppet governments.[154]

After 1937, the North China Army, not the Kantō Army, oversaw North China economic development, while the Kantō Army managed Manchuria, Inner Mongolia, and Shanxi. The opening move in these economic takeovers was the seizure of Chinese assets – a program not designed to win hearts and minds. Zaibatsu provided the necessary technical expertise, which was increasingly ignored as the Japanese military demanded investments exclusively in military industries, while the zaibatsu managers saw more promising commercial opportunities. The military took direct control over all military-related industries and encouraged the zaibatsu to develop light industry and the production of consumer goods, but the expanding war soon left insufficient resources for both military and consumer goods. In 1938 the Japanese established the North China Development Company, modeled on the South Manchurian Railway Company, which had so successfully nurtured Japanese investments up to 1931, and provided the nucleus of personnel and expertise to take over all of Manchuria thereafter. They also established a parallel Central China Development Company.[155]

Like the South Manchurian Railway Company, the North China Development Company invested heavily in infrastructure development (communications, electricity, telephone, transportation, ports), industry (chemicals, steel, textiles), resource extraction (bauxite, coal, gold, iron, manganese, salt, and tungsten), and export products for Japan. The Japanese government provided 80 percent of the capital to create a horizontally and vertically integrated organization. By 1944 the Japanese had nearly doubled the North China railway net, greatly facilitating its troop movements and resource extraction.[156]

As an indication of North China's eventual contribution to the war effort, from 1938 to 1946, under Japanese development schemes, its production increased from 12.8 to 60 million tons of coal, from 68,000 to 870,000 tons of iron, from 17,000 to 407,000 tons of aluminum, from 247,000 to 597,000 tons of cotton, and from 0 to 1 million tons of liquid fuel. Significant proportions of these resources went directly to Japan.[157]

Back in Tokyo, Finance Minister Takahashi Korekiyo cut a lonely figure. Takahashi was one of the most distinguished finance ministers in Japanese history and has sometimes been called Japan's John Maynard Keynes, for his rapid turnaround of the urban economy to full employment and full capacity by 1935–6, a decade ahead of the United States, despite a weather-induced famine in 1934. (Keynes was the brilliant British economist whose theories prescribed the antidote to economic depression that became generally accepted only after the Great Depression.) Agricultural incomes, however, did not reach their 1920 highs until after 1945, leaving a gap between urban and rural prosperity, acutely felt by the army, whose recruits were primarily from the countryside. Japanese military leaders interpreted their conquests as the reason for Japan's economic turnaround. In fact, economic indicators did not improve in 1931; they stagnated after 1937 and plummeted after 1941, the critical years of the military escalation.[158] Although military production peaked in 1944, food and basic necessity output peaked in 1937, with enormous implications for the general standard of living.[159]

Japan's economic recovery, however, fully coincided with Takehashi's final three terms (of seven) as finance minister from 1931 to 1936, when he was seventy-seven to eighty-two years of age. The hallmarks of his term were departure from the gold standard, devaluation of the yen to stimulate exports, increase of the money supply to raise consumption, deficit financing to allow government spending, public works investments, civil control over military spending, cooperation with the West, and resistance to the dismemberment of China but support for its economic development.[160] In 1935 he warned, "Our country is poor in natural resources and I doubt that we can compete in an autarkic economic environment. We must think about our position in the world and form a budget in keeping with our people's wealth. Financial trust is an intangible. Maintaining that trust is our most urgent duty. If we focus only on defense, we will cause bad inflation and that trust will collapse. Thus, our national defense will not be secure. The military should think about this."[161]

On 5 January 1936, his comments on Italy's invasion of Ethiopia contained economic advice for the Imperial Japanese Army: "If a country increases its empire and pours money into it, how big a profit is it going to have? Until the profits come in, the home country has to carry [the colony]." After restoring the urban economy to prosperity, he tried to hold firm on defense spending. Although it remained steady at 6.55 percent of the gross national product from 1933 to 1936, it grew from 27 percent of the government budget in 1931 to 46 percent of a much larger budget in 1936.[162] Takahashi argued vehemently against this trend. His ideas represented an alternative to the path demanded by the military.

Before sunrise on the morning of 26 February 1936, soldiers broke into his home, found him in bed, cut him off midsentence, and shot and slashed him to death while screaming "heavenly punishment."[163] Apparently limits to military spending constituted a sin against heaven. His death was part of the largest army uprising in modern Japanese history, the so-called February 26 Incident, also known as the Young Officers' Revolt. It lasted four days from 26 to 29 February and involved 1,027 new recruits.[164] The rebels occupied the residences of the prime minister and the war minister (i.e., the army minister), as well as the Diet, the War Ministry, and the Metropolitan Police Headquarters.[165] In addition to Finance Minister Takahashi, the hit list included Inspector General of Military Education Watanabe Jōtarō and Lord Keeper of the Privy Seal Saitō Makoto, who both lost their lives; Grand Chamberlain and retired Vice-Admiral Suzuki Kantarō, who survived severe wounds; and former Lord Keeper of the Privy Seal Makino Nobuaki and Prime Minister Okada Keisuke, who both escaped unscathed.[166] Saionji Kinmochi, the last surviving Meiji era senior statesman, known as the *genrō* (or original elders), was removed from the hit list only at the last minute.[167]

Colonel Ishiwara Kanji, a key instigator of the invasion of Manchuria, took charge of the suppression of the coup attempt. He wanted the instigators to kill themselves, but given his own record of insubordination, they refused. The rebels wanted to replace the "Control," or Tōsei, group dominating the army command with their "Imperial Way," or Kōdō, group. The Control group centered among the elite officers of War Ministry and General Staff Headquarters. Many hailed from Chōshū Prefecture. They advocated a strict military code of obedience and later would support alliance with Germany. The younger regimental officers, who formed the preponderance of the Imperial Way group, rejected Chōshū dominance, and many were from Saga or Oita Prefecture. They made a creed of nationalism, focused on Armageddon with Russia, intended to export the Manchukuo system of army rule to Japan, tried to rule by fait accompli, and were partial to terrorism against their fellow Japanese. They planned to establish a military government under the emperor – despite having just murdered his closest associates. The leaders of the Imperial Way group, Generals Araki Sadao and Mazaki Jinzaburō, soon abandoned the rebels, but not soon enough to save their careers or their group, which lost all political influence. Members of the Control group, such as Tōjō Hideki, whom the rebels abhorred, became the primary beneficiaries of the mutiny.[168]

The Imperial Japanese Navy, the Imperial Japanese Army's sworn enemy in the budget wars to hog appropriations, was more than happy to help put down the rebellion. For five months Tokyo remained under martial law. Seventeen of the ringleaders were executed, sixty-five received prison sentences, and their supporters were purged from the army with the retirement of seven of ten full generals, the transfer of seven of the most senior officers to the reserves, and three thousand more transfers during the annual August transfer period.[169]

Although the mutineers failed to achieve their objectives, they either killed or destroyed the careers of those whom Saionji and the emperor had expected to govern, namely, the pro-British, pro-American group. As a result of the February 26 Incident, all hopes of constraining the military vanished.[170] The military budget for 1937 tripled the average for the 1934 to 1936 period. In 1939 it doubled again. Rampant inflation produced a 1944 military budget seventy times larger than that of 1936. The military got the planned economy it coveted as well as the hyperinflation and the resource bottlenecks that Takahashi had predicted.[171]

The February 26 Incident was by no means unique. It differed only in scale. From 1931 to 1936, two of three finance ministers were murdered. Three of five prime ministers were assassinated, and a fourth, Prime Minister Okada Keisuke, survived the February 26 Incident only because his unfortunate adoptive brother, in a case of mistaken identity, died in his stead. The year 1932 was second to 1936 in the number of high-profile assassinations: a finance minister, a prime minister, and the head of the Mitsui corporation.[172] Prime Minister Inukai Tsuyoshi's murder on 15 May 1932, known as the May 15 Incident, marked the end of cabinets organized by political parties. The new governments euphemistically were called "national unity" governments to mask a reality of army rule by fait accompli.[173] Members of the Imperial Japanese Army conducted most of the assassinations mentioned, but civilians including representatives of farmers also freelanced, as did members of the Imperial Japanese Navy. Between 1931 and 1936 there were four attempted military coups – two called off at the last minute by the army in 1931, the May 15 Incident of 1932 assassinating Prime Minister Inukai organized by the navy, and the army's over-the-top February 26 Incident of 1936.[174] The Japanese refer to this phenomenon as "the low oppressing the high," or *gekokujō*. The term originates from the civil unrest in the fifteenth century when subordinates attacked and usurped the Muromachi Shogunate. In the 1930s and 1940s, it applied to insubordinate junior officers, who attempted to set national policy.[175]

As a result of the many coup attempts, cabinets fell apace. The rapidity itself was not unusual, since prewar cabinets generally had less than a two-year average shelf life, but the reasons for each fall were unusual and reflected a growing influence of the military, which had always been a strong force in politics. It alone of all institutions could bring down a cabinet simply by refusing to appoint an active-duty officer for either the war or the navy minister. Unlike the other cabinet ministers but like their shōgun forbears, these two met directly with the emperor. The prime minister could constrain the military only through the emperor or through the war or navy minister. His cabinet ministers were not responsible to him but to the emperor, depriving the prime minister of the ability to coordinate government policy.

The Meiji Constitution also left much unsaid. It lacked an article outlining the responsibilities of the cabinet or the prime minister.[176] The founding fathers of modern Japan, the *genrō*, deliberately embedded a special status for the military in the Meiji Constitution. The *genrō* held enormous informal power. In consultation with the emperor, they chose each new prime minister, a position virtually all had held themselves and monopolized from 1885 to 1913 (minus a five-month hiatus in 1898). As a group they followed pro-Anglo-American, anti-Communist, and pro-emperor-system inclinations.[177]

The Meiji generation compensated for the large voids in the written law and the structural weakness of the prime minister's authority with their personal ties with each other, forged in the revolution that had put them in power. These ties crossed civil and military boundaries to create interinstitutional cohesion that disappeared with their deaths in the first quarter of the twentieth century and allowed the army and navy ministers to act without accountability to the electorate, to their fellow cabinet ministers, to the prime minister, or to the emperor. In the past army and navy ministers had consulted the foreign and finance ministers. No longer and with baneful consequences.[178]

Yet the military had always delivered, first by fighting off the samurai rebellion of 1877 that threatened to turn back the clock to overturn the Meiji generation's program of Westernization by removing them from power. The military delivered even more spectacularly in two wars against Japan's oversized continental neighbors, the floundering Qing dynasty in the First Sino-Japanese War and the ailing Romanov dynasty in the Russo-Japanese War. These two wars transformed Japan into a great power, the primary objective of the Meiji generation, and, in doing so, transformed the military into the most widely respected institution in Japan. But this shifted the internal balance of power away from the civilian leadership to the military leadership. The passing of the Meiji generation then magnified the shift.

After the Russo-Japanese War the army countered the Foreign Ministry's attempt to restore the empire to civil administration with "the right of military command." The army established parallel institutions to supplant the Foreign Ministry's jurisdiction: the Advisory Council on Foreign Relations in 1915, the Colonial Ministry in 1929, and finally the Asian Development Board in 1938. On 2 November 1937, Ishii Itarō, the head of the Foreign Ministry's Bureau of Asiatic

Affairs, confided in his diary, "It seems that Fascism is happening here not by means of people but through institutions." The Foreign Ministry, with a budget of 17 million yen in 1931 in comparison to the military's budget of 590 million yen, did not have a prayer in this struggle.[179]

By the 1930s an inner cabinet system had emerged with five or fewer ministers, depending on the cabinet, who made crucial decisions. The army and navy ministers, but not necessarily the prime minister, always belonged to the inner cabinet. The finance minister and the foreign minister might serve, but again, not necessarily. The consistent army and navy attendance in contrast to the sporadic presence of the different civilian ministers shifted the internal balance of power further toward the military, making it far more powerful at home and abroad than in the Meiji era, when civil and military cabinet members and institutions had hashed out domestic and foreign policy together. Civilians, particularly after the assassination of Finance Minister Takahashi Korekiyo, feared for their lives with good reason and became reluctant to criticize the preferred policies of the army.[180]

When the Kantō Army invaded Manchuria, members of the Foreign Ministry panicked because they correctly perceived a coup d'état under way. They understood, as they observed helplessly from their consulates in Manchuria, that the Kantō Army had hijacked foreign policy and that a reversal of the new foreign policy would be impossible.[181] The invasion was a pivotal event because there could be no return to the status quo ante. The army would not withdraw, the civilian leadership could not make it do so, and indeed many civilians and the Japanese public strongly supported the invasion. An error the size of an occupation was too large to admit. No government could survive an admission of this scale.

Army leaders, their many civilian supporters, and the Japanese public perceived no alternative to an aggressive foreign policy in China in order to overcome the Great Depression and to counter Russian territorial and ideological expansion. They faced an intractable dilemma: Good citizenship in the prevailing global order promised economic disaster with the collapse of international trade caused by Western protectionism. Failure to play by the rules, however, risked diplomatic isolation and possibly war. Japanese leaders perceived communism to be on the march and their options narrowing by the minute. They had compelling reasons to intervene in China. So the Imperial Japanese Army came to the rescue.

On 24 September 1935, the newly appointed commander of Japanese forces in China, General Tada Hayao, demanded Japanese domination of North China in order to prevent the spread of communism.[182] At the post–World War II war crimes tribunal, General Minami Jirō, who had served as war minister from 1930 to 1931 and as commander of the Kantō Army from 1934 to 1936, argued, "Manchuria was regarded as a military base. Whether Japan occupied Manchuria or invaded China, the ultimate military goal was to fight Russia."[183] The tribunal imprisoned him for life. The Japanese did indeed transform Manchukuo into a military base like no other and left an infrastructure endowment still visible from its transportation grid to its flood control system.

Finance Minister Takahashi Korekiyo represented the path not taken, and his assassination silenced the last strong voice willing to speak truth to power. Japan's civil and military leaders wished Japan to remain a great power. Takahashi recommended prioritizing domestic over foreign policy because he understood that military power rested on an economic foundation. Whereas the Japanese military focused on operational success, Takahashi focused on economic performance. Whereas the military subordinated economic decisions to military decisions, Takahashi made the reverse prioritization. Before long, operational success became the Japanese military's yardstick to measure strategic success, and in doing so officers confused means with ends, with tragic repercussions, particularly for themselves and the Japan they loved and hoped to preserve.

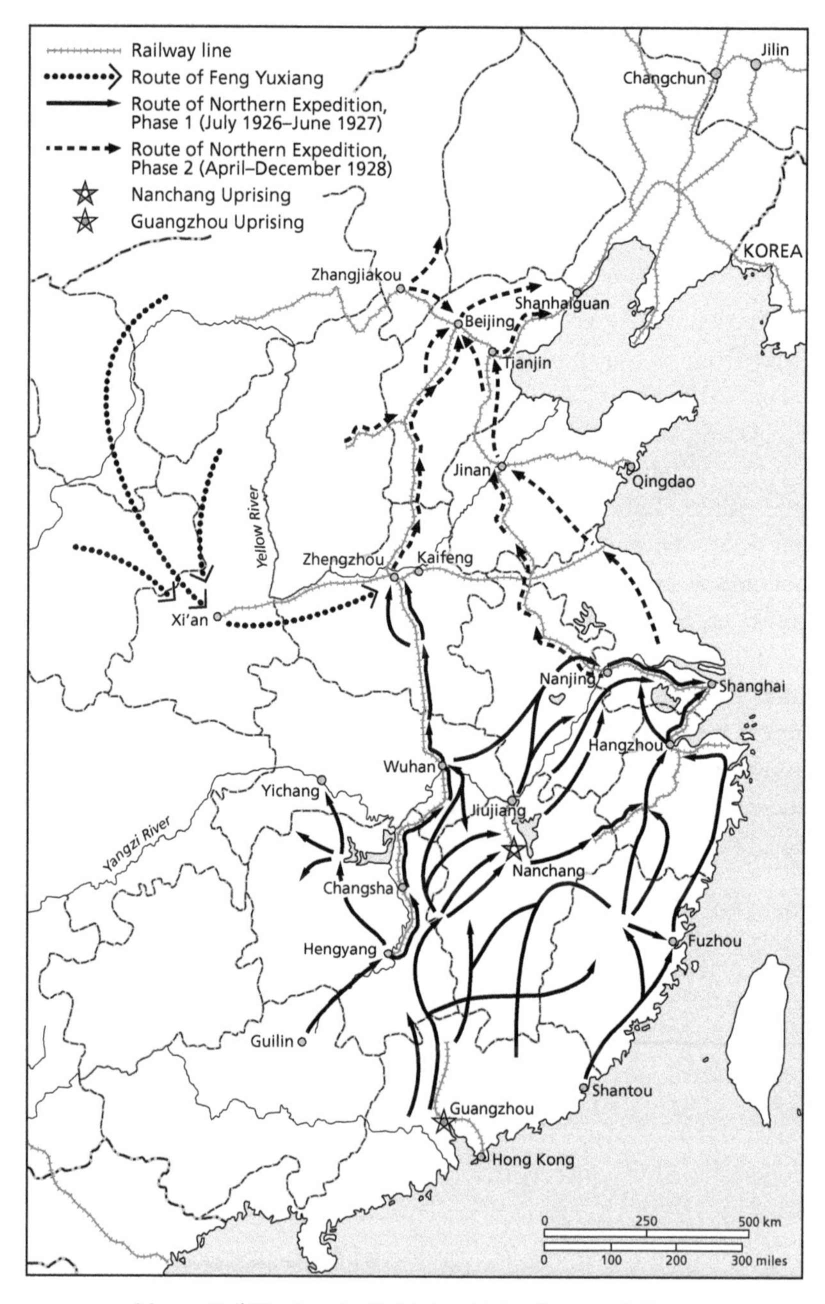

Map 2 Civil War (1926–28): Nationalist Unification of China.

3

CHINA 1926–1936

Chaos and the Quest for the Mandate of Heaven

苦撑待變
Endure bitterness, await change.
(Bide one's time.)

In Chinese history, devastating chaos characterized periods between dynasties. Prosperity resulted from unity and stable rule, while dynastic change heralded warfare on an empirewide scale, ruining provinces for decades. The Chinese have portrayed their history in terms of a dynastic cycle, consisting of the rise, the maturation, and the decline of a ruling house, followed by a chaotic interregnum before the rise of a successor dynasty. This analytical framework followed Buddhist beliefs about the birth, maturation, decay, and death of all living things, and the rebirth of life each spring after the dead of winter. According to this framework, dynasties on the rise or at their peak held the mandate of heaven, the cosmic legitimacy to rule. Those that lost their mandate could expect imminent overthrow.[1] After the fall of the Qing dynasty in 1911, China faced a long and bloody interregnum that lasted until the Communists finally reunified much of the Qing empire in 1949.

Just as Japanese leaders faced terrible dilemmas in 1930s – to work within the gridlocked international order or to take decisive action – Chinese leaders faced lethal choices. Although there was a growing consensus that Confucianism could no longer serve as the unalterable philosophical bedrock of China, there was great discord over its replacement. Everyone wanted a New China, but what sort of institutions should it have? China's ethnic minorities saw an opportunity to slip the Han-Chinese imperial leash. Tibet broke away after 1912 and remained independent until the People's Liberation Army rolled in two generation later in 1951. Outer Mongolia broke away with Russian help to become the People's Republic of Mongolia in 1924. The Muslims of Xinjiang also attempted to leave. Certain regional warlords simply wanted home rule, such as the opium-financed Yan Xishan, long the ruler of Shanxi, or the opium-financed Long Yun of the Lolo minority, long the ruler of Yunnan. Others had national ambitions such as Li Zongren of the Guangxi group in the South, the Zhang clan of Manchuria, and Feng Yuxiang, the Christian warlord of North China. The latter type desired to reunify China under their personal hegemony and so constituted alternatives to Chiang Kai-shek's government.

Many Chinese interpreted China's inability to fend off the West in the nineteenth century, its ensuing cascade of internal rebellions, and its comparative technological backwardness as indicators of Confucianism's bankruptcy as a ruling ideology. Exposure to Western ideas, often through Japanese translations, introduced a panoply of competing ideologies and analytical frameworks: republicanism, utilitarianism, liberalism, capitalism, social Darwinism, federalism, anarchism, and, most potently with the gathering economic depression, fascism and communism. With so many choices and so little experience with any of them, political debates were intense and rapidly became violent. Assassination and civil war became the default method to decide.

THE REUNIFICATION OF CHINA

When the founder of the Republic of China, Sun Yat-sen, suddenly died of liver cancer in early 1925, a competition erupted among his civil and military subordinates for leadership of his Nationalist Party. Two members of his entourage had great standing throughout urban China, Hu Hanmin, a mentor of the rightwing Western Hills group and press mogul who owned key news outlets and opposed cooperation with either Russia or the Chinese Communists, and Wang Jingwei, the brilliant orator renowned for his youthful assassination attempt in 1910 against the Manchu prince regent (Puyi's father) and miraculous escape from capital punishment. They focused on the levers of civil power, while a lesser-known figure, Chiang Kai-shek, focused on the levers of military power.[2] Chiang won the first round of the succession when he led the Northern Expedition to victory and Wang left the country for temporary exile.

Chiang Kai-shek had risen from poverty to receive a military education in both China and Japan. He returned to Japan repeatedly thereafter and became an early supporter of Sun Yat-sen, who frequented Japan as a place of periodic exile. In 1911, Chiang participated in the fighting in Shanghai on the antidynastic side, making formative contacts. Shanghai would become the center of his developing power base, which soon included the underworld Green Gang, whose power extended throughout the Yangzi River valley. As a Zhejiang man, he was from the province one removed from Jiangsu, the location of Shanghai.

In Russia, as in China, an increasingly ineffective imperial order had collapsed and the country had fallen into civil war. Because the Bolsheviks rapidly reunited the tsarist empire and created a New Russia, they seemed to offer a potential model for the Nationalist Party. Russia was also the only great power to offer China aid. In 1923 Sun Yat-sen sent Chiang Kai-shek on a three-month trip to study Bolshevik Party, military, and political institutions. Chiang returned favorably impressed and the Nationalist Party soon modeled its civil and military institutions on Bolshevik designs, insinuating party members throughout the institutional structure. In May 1924 Chiang became the commandant of the newly established Whampoa Military Academy near Guangzhou.[3] Russian military advisers and financing made Whampoa the premier military institution of China and training ground for many of the top officers and officials such as Lin Biao, Nie Rongzhen, and Zhou Enlai for the Communists, and Chen Cheng, Dai Li, Du Yuming, He Yingqin, and Zhang Zhizhong for the Nationalists.[4] It became the nucleus of Chiang's contacts within the military, later known as the Whampoa group, and source of his personal power.

In the succession struggle following Sun's death, Chiang and Wang Jingwei became the final contenders after the assassination or exile of others. They cooperated with the Chinese and Russian Communists in order to plan a Northern Expedition to reunite China from the south. On 5 June 1926 Chiang became the commander in chief of the National Revolutionary Army, soon in supreme command of eight armies, three from Hunan, two from Guangdong, and one each from Guangxi, Yunnan, and the Whampoa Military Academy, for a total of 2.2 million men. In addition allied armies in Manchuria, Sichuan, and Yunnan cooperated. Military expenditures took up 78 percent of national income. To put this extraordinary figure in perspective, during the height of World War II, military expenses consumed no more than 38 percent of the U.S. GNP.[5]

Chiang Kai-shek earned the mandate to rule in the manner of the great founding emperors by reuniting China militarily. He did so in a two-phased expedition, with a hiatus, when he took time off to annihilate his erstwhile Communist allies, line up Japanese cooperation for the second phase, and marry into one of the wealthiest families of China. The first phase followed the route of the nineteenth-century Taiping Rebellion.[6] On 1 July 1926, South China's armies set out and city after city fell before them. On 12 July, Changsha, the capital of Hunan, fell. The Yangzi River sister cities of Hanyang, Hankou, and Wuchang, today collectively known as Wuhan, fell in succession. On 6 November Hanyang fell, followed the next day by Hankou. On Double Ten 1926 (10/10/26), the fifteenth anniversary of the Wuchang Uprising that toppled the Qing dynasty, the Nationalists took Wuchang, the capital of Hubei, defeating the key Northern warlord, Wu Peifu, leader of the Zhili group based in Zhili, Hebei, Henan, and Hunan. On 5 November the Yangzi River port of Jiujiang fell. On 8 November Chiang's forces took Nanchang, the capital of Jiangxi, inflicting heavy losses on Sun Chuanfang, a defector from the Zhili group, now based in Nanjing, Jiangsu, Anhui, Jiangxi, Zhejiang, and Fujian, and defeated him by the end of the winter. Sun Chuanfang's key warlord allies, Zhang Zuolin and Yan Xishan, then defected.

With these victories, on 26 November, the Nationalists moved their capital from Guangzhou in the deep south to the central China city of Wuhan and ground zero for the death of the dynastic system. Supporters of the Nationalist left wing and the Communists, not Chiang Kai-shek loyalists, dominated this government. As the Northern Expedition continued, on 18 December, Fuzhou, the capital of Fujian, fell, followed on 18 February 1927, by Hangzhou, the capital of Zhejiang.[7] The Yangzi River cities of Shanghai and Nanjing fell on 22 and 24 March, respectively. This put the Nationalists in possession of everything south of the Yangzi, the conventional divide between North and South China. North China remained beyond Nationalist reach and mainly in the hands of the Manchurian warlord, Zhang Zuolin, whose writ extended as far south as Shandong, and his rival, Feng Yuxiang, based in Inner Mongolia, whose writ extended to Gansu, Shaanxi, and Henan. These two warlords surrounded Yan Xishan, who defied all from his strategic enclave in Shanxi.

Upon reaching Shanghai, Chiang Kai-shek took a breather to clean house. He perceived an impeding revolution from within, with his Communist allies attempting to wrest political control by dominating the Wuhan government while he was off fighting at the front. On 12 April 1927, he precipitously ended the Nationalist Party's United Front with the Chinese Communist Party, in effect since 1923. In the so-called 12 April Coup d'État and ensuing White Terror, Nationalist troops under Bai Chongxi of the Guangxi group and Green Gang members slaughtered any Chinese Communists they could find, wiping out the strong Communist presence in the Shanghai labor movement.[8]

The Nationalist Party Investigative Office, established in 1926, hit its stride during the White Terror. The organization grew rapidly to more than thirty-six hundred employees in 1937 under the baleful eye of Dai Li, its director.[9] Intelligence gathering focused inward on party loyalty, not outward against external foes. Chiang warned the Japanese of the impending butchery as they were also eager to eradicate communism.[10] Over the next few months, the White Terror left three thousand to four thousand Communist Party members and thirty thousand others dead, and twenty-five thousand imprisoned, virtually eliminating their presence in urban South China.[11] On 18 April 1927, Chiang set up a rival government in Nanjing.

The split with the Communists caused a break with Russia, the sponsor of the Chinese Communist Party and benefactor of the Nationalist Party. Russian military and financial aid had made the Northern Expedition possible. Chiang now required a great power replacement, a role that he, given his studies in Tokyo, intended Japan to fill.

At the height of his success, Chiang suddenly resigned as commander in chief, beginning a career pattern of brief resignations. The armies of both the Wuhan and Nanjing governments had continued military operations after the April purge. Wuhan troops under Feng Yuxiang had set out for Henan, while Nanjing troops had crossed the Yangzi River. Chiang had deployed his forces to Shandong in June but was forced back. The Guangxi group refused to come to his aid but turned south and then refused to coordinate with him in the Xuzhou Campaign. When he lost in July to Sun Chuanfang, the Guangxi group lobbied for his removal. Just as Chiang had used the Communists, so the Guangzi group had intended to use him to reunify China militarily, shifting power to within its reach, and then eliminate him. However, it lacked the military capability to hold land north of the Yangzi. The Guangxi leader, Li Zongren, who detested Chiang, made Chiang's resignation in August the price for cooperation against Sun Chuanfang, or so the conventional tale goes.[12]

In the fall of 1927, Chiang used his respite from national leadership to travel to Japan for secret talks with both Prime Minister Tanaka Giichi and representatives from Zhang Zuolin, the latter still alive but soon to be dead. To complete the Northern Expedition and incorporate North China and Manchuria, Chiang needed the cooperation of both the Manchurian warlord and Japan lest the Imperial Japanese Army intervene.[13] Tanaka was a man with whom Chiang presumably had something in common: Both had long army careers, had earned the rank of general, and enjoyed amassing political positions. At the time Tanaka was concurrently serving as both the foreign and prime ministers.

The Tanaka government, Chiang Kai-shek's South China government, and Zhang Zuolin's North China government all dealt bilaterally behind the back of each other. Chiang wanted Japan to stand aside while he united China and eliminated the Communists. He hoped that his anticommunism would be sufficient for the Japanese to tolerate the reunification. The Japanese preferred a divided China. They were willing to tolerate a Nationalist-controlled China up to the Great Wall but wanted Manchuria, the focus of their investments, to remain their sphere of influence, where they could contain Chinese nationalistic demands for the forfeiture of these investments.[14]

The Japanese government had been very supportive of Chiang after Chinese troops of disputed party origin had killed six foreign nationals as the Northern Expedition took Nanjing in March of 1927. The deaths caused an international uproar and became known in Chinese iconography as the Nanjing Incident. Chiang settled on foreign terms. He apologized to the countries that had lost citizens and promised to punish the Communists, whom he held responsible. The United States found the settlement so much to its liking that it declared Manchuria to be an integral part of China, not something the Japanese wanted to hear.[15] The Japanese were even more approving of the White Terror. As Tanaka explained in May, "If Chiang and his supporters can continue suppressing the Communists and can guarantee their statements concerning their own internal unification, the Japanese government will support morality and justice, and will help them realize their political goals."[16]

The Japanese were less enchanted with Zhang Zuolin, who had become increasingly hostile, promoting the development of railway lines competing with Japanese-owned lines, and whose military ambitions to dominate North China had set off hyperinflation in Manchuria.[17] Zhang was willing to tolerate a divided China so long as he got the northern half all the way south to the Yangzi River. Tanaka told Chiang he was Japan's man in China. Although the Tanaka cabinet still considered Zhang to be Japan's man in Manchuria, if he did not cooperate, Japan would trade him in for Chiang. In October 1927 Zhang caved on Japanese railway development plans for five new connector lines in Manchuria, a neuralgic point for Chinese nationalism.[18]

Upon returning to China in November 1927, Chiang also used his break from official leadership to exile his lawful wife to America and marry into one of the financially most well-connected families of Shanghai, the Soong family of the Hakka minority. Charles Jones Soong (spelled double "o" according to his preferences) had temporarily emigrated as a child to the United States, where he converted to Christianity; he then returned home to make a fortune marketing Bibles and noodles, undoubtedly a commercial first. Soong raised three sons, one a prominent Nationalist diplomat and financier, T. V. Soong, and three daughters renowned for their intelligence and two also renowned for their beauty. The eldest but least seductive was the one daughter to have children. She married Kong Xiangxi (known as H. H. Kung in the West), the financial architect for Chiang Kai-shek's government and supposedly a direct descendant of Confucius.[19] The next, Soong Chingling, had married the father of the Republic of China, Sun Yatsen, a man twenty-six years her senior, who had started the Soong-in-law tradition of exiling his legal wife without bothering about an official divorce. The youngest, Soong Mayling, married Chiang Kaishek in December 1927, just in time for Chiang to reclaim his official positions in January 1928. The marriage added money, prestige, and the flawless English of his wife to Chiang's arsenal.

In January of 1928, Chiang sent a representative back to Tokyo and promised not to deploy troops north of the Great Wall, while Japan agreed that Zhang Zuolin, then ensconced in Beijing, would withdraw his troops to Manchuria.[20] In April, Chiang resumed the Northern Expedition with the goal of uniting China up to the Great Wall, following in part a strategy laid out by the Japanese. The Imperial Japanese Army had great expertise in the proclivities of each Chinese warlord. By 1918 it had officers stationed in major Chinese cities, military advisers attached to the main warlords, and an associated intelligence-gathering service. Chiang followed Japanese advice on deployments and alliances: He allied with the remaining key North China warlords, Feng Yuxiang and Yan Xishan, each in command of an army, as well as his South China rival Li Zongren, in command of the Guangxi group army, and set out to bring Zhang Zuolin to heel.[21]

At this point the escalating politics of China and Japan's many incidents intervened. When the Nationalists took Jinan, the provincial capital of Shandong, on 1 May 1928, the Japanese responded massively to protect their investments. By the time their troops wrested control of Jinan from the Nationalists, more than six thousand Chinese had died. This became known as the Jinan Incident. As in the Nanjing Incident a year earlier, Chiang settled on foreign terms. He withdrew his troops and did not pursue the issue of the thousands of dead Chinese.[22] His countrymen remained outraged by the deaths.

His forces proceeded north. On 8 June Beijing fell, followed on 12 June by Tianjin. On 28 June the Nationalists changed the name of Beijing to *Pei-p'ing* (Beiping), literally from "Northern Capital" to "Northern Peace" with the connotation of "the pacified north," in order to demonstrate that the official capital had moved to Nanjing, literally "Southern Capital."[23] As Zhang Zuolin attempted to decamp before Nationalist troops entered Beijing, he and his railway carriage met the handiwork of Kantō Army bomb makers on 4 June on the ride home, putting a period on a long and checkered career. Zhang's son, Zhang Xueliang, after considering his rapidly shrinking options, concluded that an alliance with the Nationalists was the best among bad choices. This completed the nominal reunification of China, and on 31 December 1928, Chiang Kai-shek proclaimed the reunification complete.

Chinese terminology is misleading. The Northern Expedition was no expedition, a term suggesting a secondary military operation far from the home country. The Northern Expedition involved 1.1 million combatants, was fought in twelve of China's eighteen core provinces south of the Great Wall (in distinction to the Tibetan, Muslim, Mongol, and Manchu lands beyond), consisted of a succession of conventional battles, lasted two and a half years, and caused unknown thousands of civilian and military deaths.[24] It helped produce the 1927 famine in northwest China affecting 60 million and killing 3 to 6 million and caused the reorientation of Chinese foreign policy.[25] Russia was out. Japan was in but not in control of the Kantō Army. Whether one considers the so-called Northern Expedition a regional war or a nationwide civil war, either way it was no mere expedition.

STATE BUILDING DURING THE NANJING DECADE

Chiang Kai-shek's announcement of the success of the Northern Expedition officially ended the seventeen years of civil war since the fall of the Qing dynasty. China the failed state was no longer. Chiang had put Humpty Dumpty back together again. He had eliminated, neutralized, or co-opted his most powerful warlord rivals to complete the military requirements for state building. From 1927 until 1937, during the so-called Nanjing decade, the Nationalist government in Nanjing focused on the civil side of state building under the leadership initially of Hu Hanmin and then of Wang Jingwei.

In October 1928, the Nationalists established a five-branch government and began a period of political tutelage. Sun Yat-sen, whom the Nationalists and the Communists both credit as the founding father of modern China, envisioned a five-branch system with the three conventional Western branches – executive, legislative, and judicial – plus two branches of dynastic origin concerning the literati, the lettered class that had traditionally served as China's administrators. These two branches were the examination and control branches. The former vetted civil servants before they could assume office, while the latter oversaw them once in office. These branches harkened back to the Board of Rites and the Censorate, respectively.[26]

Sun also envisioned political development in three stages, starting with military rule in order to reunify the country (mission complete with Chiang's reflagging of Beijing to Beiping on 28 June 1928), followed by a period of political tutelage under the rule of the Nationalist Party to prepare the Chinese people for constitutional government in the final phase.[27] In practice, the period of political tutelage did not end until 2000 in Taiwan, with fully democratic presidential elections, and remains an unfulfilled promise on the mainland.

All Nationalist factions treated Sun's writings as holy text in order to legitimize their own political views. Each cited him in the manner of an ancient sage, using the archaic verb 言曰 to indicate authenticity, orthodoxy, and irrefutability. Initially Hu Hanmin played the role of "tutor in chief." In May 1931 he drafted the eighty-nine-article Provisional Constitution of the Political Tutelage Period. On the basis of this constitution, Chiang made himself the chairman of the Nationalist Party and head of the executive branch. A subsequent constitution to end the period of political tutelage was drafted on 5 May 1936, but the necessary elections and constitutional debates were delayed for years. The escalation of the war in 1937 led to the centralization of power under Chiang, and the provisional provincial assembly did not convene until 1943.[28]

The Nationalists also attempted to implement Sun Yat-sen's land-to-the-tiller program. On 30 June 1930, the 397-article land reform law originally drafted by Hu Hanmin became law. As a first step, the law called for the reorganization of land registers, in chaos after years of warfare. The law set a rent ceiling of 37.5 percent of the harvest and eliminated the many supplementary land taxes that over the years had accumulated to exceed the land tax itself. The law also returned the land tax to the localities so that the money was collected and spent locally. Land registration proceeded unevenly, but many provinces implemented these reforms at least in part.[29] The Nationalists also became more effective at borrowing money internally.[30]

In June 1931 the Nationalists introduced a comprehensive Westernized civil service system, requiring selection and promotion based on a combination of academic credentials, on-the-job ability, and Nationalist Party loyalty. In the first sitting of the highly competitive civil service examination, 2,177 persons took the test. Unlike a fully evolved Western government bureaucracy, in which most of the bureaucracy remains in place while the upper echelon turns over according to election results, the Nationalists created a bureaucracy both from the top down and from the bottom up. As the regional war with Japan went from bad to worse, party loyalty became the increasingly important determinant of government employ.[31]

As in Communist governments, the Nationalist Party had an extensive party organization carefully integrated into both civil and military institutions from the national down to the local level. No other party could possibly match it. Another extraconstitutional organization, the Military Affairs Commission, increasingly overshadowed all other institutions because, as Mao Zedong so presciently observed, "Out of the barrel of a gun, grows political power."[32] Hu Hanmin and Wang Jingwei lacked the gun and eventually found themselves out of power.

Intolerance of dissent marked Hu Hanmin's tenure from 1928 to 1931 as president of the legislative branch. In his words: "There is no party rule, only military rule." Yet he dismissed those in uniform as "having neither learning nor ability," a vulnerably arrogant point of view for a bespectacled intellectual in a time of civil war. After his resignation followed rapidly by his arrest, the Nationalists became more forgiving of dissent and opposition parties when Wang Jingwei replaced Hu as the chief political architect of civil institutions.[33] But Chiang Kai-shek's arrest of Hu created long-term and deep divisions between Chiang and the Guangdong group. Both Wang and Hu were born in Guangdong.

Chiang had long used the rivalry between Wang and Hu to strengthen his own power base while they undermined each other.[34] When Chiang had purged the Communists during the Northern Expedition and they had denounced him as a new warlord, Wang had written a letter urging Nationalist Party members to "rise up in arms and wipe away this rebel."[35] As much as Chiang despised Wang, the latter had powerful backers in the Guangxi and Guangdong groups. So, Wang Jingwei served as president of the Executive Yuan from February 1932 until November 1935, when he resigned after being nearly fatally shot.[36] During these years, Wang had a reputation for personal incorruptibility and the deep respect of many members of the Nationalist Party for overseeing comprehensive legal, fiscal, agricultural, and educational reforms that produced a surge in economic development.

In the heady early days in Nanjing, before warfare had fatally compromised civil institutions (not only in China but in Japan too), Wang introduced new codes for civil law (1929–31), civil procedure (1935), criminal law (1935), and criminal procedure (1935).[37] The day the Nationalist Party established the government in Nanjing, it simultaneously founded Academia Sinica as the country's central educational and research institution. Academia Sinica sponsored state-funded research and served as the umbrella organization to coordinate research nationwide, with heavy emphasis on the sciences. In 1931 Wang established the National Economic Council (NEC). Supporters of Chiang Kai-shek founded a competing organization, the National Resources Commission (NRC), in 1932 to promote economic modernization projects. Both institutions focused on applied science in the areas of agriculture, industry, and the military. After Wang's near-assassination, Chiang took over the NEC and subsumed it under the NRC.[38] The plans developed in this period but not implemented because of the escalation of the Second Sino-Japanese War lay on the shelves to be picked up by postwar governments eager to rebuild on both sides of the Taiwan Strait.[39]

Wang saw himself in the thankless role of China's greatest statesman of the nineteenth century, Li Hongzhang, who had made bitter but unavoidable compromises with Japan and the West because of China's military inferiority. From the invasion of Manchuria until the Second United Front in 1936, Chinese popular anger against the Nationalist strategy of appeasement of Japan focused not on Chiang but on Wang, who served at the Nationalist foreign minister from 1933 to 1935. Wang had ordered the signing of the unpopular Tanggu Truce in 1933 because Chiang's troops could not hold off the Japanese. Reinforcements were unavailable because so many troops were engaged in the Fourth Encirclement Campaign against the Communists in Jiangxi.[40]

Hu Hanmin led the antiappeasement wing of the Nationalist Party, which advocated alliance with the West.[41] The pro-Western Nationalist group also recommended gravitating toward the West in an attempt to strike a harder bargain with Japan. Prominent members included the key Soong clan members, T. V. Soong and Kong Xiangxi, and China's most famous educator, Hu Shi. Wang Jingwei, by contrast, advised caution. He regarded with contempt those who called for war but would be safely behind the lines when war began, saying that they "sang the high-flown tune" in order to rally support but offered no feasible plans. Wang belonged to the Low-Tune group, which opposed the High-Tune group's insistence upon war.[42] In 1933 he reproached: "They knew nothing about warfare, yet they attacked any peaceful settlement as traitorous ... and when the country was overrun by the enemy, they had no way to save it but could only perish with it." In a letter to Hu Shi, he drew on historical analogies of Ming and Tang dynasty generals (Yuan Chonghuan and Han Geshu, respectively) to write that he would prefer to be executed on false charges of appeasement and treason, as they were, than to send armies into hopeless battles. In the end, he essentially got his wish. Wang believed China had no choice but to negotiate with Japan because it could not fight and win.[43] As long as he remained in office, he provided political cover to Chiang Kai-shek because Chinese blamed Wang, not a general, for appeasing Japan.[44]

In keeping with Russian and Nazi practices, in 1933 the Nationalists put in place a Four-Year Production Plan. Considerable economic development took place. China lost much of its coal reserves with the occupation of Manchuria. Afterward, more than half of its remaining coal was from Shanxi, the home of the warlord Yan Xishan, one of Chiang's least reliable allies. While the privately owned coal production in unoccupied areas stagnated, government-sponsored mines made up one-fifth of China's coal production by 1945.[45] The Nationalists also made progress developing a chemical industry and expanded the rail and road systems by eleven thousand miles and sixty thousand miles, respectively.[46]

On 4 November 1935 the government implemented currency reform as a solution to three problems: the U.S. Silver Purchase Act of 1934, the deepening agricultural depression, and Japan's growing control over North China. From the 1890s until 1932, the international price of silver had declined as countries moved from the silver to the gold standard and their central banks liquidated their silver holdings. Until 1932 the price of silver in China remained higher than the international price so that silver flowed in. This had benefits since the silver inflow effectively increased the money supply of the silver-backed currency without causing undue inflation.[47]

The U.S. decision to bale out its faltering silver mining industry through the 1934 Silver Purchase Act caused silver prices to rise, leading to an outflow of Chinese silver being sold to foreigners. This contraction of the silver-backed money supply caused turmoil. The price of silver shot up, and the price of goods fell precipitously in relationship to silver. Yet taxes did not decline but continued to rise, cutting deeply into the declining general income and causing acute financial distress in rural China. A smaller supply of available silver also caused interest rates to rise, making borrowing more expensive. Those who had borrowed money in the expectation of stable or increasing asset values found themselves paying interest on purchases no longer worth their purchase price. Bankruptcies ensued. When the money dried up, so did purchases. Manufacturing declined. Unemployment rose. The Great Depression, like so many events, took on a scale of its own in China.[48]

The combination of the silver currency shortage, the decline in commodity prices, the international economic depression, the decrease in production, and the decline in credit resulted in the collapse of agriculture. A drought in the Northwest had already caused the famine of 1928–30. Flooding of the Yangzi and Huai Rivers caused another in Jiangsu and Anhui in 1931, and nationwide floods led to the famine of 1934. The acreage sown shrank, followed by a 41.7 percent decline in customs revenues exacerbating these economic effects. In Shanxi, for instance, by 1935 land prices had fallen to one-fifth of their 1927 values. Finances and investment left rural areas for the cities and then left the cities for Shanghai, explaining why Shanghai was such a crucial economic base for the Nationalists. The year 1933 was the peak year for Shanghai. Thereafter, its economy followed the rest of China and tanked.[49]

The Nationalists paid careful attention to the rural crisis. In addition to tax reform and property registration, in January 1935, they established a system of agricultural education, including a host of committees to examine key rural issues and to study agronomy. They encouraged banks to lend to farmers and promoted agricultural credit and cooperatives. Earlier, after the flood of the Huai River in 1931, the government addressed irrigation and the long-neglected infrastructure to contain rain-swollen rivers. A combination of decent weather, relative peace, and reforms produced a good harvest in 1936.[50]

Following the lead of the Western nations that had abandoned the gold standard, China abandoned the silver standard and prohibited the issuance of privately produced silver ingots as a form of currency. Previously, because China had backed its currency in silver, many people held their savings in the form of small silver ingots. The new policy allowed only three Nationalist banks, located in South China beyond the reach of Japan but under the administration of a central currency research board, to issue legal tender. The new law required the conversion of all other currencies and the exchange of all silver for cash. This put the currency of North China under Chinese not Japanese control and no longer left the effective tax rate to the vagaries of the volatile silver market.[51] The Kantō Army soon responded with military expansion, its so-called North China Operation, to transform North China into another Manchukuo.[52]

The Nationalists also reformed local and national fiscal administration. In keeping with Western, not Chinese practices, they differentiated between national and local income. In the past, the central government had collected revenues from a smorgasbord of tariffs and taxes on items ranging from salt, to cigarettes, to postal packages, to mining. Under the reformed system, the central government collected taxes on income, inheritance, stock exchanges, company and trademark registrations, agricultural production, factory production, and so on, while local governments collected taxes on business, land, employment, goods, and so on. In 1935 the Nationalists differentiated further into three levels of financial administration: national, provincial, and county. At the time of the countrywide Japanese invasion in 1937, the Nationalists had completed this differentiation in most provinces.[53]

Nevertheless, tax collection remained a festering problem. The Nationalists could not collect taxes outside their five core provinces of Jiangsu, Zhejiang, Anhui, Jiangxi, and Hunan. Instead, the other provinces in the Nationalist coalition demanded special funds from Nanjing before they would consider redeploying their own troops, whose numbers they kept secret.[54]

Despite an extraordinarily difficult international, political, and economic environment, the Nationalists fostered economic recovery and political consolidation. By 1936, Chinese imports had increased 45 percent over the previous year's figures, and its exports had increased 36 percent. Japanese trade with China, however, had suffered as a result of China's tariff increases. For instance, Japanese exports of cotton products to North China declined by 60 percent in 1933 and 50 percent more in 1934. Other products showed similar reductions. The Japanese responded by encouraging smuggling, which undermined Nationalist customs receipts.[55]

The Nationalists made their many legal, land, civil service, economic planning, agricultural, educational, currency, and fiscal reforms despite extraordinary military expenditures. From 1928 to 1934, although military expenses continued to dominate the government budget, their share declined by nearly 15 percent, from 48 to 41 percent, while civil expenses tripled from 8 to 25 percent. Debts fell as a proportion of the budget by nearly one-third from 37 percent to 25 percent.[56] Other statistics show a more precipitous decline of military appropriations from 1932 to 1935 from 57 to 27 percent of the national budget.[57]

This long recitation of the many changes implemented by the Nationalist Party should make clear the breadth of the reforms undertaken not during a decade of blissful stability but during a period of continuing civil war and gathering Japanese aggression. The conventional tale emphasizes the many shortcomings of these reforms as if anyone could solve China's litany of pressing problems within a decade. All of the institutions and laws of the Nanjing decade had only just started to function when the 1937 escalation of the Second Sino-Japanese War put civil reforms on indefinite hold.

This was the civil side of state building. There was also a military side. On the surface the Northern Expedition had produced a unified China. China has repeatedly shattered over its long history. Some dynasties ruled only the North, while others ruled only the South, and they placed their capitals accordingly. The choice of Nanjing as the capital reflected the weakness of Nationalist rule in North China. Otherwise, the Nationalists would have chosen Beijing, the internationally recognized capital ever since 1420, when the Ming dynasty transferred its capital from Nanjing to Beijing.

Chiang's influence over North China in 1928 remained tenuous. None of his three main North China warlord allies – Feng Yuxiang, Zhang Xueliang, and Yan Xishan – wished to strengthen Chiang's grip over the North, and Feng and possibly Zhang intended to unseat him. All of these warlords controlled their territory through a coalition of local warlords, who also defected when they saw their interests threatened. Warlord rule was not based on institutions that survived beyond the political life span of their leaders. Rather, rule in China was based on personalities and the loyalists such key political leaders could muster, while the loyalists depended on the followers they could muster, and so on, down a long political chain; the longer and broader the chain, the stronger the political personality on top. The complexity and secrecy of such webs of loyalty make Chinese politics murky. Warlords were uncertain of the strength of the loyalties of their own followers let alone those of the followers of their political rivals. Rule in China was personal. A hallmark of strong institutions is stable successions for leadership positions. To the present day, this problem remains unsolved in China and solved in Taiwan only in the 1990s.

Chiang's rule was not firm even in South China. Warlords in Sichuan and Yunnan jealously guarded their regional autonomy, while the leaders of Guangxi Province, the so-called Guangxi group, had national ambitions and through 1949 constituted the most important alternative to Chiang's rule within the Nationalist Party. Guangxi and Guangdong had formed the original Nationalist nucleus of support during Sun Yat-sen's time. But with the rise of the Zhejiang native Chiang Kai-shek the nucleus shifted to the north to Zhejiang and Jiangsu. Chiang attempted to split the two southernmost provinces by securing the allegiance of Guangdong with the inclusion of Wang Jingwei and Hu Hanmin, while considering Guangxi beyond hope.[58] Nevertheless, after the Japanese escalation in 1937, even the Guangxi group rallied around Chiang.[59]

Chiang commanded the loyalties of just three of the eight armies making up the National Revolutionary Armies, or about 5–10 percent of the total armed forces according to some statistics.[60] According to Japanese estimates made in the 1930s, in 1929 Zhang Xueliang controlled 365,000 troops; Yan Xishan, 129,070; Feng Yuxiang, 250,000; the Guangxi group, 75,900; and miscellaneous warlords, another 699,000 troops, against 619,300 troops loyal to Chiang. While the miscellaneous warlords were not particularly well equipped, Zhang possessed more planes than did the central government.[61]

Three key groups composed Chiang's loyalists.[62] They centered in the party, the technocratic elite, and the military, respectively. The so-called CC group, named after the brothers Chen Guofu and Chen Lifu (first letter of the surname times two), based its power within the party, and specifically, the Nationalist Party's Organization Department, which ran the party from the national level all the way down to the grass roots and was modeled on the Bolshevik Party structure. Chen Guofu headed the Organization Department, while Chen Lifu headed its Investigation

Division. The CC group asserted power by monopolizing appointments, deploying the party's secret police, controlling the press, and infiltrating the national and provincial administrative bureaucracy as well as various educational and cultural institutions.[63] Jiangsu, and particularly Shanghai, constituted its main territorial base. Members remained Confucian traditionalists in intellectual outlook. They denied the need radically to restructure China but sought to restore conventional moral and religious values. They staunchly opposed agricultural (read "land") reform, distrusted the West, and intended to expel foreigners, whom they branded as imperialists. They tried to popularize this platform through the management of educational curricula and cultural institutions. They planned to make the Nationalist Party Chiang's vehicle to power to the exclusion of other political parties.[64]

The technocrats necessary to run the modern part of the economy composed the Political Study group. It lacked a rank-and-file membership, but relied instead on an elite following of bankers, administrators, technicians, and intellectuals concentrated in the modern part of the private sector, particularly in industry and finance. It included the dominant figures of Shanghai commerce and such members of Chiang's in-law clan as T. V. Soong, who held key governmental posts concerned with finance. Other members served as ministers with economic portfolios and as provincial governors. In these positions they focused on financial and business policy and provincial administration in order to foster economic development. They favored civil not military governance.[65]

Military power formed the basis for Whampoa group, whose key members were former Whampoa Military Academy staff and students. They dominated the Military Affairs Commission in command of the Nationalist armed forces and constituted Chiang Kai-shek's praetorian guard.[66] They focused on preventing a military coup and on defeating Chiang's key enemies both inside and outside Nationalist China. Sometimes the Whampoa group worked through the Blue Shirt Society, based on Adolf Hitler's so-called brown shirts and under the leadership of Dai Li, also the head of a second secret police organization. Chiang's Blue Shirts engaged in security training, political indoctrination, mass recruitment, clandestine operations, the infiltration of regional armies, and propaganda efforts to encourage defections from these armies, particularly in provinces where the Communists were active.[67]

The CC and Whampoa groups provided the political and military underpinnings of Chiang's power. Both supported traditional and nationalistic goals. Their influence resulted from a community of vital interests concerning immediate survival. The Political Study group supplied the financial underpinnings of Chiang's power, but its ties were based on mutual self-interest of a less pressing nature: a desire to promote economic growth. Americans felt most affinity to this weakest segment of Chiang's supporters. The most vital segment was the army.[68]

Although the CC, Political Study, and Whampoa groups shared a strong loyalty to Chiang Kai-shek, they favored competing priorities. The CC group desired a Confucian revival; the Political Study group wanted to modernize the economy; while the Whampoa group focused on those military units under Chiang's direct command. The three groups were mutually hostile in their competition for Chiang's favor, while Chiang kept them divided in order to rule.

Chiang remained in power by preventing the rise of any potential political rivals. He did so not by unifying China, but by keeping divided not only his enemies but also his supporters, a strategy not of choice but of necessity. His strategy reflected the realities of China as it was, not an idea of China as it could be in the future. His predecessor, the infamous Empress Dowager, had used this strategy with great dexterity during the twilight years of the Qing dynasty, when, for four decades, this minor concubine of a deceased emperor remained in power in contravention to Manchu norms for succession. Chiang followed her divide-and-rule strategy not out of deference to the old lady, reviled by Han on both sides of the Taiwan Strait, but in response to China's political environment, which remained based on personal loyalties not on institutions with legally circumscribed jurisdictions. Such institutions had yet to be created.

In addition to factionalism among Chiang loyalists, many parts of the Nationalist Party actively opposed Chiang. The French vice chief of staff for National Defense from 1946 to 1949, General Lionel Max Chassin of the Air Force, bemoaned that Chiang did not make full use of his best commanders. Who were they? Fu Zuoyi was associated with both the Shanxi group of Yan Xishan and the Fengtian group of Zhang

Xueliang, responsible for kidnapping and threatening to kill Chiang in 1936. Bai Chongxi was a leader of the Guangxi group, which repeatedly attempted to overthrow Chiang.[69] These generals represented alternatives to Chiang's leadership, so Chiang put them in theaters where they could not stage a coup.

Such a power structure had implications: Of the troops under Nationalist command, at least half were not necessarily loyal to Chiang. Some would not deploy out of province, such as the troops of Yan Xishan in Shanxi or the armies of western Sichuan. Others had to be deployed far from their homes to minimize their ability either to stage a coup at the top or to expand their regional power base into adjoining provinces. This was the case with armies of eastern Sichuan and Yunnan, which in the final stages of the long civil war were sent to Manchuria.[70] When such troops deployed far from home, however, they did not necessarily fight well and tended to defect when the going got rough. Almost all defections, which became endemic after 1945, were provincial, not national units. Many provincial commanders believed, not without cause, that the Nationalists made them cannon fodder so that Chiang could reserve his most loyal troops to ensure his personal survival.[71]

Before concluding that this was no way to run a government or an army, it is worth reflecting on how strong institutions come into being. Through no fault of their own, the Nationalists lacked strong governmental institutions. Their government was simply too new to have any, but they were trying to create some. Institutions become strong over time through the gradual and increasing acceptance of their legitimacy or a perception of their invincibility by a growing proportion of the population. This acceptance is a spider's web spun over time, where each strand remains fragile but in combination with many, many other strands can become powerful enough to hold together a nation. Garnering enough support to spin a strong web takes decades. Strong institutions derive their strength from general acceptance and general compliance. Before the acceptance and compliance become general, however, the spider's web remains vulnerable to destruction, particularly in wartime, when opposing sides sweep aside the laws and institutional processes of their enemies.

With the collapse of not only the Qing dynasty, but the entire dynastic system of government, the Nationalists inherited an institutional vacuum. The many warlords of China attempted to spin a web of power out of their armies, and those successful enough to dominate regions attempted to spin a web of civil as well as military institutions. But power in China remained based on personalities, and loyalties remained provincial until the end of the long Chinese civil war. This late development of nationalism helps explain the longevity of Manchu minority rule. Until the end of the Qing dynasty, the primary geographic loyalties for most Chinese remained their native place, their village or perhaps their province of birth, but not their country. Chinese spoke mutually unintelligible languages. While some dialects within North China are mutually intelligible, as are some within South China, North and South Chinese dialects generally are not. This linguistic barrier contributed to the historic divide between the North and the South as well as to Chiang's difficulty uniting the two.[72]

The deep Chinese sense of nation resulted from the fifteen-year Second Sino-Japanese War superimposed over the long Chinese civil war. In the long civil war, not surprisingly, those groups that most convincingly played the nationalism card (the Nationalists and the Communists) garnered the largest national following. The Japanese unwittingly fostered the development of nationalism by choosing a military strategy that made Chinese see ever more clearly their own common bonds in the face of a brutal Japanese invasion and occupation. At the end of the Northern Expedition in 1928, this sense of nation was just beginning to spread from the cities to the countryside, where the vast majority of Chinese lived.

The Nationalists had succeeded in turning chaos into a hostile coalition system but had not created a unified government. In the absence of strong institutions, they lacked regularized means to allocate political power, resources, or anything else. The Nationalist government in Nanjing began the long process of spinning spiders' webs. On 5 May 1936, it had drafted a constitution and established a National Assembly scheduled to adopt the constitution in 1937 to end the period of political tutelage and move into Sun Yat-sen's final stage of constitutional rule.[73] The Nationalists had done this all the while facing a civil war. The regional war, however, derailed the process, freezing time in the tutelage period until the passing of the Chiang dynasty. In the meantime, the civil war, the regional war, and the global war each ripped away at the laboriously constructed web.

THE DILEMMAS OF APPEASEMENT

Historians present the Nanjing decade as the golden period of Nationalist rule. Relative to what came before and what came after, the decade between 1927 and 1937 was indeed the best decade Chiang Kai-shek ever had on the mainland, but it coincided with continuing civil wars, repeated coup attempts, and a creeping regional war with Japan. From 1929 to 1937 Chiang Kai-shek, through military campaigns, co-optation, and diplomacy, relentlessly expanded Nationalist control from more than 20 to 66 percent of the population and from 8 to 25 percent of Chinese territory. Party membership nearly doubled from 270,000 to 520,000, but control over local authorities remained difficult.[74] Chiang faced a dilemma: Elimination of the most dangerous warlords was too costly. He lacked the forces to destroy their armies, but if he bought them off with high governmental posts, he positioned his most dangerous rivals to rise up against him at a time most convenient to them, and undoubtedly least convenient to him.

In 1929, the year after the Northern Expedition, Chiang's recent ally, Li Zongren, the head of the Guangxi group, rebelled once; another recent ally, Feng Yuxiang, the Christian warlord, rebelled twice; yet another Northern Expedition ally, the Hunan warlord, Tang Shengzhi, rebelled once. Chiang deployed his armies to put down each rebellion. Whether one considers them mutinies, coup attempts, or civil wars, they indicated that Chiang's rule was anything but stable let alone generally accepted.

These rebellions coalesced into a full-scale civil war in 1930 known in China as the Great War of the Central Plains. The Central Plains comprise the mid- to lower reaches of the Yellow River. The war involved more than 1 million combatants, lasted eight months, caused 300,000 casualties (half in Hebei, Shandong, and Henan), and ravaged five provinces between the lower reaches of the Yellow and Yangzi Rivers, the heart of the modern economy south of the Great Wall.[75] Zhang Xueliang, by remaining loyal to Chiang, made the crucial swing vote that carried the day, defeating Feng Yuxiang, Yan Xishan, the Guangxi group, and Wang Jingwei, who dreamed of an opposition government in Beijing.

Chiang deployed his Whampoa-trained troops to great effect. When the dust settled, he incorporated Feng's troops into the Nationalist

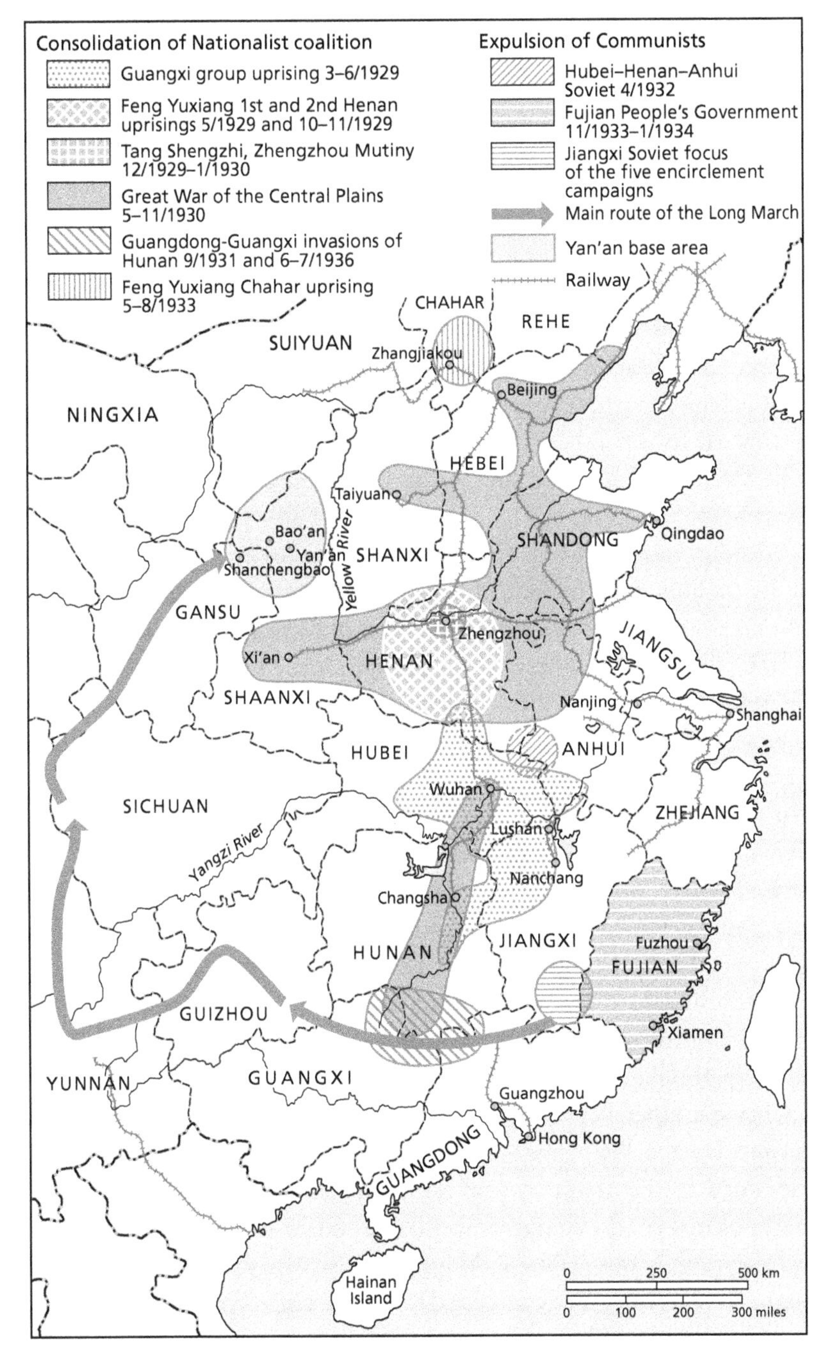
Consolidation of Nationalist coalition
Guangxi group uprising 3–6/1929
Feng Yuxiang 1st and 2nd Henan uprisings 5/1929 and 10–11/1929
Tang Shengzhi, Zhengzhou Mutiny 12/1929–1/1930
Great War of the Central Plains 5–11/1930
Guangdong-Guangxi invasions of Hunan 9/1931 and 6–7/1936
Feng Yuxiang Chahar uprising 5–8/1933
Expulsion of Communists
Hubei–Henan–Anhui Soviet 4/1932
Fujian People's Government 11/1933–1/1934
Jiangxi Soviet focus of the five encirclement campaigns
Main route of the Long March
Yan'an base area
Railway
CHAHAR
REHE
SUIYUAN
Zhangjiakou
Beijing
NINGXIA
HEBEI
Taiyuan
Bao'an
Yan'an
Shanchengbao
Yellow River
SHANXI
SHANDONG
Qingdao
GANSU
Zhengzhou
JIANGSU
Xi'an
HENAN
SHAANXI
Nanjing
Shanghai
HUBEI
ANHUI
SICHUAN
Wuhan
ZHEJIANG
Lushan
Yangzi River
Nanchang
Changsha
JIANGXI
Fuzhou
HUNAN
FUJIAN
GUIZHOU
Xiamen
YUNNAN
GUANGXI
Guangzhou
Hong Kong
GUANGDONG
Hainan Island
0
250
500 km
0
100
200
300 miles

Map 3 Civil War (1929–36): Nationalist Consolidation.

Army. Another unsuccessful rebellion in 1933 left Feng a bit player in Chinese politics until his death in 1948.[76] Yan Xishan and Li Zongren survived by retreating to their territorial bases, located on the periphery of Nationalist power. Yan returned to his home province of Shanxi, whose geography made it far more difficult to attack than to hold and whose opium crops and coal resources funded his army and his many economic development projects.[77]

This left Chiang's primary enemies separated from each other by huge distances and Chiang holding the central position, thus impeding further military collaboration. Victory added to his national stature and the legitimacy of his government and extended his effective power northward to the Yellow River. Chiang turned to what he considered to be the most dangerous threat, the Communists. Events bore out his assessment.

Within a month of Chiang's victory in the Great War of the Central Plains, he launched the first of five encirclement campaigns against the Communists, trying to eliminate them from their South China base area in Jiangxi Province, where Mao Zedong and Zhu De had set up the Jiangxi Soviet, yet another rival government. The First Encirclement Campaign from November 1930 to January 1931 failed to dislodge them. The Second Encirclement Campaign from March to May 1931 also failed. It followed on the heels of Chiang's unpopular arrest of the Guangdong-born Hu Hanmin upon his resignation as president of the Legislative Yuan on 28 February 1931.[78] The arrest outraged many Nationalists. Hu had stayed out of the Great War of the Central Plains, but as president of the Legislative Yuan he had rejected the drafting of a constitution as premature and as contrary to the principles of Sun Yat-sen. During the period of political tutelage, he believed, a party dictatorship should rule.[79]

Chiang's other key rival, the Guangdong-born Wang Jingwei, who had just backed the losing side in the Great War of the Central Plains, responded to the arrest by making common cause with other equally bad bookmakers, Li Zongren and Bai Chongxi of the Guangxi group, and Chen Jitang of the Guangdong group, to form a rival government in Guangzhou in May. They intended to reduce Chiang's civil and military power within the Nationalist Party and government. In early September they sent troops to invade southern Hunan.[80]

As Chiang faced secession from the south, he embarked on a Third Encirclement Campaign in July 1931. It went well even as the Nanjing and Guangzhou governments verged on civil war until the Japanese invasion of Manchuria caused a change in priorities.[81] The Guangzhou government dissolved in the hopes of taking over Nanjing. Chiang suspended the encirclement campaign after the Japanese attacked Shanghai in January 1932 (the First Shanghai Incident), when he redeployed and his troops valiantly fought. The Communists attributed their avoidance of encirclement to themselves, not to Japan, declaring war against Japan in April.[82]

Unlike the Chinese Communists, who only talked about fighting Japan in 1932, Chiang actually did. Although he lost in Shanghai, the Nationalist Party waged a more damaging economic war, a strategy that resonated with the Chinese population. The Japanese invasion of Manchuria fueled one of the most widespread anti-Japanese boycotts in Chinese history. The boycott had begun on 13 July 1931, before the invasion, and continued until the Tanggu peace agreement of 1933. In Fujian Japanese sales decreased on the order of 80 to nearly 100 percent. Before long, Japanese trade with China decreased by more than one-third. The invasion catalyzed the transformation of China's many Anti-Japanese Societies into National Salvation Societies to Resist Japan. Students organized an immediate boycott of Japanese goods, repeatedly petitioned the Nationalist government to declare war, and launched a campaign of escalating demonstrations that culminated in the resignation of Chiang Kai-shek on 15 December 1931 to form a national unity government, or so they thought.[83] This was his second brief resignation from power.

The Japanese may have believed that they had impeccable timing. Their invasion occurred at a particularly inconvenient moment for Chiang – when he was engaged in simultaneous fights against a rival government in Guangzhou and the Communists in the Third Encirclement Campaign. Chiang lacked the forces to deal with three enemies simultaneously. Chiang's primary North China warlord ally, Zhang Xueliang, did not even have his main forces in Manchuria at the time of the Japanese invasion, but in North China, where he harbored his father's ambitions to become the kingpin. He decided not to fight and Chiang agreed.[84] Japanese military strategy forced Chiang to call the encirclement campaign to a premature halt. Yet Japanese leaders wanted the Communists eliminated. Japanese military strategy also unwittingly reglued the Nationalist coalition, when Wang Jingwei returned to the fold and the South China groups made moves in the same direction.[85] The Guangzhou government agreed to dissolve upon the release from prison of Hu Hanmin and the resignation of Chiang Kai-shek. The Guangxi group kept its options open. Although its leaders acquiesced to Chiang's return to military command on 28 January 1932, they took out a $5 million loan from Japan in 1933 to purchase weapons.[86] Chiang's trump card remained his control over the preponderance of China's armed forces. His rivals could not fight Japan without him.

After the Shanghai truce of 5 May 1932, during the ensuing meeting of Nationalist notables at Lushan, Jiangxi in June, Chiang Kai-shek adopted a military strategy of internal pacification and external appeasement.[87] He intended to appease the Japanese while he annihilated the Communists in order to take on enemies one at a time.

In April 1932, Chiang deployed 400,000 troops to eliminate the Communist soviet on the Hubei-Henan-Anhui border area, sending the Communists on a prequel to the Long March.[88] In mid-1932, he resumed his encirclement campaigns of the mother soviet in Jiangxi, beginning his fourth, which still failed to overrun the resilient base. Again, unrelenting Japanese escalation increased the risk of concentrating forces against the Communists. The Fourth Encirclement Campaign coincided with Japan's Rehe and Great Wall Campaigns and the Tanggu Peace that ended them. Chiang appeased Japan in order to pursue the Communists. With the Tanggu Truce, he began his successful Fifth Encirclement Campaign in the fall of 1933, which continued until the following fall.[89] He employed a strategy of tightening rings of blockhouses with overlapping fire to strangle the Communist base area. The Communists then obliged by fighting from fixed positions to defend territory, rather than engaging in mobile warfare. Immobility allowed the Nationalists to move in to annihilate them.[90]

The numbers involved in the campaign speak volumes. Chiang deployed more than 900,000 men in the Fifth Encirclement Campaign against about 200,000 Communists. Chiang then halved the Communist forces to 100,000 before chasing 86,000 of them on the Long March to Yan'an, Shaanxi, where only 7,000 arrived in 1935.[91] To provide perspective on the enormity of these numbers, the United States deployed only 258,000 men against 62,000 Japanese soldiers during the Battle of Leyte Gulf in the Philippines, the beginning of one of the largest campaigns in the Pacific theater of World War II.[92] Afterward, Chiang pursued the Communist forces fleeing northward on the Long March and simultaneously prosecuted a relentless Three-Year War (1934–6) to eliminate the remaining Communist guerrilla presence in South China, where entire villages were leveled. Some say more than 1 million died. Those Communists who survived became the nucleus of the New Fourth Route Army.[93] Victory in the Fifth Encirclement Campaign marked the zenith of Chiang Kai-shek's power.[94]

Yet even at the zenith, Chiang Kai-shek had yet to assert central power over the country. Rather than a unitary government, he ruled over a coalition of warlords, whose autonomy had been reduced by the Northern Expedition, but who constantly tested his authority. His rule was weakest in the North, where Zhang Xueliang of Manchuria and Yan Xishan of Shanxi remained among his most autonomous warlord allies. Equally problematic were those in Guangdong and Guangxi in the South, who periodically attempted to wrest control over the government. Meanwhile, a growing Communist movement aimed to overturn the social order.

During the encirclement campaigns, the spectacle of Chinese massacring fellow Chinese at a time of continuing Japanese expansion horrified student activists and many others in urban China. In the spring of 1934, activists collected 900,000 signatures petitioning the Nationalists to fight Japan. Hu Hanmin piled in with the students. Until Chiang Kai-shek agreed to fight Japan, the anti-Japanese student movement continued to grow.[95] Had the Japanese limited their expansion to Manchuria, they might have be able to cut a deal with Chiang to make common cause of the containment of Russia and elimination of communism in China.

Instead, on 4 October 1935, the Japanese cabinet approved three peace conditions: (1) the cessation of anti-Japanese activities by the Chinese, (2) China's official recognition of Manchukuo, and (3) Japanese and Nationalist combined military operations against the Communists in Inner Mongolia. These became known as Hirota's Three Principles, named after Foreign Minister Hirota Kōki.[96] The first condition to halt anti-Japanese activities became a vast catchall category for anything the Japanese military did not like, and over time the geographic scope of Japanese military operations under the third demand expanded to encompass China south of the Great Wall.

When the Nationalist government ceded the Japanese de facto but not de jure recognition of Manchukuo, the Japanese military ratcheted up the military pressure. But the Nationalists would not formally cede Manchukuo.[97] Japan's generals remained equally intransigent: formal recognition or bust. The generals became intoxicated with their operational success. They kept taking lands ever farther southward, not because they had a careful strategic design but because they could, and, in anger, they did. Surely the Chinese government would fold, as had the governments of the Qing and Romanov dynasties in previous wars. Japanese military strategy forced a dilemma on the Chinese: fight and lose against the Imperial Japanese Army or appease and watch Japan gradually absorb the wealthiest parts of China. Either course entailed horrible costs.

Chiang Kai-shek, the emperor on the make during the Northern Expedition, had but one decade to establish strong civil and military institutions. He and his political rivals within the Nationalist Party, such as Hu Hanmin and Wang Jingwei, made impressive achievements, but the Japanese invaded too soon and too aggressively for these institutions to become firmly rooted in Nanjing, let alone throughout the country or down to the local level. Chiang, unlike most Communist leaders, had studied in Japan and understood the Japanese psychology as well as the lethality of the Imperial Japanese Army. This made him cautious. Perhaps Japan would serve as a buffer between Nationalist China and the Soviet Union. Perhaps Japan would support Chiang's efforts to eradicate communism in China. Chiang chose a very common military strategy against a militarily superior foe: From 1931 to 1936, he traded space for time against Japan. He then used the time to fight the Communists.

4

RUSSIA 1917–1936

Impending Two-Front War and World Revolution

坐收漁利
To profit without fishing.
(Effortlessly reap the spoils of war.)

Since the Russo-Japanese War, Japanese army war plans had focused on defeating Russia in an anticipated war to end all wars for Siberia east of Lake Baikal.[1] Army warnings about the Russian threat assumed a shrill tone after the Russian Revolution when the simple problem of Russian imperialism acquired an ideological dimension with the admixture of communism. These fears then became chronic with the post–World War I economic depression in Japan followed by the global Great Depression, which together made communism increasingly attractive to Japanese labor leaders and rank and file.

Russian revolutionaries deployed cadres around the globe to spread communism and made clear their goal not only to overturn the global order, but also to overturn the domestic orders within each country with social revolutions for all. Political and economic elites knew what to expect on the basis of the Russian Revolution – a classwide death sentence. Previously, the Russian threat to Japan had been strictly external in terms of territorial expansion abroad, but with the spread of communism, it became a domestic threat that sounded internal alarm bells throughout the Japanese government, and most particularly at army headquarters.

THE RUSSIAN REVOLUTION AND THE RUSSIAN EMPIRE

The Russian Communists, known originally as the Bolsheviks, seized power during a world war that had gone terribly wrong for their country. Russia suffered the highest casualties of any belligerent in World War I, which took the lives of 1,650,000 Russian soldiers and wounded 3,850,000 more of a total 15,500,000 mobilized. The war exhausted Russian industry. In 1915 new recruits were told to get their rifles from the corpses of fallen comrades. Sometimes entrenched front-line troops were reduced to throwing rocks at the approaching enemy.[2] Because the Entente powers ultimately defeated Germany, it is often forgotten that before the happy ending celebrated in Western history books, Germany had defeated Russia, taken much of its territory, and greatly contributed to the overthrow of the tsarist government.

In 1918, the new Communist government signed the Treaty of Brest-Litovsk ceding to the Central Powers Finland, the Baltic states, Russian Poland, the Ukraine, much of Belorussia, as well as territory in the Caucasus, which together accounted for one-third of Russia's cultivated land, half of its industry, and 80 percent of its coal production – all of this in return for a German, Austro-Hungarian, and Turkish cessation of hostilities.[3] Russia retrieved its territories only because the Entente powers, which stuck out the fight to defeat Germany, then oversaw the return or independence of all German-occupied territories. Thereafter, Russian histories emphasized, not the Entente's return of the lost territory, but two other events: first, an obscure group of 40,000 Czech soldiers, known as the Czech Legion, mainly prisoners of war in Siberia, who joined with the White (anti-Bolshevik) forces in the Russian Civil War, and second, the Entente intervention from 1918 to 1920 involving the deployment of more than 100,000 men from fourteen countries, initially to prevent German confiscation of war matériel stockpiled in Archangel and Murmansk, but, in the case of Japan, which deployed the preponderance of forces, to conquer territory. Japanese troops remained in Siberia until 1922, when the end of the Russian Civil War removed any legal pretext for lingering, and on Sakhalin Island until 1925.[4] Russians pointed to these two events as evidence of imperialism even though no territory was taken, rather than the far more important return of their German-occupied territories.

The Entente powers were appalled that Russia had violated the alliance to sign a separate peace with Germany, a fear that would then haunt them in World War II, an even more dangerous war. The Russian Communists considered the international status quo to be malevolent and hoped to overturn it as soon as possible in favor of worker-led and

Soviet-inspired revolutions. The Western powers found these plans even more appalling given their susceptibility to Soviet criticisms. In World War I the military strategies of all sides had sacrificed a generation of Europe's youth in uncoordinated battles that routinely sent young men up over trenches into oncoming machine-gun fire with predictable and tragic results. Unimaginative old men sent the young to die, rather than admit the bankruptcy of their military strategy. The Entente victory was Pyrrhic because it exacted far too great a cost. It lived up to the critique of the established social order leveled by the guru of communism, Karl Marx, who accused sheltered elites of living off the horrendous sacrifices of others.

The Communists desired no mere political revolution, but a social revolution, a far more comprehensive and deadly ordeal. Political revolutions seek to replace the people in power, while social revolutions start with a political revolution in preparation for the real agenda to eliminate entire social classes. To use the ancient Chinese military theorist Sunzi's terminology, social revolutions put both political leaders and members of certain social groups on "death ground," meaning they have no place in the postrevolutionary order.[5] At best they permanently lose their social status, and, more likely, they and their kin lose their lives. Because of the dire nature of the threat, social revolutions tend to entail bitter civil wars when those on death ground fight for their lives and those in favor of revolution fight for their ideals. Proponents of social revolution often draw strength from a lethal cocktail of ideals, jealousy, and vengeance. Elites of all ilks – political, social, economic, educational, and professional – beware. They all came to grief in communist revolutions.

The Bolshevik Revolution was a social revolution. The Romanov dynasty fell to a military coup in 1917. When officers gave Nicholas II the bitter news that his political and military incompetence required a change at the top, the tsar abdicated for himself and his hemophiliac son. The legislature arranged for a provisional government, but it fell within the year to a relatively bloodless Bolshevik coup, completing the political revolution. The Bolshevik plans for social revolution, however, met with stiff opposition from those consigned to the "ash heap of history," a turn of phrase coined by the great orator and most dangerous political rival of Joseph Stalin-Lev Trotsky. World War I, the Russian Civil War, and the ensuing famine and epidemics took the lives of 20 million Russians. Two million others fled the country.[6]

Russia's Western neighbors watched with increasing horror as the social revolution progressed and shunned the Bolshevik government, which until the mid-1920s remained diplomatically isolated. Plans to foment similar social revolutions throughout Europe elicited police dragnets to arrest revolutionaries, while the Bolshevik refusal to honor their country's significant war debts outraged Western financial circles and remained an issue until the end of the cold war, when Russia finally agreed to pay up, although on greatly reduced terms. In the meantime the Communists sought friends where they could. When plans for worker-led revolutions went nowhere in Europe, they turned to the great expanse of Asia, girding their long southern border. There they were instrumental in helping establish Communist Parties in Persia, India, and Turkey in 1920; in China and Outer Mongolia in 1921; in Japan and Palestine in 1922; in Korea in 1925; and in Vietnam, Malaya, Siam, Laos, and the Philippines in 1930.

Many people in these countries found the Russian experience compelling. Like Russia, most were old polities that had not kept up with the Industrial Revolution, the rise of the West, or the ensuing change, at their expense, of the international balance of power. Like Russia, most suffered from increasingly ineffective central governments, grinding poverty, and deep bitterness against the imperial powers, which seemed to prosper at their expense. The Bolsheviks, a tiny group of the politically committed, managed to seize power, excise the rotted old order, and invert the social pyramid to put the many in power and the loathed few out of their misery.

The Bolshevik Revolution offered instant gratification to the oppressed. It leveraged jealousy by identifying the wealthy few as the source of evil and cause for the suffering of the impoverished many. The revolution promised instant emotional satisfaction with the execution of the evildoers and financial restitution with the redistribution of their property. It also provided an easy identification process for evildoers: Anyone comfortably off lived on the wrong side of the social revolution. The Communists packaged all of this in high ideals: From each according to his ability and to each according to his needs. They extolled equality but remained silent on liberty. They treated government economic planning as a hard science, overlooking that human beings, in contrast to molecules, possess self-awareness, analytical capabilities, and an ability to game any system, not because they are evil but because they are driven to survive and, if possible, to survive in comfort. It took three generations in Russia before enough financial data piled up so that even their leaders questioned and then jettisoned this economic model.

Back in the 1920s, the model presented a compelling alternative to the West, whose greed had apparently caused yet another depression from a speculation-driven stock market crash on Wall Street that occurred within a decade of the first truly global war in human history. When a cascade of bankruptcies followed, the Western democracies could think only to beggar their neighbors by erecting towering tariff walls. This extinguished what was left of international trade and deepened the depression. Unemployment rates remained high for years, and prosperity did not return to the West until after World War II. Russian social engineering and economic planning looked good in comparison, and Karl Marx's analysis rang true to a mass audience of impoverished and fearful people around the globe.

The Soviet model for economic development and its political model for bringing the righteous to power seemed highly relevant to the literate but politically marginalized, who provided the Communists their leadership pool. The Bolsheviks had achieved the impossible. They had taken power in the greatest empire on earth, restored a militarily defeated and economically devastated country, and produced a game plan useful for the many peoples intent upon overcoming colonial domination, poverty, and dashed hopes for a better future.

Historians have killed entire forests for the paper to debate whether the Russians created the twentieth-century bloom of Communist Parties around the globe or whether these parties were primarily nationally inspired and locally directed. One can also argue at length whether a cup is half-full or half-empty. One's point of view will reflect which half of the cup one chooses to describe. The Bolsheviks provided particular ideas at a particular time when others were particularly receptive to them. The Bolsheviks made great efforts to disseminate these ideas, but others then took the ideas to places that the Bolsheviks may never have imagined. Remove the Bolsheviks and there would have been no compelling model. Remove the national leaders and there would have been no one to implement the model. Remove the catalyst and there is no chemical reaction. The fact that the catalyst can be a comparatively small additive does not diminish its importance. As Mao Zedong told a

Russian representative on the twenty-fifth anniversary of the founding of the Chinese Communist Party, "If there had been no Soviet Union, there would not have been a Chinese Communist Party."[7]

The Bolsheviks, who upon victory in the Russian Civil War gave their political party the official name the Communist Party of the Soviet Union, fervently believed that their path to political and economic development represented the culmination of history, which others were destined to follow. Given the deterministic nature of the model, it is curious that they felt so compelled to market it. Their global marketing campaign revealed their great strength and their enemies' weakness: While they excelled at propaganda, their critics fell flat. The Communists were the most brilliant propagandists of the twentieth century, convincing millions to follow their fatal footsteps. Many, many people believed the Communists and dismissed their critics for generations. Communism caught the attention of Sun Yat-sen, among others.

Before the Bolsheviks could spread social revolution to benefit humankind, they faced pressing national security concerns. First they had to defeat the armies of former tsarist generals to win the Russian Civil War. This took four years of vicious fighting during which both sides committed atrocities against civilians of all ages.[8] They also fought off the Poles, bent upon reclaiming territory lost in eighteenth-century partitions. Simultaneously they had to establish a functioning government. While Karl Marx wrote tomes analyzing the old order about to expire, he wrote remarkably little about the new order to come. He focused on destruction not creation. It fell to Vladimir Lenin, the founding father of Russian communism, to build.

Lenin and his deputy, Lev Trotsky, produced a highly effective civil-military model for rule. Communist survival depended on the military to defeat their many internal enemies and to complete the social revolution. But the military could not be allowed to stage a coup to wrest control from the Communist Party. Communism required Communist Party domination of both political and military institutions. While Trotsky created a mass army, Lenin created a mass party and put both under a political elite or revolutionary vanguard. Each military commander, known as a military commissar, had a political commissar, or "iron corset," in Trotsky's words. Military commissars focused on the operational art, while political commissars focused on allegiance through propaganda and enforced by the secret police. Programs for political indoctrination, literacy, and land reform helped cement loyalties, particularly in comparison to an enemy who invested nothing in the well-being of its soldiers.[9] Lenin's successor, Joseph Stalin, then produced the massive bureaucratic state to implement five-year economic plans of sufficient scale to administer the Soviet empire. Luckily for the Bolsheviks, the Western Europeans were in no mood for another war and so left Russia more or less to its own devices in this critical early period when the new government was most vulnerable.

The Bolsheviks took over a particular piece of real estate, Mother Russia, and this physical address came with certain geopolitical problems. Theirs was by far the largest nation on earth, spanning ten time zones. Their neighbors were numerous, often unstable, and rarely friendly. Other than the oceans in the north and east, and two landlocked seas in the south, Russia had no natural borders. Rather, the Russian Empire constituted the acquisitions of a millennium of imperial expansion. Less than half of the population was ethnic Russian.[10] Some of its provinces, in part or in entirety, had historically constituted polities in their own right and retained aspirations for independence. These included the homelands of the Ukrainians, Belorussians, Georgians, Azeris, Armenians, Kazakhs, Kirghiz, Uzbeks, Tadjiks, as well as many other nationalities. Russia had revanchist neighbors: Poland wanted the return of lost territory, Persia wished to reunify Azerbaijan, and China coveted much of Central Asia and southeastern Siberia.

The Communists not only held together all of the tsarist empire but greatly expanded it in World War II. They did so in part by relying on Russia's traditional and highly successful strategy for empire, which sought security through creeping buffer zones combined with astutely coordinated diplomacy and military operations against weak neighbors to ingest their territory at opportune moments.[11] Russia surrounded itself with buffer zones and failing states. During the tsarist period, the former were called governor-generalships, jurisdictions under military authority for a period of initial colonization and stabilization. Such areas generally contained non-Russian populations and bordered on foreign lands.

Russia repeatedly applied the Polish model to its neighbors. Under Catherine the Great, Russia had partitioned Poland three times in the late eighteenth century, creating a country ever less capable of administering its affairs as Russia in combination with Prussia and Austria gradually ate it alive. Great and even middling powers on the borders were dangerous. So they must be divided, a fate shared by Poland, the Ottoman Empire, Persia, China, and, post World War II, Germany and Korea. It is no coincidence that so many divided states border on Russia. Nor is it coincidence that so many unstable states sit on its periphery.

Russia peeled away parts of the Ottoman Empire at the turn of the eighteenth to nineteenth centuries and, had it won World War I, would have taken the Dardanelles at the highly strategic entrance to the Black Sea. In 1907 it colluded with Britain to divide Persia into Russian, neutral, and British zones. In the nineteenth century, it ingested the northern periphery of the Qing empire, taking the western coastlines of the Sea of Okhotsk and the Sea of Japan, the northern bank of the Amur River, and much of Central Asia to make all of these territories Russian outright.[12]

The Russians continued the feeding binge in Manchuria, but Japan dogged their steps, expelling them from Korea and southern Manchuria during the final years of the tsars. The rise of a powerful Japan on the difficult-to-defend Siberian frontier created deep misgivings in Russia. The protracted and slow-motion implosion of China also fed fears of disorder spreading across the border or, alternatively, of hostile powers taking over these areas. Yet the prospect of a reunified and strong China caused even deeper forebodings, conjuring Russian images of the so-called yellow peril envisioning the Chinese, like the Mongol hordes in the thirteenth century, conquering Russia or more feasibly Russian Siberia and Central Asia.[13]

The two key rules of empire were no two-front wars and, on the borders, no major powers including China. To prevent the rise of such a power, divide, influence, and, when opportune, absorb. Russia played on China's insecurities and revulsion against colonialism to keep it at odds with the West and ever more reliant on Russia to make it dependent and dependable. For these reasons, in the long Chinese civil war from 1912 to 1949, Russia funded not just the Communists but also numerous warlords. It placed bets on all horses to protract the conflict and render China prostrate.[14]

In the process, Russia continued to tear off wedges of territory from the Chinese sphere of influence. Over the years Russian diplomacy in China was remarkably successful in that Russia invested very little but got quite a lot. In the nineteenth century, tsarist Russia acquired, at

Chinese expense and without a war, sovereignty over territory exceeding all of the United States east of the Mississippi River. In the twentieth century, the Russians played an equally deft game of poker at Chinese expense. In the 1930s, they cultivated the reigning warlord of Xinjiang, China's northwest, an area greater than the combined size of Great Britain, France, Germany, Austria, Switzerland, and Italy. In the 1920s, they pealed off Outer Mongolia – an integral part of the Qing empire since the eighteenth century – to become the first member of the Communist bloc in 1921. In 1926 from northwest Outer Mongolia, Russia pealed off the gold-rich Tannu Tuva, an area almost as large as Great Britain that remains today a part of Russia, not Mongolia.[15] In 1941, Russia compensated Mongolia with territory from Manchuria that today remains a part of Mongolia, not China.[16]

Russia disguised this land grab with a brilliant propaganda campaign. Two years after the Russian Revolution, the Soviet deputy people's commissar for foreign affairs and plenipotentiary to China, Lev Mikhailovich Karakhan, issued a declaration in 1919, promising to return all tsarist railways and other concessions to China, no strings attached, as a good communist should. According to his declaration: "The government of the workers and peasants has then declared null and void all secret treaties concluded with Japan, China and the ex-Allies, the treaties which were to enable the Russian government of the Tsar and his Allies to enslave the peoples of the West and principally the people of China by intimidating or bribing them for the sole interests of capitalists, financiers and Russian generals." Then for the crucial paragraph – the one involving money: "*The Soviet government returns to the Chinese people without demanding any compensation, the Chinese Eastern Railway*, as well as all mining concessions, forestry, gold mines, and all other things which were seized from them by the government of the Tsars" and by a long list of other Russian miscreants.[17] Karakhan had served as a secretary at the Brest-Litovsk peace negotiations and went on to become ambassador to China from 1923 to 1926. He had two stints as deputy people's commissar for foreign affairs, first from 1918 to 1920, and later from 1927 to 1934.

In China, his hearts-and-minds campaign did much to popularize communism among intellectuals, who saw Russia returning its ill-gotten gains while the grasping Western powers and Japan clung to theirs. But within the year, the Russians altered the text of the declaration to deny their promise. They removed the key paragraph from subsequent versions of the Karakhan Declaration. Successive Chinese governments then kept the deletion secret lest their diplomats appear incompetent. In fact, Russia hung on to its concessions, the largest held by any foreign power, until the mid-1950s.[18] The Japanese government noticed the discrepancy between the declaration and reality. The Chinese people did not.[19]

The Russian railway concessions in Manchuria comprised 1,073 miles of track that Russia retained and 709 miles of track that it ceded to Japan in lieu of an indemnity after losing the Russo-Japanese War. These two railways, respectively, constituted the largest and the second largest foreign concessions in China. The French-owned Yunnan Railway at 289 miles ran a distant third.[20] With the exception of Hong Kong (returned in 1997) and Macao (returned in 1999), the Western powers had given up all of their concessions by 1947. In the intervening years, Chinese governments secretly demanded to no avail that Russia do likewise.[21] Instead, Russia kept the benefits of imperialism longer than the imperialist powers and did so without impairing its reputation.

In 1929, Nationalist forces under Zhang Xueliang demanded that Russia make good on the promise to return the Chinese Eastern Railway. Instead, Russia fought a five-month war, deploying tanks, bombers, and naval ships, to regain control in what the Chinese subsequently called the Chinese Eastern Railway Incident.[22] Zhang's father had repeatedly attempted to regain the concessions. Nevertheless, Russia kept both the railway and its antiimperial reputation among Chinese intellectuals. No other European country ever went to war with China over a railway concession. Russia did so twice, once under the tsars to put down the Boxer Uprising of 1900 and then under the Communists in 1929, each time deploying 100,000 men. Even during the Opium Wars, no Western power ever sent a force of a remotely comparable size. It turns out that the major critic of imperialism wielded a bigger stick and clung to the spoils longer than did those censured as imperial powers. Russia also interfered in Chinese domestic affairs far more aggressively than any other power save Japan prior to 1931, and yet it retained the sympathies of Chinese intellectuals. The power of its ideology blinded its admirers to the accumulating facts on the ground.

The 1929 Railway War had dangerous consequences for the Nationalists. No warlord in Chiang's coalition went to the aid of

Zhang Xueliang, who earned a place on Joseph Stalin's lengthy hate list for the failed attempt to recover the railway. The Russians did not lift a finger to help him when Japan invaded Manchuria two years later. Meanwhile, the Japanese perceived a growing Russian military threat and evident Nationalist military incompetence against any but warlord armies. This conclusion implied that Japan alone had the capacity to contain further communist expansion in East Asia.[23] Reinforcing this conclusion was the peace settlement that allegedly culminated in a June 1931 railway purchase agreement, which would have exempted Russian railway traffic from Chinese tariffs and applied the amount toward the eventual Chinese purchase of the railway, while continuing to levy the tariffs on Japanese traffic. This would have seriously disadvantaged Japanese trade.[24] With the Japanese invasion, the purchase agreement became moot.

In addition to manipulating Chinese elite opinion to suit Russian global interests, Stalin manipulated Chinese politics from afar to suit his own domestic interests. In 1927 he ordered the Chinese Communist Party to continue working within a united front with the Nationalist Party, the so-called First United Front that Sun Yat-sen had negotiated in 1923 in return for the Russian military aid, making possible the Northern Expedition. As the expedition approached Shanghai, Stalin was in the midst of a no-holds-barred political struggle with Lev Trotsky at home and needed events in China to vindicate his interpretation of the trends for the world revolution.

Whereas Stalin did not consider the Chinese economy sufficiently industrialized for a communist revolution and desired to focus on Russian internal development rather than to chase dreams abroad, Trotsky insisted that the Russian Revolution could not survive in isolation and so must promote world revolution. When the Chinese Communists petitioned the Russians for permission to leave the United Front, Stalin refused. Despite severe misgivings, the Chinese Communists followed the bloc-within strategy as Stalin dictated – Communists would remain a "bloc within" the Nationalist Party. However, without an independent military, the Communists could not defend themselves when Chiang turned on them. Stalin used the demise of the Chinese Communists during the White Terror as proof positive of Trotsky's errors. The massacre of Chinese Communists served Stalin's domestic purposes to prove that the outside world was unready for revolution and so Russia had better focus on internal development. He exiled Trotsky, later reconsidered, and arranged for his 1940 assassination by ice ax, an unusual murder weapon in Mexico.[25]

Continuing Russian advice to take on Nationalist main forces contributed to the catastrophic Communist defeats in the Nanchang, Autumn Harvest, Guangzhou (Canton Commune), and Barga (Hulunbuir) uprisings – the first three in 1927 and the last in 1928 – as well as in Chiang Kai-shek's Fifth Encirclement Campaign beginning in 1933, which sent the Communist remnants packing on the well-known Long March that greatly increased Chiang Kai-shek's stock in the Nationalist Party.[26] Mao Zedong, devoted Communist and future leader of China, soon started thinking seriously about a rural strategy to gain power because the Russian urban strategy had nearly destroyed the movement. Nevertheless, Russia retained its cachet among the Chinese intelligentsia and public, while the Western powers and particularly Japan became magnets for opprobrium.

Stalin also greatly contributed to the weakening of Nationalist state-building efforts, presumably to prevent the rise of a unified and powerful China on the sparsely populated Siberian frontier. Until the outbreak of World War II in Europe, Stalin continued to fund both the Nationalist Party and its most lethal enemy, the Chinese Communist Party, along with such warlords such as Zhang Zuolin, Feng Yuxiang, and Sheng Shicai.[27] These divided loyalties served to protract the civil war and weaken China, in accordance with tsarist Russia's continental strategy for empire but at variance with the supposedly fraternal relations among Communist Parties. The Chinese did not publicly complain about Russian bait-and-switch marketing practices until the 1960 Sino-Soviet split.

Japan, in turn, supported competing North China warlords in the 1920s: Zhang Zuolin, whose double dipping with Russia may have contributed to his premature demise at the hands of Kantō Army bomb makers; the Anhui group and their bitter rivals, the Zhili group, who spent the first half of the 1920s fighting each other to rule from Beijing; and Feng Yuxiang, whose double dipping with Japan may have contributed to his premature death from a particularly lethal film projector, which caught fire in 1948 aboard a Russian boat, killing him and a daughter.[28]

In the 1930s, Stalin promoted separatism in Xinjiang by supporting the local warlord, Sheng Shicai, and by establishing military bases, sending advisers, providing loans, monopolizing trade, deploying the secret police, and developing coal, oil, and tin concessions. In so doing, he transformed Xinjiang into a Russian protectorate.[29] On 1 January 1936 Russia and Xinjiang signed a treaty promising Russian financial and military aid and excluding access to third powers.[30] The German invasion of Russia in 1941, however, forced a dramatic reprioritization of resources.[31] The Russian closure of its border with Xinjiang in 1942 sent the Xinjiang economy into a tailspin.[32] This precipitated Sheng's search for a more reliable ally, his break with Russia, and the arrival of the Nationalists, who in 1943 set up in Urumqi the first Chinese provincial headquarters since 1911.[33] As part of the deal, Sheng removed and executed officials supportive of Russia, including his recent commissioner of finance, the younger brother of Mao Zedong, Mao Zemin. Sheng's shifting loyalties were too much for Chiang. In October 1944 Chiang removed Sheng Shicai from power with an offer he could not refuse, and a one-way plane ticket to Nanjing with sinecures to follow.[34] Russia responded to the growing Nationalist influence by backing a rebellion in northern Xinjiang in 1944, leading to the formation of the East Turkestan Republic, an area containing some of the province's largest and richest mineral deposits.[35] In the end, Russia did not get Xinjiang or the East Turkestan Republic, but it had invested very little and, as usual, finished up with its communist reputation intact.

The Nationalists considered three Russian initiatives to be particularly loathsome: a nonaggression pact, a railway sale, and a mutual assistance treaty with Mongolia. In response to Japan's invasion of Manchuria, on 31 December 1931 Russia proposed a nonaggression pact with Japan and in January 1932 offered to sell its enormous Manchurian railway concession. The Nationalists considered the Chinese Eastern Railway to be Chinese patrimony and not within Russia's authority to sell to a foreign power. The Japanese were not interested in either offer.[36] Nevertheless, Russia ceased paying railway remittances to the Zhang clan and starting paying Manchukuo instead.[37] In 1933, Japan rejected Russia's second offer for a nonaggression pact but had a change of heart about the railway in 1935, when Manchukuo bought it for 140 million yen, not the 1933 Russian asking price of 625 million yen.[38] The

Nationalists also looked askance at the 1936 Russian–Outer Mongolian Mutual Assistance Treaty because they considered Outer Mongolia to be an integral part of China, where Russia had no business. For analogous reasons, Russia's de facto recognition of Manchukuo also angered them. To no avail they argued that integral parts of China lacked the authority to conduct independent negotiations with foreign powers.[39] The territories involved in these disputes were not inconsequential, but huge.

MOUNTING PRESSURE FOR A SECOND UNITED FRONT

In the 1930s, international politics took a very dangerous turn for Russia. In Germany, long Russia's most dangerous European rival, the Nazi Party rose to power in 1933 on a virulently anti-Russian platform. Anyone who bothered to read Adolf Hitler's main literary effort, *Mein Kampf*, could not have missed the master plan (genocide for the Slavs in the East) for the benefit of the master race (the Aryans of Germany).[40] The German people would find *Lebensraum*, or living space, by taking over the Slavic lands and enslaving if not eliminating their population, referred to as subhumans (*Untermenschen*). The Japanese translator had tactfully edited out key racist sections of *Mein Kampf* and, therefore, Japanese readers did not grasp that Hitler had also classified them as subhumans and their government continued to maintain cordial relations with Germany.[41] The generation ruling Russia, however, vividly remembered the devastation of the First World War and Russia's inability to fight off the Germans then. In the 1930s, not only Germany was on the march, but so was Japan, which seemed poised to implement long-standing war plans to invade Siberia. The leaders of both Germany and Japan regarded communism as an anathema and Russia as the prime mover of evil in international affairs. Thus, Stalin faced prospects of war on two fronts, the Germans in European Russia and the Japanese in Siberia. By the summer of 1936, the Comintern (short for "Communist International"), Russia's international propaganda arm, pressed for a resurrection of the Communist-Nationalist United Front in order to contain Japan. But that spring Mao had made an anti-Nationalist alliance the centerpiece of his latest strategy.[42]

Matters worsened when the Germans and Japanese appeared interested in cooperation. On 25 November 1936, Japan and Germany signed a treaty portending an alliance, known as the Anti-Comintern Pact, and aimed at Russia. Because the pact set Japan on a road to membership in the Axis alliance four years later, it constituted a portentous decision, made in the wake of the attempted army coup d'état of February 26, 1936.[43] For Stalin, a combined German and Japanese attack might be fatal, since his country lacked powerful allies. None of the great powers cared to save a system bent on their overthrow. The last tsar failed to fight off Germany despite the enormous military efforts of his great-power allies, France and Britain. Russia had neither fully recovered from World War I and the ensuing Russian Civil War nor fully institutionalized its new government. How could it possibly fight off Germany let alone a German-Japanese combination? Stalin desperately needed some power to deflect either Germany or Japan, and preferably both. Yet none of the Western powers, where protectionism and domestic considerations ruled the day, showed any signs of going beyond words to contain either.

As soon as Germany and Japan signed the Anti-Comintern Pact, Stalin immediately turned to Asia, where the Chinese, who could agree on very little, shared a visceral loathing for Japan. He had contacts with the major North China political groups, which he had funded over the years. Despite bad past advice concerning the united front and associated military campaigns, and an unwillingness to return railways, both the Communists and Nationalists actually owed Russia a great deal. Not all the advice had been bad. There would have been no Chinese Communist Party without the inspiration of the Soviet example and its assistance to create effective institutions based on its political and military model. Likewise, the Nationalists could not have executed the Northern Expedition without the military training, weapons, and advisers provided by Russia through the extraordinarily influential Whampoa Military Academy. Chiang Kai-shek had developed essential parts of his support network during his tenure as commandant, when he had served as the military commissar and Zhou Enlai as the political commissar.

Both the Nationalist and Communist Parties learned institution building from the Russians and replicated the highly effective Soviet commissar system. The Military Affairs Commission for the Nationalists and the Supreme Military Soviet for the Communists (the precursor of the People's Republic of China's Central Military Affairs Commission) coordinated civil and military activities. Party members throughout their respective armies allowed for rapid expansion with the integration into the rank and file of peasants, former warlord troops, ethnic minorities, and assorted turncoats. Paired civil and military appointments assured not only civilian control over the military, but specifically party control.[44]

The Russian aid, in combination with effective Nationalist leadership and the exhaustion of the North China warlords during their own vicious infighting in the early 1920s, together had made possible the success of the Northern Expedition. Remove any one of these three elements – Russian aid, Nationalist leadership, and North China warlord exhaustion – and the reunification of China, however flawed in practice, would not have occurred.

Had Japan not chosen a military strategy to solve its problems in China, Chiang Kai-shek would have been a natural ally for Germany and Japan against Russia. All agreed that communism constituted their most important long-term threat. Japanese military strategy, however, precluded such an alliance, which would have proven fatal for Russia. Instead, unrelenting Japanese military pressure on China elicited its opposite intended diplomatic outcome by making Japan the common enemy of the Nationalists, the Communists, and the Russians, thereby providing the essential prerequisite for a strong opposing alliance.

The Chinese Communists tried to break out of their cave life in desolate Shaanxi by reaching out to an international audience. From 1938 to 1941, 7,316 foreign and Chinese visitors traveled to Yan'an, the Communists' window on China and the world beyond.[45] A succession of foreign journalists and in 1944 U.S. Foreign Service officers, paid court to Mao and went on to popularize Mao's version of events in their respective countries. These included the Americans Agnes Smedley, Anna Louise Strong, Teddy White, and, by far the most famous of all, Edgar Snow, whose *Red Star over China*, published in 1937, remains in print.[46]

The Comintern and the Yan'an leadership handpicked Edgar Snow, a young and idealistic journalist, to make a prolonged visit so that he could describe to the English-speaking world the Communist utopia under construction. Sun Yat-sen's widow and Chiang Kai-shek's sister-in-law, Soong Chingling, was the Comintern agent who put Snow in contact with Yan'an, where he arrived on 13 July 1936.

Thirty-one-year-old Snow's book *Red Star over China* would do for China what a thirty-year-old John Reed's 1919 best seller, *Ten Days That Shook the World*, had done for the Russian Revolution. Both tales transformed the Communists into heroes and communism into the salvation for those afflicted by war, poverty, and crumbling governance. Snow presented to the West the Communist version of events told to him at Yan'an that has become the conventional tale. He portrayed the Long March as a heroic period in Communist history instead of the rout that it really was. He described the horrors of Nationalist China that he had seen and found nothing comparable at Yan'an.[47]

Yet upon consolidating power, the Communist governments in both Russia and China meted out atrocities on an even greater scale (incredible though this was) than the rotting regimes they replaced. Petr Parfenovich Vladimirov, who served from 1942 until 1945 in Yan'an as a Comintern representative and correspondent for the Russian news service Tass, and who better appreciated the lethality of party politics than did Snow, took a much less starry-eyed view. According to a 1943 diary entry concerning the growing cult of Mao: "The situation in Yan'an is oppressive. Recent events have made people shun friendships, avoid contacts outside work, and distrust each other. Tension and terror are evident in people's behavior."[48] Snow could not speak much Chinese and so had relied on translators. Vladimirov, however, was not nearly the writer that Snow was.

In 1936, the Chinese Communists reassessed and decided to form a second united front, this time to fight Japan, not simply out of patriotism but out of desperation. Chiang's succession of encirclement campaigns from 1930 to 1934 had nearly obliterated them. In order to deflect the Nationalist military pressure away from themselves and on to the Japanese, the Communists played the nationalism card against both Japan and Chiang, trumping his military strategy. Chiang preferred sequential rather than simultaneous wars. He regarded winning the civil war as the prerequisite for winning the regional war. Rather than fighting two lethal enemies simultaneously, he wanted to finish off the Chinese Communists before taking on the Japanese. So he appeased the latter while lacerating the former. It was sound military strategy but an increasingly unfeasible political strategy.

China's privileged and mainly first-generation university students, propelled by idealism unconstrained by experience, regarded the appeasement of Japan with increasing outrage.[49] A keen sense of injured nationalism drove their demands for the Nationalists to cease fighting other Chinese (read Communists) to set their sights on Japan. In December 1935, against the backdrop of Japan's de facto partition of North China and its arrest of the president of Beijing University, students petitioned the Nationalists to resist Japan and save the motherland. Massive student demonstrations in Beijing denounced both Japanese and Nationalist foreign policy. The Chinese Communists paid careful attention to the growing student movement, encouraging it when they could and capitalizing on any Nationalist blunders.

Over the winter of 1935–6, the many local National Salvation Committees united under an executive organization, the Union of National Salvation Associations, to put enormous pressure on the Nationalists by keeping urban China churning with continuing demonstrations.[50] In July 1936, members of the association's executive council jointly signed and published a petition aimed at Chiang and entitled "A Number of Essential Conditions and Minimum Demands for a United Resistance to Invasion." It called for an end to the civil war against fellow Chinese for a united struggle against Japan. The following month, Mao Zedong responded with his agreement to make common cause with the Nationalists against Japan. In late November 1936, members of the Union of National Salvation Associations supported labor strikes against Japanese-owned factories in Shanghai, the center of Chiang's personal power. On 23 November Chiang responded to the worker walkout by arresting seven of the petition writers, eliciting a nationwide public outcry.

Among the seven were Zhang Naiqi, who had aided strikers in Japanese factories in Shanghai; Shen Junru, the dean of the Shanghai Law School and chairman of the Shanghai Lawyers Association; Zou Taofen, a journalist, whose anti-Japanese diatribes had attracted a large readership for his many publications; and Wang Zaoshi, a holder of a U.S. doctorate in political science, who returned home to practice law and journalism and to organize the likeminded – the latter activity at the Shanghai Writers' Association.[51] Two others, Sha Qianli and Shi Liang, were also lawyers, and the final member of the seven, Li Gongpu, was an educator. Their diverse professional backgrounds indicted the extent of public dissatisfaction with Chiang's strategy of internal pacification and external appeasement. The name of the incident in the public lexicon indicates Chiang's plummeting national popularity – the Seven Gentlemen against Japan Incident.[52] Given the traditional prejudices in China against soldiers and reverence for scholars, the word choice contained an implicit subtext: those in khaki do not arrest those in scholars' gowns. As domestic criticism mounted, Chiang must have wondered how long he could retain power if he did not fight Japan. Yet his reluctance to do so reflected a difference of strategy not policy. He shared their objective to expel Japan from China, but he did not believe his troops could fight those of Japan and win. He was right. Hundreds of thousands of Chinese soon died, demonstrating his point.

Meanwhile, over the spring and early summer of 1936, the powerful South China Guangdong and Guangxi groups added military pressure to the mix. Under the banner of "fight Japan to save the nation," the Guangdong warlord, Chen Jitang, and the Guangxi warlords, Li Zongren and Bai Chongxi, again deployed their forces into Hunan in the direction of Nanjing during the so-called Guangdong-Guangxi Incident, as they had in 1931 on the eve of Japan's invasion of Manchuria. Although Japanese military escalation then had pushed them back into the Nationalist fold, Chen, nominally the Nationalist military commander in charge of Guangdong, had focused not on cooperation with but on autonomy from Nanjing. He had implemented his interpretation of Sun Yat-sen's political, economic, and ideological program.

Li Zongren and Bai Chongxi, respectively, first and second in command of the Fourth Group Army during the Northern Expedition, likewise had visions for autonomy not subordination and had implemented an alternative to Sun Yat-sen's program in their home province of Guangxi. Instead of the Three People's Principles, they promoted the Three-Self Policy – self-government, self-defense, and self-sufficiency – the province of civil institutions under Li Zongren – and the Three-Reservation Policy – the jurisdiction of military institutions under Bai Chongxi. The latter emphasized the threefold duties of militia leaders to administer, command, and teach.[53] They initiated a series of legal, political, financial, tax, agricultural, and educational reforms in Guangxi.[54] But they lacked the military superiority to take on Chiang, let alone Japan, so they pushed for a united front. During the Guangdong-Guangxi Incident, the Comintern and the Chinese Communists pressured all parties to unite against Japan.[55]

Chiang had other ideas. In May 1935 Japan reiterated its perennial demand that China and Japan coordinate to eliminate communism and upped the ante to require that Zhang Xueliang's forces remove themselves from Japan's expanded sphere of influence. Chiang sought a win-win solution. He redeployed Zhang's Northeastern Army from North China and Yang Hucheng's Northwestern Army to Shaanxi for a sixth and final encirclement campaign to annihilate the Communists in their new base in Bao'an (Zhidan), Shaanxi, where Mao Zedong had just arrived in October at the end of the Long March.[56] In September, less than fifty miles away in Xi'an, Chiang had already established his main headquarters for bandit suppression, his euphemism for Communist annihilation, and made himself the commander in chief of the armed forces of the Northwest and Zhang Xueliang his lucky deputy. In this capacity, Zhang commanded the Northwest Encirclement Campaign while Chiang put Yang Hucheng in charge of the Xi'an Pacification Office.[57]

Chiang expected his North China warlord allies to provide the main forces for the campaign. He had a habit of deploying the troops of allied but potentially mutinous warlords to the front lines, where their troops weakened his primary adversary while any losses weakened them as potential political rivals within the Nationalist coalition. If Zhang, Yang, and neighboring Yan Xishan were aware of this strategy, they must have found Chiang's latest plans unsettling.

Over the summer and fall of 1935 the Communists defeated Zhang's forces in Shaanxi, destroying two divisions. The Japanese then cut off Zhang's escape route, leaving the beleaguered Manchurian warlord – no longer in possession of a regional base since 1931 – in danger of losing his army as well. To escape from the Communists or to fight the Japanese, either way Zhang needed allies. He did not have any good choices. The Japanese had murdered his father, leaving as potential allies Russia, the warlords of North China, and the Communists. He tried all three.[58]

Beginning in late 1935, Zhang Xueliang approached Russia for military assistance. It turned him down for an independent government in Northwest China. Not only did it have a client state already in place under the Xinjiang warlord, Sheng Shicai, but Zhang's gambit to expropriate the Chinese Eastern Railway in the Railway War of 1929 presumably did not endear him to Stalin, a man not known for the capacity to forgive.[59]

Zhang also approached Yan Xishan, holed up in Shanxi after his defeat in the Great War of the Central Plains in 1930.[60] Between January and October 1936, he traveled there five times for talks. Prior to the invasion of Manchuria, Yan had preferred to alternate between using Chiang and the Japanese to ward off the Communists. Then the Long March sent the Communist main force flooding into neighboring Shaanxi and Communist forces began attacking Yan's troops in May of 1935, leaving the latter worse for wear.[61]

Mao Zedong favored a strategy of eastward expansion to absorb Shanxi and then a move northward to take Suiyuan in the hopes of linking up with Russia. On 20 February 1936, the Communists suddenly sortied their main force from Shaanxi on an Eastern Expedition to attack Shanxi, shocking both the Japanese and the Nationalists, not to mention Yan Xishan, who now had problems from three directions. The Communists made public that they were off to fight the Japanese. Although Chiang's deployment of his Central Army into Shanxi caused the Communists to call off the campaign on 5 May, this left Yan with uncomfortable numbers of Chiang's forces deployed in his province.[62]

Then in November 1936, Japan orchestrated an Inner Mongolian attack, nominally under Demchugdongrob, on neighboring Suiyuan, where Yan had served as the Nationalist pacification commissioner since 1932. Yan must have wondered whether his province would be next.[63] He needed to relieve Communist pressure on Shanxi, while retaining his regional autonomy from the Communists, Japan, and Chiang Kai-shek. Before long Yan deputized Zhang Xueliang to approach the Communists for him and dealt directly with Yang Hucheng in search of a solution.[64] By early December 1936, as the anti-Japanese student demonstrations were reaching a crescendo in urban China, Yan allied with the Communists against Japan. He lifted the ban on their activities in Shanxi, where they soon began organizing.[65] As he observed, "There is some risk in a united front.... But if we don't collaborate with the Communists, what else can we do?... Otherwise we cannot hold off the Japanese and Chiang Kai-shek."[66]

The Shaanxi warlord, Yang Hucheng, was no happier than Yan Xishan about the recent turn of events. His end of the Sixth Encirclement Campaign had not gone well. During the first half of 1935 the Communists had destroyed three of his brigades.[67] For some years, Yang had favored a more aggressive course against Japan, not the

Communists, with whom he had signed a nonaggression pact around the time of Japan's Rehe Campaign. In the fall of 1935, Mao Zedong approached him in Xi'an and they met repeatedly thereafter.[68]

In February 1936 Yang made the arrangements for Zhang Xueliang to negotiate with the Communists in Yan'an, where on 9 April 1936, Zhang concluded an anti-Japanese military cooperation agreement with Zhou Enlai, who became famous in the West as China's diplomat in chief for the next forty years. They did not resolve whether to include Chiang in the united front – the Communists preferred him dead.[69] Over the summer radio contact, disrupted for two years, was restored between Russia and the Chinese Communists.[70]

Meanwhile, Wang Ming bent the ear of his Russian handlers in Moscow, where he resided in quasi-exile. In early 1936 he recommended Chiang's inclusion in the developing united front. Wang was one of the so-called Twenty-Eight Bolsheviks – the Russian-educated Communists, who had dominated the Chinese Communist Party leadership in the early 1930s but who had lost out to Mao.[71] The Russians saw the realpolitik advantages of including in the united front the man with the largest army. After the Guangdong-Guangxi Incident, the Comintern continued to meet with the Chinese Communists over the summer of 1936 to formulate their strategy and pressured them to cooperate with the Nationalists.[72]

The Chinese Communists agreed to join a united front only if Russia guaranteed military aid and if Zhang lined up either Chiang or (preferably) some other combination of Nationalist warlords to join.[73] Meanwhile Mao Zedong and Wang Ming engaged in secret negotiations with Nanjing.[74] The Nationalists made their conditions Russian military aid and a unified military command, with the full integration of Communist and Nationalist military forces.[75]

Over the fall, Zhang worked out the details of the united front, and in November he proclaimed the creation of the Northwest National Defense Government and the Northwest United Army to Resist Japan. Zhang served as the commander in chief, while Yang Hucheng and Zhu De, the Communist representative and later renowned general, served as his deputies. Zhang as commander of the Army of the Northeast (Manchuria), Yang as commander of the Army of the Northwest (Shaanxi), and Zhu De in command of Communist forces planned to take Shaanxi and Gansu with their 250,000-man combined force. The three coordinated their deployments to maximize the pressure on Xi'an, the provincial capital of Shaanxi and Chiang's base of operations.[76]

PREVENTING A TWO-FRONT WAR

On Chiang Kai-shek's fiftieth birthday party held at Xi'an on Halloween 1936, Yan Xishan and Zhang Xueliang both urged him to fight Japan, not the Communists.[77] The thought had already occurred to him. Ever since the invasion of Manchuria, he had tried to improve relations with Russia as a counterbalance to Japan. He had unsuccessfully worked through a Canadian intermediary, Harry Hussey, to restore diplomatic relations.[78] Later Stalin begrudgingly agreed on 12 December 1932.[79] Chiang also tried to improve relations in 1934, sending an emissary to Russia.[80] As the Japanese continued expanding southward, the Nationalists and the Russians started to work out the terms for a Second United Front. These discussions began at least as early as February of 1935, when Chiang again sent representatives to Moscow. Negotiations continued in China and Russia into 1936 and included Nationalist-Communist talks in Moscow.[81]

Under an alleged Sino-Russian treaty concluded on 1 July 1935, Russia recognized Xinjiang as under Nationalist administration and agreed to stay out of South and Central China in return for a Nationalist agreement to allow the Chinese Communists to move to and remain in Northwest China, specifically Shaanxi, Gansu, Shanxi, Qinghai, Ningxia, and Inner Mongolia, but no farther east. In the event of an invasion by a third-country (i.e., Japan), the Nationalists and the Russians agreed to cooperate.[82] In October 1935, Kong Xiangxi, Chiang's brother-in-law, met with the Russian ambassador to Nanjing, Dmitrii Vasil'evich Bogomolov, to negotiate Russian military assistance to fight Japan. Meetings continued in January 1936 with further discussions in Russia.[83]

Prior to February 1936, the Nationalists allegedly concluded another secret agreement with Russia. The provisions included a Nationalist cessation of their anti-Communist encirclement campaigns in exchange for an end to Russian aid to the Chinese Communists. Russia would assume responsibility for defending Inner Mongolia, which would be administered by the Mongolian Communist Party, and promised not to enter North China. In the event of a Russian-Japanese War, the

Nationalists agreed to tolerate a Russian-administered Manchuria.[84] In August the Nationalists even entered into secret negotiations with the Communists, but they failed to finalize their draft united front agreement.[85]

Chiang's preferred strategy remained Communist annihilation. On his birthday trip to Xi'an, he had conferred with Yang Hucheng and Zhang Xueliang about the Sixth Encirclement Campaign, but they were unenthusiastic, as their birthday advice had indicated. Chiang had forged ahead, despite his awareness of their negotiations to create a united front and of Zhang's truce with the Communists. Communist forces soon defeated Chiang's troops under Hu Zongnan on 22 November 1936 at Shanchengbao, Gansu, stymieing their campaign to take the Communist headquarters at Bao'an.[86] Zhang Xueliang requested that Chiang allow him to use the Northeast Army, deployed in Xi'an, to counter the Japanese in Suiyuan. This precipitated a second trip to Xi'an to press Zhang to finish the Sixth Encirclement Campaign instead,[87] Chiang threatening to cashier Zhang and to deploy the troops far, far away to Fujian if he did not encircle.[88] Chiang had already sent a loyalist, Jiang Dingwen, to assume command of the Bandit Suppression Army.[89] On this trip Chiang became the centerpiece of the so-called Xi'an Incident.[90]

A week prior to the trip, Japan and Germany had concluded the Anti-Comintern Pact, which Russia's master spy in Tokyo, Richard Sorge, immediately photographed and forwarded to Moscow.[91] The Japanese had misjudged Sorge, who kept Stalin well informed of their intentions from 1933 until his arrest in 1941. Sorge was the son of a German father and a Russian mother. Apparently the Japanese assumed patrilineal loyalties to the German side of Sorge's family, rather than matrilineal loyalties to the Russian side. The Japanese also missed a beat on the German side. His paternal great uncle had been a secretary to Karl Marx.[92] They should have recalled that Germany was the birthplace of both Nazism and Communism. The Japanese tried and then executed Sorge on 7 November 1944.

According to the conventional tale, in early December, a blissfully ignorant Chiang Kai-shek breezed up to Xi'an to confer with his generals for the prosecution of the Six Encirclement Campaign. In Xi'an they kidnapped and threatened to kill him unless he repented and fought Japan instead. He did a sudden about-face and agreed. They let him loose. He went home, honored his promise, and his troops suddenly turned on Japan. The conventional tale portrays Chiang as a man without honor, who inexplicably honored a coerced pledge.

It turns out that Chiang had been trying to line up Russian military aid for a long time. Given his industrial base, how could he fight Japan without heavy weapons from somewhere else?[93] The Chinese Communists did the talk, but Chiang would have to do the walk. Chiang's conventional armies, not Communist guerrilla units, would fight Japan's armies because guerrilla forces always lose toe-to-toe engagements against conventional main forces. Guerrillas can escalate the costs of fighting, and they can deny the enemy victory by precluding pacification, but they cannot deliver a war-winning military victory. At best, they can achieve a political victory after a protracted and costly war, if and only if the intervening power decides the costs are too high and so withdraws for political and economic reasons.

As Chiang weighed the merits of fighting or continuing to appease Japan, domestic changes in Japan propelled him to take the more aggressive course. The February 26 Incident in 1936 killing Finance Minister Takahashi Korekiyo and selected others had produced a new cabinet under the ultranationalist Prime Minister Hirota Kōki (formerly the foreign minister with the three principles), who favored the formation of an autarkic zone out of Japan, Manchuria, and China. Under his stewardship, Japan signed the Anti-Comintern Pact with Germany. His accession to the prime ministership confirmed the trend in Japan favoring military not political solutions to problems in China.[94] As the years went by, the Rehe Campaign, the Great Wall Campaign, the invasion of Inner Mongolia, and a proliferation of puppet states in Inner Mongolia and North China drove Chiang Kai-shek to the conclusion that Japan's objectives were unlimited, with no place for an independent Chinese government. If so, there was nothing to negotiate since Japan wanted all of China. Even worse, any further compromises would simply position Japan more favorably to achieve its unlimited objective to absorb China into the Japanese empire.

If Chiang concluded that the new Japanese government intended to put his own government on death ground, this would leave him two choices: fight or be annihilated. The question became not whether to fight Japan but when. His preferred strategy of taking on enemies sequentially, not simultaneously had been vetoed in multiple quarters: by key members of the Nationalists coalition in both North and South China, by the student movement throughout urban China, and, most importantly, by Japan. But Chiang still required military aid from a major arms producer in order to take on Japanese conventional forces. The conclusion of the Anti-Comintern Pact propelled Russia to play every one of its carefully cultivated contacts in China in order to avoid a two-front war.

By the time Chiang arrived in Xi'an on 4 December 1936, a united front had been in the works for two years.[95] Both the Chinese Communists and the Nationalists had made Russian military assistance a precondition for cooperation, while Russia had made a formal united front a precondition for any military assistance against Japan. The day before Chiang's trip, his negotiations with Japan had collapsed. Japan had pressured the Nationalists to join their Anti-Comintern Pact with Germany along with other demands that the Nationalists considered excessive.[96]

After Chiang's arrival in Xi'an, his generals mutinied, took him hostage on 12 December, and were weighing the pros and cons of executing him. This became known as the Xi'an Incident.[97] The Chinese Communists sent Zhou Enlai, in order to broker a Second United Front. Zhou Enlai wanted a show trial for Chiang, presumably like the ones then going on in Russia that delivered death sentences to Stalin's political rivals with predictable regularity. Mao also looked forward to an execution, but Russian pressure changed their minds.[98] The Russian press excoriated Zhang Xueliang and Yang Hucheng for playing into Japanese hands with threats to kill Chiang, whose loss would eviscerate Chinese military power by eliminating the only person capable of holding together Nationalist China or, worse yet, might produce a pro-Japanese government. On 13 December, Kong Xiangxi, acting as the representative of the Nationalist government, told the Russian representative in Chongqing to inform Moscow that the Nationalists saw a Communist hand in the kidnapping, and if Chiang died, the Nationalists would unite with the Japanese to turn on the Soviet Union. Wang Jingwei seized the moment to meet with Hitler about China's joining the Axis as soon as Wang replaced Chiang. The Japanese saw Russian machinations behind the incident and threatened Chiang with harsh reprisals if he allied with the Communists.[99] They kept their promise.

The Russians brokered the settlement that saved Chiang's life and created the Second United Front so that Chinese not Russian soldiers would die fighting Japan. A Comintern telegram demanded the release of Chiang.[100] Chiang agreed to join the armed resistance against Japan, free his many political prisoners, end the encirclement campaigns against the Communists, include all anti-Japanese parties both at home and abroad in the united front, and formulate a strategy to expel Japan from China.[101] Under Russian pressure, the mutineers released Chiang on Christmas Day of 1936. Zhang personally escorted Chiang to the airport and flew away with him without telling the Chinese Communists of their departure plans. Zhang's survival to old age, mostly under house arrest in Taiwan, suggests that Chiang Kai-shek begrudgingly honored Zhang, who had remained loyal during the critical Central Plains War and personally guaranteed his safe return from Xi'an.[102]

The Russian strategy worked like a charm when the Japanese reacted viscerally with a full-scale invasion of China. By joining the Second United Front, the Nationalists acquired guilt by association. The Japanese saw spreading communism in China, their perennial nightmare, and were determined to stop it with their usual military solution of escalation. They failed to see that their military strategy had conjured an unnatural hostile coalition composed of parties that, under normal circumstances, would have focused on fighting each other. These Chinese agreed that they hated Japan even if they could agree on nothing else. In 1937 all parties made good their promises.

At long last Chiang met the demands of the increasing numbers of Chinese who believed their country had to ally with Russia to fight Japan. Both Mao and Chiang expected Russia to join the war. They got it backward: Once they were in, Russia was out. For very powerful geopolitical reasons, Stalin intended to have China fight Japan so he would not have to do so.[103] After the escalation of hostilities in July 1937, Chiang repeatedly requested Russia to send troops, apparently not realizing that once he and the Communists had done so, Stalin had no need to send any.[104] Mao and Chiang had swallowed the Russian bait and would fight Japan alone. In a buck-up talk on 18 November 1937 as the Nationalists were evacuating Shanghai, Stalin told Chiang's representatives, "Even if Japan defeats China now, China will get revenge. Great peoples do not die. That's my opinion." He promised Russian troops only if Japan seemed poised to overthrow the Chinese government.[105]

He would make good this promise during two brief but essential battles at Zhanggufeng and Nomonhan in 1938 and 1939, respectively, that relieved Japanese military pressure at critical moments.

On 21 August 1937, Russia made good on its end of the bargain by concluding a nonaggression pact with the Nationalist government. This promised all quiet on the northern front.[106] Since 1932 the Nationalists had been trying with no success to conclude such a treaty. It guaranteed that neither China nor Russia would cut a separate deal with Japan, alleviating Chiang's fears of a Russian-Japanese partition of China in the manner of past partitions by the *genrō* and the tsar.[107] The Russians also returned Chiang's only legitimate son, Chiang Ching-kuo, who had gone to Russia for higher education in 1925 but who had not been allowed to return home after Chiang senior's purge of the Communists in 1927. In the meantime, the son had become irreplaceable after Chiang's childless marriage to Soong Mayling in 1927 preceded by a succession of childless mistresses, confirming that Chiang could no longer father children.[108] Chiang's dynasty depended on the son's return. The Chinese Communists also made good on their end of the bargain: They put their troops at least nominally under Nationalist command by consolidating their forces into two armies: the Eighth Route Army and the New Fourth Route Army.

Chiang did not publicly announce the Second United Front until 23 September 1937, after he had received the first arms shipments from Russia earlier that month.[109] By then he had already proven his mettle by standing up to the Japanese during the so-called Marco Polo Bridge Incident on 7 July, which marked the massive escalation of the Second Sino-Japanese War throughout coastal China and up the Yangzi River toward the Nationalist capital. Much more Russian aid followed.[110]

The Xi'an Incident was the most successful act of Soviet diplomacy between 1917 and 1991, when the Soviet Union was no more. It foreclosed a fatal combined German and Japanese attack. Japan, once deeply embroiled in China, lacked the capacity to invade Siberia, freeing Stalin to concentrate on Germany, where his diplomacy lost its magic. The expanded war damaged the Japanese economy much more quickly than anticipated. Signs of economic distress became evident by the winter of 1937–8.[111]

The escalating war was even more damaging to the Chinese economy. China's idealistic and privileged students got the war they demanded, fought by China's legions of underprivileged peasant youth. Japan's warlords passed a point of no return, setting an irreversible course for military overextension, an error for which we are all still paying the price. Years later, when all the fighting ended (for a few months anyway before the onslaught of the Korean War), the political face of Asia was unrecognizable and, in many ways, grotesque from the point of view of both Japan and the West.

PART II

NESTED WARS

A Civil War within a Regional War within a Global War

借刀殺人
Kill with a borrowed knife.
(To kill someone by another's hand.)

5

FLASHBACK TO 1911 AND THE BEGINNING OF THE LONG CHINESE CIVIL WAR

話說	It is said that
天下大勢	the world
分久必合	long divided must unite,
合久必分	and long united must divide.[1]

Luo Guanzhong (c. 1330–1400), *Romance of the Three Kingdoms*

Understanding the magnitude of Chiang Kai-shek's accomplishment with the Northern Expedition's reunification of China and the magnitude of the task still lying ahead at the time of the Xi'an Incident requires a retrospective on China's long civil war of the twentieth century that lasted from 1911 to 1949. This was a dreaded interregnum period between the Qing dynasty and its successor system of government. In Chinese history, periods of dynastic change, when central authority collapses and war ravages the land until the restoration of authority, typically last decades and are characterized by chaos, or 亂 (*luan*) in Chinese. The word resonates with evil foreboding.

In 1936, the chaos had been escalating for a century. Like the Japanese euphemism of "incidents" for wars, the Chinese apply the misnomer of "rebellions" to their civil wars. In the nineteenth century, China faced numerous and overlapping civil wars – the Taiping, Nian, and Donggan Rebellions – to name just the largest. These three alone may have taken up to 50 million lives.[2] To put the figure in perspective, more than 57 million people died in World War II.[3] These rebellions devastated virtually every province of China. The peak period lasted more than twenty years in the third quarter of the nineteenth century.

China also simultaneously fought and lost a succession of regional wars against the colonial powers: the Opium Wars (1839–42, 1856–60), the Sino-French War (1883–5), the First Sino-Japanese War (1894–5), and the Boxer Uprising (1899–1901). The Boxer "Uprising," another misnomer, was a civil war overlaid by a multinational invasion by all the great powers plus some.

The Industrial Revolution overturned the international balance of power, and the industrial powers soon imposed a global maritime trading system. In response, Japan, Russia, and China all implemented aggressive plans for state building. In Japan this process took place during the Meiji Restoration period (1868–1912) and proceeded with minimal bloodshed – a short civil war that overthrew the last Tokugawa shōgun and a short-lived samurai rebellion in 1877 against the Westernizing reforms. In Russia state building under the Communists cost millions of lives. Lenin imposed party rule over closely linked civil and military institutions during a five-year civil war. Stalin then implemented the first five-year plan in 1928, mandating forced-draft industrialization and collectivizing agriculture, beginning in 1929 and completed by 1937. Together these events produced a strong Soviet state fully in control of the economy but at the cost of a searing postcollectivization famine and the forced deportations to prison camps of the many who resisted these plans. Chinese state building was even bloodier and far more protracted than either the Soviet or Japanese experiences, and far less economically successful.

As in Russia and Japan, there were deep divisions among Chinese concerning what institutional framework their country should have. As in Russia and Japan, this disagreement was resolved through civil war. Both the Bolsheviks and the Meiji generation used their armed forces to assure the implementation of their plans domestically and regionally. China's many warlords, when not fighting each other, dabbled in state building to impose a kaleidoscopic array of local laws and short-lived institutions.

Like the Russians of Joseph Stalin's generation, the Chinese of Chiang Kai-shek's and Mao Zedong's generation inherited a shattered country. Japan, in contrast, had not been shattered; rather, prior to the Meiji Restoration, it had never fully been glued, but had been composed of hundreds of semiautonomous fiefdoms over which the Meiji generation finally asserted full central control. Russia and China had the task of reassembling the many pieces to restore once-great empires and, in China's case, a brilliant civilization that had served as the benchmark for Asian achievements in all fields for millennia.

After the energetic founding emperors, the Qing dynasty reengaged in state building only late in the game. Observers had been pronouncing the death of the Qing dynasty throughout the last fifty years of Manchu rule.[4] Foreign and local commentators alike considered China to be a mess. It suffered from appalling levels of starvation, disease, unemployment, drug addiction, misappropriation of public funds, and fatalities attributable to a combination of natural disasters and the government's failure to maintain basic infrastructure. When the Qing dynasty in the last decade of its rule belatedly tried to emulate Meiji Japan's highly successful modernization program, the new Westernized army mutinied against Manchu minority rule, brought down the dynasty, and ushered in a period of even greater chaos. The revolutionaries achieved their negative objective very rapidly – they destroyed what they did not want – but failed to construct a viable replacement. The mutiny took place in 1911, setting off a cascade of provincial secessions that culminated in the abdication in 1912 of the last Manchu monarch, a bewildered six-year-old child, whom the Japanese would later make their puppet monarch of Manchukuo. The fall of the dynasty became known as China's First or Xinhai Revolution.

The highly incomplete late–Qing dynasty reforms included the creation of a National Assembly that had first convened in 1910. As in Russia, where the last tsar created a national assembly a decade before his own overthrow, the new legislative branch of government became the basis for each country's first postdynastic government. In Russia that provisional government fell within the year to a Communist coup, the October Revolution versus the earlier February Revolution, both in 1917. In China the national assembly lasted in one form or another throughout the republican period. In Japan, the full array of Meiji civil and military institutions, including the constitution and the Diet, remained in place until the loss of World War II, and even then, their successor institutions relied heavily on their Meiji antecedents. China, even more so than Russia, disintegrated with the fall of the imperial system and could not be reassembled for decades.

The republican period refers to the Republic of China created upon the demise of the Qing dynasty and lasting in mainland China until the

Communist Revolution of 1949. The Nationalists claimed, when they fled to Taiwan that year, that their country constituted the Republic of China, the official name for the government of Taiwan. The republican period corresponds both with the interregnum between the Qing dynasty and the People's Republic of China, and with China's long civil war.

At the time of the collapse of the Qing dynasty, high-ranking North China officers of the new military held the balance of power because they could deploy troops to the capital. General Yuan Shikai, who had created the Qing dynasty's new Westernized military, became the new president. The rest of the country, however, did not go along. A Second Revolution took place in 1913, when Yuan Shikai refused to accept a landslide legislative victory of the predecessor party to Sun Yat-sen's Nationalist Party. Instead, Yuan banned the party, closed the legislature, and apparently assassinated key opposition leaders. Seven South Chinese provinces unsuccessfully attempted to secede, but North China's conventional military trumped South China's political aspirations. When Yuan attempted to make himself emperor in 1915, a Third Revolution erupted in 1916, when eight predominantly South China provinces again seceded. Yuan's sudden death in June left the country in chaos and lacking a leader with sufficient military power to hold it together.

Yuan's two most important subordinates immediately fell out to lead two of North China's three most important warlord groups, the Zhili group and Anhui group, named in reference to the place of origin of their founders. Zhang Zuolin led the third warlord group, known as the Fengtian group. ("Fengtian" is one of the many names for the city also known as Shenyang or Mukden as well as for its province of location, known also as Liaoning.) The North China warlords fought a succession of wars to dominate Beijing and the central government: the July 1920 Zhili-Anhui War, the April–June 1922 First Zhili-Fengtian War, and the September–November 1924 Second Zhili-Fengtian War. These wars were not minor fracases, but entailed World War I–style combat. Each involved more than 100,000 combatants, and seven to ten provinces. The last involved 450,000 soldiers and produced a Fengtian victory. Zhang Zuolin then took control over Beijing in the Fengtian-Feng Yuxiang War running from November 1925 to March 1926, involving 600,000 combatants, and affecting eight provinces.[5] The numbers of belligerents, wars, and affected provinces should convey a picture of national devastation. To give perspective to Americans of the 9/11 generation, who also experienced violence in their homeland, 9/11 was a day, four planes, three buildings, a field, and three thousand deaths, whereas New China's postpartum civil wars consumed more than a decade and much of the country, and killed tens of thousands.

While the North China warlords exhausted each other, Sun Yat-sen attempted to organize a government in South China based on civilian, not military rule. He created three different governments in Guangzhou between 1917 and 1923. The first two fell for the lack of adequate military forces to protect the government from various South China warlords. The third, formed in 1923, lasted until Sun's death in 1925. In the early 1920s, he became the only leader with a national following. Unlike the many warlords of China, Sun Yat-sen produced an ideology capable of transcending provincial boundaries and a political party, the Nationalist Party, capable of organizing nationwide political support. Both endured beyond his death.

The ideology centered around the Three People's Principles or Threepeopleism (三民主義), which are usually translated into English as "nationalism" (民族主義), "democracy" (民主主義), and "the people's livelihood" (民生主義). A more literal translation would be "people's tribes," "people's leadership," and "people's life." Significant is the word choice of 民族, which has racial overtones absent in the English word "nationalism," but present in the word "nationality." The three principles were simple and catchy, and they caught on.

The Nationalist Party became embroiled in the struggles between the executive and legislative branches of government, and among the warlords competing to dominate the incapacitated but nevertheless internationally recognized government in Beijing. Reunification required the power to compel. In Sun's final three years, he began to acquire this power through an alliance with Russia. He had approached the West and Japan, but only Russia offered significant military aid. This aid produced the Whampoa Military Academy and eventually made possible the Northern Expedition.[6]

With the success of the Northern Expedition, China's seventeen-year interregnum seemed to be over. But as Carl von Clausewitz, the military guru of the West, observed, the result in war is never final.[7] Chiang Kai-shek's warlord rivals remained suspicious of Nanjing dominance, and

Chiang fought off a succession of uprisings to unseat him in 1929, followed by the nationwide Great War of the Central Plains from May until November of 1930. The Communists did not give up after the White Terror of 1927. Expelled from the cities, they moved to the ungoverned and difficult terrain along provincial boundaries and between warlord spheres of influence. Russia provided assistance to establish soviets in Hunan, Jiangxi, Fujian, Hubei, Zhejiang, Henan, Anhui, Guangdong, and Guangxi.[8] Soviets were Communist states within states, an attempt to create the nucleus of a rival government that would grow from within to supplant the host government.

Like the Nationalists, the Communists had an ideological program capable of attracting a national audience. Whereas the Nationalists emphasized Sun Yat-sen's Three People's Principles, the five-power constitution, and three stages of political development, the Communists focused on the party in the vanguard of the revolution, class warfare, the political education of the powerless, the mobilization of the peasantry into guerrilla units and logistical support activities, and the inevitability of a Communist victory. The Communists took advantage of Chiang's divided attention to establish a proliferation of base areas. In March of 1930 Mao Zedong and Zhu De had founded what became the central soviet on the inaccessible Jiangxi-Fujian border. They had started with just 10,000 mostly unarmed peasant-soldiers, a small number compared to a typical warlord army. Zhu De commanded the original Fourth Route Army and Mao Zedong served as its political commissar, in keeping with the Soviet model for party control over the military. This system recognized the politics to recruitment, morale, and retention. Mao and Zhu emphasized the ideological bonds among party members, the peasantry, and the recruits and implemented land reform to reinforce the bonds with vital interests. Land gave the peasants a stake in the soviet, and they were willing to fight for it. So land produced recruits, strengthened morale, and stemmed desertions. The redistribution of land also eliminated the old social order based on gentry control of the land, tenant farming, and local governance through the gentry. The Communists decapitated and then overturned the old social pyramid, taking advantage of the massive base to excise the small apex.

Over the years, the Nationalists and the Communists either absorbed or eliminated the many warlord factions fracturing China so that the multilateral civil war gradually transformed into a bilateral Nationalist-Communist fight. The Communists and the Nationalists each had the unlimited objective of eliminating the other from the political map. Neither sociopolitical system could accommodate the other; rather, they were mutually exclusive. If the Communists had their way, entire social classes were slated for death and the Communist Party would dictate policy. If the Nationalists had their way, property would remain private, all Communists would be executed, and the Nationalist Party would dictate policy. Both parties understood that regardless of any truces and negotiations, in the long run theirs would be a merciless fight to the finish. When the United States began to intervene in the long Chinese civil war, policy makers in Washington missed this element of the struggle and kept trying to peddle democracy to a society where it was mainly favored by powerless (but often English-speaking) bookworms.

The Nationalists deeply feared the Communist agenda of social revolution and its growing popularity among China's population caught among the Great Depression, Japanese aggression, and civil war. Peasants struggled to evade military recruitment by warlord armies on the road, to protect their harvests from warlord requisition squads, and to pay the taxes demanded by the gentry. The gentry may have been at the top of the local social pyramid, but marauding warlord armies forced them to take sides, form armies of their own, flee their home village, or submit to the men wielding the guns. The depression, Japanese aggression, and the civil war threatened not only peasant livelihoods, but gentry livelihoods as well. Famine soon followed in the wake of endemic warfare. Yet no matter how many Communists the Nationalists killed, they could not eliminate the idea of communism, which resonates most compellingly in times of chaos.

In the Fifth Encirclement Campaign, the Nationalists flushed the Communists out of South China on the Long March to the far North. The Communists portray the Long March as a heroic era, but the military realities do not match the conventional tale popularized in the West by Edgar Snow.[9] Like the British evacuation of Dunkirk in the early part of World War II in Europe, the Long March (really the Great Escape) was heroic, but it reflected a disastrous military strategy. The British were lucky in that their evacuation required just a short boat ride, not a six-thousand-mile trek under appalling conditions. The Long March did not merely decimate Communist forces – decimate means the loss of one-tenth. The Communists lost 93 percent of an army already reduced by half, which means an attrition rate of 96.5 percent. For the mathematically inclined: after the original army of 200,000 was halved to 100,000 defending the Jiangxi Soviet, only 7,000 survived the flight to Yan'an.[10]

Mao chose the far North for his getaway because it abutted the Russian sphere of influence in Mongolia, putting him within reach of foreign aid.[11] In Yan'an, Mao turned from the gun to the pen and wrote some of his most famous essays. These were buck-up works to the men around him living in caves in one of the most desolate parts of China. These writings emphasized the essential role he anticipated Russia would play.[12] In *On Protracted War*, written in 1938, he called the Soviet Union a "vital factor" and anticipated "large-scale direct assistance" in the future. In *On New Democracy* written in 1940 he made clear: "The assistance of the Soviet Union, is the indispensable condition for the final victory in the war of resistance.... Refuse the assistance of the Soviet Union and the revolution will fail."[13]

For both Mao Zedong and Chiang Kai-shek, the key fight remained their duel to the death. They thought of the unfolding regional war with Japan and later the global war involving the United States in terms of the effect on the outcome of the civil war. They knew the civil war would resume full throttle once Japan left – and they knew Japan would leave because it lacked the finesse for empire demonstrated by either the Mongol Yuan dynasty or the Manchu Qing dynasty. Japan's civil leaders understood economic development, not coalition building, and its military leaders understood neither.

The Long March was a Communist military disaster that Chiang Kai-shek failed to leverage because Japanese leaders constantly interfered. Each time he fought the Communists, the Japanese moved deeper into Chinese territory, forcing him to call off the latest encirclement campaign to discourage Japan from advancing even farther south. The Japanese were unwilling to bide their time while Chiang took care of the Communist problem for them.

Japanese actions repeatedly unified the Nationalist coalition just as it was falling apart, reglued South China to Central China, and eventually epoxied North China as well. The invasion of Manchuria in 1931 temporarily sent the Guangxi group back into the fold when it had been poised to set up a rival government. Japan's continuing southward advance through North China gave life to a nationwide anti-Japanese student movement in urban areas and rallied Chinese of all backgrounds around the flag. As the Nationalist coalition again began to fray and the Guangxi group made moves to resume its separatist ways, the military escalation in 1937 again propelled it back to the Nationalist fold. Because Japan presented a military threat, it required a military counter, which made Chiang Kai-shek essential for any effective countervailing coalition, no matter how much the many warlords and political groups distrusted or detested him. Japanese military strategy forced the Chinese to coalesce around him as the man with the most proficient military. Incredibly, Japanese strategy even returned the Communists for a Second United Front after the nearly fatal first one.

Japanese strategy also delivered vital foreign aid. In November 1935, one year before the Second Nationalist-Communist United Front, the Japanese ambassador to Nanjing, Ariyoshi Akira, informed Chiang Kai-shek, "If the central government [i.e., you] uses coercive or military measures, etc. [in North China], this cannot but cause disputes and undermine law and order; furthermore, it can have serious consequences for Japan and Manchukuo, which have close connections with this area." He warned, "In particular, the Kantō Army, which bears responsibility for Manchukuo's security, will definitely not stand idly by. This point cannot escape Your Excellency's attention."[14] Given the Japanese preference for extreme politeness in diplomatic settings, an English translation more faithful to the conveyed meaning would be "If you so much as lift a finger in North China, we will obliterate you." The warning elicited the opposite of the intended reaction. Chiang made renewed efforts to find a big friend and Russia immediately came to mind. The Second United Front then seemed to promise the Japanese nightmare scenario of a Russian-Nationalist alliance and an accelerating spread of communism in China. Increasing border incidents with Russia between 1935 and 1936 heightened these fears.[15]

Chiang understood the likely outcome of Japan's coercive diplomacy better than did Japan's diplomats, let alone Japan's military officers. Chiang wrote in his diary: "If one examines the violent and unreasonable temperament of the bandits, war is unavoidable, but since the dwarf bandits [the standard Classical Chinese term for the Japanese] still do not comprehend but provoke disputes, no opportunity to negotiate a peace will ever arise; it shall not be my demise, but theirs; from the logic of power this too is obvious."[16] In other words, Japan's insatiable appetite for Chinese territory was bad strategy because it guaranteed a war, which, given the size of China, promised a protracted conflict that Japan, given its resource and manpower constraints, could ill afford to wage but that the Chinese could ill afford not to wage. The Japanese mistook Chiang's reluctance to fight over Manchuria for a defeatism that they assumed would extend to the rest of China as well.

Prime Minister Konoe Fumimaro, who rose to power on the eve of the escalation of 1937, described his cabinet's foreign policy as follows: "International justice cannot fully be realized until the territory of the globe has been equitably distributed.... Our Japan belongs to the ranks of countries without natural resources; we must guarantee the right to survival of our race. Guaranteeing this vital right to survival forms the foundation of Japan's China policy. International justice has yet to be achieved. This situation also forms the backdrop to the China policy followed by our country."[17] In other words, the Japanese attached an extraordinarily high value to victory on their terms in China, a value on a par with national survival. Alas for the Japanese, victory in China on Chinese terms was even more highly prized by the Chinese, who, unlike the Japanese, lived in the theater. A high value attached to victory by both sides guaranteed a bitter fight even between unevenly matched belligerents.

Those who study warfare identify three levels: the tactical, the operational, and the strategic. The tactical level involves the use and capabilities of particular weapons or deployments of particular types of formations. The operational level combines tactics and formations to conduct a battle or a campaign (a series of battles) generally, but not always, in pursuit of military objectives, such as taking or defending certain territory, or eliminating certain enemy forces. The strategic level of warfare concerns the national objectives for which the war is fought and usually entails marshalling multiple elements of national power, of which the military is but one. Other elements of national power include economic wealth, productive capacity, technological capabilities, resource access, transportation and communication networks, cryptographic skills, espionage, political stability, diplomacy, alliances, political support at home and abroad, to name just the most obvious. Grand strategy entails marshalling all the relevant elements of national power in order to achieve national objectives. Grand strategy is strategy at the strategic level. Military strategy is strategy at the operational level, and strategy at either level requires the balancing of ends and means.

Japanese leaders focused on the operational level of war – winning the battles. They did not adequately consider the strategic effects of these military operations. Victory at the strategic level required stability in China, its economic integration with Japan, the elimination of communism and Soviet influence in China, trade with the West, and the end to foreign interference with Japan's plans for China. Japanese military operations did not further these strategic goals. Quite remarkably, Japanese military operations precluded their achievement.

Chiang did not want to fight Japan at all, but Japanese military strategy then left him no other choice. Japan's forays into Inner Mongolia, an economic backwater unlikely to produce meaningful resources for Japan, unified the North China warlords against Japan. As part of the unintended consequences of 1936, Chiang Kai-shek deployed more than 200,000 soldiers northward ostensibly in preparation for the final encirclement campaign against the Communists holed up in Shaanxi, but also positioned to contain Japan.[18] These outcomes – the survival of the Communists, the rallying of the Nationalist coalition in order to fight Japan, and the outbreak of a virulently anti-Japanese Chinese nationalism – were outcomes antithetical to Japanese goals.

Japanese military strategy had unintended consequences beyond China. After the invasion of Manchuria, the U.S. president, Herbert Hoover, threatened to cut credit to Japanese businesses, and Secretary of State Henry L. Stimson inclined toward a naval buildup.[19] On 7 January 1932, the United States made official its nonrecognition of Manchukuo in a document that became known as the Stimson Doctrine.[20] Prior to 1937, other than Japan, only El Salvador and the Vatican recognized Manchukuo.[21] Until the bombing of Pearl Harbor, Japan would focus its diplomacy with the United States on rescinding the doctrine.

Meanwhile, Russia responded to Japan's military strategy with a military buildup that included the creation of a Pacific Fleet in 1932, reinforcement of Siberian border defenses, and the double-tracking of the Trans-Siberian Railway by 1937.[22] By 1935 Russia had added six divisions to its original eight in Siberia as well as 750 planes to its original 200. These included long-range bombers capable of hitting Tokyo, a capability that Japan could not match. In comparison, Japanese ground forces and air assets in Manchuria were just 36 percent and 23 percent, respectively, of these Russian figures.[23] The Russian buildup continued through 1939.[24] Thus, Japanese military strategy made the Imperial Japanese Army comparatively less prepared for its nightmare scenario of a Russian invasion of Manchuria.

Japanese leaders of the 1930s lacked the brilliance of their Meiji generation predecessors, who had understood that a quick victory in war required a generous peace so that the enemy would lay down its arms instead of fighting for better terms. In the 1930s, the Japanese military consistently demanded far more military gains than any Chinese government could ever grant and hope to remain in power. Yet China was much too large a theater to be garrisoned in the absence of Chinese cooperation. So the costs of war escalated for all sides.

The Japanese are known worldwide as a very enterprising people. Theirs was the only non-Western country to match European levels of economic development in the early twentieth century. They did so inside two generations, an enormous achievement by any measure. The Japanese knew a great deal about China, and yet they followed military strategies antithetical to their own interests. Why?

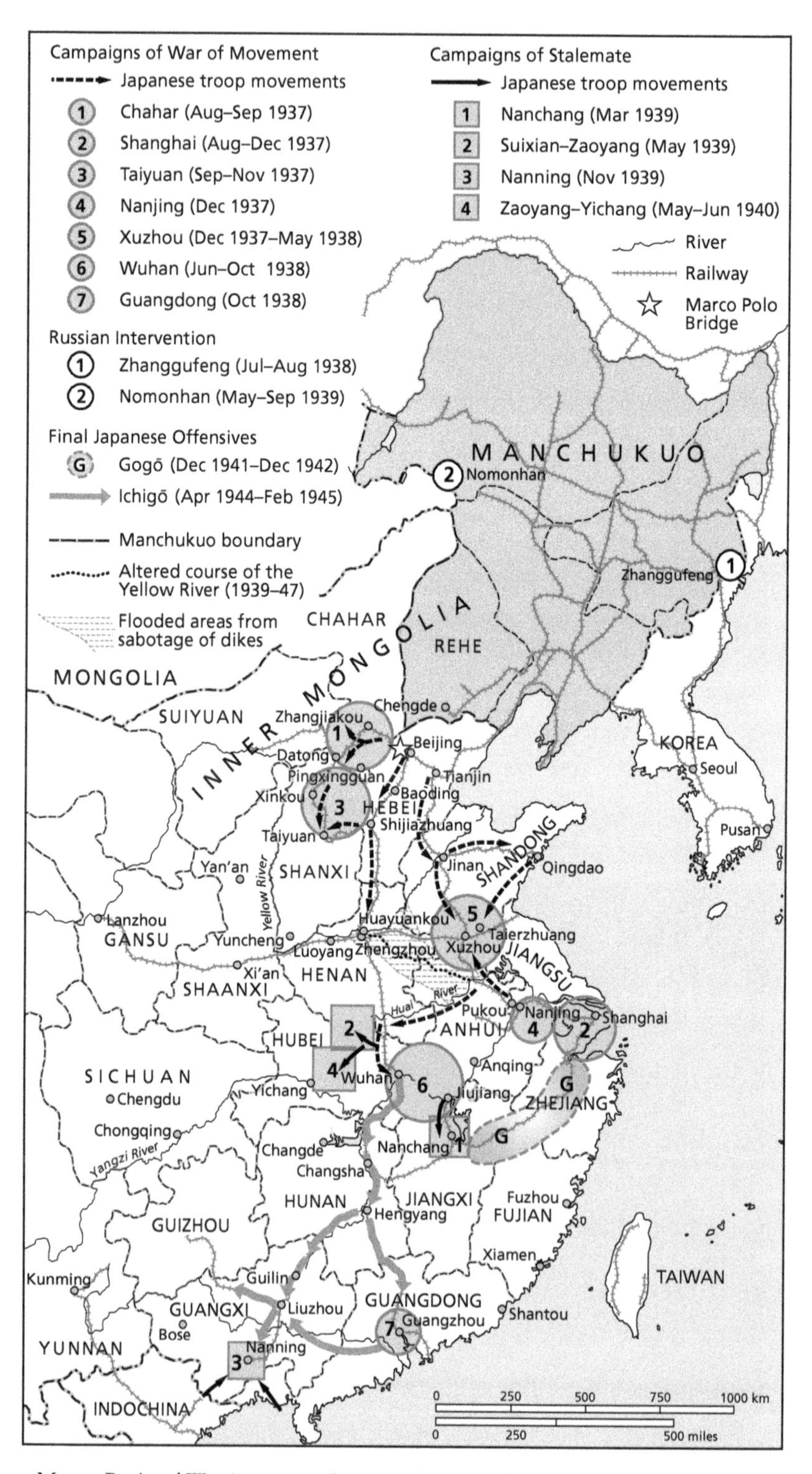

Map 4 Regional War (1937–45): Japanese Invasion of Central and Southern China.

6

REGIONAL WAR

The Second Sino-Japanese War

得寸進尺
Get an inch, advance a foot.
(Insatiable.)

Historical convention in both East and West dates the Second Sino-Japanese War as beginning in 1937. From the Chinese Communist Party point of view, this dating emphasizes that the Nationalist armed resistance to Japan began only in 1937 – contemptibly late in the game. From the Nationalist Party point of view, the dating emphasizes the Japanese campaign to occupy its capital and the bitter fighting between its conventional forces against those of Japan. From the Japanese point of view, the conventional dating implies that Manchuria was not a part of China, and therefore the hostilities emanating from Manchuria were separate from the war between Japan and China, so Japan was not so bad after all because Manchuria was up for grabs. Yet both the Nationalists and Communists agree that Manchuria was and is an integral part of China, and, since World War II, Japan has also recognized this fact. If so, then basic logic reveals a war that began in 1931, not 1937.[1]

In 1931 Japan invaded Manchuria and fought against local resistance that it did not largely suppress until 1933. While Japanese and Chinese historians referred to these events as the Manchurian Incident, the facts on the ground fit the narrowest definition of a war even if the parties involved were too polite to call it such. Although Nationalist troops did none of the fighting, other Chinese did, mainly Manchurians, most of whom were ethnic Han Chinese, not Manchus. The occupation of Manchuria did not sate the Japanese, who continued to expand their zone of occupation in North China from 1933 to 1936, what

I impoliticly call the North China Campaign. Again, although the Nationalist armies did not fight the Japanese, North Chinese did. So again even under the narrowest definition of warfare, war continued between Japanese main forces and Chinese insurgents from 1933 and 1935, and the battlefield was located on Chinese territory.

Although the Japanese were not always fighting the Nationalists from 1931 to 1945, they were always fighting Chinese forces of one denomination or another, hence the term "Sino-Japanese War" (not Nationalist-Japanese War or Communist-Japanese War) and hence the dating of 1931 to 1945. It turns out that the Nationalists did not control all of the armed forces of China by a long shot. This should not be very surprising since the condition of civil war, by definition, means that no one side does. Different sides took up arms against Japan at different times, but, beyond some Korean Communist insurgents in Manchuria, they were all Chinese, so Sino-Japanese War is the accurate designation. It was the second such war between China and Japan. The First Sino-Japanese War had occurred between 1894 and 1895. So the Second Sino-Japanese War is the accurate terminology. Confucius might approve of a name rectified at last.[2] Its misidentification by so many with such varied political agendas illustrates the problem he sought to solve with accurate terminology. To do otherwise distorts reality and impedes understanding.

Accurate periodization emphasizes that warfare continued in China from 1931 onward, so 1937 constituted an escalation, not a beginning. Using 1937 as a starting date sanitizes Japanese activities. Japan deployed full-scale conventional armies throughout Manchuria and North China from 1931 on. These armies killed insurgents and civilians, torched villages, and took over the economic assets of the occupied areas. For those at ground zero, it was war. Likewise it was war for their respective governments and insurgent forces, which were actively trying to craft a winning strategy.

Manchurian and North Chinese resistance to Japan in the early 1930s, in contrast to Nationalist inaction, reflected the antebellum disposition of power. The Northern Expedition and the Great War of the Central Plains produced a Nationalist coalition that embraced North China, but the coalition remained fragile. The Nationalists did not physically control the North; rather their various coalition partners – Zhang Xueliang, Yan Xishan, and Yang Hucheng – did, and even their control was incomplete as long as the Communists remained in Shaanxi and the Russian puppet, Sheng Shicai, remained aloof in Xinjiang. Moreover, Chiang Kai-shek's North China allies wished to maximize their regional autonomy and so viewed the Nanjing government with suspicion. The Nationalists were a predominantly South China force and Chiang really a Central China force, although with ambitions to assume power over the North. The Japanese invasion disrupted these plans.

JAPAN IN SEARCH OF A QUICK DECISIVE VICTORY

The war from 1931 to 1936 entailed what today is called "asymmetric warfare," a clumsy term since no two sides are perfect reflections of each other, and any military strategy should leverage the differences to predispose desired outcomes. Asymmetric refers to the conventional war the Japanese wished to wage (because they knew they would win it) in juxtaposition to the insurgency their enemies delivered (because the latter lacked the equipment to fight conventionally but knew the Japanese could ill afford to wage a protracted war). Conventional warfare is expensive: It entails armies, parking lots of heavy equipment, massive firepower, and gluttonous logistical lines. Insurgencies are cheap: They require people willing to fire a weapon from time to time or to perform an act of sabotage or two. Often a packed lunch and a grenade will suffice. Conventional strategies usually seek quick decisive victories to keep the costs of warfare down. Insurgent strategies, generally favored by the weak precisely because the weak lack the capability to win a conventional fight let alone deliver a quick decisive victory, seek to protract hostilities to remain in the game long enough for the strong, but increasingly insolvent, to call it quits. Conventional warfare usually relies on a deliver-victory strategy, while insurgencies often pursue a prevent-defeat strategy – the operative concept of the latter being to survive to fight another day so that the impoverished long-distance runner can defeat the rich sprinter.

Successful insurgencies often require an asymmetry in the value that each side attaches to victory. If the weak attach a much higher value to victory than do the strong, the strong may give up before the weak succumb to exhaustion. Fighting a protracted insurgency exacts an enormous human toll under the most appalling conditions; therefore, the weak must value victory sufficiently to muster a constant flow of those willing to take the risks of part-time soldiery and sabotage, and willing to pay the terrible price when caught by the far better equipped but increasingly frustrated opponent.

While the Manchurians and North Chinese fought Japan from 1931 to 1936, Nationalist armies were not ensconced in their barracks. Rather, the Nationalist government employed a strategy of nonresistance against Japan in order to focus on winning the long Chinese civil war. The Nationalists focused on fighting the Communists in the expectation that upon victory in the civil war, they would turn their attention to Japan. In the meantime, the Nationalists used diplomacy to contest Japanese expansion. On 21 September 1931, three days after the Japanese invasion, the Nationalists appealed to the League of Nations to take action. This led to the Lytton Commission, the subsequent Lytton report demanding that Japan withdraw from Manchuria, and Japan's withdrawal from the League of Nations instead. As Joseph C. Grew, the U.S. ambassador to Japan from 1932 to 1941, wrote in his memoirs, "Nobody could miss the political significance of Japan's decision to quit the League of Nations. It marked a clear break with the Western powers and prepared the way for Japan's later adherence to the Axis."[3]

The Nationalists described their strategy in the early 1930s with the slogan "internal pacification, [before] external resistance" – a turn of phrase vilified in subsequent Communist histories of the period.[4] In July of 1931, two months before the Manchurian invasion, Chiang Kai-shek explained the logic of the strategy: "If we do not first annihilate the Red Bandits [his term for the Communists] and restore the people's capacity for survival, we will be unable to resist foreign aggression. If we do not first suppress the Guangdong-Guangxi traitors [his term for the Guangdong and Guangxi groups] and complete national unification, we will not be able to resist foreign aggression." He insisted: "Now is not the time to go to war against Japan.... The central government considers suppression of internal disorder [read victory in the civil war] to be the priority."[5]

The Communists juxtaposed this capitulationist strategy to their own patriotic plan of "opposing Chiang [and] resisting Japan" from the very beginning.[6] The words in the brackets are all-important – internal pacification [before] external resistance versus opposing Chiang [and] resisting Japan. Chiang Kai-shek anticipated sequential operations, civil war *before* regional war. The Communists planned to take on all at once civil war *and* regional war – or so they later claimed. They portrayed Chiang as a black-hearted traitor for failing to fight Japan the moment it invaded Manchuria. It is true that Communists fought the Japanese in Manchuria, and it is also true that the Japanese soon reduced them from a threat to a nuisance concentrated along the Korean border. In 1929, the Comintern had organized Koreans to participate in the Chinese Revolution and to foment revolution in Korea. As it turns out, the Communists fighting in Manchuria were mainly Korean, not Chinese. Kim Il Sung, the future leader of North Korea, not Mao Zedong, was very active in this guerrilla movement.[7]

Unlike Mao, Chiang actually took on Japanese main forces in 1932 in bitter fighting during the so-called First Shanghai Incident. In the 1930s, Chinese Communists were mostly bluster, taking credit for resistance by Korean Communists and the provincial armies of Manchuria and North China that actually fought Japan. For the duration of the Second Sino-Japanese War, the Chinese Communists remained mainly an insurgency. They developed large conventional forces only after the end of World War II, when Russia finally delivered sufficient armaments to engage in conventional military operations. Rural China simply could not produce such weaponry.

This left the Nationalists, who prior to 1945 alone possessed large and comparatively well-equipped conventional armies, with the honor of going toe to toe with Japanese main forces until the United States and the British Commonwealth joined the fight after 1941.[8] In military strategy it is generally considered prudent to eliminate adversaries sequentially rather than to risk overextension by taking on all foes simultaneously. The domestic politics of China, however, forced Chiang Kai-shek, during the events at Xi'an, to abandon his strategy of appeasement of Japan. As Feng Yuxiang summed up the domestic situation in 1935, "If we fight Japan, sworn enemies can become comrades; if we do not fight Japan, comrades will become sworn enemies."[9]

Because of domestic considerations, Chiang wound up fighting all foes at once, with predictably bad military results. From both the Russian and Chinese Communist points of view, it was good strategy to set up Chiang to fight the Japanese in order to reap the spoils after Chiang and Japan fatally weakened each other. From the point of view of the Chinese civilians living in the growing theater of battle, the escalation of the Second Sino-Japanese War was a nationwide catastrophe.

On 7 July 1937, a Japanese company lost track of a single soldier during night maneuvers near the Marco Polo Bridge, a beautiful Song dynasty stone structure crossing the Yongding River on the southwestern outskirts of Beijing. To find him, the Japanese demanded to search the position of China's 29th Army. The Chinese refused. Someone fired and then both sides fired. The Japanese called in reinforcements and attacked Chinese troops at the Longwang Temple and the Wanping county garrison. Meanwhile, the missing soldier turned up unharmed. No matter. The Japanese demanded that the Chinese withdraw the garrison. They began to do so, but with inadequate dispatch, so the Japanese bombarded it on 9 July.[10] These events became known as the Marco Polo Bridge Incident in Chinese and the North China Incident in Japanese.

The 29th Army was nominally under the command of General Song Zheyuan, the former subordinate of Feng Yuxiang most recently fighting the Japanese in Chahar. Since December 1935, Song had served as the Nationalist chairman of the Hebei-Chahar Political Council, charged with slowing the southward advance of Japan with measures short of full-scale war. The events at the Marco Polo Bridge differed from past altercations in that the Chinese did not back down. At the time of the initial hostilities, Song was off being filial, sweeping the tombs of his ancestors, but he hurried back to reject Japan's diplomacy by ultimatum.[11] On 13 July a telegram from the Japanese embassy in China informed Chiang Kai-shek: "This time when Japan sends troops, the central government [i.e., you] will be the target."[12]

But Chiang had already concluded, "If we do not accomplish this [standing up to Japan], after taking an inch they will reach for another foot with no end to it."[13] He made his stand over a skirmish at a bridge outside the historic capital of Beijing on the seventh day of the seventh month of the seventh year of the 1930s. In Chinese philosophy the number 7 is associated with fire, bitterness, burning, war, blood, and the color red.[14] The Japanese got the message and reacted viscerally; they sent reinforcements of three army divisions in July, followed by two more in August after the hostilities spread to Shanghai. Over the course of 1937, Japan doubled the number of divisions deployed in China and committed 600,000 men so that by year's end, it had twenty-one divisions in China and Manchuria plus two more in Korea and Japan, totaling 950,000 men.[15]

Many of Chiang's respected military advisers argued that China was not ready. Xu Yongchang, at different times a subordinate of Feng Yuxiang and Yan Xishan, presciently advised: "If one can stomach it, it would be best to make the utmost effort to stomach Japan. Because if a major war breaks out, regardless of whether or not a third country intervenes, at best both sides will lose."[16] In the end, both Imperial Japan and Nationalist China did lose.

Other Nationalist military advisers correctly anticipated that the Chinese Communists would take advantage of the escalation to expand at Nationalist expense. Wang Jingwei and Hu Shi, China's most famous intellectual, believed fighting Japan would be far too costly so that Chiang should meet Japan's primary demand to recognize Manchukuo as the price for peace. However, under international law, once a country recognizes a territory as independent or belonging to another, it can never reverse the decision, while a country promising peace can resume hostilities. Even though Chiang was not optimistic about the outcome of a countrywide war, he believed Japanese military strategy had put him on death ground: "This round of the Sino-Japanese War puts our national survival at stake!"[17]

The Japanese did not anticipate a dire struggle. In a cabinet meeting on 11 July, four days after the original skirmish at the Marco Polo Bridge, War Minister Sugiyama Gen recommended that only a limited number of troops – a mere five divisions – would be necessary to stabilize China. He informed Emperor Hirohito: "The incident probably can be resolved within a month."[18] Others in the Imperial Japanese Army predicted that three divisions, 100 million yen, and three months would allow Japan to eliminate Chiang's army and force him to come to terms. The estimates had no connection with reality. By the end of 1937 Japan suffered 100,000 casualties. A year later, Japan was struggling to raise twenty new divisions and more than 2.5 billion yen out of a total government budget of 2.8 billion for fiscal 1937–8.[19] And by the end of 1938 Japan had thirty-four divisions totaling 1.1 million men, and by 1941, fifty-one divisions.[20]

The optimistic predictions reflected the Japanese understanding of their recent military history. In the First Sino-Japanese War, Japan had defeated the Qing empire in a matter of months and acquired, in addition to the initial war aims of expelling China from Korea, a massive indemnity and sovereignty over Taiwan. Thus, Japan profited from the war both financially and territorially. In the Russo-Japanese War, Japan again achieved its main objective, this time of keeping Russia out of Korea. It also acquired the extensive Russian railway concession in southern Manchuria and the southern half of Sakhalin Island. In both instances, Japan fought relatively short wars against dramatically larger continental adversaries and achieved all of its war objectives plus some. In 1931 Japan pacified Manchuria in short order, restoring its own economy in the process. Japanese leaders saw no reason why invading the rest of China would not proceed swimmingly.

The Japanese had studied their own military history in terms of what they had done right, not in terms of what their enemies had done wrong. Japan had not so much won these wars as its enemies had lost them. China in the final years under the Qing dynasty and Russia in the final years under the Romanov dynasty both had increasingly intractable domestic problems that had nothing to do with Japanese military prowess but that greatly facilitated Japan's victory. Neither the Han Chinese nor the Great Russian recruits were interested in shedding their blood to prop up dynasties bent on imperial adventures remote from their daily concerns.

Neither Qing China nor Romanov Russia employed military strategies taking advantage of their country's massive superiority over Japan in terms of resources, population, and strategic depth. Both could have deferred fighting until they had drawn Japan's forces inland, overstretched its logistical lines, and taken advantage of the harsh Manchurian winter to give the Japanese a fight they would have regretted, regardless of their soldier-for-soldier military superiority. To repeat a quotation variously attributed to Vladimir Lenin or Joseph Stalin, quantity has a quality of its own. But for incompetent military strategy, Chinese and Russian material superiority should have yielded victory. Thus, Japan had not won these wars because its leaders were so very clever, though they were, but because its adversaries were so very inept. So Japanese military strategy of the 1930s and 1940s emphasized the ability of willpower to trump technological or material limitations and to deliver quick decisive victories. Logistical issues such as providing rations, transport, and protection for merchant ships or the ability to garrison large areas received scant attention.[21] Japan's military strategy gave no consideration at all to the defeated, but assumed Japan could dictate the peace terms.

On 28 July 1937, Japan began its general attack on China over an area roughly equivalent to the United States east of the Mississippi River. Japanese troops occupied Beijing that day and took Tianjin two days later. The main thrust followed two parallel railway lines southward: Japan's First Army followed the Beijing-Wuhan Railway toward the inland center of industry in Wuhan, while the Second Army followed the Tianjin-Pukou Railway toward the capital in Nanjing, and, for logistical reasons, both lines of attack remained within 150 to 180 miles of the tracks. No bridge spanned the Yangzi, so a ferry service linked Nanjing on the southern bank with Pukou on the facing northern bank. On 26 August 1937, the North China Area Army was activated to assume overall command. A third, smaller campaign left from Beijing northwest along the Beijing-Suiyuan Railway into Chahar, Inner Mongolia, toward Communist country. Elements of the Kantō Army and the First Army launched the Taiyuan Campaign to take the capital of Shanxi and location of Yan Xishan's General Staff. The Communist Eighth Route Army participated in the fighting in order to defend the base area in neighboring Shaanxi Province. On 13 September Datong fell, followed by a three-week battle to take Xinkou, which fell on 13 October, and Taiyuan on 9 November, putting most of the Shanxi railway system in Japanese hands. In early 1938, the Nationalists and Communists responded by establishing the Border Government of Hebei, Shanxi, and Chahar, with Hebei under the authority of the Nationalist general Chen Cheng, Shanxi under Yan Xishan, and Chahar under the Communist Eighth Route Army. Together they sponsored numerous guerrilla attacks to harass the Japanese.[22]

The main lines of Japanese attack, however, headed due south into Nationalist country. Chiang Kai-sek dreamed of destroying the Japanese in one blow at Shanghai, where his own troops greatly outnumbered those of Japan. This best-case scenario would have preserved his own political power base and the Nationalist economic base, but he was under no illusions about its likelihood.[23] Fighting in Shanghai would threaten Western investments and would perhaps even draw a Western ally into the war. Unless he diverted Japan's attention from the North, it might cut his supply route to Russia, which was on the verge of making good its promise to provide essential military equipment. So in August

1937, Chiang disrupted Japanese plans by opening a second front in Shanghai, the so-called Second Shanghai Incident.

On 14 August, the Nationalist Air Force's opening salvo targeting Japanese warships anchored in the Shanghai harbor bombed the International Settlement and French Concession instead, killing or injuring thirteen hundred civilians. The Nationalists blamed Japanese bombers. Their air force missed again on 22 August, killing more people in the International Settlement, and again they blamed the Japanese.[24] The bombing had the important strategic effect of transforming the Imperial Japanese Navy, normally skeptical of the Imperial Japanese Army's continental adventures, into a proponent of a march on the Nationalist capital in Nanjing.[25] This time Chiang missed the strategic effects of military operations. He seems to have had little sense of the deep rift separating the Imperial Japanese Army and Navy.

On 11 July the Japanese army and navy had divided their responsibilities, with the army in charge of North China and the navy of the air war over Central and South China. The day of the bombing, the Japanese Third Fleet, based in Shanghai, seized the opportunity to showcase its aviation capabilities, which were far superior to those of the army. On 14 August, Vice Admiral Hasegawa Kiyoshi who had just completed the navy's unofficial war plan, escalated the war on his own initiative by sending planes from carriers to target air bases on the central China coast. On 15 August, the day after the first Nationalist air raid, Imperial Japanese Navy planes began bombing Nanjing, and the Nationalists ordered a general mobilization. On 16 August Japan blockaded Shanghai and Guangzhou, on 25 August it extended the blockade to China's entire east coast with the exception of foreign treaty ports, and over the fall it bombed dozens of Chinese cities. In October, Japan established the Central China Expeditionary Army to assume command of what had become the Shanghai Campaign.[26] By late October, Japan had more troops deployed in the Shanghai Campaign than in all North China.[27] By this time, the Japanese retroactively upgraded the North China Incident to the China Incident.[28]

From 13 August until 12 November, fighting raged in Shanghai, destroying 2,900 of its 5,255 factories and cutting the east-west railway lines.[29] The campaign was among the largest of the war. The Japanese employed poison gas at least thirteen times even though they had signed the 1899 and 1907 Hague Conventions, whose article 23 banned its use.[30]

By the time Shanghai fell, 9,115 Japanese soldiers had died and 31,257 had been wounded. Chinese forces suffered 187,200 casualties, including 70 percent of Chiang's young officers. Afterward, he concluded that he should have retreated sooner.[31]

Provincial capitals fell like dominoes: Baoding (Zhili) on 24 September, Shijiazhuang (Hebei) on 10 October, Taiyuan (Shanxi) on 9 November, Hangzhou (Zhejiang) on 24 December, and Jinan (Shandong) on 26 December. Provincial capitals were important: They were transportation hubs. Upon taking Shanghai, Japanese troops moved up the Yangzi, launching the Nanjing Campaign on 1 December and occupying the former capital on 13 December. In November, the Nationalists had transferred their capital farther up the Yangzi River briefly to Wuhan and in 1938 to Chongqing, located beyond the railhead that the Japanese required to deploy and sustain their troops. The Chinese, rather than capitulate, as the Japanese had assumed, traded space for time in keeping with plans developed after the first Battle for Shanghai in 1932. These plans anticipated a protracted war of attrition fought deep inland to force Japanese overextension and impose unsustainable costs.[32] As the Japanese pursued ever farther from the sea and from China's limited railway network, they extended their logistical lines and expanded the territory to garrison. While the Chinese could not defeat Japan, they could deny Japan victory. Their prevent-defeat strategy negated the Japanese strategy for a quick decisive victory.

Japan's tremendous operational success exacted a cost that the Japanese military failed to appreciate. The fighting tanked trade. In October, Shanghai trade, which had totaled $U.S.31 million a month before the escalation, sank to $U.S.6.7 million, settling at a monthly average of $U.S.8.3 million for the first half of 1938. Japan sought resources and commerce in China; instead it reaped collapsing trade and mushrooming military expenditures. Its military strategy not only undercut its economic goals, but undermined its relations with the Western powers, which protested in vain against Japan's closure of the Yangzi River to their commercial traffic and their increasing exclusion from the China market.[33]

Japanese officers also missed the nationalism that their strategy fed, not in Japan, where they encouraged and leveraged it, but in China, where nationalism undermined their military strategy in a malignant synergy. When the Manchus had ruled, they had done their utmost to keep their Han subjects divided, correctly guessing that the opening move of a united Han Chinese people would be the overthrow of Manchu minority rule. As the Chinese fought their long civil war and soldiers deployed outside their home province, as more Chinese became literate, and as a mass media developed and was written more often in the accessible vernacular instead of the arcane Classical Chinese language, as China's railway system spread to interconnect communities, and as the Japanese committed ever widening acts of violence, the Chinese acquired a deepening sense of nationalism. Every Japanese coercive act against a Chinese, now reported in the media and retold by travelers on the trains, heightened that sense of nationalism.

The Japanese decision to have their armies live off the land – in their words, "providing for the war by war"[34] – reflected an imperative to economize without consideration of the effects on Chinese public opinion. In the First Sino-Japanese War and the Russo-Japanese War, Japan had very carefully provided for its troops, had paid Chinese producers for what it took, and so did not alienate the local population.[35] Living off the land apparently worked in Manchuria, which Japan rapidly pacified, developed, and transformed into a supplier of war matériel. Pacification proved much more problematic in China south of the Great Wall. The Japanese soon turned to drug trafficking to raise funds. The Rehe Campaign in 1933 put one of China's main opium producing areas under Japanese administration. The army, the government, and the great holding companies of Mitsubishi and Mitsui oversaw its sale along with imported Persian opium and spread opium cultivation from Mongolia to Hainan Island in the far south.[36]

The Japanese also turned to poison gas and germ warfare to economize.[37] To develop these weapons, they experimented on prisoners of war and civilians at their notorious Unit 731 in Manchukuo.[38] They equipped units with biological and chemical weapons and used them throughout China.[39] In 1938, they employed poison gas thirty-nine times in Jiangxi and twenty-one times in Henan.[40] They tried to spread anthrax, the plague, typhoid, and cholera, sickening their own and the enemy alike.[41] As the belligerents in World War I had discovered, poison gas was not particularly effective because it often killed its deployers instead of its intended victims. So Japan used gas less frequently after 1938, but by then the damage had been done.[42] Its use appalled Chinese and Western public opinion. Whatever savings Japan generated from cheap provisions, narcotics sales, and exotic weapons, the savings did not offset the hatred these actions caused. The hatred then fueled recruitments for the Nationalists and Communists and heightened Japan's diplomatic isolation. Whereas the Han had been unwilling to fight in support of Manchu minority rule in the First Sino-Japanese War, they became determined to defend their homeland in the Second Sino-Japanese War. This change in public attitude meant the war would not be short. Yet the longer it lasted, the stronger Chinese nationalism became.

In military terminology, the Japanese determined that either the Nationalist economy or Chiang's conventional forces (and certainly both together) constituted China's "center of gravity."[43] They believed that if they targeted that center of gravity the edifice of Nationalist control would collapse like a building with charges correctly laid at the foundations. The Chinese economy and, by extension, the tax base was concentrated, as it is today, in the coastal cities and along the Yangzi River, China's greatest internal waterway. This was the maritime world of sea-lanes connecting domestic and international markets. China had five key centers of economic activity: Japan had already taken Manchuria and soon took the Beijing-Tianjin and Shanghai areas. This left two outstanding: the inland center at Wuhan and Guangzhou in the far south. By the fall of 1938, Japan had taken all five.[44]

The escalation of 1937 did indeed cause an implosion of the Nationalist economy. The Nationalists tried to move their industrial base with them, relocating factories from occupied China to the two main cities of Sichuan, Chongqing and Chengde, whose populations between 1934 and 1945 nearly quadrupled for the former and doubled for the latter.[45] The Nationalist Party opened numerous new factories so that by 1944, it controlled more than half of those in Chongqing, the focus of government investments, and managed more than 60 percent of capital nationwide.[46]

Despite the heroic effort, the Nationalists could restore only a fraction of the former economic activity.[47] The move inland cost them nearly 87 percent of their productive capacity.[48] Shanghai had the greatest concentration of large and efficient firms in China south of the Great Wall. In category after category of industry, Shanghai firms dominated China. The city had the best urban infrastructure in terms of electricity and water supply.[49] In comparison, Nanjing and Chongqing were commercial and industrial backwaters. Although the Nationalists gradually increased production in their new inland stronghold, they reached only 41 percent of the preescalation capacity.[50]

The Japanese had long tried to undermine Nationalist finances through officially sanctioned smuggling, much of it under the protection of the Imperial Japanese Army.[51] After the 1937 escalation, there was no need to continue since Japan eliminated the hated 1933 Nationalist tariffs in its expanded zone of occupation, shrinking Nationalist customs receipts in the process.[52] The creeping Japanese occupation deprived the Nationalists of 90 percent of their former tax revenues from customs, salt, excise, alcohol, cigarettes, and the like.[53] Nationalist local government income plummeted by nearly one-quarter between 1936 and 1940, and the loss of China's main grain producing areas meant that Nationalist requisitioning to feed the army produced severe deprivation among farmers.[54]

In 1937, the Nationalists were already running a 37 percent government budget deficit.[55] Then from 1937 to 1939, expenditures rose by one-third, while revenues fell by two-thirds.[56] From 1927 to 1937, they had relied ever more heavily on borrowing to sustain government funding. As the war escalated, the borrowed money no longer financed investment but consumption – primarily in the form of military expenses – so that the borrowing did not promise future income but only future interest payments as well as inflation when they turned to the printing presses to meet expenses.[57] The value of the Nationalist yuan plunged against the U.S. dollar from about thirty cents in 1937 to about four cents in 1941.[58] When the government tried to cap civil service and military salaries, the purchasing power of those people vital for regime survival plummeted.[59] The Nationalists, like the Japanese and such warlords as Yan Xishan, turned to the opium trade for government finance. In 1927 they had planned to eradicate opium cultivation within three years. They forbade its private sale but levied a tax on its use for medicinal purposes with the consequence of legalizing the opium trade and making the taxes on this trade a source of government revenue, which the government then used to finance the encirclement campaigns.[60]

In addition to the economy, the Japanese believed that Chiang's conventional forces constituted a second center of gravity. Destroy these forces and he would have to capitulate. So Japan blockaded China, occupied its coastal cities, and moved up the Yangzi River in pursuit of Chiang's most loyal and proficient conventional forces. Chiang did not follow the Japanese script to sue for peace, but retreated inland.

The Japanese soon focused on a third presumed center of gravity, the Chinese will to resist. Bushido, or the code of the samurai, which so captivated Japan's military, treated willpower as the trump card in warfare. In addition to believing their own willpower to be superior, they brutalized occupied populations to undermine the will to resist. On the road from Shanghai to Nanjing, Japanese troops had orders to treat all Chinese outside Shanghai as belligerents, kill them, and destroy their homes.[61] They burned Zhenjiang, a city left undefended by the Nationalists and located on the Yangzi between Shanghai and Nanjing. It burned for ten days. The Japanese burned wounded Chinese soldiers alive and raped women and girls. A city resident explained such actions in his memoirs: "The main reasons why the entire city was burned so extensively had to be their intention to destroy our property. Everywhere a fire was set, it was on their orders." Those trying to douse the fires were executed.[62]

When Japanese forces under the command of Lieutenant General Prince Asaka Yasuhiko, Emperor Hirohito's paternal granduncle, entered Nanjing, they massacred tens of thousands, some say hundreds of thousands, over the next year. Whatever the numbers, Japanese troops committed an atrocity of horrific proportions.[63] This became known as the Rape of Nanjing. The massacre attending the Xuzhou Campaign in 1938 also lasted for several months.[64] Likewise, the Japanese intended their bombing campaigns to terrorize civilians into submission.

As a result, between 1937 and 1945, more than 95 million Chinese, or 26 percent of the population, became refugees. The economies of Taiyuan, Jinan, Changsha, Wuhan, and Nanjing required decades to recover.[65] Major epidemics ensued and continued throughout the war – cholera, malaria, and the plague.[66] It takes little imagination to realize that such actions instilled a deep and enduring Chinese hatred of the Japanese. Far from laying down their arms, the Chinese fought on.[67]

Unwittingly, the Japanese strategy landed Japan in a protracted war whose costs rapidly undermined the home economy. Whereas from 1931 to 1936, Japanese economic statistics show flourishing growth both on the home islands and in the greater empire, from 1937 onward, key economic statistics plateaued. Territorial expansion no longer benefited the economy. On the contrary, it constituted an increasing burden so that by 1940 the Japanese home islands faced food shortages.[68]

OPERATIONAL VICTORY AND STRATEGIC STALEMATE

Over the course of 1937 and 1938, the Imperial Japanese Army won an uninterrupted string of victories on three fronts – Inner Mongolia, North China, and the Yangzi River valley – in the expectation that surely the Nationalists would fold.[69] The two major campaigns had focused on Nationalists forces in North China and Shanghai, while the much smaller Chahar Campaign targeted the Communists. Suicide, however, did not figure as prominently in Chinese as in Japanese culture. The elusive Nationalists continued to trade space for time in the belief that they, as the residents of China unified by a common hatred of Japan, were better positioned to hold out for the long haul than Japan's expensive armies of occupation.

After the fall of Nanjing, Japan's North China Area Army again deployed southward on two axes following the main north-south railway lines, one toward the junction at Zhengzhou and the other toward the junction at Xuzhou, where the Central China Expeditionary Army converged from the south. The Xuzhou Campaign, fought between March and 19 May 1938, was one of the largest campaigns anywhere in the 1930s or 1940s, involving some 600,000 combatants. The city sits at the midpoint of the north-south Tianjin-Pukou Railway connecting Manchuria with Shanghai and serves as the junction with the major east-west railway line, connecting Zhengzhou with the sea (at Shanghai) and linking up with the other north-south line, the Beijing-Wuhan Railway. After taking Xuzhou, Japan's plans called for a second pincer movement, this time on Wuhan, approaching it from the north and from the east along the Yangzi River. The Nationalist counterstrategy in combination with essential Russian weapons plus a Russian diversion in the far north, however, transformed Japan's war of rapid movement into a stalemate.[70]

Chiang Kai-shek had lost his army during the Shanghai and Nanjing Campaigns. Li Zongren, the leader of the Guangxi group, recreated a Nationalist army out of a motley array of poorly trained regional forces, mostly from areas far to the south of the fighting. Although Li's troops had inferior training compared to Japan's, their heroism in combination with Russian tanks and guns inflicted Japan's first major defeat in modern history at Taierzhuang in April of 1938. Earlier during the Taiyuan Campaign, on 25 September 1937 at Pingxingguan, Shanxi, the legendary Communist commander Lin Biao, who became famous during the postwar phase of the long Chinese civil war and infamous in his subsequent power struggles with Mao Zedong, had defeated the Japanese when the latter had been arrogant enough to enter, without prior scouting, a several-mile-long defile with no egress except the one road. Three thousand Japanese lost their lives.[71] This victory had elated the Communists, providing a much-needed boost to morale, but the Japanese had occupied the provinces of Chahar and Suiyuan, along with the northern half of Shanxi. The scale of the two Chinese victories, however, was not comparable. At Taierzhuang, General Li Zongren eliminated two of Japan's finest divisions and dispelled the myth of Japanese invincibility, greatly boosting Nationalist morale.[72]

The scale of the equipment was not comparable either. Li Zongren had heavy military equipment that Lin Biao simply did not. In February two transports of Russian arms had arrived in Haiphong and Hong Kong including 82 tanks, 20 antiaircraft guns, 50 antitank guns, and numerous other weapons and ammunition. Another large delivery followed, including 400 motor vehicles, 297 planes, artillery, millions of rounds of ammunition, and a long list of other weapons and ammunition.[73]

To break Chinese morale, the Japanese promised to give no quarter to those fleeing the field. Instead of creating paralysis, the threats apparently steeled the will to resist. Tens of thousands of Chinese died during the Xuzhou Campaign including nine generals, but only one from Shandong, the location of the fighting. In other words, the Chinese were fighting for China, not, as in the past, strictly for their native place.[74] The surviving Chinese generals, such as Li Zongren, Bai Chongxi, and Tang Enbo, became national heroes.[75]

But willpower alone could not defeat modern weapons, as the Japanese would later learn for themselves in their fight against the United States. After the Russian equipment ran out, Xuzhou fell on 19 May 1938, but unlike the disorderly retreats after the fall of Shanghai, Nanjing, and Jinan, Chinese troops conducted an orderly retreat. In an act of desperation to halt the Japanese progress inland, on 5 and 7 June 1938, the Nationalists, not the Japanese, committed one of the worst atrocities of a war famous for atrocities. Chiang Kai-shek ordered the breach of Yellow River dikes at Huayuankou, Henan, near the key railway junction at Zhengzhou.[76] The dikes were actually breached in multiple places including at the junction with Grand Canal and inundated 70,000 square kilometers of mainly prime farmland.[77] Nearly an estimated 900,000 perished, 325,589 in Henan, 407,514 in Anhui, and 160,200 in Jiangsu. The statistics for refugees are equally heart-rending: nearly 3.9 million with 1,172,639 in Henan, 2,536,315 in Anhui, and 202,400 in Jiangsu.[78] In this one act, Chiang Kai-shek killed more Chinese than had the Japanese despite all their atrocities.[79] For the next decade the Yellow River ran outside its dikes, leaving a wake of misery.[80] Although the flood prevented the Japanese from taking the railway junction at Zhengzhou to reach Wuhan by rail, they improvised to reach the city by boat via the Yangzi River.[81]

With the failure to surround and annihilate the Nationalist army at Xuzhou, the Japanese again targeted the economy and the transportation network. Wuhan was the great distribution and processing center for China's agricultural commodities as well as an inland industrial center.[82] It was also the point where the Yangzi River became wide – with the confluence of the Hanshui River – and could be easily crossed only to the west, but all the way east to Shanghai, it formed a powerful barrier between North and South China and the armies caught on either bank. No bridges spanned the Yangzi until 1957, with the completion of the railway bridge at Wuhan, and a decade later, with a second railway bridge crossed at Nanjing.

In 1938 Wuhan became the staging area for the 2 million Nationalist troops defending the central Yangzi Valley.[83] The Japanese launched a triple pincer, with one prong sweeping up the Yangzi River toward Wuhan and the capital farther upstream, another prong reaching down the coast to Guangzhou in order to cut the railway terminus in the south, and the last sweeping southward down the railway system to break Nationalist control from Wuhan south to Guangzhou and east to the coast.[84]

Japan took Yangzi River cities in succession: On 12 June 1938 Anqing fell, followed by Jiujiang on 26 July. Meanwhile in May, the Imperial Japanese Navy launched an air campaign on Chongqing, which it bombed more than any other city, mainly between the months of May to October when the cloud cover lifted. The city suffered more than two hundred air raids between February 1938 and August 1943.

Japanese pilots called their route the "Chongqing Milk Run," when they dropped incendiary bombs and watched Chongqing burn, little dreaming of how much more flammable their own cities were should anyone return the favor. According to the logic of strategic bombing, either the capital or the will of the civilians to resist was the key center of gravity to target, so terrorize with relentless bombing. It turns out bombing a capital city rarely cows but often enrages.[85]

A month after Chiang Kai-shek breached the Yellow River dikes, Russia took action in the north, with the probable intent to disrupt Japanese plans by forcing a redeployment north. Japan suspended the Wuhan Campaign not because of the flooding but because of fighting on the Korean-Russian-Manchukuo border at Zhanggufeng, where from 11 July to 10 August 1938, Japanese and Russian troops fought a pitched battle. This became known as the Zhanggufeng (Chōkohō) Incident for the Chinese and Japanese or the Battle of Lake Khasan for the Russians. Russian-Japanese border incidents had occurred with regularity since 1931.[86] This time the Russians chose to escalate at a place of their choosing, seventy miles south of Vladivostok.[87] Events seemed to be moving toward Chiang Kai-shek's long-awaited Russian-Japanese Armageddon. The Russians deployed a force of 21,000 against 3,000 Japanese with predictable results.[88] They accused Japan of territorial encroachments, they deployed the air force, but after a month of fighting the Japanese withdrew, and both sides signed a cease-fire agreement. The Russian price for peace was a piece of Chinese territory. Afterward, the Russians deported to Kazakhstan 200,000 Koreans, who had farmed the area and given cover to Japan's main espionage base in Siberia.[89]

Despite this delay, in the fall of 1938 Japanese forces closed in on Wuhan via the Beijing-Wuhan Railway from the north, the Yangzi River from the southeast, and overland from the east. Russia had provided 602 planes in early September, but by 28 October only 87 remained. While the military equipment lasted, the Chinese fought well.[90] The Nationalists removed Wuhan's munitions factories to Sichuan before the city fell on 25 October.[91] Again the Nationalists conducted an orderly retreat after a hard-fought ten-month campaign. Their attrition strategy had done what it was designed to do: survive to fight another day and overextend the Japanese militarily and financially in the meantime.[92]

Victory put Japan in possession of all of North China and the Yangzi River valley, the most prosperous and developed parts of the country. Japan set up two major air bases, one in Wuhan and the other in Yuncheng, Shanxi. The former facilitated the bombing of Nationalist interests in Chengdu, Chongqing, Kunming, and Guilin, while the latter facilitated the bombing of the Communist headquarters in Yan'an and Lanzhou, the terminus of the 1,816-mile highway specially built by the Russians to convey their aid and the location of their air base to train Chinese pilots.[93] Yet still the Chinese fought on.

The Japanese had begun to perceive another possible center of gravity – China's trade and aid from the outside. After the fall of Shanghai, half of unoccupied China's trade traveled along the Guangdong-Wuhan Railway.[94] Therefore, in May 1938 Japan also launched amphibious expeditions to take the treaty ports of Xiamen (Amoy), Fuzhou (Foochow), and Shantou (Swatow),[95] followed in October by the Guangdong Campaign. On 21 October the great port of Guangzhou fell and on 10 February 1939 the navy took Hainan Island, indicating ambitions even farther south.[96] Together these victories put Japan in possession of the main ports from Guangdong north and allowed it to tighten the naval blockade. Yet as Japan reached the limits of the Chinese railway system, it also reached the logistical limits of the Japanese way of war.[97]

As events went from bad to worse, Chiang Kai-shek simultaneously pursued a diplomatic track to induce the United States, Britain, or Russia to intervene militarily. Earlier, the U.S. Congress had tried to claim the moral high ground by prohibiting arms sales to either side on 14 September 1937. This of course had done nothing to slow Japanese expansion, since Japan produced its weapons domestically. It did, however, cut off a key potential source of arms to Chiang Kai-shek, who, once ejected from Shanghai, Xuzhou, and Wuhan, had little ability to produce weapons internally. From 1933 on, the United States had been an important arms supplier for the Nationalists, providing 150 planes in 1933, 79 in 1934, and 110 in 1935, but virtually nothing in 1936 and 1937.[98] The United States did not prohibit oil exports, however. Until 1941 U.S. oil kept both the Japanese army and navy on the move and its bombers airborne.

As Japanese forces had moved down the China coast, President Franklin D. Roosevelt had made his famous quarantine speech on

5 October 1937, urging the quarantine of Japanese and German aggression.[99] The speech reflected a perception of fascism on the march in many parts of the globe. In 1935 Italy had begun expanding its empire in North Africa with the Ethiopian War. On 7 March 1936, Adolf Hitler had disregarded the provisions of the Versailles Peace Treaty terminating World War I, to remilitarize the Rhineland, securing his hold over the heavy industry and key resources essential to wage war. In July 1936, civil war had erupted in Spain; three years later it resulted in the overthrow of the government by a Fascist dictatorship under General Francisco Franco. Foreign intervention by Germany and Italy and studied nonintervention by Britain, France, and the United States had greatly contributed to this outcome. On 25 October, Germany and Italy had allied. On 25 November, Germany and Japan had signed the Anti-Comintern Pact, which within the fortnight had propelled Russia into action at Xi'an to broker the Second United Front.

American voters, however, remained isolationist. There was also no natural political affinity between the United States and the Nationalist Party, which had far more natural affinity with the European Fascists, who also emphasized military over civilian leadership, an oppressive secret police, and pervasive state intervention in the economy. Chiang soon sent his adopted son, Chiang Wei-kuo, to the German Army, where he participated in the invasion of Austria in 1938.[100] So Chiang Kai-shek received no aid from the United States.

Germany had been Chiang's most reliable foreign supporter after the breakdown of the First United Front. From 1928 until 1938, the Nationalists maintained cordial relations with Weimar and then Nazi Germany. Weimar Germany had recognized Chiang's government, fresh from the Northern Expedition, right after the United States did. In 1927 Germany had begun sending military advisers, reaching a peak of seventy in 1935. These men had trained Chiang's elite units, which he had deployed during the encirclement campaigns, but which Japan had then destroyed in the Shanghai Campaign in 1937. Relations had improved after Adolf Hitler had become chancellor. In 1936 Germany had become the first Western country to give the Nationalists substantial financial aid. Germany had provided four-fifths of the Nationalists' imported weapons in return for tungsten, a critical war matériel for producing heavy metal alloys for armaments, machine tools, and light bulb and vacuum tube filaments. Germany had bought half of the world's tungsten. Nearly three-quarters was from China.[101] The weapons produced would soon train on Allied soldiers.

German leaders had deplored the 1937 escalation of the Second Sino-Japanese War in the belief that the conflict would disrupt commerce with China and German war plans that depended on numerous imported resources. The escalation ruined German plans to maintain cordial relations with both China and Japan and reduced Japan's military pressure on Russia that had kept Russian attentions divided. Japan deplored continuing German military aid to China. In the sixteen months following the escalation, Germany provided 60 percent of Chinese arms imports at a rate of sixty thousand tons per month that the Chinese used to take Japanese lives. Although Germany rejected Japanese requests for its support under the Anti-Comintern Pact, it reluctantly cut off its aid to the Nationalists to preserve working relations with Japan.[102]

As Germany faded from the scene, Russia took its place to provide the Nationalists with the armaments to conduct conventional military operations. On 31 July 1937, three weeks after the events at the Marco Polo Bridge, Russia had agreed to supply China with arms worth up to 100 million Chinese dollars in two installments within the year as well as Russian artillerists and pilots, the latter to fly combat missions and to train pilots. The first aid had arrived in early September, the first promised planes had reached Xinjiang on 22 October, 450 Russian pilots and aviation personnel along with other military advisers had arrived by year's end, and soon they were targeting Japanese traffic on the Yangzi River. Russia supplied arms sufficient for twenty divisions.[103]

In January 1938 the Nationalist government sent a representative to negotiate the details of a second Russian aid package. Russia agreed to loan China $50 million on 1 March, and that same month the deliveries began arriving. Four-fifths of the money went to acquire airplanes. Between this 1 March loan and 13 June 1939, Russia extended three loans totaling $250 million, but actually delivering only $173 million.[104] Military aid went mainly to Nationalist, not Communist forces. China repaid the loans in tea, wool, and tungsten.[105] From 1937 to 1941 Russia sent 1,235 planes, 1,600 artillery pieces, more than 14,000 machine guns, 50,000 rifles, more than 300 advisers, more than 2,000 pilots, more than 3,000 engineers and technical experts, and thousands of drivers to deliver the goods. By the beginning of 1939, Russia had sent 5,000 military experts. Russian pilots flew from Nanjing, Wuhan,

Chongqing, Chengdu, Lanzhou, Xi'an, and other places.[106] More than 200 Russian pilots died in China.[107] The Nationalists relied on Russian planes until 1942, when U.S. generosity took over.[108]

Britain and the United States did not become interested in helping until early 1939. British diplomacy in Europe and the U.S. arms embargo in Asia did not slow the march of fascism in either theater. Italy joined the Anti-Comintern Pact on 6 November 1937. On 1 November Italy had recognized Manchukuo, on 2 December Spain soon followed, while Germany dithered until 20 February 1938 – stalled by its desire to maintain friendly relations with both Japan and China.[109] On 12 March Hitler annexed Austria in what the Germans called the *Anschluss*, or "connection." On 29 September, Britain capitulated to German demands at Munich, by allowing Germany to annex the Sudentenland, where the preponderance of German speakers lived in Czechoslovakia. In March 1939 Germany annexed the rest of Czechoslovakia for good measure. When it invaded Poland six months later in September, France and Britain, like Chiang Kai-shek before them, finally abandoned their strategy of appeasement and declared war, the conventional date for the outbreak of World War II.

It turns out that a strategy of appeasement for an enemy with the unlimited objective of regime change, rather than appease, allows the enemy to gather strength. With the invasion of Poland, Neville Chamberlain, the British prime minister who had negotiated the Munich agreement, belatedly realized that Hitler did not share his predecessor, Otto von Bismarck's, limited political objective of unifying the Germanic-speaking lands, but ultimately had the unlimited objective of overturning the global order to replace it with Nazism for the master race and death to subhumans, whom Hitler defined as Jews, Gypsies, the handicapped, and Slavs initially, with other groups presumably left for later. Targeted for demolition were both Britain and Russia.

As British and American leaders mulled over the meaning of the 1938 Munich agreement, in 1939 they began extending loans to the Nationalists, the enemy of Germany's Asian ally, Japan. On 8 February, the United States loaned the Nationalists $25 million, and on 15 March, Britain provided $750,000. By this time, the Japanese had advanced so rapidly and so deep into China that if the trend continued, the Nationalist government would soon lose its toehold in China. Britain responded to the Guangdong Campaign of October 1938 by building the Burma Road to supply the Nationalists. The Burma Road connected Kunming, Yunnan, to the railhead in Lashio, Burma, then part of the British Empire. It provided key but very limited military supplies to the Nationalists from December 1938 until July 1940 and again from October 1940 until March 1942, when the Japanese closed it for good.[110]

Meanwhile, in 1939 Japan's rampage through China reached its logistical limits as Japan ran out of easy targets. After the destruction of the Nationalist economy proved insufficient to bring the Nationalists to terms, the Japanese made a renewed attempt to occupy the new capital. In March of 1939 Japan won the Battle of Nanchang, taking the railway spur connecting Nanchang, the capital of Jiangxi, to the Yangzi River between Wuhan and Nanjing and to the east-west Zhejiang-Jiangxi Railway. Japan engaged in successive battles farther west in May 1939 at the battles for Suixian-Zaoyang, Hubei, and in the fall of 1939 for Changsha, Hunan.[111]

Stalin interrupted the rampage. After Wuhan crumbled, again he relieved pressure on the Nationalists by opening a second front. In March of 1939, his protégé, Choibalsan, assumed power in Mongolia.[112] Choibalsan apparently was amenable to large Russian troop deployments. In May 1939 fighting again broke out between Japanese and Russian forces, this time in Nomonhan, Mongolia. This became known as the First Nomonhan Incident among the Japanese and the Battle of Khalkhin-Gol among the Russians. In June renewed fighting at Nomonhan escalated into pitched tank battles that raged until the exchange of a cease-fire agreement in September. The Russian price was another piece of Chinese territory. The battle became known as the Second Nomonhan Incident. Russian tanks under the command of the soon-to-be-legendary Georgii K. Zhukov, future savior of Russia, obliterated Japanese forces, killing or wounding an astounding 79 percent of frontline Japanese troops and, in the process, gutted the Imperial Japanese Army's long-standing war plan (really its only war plan), the so-called Northern Advance on Russia.[113] The plan had called for a rapid conquest of Siberia as far west as Lake Baikal to eliminate the Communist threat to Asia. Stalin observed after learning of the estimated twenty thousand Japanese deaths among the seventy-five thousand deployed at Nomonhan: "That is the only language these Asiatics understand. After all, I am an Asiatic too, so I ought to know."[114]

Back in June 1926, the Japanese army and navy had arranged a fateful compromise in their incessant feuding over military budgets and war plans, allowing each to concentrate on its preferred main enemy. The navy had never liked the Northern Advance plan, which left it with a less-than-heroic supply-service role, transporting war matériel and troops from Japan to the Asian mainland. So the navy came up with its own war plan, the so-called Southern Advance, which showcased naval assets to project empire southward overseas.[115] While the army plan focused on Russia as the main enemy, the navy plan targeted Britain and the United States. This resulted in mutually irrelevant and mutually nonsupporting war plans.

Neither plan emphasized China, the actual theater for most of the fighting. Each service envisioned a symmetrical fight against its enemy opposite number, but, in the event, Japan's enemies fought asymmetrically. China launched a massive insurgency, the United States targeted Japan's undefended civilian merchant marine, and Russia used diplomacy to set up proxies. In Japan's successful wars against the Qing and Romanov dynasties, the army and navy had developed war plans jointly and fought jointly. The 1926 plans envisioned sequential operations first eliminating Russia in Asia before embarking on a resource grab throughout the South Pacific that would touch off war with Britain and the United States.[116] After Nomonhan, the Southern Advance was the only war plan left on the shelf.

Worse still, in the midst of the fighting at Nomonhan, Germany stunned Japan by violating their 1936 Anti-Comintern Pact to sign a credit agreement and a nonaggression pact with Russia on 19 and 23 August 1939, respectively. The agreement allowed Russia to provide Germany with raw materials in return for weapons and machinery. The nonaggression pact was concluded one week before Germany invaded Poland and is known variously as the Nazi-Soviet Pact or the Molotov-Ribbentrop Pact, in honor of its two signers.[117] Not only did it hang Japan out to dry, but a secret protocol divided Poland between Russia and Germany and ceded Finland, Estonia, Latvia, and Bessarabia to Russia.

As a result of the Nazi-Soviet Pact, the Japanese cabinet fell. A week and a half later, on 3 September, World War II broke out in Europe when France and Britain declared war on Germany for its invasion of Poland two days earlier.[118] On 17 September, the day after Nomonhan ended, Russia joined the German attack on Poland and soon negotiated

German recognition of Russian domination over Lithuania. Russia occupied not only eastern Poland, but before long Latvia, Estonia, Lithuania, Bessarabia, and only eastern Finland because of stiff resistance during the Finnish-Russian War of 1939–40.

Foreign Minister Matsuoka Yōsuke tried to pick up the pieces by strengthening Japan's ties with both Germany and Russia through a formal alliance with Germany and Italy signed on 27 September 1940, the so-called Tripartite Alliance, more commonly known as the Axis, and a neutrality pact with Russia signed on 13 April 1941 that made the Germans fume, but these two centerpieces of the strategy soon became mutually exclusive when Germany invaded Russia in June. This part of the story, however, concerns the war in Europe and brewing global war.

Following Nomonhan, over the winter of 1939–40 the Nationalists launched the Winter Offensive, a massive counterattack involving eighty divisions in southern Shanxi and along the Yangzi that widened into South China when the Japanese threatened Sichuan from the south in the Battle of Southern Guangxi. In Shanxi, Yan Xishan soon cut a separate peace with the Japanese in return for arms and agreement to turn on the Communist Eight Route Army, which he attacked in December 1939. On 24 November, Japan won the Nanning (Yongning) Campaign far to the south in Guangxi in an attempt to sever trade via Hanoi. Trade was not cut but only diverted to Bose (Baise or Paise), Guangxi. The Nationalist victory in the Battle of Kunlun Pass saved the supply route, when Chiang deployed his only formation equipped with tanks and these forces killed the opposing commanding major general, Nakamura Masao, and annihilated Nakamura's most elite unit.[119]

The Japanese also lost the Battle of Changsha, near the southernmost point on the north-south railway line from Beijing to Changsha via Wuhan. South of Changsha, the railway connected with the major east-west line running from Shanghai to Liuzhou. On 12 November 1938, Changsha, the capital of Hunan, had been the scene of one of the great atrocities of the war, again committed not by the Japanese, but by the Nationalists, when General Zhang Zhizhong, the governor of Hunan, mistakenly thought the Japanese were about to take the city and so ordered it torched. It turns out that the Japanese had other plans. The city burned for four days, forcing the flight of a population swollen by refugees to 800,000. Chiang had three officials executed but not his primary political ally and key Whampoa group member, Zhang Zhizhong, the man in charge.[120]

Zhang Zhizhong correctly understood the strategic position of Changsha and the certainty that it would become the object of a Japanese attack. He got the timing wrong. Thereafter, the Japanese repeatedly tried to take the city. The Nationalists successfully defended it three times, from September to October 1939, from September to October 1941, and from December 1941 to January 1942. These are known as the First, Second, and Third Battles of Changsha. The Nationalists did not lose the city until 1944 in Japan's Ichigō Campaign.[121]

In the spring of 1940, the Japanese launched a major offensive up the Yangzi River toward the capital in the Zaoyang-Yichang Campaign.[122] On 12 June, the Nationalists halted the Japanese advance at the Yichang rapids in the Yangzi gorges, the gateway to Sichuan and Chongqing, but the campaign cost them much of Hunan, a key source of rice. They also suffered high losses – fifty-one thousand killed – but they made clear that the Japanese were no nearer to victory. Despite numerous Japanese offensives, after 1938 they failed to hold the new territory. As soon as their main units departed for battles elsewhere, Chinese forces returned.[123]

Outbreak of war in Europe offered Japan hope. With the fall of France in June 1940, Japan pressured Britain to close the Burma Road in July, putting Chiang Kai-shek in his worst situation since the beginning of the Second Sino-Japanese War.[124] Although Britain reopened the road three months later in October, in March 1942 Japanese troops took the railhead at Lashio, Burma, eliminating the Burma Road as a land route to China until early 1945.

Japan conducted three offensives in 1941, the fruitless Battle of Southern Henan in which it gained no territory, the unsuccessful Battle of Shanggao in which it lost nearly half its force, and its only operational success, in the Battle of Southern Shanxi, when it forced the Nationalists to withdraw at the cost of opening North and Central China to Communist infiltration. In doing so, Japan inadvertently relieved the Nationalist blockade of the main Communist base areas – a strategic blunder. Russia, Britain, and the United States responded to Japanese advances by intervening ever more aggressively. Although Chiang's diplomacy failed to convince any of the great powers to deploy troops, he secured vital military aid that the Japanese increasingly saw as the surviving center of gravity.[125] Japan's fixation on the regional war and the operational level of warfare without consideration to the civil war and brewing global war made strategic victory – the restoration of prosperity and stability to Asia – ever more unlikely.

INSURGENCY AND PACIFICATION

As the Nationalists continued to lose the conventional fight, they increasingly turned to a strategy often favored by the weak, guerrilla warfare. On 23 May 1938, Stalin advised Chiang's representative and son of Sun Yat-sen, Sun Fo, of the necessity to engage the entire civilian population in a massive partisan movement behind Japan's lines to make life unbearable for the Japanese.[126] Chiang became caught between the conventional campaigns he wished to fight and the insurgency that his defeated troops were capable of waging. As early as the winter of 1937–8, he began following the advice of one of the most brilliant Nationalist generals, Bai Chongxi of the Guangxi group, who recommended combining guerrilla forces with mobile operations in order to score small victories that would help maintain morale while eroding that of the Japanese. Chiang concurred, "As politics transcends military affairs and guerrilla warfare transcends conventional warfare in that it transforms the enemy rear into the front line, and so one-third of our forces shall be deployed to the enemy rear." The Nationalists transformed elements of their defeated armies into guerrilla units that remained in Japanese-occupied territories to make life miserable for the occupiers. By 1938, the Nationalists had between 600,000 and 700,000 guerrillas harassing Japanese operations. Most deployed in Central China, while in North China warlord troops performed equivalent functions.[127] After the loss of the Wuhan Campaign and virtually the entire railway system outside South China, he reorganized the country into ten war zones and increasingly changed his focus from positional warfare in the defense of cities to mobile warfare aimed to attrite Japanese troops, and from conventional to guerrilla operations.[128]

The combination of guerrilla and conventional forces proved lethal. The new strategy impeded the Japanese ability to launch major new offensives.[129] Japan's conventional army needed to concentrate to fight Chiang's armies but had to disperse to fight the insurgency. Yet it could not do both simultaneously. When Japanese troops dispersed, Nationalist main forces concentrated to eliminate these isolated elements. As Chiang anticipated, the insurgency undermined security in Japan's rear, blurred the front lines as the boundary between hostile and safe territory, and stymied economic development in Japanese-occupied China, the rationale for Japan's invasion.[130]

The insurgency forced Japan into a point-line strategy of defending cities and the railway lines connecting them. But this left the countryside to the guerrillas and to the Communists, who remained to organize the peasantry with promises of landownership. Japan simply lacked the forces to garrison a country of China's size. Chiang believed that Japan would eventually choke on its conquests, when overextension and exhaustion would force it to withdraw. The commander of Japanese forces in South China dismissed Chiang's guerrilla strategy, saying it "invites only contempt and is not in keeping with a soldier's honour" (as if the rape of Nanjing were).[131] The Japanese conducted a vicious counterinsurgency that together with the Communists, who were conducting their own anti-Nationalist counterinsurgency, eliminated most of the Nationalist base areas north of the Yellow River by 1941 and most of their guerrilla areas by 1943.[132]

Chiang further centralized his control over military and political institutions. In 1938 he had the Nationalist Party National Congress elevate him to *zongcai,* or general director of the party, a title held by the founding father, Sun Yat-sen. He became known as the Generalissimo and pompously, if accurately, observed, "Wherever I go is the Government and the centre of resistance.... I am the State."[133] Further centralization occurred at a party meeting in January 1939.[134] At one point during his tenure in Chongqing, he simultaneously held up to eighty-two posts, down to such irrelevancies as the presidency of the National Glider Association.[135]

Over the course of the Second Sino-Japanese War, Chiang also eroded warlord autonomy. He executed General Han Fuju, a former Feng Yuxiang loyalist, in January 1938 for the failure to defend Jinan, Shandong. Han remains the highest-ranking Chinese officer ever to be executed for cowardice. On his way to his execution, he allegedly observed: "I take responsibility for losing Shandong. But who takes responsibility for losing Nanjing?"[136] Chiang had the troops (i.e., the power base) of the Guangxi group warlords, Li Zongren and Bai

Chongxi, fight the Xuzhou Campaign, where they became national heroes at the Battle Taierzhuang but were subsequently annihilated in the campaign end game. Chiang consistently sent warlord troops to the front and held his loyal troops in reserve – prudent politics in a cut-throat land.[137]

His scorched-earth tactics were less successful. General Xue Yue, the man in charge of breaching the Yellow River dikes and subsequently governor of Hunan, described the "scorched earth policy" as his "major strategy" in order to make the Japanese "weary of their invasion" during the defense of Changsha. "We have destroyed China – removed every stone, burnt down every farm, torn up every railway track upon which we could lay our hands." His breaching of the Yellow River dikes, in a stratagem called "using water as a substitute for soldiers," became a powerful symbol of Nationalist callousness and unfitness to govern that became grist for Communist propaganda mills.[138] The Communists followed a very different trajectory to power. According to their conventional tale, they deliberately and wisely ceded the cities to the Japanese in order to focus on the countryside. In reality, they could not hold the cities against the Nationalists, let alone the Japanese. The Long March had proven this. Nevertheless, adversity forced the Communists to think creatively to develop a prevent-defeat strategy focusing on survival in the countryside.[139]

Mao Zedong made the stunning transition from a junior librarian at Beijing University to leader for life of the People's Republic of China. Over the years, the Chinese Communist Party gradually expanded from a political party into a government. Mao and others transformed small groups of the likeminded into cadres and guerrilla forces and eventually into vast conventional armies capable of wresting control from Chiang Kai-shek and performing the impossible task of putting Humpty Dumpty back together again. Mao took Vladimir Lenin's strategy of a revolutionary party in the vanguard of political and military institutions but abandoned the urban focus for a rural twist with much heavier emphasis on literacy, propaganda, land, and tax reform programs.[140] As early as 1925, the key Communist government body was, as it is today, the Central Military Affairs Commission, because when push came to shove, he who controlled the gun won in China. The name of the organization has changed over the years, but not its centrality to the retention of power. From the very beginning, the military has served as the guarantor of the Chinese Communist Party. From 1927 on, Zhou Enlai remained a key member of this commission.[141] Mao was always on it.[142]

The Communists had two armies to their name, the Eighth Route Army that operated in North China and the New Fourth Route Army that operated in Central China south of the Yangzi River.[143] The Nationals, by contrast, had forty army groups.[144] The two Communist armies were created as a result of the Second United Front that consolidated Communist units. On 22 August 1937, the Communists' 30,000-strong Northwest Army in Shaanxi became the National Revolutionary Army's Eighth Route Army under the command of Zhu De and his subordinate Peng Dehuai, two of China's greatest generals of the civil war period. By 1938 it had grown to 156,000 men. Mao eventually based the Eighth Route Army in Shanxi, which became the staging area for his military operations in North China. On 12 October 1937 Communist remnants south of the Yangzi River were amalgamated into the New Fourth Route Army under the command of Ye Ting and his deputy Xiang Ying, the political commissar and so the actual superior. By 1938 it had grown from 10,000 to 25,000 men.[145] These latter two cadres are not nearly as well known as generals Zhu and Peng because over the winter of 1940–1, the Nationalists captured Ye Ting, and a bounty hunter then killed Xiang Ying, who had the New Fourth Route Army bank account on him in the form of ingots and cash. After their demise the army, which had a strong student, urban, and intellectual presence, was absorbed into the Maoist-modeled, peasant-centric Eighth Route Army.[146]

There is another reason why the New Fourth Route Army is less well known than the Eighth Route Army. The Communist leadership used the New Fourth Route Army as a disposal force.[147] This army constituted the manpower that the Communist Party could afford to lose without jeopardizing command central in Yan'an and so could afford to risk. It was not a disposable force on a suicide mission, but a force that could be sent on high-reward, but high-risk missions. Hanging around in Central China in the heartland of Nationalist control to maintain a Communist presence was one such mission, very costly to the Nationalists and Communists alike. In a similar fashion, Chiang Kai-shek treated his warlord armies as disposal forces, while keeping his most loyal formations in reserve as his praetorian guard.

The primary duty of the two Communist armies was not fighting, but the mobilization and organization of the countryside in preparation for fighting the decisive phase of the long Chinese civil war.[148] Despite the Second United Front, during the Second Sino-Japanese War the Communists spent more time fighting the Nationalists than the Japanese.[149] And rather than fighting at all, the Communists took advantage of the Nationalist preoccupation with Japan to organize behind Japanese and Nationalist lines. In the fall of 1937 the Eighth Route Army was ordered to devote 70 percent of its effort to organizing the countryside, 20 percent to fighting the Nationalists, and only 10 percent of its effort against Japan.[150] Nationalist not Communist forces engaged in the bitter fighting in Central China in 1939.[151] Russia provided the Communists enough military aid so that the Eighth Route and New Fourth Route Armies could move beyond guerrilla attacks to operate as armies at all.[152] Petr Parfenovich Vladimirov, the Russian representative in Yan'an, recorded in his diary in 1942 that Mao Zedong's armies "have long been abstaining from both active and passive action against the aggressors." Vladimirov concluded that "the years of inactivity have had a degrading influence on the armed forces" of the Communists. In the spring of 1945, a U.S. mission to Hebei likewise reported that fighting by the Eighth Route Army was "grossly exaggerated."[153]

In January 1940, Zhou Enlai estimated that of China's 1 million plus military casualties from 1937 to August 1938, only 31,000 were Communists. By December 1944, the total number of Communists killed in action remained shy of 110,000.[154] With limited attrition and much recruitment, the Communist armies grew rapidly over the course of the Second Sino-Japanese War from 40,000 men in 1937 in possession of 92,000 square kilometers of territory with a population of 1.5 million, to 310,000 soldiers for the New Fourth Route Army in 1945 and 1,028,000 million soldiers for the Eighth Route Army, which, respectively, controlled 34 million people inhabiting 250,000 square kilometers of territory in Central China and 90 million people inhabiting 800,000 square kilometers of territory in North China. Communist Party membership increased from 40,000 to 2.7 million.[155] In contrast, unrelenting conventional warfare diminished Chiang's armies so that after 1941 additional recruitments required extreme coercion and undermined the already beleaguered civilian economy.[156]

Between Nationalist and Communist guerrilla activities, the Japanese had to reconquer previously occupied territories in their rear.[157] By the fall of 1940 the Chinese Communists had built up their conventional forces sufficiently to wage their only major offensive of the Second Sino-Japanese War. They suffered the kind of enormous casualties that the Nationalists had endured throughout. The Hundred Regiments Campaign from August to September 1940 contested the territory that Japan had taken in the Xinkou-Taiyuan Campaign in the late fall and winter of 1937. The attacks focused on the North China railway system in the hopes of cutting Japanese supplies of high-quality coking coal.[158] Like the Nationalists, the Communists lost their campaign.

The Nationalists contributed to the loss by cutting their support for the Eighth Route Army in September, midcampaign. The terms of the Second United Front required the Nationalists to subsidize the Chinese Communist government in Yan'an. In 1937 the Nationalists had provided the Eighth Route Army with 600,000 yuan. Such subsidies plus remittances from overseas Chinese accounted for 70 percent of the Eighth Route Army budget during the 1937–40 period and the subsidies made up half the budget for the Shaanxi-Gansu-Ningxia Base Area.[159] But from 1939 on, the Nationalists increasingly targeted Communist forces.[160]

The Eighth Route Army reportedly sustained 100,000 casualties during the Hundred Regiments Campaign, which boomeranged as badly as any Japanese strategy. General Okamura Yasuji responded with the Three Alls Campaign, the Chinese abbreviation for "kill all, burn all, and pillage all," but which the Japanese insisted was actually the Three Prohibitions Campaign, admonishing the Chinese not to burn, commit crimes, or kill. Whatever the name, the Japanese waged a war of annihilation, including the use of poison gas. Beyond all the killing, they stripped the countryside of all food, causing indescribable civilian misery, while temporarily reducing the population under Communist control from 44 million to 25 million.[161] Again Japan lacked the forces to garrison the land they took. Over the course of 1941 and into 1942, in preparation for a broadening of the war against the United States and Great Britain, Japan doubled its forces and launched five campaigns to pacify the North China provinces of Shanxi, Hebei, Shandong, Henan, and Chahar.[162] Pacification campaigns continued until March of 1945, but North China remained unpacified.[163] In the process, they took the lives of 2.7 million Chinese noncombatants, who bore the brunt of Japanese retribution, not the mobile Communist military units.[164]

The Japanese continued to hammer Nationalist conventional forces, both weakening the Communists' primary enemy and protecting the Communists' North China base areas. Chiang's protracted-war strategy entailed ceding North China and redeploying to the course of the Yangzi River.[165] With the growing influence of the Communists in the countryside, the Nationalists restricted Communist political activities, outlawed their sponsorship of mass organizations, and criticized them for reneging on their promise under the united front to put their forces under Nationalist command.[166]

Increasing tensions became visible with fighting over Communist incursions into Shanxi in the fall of 1939 and the suspension of Nationalist aid to the Communists. From 1938 to 1939 the Nationalists often fought the Communists, concentrating on the Eighth Route Army, a period the Communists called the first anticommunist high tide. Although the Russians brokered a truce to rescue the united front, the growing tensions culminated in the so-called New Fourth Army Incident (also known as the South Anhui Incident) in January 1941, when the Communist-led New Fourth Route Army defied Chiang's orders to deploy north of the Yangzi River.[167]

In 1940, the New Fourth Route Army had destroyed the Nationalists' largest army operating behind Japanese lines. Nationalist forces retaliated and tried to drive the New Fourth Route Army into the Japanese-dominated North. They wiped out a ten-thousand-man column, captured the commanding officer Ye Ting, but proved unable to disband the army. Guangxi group forces played an indispensable role, horrifying the Communists, because up until that point the Guangxi group had sided with them against the Nationalists.[168] Russia threatened to cut off aid if the Nationalists did not cease and desist and put simultaneous pressure on the Communists to keep working within the united front.[169] The Russian advice outraged Mao, who thereafter struck a line as independent from Moscow as his finances would allow.[170] Later that year, when Stalin pleaded with Mao to launch offensives against the Japanese to prevent them from piling on with the initial German invasion of Russia and then during the near-run Battle of Moscow, Mao declined.[171] To the Communists the New Fourth Route Army Incident became known as the second anticommunist high tide.

The New Fourth Route Army Incident like the Long March was a military disaster for the Communists. However, both became propaganda victories, when the spectacle of Chinese fighting Chinese while the Japanese deployed at will alienated many, who blamed the Nationalists.[172] As the incumbent government, the Nationalists also reaped the blame for their failure to fight off the Japanese, for the rampant inflation that left the middle class in poverty and the poor verging on starvation, and for the misery of the tens of millions of refugees fleeing the hostilities. The Communists, who rarely fought the Japanese, emerged image intact despite wiping out Nationalist guerrilla areas behind Japanese lines in Shandong and elsewhere.[173]

After the New Fourth Army Incident, negotiations between the Nationalists and Communists ceased; the subsidies ended; the Nationalists tried to cut off supplies to the Communist armies; and handpicked government troops blockaded the Communist base in northern Shaanxi. The united front limped along in name only. This uneasy stalemate continued through May 1944, when U.S.-brokered discussions in Xi'an – apparently the preferred venue for Nationalist-Communist deal making – renewed negotiations between Nationalist and Communist representatives.

According to Mao, the loss of Nationalist subsidies reduced the Communists to penury: "The Nationalists' two anti-Communist clashes were both in the 1940 to 1941 period. We had already reached the point of having virtually no clothing to wear, no cooking oil to eat, no paper, no vegetables, soldiers had no socks, in winter workers had no quilts. The Nationalists used the termination of funds and an economic blockade to deal with us. They planned to surround and starve us. We were in the most extreme difficulties."[174] Mao neglected to note that Russia's 1941 Neutrality Pact with Japan entailed an end to Russian aid to both the Communists and Nationalists. The German invasion of Russia two months later then eliminated any possibility of further Russian aid. From 1937 to 1940, Russia had provided 71 percent of the Yan'an government's income.[175]

To compensate, the Communists became extremely adept at tax collection. They ceased circulating Nanjing's currency and issued their own.[176] Over the course of the 1940s, they transitioned from financial dependence on revenues from salt to a more diversified tax base expanded to include taxes on trade.[177] Like the Nationalists, they resorted to the drug trade.[178] Mao took advantage of his location in the heart of opium-growing country to encourage the cultivation and sale of opium and to profit from the lucrative opium trade passing through Ningxia and Gansu to Beijing and Tianjin.[179] North China became the center of China's heroin production.[180] By 1942, opium constituted the most important source of Chinese Communist Party income.[181] As in the Nationalist-controlled areas, the Communists printed money without adequate underlying economic activity, producing equally rampant inflation.[182]

According to the conventional tale, the Nationalist-controlled areas alone suffered inflation, and this inflation reflected Nationalist corruption. Yet Communist-controlled areas suffered equal rates of inflation for the same reasons that the Nationalist-controlled areas did: The Japanese had taken the productive parts of the Chinese economy and launched a massive war, leaving the defending Chinese, whatever their political persuasions, little choice but to print money and let inflation rip.[183] The Japanese caused China's inflation, the implosion of its economy, the destruction of its cities, and the ensuing rampant corruption among its increasingly desperate population. Spiraling corruption was the effect not the cause of China's economic maladies. Japan was the cause.

FROM A LIMITED TO AN UNLIMITED POLICY OBJECTIVE

Carl von Clausewitz earned the reputation as the most brilliant Western theorist of war in large part because of his counterintuitive observation that the essential distinguishing feature among wars is not the level of effort made by each side, but the limited or unlimited nature of the political objective for which each side fights. The victor in an unlimited war dictates the peace terms including the survival or annihilation of the defeated government and population. Wars for unlimited objectives concern the highest stake there is – survival – and the side on death ground tends to fight with awesome tenacity. Counterintuitively, even failed states, if facing extinction, can become deadly foes. Wars for more limited objectives, by contrast, can often be settled through negotiations because both governments survive the war to fight another day if they choose.[184] Japanese actions over the course of the Second Sino-Japanese War moved steadily along a spectrum from the limited objective of the transfer of Manchuria to Japanese sovereignty to creeping Japanese control over territories ever farther south. As time went on, Japan's goals expanded to the unlimited objective of regime change in Chongqing.

On 4 September 1937, when War Minister General Sugiyama Gen declared that "this war has become a total war,"[185] he failed to consider the impact on the Chinese population of escalating from a limited war – limited to a territorial concession – to an unlimited war that entailed the overthrow of the Nationalist government and the murder of the dissenting civilian population. The military strategy of unrelenting expansion unwittingly herded Chinese of all political persuasions toward an inescapable conclusion: Either cooperate with each other to fight Japan or become a servile population in their own land. As much as the many factions of China disagreed with each other about the form future Chinese institutions should take, they agreed that Japan had no place at the table to resolve the matter.

Japanese military strategy transformed a multilateral civil war among the many warlords of China into a bilateral Communist-Nationalist fight, and even the Communists and Nationalists ceased fighting each other for a long time. Japan, the alien "other" and lethal external threat, became the catalyst to create a shared sense of community, which previously had been hopelessly fractured by countervailing clan and regional loyalties. The Japanese failed accurately to assess the value of victory to the Chinese, which was enormous, making the Chinese unlikely to give up. Economists speak of sunk costs. Such costs cannot be recouped unless the investment pans out. Bankrupt policies lose sunk costs. The more resources the Japanese expended on their military efforts, the more they demanded from China to help recoup their sunk costs, but such escalating demands precluded the negotiated settlement they required. Unlimited objectives left every Chinese including Chiang's many internal enemies with no choice but to rally around the flag in a desperate fight for survival. Japan's escalation of its policy objective transformed a country wracked by civil war into a lethal adversary. Ishiwara Kanji, the instigator of the invasion of Manchuria, accurately predicted that the 1937 escalation throughout coastal China "will be what Spain was for Napoleon … an endless bog."[186]

Some of Japan's civilian leaders tried to no avail to limit their military's appetite for territorial expansion. From the invasion of Manchuria onward, the military deployed in China presented the cabinet with one fait accompli after another. At the time of the Marco Polo Bridge escalation, an Imperial Conference as well as Prime Minister and Prince Konoe Fumimaro urged the military to contain the hostilities. When the war escalated to encompass virtually all of coastal China and the Chinese still showed no signs of capitulating, Konoe complained, "A person such as myself is like a fashion model; I am not allowed to know anything but am led around by the nose. What an impossible situation!"[187]

Yet before he resigned in frustration, he made the critical foreign policy pronouncements that signaled Japan's change from a limited to an unlimited policy objective. On 16 January 1938, Konoe announced that the Japanese government no longer would deal with Chiang Kai-shek beyond trying to kill him: "The Imperial Government will hereafter have no dealings with the Nationalist Government and will await the formation of a new Chinese Government that will cooperate sincerely with the Japanese Empire."[188] Thus, Konoe made clear to the Chinese that the Japanese political objective had become regime change. On 3 November, Konoe then announced the formation of a New Asian Order encompassing Japan, Korea, Manchuria, and China. He considered Woodrow Wilson's Fourteen Points concerning self-determination to be a ploy by the old empires to deny territories to newcomers.[189] His new order put the old order in Asia on death ground, attracting the attention of all the colonial powers as well as the United States, which had strong vested interests in the international legal and institutional status quo. As a result, Chiang's pleas for their aid no longer fell on deaf ears – very bad news for Japan.

Japanese actions also indicated an expanding policy objective. Wherever Japanese troops took territory, they set up new puppet governments. In 1937, Japan turned to remnants of the North China warlords defeated by Chiang Kai-shek in the Northern Expedition and Central Plains War to head its expanding inventory of puppet governments.[190] At different times, the Japanese tried to win over Chiang's most restive generals such as the leader of Shanxi, Yan Xishan, and the leaders of the Guangxi group Li Zongren and Bai Chongxi, as well as the aging former head of the Zhili group, Wu Peifu. They all spurned the Japanese advances.[191] So Japan turned to second-tier defectors, whose decision to collaborate with Japan overshadowed every other decision they ever made. It is impossible to keep track of Japan's proliferation of puppet states. North China puppet governments created in 1937 included the South Chahar Autonomous Government, the North Shanxi Autonomous Government, and the Mongol League Autonomous Government (under Demchugdongrob), which by 1939 were combined into the Mongolian Border Region Unified Government (so-called Mengjiang under Demchugdongrub).[192] Central China puppet governments established in 1937 included the Henan Autonomous Government and the Provisional Government of the Chinese Republic based in Beijing. The latter gradually absorbed the others.[193]

The Provisional Government of the Chinese Republic, established by the North China Area Army on 14 December 1937, the day after the fall of Nanjing, signaled the unlimited objective of regime change in China. The North China Area Army, under the command of Count, General, and later Field Marshal Terauchi Hisaichi, planned to use Manchukuo as its model for North China.[194] By October 1937, the army had set up the North China Development Company to dominate North China's resources. For the civilian leader of the new government, the army dusted off Wang Kemin, a Japanese-educated, recycled former Zhili group financial expert. Before long, Wang resigned. The Provisional Government of the Chinese Republic absorbed the proliferation of puppet governments initially formed in Beijing and Tianjin right after the 1937 escalation and soon expanded into Hebei, Shanxi, Shandong, and Henan and linked up with Chahar and Suiyuan.[195]

The North China Area Army and its paired civil institution, the Provisional Government, dominated China north of the Huai River. Soon it established two banks to issue notes distinct from those of the Nationalists in order to control North China's finances. In doing so, it opened a new theater in the war, the theater of finance, with competing currencies and resource development corporations and schemes to undermine the Nationalist yuan.[196] The Japanese even tried to create a potable ideology, the New People's Principles, as an antidote to the Nationalists' Three People's Principles, and a People's Association to promote them. The New People's Principles' heavy reliance on Confucianism seemed remarkably unnew.[197]

Not to be outdone, on 28 March 1938, the Central China Expeditionary Army under the command of General Matsui Iwane set up an additional puppet government in Nanjing, pointedly called the Restoration Government of the Republic of China, under Liang Hongzhi and the Central China Development Company, with jurisdiction over Jiangsu, Zhejiang, and Anhui. The name of the government – the Restoration Government – conjured images of the Meiji Restoration, which had restored good governance. It soon became known as the "Hotel Government" because, although based in Nanjing, its employees often commuted from Shanghai. Shanghai turned out to be an unsafe residence. A wave of terrorism followed in early 1939 with the puppet foreign minister falling to an assassin's bullet. Given the presence of foreign concessions in Shanghai and throughout Central China, General Matsui stuck with Nationalist currency.[198] Matsui had led the attack on Shanghai and follow-on campaign against Nanjing that had earned him the sobriquet "the Butcher of Nanjing,"[199] while the Japanese-educated Liang Hongzhi had been a stalwart of the North China Anhui group in the 1920s.[200] The North China Area Army regarded the Central China Expeditionary Army's government as a rival to its Beijing Provisional Government.[201]

It remains unclear whether Japan's civil and military leaders fully examined the implications of their decision to transform a limited war into an unlimited war. One suspects not. The former prime minister Konoe Fumimaro later remarked, "No large amount of intelligence is necessary to point out that the policy [of not dealing with Chiang Kai-shek] was a serious mistake."[202] Back in early June of 1935 the former foreign minister Shidehara Kijūrō, who was known for a foreign policy of engagement with the West and China, wrote, "It looks as though not only the foreign minister but also the prime minister are busy waving white flags [to surrender to the army]." At the end of the month, he elaborated: "Kasumigaseki [the address of the Foreign Ministry] and the prime minister's office at Nagata-chō are being superseded by the military. There seems to have been surprise at army headquarters at Miyakezaka that the anxiety this has generated at home and abroad should be so great. It persists in explaining that this was based on a decision between the 'three ministries' but, when one looks further into it, one finds that Kasumigeseki was not among those consulted."[203]

Throughout the Second Sino-Japanese War, the Japanese repeatedly sought a diplomatic solution. They generally made four diplomatic initiatives per year from 1937 to 1940, and eleven in 1938 – the peak year for diplomacy – when Japan combined aggressive military operations with aggressive diplomacy, a technique that had borne fruit in the First Sino-Japanese War and the Russo-Japanese War.[204] Unlike in those wars, however, Japan did not offer generous but punitive peace terms.

As Japan's military costs escalated in China, so did the ultimatums that constituted its diplomacy. Japanese peace demands became a function of their sunk costs. The more the military spent, the more it required to justify the sacrifice to the Japanese public. Back in October 1935, Japan had demanded that the Chinese government cease seeking Western aid and slandering Japan, start cooperating on both North China economic development and the eradication of communism, and tacitly accept Manchukuo's independence. On 17 July 1937, immediately after the escalation at the Marco Polo Bridge, Japan upped the ante to include respect for Japanese territorial privileges; participation in a coprosperity zone encompassing Japan, Korea, Manchukuo, and China; and agreement to transform North China into a special buffer zone against the spread of communism. When China refused, Japan responded by deploying three more divisions to North China. Two and a half weeks later – after Japan had occupied Beijing and Tianjin, and after bitter fighting had erupted in Chahar, Suiyuan, and Shanxi, but before the Shanghai Campaign – the Japanese were not so generous. On 7 August, they added new demands to the old. These included Japanese freedom of action in Inner Mongolia (i.e., Chahar and Suiyuan), adjustment of the terms regulating their troop presence in Shanghai, and a reduction in Chinese tariffs.[205]

Three months later, just before Shanghai fell, the Japanese turned to German mediators to convey additional demands. (None of the old demands ever disappeared.) These included Inner Mongolian autonomy, a demilitarized zone on the North China–Manchukuo border as well as in Shanghai, and Japanese administration of North China. Chiang Kai-shek dryly noted that if he accepted such conditions, the Chinese people would stage a revolution. A month later Nanjing fell and the Japanese expanded their list accordingly.[206] By the end of 1937, Japan had 600,000 troops deployed in the Beijing-Tianjin area. The Nationalists were willing to make concessions concerning Japanese dominance of Inner Mongolia and to tolerate joint Sino-Japanese development of China's resources but would not accept Japanese control over North China.[207] Yet as the war dragged on, the Imperial Japanese Army leadership became increasingly intent upon detaching North China as the required compensation for its military sacrifices.[208] By January 1938, Japanese demands were too much even for the Nazis, who also had a fondness for ultimatums. The Germans threw up their hands and abandoned their mediation efforts.[209]

After the victory in the Xuzhou Campaign in May 1938, Japan required China to recognize Manchukuo, cooperate against the Communists, set up demilitarized zones south of the Great Wall and around Shanghai, and give Japanese specific rights to deploy troops northward from Central China. In return, Japan would remove its many puppet governments on the condition that Chiang Kai-shek also step down. The Asia Department chief of the Japanese Foreign Ministry, Ishii Itarō, disagreed to no avail that Chiang was a national hero, who served as a useful means to hobble Chinese hard-liners, and whose removal would cause the Nationalist Party to collapse. In the secret negotiations in June and July 1938, the Nationalists refused to discard Chiang, allow Japan to transform North China into a special region, grant Inner Mongolia autonomy, or pay any indemnity. China would be willing to sign a Sino-Japanese Treaty, which would serve as indirect recognition of Manchukuo. China appealed to the United States and Britain for assistance, but there was little they could do. When these Sino-Japanese negotiations failed in September 1938, Foreign Minister Ugaki Kazushige resigned.[210] He had lasted four months on the job.[211]

In early October of 1939, after Japan's defeat at Nomonhan and the outbreak of war in Europe, Chiang tried to take advantage of the changed regional and international situation by turning again to the Germans to broker a Sino-Japanese peace. Chiang offered Nationalist de jure recognition of Manchukuo and de facto recognition of Japan's privileged position in North China, and a general improvement in Sino-Japanese relations in return for a Japanese withdrawal from the Yangzi River valley but not necessarily from North China. In return for diplomatic assistance, Chiang promised Germany a privileged position in China for the next fifty years and the sale of raw materials to Germany instead of Britain. Japan, however, rejected German mediation in anger over Germany's nonaggression pact with Russia, signed less than two months prior. Chiang enlisted German help one last time in November of 1940 when he proposed trading Japanese recognition of his government and a troop withdrawal for Chinese recognition of Manchukuo, protection of Japanese privileges in North China, and Japanese naval basing rights in Shanghai, Qingdao, Fuzhou, Hong Kong, and Shantou.[212] At that time, the Japanese were not thinking in terms of deescalation of the conflict, but of escalation. With the outbreak of the War in the Pacific in 1941, Japan abandoned the diplomatic track.

When diplomacy by ultimatum failed, Japan turned again to puppet governments, this time moving in the direction of consolidation rather than fragmentation.[213] In March of 1940, it set up a consolidated puppet government in Nanjing under Wang Jingwei called the National Government of the Chinese Republic. The Japanese government then made it official by recognizing it as the government of China on 30 November 1940.

Wang Jingwei had a long and bitter history with Chiang Kai-shek. In 1929, two years after Chiang's purge of the Communists and break with Russia, Wang had favored a restoration of relations with Moscow; a populist domestic agenda focusing on organizing peasants, workers, and trade people; a reorganization of the Nationalist Party based on democracy and law; and an antiimperialist foreign policy. But Wang had gone down in flames during the Great War of the Central Plains of 1930 when he had supported the losing side against Chiang.[214] Although he had become president of the Executive Yuan as part of the political deal to unite South and Central China against Japan in 1931, a nearly successful assassination attempt on 1 November 1935 forced him to resign. Apparently, a second assassination attempt in 1938 by Chiang's secret police, while he was in Hanoi, convinced him to abandon the Nationalists and, rather than going into exile, to work with the Japanese.[215]

The course of the Second Sino-Japanese War had confirmed Wang's worst forebodings. He had consistently argued that China should not fight Japan because it would lose and cause unspeakable human suffering in the process. Both he and Chiang's other key civilian rival, Hu Hanmin, had been out of power at the time of the events in Xi'an. Several months before the Second United Front negotiations at Xi'an, Hu Hanmin had conveniently died of a cerebral hemorrhage in May of 1936 at the age of fifty-seven.[216]

In 1938 Japan started cultivating Wang, who signed an agreement with General Kagesa Sadaaki, the head of the War Ministry's Military Affairs Department, promising cooperation on national security and economic development and diplomatic recognition of Manchukuo in return for a Japanese promise to withdraw its troops after the restoration of order.[217] On 8 December 1938, Wang announced his break with Chiang, but he soon became disappointed when his South China government in Guangdong became just another stall mate in Japan's pre-existing stable of puppet governments.[218] The Japanese simply changed the name of the Provisional Government of the Chinese Republic in Beijing to the North China Political Affairs Commission, and Inner Mongolia remained under Kantō Army rule.[219]

On 1 November 1939 Wang Jingwei moved his government to Shanghai.[220] But Japan soon resumed negotiations with Chiang to pressure both Chiang and Wang to see who would offer the better deal. As an appetizer, Chiang demanded Japanese renunciation of Prime Minister Konoe Fumimaro's policy of not dealing with him and an annulment of all treaties with Wang. The demands did not sit well in Tokyo. This is when Prime Minister Konoe and Foreign Minister Matsuoka made the stellar diplomatic move of officially joining the Axis on 27 September 1940 and thereby putting Japan's war in Asia front-row-center in Western security calculations. Chiang suddenly saw the prospects of U.S. military intervention on the horizon, obviating the need for further compromises with Japan.[221]

So on 30 November, Japan concluded that Wang offered the better arrangement and officially recognized his government, which in turn recognized Manchukuo and permitted the continuance of North China autonomy and the stationing of Japanese troops throughout Wang's China. He made these concessions because Japan seemed to be on the verge of fulfilling his ardent wish for his government to absorb the other puppet governments.[222] It did absorb the Restoration Government, and the Provisional Government in Beijing was downgraded to a part of the North China Political Affairs Commission.[223]

In May 1941 Wang's military joined Japanese forces north and east of Suzhou to attack the Communist New Fourth Route Army, already weakened by the New Fourth Route Army Incident and capture of its commander the preceding January. In July and August, they then targeted the army's base area in northern Jiangsu but failed to overrun it. The combined Japanese–Wang Jingwei attack surprised and forced back the New Fourth Route Army with heavy casualties.[224] From February 1941 to early 1944, troops loyal to Wang combined with Japanese forces in a major campaign to eliminate the Nationalist insurgency in the area between Hangzhou and the Yangzi River.[225] Yet the Japanese refused to allow Wang to establish a strong military, so that they could dispose of him the moment that Chiang finally came to his senses.[226]

Postwar histories have excoriated Wang Jingwei as a traitor. They ignore the terrible national dilemmas facing all Chinese leaders. While there were compelling reasons to resist Japan, there were also compelling reasons to seek an accommodation instead. Wang tried and failed. He misjudged the Japanese, just as the Japanese misjudged the Chinese. For the Japanese, he was a piece to be played.[227] Japan used him to gain leverage over Chiang by raising the prospects of a replacement government.[228] Disagreements between Wang and Japan proliferated over a full range of issues. To Wang's great disillusionment, Japan compromised on none of them.[229] Throughout his tenure as senior Japanese puppet south of the Great Wall, the Japanese repeatedly offered him up to the Nationalists in return for concessions too extreme for Nationalist tastes.

Occupied China (excluding Manchuria) remained divided in thirds, with Wang in nominal control over the Yangzi River valley provinces, the North China Political Affairs Commission in control of North China, and the Mongolian Border Region Unified Government under Demchugdongrob in control of Inner Mongolia from his capital in Zhangjiakou (formerly Kalgan). Wang focused on negotiating with the North China Political Affairs Commission in the hopes of unifying. Japan rejected these initiatives.[230] Despite Wang's misjudgment of Japan, he correctly predicted that a protracted Sino-Japanese war would deliver not only a Nationalist defeat, but a Communist victory in the long Chinese civil war – an outcome the Japanese failed to anticipate. He chose collaboration with Japan as the lesser evil compared to a Communist victory. He did not foresee the Allied defeat of Japan.[231]

Japan had invaded China in pursuit of national security through autarky. Yet its military strategy made its economic goals unattainable by causing the collapse of the Chinese economy. Given all that happened from 1937 to 1941, it is amazing that the Nationalists survived at all. Within a year of the 1937 escalation, Japan took all or pieces of twenty-one provinces.[232] By 1939 it occupied one-third of China, comprising 40 percent of its agriculture, 92 percent of its modern industry, and 66 percent of its salt fields (the latter a major source of tax revenues). Together this produced a Nationalist loss in tax revenues of more than 80 percent.[233]

A lethal combination of extraordinary military expenditures and crippled production in all sectors caused the corrosive inflation of the civil war period. Bumper crops from 1937 to 1939 mitigated the growing inflationary spiral. From 1937 to 1942, the thirteen (mainly) unoccupied provinces suffered a loss of 17 percent of the acreage sewn and a 13.3 percent decline in production. From 1937 to 1944 professionals suffered a 68 percent loss of purchasing power, while industrial labor suffered a 43.2 percent loss. The pay of soldiers collapsed. In 1938 they were earning 95 percent of their 1937 income, but this plummeted to 10 percent by 1942. By 1944 the Nationalists started handing out goods in lieu of pay. Intellectuals suffered a similar collapse in purchasing power, making both them and soldiers fodder for communism. The pay differential between a full general and a private second class took inequality into the stratosphere from a highly skewed 80 to 1 differential in 1931 to a jaw-dropping 320 to 1 by the end of 1944. Business people and landowners fared the best because they had real goods, whose value tended to keep closer pace with inflation. As a result of the inflation and the desperation it caused, government corruption metastasized. Bank deposits disappeared, paralyzing many normal economic transactions and business activities. Inflation destroyed military morale as it indicated a government out of control and incapable of paying those who risked and gave their lives.[234]

Not only did Japan's military strategy destroy the Chinese economy, it also undermined the home economy. From 1936 to 1945, the Japanese government implemented a wide variety of measures to take control of production but that strangled the economy instead, just as the assassinated finance minister, Takahashi Korekiyo, had predicted.[235] Before long central planning in Tokyo mimicked the reviled Soviet system. In September 1937 Japan jettisoned the market economy in favor of central planning with the Diet's passage of the Temporary Capital Adjustment Law, the Law Relating to Temporary Export and Import Commodities, and the Law for the Application of the Armament Industry Mobilization Law [of 1918]. The first took over capital allocation, the second commodity allocation, and the third allowed the military to commandeer factories. In October 1937 the government set up the Planning Board and soon regulated prices. In 1939, it responded to inflation with price and wage freezes, and in 1940, even before the bombing of Pearl Harbor, it imposed rationing.[236]

The percentage of the government budget devoted to military expenditures rose from 30.8 percent in 1931, to 69.2 in 1937, to 75.6 percent in 1941, to an economy-busting 85.3 percent in 1944.[237] The structure of the Japanese economy changed in tandem with these expenditures. In 1930 the division between heavy and light industry was 38.2 percent devoted to heavy industry. This rose to 57.8 percent in 1937 and to a standard-of-living-killing 72.7 percent in 1942.[238] No light industry meant no consumer goods.[239] Real wages in Japan plummeted. Wages indexed to buying power and set at 100 for the 1934–6 period, fell to 79.1 in 1941 before shriveling to 41.2 in 1945.[240] After the hostilities with the United States began, the calorie intake of Japanese civilians dropped precipitously from 2,195 calories per day in 1941 to 1,793 calories per day in 1945. Inflation rose from 1935 to 1945 by 300 percent at official prices.[241]

As Japan imposed economic controls, it became progressively less democratic. In 1940 opposition parties were all but eliminated, and the introduction of the Chinese method of collective responsibility, the *baojia* system, put Japanese under the Ministry of the Interior and the police. As Foreign Minister Mastuoka noted, "To wait for political parties to improve is like waiting for pigs to fly."[242] In 1941 General Tōjō Hideki, who had started out as the war minister, added to his portfolio prime minister and minister of the interior and took over the military police, for an unprecedented concentration of power in one man's hands.[243]

The 1937 escalation also made Japan more, not less, reliant on imports. Whereas Japan had imported 67 percent of its oil in 1935, this grew to 74 percent in 1937 and to 90 percent in 1939.[244] Thus, Japan's means to produce autarky (i.e., war) precluded the ends by making the Japanese military's consumption of imported resources skyrocket and Japan more not less dependent on trade.[245] Japan was also becoming less capable of executing its military strategy. By 1940, it was running out of troops to conduct endless campaigns in China.[246] In the second half of 1937, Japanese forces had advanced 17.4 kilometers per day; this declined to 7.6 kilometers per day in 1938, to 1.1 kilometers in 1939, to 0.6 kilometers in 1940.[247] The Second Sino-Japanese War had stalemated.

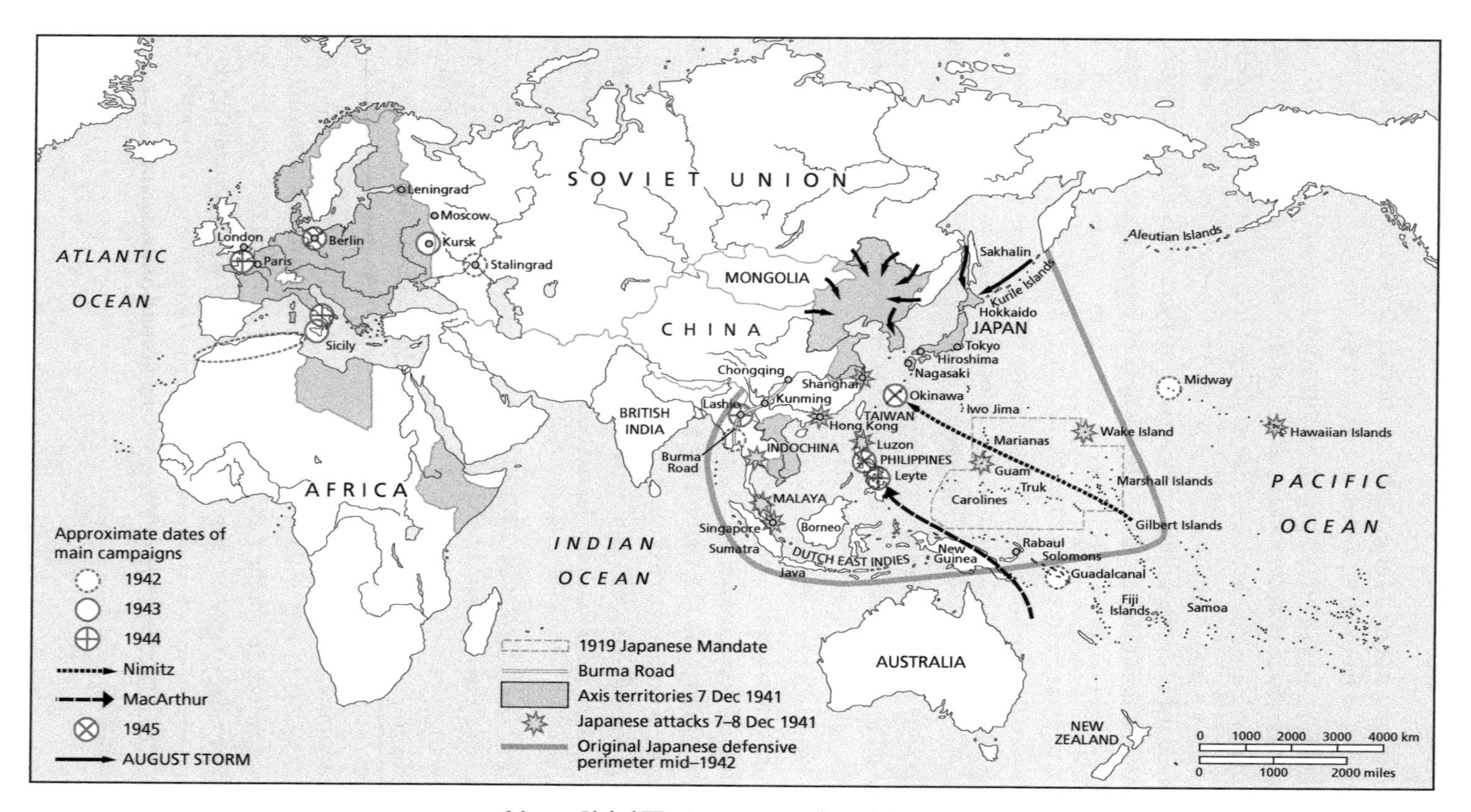

Map 5 Global War (1939–45): Defeat of the Axis.

7

GLOBAL WAR

World War II

孤注一掷
Concentrate on one throw alone.
(Stake everything on one move.)

Until World War II, the United States remained a bit player in Asia, where the European powers had apportioned themselves spacious colonies and spheres of influence. The United States had arrived late on the colonial scene with the Spanish-American War of 1898, which netted it Puerto Rico, the Philippines, and Guam, and, the month the war ended, it annexed Hawaii. The following year, the United States, now a rising power with great power aspirations, made a major foreign policy pronouncement, the Open Door Policy, which strongly suggested that all powers should respect China's territorial integrity and not attempt to carve out exclusive zones. The other powers had reacted to Chinese political and military incompetence in the First Sino-Japanese War with a postwar feeding frenzy, the so-called scramble for concessions, when they had vivisected China into a welter of exclusive spheres of interest. Americans, as usual, wanted markets open to trade, and exclusive zones threatened this plan. Americans also believed that exclusive zones threatened Chinese interests.

For better or for worse, the ideas of free trade and free access underlying the Open Door Policy have remained consistent themes in American foreign policy ever since. The policy contained an assumption, which Americans did not consider necessary to state because they assumed it to be obvious to all. This was freedom of the high seas, which were assumed to be a commons for all to use up to a few miles from the shore. These two principles, free trade and freedom of navigation, underlie the outlook of a maritime power, but not necessarily of a continental power, which may consider seas as territory to be claimed, divided, and closed off. The Western order of global trade, however, depends on freedom of the seas. The whole edifice crashes down without it.

Up until World War II, although American traders had long plied Asian waters, the British and the Japanese dominated the China trade and the other powers dominated the trade with their respective colonies. The United States did comparatively little commerce with Asia. In 1930, Europe and Latin America each accounted for one-third of U.S. trade, Canada for one-quarter, and Asia a mere 6.5 percent.[1] These were the years of relative resource self-sufficiency for the United States. Its main vital imports from Asia were rubber and tin, and to a lesser degree tungsten and chromite, but not oil, in those days a U.S. export not an import.[2]

Yet a surprising number of Americans remained captivated by China, as they are today. Perhaps it was the missionary presence. Many American missionaries went to China and returned with a love of the people and a despair about the conditions in which they lived. Rich Americans developed a taste for the artwork reflected in their major museums, which tend to have particularly strong collections in Chinese art. In contrast, Islamic, Indian, Sub-Saharan, Southeast Asian, and pre-Columbian art are comparatively underrepresented. For whatever reasons, many Americans have long had a soft spot for the Chinese and have considered China to be a great power regardless of its fortunes.[3]

During the peace negotiations following World War I, President Woodrow Wilson submitted his Fourteen Points to the other powers in the hope that this agenda would form the basis for the settlement. His failing health prevented him from seeing the matter through, but his ideas left an indelible mark on the guiding principles of U.S. foreign policy, namely, that U.S. foreign policy should support democracy and national self-determination abroad. At the Versailles Peace Conference terminating World War I, the United States played a central role in determining the future of Germany's former colonies, including its concessions in China, at the time in Japanese possession. The Chinese were unhappy about the method of return, through Japan as an intermediary rather than directly from Germany, and many blamed the United States, whose negotiators felt hamstrung by China's own treaties and loan agreements with Japan.[4]

Those who argue that the United States lacks a consistent foreign policy overlook its three guiding principles from 1918 to the present: free trade (dating to the Open Door Policy of 1899), self-determination (dating to Wilson's Fourteen Points of 1918), and anticommunism dating to the Truman Doctrine enunciated in 1947. In reality, the Truman Doctrine simply recognized communism as a negation of the other two principles, which form the bedrock of the global order that the United States has promoted ever since. In the 1930s, the United States applied these principles to China and Japan, with unanticipated results.

In the Washington Naval Conference that concluded in February 1922, the United States and the other great powers signed the Nine-Power Treaty upholding the Open Door Policy. In addition, Japan, the United States, and Britain signed the Washington Naval Limitation Treaty, whose naval tonnage caps the Imperial Japanese Navy considered to be so outrageous. Like the United States, Japan was a rising power, intent upon upgrading its position in the hierarchy of nations. The London Naval Conference in 1930 raised the Japanese tonnage ratio slightly but not close to the requirements of the Imperial Japanese Navy leadership. Within the year the responsible Japanese prime minister had been fatally shot. By the 1935 London Naval Conference, the Imperial Japanese Navy forced a Japanese walkout from the negotiations; the arms limitations then expired at the end of 1936; and Japan began building its superbattleships, *Yamato* and *Musashi*, which had nearly twice the displacement of any existent ship.[5]

THE PEARL HARBOR SOLUTION TO THE CHINA QUAGMIRE

Over the course of the 1930s, as the U.S. newspapers covered events in China that went from bad to worse, the U.S. government increasingly chimed in to make pronouncements concerning Japanese behavior, mostly in the negative, and suggestions, mostly in the imperative. On 7 January 1932, U.S. Secretary of State Henry L. Stimson circulated the Stimson Note, soon to become known as the Stimson Doctrine, which broadcast the U.S. refusal to recognize Manchukuo and its demand for adherence to the Open Door Policy in China – a pointed and public rebuke of Japan.[6] U.S. appraisals of Japanese foreign policy did not become any more flattering over the years as Nationalist diplomatic representatives kept calling Japanese actions to U.S. public and political attention.[7] The year 1933 was not a good one for the League of Nations, as both Japan and Germany withdrew, signaling their rejection of the prevailing international order. Rejection of the order implies plans for another and can be a harbinger of an impending attack on the status quo. Shortly after Japan's withdrawal, the United States provided the Nationalist government a $50 million loan to purchase U.S. cotton and wheat. Japan responded by banning U.S. cotton from its mills in China.[8] In May 1936, the United States slapped a 42 percent tariff on cotton cloth.[9] Despite Japanese and Chinese anger at U.S. foreign policy, American leaders believed themselves to be fair and principled in their dealings with both countries.

Three items caused consternation in the Imperial Japanese Navy: the passage by the U.S. Congress of the Fifteen-Cruiser Bill in 1929, the decision to signal U.S. displeasure over the invasion in Manchuria by leaving the Scouting Fleet on the California coast after the annual fleet exercise in 1932, and the passage in 1934 of the Vinson-Trammell Bill authorizing but not funding a buildup of the U.S. Navy to the limits set in 1930.[10] Meanwhile in 1935, at a time when the Imperial Japanese Army was implementing smuggling schemes to undermine the Nationalist currency, the United States provided financial assistance to stabilize the currency.[11] The day after the 1937 escalation at the Marco Polo Bridge, the United States provided further support for the Chinese currency, including a proposed loan, but soon restricted arms shipments to both China and Japan in an attempt to remain neutral.[12] The next notable example of American rhetoric occurred in October of 1937 in President Franklin D. Roosevelt's famous quarantine speech, signaling the U.S. judgment that Germany and Japan were pariah states, lying outside the international order.

On 12 December 1937, during Japan's Nanjing Campaign up the Yangzi River, its naval air force sank USS *Panay* near Nanjing, outraging Americans. As a Christmas Eve present, Japan made a formal apology and offered to pay an indemnity, both of which Roosevelt accepted. During the two-week diplomatic crisis, however, he ordered the drafting of secret plans to blockade Japan from the Aleutian Islands to Hong Kong and tried to secure British cooperation. Roosevelt intended to implement the blockade upon the next provocation. Britain noted that doing so would lead to war, while the United States disagreed and began building a fleet capable of conducting the blockade. In 1938 the second Vinson naval bill finally funded the construction plans authorized under the original bill for the first expansion of the fleet since World War I. In the four years intervening between the two bills, the ceilings established in London in 1930 had lapsed.[13]

On 22 July 1939, Britain caved to Japanese demands in what Chiang Kai-shek coined as "the Far Eastern Munich" when it allowed Japan to take over the Tianjin foreign concession area, where the presumed Chinese murderer of an assassinated Japanese customs official was said to be hiding. The Japanese blockade of the British Settlement in Tianjin leading to Britain's capitulation had produced bad publicity for Japan in the United States and an unintended side effect: On 26 July, the United States confirmed its judgment made in the quarantine speech with the announcement of its intended abrogation of the 1911 U.S.-Japanese Commercial Treaty, in effect giving Japan six-months' notice of trade restrictions to come when the renunciation went into effect in January 1940.[14]

In 1931 the United States had been Japan's most important trading partner and a multiple of Japan's second- and third-most important markets, China and British India. Prior to hostilities, the United States had bought 40 percent of Japanese exports and had provided 34.4 percent of Japan's imports, 49.1 percent of its iron imports, 53.6 percent of its machine tool imports, and 75.2 percent of its oil.[15] Japan depended on the United States for manganese and molybdenum, and its aluminum and nickel were also imported from overseas. Despite growing tensions, Japan's economic plans assumed continuing revenues from textile exports to the United States made from imported U.S. cotton.[16] Japan was fatally reliant on imports of two of the most critical war matériel; 95 percent of its oil and 88 percent of iron ore originated overseas and 90 percent of the imported iron was from China and Malaya.[17] Japan's rapidly deteriorating relations with its most important trading partner were fraught with problems.

In May 1940, after the annual fleet exercises in the Pacific, Roosevelt ordered the U.S. Navy not to return to its home base in California, but to remain forward-deployed in Pearl Harbor.[18] Japan tracked the U.S. wireless traffic and soon realized the weakness of the U.S. position in Hawaii.[19] On 28 June, less than a week after the fall of France on 22 June, the U.S. Congress passed the third Vinson naval bill, funding naval expansion 11 percent beyond the lapsed London naval limits. On 2 July it passed the Export Control Act, which allowed the restriction of exports of potential war matériel to Japan. Three days later Roosevelt invoked the act to cut the export to Japan of key minerals and chemicals and aircraft engines. On 19 July he signed into law the Two-Ocean Navy Act. This fourth Vinson bill authorized a 70 percent naval expansion to build a two-fleet navy, one for the Atlantic and the other for the Pacific, creating a navy with four times the tonnage and four times the air power of Japan's. This meant Japan's relative naval strength would peak in late 1941 at near-parity with the U.S. Navy before rapidly declining.[20] On 26 July, on the first anniversary of the U.S. abrogation of its commercial treaty with Japan, Roosevelt again invoked the Export Control Act to cut the export to Japan of aviation gasoline and various categories of iron and steel scrap.[21] On 16 September, the United States introduced the first peacetime conscription in its history. By this time it had effectively abandoned its strategy of arming neither side in the Sino-Japanese War. It had loaned the Nationalists $25 million in February 1939, followed by a second loan in April 1940, with many more to follow.[22] The emerging pattern focused Japanese attention on foreign aid as the last prop sustaining Chiang Kai-shek.

The mastermind behind Japan's diplomacy was Matsuoka Yōsuke – the talkative alumnus of Oregon Law College and of the South Manchurian Railway administration – whose walkout from the League of Nations in 1933 had made him internationally famous.[23] Upon becoming foreign minister in July of 1940, he smugly told U.S. reporters, "In the battle between democracy and totalitarianism the latter adversary will without question win and will control the world. The era of democracy is finished and the democratic system bankrupt. There is not room in the world for two different systems or for two different economies."[24] The man had a way with words. He had coined the term "Greater East Asia Co-Prosperity Sphere," a matching concept for Prime Minister Konoe Fumimaro's equally ill-conceived New Asian Order.[25]

On 21 May 1939, Japan had declined Germany's original invitation to ally. The following day Germany and Italy had allied without Japan in their "Pact of Steel."[26] On 23 August, as Japan lost to Russia at Nomonhan, Germany paid Japan back by signing the Nazi-Soviet Pact promising mutual nonaggression and an amicable division of Eastern Europe. This preparation for Germany's invasion Poland nine days later breached article 2 of the secret protocol to the Anti-Comintern Pact, rendered the alliance under the pact useless, outraged Japan, and caused the immediate fall of the cabinet.[27]

Matsuoka and the military increasingly saw foreign aid as Chiang Kai-shek's last remaining center of gravity. On 27 September 1940 Japan signed the Tripartite Pact with Germany and Italy in the mistaken belief that this would deter the United States from risking war with Japan and in the false hope that Russia would soon join the Axis, cutting off aid across China's northern border.[28] Navy Minister Yoshida Zengo was the sole strong opponent of the alliance, arguing that it would produce a war with the United States for which Japan was not prepared. In early September he had a nervous breakdown and stepped down.[29] The week Japan signed the Tripartite Pact, it invaded northern French Indochina to cut off Nationalist supplies from the south. On 17 October, Britain responded to the Axis alliance by reopening the Burma Road, and on 22 October the United States offered the Nationalists another loan.[30] From the British and American point of view, the alliance with Germany transformed Japan from regional irritant into a key player in the worldwide threat to overturn the global order.

In the early spring of 1941, Matsuoka then made a fateful trip to Europe. He arrived on 24 March in Moscow, spent 26 to 29 March in Berlin, 1 April in Rome, back to Berlin on 4 April, and 7 to 13 April in Moscow again. While in Germany he told the Germans of his desire to come to diplomatic terms with Russia (logical to him since the Germans had signed a nonaggression pact with Russia). He expressed his wish to include Russia in the Axis alliance but learned of Germany's massed troops on the Russian border. When Hitler hinted on 27 March of an impending German attack on Russia, Matsuoka predicted that Japan would join in. Yet on his way home, on the inauspicious date of 13 April 1941, he concluded a neutrality pact with Russia to the irritation of Germany, which expected Japan to keep pressure on Russia while attacking Britain's Asian colonies.[31] Perhaps Matsuoka believed he was paying Germany back for its neutrality pact with Russia concluded during the Battle of Nomonhan, when Japan would have greatly appreciated Germany's opening a second front on Russia.[32] More likely, Matsuoka hoped to cut Soviet aid to Chiang Kai-shek – he saw the regional war, not the developing global war.[33]

The pact also outraged both the Chinese Nationalists and the Communists because, as Matsuoka anticipated, Russian neutrality entailed halting aid to China. The Nationalists accused Russia of nullifying the Sino-Russian Non-Aggression Pact of 21 August 1937 as well as violating article 4 of the 1924 Sino-Russian Treaty forbidding either to sign a treaty prejudicial to the interests of the other.[34] In fact, Russia had already sold them out six months prior, when it traded cutting off its aid to the Nationalists for a Japanese promise to allow the survival of the Chinese Communist Party. On 3 October 1940, Russian and Japanese diplomats apparently agreed that "the USSR will abandon its active support for Chiang [Kai-shek] and will repress the Chinese Communist Party's anti-Japanese activities; in exchange, Japan recognizes and accepts that the Chinese Communist Party will retain as a base the three [Chinese] Northwest provinces (Shaanxi, Gansu, Ningxia)."[35]

On 16 April 1941 Lieutenant-General Ōshima Hiroshi, Japan's ambassador to Germany, good friend of numerous high-ranking Nazis, and fluent German speaker, wired Matsuoka that Hitler intended to attack Russia. He sent repeated reconfirmations thereafter. These all became known to the United States, which had broken the Japanese diplomatic code in September 1940, in the decryption effort known as MAGIC. When the Russians later reconstructed events, they believed that by February or March the Japanese were aware of German plans to invade Russia. The decryptions transformed Ambassador Ōshima into the most reliable Allied informant of German battle plans for the duration of the war. The information included the details of the German defenses at Normandy, essential for the success of the Allied invasion of France in 1944.[36] The United States also broke parts of the Japanese navy and army codes, in a decryption effort known as ULTRA. It passed on the warnings of the impending German invasion of Russia to Stalin. These fell on deaf ears: Stalin made no preparations. When Stalin had a chance to reciprocate, he chose not to pass along information from his spy in Tokyo, Richard Sorge, of Japan's plans to attack Hawaii. Japan arrested Sorge in October 1941, so Stalin had ample warning about Pearl Harbor.[37]

Apparently Foreign Minister Matsuoka missed the cross-cutting logic of his alliance with Germany and his neutrality pact with Russia. He concluded the neutrality pact with the main enemy (Russia) of his own main ally (Germany). The diplomacy was tenable only as long as

Germany and Russia remained at peace with each other. When Germany invaded Russia, Russia immediately allied with Japan's potentially most lethal enemies (Britain and the United States). Although Matsuoka knew of the imminent German invasion, he signed the neutrality pact with Russia anyway. Afterward, some Japanese leaders belatedly wondered whether the agreement was compatible with their Tripartite Pact with Germany and Italy – particularly if Germany were to attack Russia.[38] Others understood the illogic of the two documents. Within a month of the German invasion of Russia, yet another cabinet fell, leaving Matsuoka out of a job, and the cabinet fell again in October because no one could figure out an exit strategy. Japan was stuck with the combined handiwork of Matsuoka's diplomacy and the army's military strategy that had required his diplomatic acrobatics.[39]

Hitler launched Operation BARBAROSSA with lethal efficiency on 22 June 1941. Russian defenses fell before him. Within three months the Germans had taken nearly 1.5 million prisoners including nearly 665,000 in the Ukraine in the largest largest mass surrender in history. By December the Germans arrived within twenty-five miles of Moscow.[40] With Germany's rapid success, Foreign Minister Matsuoko, prior to his departure from office in mid-July, turned on a dime, to recommend breaching his neutrality pact with Russia, signed half a year prior, and joining the attack on Russia.[41] This was too duplicitous for his colleagues.

German-Japanese relations did not improve. In late July, his replacement, Foreign Minister and Vice-Admiral Toyoda Teijirō, blamed Germany for starting "a war with Russia because of her military expediency when it was least desirable on our part."[42] On 22 August, Hitler confided to his generals, "The Emperor [of Japan] is a companion piece of the later Czars. Weak, cowardly, irresolute, he may fall before a revolution. My association with Japan was never popular.... Let us think of ourselves as masters and consider these people at best as lacquered half-monkeys who need to feel the knout."[43] The Germans and the Japanese had long failed to have a meeting of minds. Their alliance was one of words, not deeds.

Over the summer, the Germans urged the Japanese to join the attack but Japan declined.[44] The Imperial Japanese Navy remained adamant not to take advantage of the German invasion.[45] Although from 1941 to 1942 the army increased its troop strength in Manchuria from

300,000 to 1 million men, it did not plan to cross the border until a German victory at Stalingrad and a removal of Russian border forces that never occurred. The Japanese anticipated the role of a jackal state, ready to jump in for the choice pickings of a kill made by others. This was a fatal error of strategy. Russia barely won the Stalingrad Campaign. Had Japan launched an attack in Siberia simultaneous with BARBAROSSA, let alone deferred from escalating against China in 1937, this might have tipped the balance.[46]

The Allies worked to preclude this possibility. On 2 August 1941, the Russians inhibited any Japanese plans to cross the border by blowing up key ammunition and fuel supplies in Manchukuo.[47] The United States understood Russia's predicament and in November responded with the astronomical sum of $1 billion in Lend-Lease aid, which arrived in Siberia unmolested by Japan courtesy of the Japanese-Russian neutrality pact.[48] Russians would soon be killing Germans with the aid. From the summer of 1941 until early 1945, Japan repeatedly tried to broker a peace between Germany and Russia so that Japan and Germany could focus on fighting Britain and the United States.[49] Just as Japan did not want Germany to fight Russia, Germany did not want Japan to fight China. Each wished the other had a different primary enemy.

The Imperial Japanese Army was torn by a desire to prosecute both the Northern and Southern Advance plans as if it were not already adequately overextended in China, so the compromise was to do a little of both, starting with the southern offensive.[50] As usual when major policy differences arose, Japanese leaders did not choose, synthesize, or compromise. They amalgamated, expanded, and piled on diverse war objectives. Japanese leaders believed that the changed international situation offered a unique window of opportunity to resolve the China quagmire by expanding the Japanese empire to gain sufficient winnings to justify the costs. By 1941 Germany occupied virtually all of the Western European continent, putting the Western colonial powers on the run. The European powers had no ability to protect their Asian colonies.[51] Why not defeat China by filling the power vacuum?

Japan had already attacked multiple presumed Nationalist centers of gravity – the army, the changing capitals, the economy, and the will to resist – but still the Chinese fought on. In 1940, Japan turned to the remaining presumed center of gravity, foreign aid.[52] After the fall of Guangzhou in October 1938, Indochina had become the Nationalists' main supply route. In June of 1940, the Japanese military estimated that the Nationalists received 1,000 tons of aid per month from Russia via Xinjiang, 9,000 tons per month via South China, 3,000 to 4,000 tons per month via Burma, and 25,000 to 30,000 tons per month via French Indochina.[53] After pressuring Britain to sever the Burma Road in July, on 22 September, the Japanese pressured the French governor of Indochina to allow their troops to land in Haiphong, and they did the following day.[54]

Three days later, the United States responded by embargoing scrap iron to Japan. Following Roosevelt's reelection in November 1940, he made his arsenal-for-democracy speech on 30 December, promising that America would arm democracies beset by aggressors and thereafter interpreted "democracy" broadly to include the Nationalists, whose politics by assassination were well known to the U.S. State Department, and Stalin, whose politics of show trial, purge, and gulag were in a class of their own. On 11 March 1941 Roosevelt made good his promise by signing the Lend-Lease Act, extending military aid, particularly to Britain and soon to China and Russia.[55] In 1941 the Nationalists received $26 million in Lend-Lease aid, or 1.7 percent of the total. This rose to $100 million in 1942 but just 1.5 percent of the total, and then fell by half for the following two years to just 0.4 percent, but rising to 8 percent or $1.1 billion in 1945 once the Burma Road reopened.[56]

The Japanese blockade precluded the delivery of much aid to China – 60 percent in 1945 was gasoline and oil, not the heavy conventional arms the Nationalists so desperately needed. American military personnel deployed to China consumed 73 percent of the airlifted Lend-Lease aid and burdened a fragile economy. Their demands for beef decimated the stocks of water buffalo essential for farming. Unable to get military equipment in, the Nationalists used U.S. loans to import gold bullion for corruption schemes instead.[57] Even so, the military expenses, which had consumed between 55 and 71 percent of the Nationalists' national budget between 1937 and the U.S. entry into the war, dropped to between 33 and 46 percent of the budget thereafter.[58]

After the German invasion of Russia in June 1941, the United States had feared that Russia might fall and, if this happened, Britain would be next. President Roosevelt told Secretary of the Interior Harold L. Ickes that the United States must strive not to "tip the delicate scales and cause Japan to decide to attack Russia." Probably on the basis of the MAGIC intercepts of Japan's ambassador in Berlin, Roosevelt captured the heated policy debate among Japanese leaders, "trying to decide which way they are going to jump – attack Russia, attack the South Seas ..., or whether they will sit on the fence and be more friendly with us. No one knows what the decision will be."[59] So the United States ratcheted up the pressure on Japan to make sure it did not jump north.

While Germany invaded Russia, Japan redoubled efforts to sever outside support to the Nationalists. From 24 to 27 July 1941, Japan occupied southern Indochina. The United States immediately retaliated on 26 July by freezing Japanese assets worth 500 million yen. (In June it had already frozen German and Italian assets.) On 26 July Britain followed suit along with the Netherlands on 27 July. In July the United States also provided the Nationalists with $240 million in military aid, followed by an additional $500 million in 1942.[60] From the initial 8 February 1939 loan to 21 March 1942, the United States provided six aid packages, totaling $620 million, but actually delivered $606 million. Britain made four loans from the initial 21 March 1939 offering to 2 May 1944, promising $290 million but delivering only $77 million.[61]

On 26 July 1941 the United States appointed General Douglas MacArthur as commander in chief of U.S. forces in East Asia and made plans to improve defenses in the Philippines.[62] On 1 August, it embargoed oil exports to Japan – if the Japanese had no oil, they could no longer fight, or so the logic went. At the time Japan had reserves of 9.4 million kilotons and consumed 450,000 kilotons per month, giving it about a one-and-a-half-year supply at stable consumption rates.[63] Japanese leaders construed this as a deadline for making alternate arrangements for fuel. Thus, the escalating embargoes, far from deterring Japan, acted as an accelerant as its leaders put the finishing touches on their plans to expand the war throughout the Pacific.

Admiral Yamamoto Isoroku, the commander of the Combined Fleet, developed the operational plan to eliminate the U.S. Pacific Fleet based at Pearl Harbor so that Japan could both cut the last avenues of foreign aid to Chiang Kai-shek and prevent U.S. interference with Japan's seizure of the oil fields of the Dutch East Indies. Yamamoto was one of Japan's leaders most knowledgeable about the United States, where he had spent more than five years in the 1920s, two at Harvard University and three as a naval attaché in Washington. He opposed war with the West.[64] He, like the former navy minister Admiral Yoshida Zengo and Admiral Yonai Mitsumasa, who served as navy minister and then prime minister, all opposed Japan's formal membership in the Axis alliance because they correctly predicted that the United States and Britain would respond by ratcheting up their aid to Chiang Kai-shek. Meanwhile, the army, through Japan's ambassador to Berlin, Lieutenant General Ōshima Horoshi, worked to strengthen ties with the Axis. In the end, the navy traded its acquiescence to the alliance in return for a larger proportion of the military budget.[65]

Great powers routinely maintain war plans against the other great powers in order to prepare for all eventualities, no matter how remote. From September 1939 on, Admiral Yamamoto had been working on navy war plans targeting the United States. In the fall of 1940, he warned Prime Minister Konoe: "If you order us to do so, we will show you how ferocious we can be for six months to a year of battle. The Tripartite Alliance has been agreed and it can't be altered now, but I beg you to do everything within your power to avoid war with the United States, whatever else may happen."[66] After the oil embargo a year later, he apparently assumed that Japan could not take Dutch East Indian oil fields without provoking war with the United States, whose role as imperial overlord of the Philippines put it astride the sea-lanes between Japan and the oil. This assumption, which was probably correct, had enormous consequences because it led to attacking rather than bypassing U.S. territories.[67] Since Yamamoto understood that Japan could not win a protracted war against the United States, his hopes lay in a short war.[68] Given the ongoing U.S. military buildup in the Philippines over the summer of 1941 and the naval buildup under the Vinson bills, Yamamoto realized that time was not on Japan's side; U.S. military strength would wax as Japan's waned.[69]

His country could not match U.S. production. In 1941 the United States had a GNP twelve times that of Japan.[70] It produced 105 cars for each Japanese car. It could generate 1 million kilowatts of electricity for every 5.5 kilowatts in Japan.[71] Nevertheless, both Admiral Yamamoto and General Tōjō Hideki concluded that Japan would be better off acting preemptively to engage the U.S. fleet.[72] With the U.S. fleet out of action, Japan would rapidly occupy the vulnerable colonies of the Western powers, now either themselves occupied or besieged by

Nazi Germany, and build an impregnable defensive perimeter on the islands at the outer edges of the empire. Yamamoto's war plan then scripted a showdown with the U.S. Fleet to take place from these fortified positions while the United States scrambled to supply itself over lengthy logistical lines.

His strategy reflected a long-standing strand in Japanese thinking about their country's foreign policy. Some Japanese, particularly the military, favored an increasingly exclusive relationship with China from the Twenty-One Demands of 1915 onward, what they called the Asian Monroe Doctrine. Just as the U.S. president James Monroe had informed the great powers in 1823 that they had better stay clear of Latin America, likewise increasing numbers of Japanese favored making East Asia the exclusive preserve of Japan.[73]

Within the week of the total oil embargo, just as the British had predicted, the Imperial Japanese Army favored going to war in the Pacific. The total oil embargo meant the Greater East Asia Co-Prosperity Sphere had to be expanded to include the oil fields of the Dutch East Indies. In September the cabinet and then an Imperial Conference confirmed the Imperial Japanese Army and Navy's recommendation for the Southern Advance war plan to exploit the window of opportunity opened by the war in Europe to take over Europe's colonies in Asia, while neither the colonial powers nor Russia could interfere. The navy, not the army added Hawaii to the list of targets.[74]

Many blame Japan's military leaders for Japan's national tragedy of the 1930s and 1940s. The case is indisputable as far as it goes, but Japan's problems went deeper than mere military men out of control. Matsuoka, the diplomat, and Konoe, the aristocrat, also contributed fatally to Japan's tragedy in their civilian role conducting ruinous diplomacy. Their best bet was not to betray all the great powers sequentially. A coordinated attack with Germany to defeat Russia would have eliminated Japan's primary threat, which its leaders believed was the spread of communism in Asia. The Chinese Communist Party would have lost its essential benefactor. Most striking were the bankruptcy of Japanese leadership in virtually every sphere from the late 1930s until the end of the war and the utter dedication with which Japanese citizens carried out a ruinous strategy. A country whose leadership in the late nineteenth century had dazzled the world proved unable to cope with the Great Depression. Its citizens suspended their capacity to analyze and they and everyone they touched paid the price for their unquestioning obedience to their leaders.[75]

Prior to the Pearl Harbor attack, Japan had suffered 600,000 casualties in China, a sunk cost of stupendous proportions that its leaders found difficult to justify to the Japanese people.[76] Japan's situation was reminiscent of that of great powers in World War I that were equally incapable of reassessing flawed military strategies, which were consuming the lives of a generation of young men so that old men could pretend that they knew what they were doing. At an Imperial Conference in September of 1941, General Tōjō Hideki, who had become prime minister as negotiations with the United States went from bad to worse, argued that together the U.S. oil embargo, its Lend-Lease aid to Russia, and its increasing military aid to Chiang Kai-shek constituted an attempt to encircle and put Japan on death ground. General Tōjō and Japan's other leaders – civil, army, and navy – who rarely agreed on much concluded that peace on American terms, entailing a withdrawal from China, would lead to the gradual impoverishment of Japan and would undo the efforts of generations of Japanese to transform their country into a modern power. War with the United States, on the other hand, offered a 50-50 chance of success. Finance Minister Kaya Okinori alone repeatedly raised economic concerns indicating the infeasibility of Tōjō's plans. They ignored him. At least, unlike his predecessor, Takahashi Korekiyo, no one murdered him.[77] On 5 November, Tōjō predicted, "America may be enraged for a while, but later she will come to understand [why we did what we did]."[78] He argued that risking war with the United States was better than "being ground down without doing anything."[79]

As it turns out, Japanese leaders did not perceive the U.S. strategy as one designed to deter. They concluded that U.S. demands put on death ground not only their country, but themselves personally as those responsible for Japan's China policy, leaving them a stark choice of fight or perish. Americans would have disagreed that their demands threatened Japanese survival. They did not perceive the tremendous value that the Japanese attached to stability in China or the extreme fear the Japanese leadership had of the spread of communism. Americans would have argued that the Japanese invasion greatly exacerbated Chinese instability, to which the Japanese would have used Manchukuo as a shining example of what was possible, if only the Chinese would cooperate. The Japanese perceived an overarching Russian threat, which the United States overlooked at this juncture. For two generations after the war, however, U.S. leaders would frame foreign policy in terms of the very Russian threat that had so consumed the Japanese in the 1930s. Unimaginative strategy by both the United States and especially Japan, which used military escalation as its universal remedy for all ailments, produced a U.S.-Japanese war that benefited neither.

In the continuing dialog of the deaf, on 26 November 1941 the United States delivered another ultimatum to Japan, the Hull Note, named after U.S. Secretary of State Cordell Hull. It required Japan to evacuate Indochina and China including Manchuria, and to repudiate both its puppet government under Wang Jingwei and its Tripartite Pact with Germany and Italy. Within the fortnight, Japan attacked Pearl Harbor, not the desired outcome for a strategy of deterrence. In the end, the United States succeeded in deterring a Japanese attack, not against itself but against Russia – the Kantō Army finally gave up its long-standing war plan to invade Russia as relations with the United States deteriorated.[80] After Pearl Harbor, Americans focused on delivering disaster to Tokyo. There was no time to reflect on why the American strategy had failed to deter the Japanese from attacking Americans.

A WAR OF MANY FRONTS

The conventional tale focuses on one day that shall live on in infamy, when the Japanese became clinically insane and attacked Pearl Harbor. This pushed the United States into World War II, and Americans were off to make the world safe for democracy. As it turns out, Japanese military planners conceived of Pearl Harbor as a peripheral operation to secure victory in the primary theater, which remained China. As it also turns out, the Japanese did not attack just Pearl Harbor – a breathtakingly America-centric view of World War II – but on that same infamous day simultaneously attacked Thailand, Malaya, the Philippines, Wake Island, Guam, Hong Kong, and the International Settlement in Shanghai – theaters scattered over the wide Pacific. Japan attacked not only U.S. interests but also British and soon Dutch interests. Australia and New Zealand as part of the British Commonwealth immediately joined the hostilities too. Occupying these scattered areas in order to solve "the Manchuria-Mongolia problem" had been under discussion in Japan since at least 1934. Evidently the failure to balance ends and means, and risks and rewards, was a long-standing lapse in army thinking.[81]

Analytical thinking was not much better in the navy. At a 1 November 1941 liaison conference of Japan's top leadership, Navy Chief of Staff Admiral Nagano Osami supported expanding the war to Great Britain and the United States: "In general, the prospects if we go to war are not bright." (In other words, Japan would lose.) "We all wonder if there isn't some way to proceed peacefully. There is no one who is willing to say: 'Don't worry, even if the war is prolonged. I will assume all responsibility.'" (And no one had any good ideas.) "On the other hand, it is not possible to maintain the status quo. Hence one unavoidably reaches the conclusion that we must go to war."[82] (So Japan would fight, but it was not Japan's fault that the status quo was intolerable.) Unconditional surrender was going to be better? How many young men had to die for the old men to save face?

The conventional tale skips another important beat. The attack on Pearl Harbor did not draw the United States into the war in Europe, only into Japan's war in Asia. Although Hitler wanted the United States bogged down in Asia, his declaration of war – a diplomatic blunder of suicidal proportions – drew the United States into the war in Europe. Without the Japanese attack precipitating the German war declaration, the United States would not have joined either war, wars that both China and Europe were losing spectacularly, at that time.

The Japanese execution of their war plan was impressive: On 7 December 1941 (Hawaii time), their forces landed in Thailand and half an hour later on the Malay Peninsula. An hour later, the Imperial Japanese Navy began the attack on Pearl Harbor. Two hours later the Japanese bombed Singapore. One hour later, the Japanese landed on Guam and began bombing Wake Island. Six hours later they attacked Clark Air Base in the Philippines. Japanese forces also bombed Hong Kong and overran the International Settlements in Shanghai and elsewhere in China.[83] Emperor Hirohito's naval aide, Lieutenant Commander Jō Eiichirō, confided in his diary, "Throughout the day the emperor wore his naval uniform and seemed to be in a splendid mood."[84]

Operationally, Japan achieved stunning success. The Imperial Japanese Navy took the United States by surprise, sinking four of eight battleships at anchor in harbor, destroying 180 aircraft, and damaging

128 others, many of them parked in close rows on the tarmac. Japan, in contrast, lost just 29 planes and five midget submarines.[85] Thailand folded within two days. On 15 December Japanese troops invaded Burma. On 16 December Japan occupied the vital Dutch oil field in Borneo. On 25 December Hong Kong fell, followed by Manila on 2–3 January 1942, the Australian military bases at Rabaul on 22–3 January, Malaya on 31 January, Singapore and the Palembang oil fields on Sumatra on 15 February, and Lashio, Burma, on 8 March, closing the Burma Road.[86] In the first five months of 1942, Japan took more territory over a greater area than any country in history and did not lose a single major ship.[87] The statistics overwhelm. Japan took 250,000 Allied prisoners of war, sank 105 Allied ships and seriously damaged 91 others, while it lost only 7,000 dead, 14,000 wounded, 562 planes, and 27 ships, but no cruiser, battleship, or carrier.[88]

Japan's conquests followed two prongs, one through the Southeast Asian mainland to invade Thailand, Burma, Malaya, and Singapore, and the other through the Pacific to take the Philippines, Guam, Borneo, Java, and Sumatra. Thereafter the army wished to consolidate its winnings, while Admiral Yamamoto insisted that success depended on maintaining the military pressure in the hopes of breaking American will. The army and navy compromised to take Fiji and Samoa in order to cut U.S. links to Australia.[89]

Some quibble that Admiral Nagumo Chūichi, the operational commander of the attack at Pearl Harbor, should have sent in a third wave of bombers to take out the refitting facilities, the submarine base, and especially the oil tanks, which contained more oil than the entire Japanese strategic reserves at the time. Like Yamamoto, who was no fan of attacking the United States, Nagumo was not in favor of Yamamoto's plan to attack Hawaii. Others noted that Japan sank none of the U.S. aircraft carriers that just happened to be out of port. But at the time battleships were considered the core capital ships of navies. Carriers acquired their cachet only as a result of the war for the Pacific. Nagumo may have believed he could not afford to risk losing capital ships in another bombing run that might have roused a posse of carriers in close pursuit. His country lacked the capacity to build a replacement fleet in any militarily useful time frame – another limitation of its strategy. Also the smoke from the burning U.S. ships impeded the vision of his pilots. So Nagumo decided against a third wave of bomber attacks.[90]

It remains unclear how many months the loss of the oil storage facilities on Hawaii would have delayed the U.S. counterattack and thereby extended Japan's breathing space to reinforce its defensive perimeter and to access to the key resources within. The loss of the oil alone would have delayed the United States by many months. In any case, stunning operational successes did not produce the desired strategic outcome of a negotiated peace.

On the strategic level Pearl Harbor was a disaster because it metastasized a malignant quagmire in China into a terminal disease for Japan with little likelihood of remission. The Japanese misjudged the intangibles of warfare – what motivated the Chinese and what motivated the Americans. The attack on American sailors in Hawaii instantly galvanized the population to fight an unlimited war, with Tokyo as the ultimate destination of the counterattack. Americans remember one infamous day in Hawaii because the Japanese actions there, not the many other attacks across the Pacific, instantly transformed American isolationism into a march on Tokyo.

Whatever the problems in the China theater, the Chinese lacked the capacity to threaten the Japanese home islands. The United States, of course, could and did. In military strategy, it is sometimes wise to open a new theater in order to attack an enemy from an additional and unexpected direction. Opening a theater that introduces a new adversary is particularly unwise in a war that has already caused overextension. The day that Roosevelt accurately predicted would live on in infamy introduced numerous new adversaries into the fight: the United States, Britain, Australia, New Zealand, and the Netherlands. Chiang Kai-shek understood the magnitude of Japan's blunder. Upon learning of the attacks, he celebrated by playing "Ave Maria" on his gramophone.[91] He knew that the United States would defeat Japan for him. The Imperial Japanese Navy had already removed its aircraft carriers from Chinese waters.[92]

Chiang seized the opportunity to ally with a strong power against Japan, by declaring war against the Axis the following day. He had already severed relations with Germany on 2 July 1941, the day after Hitler's recognition of the Wang Jingwei puppet government. Hitler had done so to appease Japan in the hopes that it would finally implement the Southern Advance to attack British interests in Asia.[93] Instead the United States recognized Chiang's command of the China, Thailand,

and Indochina theaters but assigned a handler, Lieutenant General Joseph W. Stilwell, with authority over the flow of Lend-Lease aid as his control mechanism.[94]

Back in Europe, in less than a year and a half, Germany had taken Czechoslovakia, Poland, the Netherlands, Belgium, Norway, Denmark, and half of France and starting in July 1940 had begun to strangle Britain's trade with a maritime blockade and a bombing campaign. Had Hitler not reacted to a British bombing raid on Berlin by suddenly changing the German Air Force's target sets from the Royal Air Force, Britain's key line of defense, which it was destroying, to London, Germany might have opened Britain to invasion.[95] As Britain tipped closer to the abyss, the United States did very little.

Over the summer of 1941 during the Russian invasion, Hitler promised Ambassador Ōshima that Germany would join a Japanese war against the United States.[96] He made good the promise immediately after the attack on Pearl Harbor. Technically he needed to aid Japan only if it became the victim, not the perpetrator of an attack. Hitler chose to bring the European conflict to isolationist America. Often countries do not have the luxury of determining when or whether they will go to war because others act first to visit war upon them. Had Hitler chosen not to honor his alliance with Japan, Roosevelt would have been hard-pressed to justify hostilities against any power but Japan. Under such circumstances, Britain might have fallen. If Britain had fallen, Russia might have fallen too. Russian success against the Germans depended not only on its extensive manpower, growing industrial base, and grim determination, but also on vital Lend-Lease aid to feed and transport its armies, and on U.S. and British military operations in North Africa and their aerial bombing campaign over Germany, which diverted Germany's forces – particularly its air force and artillery – away from Russia.[97] How Hitler would have garrisoned Russia is another matter, but for a time, perhaps generations, there might have been a German empire in Europe. Japan's actions and the German reaction to them, however, sent the war in a different direction altogether.

U.S. policy makers believed Germany posed a lethal threat to long-term U.S. interests and therefore agreed with Britain and Russia to pursue a Germany-first strategy. The German economy was a multiple of that of Japan. Germany had just taken over most of the industrialized world; it could cut off key U.S. markets, which were in Europe, not

Asia, and it could threaten U.S. merchant shipping in U.S. waters, as it had done to such great effect in World War I. Japan, on the other hand, could not strike the United States, except in remote outposts such as Hawaii or the Aleutian Islands, and was already bogged down in an endless war in China.

Japanese leaders understood these differences clearly and so could not fathom why the United States would ever engage in an unlimited war in Asia – U.S. stakes were simply not high enough to warrant a protracted war. The Japanese had been careful to strike strictly military targets in Hawaii, then a U.S. territory. Hawaii did not become a state until 1959. The Americans remained hopelessly isolationist as they floundered in the aftereffects of the Great Depression. American leaders, however, correctly interpreted Japanese actions as an attack on the global order, which meant the stakes were actually very high. Japan's quest for a sphere of influence eventually extending to the Middle East negated the two foundational principles of U.S. foreign policy: the Open Door and self-determination.[98]

Japan and Germany gave Roosevelt the provocation he needed to galvanize the nation to intervene massively in both the European and Asian wars, which after Pearl Harbor became linked. The logic of the European theater would extend to the Asian theater: The Allies would demand unconditional surrender in both, a turn of events unsuspected by Japanese leaders, who never thought that they could win a protracted war against the United States. As in all their past modern wars, they planned a quick decisive victory with a cost-efficient negotiated settlement to wrap it up. Like the Germans, the Japanese dismissed the fighting ability and willpower of others. Both also grossly underestimated U.S. productive capacity and the implications for a protracted war.

It took months before the United States could muster the forces for a major battle. In the meantime, on 18 April 1942 it improvised to conduct a one-way aircraft carrier bombing raid over the Japanese home islands, the so-called Doolittle Raid, under the command of Lieutenant Colonel James H. Doolittle. The heavy bombers were too large and lacked the fuel capacity to return to their ships and so had to ditch in China. The raid was not meant to do real damage but to bolster American morale at home while letting the Japanese know that Americans were thinking about them.[99] Americans brushed off Chiang's criticism of the raid. He strenuously objected because he correctly predicted the Japanese would retaliate on him. When the Japanese deployed 140,000 men to eliminate U.S. air bases in Zhejiang and Guangxi, where they believed the planes had launched, waves of reprisals focused on those suspected of aiding Doolittle's men and China suffered 30,000 military casualties.[100]

The Doolittle Raid, by mortifying the Imperial Japanese Army for its inability to protect Japanese skies, induced a major although unanticipated Japanese blunder. The Imperial Japanese Navy had been pushing for an attack on Midway in the expectation that it would sink the rest of the U.S. Fleet, which would surely defend the U.S. base there. Yamamoto, the planner of both the Pearl Harbor and Midway attacks, threatened to resign if the army did not go along, but the army would not budge until the Doolittle Raid, when army leaders reversed themselves to support revenge forthwith at Midway.[101]

Unknown to the Japanese, the United States had broken their diplomatic and naval codes and so knew the itineraries of the ships converging on Midway, where it sank four, or one-third, of Japan's twelve difficult-to-replace aircraft carriers.[102] In doing so, it overturned vague German and Japanese plans to join up in India and precluded further Japanese expansion in the Pacific. Midway was Japan's first major defeat since the beginning of the Second Sino-Japanese War. Henceforth the Japanese would have to defend what they had. For many months the Imperial Japanese Navy concealed its aircraft carrier losses from both the army and the civilian leadership.[103] It did inform Emperor Hirohito, who kept the bad news to himself as if it would go away.[104] So, no one examined how the United States, with inferior naval assets, had miraculously managed to converge them at just the right spot in the expansive Pacific theater to sink one Japanese carrier after another and the army maintained its war plans on the assumption that Japan still had twelve carriers.

Simultaneous with the infamous day in Hawaii, the Imperial Japanese Army launched the first in a sequence of battles, running from December 1941 through December 1942, intended to take over the Central China railway system south of the Yangzi River and to culminate in the war-winning Gogō Campaign in Sichuan, flushing the Nationalists from the capital in Chongqing. But now the Nationalists had some Lend-Lease arms to fight conventionally and U.S. aviators, while the Imperial Japanese Navy, which had conducted most of the bombing in Central China, had redeployed planes to the Pacific, reducing the bombing of Chinese cities by more than half in 1942. So Japan no longer owned the skies over China. Before long Japan began transferring troops from the China theater to the Pacific. During bitter fighting, cities repeatedly changed hands. The battles preceding the Gogō Campaign included the Third Battle of Changsha, Hunan, from December 1941 to January 1942, which failed, and the Battle of Zhejiang and Jiangxi from May to September 1942, taking the Zhejiang-Jiangxi Railway connecting Shanghai and Nanchang. The losses suffered in distant Guadalcanal, however, compelled Japan to call off the Gogō Campaign, scheduled for the spring of 1943. Instead, Japan fought the Battle of Western Hubei from May to June 1943 and the Battle of Changde, Hunan, from November through December. Throughout 1943 Japan conducted offensives on broad fronts, taking territory only temporarily for a lack of men to garrison the vastness of China.[105]

As U.S. military capacity grew but remained insufficient to engage the main armies of Germany on the main front in continental Europe or to conduct sustained military operations against the Japanese home islands, the United States turned to peripheral theaters. It took what assets it had to engage elements of the German and Japanese armed forces in locations comparatively more inconvenient for its enemies than for itself. This allowed the United States to leverage its naval assets to bear down on theaters neither enemy would naturally have chosen.

In 1942, President Roosevelt opened two peripheral theaters, one in the European war and one in the Asian war, as an indirect way to relieve pressure on the main theaters that the United States could not yet reach to support its Russian and Chinese allies who were fighting the enemies' main forces at such great cost. For Europe, he followed British Prime Minister Winston Churchill's advice to choose North Africa, where the Germans and British were already engaged. Allied naval superiority in combination with a theater separated from Germany by sea allowed the Allied armies to win against the Desert Fox, General Erwin Rommel, one of Nazi Germany's finest generals. Rommel lost not for want of good soldiers or generalship, but for want of adequate supplies, sunk at sea before they could reach him. For Asia, President Roosevelt supported Guadalcanal, a tropical nightmare, which was bad for all sides, but worse for the Japanese, again because of an inferior ability to protect their logistical lines by sea to supply their men on land. Roosevelt believed that U.S. resource superiority over Japan should yield victory in the end, so he chose resource-intensive theaters.[106]

Japan's Southern Advance strategy required a heavily defended outer perimeter of airfields on far-flung islands to parry the expected Allied counterattack. The Imperial Japanese Navy had failed to inform the Imperial Japanese Army that, as attractive as its strategy was, it had not yet built the required Maginot Line of airfields. One of the airfields under construction was at Guadalcanal, which the United States discovered and then attacked on 7 August 1942.[107] The Imperial Japanese Navy desperately called on the Imperial Japanese Army for help. From August 1942 to February 1943, Japan tried in vain to defend Guadalcanal, where U.S. forces pierced the defensive perimeter, halted the advance toward Australia, and forced the Japanese remnants to withdraw. Japan also lost its vital elite cadre of naval aviators, on whom its defense rested.[108] From the second half of 1942 to the first half of 1943, Japanese pilots from land-based craft suffered an 87 percent casualty rate, and carrier-based aircraft had an astounding 98 percent casualty rate. Although these numbers dropped in the second half of 1943 to 60 and 80 percent, respectively, Japan could never replace its lost elite pilots.[109]

Guadalcanal drained so many Japanese resources that midcampaign in December 1942, Japan called off the Gogō Campaign.[110] If these losses had not forced deployment of soldiers from the China theater to the Pacific, Chiang might have lost his last foothold in China. The Long Boat Ride up the Yangzi River might have ended at the headwater in Tibet or Burma, neither a promising location for a comeback. The Nationalists had fled from Shanghai in 1937 all the way upriver to Chongqing and were on the verge of reembarking in 1942 until Guadalcanal saved them. The Long Boat Ride was the Nationalist equivalent to the Communists' Long March, which the latter were better at marketing.

In 1942 the tide of battle turned in both the European and Asian wars. In Europe, Russia won the Stalingrad Campaign, which raged from 13 September 1942 until 2 February 1943. Stalingrad was the largest and bloodiest battle of World War II and Germany's greatest defeat. Combined casualties for both sides exceeded 750,000.[111] Henceforth, Russian troops moved westward. Again Germany unsuccessfully pressured Japan to open a second front on Russia.[112] Britain and the United States defeated Italy in September. In 1943 the United States began a two-pronged offensive, one led by General Douglas MacArthur to reclaim the Philippines, which he had lost in May 1942, and another led by Admiral Chester Nimitz to follow the island chains to establish bomber bases within range of Japan.[113] Japanese forces scrambled to maintain their defensive perimeter in the campaigns for the Solomons and New Guinea.

The Japanese assumed that the United States would take each position on the way to Tokyo. They planned to fight to the death at each one, understanding that more men are required to storm a well-fortified position than to hold it. They believed that the United States would not have the stomach to continue but would agree to a negotiated settlement long before reaching Tokyo. Instead the United States bypassed many islands, taking only those necessary for naval logistics, and, more importantly, for bomber bases to take the air war to the Japanese home islands. Simultaneously, the United States used its submarine service to eliminate the Japanese merchant marine, an unexpected primary mission from both the Japanese and the U.S. submariners' perspective.

The Imperial Japanese Navy fixated on the heroic task of fighting the U.S. Navy, not picking off sitting-duck merchantmen that posed no match for naval vessels.[114] It fought the symmetric fight, conventional force on conventional force, while the United State also fought the asymmetric fight of naval ship on merchant vessel. Code breaking allowed the United States to predict the location of Japanese supply ships and troop transports, which submarines destroyed with great regularity once they received working ordnance. The original Rhode Island–designed torpedoes were defective, and only after a U.S. captain defied orders to open one up and figure out the problem did the manufacturer finally acknowledge and correct its error in October 1943. During the Pacific Ocean war, U.S. submarines sank 201 warships of 686, including 1 battleship, 8 carriers, 12 cruisers, 23 submarines, 43 destroyers, and 60 escort ships.[115] Of the 2,117 Japanese merchant ships sunk in the war, U.S. submarines accounted for 1,314, or 56 percent.[116] By war's end Japan's merchant marine had been reduced to one-ninth its pre–Pearl Harbor capacity, and only half the men and supplies sent from Japan and Manchuria reached the Pacific theater. These statistics are particularly notable, given the tiny numbers of submariners compared to the other services and specialties.[117] The Japanese empire depended on resources and their transport home. Japanese expeditionary forces scattered throughout the Pacific required supplies delivered by sea. U.S. submariners increasingly prevented this, starving both Japan's expeditionary forces and the home islands.[118]

Apparently Japanese army and navy leaders suffered from the same lack of imagination paralyzing the civilian leadership. Like the major belligerents in World War I, which responded to the terrible costs of a nonperforming military strategy with increasing doses of the same, Japan responded to Chinese intransigence with escalation. Japanese conquests became a function of both operational success and strategic failure. The Japanese took territories because they could, but the more they took and the harder they fought, the more militarily and financially overextended they became. Japanese leaders never seemed to ask the question: How much territory could Japan take before the garrisoning costs exceeded the value of the resources that could be extracted? The answer to this question was probably Manchuria.

Japan also lacked an exit strategy. China's response to conventional defeat – an insurgency in order to outlast the enemy – was not original, but time honored. The United States won its independence from Britain using this strategy. At that time American forces lost virtually every major conventional engagement, but they delivered a costly insurgency, convinced the French and others to intervene, and, relying on French conventional land and especially naval forces, won at Yorktown, by which time the British government, propelled by elections, refused to waste any more money on the insurgency, and the thirteen colonies gained their independence.[119]

THE GENERALS' WAR

From January 1942 to October 1944, Lieutenant General Joseph W. Stilwell served as U.S. commander for the China-Burma-India theater and Chiang Kai-shek's chief of staff for Allied forces. From the start Stilwell believed that victory in World War II required the prior defeat of Japan in China and a supply route through Burma – a plan that gave him a starring role in the war. Admiral Nimitz and General MacArthur saw different starring roles – for themselves, the former in an island-hopping campaign to bomb and blockade the Japanese home islands into submission, and the latter in a land campaign to make good his promise to return, victorious, to the Philippines after losing them in 1941, when ten hours after the Pearl Harbor attack, Japan caught his bombers still stationary on the tarmac. Unlike Admiral Husband E. Kimmel, the commander of the Pacific Fleet, who was cashiered within days of Pearl Harbor, MacArthur – who failed to take advantage of his advance warning and whose seventy-five thousand abandoned surviving troops eventually made the largest surrender in U.S. history – was transformed into a national hero in newspaper coverage that portrayed the fighting in the Philippines as heroic instead of the unmitigated disaster that it was.[120]

In China, the ranking American military advisers, Generals Stilwell and Chennault, vehemently disagreed over priorities. On the surface Stilwell had one of the most impressive army service records at the time of his appointment to the China theater and even spoke Chinese, yet he had never commanded troops, attended the command course at Leavenworth, or engaged in combined operations. Major General Claire L. Chennault had retired from the army reserve at the modest rank of captain, then promoted himself to colonel when serving under Chiang Kai-shek in 1937 as a mercenary to develop an air force, and was catapulted to the rank of brigadier and then major general when the U.S. government took him over after Pearl Harbor and in 1943 made him commander of the Fourteenth Air Force, formerly known as the Flying Tigers of China. Stilwell despised the Chiangs, both Generalissimo and Madame, while Chennault was devoted to them.[121] Stilwell and Chennault also despised each other and had friends in high places, Marshall and Roosevelt, respectively, who kept them in their positions long after their personal vitriol damaged rather than furthered U.S. foreign policy.[122]

While Chennault promised that the war could be won from the air, with bombers and fighters under his command (naturally), Stilwell fixated on Burma and envisioned a war-winning battle between Japanese and Chinese ground forces, the latter under his command – naturally. The U.S. Army chief of staff, General George C. Marshall, pointed out that U.S. strategy should leverage its maritime position to avoid such large and costly battles. Stilwell had the secondary objective of wishing to show up Chiang as publicly as possible. He saw only the global war and his personal quarrel with Chiang, not the regional war and civil war that explained Chiang's actions. So Stilwell exerted enormous pressure on Chiang to fight the North Burma Campaign in 1944.[123]

Stilwell was nothing like the future five-star general and postwar president Dwight D. Eisenhower, whose enormous diplomatic skills helped keep the Anglo-American alliance solid, in part by humoring some of Britain's greatest egos, such as Field-Marshal Bernard Law Montgomery, while reining in some of America's, such as General George S. Patton. General Stilwell, upon assuming his assignment in China, told Teddy White of *Time* magazine, "The trouble with China is simple.... We are allied to an ignorant, illiterate, superstitious, peasant son of a bitch." He referred to Chiang by animal and vegetable epithets – rattlesnake or peanut – depending on his mood.[124] By 1943 he was working on a contingency plan to assassinate Chiang.[125] Small wonder the two men detested each other.

Roosevelt and Marshall supported a Burma Campaign and the construction of airfields in Asia not to help China in the regional war but to support Britain in the global war by preventing the fall of India and to defeat Japan via the Pacific.[126] Japan had hoped that its operations in Burma would lead to an invasion of India and an Indian uprising against British rule.[127] After Churchill had rejected an Indian offer to support the war effort in return for independence, in 1942 Indians responded with organized civil disobedience known as the Quit India Movement to sit out the war. The movement posed a direct threat to British rule. In January right after Pearl Harbor, Chiang Kai-shek had flown to India in the hope of opening a supply route via Tibet and to urge Mahatma Gandhi and Jawaharlal Nehru's Congress Party not to undermine the British fight against Japan. Gandhi agreed. The tortuous supply route, known as the Ledo Road, would link India to the northern part of the Burma Road but did not open until early 1945.[128] Meanwhile, Japan cultivated Subhas Chandra Bose, the charismatic orator, who supported a violent campaign for independence and who established the Provisional Government of Free India on 14 October 1943.[129] The British deeply felt the Japanese threat to India.[130]

In 1942, Chiang had made three demands to the United States: three U.S. divisions to Burma to reopen the Burma Road, five hundred planes to China, and five thousand tons of supplies per month flown in. If not, Soong Mayling, translating for her husband, implied, China might seek a separate peace with Japan.[131] America's other continental ally, Stalin, also apparently tried to arrange a separate peace, but he had the brains not to let the United States know. In the spring of 1943, the Russians allegedly approached Germans via the Japanese naval attaché in Stockholm for a restoration of the territorial status quo of June

1941.[132] The Germans were not interested. By the summer of 1943, Chiang made good his threat but found the Japanese terms – as usual – too harsh: Japan offered peace in exchange for a Nationalist promise to join Japan to fight Britain and the United States.[133]

Meanwhile, Chiang had reluctantly deferred to Stilwell's campaign plan to counter the Japanese invasion of Burma in January 1942 that threatened to keep the Burma Road cut indefinitely and to unsettle India. The Allies lost. The Japanese took Burma and destroyed two of Chiang's only armies with the full complement of heavy equipment along with his only motorized heavy artillery. Without the Burma Road, no more heavy equipment would be forthcoming, positioning Chiang poorly to fight either the Japanese or the Communists.[134]

To placate Chiang, Roosevelt dangled future prospects. At the Cairo Conference in December 1943, the Allies agreed to open a second front in Europe and a campaign in Burma in 1944. For the first time in modern history China was treated as a great power with its inclusion among the "Big Four" (Britain, Russia, the United States, and China) on the invitation list to Cairo – although Russia refused to appear, allegedly because China was attending. Sir Horace J. Seymour, the British ambassador to China, reported that "the picture of China as a leading world Power corresponds less to facts than to a promissory note drawn on 'prospects.'"[135] Churchill, ever blunt, called it "an absolute farce."[136] Anticipated Russian participation in the war in Asia then diminished the importance of Chinese cooperation.

At Cairo, Chiang annoyed his allies with insatiable demands for aid and his insistence that he have full control over its allocation. Marshall responded: "Now let me get this straight. You are talking about your 'rights' in this matter. I thought these were *American* planes, and *American* personnel, and *American* materiel. Don't understand what you mean by saying we can't do thus and so."[137] Chiang failed to appreciate that the United States, alone of all the powers, was simultaneously fighting enemies and supporting desperate allies in both the European and Pacific theaters and that from the U.S. point of view Germany, not Japan presented the more dangerous threat, making China a secondary priority. Hitler had not believed that the United States could conduct strategically significant campaigns in both theaters, whereas Chiang apparently felt entitled to first dibs on U.S. aid. In return for a U.S. promise to equip and train ninety Chinese divisions, and another promise that Taiwan and Manchuria would be restored after the war, Chiang agreed to participate in the Burma offensive.[138]

But in early 1944, a shortage of landing craft needed for the invasion of France caused the Allied cancellation of the promised major amphibious operation in the Bay of Bengal to open a land route to China. This meant that at war's end, Russia would have the only powerful army in China. Chiang became angry when the United States then transferred its Lend-Lease aid stockpiled in India to other campaigns. He demanded a gold loan for the extraordinary sum of $1 billion; otherwise, he would seek terms with Japan. Roosevelt threatened to cut off all Lend-Lease aid unless Chiang cooperated in Burma.[139]

Japanese peace terms did not improve. In the summer of 1944, after the fall of the Tōjō cabinet, in exchange for peace, Japan offered to tolerate the existence of Nationalist diplomatic relations with the United States and Britain, allow the Nationalists to return to their capital of Nanjing, and deal with the Wang Jingwei puppet government as they saw fit, if they agreed to have Britain and the United States maintain strict neutrality in China. The price remained too high.[140] However much Chiang double-dealt, the United States always offered him better terms than did Japan.

Like MacArthur, who saw the war through the prism of his defeat in the Philippines, Stilwell remained determined to win back Burma after his defeat in 1942. The 1944 North Burma Campaign poisoned Sino-American relations. Chiang saw some of his best remaining troops deployed in a theater that had become irrelevant to his survival, while Stilwell portrayed Chiang as hoarding U.S. military largesse for other purposes. Chiang had warned that Japan would take advantage of the Allied preoccupation with the impending invasion of France: "It may therefore be expected that before long Japan will launch an all-out offensive against China so as to remove the threat to their rear." As predicted, in March 1944 the Japanese launched the Ugō Campaign against India, known in the West as the Imphal Campaign, and in April, the Ichigō Campaign against China, for which they had stockpiled ammunition for two years and aviation fuel for eight months. Chiang required Chennault's air force to survive Ichigō. But mid-Ichigō Stilwell tried to have Chennault cashiered for his obstreperous demands for supplies. Chiang could not see why he should be fighting a two-front war – one in Burma, of all places – at a time like this.[141] In Europe, Britain and the United States had put off

Stalin's urgent demands for a second front on the Continent for years because the timing was wrong for them. Chiang was in a much more desperate position. This was not the time for Burma.

The Ichigō Campaign was the final and the largest campaign ever conducted by the Imperial Japanese Army. It ran from 17 April 1944 to early February 1945 and followed the Beijing-Wuhan, Guangdong-Wuhan, and Hunan-Guangxi railway lines. The campaign had multiple objectives: It attempted to carve a passage through central South China to create an inland (and submarine-proof) transportation route between Pusan, Korea, and Indochina; to take the airfields in Sichuan and Guangxi to preclude U.S. bombing of Taiwan and Japan; and to target elite Nationalist units to cause the Nationalist government to collapse.[142] Japan deployed twenty divisions composed of 510,000 men against 700,000 Nationalist soldiers. From April to December 1944, the Nationalists lost most of Henan, Hunan, Guangxi, Guangdong, and Fujian and a large part of Guizhou.[143] Key battles included the Battle of Central Henan from April to June, the Battles of Changsha and Hengyang from May through August, and the Battle of Guilin-Liuzhou from September to December.[144] By the time the Nationalists realized that they did not face another Japanese "cut-short" operation, intended to attrite Chinese forces and hold territory temporarily, but the largest Japanese campaign of the war, it was too late.[145]

In the first phase of the campaign, lasting until late May 1944, Japan launched a north-south pincer to take Luoyang, Henan, and to clear the southern Beijing-Wuhan Railway all the way to Wuhan. Luoyang fell on 25 May. In the second phase, from May to December 1944, Japanese forces cleared the Guangdong-Wuhan Railway, the Hunan-Guangxi Railway, and their junction at Hengyang, the location of the largest air base in Hunan. On 18 June Changsha finally fell in the Fourth Battle of Changsha, followed on 8 August by Hengyang, on 11 November by both Guilin (the capital of Guangxi) and Liuzhou, and on 24 November by Nanning. Chiang lost Changsha when he refused to resupply General Xue Yue, a member of the Guangdong group, whom Chiang saw as a southern autonomist. Disagreements between Stilwell and Chennault undermined coordination on the U.S. side, not to mention between U.S. and Nationalist planners at the Battle of Hengyang, which fell to Japan after seven weeks of fighting. In early 1945, Japanese forces broke through to Indochina, opening a continuous land route and eliminating many but not all U.S. air bases.[146] The Nationalists torched Guilin as they retreated.[147]

The Nationalists lost more than 130,000 killed in action, ten major air bases, thirty-six airports as well as their key remaining source for food and recruits with the occupation of Henan, Hunan, and Guangxi.[148] Japanese killed from twenty to forty Chinese soldiers for each one of theirs – a kill ratio attributable to superior conventional equipment. Given the rapid approach of the U.S. Navy to the Japanese home islands – the Gilbert Islands in November 1943, the Marshall Islands in January 1944, and the Marianas ongoing – a win in the regional war in China at this late date contributed nothing to the defense of the home islands in the global war.[149]

In the midst of the campaign, in September of 1944 Japan again attempted to make peace with the Nationalists. Japan agreed to withdraw all of its troops from China in return for a withdrawal of the U.S. Air Force, whose planes based in Chengdu, Sichuan, on 15 June for the first time since the Doolittle Raid had started bombing Kyūshū, the southernmost of Japan's main home islands. Japan would let Chiang determine his relations with the United States, Britain, and the Wang Jingwei puppet government.[150] Chiang Kai-shek continued to negotiate but agreed to nothing. Within a month Wang died in a Tokyo hospital.

Meanwhile Admiral Nimitz's Central Pacific Campaign, not General MacArthur's high-casualty campaign in the direction of the Philippines, delivered airfields in the Marianas, much closer to Japan than the bases in Sichuan. From 16 June 1944 to 9 January 1945, the United States had been able to launch one bombing raid per month from Chengdu with an average of 53 planes. Beginning on 24 November 1944, the United States began bombing raids from the Marianas, running an average of four raids of 68 planes per month. From March through August 1945, the bombing raids intensified, with daily raids of more than 100 planes.[151] As a result, the China theater became irrelevant to the outcome of the U.S. war against Japan. Likewise, Ichigō lost its rationale as the Japanese home islands became the main theater, under air attack not from China, but from the inaccessible Marianas. At the end of 1944, the Japanese called off the Ichigō Campaign in order to redeploy as many troops as possible to defend Japan.

Ichigō had a greater impact on the civil war than on the global war by making the Nationalists look militarily incompetent, wiping out formations vital to defeat the Communists, and leaving Central China wide open to Communist infiltration. Vladimirov, the Russian representative in Yan'an, wrote that Ichigō exceeded Mao's "most optimitistic forecasts." The Allied victory in March 1945 in the simultaneous Imphal Campaign resulted in the reopening of the Burma Road supply route, breaking Japan's eight-year creeping blockade of China, but doing so too late to affect the outcome of either the regional or the global war. Lend-Lease aid started arriving in quantity for a Nationalist army gutted by the Ichigō Campaign.[152]

During the North Burma Campaign, Stilwell had maneuvered Roosevelt into demanding that Chiang put all Nationalist forces under Stilwell's command, which greatly flattered his own ego as evidenced by his flight into poetry – "I've waited long for vengeance – / At last I've had my chance. / I've looked the Peanut [Chiang] in the eye. / And kicked him in the pants." Both bad poetry and bad policy. The plan was a nonstarter since Chiang's power rested on his military, and since however distinguished Stilwell's career may have been on paper, it did not measure up in practice. His only campaigns had been in Burma, which he lost when it counted, and then won when it did not. Both the British and the Nationalists demanded Stilwell's recall.[153]

Like the relations among the Axis powers, U.S.-Chinese relations remained fraught throughout the war as each focused on different primary enemies. Chiang had to position his troops to win the long Chinese civil war, which the Nationalists and the Communists planned to resume as soon as Japan capitulated. The United States promised Chiang far more aid than it could deliver over the Hump, the treacherous air route over Burma, known as the "Skyway to Hell," which was the only way in until the expulsion of Japan from Burma. Massive aid requires ports or railways – both of which Japan blocked. What little aid there was went mostly to support Chennault's air force, leaving a very angry Stilwell. By May 1944, a little more than ten thousand tons of war matériel had reached Chinese forces. Most aid went to American-trained troops to be used for Burma, leaving a very angry Chiang.[154] The Chinese then played games with the exchange rates to charge the United States exorbitant prices for any labor done at U.S. air bases, leaving very angry Americans.[155] Although Chennault helped provide air cover, Chiang largely fought the Japanese without any U.S. aid.

During the Stilwell-Chiang and Stilwell-Chennault spitting contests, Zhou Enlai made hay. In his capacity as Communist representative in Chongqing, Zhou regularly visited the U.S. Embassy, where he confirmed Stilwell's criticisms to portray the Nationalists as failing to fight the Japanese and hoarding U.S. Lend-Lease supplies for use against the Communists in the civil war. His "smiling diplomacy" was highly effective. In his student days, he had been a Chinese opera actor; in his professional life he used his acting skills to great advantage. The Americans believed him even though the Japanese blockade prevented much aid from entering the country, leaving little to hoard.[156] Journalists instinctively gravitated toward Zhou. Teddy White of *Time* and *Life* magazines described how he and Zhou had "become friends."[157] Vladimirov described White as Zhou probably also saw him, as another "young bourgeois journalist" to be played. Before returning to Russia from Yan'an in 1945, Vladimirov summarized Mao's strategy as leaving the fighting of Japan to others in order to position himself to seize power after Japan's defeat, a strategy Mao successfully and inaccurately (after 1936) pinned on Chiang. Mao's crowning diplomatic achievement during the long Chinese civil war was his victory against Chiang in the media theater, which corroded the U.S.-Nationalist alliance.[158]

WAR TERMINATION

When U.S. precision bombing of Japan proved ineffective, the new U.S. commander of the air war over Japan, "bombs-away" General Curtis E. LeMay, who took over on 19 January 1944, realized that Japan's cities filled with wooden housing and narrow streets made excellent tinder. Despite the shameless false advertising from air power buffs, precision bombing did not become technically feasible for nearly three decades, until late in the Vietnam War. In the meantime, civilian populations bore the brunt of bombing. The U.S. firebombing of Japan deliberately targeted civilians, who were the overwhelming majority of its victims. It proved brutally successful. During the night of 9–10 March 1945, firebombing destroyed sixteen square miles of central Tokyo, where the temperatures made the canals boil. More people died that night – an estimated eighty-four thousand – than were killed during the atomic bombing of Nagasaki. Over the following ten days, firebombing destroyed the four next largest cities: Kobe, Nagoya, Osaka, and Yokohama. By the end of the war sixty-six Japanese cities lay in ruins, leaving 9.2 million homeless. Only Kyoto, Nara, and Kanazawa survived.[159]

By this time, American military planners understood that Japanese soldiers fought to the death, treated prisoners of war with appalling and also pointless cruelty, and meted out cutthroat treatment to occupied civilian populations. So they focused on minimizing Allied casualties and putting the maximal pressure on Japan in order to end the war as soon a possible. Firebombing met these criteria, but it gave no quarter to the young or old, the innocent or the guilty, the powerful or the powerless.

Emperor Hirohito made one decision of consequence during the war – the decision to throw in the towel. When he assumed the throne in 1926 after the death of his mentally ill father, he took the reign title of *Shōwa*, the name Japanese use for the man and more often for the era lasting until his death in 1989. The two characters composing *Shōwa* translate separately as "brightness" and "harmonious" and together as "illustrious peace" or even "enlightened peace." His reign was anything but. Japanese emperors safeguard three pieces of imperial regalia, a sword, a jewel, and a bronze mirror, symbolizing, respectively, courage, intelligence, and benevolence and allegedly given to the imperial line by the sun goddess, Amaterasu Ōmikami. Above all, Emperor Hirohito sought to preserve these treasures and the imperial line, which had ruled longer than any other dynasty, since 660 B.C., or so the conventional tale goes.[160]

In Japan, emperors reign but do not rule.[161] They are symbols of legitimacy for power exercised by others, in traditional Japan by the shōgun or general, and in Meiji Japan forward through the government bureaucracy. According to Nakamura Takafusa, the eminent postwar Japanese historian of wartime Japan:[162]

> The decision-making process within the Japanese bureaucracy, now as in the past, is that middle-level managers formulate policy proposals, which are then passed up through the hierarchy one stage at a time for approval until they eventually reach the top and are adopted as official policy. Of course, someone higher up may occasionally indicate a preference in advance, and proposals are sometimes revised along the way, but these are exceptions to the general rule. Even such fateful decisions as whether or not to take Japan into war were determined according to the traditional pattern, by officers of middle rank.

This governmental system has been called variously "government by acquiescence"[163] or a "system of irresponsibility"[164] because if everyone is responsible for policy, then policy formation becomes anonymous so that no one is actually accountable. The primary value emphasized in decision making was consensus reached through informal procedures.[165]

General Tōjō Hideki, who became prime minister just in time to give his support to the strategy to attack Western interests across the Pacific, and who remained in office until U.S. bombs began raining down on the home islands in mid-1944, was powerful not in himself personally but because he combined at least three offices, prime minister, war minister, and munitions minister, as well as short stints as foreign minister, home affairs minister, and education minister.[166] He demonstrated no profound powers of perception. At the critical time before the decision to expand the war in 1941, he had observed: "At the time of the Russo-Japanese War, we took our stand with no prospect of victory, and that was the situation for one year from the Battle of the Yalu River. Yet we won."[167] Pushing Japan's luck for a second risky roll of the dice was not the appropriate conclusion to draw from Japan's extraordinary good fortune the first time around.

Back in the 1920s, the passing of the *genrō* generation left the government without persons with broad experience in both civil and military affairs and close personal connections beyond the confines of their own specialization. While the post-Meiji generation of leaders may have received greater formal training, their knowledge ran in narrow channels, with the boundaries between civil and military institutions clearly defined and the divisions between the army and navy equivalent to battle lines in their fight over the military budget.[168]

As the war went badly and the military needed to spread the blame, the Imperial Conference was resurrected on 11 January 1938 after a more than thirty-year hiatus.[169] Select civil and military leaders of the cabinet met together to present unanimous recommendations to the emperor. As the war went from bad to worse, Imperial Conferences met more frequently so that the emperor could personally approve major policy and strategy shifts. Some postwar historians have excoriated Emperor Hirohito for not stopping the military escalation.[170] This argument rests on the assumption that the emperor had the power to force his generals to do what they did not wish to do. In major matters of state, Emperor Hirohito rubber stamped the advice provided, just as he did after the war when he rubber stamped General Douglas MacArthur's fiats concerning the terms of the occupation and, more importantly, the nature of the postwar Constitution, written by U.S. military lawyers in one week, which has remained the unamended fundamental law of Japan.[171]

Only when the dynasty faced extinction did events force Emperor Hirohito to take a more active role in governance regardless of any fears of army reprisals. The loss of Okinawa on 22 June 1945 made the invasion of the home islands imminent. The bombing of the Imperial Palace must have made the threat concrete to Emperor Hirohito. The United States rained down 7 million leaflets on Japan containing the peace terms and dangled the prospects of survival for the emperor with the tantalizing line "Even the powerful military groups cannot stop the mighty march for peace of the Emperor and the people."[172] Emperor Hirohito apparently read one that landed in the palace grounds. It outlined both the Potsdam Declaration and Japan's official response to it.[173] The day Okinawa fell, Hirohito informed the Supreme War Leadership Council that it was time to take the necessary diplomatic actions to end the war.[174]

On 26 July, on the sixth anniversary of the U.S. abrogation of its commercial treaty with Japan, the United States, Britain, and China, but not Russia had issued the Potsdam Declaration. It called for the unconditional surrender, demilitarization, democratization, and occupation of Japan; the prosecution of war criminals; and the payment of reparations. The former ambassador to Japan from 1931 to 1941 Joseph C. Grew unsuccessfully urged senior U.S. policy makers to guarantee the survival of the Japanese monarchy as a useful tool for the anticipated U.S. postwar occupation. He considered Emperor Hirohito to be the "queen bee in a hive ... surrounded by the attentions of the hive."[175] U.S. policy makers left the fate of the dynasty ambiguous until after the capitulation, when they ultimately followed Grew's advice. Because Russia had not signed the declaration, the Japanese hoped for a separate peace with Russia or Russian mediation of the end of the war.[176] Since at least August 1944 and continuing into June of 1945, the Japanese had secretly but ineffectively negotiated with Russia.[177]

For a short but critical period between 7 April and 17 August 1945, the seventy-eight-year-old baron and vice-admiral Suzuki Kantarō, who had been seriously wounded in the 26 February 1936 coup attempt, served as prime minister. As a former grand chamberlain he had close ties to Emperor Hirohito. On 28 July, he held a press conference in which he said he intended to "ignore" the Potsdam Declaration. The United States interpreted this as rejection. So atomic bombs followed. On 6 August, 100,000 to 140,000 Japanese perished at Hiroshima followed by another 100,000 over the following five years from radiation sickness. On 9 August, 35,000 to 40,000 died at Nagasaki.[178] Right after the war, an employee at the Mitsubishi torpedo plant in Nagasaki observed: "This is where we made the first torpedoes, the ones dropped on Pearl Harbor ... and in the end here's where we were stabbed to death. We fought a stupid war."[179] Secretary of War Henry L. Stimson had removed the historic city of Kyoto from the target list under the strenuous objections of the head of the Manhattan Project, Brigadier General Leslie R. Groves. Groves believed that Japanese surrender would require a minimum of two atomic bombs, one to demonstrate the effects, and a second to prove there were more.[180]

Starting in February 1945 Russia began transferring troops and equipment from European Russia to Siberia. On 5 April, Stalin declined to extend the Russian-Japanese Neutrality Pact, which legally remained in force for one year after the renunciation.[181] Regardless, in the opening minutes of 9 August battlefield time, Russia attacked Manchuria just ten minutes after it informed Japan's ambassador, on 8 August at 5:00 p.m. Moscow time, of its declaration of war effective 9 August.[182] One and a half million troops crossed the border.[183] Russia's invasion, known as Operation AUGUST STORM, broke two treaties, its Neutrality Pact with Japan, by failing to wait the stipulated full year, and the Yalta Agreement, requiring a prior treaty with China.[184] At the Yalta Conference from 4 to 11 February 1945, Stalin, Roosevelt, and Churchill had agreed on strategy for the final campaigns of the global war. This included Stalin's promise to declare war on Japan after the defeat of Germany.

Operation AUGUST STORM was the Russian Army's most ambitious campaign of World War II over extraordinarily difficult terrain. From 9 to 18 August, Russia took territory exceeding the combined area of Germany and France. Within nine days Russian troops drove from 310 to 590 miles (500 to 950 kilometers) into Manchuria and put to flight Japan's million-man army stationed there.[185] When Japan formally capitulated on 15 August, all military operations should have ceased. At 7 p.m., President Harry S. Truman ordered a cease-fire for U.S. military operations. Japan dithered for two days before ordering its own cease-fire, giving Russia an excuse to press on, but by 17 August Russia still had yet to take the major cities. Meanwhile on 16 August, Lieutenant General Hata Hikosaburō, the Kantō Army chief of staff, despite having received no official instructions from Tokyo, ordered an end to hostilities and concluded a cease-fire agreement with the Russians on 19 August. Nevertheless, Russian forces pressed on from 18 to 20 August, occupying Harbin, Qiqihaer, Changchun, Shenyang, Chengde, Lüshun, and Dalian. Meanwhile the battle to take Sakhalin Island continued from 11 to 25 August.[186] Wherever the Russians went, they raped, looted, and murdered civilians, angering even the Chinese Communists.[187]

Until 22 August, Stalin remained intent upon occupying the northern half of Hokkaido, before bowing to strong U.S. opposition.[188] At Potsdam, Russia and the United States had agreed that the U.S. occupation zone included all the Kurile Islands save the northernmost four, but once Stalin confirmed that the United States would not intervene over the islands north of Hokkaido, he ordered their occupation on 19 August, taking Etorofu on 28 August, and Kunashiri and Shikotan both on 1 September. These islands had never been tsarist or Soviet territory. (In the 1875 Treaty of St. Petersburg, Japan had negotiated sovereignty over the northern Kuriles in exchange for giving up the southern half of Sakhalin Island.) On 2 September, Japan formally surrendered by signing the capitulation documents in a grand ceremony in Tokyo Bay aboard USS *Missouri,* a ship named after the home state of President Truman. It flew the flag that Commodore Matthew C. Perry had flown when he forced the unequal treaty system on Japan in 1854 and 1855. This was the official ending of the four-year war in the Pacific and the fifteen-year Second Sino-Japanese War in China. Three days later, Russia completed its occupation of the Habomai Islands.[189] Its seizure of land after the surrender left an enduring territorial dispute and the absence of a peace treaty between Japan and Russia.

The Japanese cabinet had remained split on the subject of capitulation even with the two atomic bombs dropped three days apart on 6 and 9 August 1945, the Russian declaration of war on 8 August, and the bluff that the U.S. would rain down more atomic bombs (when it could not finish a third until 22 August and could produce only seven by the end of October).[190] War Minister Anami Korechika believed the bluff, thinking the United States might possess more than 100 atomic weapons, yet he remained adamant on rejecting the Potsdam Declaration. General George C. Marshall thought Japan would not capitulate before both U.S. and Russian troops had landed on the home islands.[191]

A decision to surrender required unanimity among the so-called Big Six: the prime minister, the foreign minister, the war minister, the navy minister, the naval chief of staff, and the army chief of staff. In other words, the military had four votes to the civilian side of the government, which had two. No one with economic expertise, such as the finance minister, participated. The requirement for unanimity gave each of the Big Six veto power.[192] In the terrible four days when atomic bombs fell and the Russians invaded, the Big Six fixated on four peace conditions: an independent military, Japanese (not foreign) prosecution of any war criminals, no foreign occupation of Japan, and the retention of the imperial system. When the Big Six deadlocked, Prime Minister Suzuki Kantarō requested Emperor Hirohito to cast the tie-breaking vote. On 10 August, Emperor Hirohito supported acceptance of the Potsdam Declaration and left the army out to dry by dropping the first three conditions protecting the military and concentrating on the fourth to save the imperial system and, by extension, his own skin. War Minister Anami Korechika, Chief of Army Staff Umezu Yoshijirō, and Chief of Navy Staff Toyoda Soemu remained opposed.[193] On 12 August, the imperial clan gathered in an unprecedented meeting.[194] That day the emperor recorded a speech to be broadcast to the Japanese people announcing Japan's surrender.[195]

Emperor Hirohito's intervention would have been meaningless unless the military agreed to comply. With the Russian invasion of Manchuria, there were discussions at the army general staff headquarters about making itself the government.[196] A coup attempt brewed, with the brother-in-law of War Minister Anami, Lieutenant Colonel Takeshita Masahiko, one of two key instigators.[197] On 13 August, the coup leaders murdered General Mori Takeshi, the officer in charge of defending the Imperial Palace, and forged orders in his name but could not find the emperor's taped speech. General Mori's successor, General Tanaka Shizuichi, put an end to the coup, the so-called August 15 Incident.[198] If the rebels had kidnapped the emperor as planned, the war would have continued. While army officers intrigued and Emperor Hirohito and the Big Six dithered, the United States firebombed seven more Japanese cities.[199]

Immediately before the Imperial Conference on 14 August, War Minister Anami had three marshals petition Emperor Hirohito to reject the Potsdam Declaration. Instead, the emperor rejected their petition. At the ensuing Imperial Conference a tearful Emperor Hirohito implored Anami to honor the Potsdam Declaration. Afterward, Anami no longer supported the coup attempt.[200] That same day Emperor Hirohito dispatched members of the imperial family to communicate the surrender to Japan's armies in the field: Lieutenant Colonel Prince Takeda Tsunenori went to Korea and Manchuria to inform the Chōsen and Kantō Armies; Colonel Prince Asaka Yasuhiko went to China to inform the China Expeditionary Army Group; Prince Kanin Haruhito went to China, Indochina, and Singapore to inform the Southern Army Group; and Emperor Hirohito's younger brother, Prince Takamatsu Nobuhito, who had served as a navy captain, ordered the Special Attack Corps not to resist the U.S. landing in Japan.[201] Still the Southern Army Group stalled on surrender until 23 August, after it learned all other commands had complied.[202]

In the early hours of 15 August, War Minister Anami committed ritual suicide. Emperor Hirohito's speech accepting the Potsdam Declaration, the so-called Jade Voice Broadcast, was aired at noon, and the two coup leaders, Major Hatanaka Kenji and Lieutenant Colonel Shiizaki Jirō, committed suicide. The cabinet resigned and Emperor Hirohito made his paternal uncle, Major General and Prince Higashikuni Naruhiko, prime minister.[203] The Jade Voice Broadcast obliquely referred to the atomic bombs but made no mention of the Russian invasion. On 17 August, the emperor issued a rescript to the armed forces ordering them to lay down their arms. The rescript emphasized the Russian invasion but made no reference to the atomic bombs. In this way, he left ambiguous which factor, the atomic bombs or the Russian invasion, had decisively influenced his own thinking.[204]

The conventional tale does not give adequate credit to Russia's role in Japan's unconditional surrender. While Russia did not join the Pacific War until very late in the game, only during the final month (and then stayed too long, taking territory after Japan's surrender), its massive deployment of 1.5 million men in Manchuria delivered the Imperial Japanese Army a morale-breaking nightmare scenario of Communist forces sweeping toward Japan. Stalin proposed to the United States a divided Japan with his country in possession of the northern half of Hokkaido, Japan's northernmost main island.[205] The Japanese had a choice: capitulate immediately to the Americans or capitulate potentially to the Russians with their well-known appetite for other people's territory. Americans lived far away and could be expected to leave, but Russians had no history of willingly returning their conquests. Prime Minister Suzuki Kantarō preferred to conclude the peace with the United States rather than with Russia because he believed that the longer the war continued, the more territory Russia would occupy – a powerful incentive to capitulate immediately after Russian entry into the war in Asia.[206] Russian atrocities in Manchuria gave the Japanese a taste of things to come should Russian troops reach the home islands.[207]

Navy Minister Yonai Mitsumasa and the former prime minister Prince Konoe Fumimaro favored acceptance of the Potsdam Declaration. Both considered the atomic bombs in combination with Russian entry into the war in Asia as a "gift from heaven," in Yonai's words, to force the army to comply with war termination. They and others feared a social revolution from below if the war continued and an army rebellion if Japan surrendered. Thus, the atomic bombings and Russian entry affected different groups differently. The Imperial Court feared for the survival of the royal house, while Russian entry particularly affected the army.[208] Without ships or fuel to fight, the navy could do nothing.

Postwar analysts debate the ethics of dropping atomic weapons on Japan. More people actually died in the firebombings. Not only the Japanese and Germans targeted civilians, but so did the Allies. They did so because alternative strategies would have caused far more deaths of their own armed forces and would have prolonged the war, causing further civilian deaths from starvation in the occupied areas and, in the case of Japan, would have yielded a divided Japan with Russia in possession of at least the northern half of Hokkaido. Such alternate strategies might have produced an enemy capitulation, but not unconditional surrender with the utter destruction of both the Japanese empire and the regime that went with it. The Japanese government barely capitulated after two atomic bombings. During the war, Americans experienced no angst over the enemy civilian death toll from the air war or even over the atomic bombs. They had lost too many of their own children and wanted a victory that minimized their own children's deaths. Only from the security of a postwar world, no longer under threat of imperial Japanese or Nazi German aggression, have subsequent generations criticized the air war.[209]

By war's end, the Japanese had earned a legendary reputation for atrocities. It turns out that they were not particularly good even at taking care of their own. When representatives of the International Red Cross visited a Japanese field hospital outside Wuhan after its fall in October 1938, they saw patients with only minor wounds. None was in splints, but a cemetery was located alongside the hospital. According to the Red Cross representative, Bob McLure, "There wasn't a shadow of a doubt that the Japanese were doing away with their badly wounded men.... Crippled men back in Japan would have spoiled the picture of easy conquest the High Command was painting."[210] After the war, Japanese veterans and witnesses described the common practice of executing their own men who could not keep up and encouraging if not requiring Japanese civilians to kill their families and themselves rather than surrendering.[211]

The Imperial Japanese Army leadership did not look kindly on those who failed in combat – either enemy prisoners of war or their own soldiers. According to the 1908 Army Criminal Code: "A commander who allows his unit to surrender a strategic area to the enemy shall be punishable by death." "If a commander is leading troops in combat and they are captured by the enemy, even if the commander has performed his duty to the utmost, he shall be punishable by up to six months confinement."[212] It was illegal for Japanese forces to withdraw or surrender. This meant that officers who were careful of their men's lives were considered cowardly. So the profligate were promoted instead.[213] The 1941 Field Service Code ordered Japanese soldiers, "Do not be taken prisoner alive."[214] So often they did not take others alive either, and their enemies responded in kind. Such rules and the attitudes embedded in them made for a brutal war and a historical legacy that haunts the Japanese, despite all their numerous achievements in other eras. As the Second Sino-Japanese War protracted and then metastasized into a world war, the Imperial Japanese Army became increasingly brutal with the Three Alls strategy, depopulated zones, blockade, massacres, death marches, internment camps, germ warfare, and biological experiments on prisoners.[215] When the tables turned, others felt little compunction about raining down firebombs on them.

Japan's brutality proved singularly counterproductive. If the goal was empire and autarky, making the colonies ungovernable by leaving the colonial population no alternative but resistance indicated a stunning lack of perception. Everywhere the Japanese went, they alienated those whom they encountered. They conducted serial diplomacy with the United States, Germany, China, and Russia, alienating each in turn. Their cruelty in China transformed a fractured people into a lethal enemy. Despite great expertise in the technical aspects of economic development demonstrated in Manchukuo, Japan's gratuitous brutality transformed potential sympathizers into bitter enemies. For a short time Asians living in the Pacific theater looked upon Japan as their liberator from the colonial powers, but Japanese actions rapidly made clear their own colonial ambitions, and their oppressive rule soon outdid all powers save Russia, Germany, and China, the record setters for mass murders in the twentieth century.[216]

Japan's quest for national security via war destroyed 66 percent of its national wealth,[217] 25 percent of its fixed assets, 25 percent of its building stock, 34 percent of its industrial machinery, 82 percent of its merchant marine, 21 percent of its household property, 11 percent of its energy infrastructure, and 24 percent of its production.[218] Japan suffered 28,000 military deaths in 1941, 66,000 in 1942, 100,000 in 1943, 146,000 in 1944, and a stunning 1,127,000 in 1945. If it had surrendered in 1944, it would have prevented the vast majority of Japanese fatalities. Between 3 and 3.5 percent of Japan's population died in the Pacific War, which, including all sides, took 20 million lives.[219] From 1937 to 1945, 410,000 Japanese soldiers died in China – 230,000 after December 1941. Nine hundred thousand were wounded. They killed at least 10 million Chinese soldiers and civilians – a conservative estimate. Some triple this number. Whatever the toll, China suffered far more casualties than any other part of the Pacific theater of World War II. In fact, Japan's military operations threatened or occupied lands with nearly twice the population of those so abused by Germany.[220]

In 1946, the Nationalists estimated that China had suffered $5.6 billion in economic losses, 12.8 million casualties, 9.1 million of whom were civilians, for the years between 1937 and 1945.[221] Japan had occupied thirteen provinces plus parts of eight others and taken 90 percent of Chinese industry, resulting in huge wartime economic and agricultural losses. Japan forced laborers to man the factories of Manchukuo and North China. Total financial losses from 1937 to 1945 were 6.5 billion yuan in raw materials, 31 billion in private and public capital, 4.5 billion tax losses from the occupied areas, and 1.6 billion yuan in military expenses for the Nationalist government.[222]

The costs for Japan did not end with the war. Russia took 639,635 Japanese prisoners including 148 generals, and kept most of them for four years of forced labor in violation of article 9 of the Potsdam Declaration. The last prisoners did not return home until the 1990s and 62,068 died in captivity.[223] Although Japan released thousands of Western prisoners held in its internment camps, which were known for their brutality and high mortality rates, it held virtually no Chinese prisoners of war. Apparently, those captured alive and not summarily executed became forced laborers, often sent to Manchukuo. Despite fifteen years of warfare in China, the Japanese allegedly held only 56 Chinese prisoners of war at the end of World War II – a death rate outdoing even the extermination camps of the Germans, a hard record to beat. The Chinese did not necessarily take prisoners of war either, as was often their practice in their own civil wars.[224]

Had Japan failed to capitulate when it did, U.S. planners envisioned a full-scale invasion of the home islands, where they had grossly underestimated the number of Japanese troops awaiting their arrival. By 15 August 1945, unbeknownst to the United States, Japan had redeployed more than 1 million men out of the China theater to the home islands.[225] On 18 June, when Truman approved Operation OLYMPIC to invade Japan, General Marshall estimated that Kyūshū, the southernmost main island, had no more than 350,000 men to face an onslaught of 766,700 Americans. In fact, by mid-August, the Japanese had 625,000 soldiers on Kyūshū, or nearly double Marshall's estimate, as part of Ketsugō, their so-called Decisive Operation.[226]

Given what Americans had endured to take Okinawa, a mere 454-square-mile island compared to Japan's 142,811 square miles, the invasion of the home islands would have yielded an American and Japanese bloodbath, and perhaps a permanent blockade of Japan instead of the unconditional surrender. Okinawa, one of the greatest battles in the Pacific theater, in which 182,821 Americans fought 100,000

Japanese, was a mere fraction of the Shanghai or Ichigō Campaigns that China had endured, let alone what the United States would have faced invading the home islands.[227] On Okinawa, 12,520 U.S. soldiers died along with 65,908 Japanese soldiers and 122,228 Okinawan soldiers and civilians.[228] The Japanese officers in charge of the defense, veterans of the rape of Nanjing, treated the Okinawans with contempt, expecting them to commit suicide rather than surrender.[229]

Chinese histories credit the Chinese with defeating Japan, while U.S. histories credit Americans. Australians and New Zealanders agree with the U.S. win but highlight their own contributions to the bitter New Guinea Campaign. These versions of events leave out a great deal. It took the combined efforts of China, the United States, Australia, New Zealand, Britain, and Russia to defeat Japan, and this alliance did so just barely. The Nationalists and the Communists could not have defeated Japan without the U.S.–British Commonwealth war in the Pacific. Although the Nationalists and the Communists each won an occasional battle against Japan and the Nationalists often successfully defended cities from Japanese attack, neither ever won a conventional campaign. Japan might have been stuck in a quagmire, but without U.S. intervention, it would have remained stuck but undefeated. However badly off the Japanese were, the Chinese were worse off.

Although it is also true that the United States did defeat the Imperial Japanese Navy without Chinese assistance, it never fought more than a fraction of the Imperial Japanese Army. At the end of the war, Japan still had nearly one-third of its total armed forces deployed in Manchuria and China, or 1.8 million men, while another 2 million men defended Japan, Korea, and Taiwan, the nucleus of the prewar Japanese empire. This left about 1 million men facing the United States. Thus, China played a crucial role in keeping nearly 1.8 million Japanese soldiers fully occupied and far away from U.S. forces. The theaters where U.S. fighting concentrated had comparatively small numbers of Japanese troops, 100,000 in the Philippines and 186,100 in the Central Pacific. Japan remained fundamentally a land power with its armies concentrated at home or on the Asian mainland.[230]

For most of the Pacific Ocean war, China pinned down more Japanese land forces than did any other theater. From 1941 to 1942, Japan deployed about 60 percent of its army to China. This fell to 44 percent in 1943, and to 31 percent for the final two years when Japan redeployed its forces initially to the South Pacific and then to the home islands. Deployments in the South Pacific rose from 21 percent of the army in 1942, to 32 percent in 1943, and to 40 percent in 1944, when the home islands came under attack and Japanese forces in the Pacific could no longer alter the course of the war because so much of the navy and merchant marine lay at the bottom and could not easily resupply or redeploy the army. Likewise most of Japan's army expenditures focused on China and Manchuria – 77 percent in 1941 and falling to 68 percent in 1945.[231]

The United States could not have won the Pacific War at an acceptable cost without China's tying down one-third of available Japanese forces. The Chinese fought bitterly, requiring the efforts of Japan's best forces. China as an enormous continental power became a sinkhole for Japanese manpower, much in the same way that Russia's vast and inhospitable theater became a sinkhole for German manpower. Without either continental power's participation in the war and the gross overextension this caused for Germany and Japan, it is hard to imagine unconditional surrender by either. The maritime powers, Britain and the United States, ate away at the periphery, but the continental powers fought on the main front at great cost from the beginning to the end.

Stalin had been alive to this problem and made diplomacy his primary defense before BARBAROSSA. Diplomacy turns out to be a high-risk profession. American and Japanese diplomats seeking to deter actually precipitated the very actions they intended to stop. The Japanese construed the U.S. oil embargo not as a deterrent but as a looming deadline for war, while the Americans construed Japan's alliance with Germany not as a deterrent but as a threat to the global order that required immediate attention. In the 1930s, when Stalin observed the growing danger posed by Germany, he cut a separate peace, the Nazi-Soviet Pact, which traded other people's space for time (for him). The division of Eastern Europe and accompanying trade agreements unwittingly provided Germany with the necessary resources and the geographic position to invade Russia. To fight a global war, Germany required metals, manufactures, fuel, food, and manpower, much of which it gained from its conquests.[232] Russian diplomacy facilitated this outcome.

When war began, Russian not British or U.S. armies bore the brunt of Germany's land forces. In the initial German invasion, Russia faced 142 Axis divisions, 20 percent more than the 119 divisions that overran

France.[233] During the Normandy landings, when the United States and Britain finally conducted a cross-channel invasion of the European continent, they faced only 58 Axis divisions compared to the 228 divisions then deployed against Russia on the Eastern Front.[234] Russian diplomacy in Europe did not match the brilliance of its diplomacy in Asia, where the Russian-brokered Second United Front saved it from a two-front war by setting up China to fight Japan. The same plan in Europe, to set up others to fight the main adversary, backfired at great cost.

Japanese military strategy was even more counterproductive than Stalin's European diplomacy. Japanese leaders greatly feared the spread of communism in Asia. They invaded Manchuria, in part, to contain Russian expansion. Yet their strategy heightened rather than reduced the threat. Russia responded by increasing its troop deployments in Asiatic Russia from 230,000 to 370,000 men by 1937, and reaching 700,000 by 1940. The Kantō Army could not match these numbers. In 1941 it had 300,000 to 350,000 men, or less than half the Russian force strength. Although Russian numbers fell after the German invasion to 500,000 by 1942, as Russian forces rolled toward Berlin, the number again reached 700,000 in 1944 and 1,600,000 for the invasion of Manchuria in 1945.[235]

The great gambit for oil also failed. In short: Japan ramped up merchantman and tanker construction, the United States ramped up submarine warfare, and Japanese oil imports plateaued before falling to zero. In detail: Once the war with the United States broke out, Japan's merchant marine construction could not keep pace with combat losses. Although ship production reached its highest point in 1944, the total number of ships in service peaked in the first half of 1942 at 3,130,000 tons, stabilized at about 2,600,000 tons until early 1944, and then plummeted over the winter of 1944 to 1945 to 1,840,000 tons.[236] Oil tanker capacity did better in that it increased through the end of 1943, dropped but remained at a high plateau for the next two years, and then fell catastrophically in 1945 from a capacity of 800,000 tons to about 250,000 tons. Allied sinkings of oil tankers grew from 170,000 tons in 1943 to 825,000 tons in 1944, before falling back to 323,000 for 1945 for lack of targets. Although oil imports increased from 1,489,000 tons in 1942 to 2,646,000 tons in 1943, they plunged to 1,060,000 tons in 1944 for lack of oil tankers. Home energy production remained flat at about 265,000 tons.[237] Most of the oil was from the Dutch East Indies, which provided Japan with 8.1 million barrels in 1942, 9.8 million barrels 1943, but only 1.6 million barrels in 1944 as a result of losses from U.S. submarine attacks. Simultaneously, Japan's oil consumption in the southern theater exploded from 15.4 million barrels in 1942 to 35.1 million barrels in 1943. Inability to access supplies reduced consumption to 32.0 million barrels in 1944.[238]

Japanese naval ship losses followed the pattern of merchant marine losses. Sinkings increased in the second half of 1942 and then snowballed from the second half of 1943 onward.[239] In the largest naval battle of World War II at Leyte Gulf in the Philippines from 23 to 26 October 1944, the United States sank forty Japanese ships, damaged forty-six, and destroyed 405 planes, crippling the Imperial Japanese Navy.[240] After May 1944, the shipping routes for oil from the Dutch East Indies were cut. In 1945 all Japan's sea lines of communication were under assault so that even transportation to Korea became dangerous.[241]

Although war matériel production continued to rise until 1944, food and daily basic necessity output peaked in 1937.[242] The loss of transport for oil and metals undermined steel and aluminum output after 1943. Plane production took precedence for resources and increased until 1944, but then imploded in 1945. Even so, the United States outproduced Japan by a margin of more than three to one for airplanes.[243] Although Japan's strategy to blockade China succeeded at the operational level, its complementary strategy to secure resources in the global war consumed more resources in gluttonous military operations than it provided and yielded defeat in both the global and regional wars.[244]

Thus, Japanese operational strategy produced strategic disaster throughout the war. By focusing on military operations, the Japanese failed to give adequate attention to the social, diplomatic, and economic repercussions. Atrocities fed animosities and conjured countervailing alliances. Unrelenting warfare undermined first the Chinese and then the Japanese economy. Japan went to war to secure resources, first in Manchuria, then in China south of the Great Wall, and finally throughout the Pacific theater. It sought resources to ensure prosperity at home. Yet each phase of the escalation made Japan more not less resource dependent, burdened rather than strengthened the home economy, and expanded rather than decreased Japan's list of enemies. Japanese leaders proved singularly incapable of cutting losses, so in the end they bet all and lost all. In the process, from 1931 to 1945, Japanese actions caused the deaths of 17.2 million people throughout Asia.[245]

They also set the stage for a very unpromising postwar regional balance of power. They gutted Chiang's conventional forces; destroyed 55 percent of Nationalist China's industry and mining, 72 percent of its shipping, and 96 percent of its railways; and shifted the internal balance of power in China in favor of the Communists.[246] In the end, the Japanese did achieve one of their major war aims: They booted the European colonial powers from Asia, but at extraordinary cost to the civilians caught in the war zone.[247] Although the Netherlands, Britain, and France would attempt to retrieve their colonies, they all failed. Japan did indeed create a new regional order in Asia, although not the one its leaders had in mind.[248]

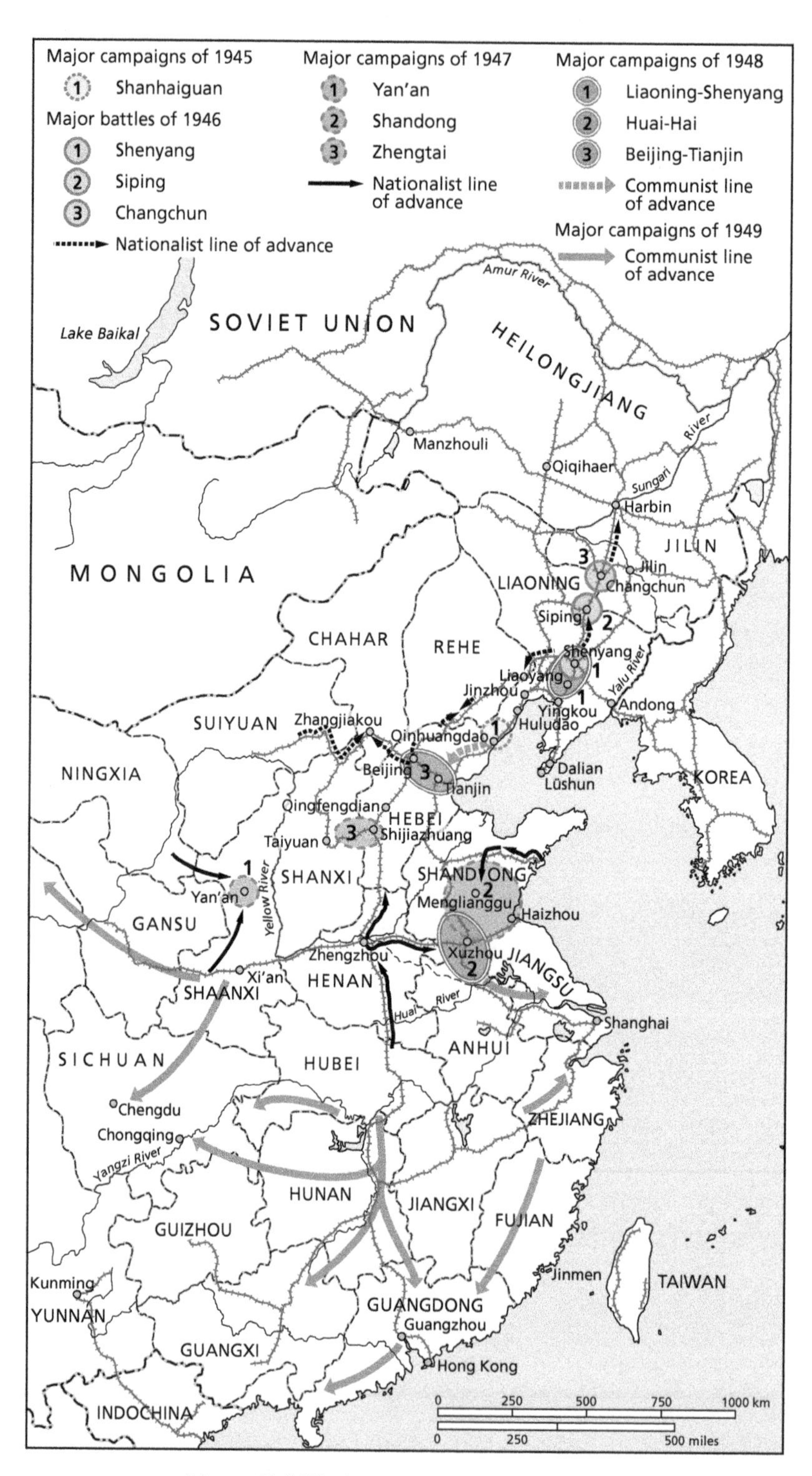

Map 6 Civil War (1945–49): Communist Victory.

8

THE FINAL ACT OF THE LONG CHINESE CIVIL WAR

一山難容二虎
It is difficult for one mountain to hold two tigers.
(Great rivals cannot coexist.)

The global war brought an end to the regional war, but not before the Second Sino-Japanese War had altered the balance in the long Chinese civil war. The long regional war destroyed not only the Nationalist army, but, more importantly, the sociopolitical fabric of Chinese society, which previously had prevented Communist expansion in rural areas. Japanese actions uprooted communities, turned peasants into refugees, and left a political vacuum, which it lacked the capacity to fill. The vacuum created an opportunity, which the Communists recognized and seized. The Japanese military strategy of relentless expansion and brutality catalyzed a countervailing Chinese nationalism. This viscerally anti-Japanese nationalism increasingly united a chronically divided peasantry, the often forgotten force in Chinese politics, whose influence becomes decisive in periods of dynastic change. As General Peng Dehuai told Edgar Snow in 1936, the peasantry required only leadership.[1]

While the Communists recognized and filled the leadership vacuum in rural China, the Nationalists fixated on the illusive pursuit of operational victory that had also consumed the Japanese. Like the Japanese the Nationalists tried to kill their way to power without adequate attention to the sources of allegiance. Japanese military strategy created a nationalistic community increasingly loyal to the Chinese Communist Party as the only political force offering any hope for rural China, where the vast majority of Chinese conscripts lived.[2] In rural and urban areas, the Communists relied on the youth – a neglected group in Confucianism, where youth deferred to age. They harnessed the idealism of the young with a promise of leadership in the vanguard of New China.

STATE BUILDING AND UNBUILDING

Back in 1935, the Communists were holed up in Yan'an on the verge of defeat. Less than 10,000 Communist Chinese forces had survived the Long March.[3] Yet from 1937 to 1940 party membership expanded from 40,000 to 800,000, and its military forces grew from 45,000 to 500,000.[4] By 1945 the Chinese Communist Party claimed a membership of anywhere between 1.2 and 2.7 million, depending on one's source, and the New Fourth Route and Eighth Route Armies had grown to 1.3 million men.[5]

Although Nationalist troops still numbered in the millions, Japan's repeated destruction of Chiang Kai-shek's armies cost him his reputation as a great military leader gained in the Northern Expedition and the Nationalist Party its reputation as a force for reform gained during the Nanjing decade. Instead Chiang and the Nationalist Party became synonymous with defeat in the field of battle and economic disaster on the home front. During the Second Sino-Japanese War, the Nationalists had repeatedly lost and then rebuilt their armies: at Shanghai in 1937 when Japan decimated Chiang's German-trained troops, at Nanjing also in 1937 when Japan chased Chiang's forces up the Yangzi River and massacred those captured, at Xuzhou and Wuhan in 1938 when General Li Zongren built and then lost a new Nationalist army, in Chiang's Winter Offensive of 1939–40, in the battles of 1941–3, and most critically, during the Ichigō Campaign of 1944. This virtually uninterrupted string of defeats left Chiang with a very different group of men under his command. Millions had died in the intervening years. One can speculate that the brave and true undoubtedly died first, leaving behind the brutal, the cynical, and the desperate.

The Japanese economic strategy to wipe out the Nationalist economy then destroyed Chiang's credentials as a civil leader. Without an economic base, the Nationalists printed money to pay their civil servants and soldiers. Predictably inflation spiked, sending businesses into bankruptcy and devouring the savings of ordinary people. Statistically, Nationalist- and Communist-controlled areas suffered from comparable levels of inflation from 1937 to 1942. As U.S. aid arrived, it helped prevent the stratospheric levels reached in Yan'an in 1943–4.[6] The political effects, however, differed.

As the incumbent government, the Nationalists reaped the blame for the cascading effects of Japanese military operations. Moreover, inflation hurt the rural less than the urban population, because the former produced goods that could be consumed or traded, while the latter lived on increasingly worthless paper money. Soldiers, civil servants, white-collar workers, and urban laborers suffered the most – people whose wages the government froze or neglected to pay and whose buying power plunged with inflation. Yet Nationalist rule depended on these critical groups. By 1943, Nationalist soldiers and public servants were making 6 and 10 percent, respectively, of what they had earned in 1937.[7] Labor unrest grew.[8] Inflation became politically debilitating by alienating loyalties.

The Guangxi group remained eager to replace Chiang with Li Zongren, whose heroic victory at Taierzhuang and whose leadership of the Xuzhou Campaign had earned him great admiration.[9] As loyalty became a scarce commodity, Chiang, well known for a reliance on brutality since the White Terror of 1927, increasingly turned to his secret police under the nefarious Dai Li to maintain order through terror on the home front. Arbitrary arrests and assassinations became the hallmarks of Nationalist wartime rule.[10]

In an environment of cascading military defeats and economic collapse, increasing numbers of Nationalist officials took a devil-may-care, seize-the-moment attitude to live in comparative splendor while waves of refugees lived and often died in squalor. Instability removed the incentive to save, so that those who had, consumed while they could, often flaunting what they had before those who had nothing. Famine followed in the wake of war and ravaged Henan repeatedly. The 1937 famine afflicted 30 million people in Henan, Shaanxi, and Sichuan.[11] From the fall of 1942 through 1943, 2 to 3 million again starved to death in Henan, followed by another famine in 1944 coinciding with the Ichigō Campaign.[12] The breached Yellow River dikes in Shandong and changed course of the river remained a constant reminder of Nationalist ruthlessness toward the population they claimed to protect. The dikes were not restored and the river did not return to its course until 1947 and then only with aid provided by the United Nations Relief and Rehabilitation Administration, employing nearly 200,000 laborers to undo what Chiang had done. The end of the Second Sino-Japanese War then brought a nationwide famine in 1946 affecting 30 million persons. Four million died in Hunan alone.[13]

In contrast, Mao Zedong's reputation emerged from the Second Sino-Japanese War greatly enhanced from his sheer ability to survive and his appealing message of revolution for a ruined land. During the war, the Communists played the gadfly role of incessant criticism of the proliferating and obvious ills of China, which they blamed on the incumbent government. In fact, Japan deserves the credit for upending the Nationalists' extensive domestic reform program and causing the economic collapse. The collapse then brought to the fore the worst characteristics of human beings, transforming the Nationalist government by 1945 into a kleptocracy, incapable of stirring allegiance, only revulsion.[14] As a result of horrendous facts on the ground and the interpretation of these facts through a Communist lens, the Nationalists gained a national and soon a global reputation for economic incompetence, shameless corruption, and unspeakable cruelty to their own. They were fast losing their mandate to rule, while in Yan'an a new emperor was emerging with a message of hope for the desperate, promises of land to the tillers, and a leadership role for China's idealistic youth. Striking in Edgar Snow's account of Yan'an is the youth of the Communists – half below the age of twenty and virtually no one above the age of thirty.[15] Mao Zedong leveraged the power of youthful idealism unrestrained by a skepticism imparted by broad experience. These youthful cadres believed the Communist promise of the utopia soon to come.

The Communists used their time well in Yan'an, which became the central Communist cadre training school. Mao devoted himself to writing as well as organizing. His efforts distilled the collective wisdom of his generation of Communist leaders and explained to others how to organize: The threat of force was embedded in the practice of politics. There was no sacred line separating combatants from noncombatants. Killing the young or the old, men or women, those in uniform and those not – all were fair game because all could contribute to the war effort. Indeed the transformation of peasants into cadres and guerrillas, and guerrillas into conventional military forces held the key to victory. This transformation required a Leninist party, whose members infiltrated all organizations, and whose paired civil and military cadres controlled the military. This was Mao's strategy for the weak to take over a country from within in anticipation of the climactic overthrow of the incumbent government from without. Chiang Kai-shek correctly identified the Communists as "a disease of the heart" like a cancer growing undetected from within, in comparison to the Japanese, whom he likened to a "disease of the skin" – visible and repulsive, but external and not fatal.[16]

During the Yan'an years Mao wrote his most famous works on military strategy, propaganda, civil-military relations, mobilization of the peasantry, land reform, social classes, and social and political revolution. Mao broadcast a powerful message for those seeking independence after World War II.[17] While he lived, he claimed exclusive credit for these innovations. The Yan'an period marks the beginning of the cult of Mao, which reached stupendous proportions as a result of the Korean War, when Mao presented himself as the victor over a coalition of all the greatest non-Communist powers. Since Mao's death, Chinese authors have become more egalitarian in attributing victory in the civil war to the contributions of others as well. It turns out that General Zhu De, the founder of the People's Liberation Army, not Mao, developed so-called sparrow warfare, entailing flocks of little forces swarming around the main enemy force to land briefly here and there on harassment missions to cause attrition and demoralization. Zhu De also emphasized war against the enemy's logistical lines; the destruction of railway lines and bridges; the removal of the population, animals, and food; the collection of intelligence from the community; the careful preparation of the battle space before moving in for the kill; and the conduct of political work in the population to organize the entire community.[18]

It turns out that General Peng Dehuai, the future commander of Chinese forces in the Korean War, developed mobile guerrilla warfare. He emphasized the desperation of the peasants awaiting only leadership to coalesce into a powerful military force, and the imperative to address their main grievance immediately – principally land reform – in order to cement rural loyalties. Partisan warfare rallied the surplus manpower of the countryside under Communist military leaders, who divided their time equally among organizing, propagandizing, and fighting, and in doing so, they filled the rural power vacuum left by the Nationalists and the Japanese.[19]

During the final phase of the civil war, Liu Shaoqi pushed the Communist leadership to focus on Manchuria instead of South China, and then to follow the strategy of "Ceding the Highways, but Taking Both Sides" as a way of making the best of the Russian demands in 1945 that the Communists evacuate Manchuria's cities. His strategy positioned his forces to cut the transportation arteries linking the cities in order to strangle them economically.[20] In civil affairs, Liu also apparently made far greater contributions than Mao allowed.[21]

So the conventional tale is overly Mao-centric. He was the great propagandist, who carefully put himself front-row center. Indeed his literary skills and ability to rivet the attention of disparate audiences were unrivaled certainly in twentieth-century China and perhaps unrivaled in Chinese history: His homilies to the peasantry in vocabulary they could understand and his elegant poetry to the educated demonstrating literary skills they admired cemented loyalties among two normally mutually exclusive groups. Chiang also wrote well, but not brilliantly, and often in the Classical style attractive only to those with sufficient education to understand it, leaving out the majority of Chinese people, who were illiterate. Unlike Mao, Chiang could not speak Mandarin, the dominant North China language, but only the Zhejiang dialect of Shanghai, and so required an interpreter to communicate with Chinese from elsewhere.[22]

The strategies of Zhu, Peng, Liu, and Mao required sanctuary for survival and a bully to blame for the hardships. The Japanese and the Nationalists provided the bullies and the Russians negotiated the sanctuary. For the duration of the Second Sino-Japanese War, Russian diplomacy protected the Communists from Japanese attack as long as they remained in Shaanxi. The terms of four agreements – the alleged Nationalist-Russian agreement of 1 July 1935, the other alleged Nationalist-Russian treaty concluded before February 1936 (both negotiated during the lead-up to the Xi'an Incident), the Second United Front, and a secret Russian-Japanese agreement of 3 October 1940 – all guaranteed the Communists sanctuary from Nationalist persecution in Yan'an. Within months of the New Fourth Route Army Incident, which resumed the civil war, Russia and Japan signed their Neutrality Pact, whose terms also promised the Chinese Communists sanctuary in Yan'an, under both Russian and Japanese protection.[23] Japan's spreading invasion gave the Communists a long breather in the civil war that Chiang had so nearly won with the Long March. Japan broke his blockade of Yan'an in May 1941 in the Battle of Southern Shanxi, easing Communist expansion southward. Chiang's efforts to fight the Communists then became episodic as he struggled to survive the impending Gogō and then Ichigō Campaigns.

Outside Shaanxi, the Communists found sanctuary in the rural hinterland between and beyond China's sparse railway net in North China. The Communists rallied the population to oppose and provide intelligence on both the Japanese and the Nationalists, to smuggle goods and people, and, over the course of the war, to create a full-fledged party organization throughout the North China countryside, to build extensive guerrilla forces, and to man large armies. During this period, the Communists cooperated with all anti-Japanese or anti-Nationalist groups, but with the ultimate objective of reducing all Chinese to one flavor: Communist.[24]

Shaanxi, the location of the main Communist base area at Yan'an, was one of the poorest provinces, largely deforested and perennially afflicted with drought. The Shaanxi peasantry lived in desperate conditions, which the Communist message of hope, blame, and retaliation seemed to explain and resolve.[25] In the mid-1930s, the Communists expanded the main base area into neighboring Ningxia and Gansu Provinces, the homeland of China's Mongol and Muslim minorities, well outside the core areas of Nationalist rule. Again, these were some of the poorest provinces, far from the lucrative trade brought by sea that had enriched coastal areas and far from the most productive agricultural lands, located on the coast, South China, the Yangzi River valley, and Manchuria. The Communists developed key petroleum, shale oil, and coal reserves in the vicinity of Yan'an. They started with light industry (textiles, paper, and soap) and resource extraction (coal and oil), but their munitions production remained primitive.[26]

Over time, they became increasingly cognizant of the economic dimension of warfare – they could not fight if the population was too poor or alienated to produce the food to sustain their guerrilla forces, the cloth to clothe them, and the weapons to arm them.[27] Victory in the post–world war long Chinese civil war required the financial resources to field mass armies. These resources would have to come from the land and the peasantry, who worked the land, since the Communists had virtually no urban presence in 1945. They intended to organize a government, an army, and a working economy out of the people of rural China, and this process had to start from the ground up, beginning with the land to produce the agricultural products to fund the plans and to build the loyalties to support them. Therefore, land reform was critical for the Communists not only to rally popular support but also to mobilize the resources to continue fighting the protracted war against the Nationalists.

Landownership in the key Communist base area in Shaanxi, Ningxia, and Gansu was highly concentrated. In general, the least productive lands had the most concentrated ownership because a living income required more acreage.[28] This of course left many landless. Ownership tended to be more concentrated in North China, where the Communists had retreated, than in South China, where the Nationalists dominated. The Communists set to work reversing this pattern in the Shaanxi, Ningxia, and Gansu base area, where they differentiated social classes by property ownership in the late 1930s and began to redistribute land in 1940 and 1941 as the Second United Front broke down.[29] From 1940 to 1943, they implemented tax reform in the Shanxi-Chahar-Hebei border area. Through trial, error, and revision, they developed a progressive rural tax bracket scheme, calibrated not to alienate any but the largest landowners, but embracing a large enough proportion of the population to generate adequate revenues to fund military operations.[30] In some areas, the Communists focused on rent and interest reduction instead of the elimination of private property, again to retain sufficient smallholder support to win the civil war.[31] In other areas, they took advantage of Japan's growing preoccupation with homeland defense, to promote rural reform more aggressively.[32] In April 1944, they ordered the confiscation of all Manchukuo government lands, colonized lands, and collaborator holdings, and their redistribution to the rural population.[33] By the end of 1946, the Communists had completed their first North China–wide redistribution of land to the tillers.[34]

Wherever the Communists went, they implemented land reform not only to cement loyalties, but also to implicate the peasants in a social revolution. Peasant involvement in the act of expropriation precluded their return to the Nationalist fold as anything but dead men. An observer in Nationalist-held areas commented in 1946: "After the farmer receives his share of the land, he will naturally think that the only way to preserve his share of land is to follow the CCP [Chinese Communist Party] to the very end. As a matter of fact, farmers are fearful of measures of revenge from the landlords."[35] The peasants became fearful of the Communists as well. Those benefiting from the original round of Communist expropriations then became victims of the second round, when they were perceived as landowners. They also became the focus of Communist grain requisitions and their sons the target of conscription.[36]

The Communists tried to unite all potentially sympathetic groups under their leadership initially against the Japanese and then after 1945 against the Nationalists. To create civil and military institutions out of nothing, Mao Zedong focused on winning over popular loyalties, not the elite loyalties that consumed Chiang Kai-shek's attention. The Communists leveraged tensions between landlords and tenants, creditors and debtors, and the government and the governed to garner loyalties through rent reduction, antiusuary laws, wage increases, and the prosecution of local bullies. The accused faced struggle meetings, where the aggrieved could vent their anger on their oppressors and the weak could take down the strong.[37]

Mao's strategy, called the Three-Thirds System, enunciated in March of 1940 and implemented throughout the Communist base areas in February 1941, divided the potentially sympathetic part of the population into three groups – Communists, members of other left-leaning parties, and potential progressives – and reserved one-third of all government and administrative positions for each group. This relieved local fears of outside domination, gave people a sense of inclusion, and became a vetting mechanism to expand local government with loyal cadres. Training such a broad group of people yielded a shadow government and armed force. In 1945, the Communists held local elections, officially unseating the traditional power holders, many of whom had fled rural North China.[38] They established government administrative institutions from the village upward to the area, district, and base-area levels and at each level created parallel popular front organizations to rally public support and to perform public services.[39]

The popular front was the public face of a covert organization in command of a rebel military. Popular front organizations operated under the law and so could be public, yet the goal of the covert shadow government and rebel force remained regime change. The organizational division was clever: It enabled the Communists publicly to leverage any legal protections against the Nationalist government while working covertly to subvert the legal system.

Weeding out unsatisfactory party members went in tandem with party expansion. The Communists maintained ideological unity through rectification campaigns to expel, punish, and possibly kill the unorthodox – whom others might call independent thinkers. The intense rectification campaign of 1942–4 led to the demotions and deaths of many. It followed a rapid expansion of the party, whereupon Mao asserted his ideological dominance; unseated those closest to Russia, such as Wang Ming; and cleared the way for the cult of Mao, Mao's Sinification of Marxism. He remained loyal to the great northern benefactor in word but ever less so in deed.[40]

While Mao focused on the people as the basis for creating a shadow government and military, Chiang concentrated on the military foundations of power and offered nothing to the peasantry but unrelenting conscriptions and requisitions at gunpoint.[41] As his vice-minister of agriculture had observed in late 1944, those who tilled the land had borne "almost the whole burden of the war" against Japan.[42] Chiang intended to fight and then reform, whereas Mao understood that he had to reform in order to win. This difference in the sequencing of reform and military operations became critical to the outcome of the long civil war. When discussing the peasantry, Peng Dehuai told Edgar Snow, "[I]t is possible to develop partisan warfare only by the *immediate* satisfaction of their most urgent needs."[43] Whereas Chiang offered only promises to his peasant conscripts, Mao implemented literacy and public health programs, provided basic social services in the long-neglected countryside, included local residents in local governance, and, most importantly, implemented land and tax reform. From Yan'an, the Communists gradually spread their influence into neighboring areas.[44]

During the Nanjing decade, the Nationalists had discussed, drawn up laws, but only begun to implement land and tax reform. With the escalation of the war in 1937, they never again devoted much attention to land reform until after their flight to Taiwan, where they did so by redistributing the property of others. In the meantime, the coalitional nature of their rule and the increasingly desperate military situation made such reforms politically unfeasible. Land reform on the mainland would have required taking property from key generals and key Nationalist supporters.[45]

The Communists, however, had no vested interest in any part of the status quo. They constituted a coalition of politically excluded social groups – intellectuals, students, workers, and peasants – none of whom owned land, whereas many of the key players in Nationalist China were landowners unwilling to divest themselves of their power base. Land reform for the Communists undermined the Nationalist power base at no cost to themselves, so they enthusiastically redistributed the property of others. But communism had no place for private property. The strategy was a classic bait and switch. The Communists used land reform as an expedient to buy peasant loyalties long enough to win the civil war. Afterward, they turned the army on the peasantry to reclaim all the land for the state. This Big Lie had worked in the Russian Civil War, when promises of land reform caused waves of desertions from the tsarist armies and bound peasant loyalties to the Bolsheviks during the fighting. Within a decade of the civil war, Stalin collectivized agriculture at gunpoint, sending those who resisted to prison camps in Siberia and causing a nationwide famine. The Chinese Communists followed the Russian example with similar results.

Although it is unclear whether land reform earned the Chinese Communists the full support of the peasantry, it is clear that an increasing percentage of rural and urban Chinese loathed the Nationalists. According to Chiang Kai-shek, in the Battle of Hunan during the Ichigō Campaign, "The local population attacked our own forces and seized their arms, just as happened with the czar's army in imperial Russia during World War I. Such an army cannot win! Our military trucks and horses carry smuggled goods, not ammunition.... During the retreat, some troops lost discipline, looting and raping women."[46]

Peasant support was necessary but insufficient for a Communist victory. The conventional tale does not explain how the Communists won the conventional war with tanks and artillery, not the normal products of rural areas. As the Japanese and the Nationalists had anticipated, the war-winning battles of the long Chinese civil war were all conventional.

RESUMPTION OF THE CIVIL WAR

World War II ended much sooner than expected in a firestorm of atomic bombs and a Russian invasion. Neither the Communists nor the Nationalists were ready. The most well-trained Nationalist forces were in Burma, and there had been no time to replace the losses suffered during the Ichigō Campaign. As of August 1945, the United States had fully trained sixteen Nationalist divisions, half-trained another twenty-two divisions, and provided more than 80 percent of the equipment for twenty divisions. The Communists, by contrast, lacked adequate base areas in the South, and their armies were not sufficiently developed to defend those in the North.[47] The presence of a common enemy, Japan, had made the united front possible. With its defeat any remaining glue holding together the coalition disappeared just as the defeat of Germany dissolved the glue holding together the Anglo-American and Russian alliance.[48] In the absence of a common enemy, U.S.–Chinese Communist Party relations quickly unraveled.[49]

From 1941 to 1944 the Chinese Communists had cooperated as much as possible with the United States because they had determined that of the three Allies – Britain, Russia, and the United States – the United States had the greatest ability to fight Japan. In other words, their primary ally, Russia, was useless once attacked by Germany. Problems like this might have impelled others to reconsider their alliances, but a shared vision of the world order to come bound the communists together.[50] The Chinese Communists repeatedly invited U.S. representatives to Yan'an. In June 1944 President Roosevelt sent Vice President Henry Wallace to pressure the Nationalists to allow a U.S. Army Observer Group to accept the invitation. Since September 1943, despite Chiang Kai-shek's strenuous objections, General Stilwell had recommended arming Communist troops to fight Japan, an opinion reinforced by the Ichigō Campaign. Chiang understood that any arms the Communists received would eventually train on Nationalist targets. Wallace reported to Roosevelt that Chiang was a "short-term investment" lacking "the intelligence or political strength to run postwar China."[51]

Wallace did organize a trip to hostile "Confederate" territory in Yan'an, the so-called Dixie Mission, which found Communist governance there superior to the misgovernance in Nationalist-controlled areas. He recommended military aid to the Communists to the horror of Roosevelt's second emissary to China, Patrick J. Hurley, a retired general, former secretary of war, and active lawyer. Ambassador Hurley replaced the outgoing ambassador Clarence E. Gauss, whose parting shot had been a recommendation that the United States "pull up the plug and let the whole Chinese government go down the drain."[52]

Hurley arrived in China in September 1944 and remained until November 1945. Roosevelt wanted him to patch up the tattered relations between the Generalissimo and the general. Hurley supported Chiang's demands for General Stilwell's recall, deep-sixed the Dixie Mission, and pushed the Communists and Nationalists to form a coalition government. Vladimirov, Russia's representative in Yan'an, believed that Hurley had "fallen into a trap" because Chiang would never voluntarily cede power, as required by any agreement for a coalition government, yet his failure to do so would follow Mao's script to portray Chiang to the world as "a dimwitted obstructionist." Whether or not Chiang supported a coalition government, he lost power either way.[53]

Mao had been playing this particular game for several years. In 1943, he had crowed about his successful propaganda campaign. According to Vladimirov, by then foreign reporters directed "tough questions" to Nationalist spokesmen and, better yet, "the ambassadors of Britain, the U.S., and the Soviet Union also warned Chiang that if he started a civil war, international aid would stop coming in."[54] Hurley's blunder left Chiang politically isolated and furious at Americans. Although an army observer group remained in Yan'an until July 1946, its role transformed from coalition building to intelligence gathering. Meanwhile, four waves of student protests erupted across urban China from 1945 to 1949. Each one was increasingly critical of the Nationalists for pursuing civil war instead of a coalition government and of the United States for supporting the Nationalists. Mao called the student protests a "second front." The second front depended on a degree of tolerance for youthful protesters and a degree of press freedom. When the Communists took power, they would tolerate neither.[55]

Hurley's expertise in U.S. politics did not apply in China, where he addressed the Generalissimo as Mr. Shek and greeted Mao with his version of a Choctaw native American war whoop. It is unclear whether he chose the latter mode of introduction out of racism or stupidity. The Nationalists called Hurley "The Big Wind"; Mao named him "The Clown"; and Chiang Kai-shek considered him "an idiot!" The China hands in the State Department also looked down on Hurley, whom some considered to be senile, but they shared his dream of a coalition government.[56] There was a fundamental problem with these plans for a coalition government and the U.S. demand for a cease-fire in order to negotiate one: This very American approach to politics was a nonstarter as long as the primary objective of both the Nationalists and the Communists remained the annihilation of the other.[57] The Americans did not wish to see that both sides planned to rule China in a way guaranteed to turn American stomachs. The then-undersecretary of state, Dean Acheson, who later served as secretary of state during the Korean War, noted in his memoirs: "Only later did we understand that we were, in effect, seeking the reconciliation of irreconcilable factions."[58] By then it was too late.

When the resumption of the civil war dashed the hopes for a coalition government, the Americans blamed each other – rather than the Chinese who deserved the credit. Hurley resigned amid a flurry of accusations. His parting shot was to accuse the State Department's China experts of sabotaging his mission. The gathering witch hunters of the McCarthy era soon hunted the China hands of the State Department to virtual extinction on the flimsy logic that their correct analysis of the strength of communism in China made them communists. John S. Service of the State Department, who served on the Dixie Mission, reported to his superiors that Hurley had threatened that if "I 'ever interfered with him' he would 'break me'. It was never made clear to me just what he considered 'interference.'"[59] Service was among those purged.

After the death of Roosevelt, and the surrenders of Germany and Japan, President Harry S. Truman faced pressing concerns in all theaters. It was unclear how to transform operational victory into a better peace. Truman also envisioned a coalition government in which Nationalists, Communists, and other political parties all participated and promoted a political not a military solution for China's internal problems.[60] At the time, he was negotiating with Russia on the postwar disposition of Europe, where he hoped that Russia would support coalition governments. Undoubtedly he worried that if the Nationalists annihilated the Communists, the Russians would be less likely to tolerate non-Communist parties in Eastern Europe, a region far more important than China to the United States, but occupied by Russian troops. In order to settle the civil war and prevent events in China from undermining the situation in Eastern Europe, Truman replaced Hurley with a mediator of enormous skill and prestige, General George C. Marshall, fresh from his key role in the Allied victory in World War II. Marshall led a mission to China from December 1945 until January 1947.

The Marshall Mission gets enormous play in the historical literature to the neglect of other negotiations, such as Chiang's repeated attempts to arrange a separate peace with Japan during the World War II phase of the Second Sino-Japanese War, let alone Russia's negotiations through its ambassador, Lieutenant General Nikolai V. Roshchin, during the endgame to the long Chinese civil war. This uneven coverage does not reflect the relative importance of the topics, but rather the publication of U.S. diplomatic records and the public access to U.S. archives.[61]

In the spring of 1945, at the Seventh Congress of the Chinese Communist Party, General Zhu De, the commander of the Eighth Route Army, which became the People's Liberation Army after the defeat of Japan, recommended turning from guerrilla to mobile warfare. This required deploying conventional forces, not to hold territory, but to destroy enemy forces. He recommended relying on interior lines of communication and mobile defense in the North China base areas.[62] In terms of the military strategy enunciated by Mao in May 1938 in his famous essay *On Protracted War*, Zhu was recommending phase transition.

During the Second Sino-Japanese War, the Communists had remained primarily a guerrilla force. According to Mao's three phases of people's war, the Communists had long remained in phase one, the strategic defensive, focusing on organizing support and conducting small guerrilla operations to maintain morale with little victories here and there. The second phase, recommended by Zhu De in 1945, entailed a transition to occasional conventional battles to wear down the enemy against a backdrop of continuing guerrilla operations and ongoing rural organization. During phase two, the Communist forces would approach military parity with their enemies, in preparation for phase three, when at long last they would go on the strategic offensive to win the war through sustained conventional battles.[63]

Although Mao presented these phases as a three-staged linear progression to victory, the three stages were more useful as a measure of military effectiveness.[64] Premature transitions to phase-two operations during the Fifth Encirclement Campaign and the Hundred Regiments Campaign produced costly and nearly fatal defeats that twice threw the Communists back to phase one. Sustained phase-three operations did not take place until 1947 – two years into the post–World War II resumption of the long Chinese civil war.

In preparation for a transition to phase two, on 11 August 1945, Zhu De ordered Communist cadres into Manchuria. By mid-September 20,000 political cadres and 100,000 soldiers were on their way. Peng Zhen, the political commissar paired with Lin Biao, the commander of Communist forces in Manchuria, arrived aboard a Russian plane. Peng served on the Politburo and soon became the secretary of the Chinese Communist Party Northeast Bureau.[65] Critically, 100,000 to 150,000 troops from the Eighth Route and New Fourth Route Armies left all their equipment behind in Shandong, expecting to use that left by the Japanese and promised by the occupying Russians, but the Russians reneged and troops of the former Manchukuo army walked off with the best weapons.[66] The New Fourth Route Army, even with its weapons, was very poorly armed.[67]

Stalin, like Truman, could not have wanted events in China to undermine his far more pressing national security agenda in Europe.[68] In November and December 1945, Russia repeatedly ordered the Communists out of Manchurian cities, but the Chinese Communists tried to retain control over them.[69] Only cities had the industrial base to manufacture the conventional weapons necessary for phase transition.[70] But if the Chinese Communists were too aggressive in Manchuria, the Western Allies might become intransigent about issues in Europe. World War II left Russia in occupation of Eastern Europe and all of Manchuria, where the presence of the Red Army gave Russia great leverage over events in its zone of occupation. In 1944 Stalin had told Hurley that the Chinese Communist Party had no real Communists, just "followers of margarine communism."[71] Stalin continued to play a double game in China as he always had with the many countries on his borders. By negotiating with and playing off the many sides, he positioned himself to assume the role of grand puppeteer over increasingly factionalized adversaries.

Lieutenant General Roshchin, who served as a military attaché to the Russian Embassy in China from 1942 to 1948 and as ambassador from February 1948 until 1952, advised the Communists to wall off Manchuria by defending at the line defined by the Great Wall running westward from the sea at Shanhaiguan to Gubeikou, the pass where the Chao River intersects the Great Wall just north of Beijing, and on to Zhangjiakou near the Hebei-Shanxi border. Roshchin served in China on a mission parallel to Marshall's – to influence events so that the outcome of the Chinese civil war enhanced his country's interests. For Marshall, U.S. interests required a unified non-Communist China. Roshchin's goal may have been a divided China to eliminate the possibility of a great power bordering on Russia.[72]

On 17 September 1945, the Russian Politburo telegrammed Mao to follow the strategy of "expanding toward the north and defending toward the south." Two days later, the Chinese Communist leadership agreed to follow the strategy.[73] Liu Shaoqi, who after Mao was the most important Communist civil leader, also recommended a reorientation to Manchuria, the abandonment of the bases in the South, and the redeployment of troops to the North.[74] On this advice, Mao reversed his preferred strategy from "Hold in the North, Advance in the South" to "Advance in the North, Hold in the South."[75] On 4 October, the Russians advised the Communists to deploy up to 300,000 troops in Manchuria within the month on the promise that Russia would provide the necessary arms.[76] In other words, the Communists would give the Nationalist government easy wins in the South as they withdrew northward, where they would lure the Nationalists in deep and then spring the trap. As China's preeminent military strategist, Sunzi, advises: Where the enemy "is strong, avoid him."[77]

General Albert C. Wedemeyer, General Stilwell's replacement, retaliated against the Communist redeployment to Manchuria that began in the early fall of 1945, by transporting Nationalist troops to North China, positioning them to reoccupy the major cities.[78] Nevertheless, in November, Wedemeyer advised Chiang to refrain from sending large forces to Manchuria.[79] Wedemeyer's fact-finding commission concluded that the Nationalists should be able to stabilize South but not North China and could not possibly recover Manchuria without agreements with the Communists and the Russians, which, as predicted, would not be forthcoming, since the Chinese Communists were well positioned to take over both Manchuria and North China.[80]

Full-scale civil war had resumed in October 1945, the month after Japan's formal surrender, and by December hostilities had broken out in eleven provinces. Chiang Kai-shek sent more than 70 percent of his troops to North China, deploying them to the Central Plains, Manchuria, Hebei, Shandong, Henan, Shaanxi, Gansu, and Ningxia.[81] He was confident that he could restore control over Japanese-occupied South China and so focused not simply on the prewar task of fully reuniting North and South China, but on the imperial task of reclaiming the entire Qing empire. The last emperors of China, the Manchus, had transformed the way the Han Chinese defined their homeland. Henceforth, the Han thought of China not just as the eighteen core provinces south of the Great Wall, where the Han ethnic group and settled agriculture predominated, but as a great empire including the nomad lands of Manchuria, Inner and Outer Mongolia, Inner and Outer Tibet, and Xinjiang. The Manchus had conquered and added these lands to the central Han Chinese provinces to create the second largest empire in Chinese history – second only to the Mongol empire, the creation of another occupation dynasty of non-Han rulers, the Mongol Yuan dynasty.

When the civil war resumed, Russia refused to allow Nationalist troops to land in Dalian, Manchuria, so that in October 1945 the Nationalists tried to land at Huludao (at the midway point between Shanhaiguan and the former Manchurian treaty port of Yingkou), as well as on each side of the Liaodong Peninsula at Yingkou and at Andong (near the mouth of the Yalu River). All locations connected with the railway lines. By 7 November Russia had closed all Manchurian ports, forcing the Nationalists to use the port of Qinhuangdao in Hebei and take the railway north via Shanhaiguan.[82] Shanhaiguan was the critical bottleneck where the Great Wall meets the sea and the traditional entryway into Manchuria.

Russia also rejected the Nationalist request to transfer Japanese and Manchukuo factories to Nationalist administration. Instead, in September 1945, Russia had started shipping confiscated industrial equipment across its border and belatedly notified the Nationalists on 17 October that it considered all Manchuria industry to be a prize of war. This followed a pattern established in Germany, where the Russians had also removed factories and heavy equipment. The Chinese, however, believed these investments should be part of Japan's indemnity to China.[83] In effect, Russia exacted reparations from China for a war against Japan in which it had barely participated. The Russians also commandeered the railway system.[84]

They soon took 83 percent of Manchukuo's electrical power generation equipment, wiping out 71 percent of its electrical capacity, 86 percent of its mining equipment, 82 percent of its cement production equipment, 80 percent of its metalworking industry, 65 percent of its liquid fuels and lubricant production, and so on.[85] All told, Russia removed 70 to 90 percent of Manchuria's industrial capacity.[86] It also commandeered fifty thousand railway cars to move the loot home.[87]

These statistics are from the Pauley Commission. After World War II, President Truman assigned the wealthy oilman Edwin W. Pauley as the special representative to the Allied Reparations Committee. Pauley organized a fact-finding mission to Manchuria in 1946 and produced a report detailing the Russian expropriations. The report estimated that the Russia's "prize of war" constituted U.S. $895 million in damage to Manchurian industry. This plus additional damage suffered from the Russian occupation totaled the extraordinary sum of U.S. $2 billion.[88] Worse still for the Chinese, the replacement cost for the equipment was two and a half times greater than the physical loss.[89]

A member of the Pauley mission noted the lack of care taken during the equipment removal as well as additional gratuitous looting. At the Fushun coal mines, the largest in Manchuria, he observed: "[The] size and types of material involved refutes any contention that the chaos was the result of local Chinese looting. There was an abundance of evidence of unnecessary destruction of the remaining facilities and equipment." The removal had been conducted in such haste and inexperience that "it seemed improbable that this equipment would have little more than scrap value by the time it reached its destination.... The damage to the coal mine as a result of the lack of power was many times the cost of the electrical equipment removed."[90]

Despite the large Russian troop concentrations, in late 1945, Chiang made the pivotal decision to deploy his best forces to Manchuria to complete, at long last, a Sixth Encirclement Campaign to annihilate the Communists. The United States abetted Chiang's plans to contest Manchuria. It circumvented the Russian naval blockade by flying his troops to Changchun and Shenyang, two key railway junctions otherwise isolated in the Manchurian interior. Although the two cities lay on the trunk line to Shanhaiguan, the railway ran through a sea of Communist-held territory.[91] Russia's naval blockade should have been interpreted as proof positive that it planned an obstructionist path. Nevertheless, Chiang soon deployed 85 percent of his army to Manchuria.[92] Since the Japanese had neutralized the Communist insurgency in Manchukuo, Chiang may have thought he could take it over before the Communists could redeploy from Yan'an. He may also have believed that the Russians, despite their record of breaking treaties at their convenience, would honor their 21 August 1937 Non-Aggression Pact and the brand-new Sino-Russian Friendship Treaty.

Back in August 1945, as Russian troops poured over the Manchurian border, Nationalist negotiators must have felt extreme pressure to sign a treaty as soon as possible to control the unfolding situation. On 14 August, the Russian and Nationalist governments had signed a whole series of documents, including the Sino-Russian Friendship Treaty, a longer treaty regulating the Manchurian railway system, and a note concerning elections in Outer Mongolia. Altogether, Chiang Kai-shek traded Chinese sovereignty over Outer Mongolia for the return of Manchuria.[93] When this did not pan out, he blamed his loss of Mongolia on bungled American diplomacy at the Anglo-Soviet-U.S. Yalta talks in February 1945.[94]

THE MANCHURIAN THEATER

Manchuria became the object of Chiang's ambitions for very compelling reasons. Despite Russian predations, Manchuria was the least war-torn part of China. It had been the crown jewel of the Japanese empire, the focus of Japan's external investments that had transformed it into the most industrialized part of Asia outside the home islands. Japanese holdings in Manchuria exceeded all of its investments in Korea, Taiwan, and China south of the Great Wall. Half of China's railways lay in Manchuria, creating its densest network, ideal for moving armies and meeting their enormous logistical needs, and it had traditionally produced an agricultural surplus, giving it the potential to feed large armies.[95] The Japanese had built the railway grid, not primarily with commerce in mind, but with military and military-industrial goals – to impose control and deliver resources for heavy industry.[96] The power in possession of Manchuria gained a large industrial base and extensive transportation network geared for the production and transport of war matériel and the movement of troops, and ideal for fighting a civil war and rebuilding the rest of the country thereafter.

In addition to these economic and military considerations, Chiang could not easily relinquish claims for political reasons. A fifteen-year Sino-Japanese War had just been fought over Manchuria. Japan had demanded Chinese recognition of Manchukuo; Chiang had refused; and

Japan had escalated the war to compel him. Chiang never did and the Chinese people had paid an enormous price. Chiang's failure to contest Japan's occupation of Manchuria from 1931 to 1936 nearly cost him his leadership then, when his position was far more secure. In 1945 he had an opportunity to reunify China and realize not only his own dream, but the dreams of many Chinese to restore the entire Qing empire. After all the human suffering of the fifteen-year war with Japan, Chinese sovereignty over Manchuria would have greatly enhanced his prestige and the legitimacy of his government.

The Communists focused on the Manchurian theater for all reasons motivating Chiang Kai-shek, plus some. Communist forces were already concentrated in North China. Except for Yan'an and Manchuria, Nationalist forces outnumbered them everywhere else. Unlike the Nationalists, the Communists had virtually no industrial base and therefore could not manufacture the necessary war matériel to prosecute a protracted conventional war. Manchuria offered an important arms industry as well as large Japanese arms depots. Russia, the most promising foreign benefactor for the Communists, bordered on Manchuria. Russia could easily supply only areas on its borders, and Manchuria alone had the railway network to do so. If the civil war had focused not on North China, but on South China, Russia could not have supplied the Communists given the long distances and the U.S. command of the sea lines of communication. Thus, there were compelling reasons for both sides to contest the Manchurian theater.

Alas for the Nationalists, Manchuria was the optimal theater for their enemies but a difficult theater for them, located far from South and Central China, the center of Nationalist loyalties and the origin of their supply lines. Geographically, Manchuria was a salient, projecting deep into Communist-held territories with Communist-held North Korea on the east, Russia on the north, Russia's Outer Mongolian puppet state on the west, and the Chinese Communists in Shaanxi on the southwest. Under the best of circumstances, the Nationalists had limited geographic access to the theater. Without the Russian blockade of Manchuria, Chiang would have retained multiple access points through the ports of Huludao, Yingkou, Dalian, Lüshun, and Andong. Instead the blockade left him with a single highly vulnerable rail link from Shanhaiguan northward to run a gauntlet through massing Communist forces.[97] In effect, Manchuria was a peninsula surrounded by a Soviet sea, where Nationalist movements would be predictable, along a lone railway line that the Communist could attack anywhere.

Moreover, the social and economic structure of Manchuria matched Communist not Nationalist needs. Manchuria was the only theater where the Japanese had completely eliminated the Nationalist presence, which had never been strong. Throughout the Second Sino-Japanese War, the Nationalists had tried to cultivate support in Manchukuo so that upon the defeat of Japan, there would be a receptive local population. The Japanese, aware of this strategy, arrested Nationalist supporters in periodic dragnets. In particular, they arrested many immediately after the attack on Pearl Harbor, again in 1944, and immediately after Germany's capitulation in 1945.[98] In doing so, the Japanese unwittingly cleared the decks for the Chinese Communists so that the only Chinese elites remaining in Manchukuo were collaborators, creating the perfect power vacuum for the Communists to fill.[99] The economic structure of the agrarian economy was also uniquely conducive to the growth of communism. Unlike South and Central China, Manchuria had an unusually skewed land distribution that much more closely fit the Communist explanation for the inequities of rural life than did the rest of China and allowed the Communists to satisfy land hunger comparatively easily by breaking up large holdings.[100]

Russian actions then magnified these Communist advantages. The Russian rape of Manchuria required a working railway system.[101] In mid-May 1948, Lin Biao requested Russian assistance to repair the railways. Stalin thought the task so important that he sent the people's commissar of transportation, Lieutenant General Ivan Vladimirovich Kovalev, who had been instrumental in keeping Russian railways running during World War II. By the end of 1948, his team, which grew to three hundred engineers and technicians, had repaired thirteen hundred kilometers of track and sixty-two bridges and had trained thousands of Chinese to operate the trains in time for the decisive Liaoning-Shenyang Campaign.[102] Whereas the system had carried 9.1 million tons in 1947, it transported 15.7 million tons in 1948 for the decisive campaigns of the war, and 19.6 million tons in 1949.[103] Control over the Manchurian railways gave Communist troops the mobility that the Nationalists lacked.

When the Russians had invaded, they had seized Japanese weapons depots as they went. Statistics vary in the particulars but not in the magnitude. On the Trans-Baikal front on the west and the First Far Eastern front on the east, Russian sources document that their armies seized 679 arms depots, more than 2,000 motor vehicles, 600 tanks, 861 planes, 12,000 machine guns, and 3,700 guns, mortars, and grenade launchers. These statistics do not include war matériel seized on the Second Far Eastern front through central Manchuria or in military operations in Korea. Eventually the Russians turned over virtually all of it to the Chinese Communists.[104]

Russia maintained a careful inventory of what it supplied and to whom, suggesting a transaction. A Russian inventory of Japanese arms made one month after the end of World War II listed 925 planes, 369 tanks, 35 armored cars, 1,226 field artillery pieces, 1,340 mortars, 4,836 machine guns, 300,000 rifles, 133 radios, 2,300 vehicles, 125 tractors, 17,497 horses, and 742 armories containing more bullets, weapons, equipment, and food. According to Nationalist sources, Russia supplied the Communists with the following Japanese war matériel: 1,436 field artillery pieces, 8,989 machine guns, 11,052 grenade launchers, 3,078 trucks, 14,777 horses, 21,084 supply vehicles, 815 specialized vehicles, and 287 command cars. Russia also supplied the Communists with its own war surplus and helped reopen Manchukuo's extensive armaments factories. These weapons allowed the Communists to reorganize their light guerrilla units into conventional armies and, after decades of civil war, finally to transition to sustained phase-three conventional operations.[105]

At the beginning of the Manchurian Campaign, the Russians provided the Communists with Japanese, Russian, and Czech light arms.[106] They did not transfer tanks and heavy artillery until the fall of 1947, when they turned over the weapons depots at Manzhouli with sufficient armaments including tanks and artillery for 600,000 soldiers.[107] Not until November 1948 did the Communists take over Manchuria's industry, including 160 factories, 74 mines, and 26 lumber areas. Despite Russian expropriations, by 1949 the Communists had restored industrial production to 35 percent of is pre-1945 capacity.[108] In other words, the Communists received arms only gradually and mostly not until two years into the fighting in the fall of 1947.

In addition to weapons, the Russians eventually shared their mastery of conventional warfare acquired at such great cost fighting Germany. Whereas U.S. military advisers to the Nationalists, such as Stilwell,

Chennault, and Wedemeyer, had no significant combat experience prior to their long assignments in China, the Communists' Russian advisers were fresh from long combat tours fighting and defeating the world's most lethal army. Thus, the Russian advisers arrived at the top of their game, whereas the Americans arrived green. The Russians provided key training in logistics, battle formations, and armored warfare. Before Lin Biao began his successful Winter Offensive of 1947–8, he awaited Russian railway technicians to repair the north-south railway lines. Over the summer of 1948, Russians trained his army in the use of heavy artillery in preparation for the Battle of Jinzhou in October.[109]

Mao's writings on people's war did not explain how rural peasant armies could acquire the heavy equipment to transition to phase-three operations. In earlier writings, however, he had emphasized in very general terms the critical role he expected Russia to play.[110] In comparison to Russia's assistance to the Communists, the United States provided far more aid to the Nationalists from 1945 to 1949 – more than U.S. $1 billion of military aid, equipping thirty-nine divisions and greatly expanding their navy, plus an additional billion in economic aid.[111] If aid alone were decisive, the Nationalists would have won. Although aid does not explain why the Communists won the civil war, it does explain why they did not lose. Without enormous supplies of conventional weapons, the Communists would have remained at best a phase-two military problem and more likely a phase-one insurgency in a very inhospitable climate, where winters kill insurgents in disproportionate numbers.

On 15 November 1945, the Nationalist general Du Yuming began to extend Nationalist control over Manchuria by attacking Shanhaiguan and dislodging the Communists the next day. The Communists had not expected such a rapid defeat. Whereas Nationalist units had been engaging in conventional operations throughout the long war against Japan, the Communists had little experience. As U.S. forces later discovered in the long Vietnam War, conventional and guerrilla operations are different items; expertise in the one form of warfare does not translate to the other. As a potentially decisive battle impended, Mao Zedong fell ill and remained confined to his bed until mid-December. On 17 November, the Russians stepped in to request a delay in their troop withdrawal to "assist" the Nationalist takeover. Their expulsion of the Chinese Communist authorities from the cities suggested an intent to honor their treaties. So Chiang accepted their offer in return for cooperation with his troop deployments along Manchuria's railways and to Shenyang and Changchun (formerly the puppet capital of Xinjing). Although the Communists removed their military forces from the cities, a covert political presence remained. Peng Zhen favored defending urban areas. Liu Shaoqi, however, gave orders to let the Nationalists move unimpeded along the railways and into the cities to encourage their overextension and directed the Communists to conduct military operations from three rural base areas.[112]

Du Yuming's troops immediately entered southern Manchuria and took the important railway junction at Jinzhou, as the first phase in asserting Nationalist sovereignty, but the Russians refused to evacuate Shenyang or northern Manchuria. Instead they demanded economic cooperation in return for a troop withdrawal agreement.[113] In subsequent negotiations, they offered the Nationalists joint management of Manchurian enterprises, with Russians serving as all company presidents paired with Nationalists in the number-two, vice-presidential slots. When these negotiations foundered, the Communist Eighth Route Army contested the Nationalist deployment to Manchuria, causing the Nationalist civil administration to flee.[114]

Despite the Friendship Treaty, the Russians made a parallel offer to the Chinese Communists for joint ownership of 80 percent of Manchurian heavy industry. The Chinese Communists coyly proposed discussing the matter after the Russian troops had returned home. Stalin even more coyly informed the Chinese Communists that his troops would be taking with them all portable parts of the Manchurian industrial base as reparations.[115] The document trail ends here.

Both the Communists and the Nationalists remained uncharacteristically silent about the rape of Manchuria.[116] In the past, both had excoriated the imperial powers for making not taking investments. Their silence suggests some kind of political deal. The Nationalists apparently agreed to the expropriation of half of Manchurian industry in return for Russian assistance to Nationalist troops entering Manchuria, while the Communists may have bartered away the lost infrastructure to pay for the conventional arms Russia soon provided. This might account for Russia's delay in providing the best equipment.[117]

Before the Communist troops marched into Beijing on 31 January 1949, they replaced these Japanese and Russian weapons with those of U.S. manufacture as evidence that they won the war by taking

U.S. weapons from fleeing Nationalist soldiers.[118] This informed the conventional tale that the Nationalists subsisted on infusions of aid from their odious big friend the United States. The Communists omitted their own odious big friend Russia, whose aid was not donated, but apparently paid for with the infrastructure of Manchuria. In Karl Marx's economic model, imperialists do not deindustrialize their colonies. They build infrastructure; they do not cart it away. The Communists also neglected to compare the numbers of foreign troops deployed on Chinese soil: 1.5 million Russian troops to 20,000 U.S. army, navy, and marine personnel.[119]

Even as Russia secretly assembled the weapons enabling the Communists to transition to conventional military operations, the Nationalists apparently assumed it would honor its treaties not to aid the Chinese Communists. As the 3 December 1945 Russian withdrawal date approached, the Nationalists requested a second Russian delay, extending its occupation to 1 February 1946. Presumably they did so on the assumption that a continuing Russian military presence would prevent a Chinese Communist takeover before they could organize the forces to go north. Then as the 1 February deadline loomed, the Russians, experts in winter, alleged wintertime logistical difficulties would prevent their departure until 1 March 1946, another deadline they failed to meet.[120] When Russian-Nationist negotiations on economic cooperation broke down, the Nationalists sponsored anti-Russian demonstrations, a belated protest against Russia's deindustrialization of Manchuria.[121]

Back in January and February 1946, the Nationalists massed troops in Jinzhou, where they left on three routes heading northward on 8 February. Previously there had been few Communist-Nationalist clashes in Manchuria.[122] On 10 January, Marshall had negotiated a cease-fire in Manchuria and soon turned to the framework for a coalition government. China's many small political parties had joined to create the Democratic League in 1944, but by 1945 it had split along Nationalist-Communist lines. On 25 February 1946, Marshall negotiated troop reductions with the Nationalists and Communists, to fifty and ten divisions, respectively. As an indication of the relative Communist weakness at that time, their opening position had granted the Nationalists a 9-to-2 troop superiority, while the Nationalists had sought a 6-to-1 ratio.[123]

As soon as Marshall returned to the United States to negotiate an aid package from 11 March to 18 April 1946, Russia suddenly began withdrawing its troops, completing the evacuation of Shenyang on 12 March, the day after Marshall's departure.[124] As they moved out, the Chinese Communists moved in, reaching Shenyang before the Nationalists. The day after the Russians evacuated, all-out war broke out when the Nationalists took the city, a railway junction servicing southernmost Manchuria.[125] Marshall blamed the Nationalists for taking advantage of his return to the United States to renew the civil war. Actually, Russia had taken advantage of his absence to set the conditions.

These events coincided with a rapidly developing cold war – a new global war replacing the global hot war that had ended less than a year prior. On 9 February Stalin gave his inevitability-of-war speech. On 22 February, George Kennan, the famous U.S. State Department Russia expert, sent his long telegram outlining his containment strategy that became the bedrock of U.S. foreign policy until the fall of the Soviet Union in 1991. And on 5 March the former prime minister Winston Churchill gave his Iron Curtain speech in Fulton, Missouri, describing the division of Europe that prevailed for the duration of the cold war.[126]

On 15 March, the Russians completed the evacuation of Siping, the railway junction linking the north-south and east-west trunk lines servicing south-central Manchuria, and promised to evacuate all of Manchuria by the end of April.[127] Three days later, on 18 March the Communists took Siping, which the Nationalists contested. Mao ordered Lin Biao to hold Siping at all costs on the expectation that Marshall would call another truce that would allow the Communists to dig in. After a month of fighting, the Nationalists occupied Siping on 19 May.[128] On 14 April, Russian troops left Changchun, the railway junction linking Manchuria to Communist supply lines in Korea.[129] Four days later on 18 April, the Communists took Changchun, but after a month of fighting, it fell to the Nationalists on 23 May, completing the Nationalist occupation of southern Manchuria.[130]

On 3 May, the Russians informed the Nationalist government that their full evacuation would be delayed until 23 May. Thereafter, Russian forces remained in Lüshun, the main Manchurian naval base.[131] They had failed to supply the Communists with weapons in sufficient quantity and in time to train for conventional military operations.[132] This allowed the Nationalists to conduct a rapid offensive. In June, when Nationalist troops crossed the Sungari River heading for Harbin, the railway junction connecting northern Manchuria both to Russia and to Lüshun, Marshall pulled out all the stops to make Chiang agree to another cease-fire on 6 June. Later, Chiang called this agreement his "most grievous mistake."[133]

On 27 June Zhou Enlai told the Russian ambassador, Apollon Aleksandrovich Petrov, that by the time of the truce, Communist forces were down to no more than three bullets per soldier in an exhausted and severely weakened force. Lin Biao had even prepared the order to evacuate Harbin, when the truce made this unnecessary.[134] The Communists used the breathing space afforded by the truce to regroup, amass weapons, train, and transition from a guerrilla to a conventional force.[135] The Nationalists estimated that Communist forces had grown from 30,000 in September 1945 to 500,000 by June 1947.[136] The Nationalists never recaptured the momentum of their spring 1946 offensive lost with the cease-fire demanded by Marshall. When the Russians finally decamped, the Communists controlled the northeastern two-thirds of Manchuria, which, surprise, surprise, was the old Russian sphere of influence under the Qing dynasty.[137]

Stalin's actions indicate that he did not actually desire a strong, unified China. He timed his troop withdrawal so that neither the Communists nor the Nationalists became firmly entrenched. Before the ink had dried on the 14 August 1945 Treaty of Friendship with the Nationalists, he violated the terms by providing military aid to the Chinese Communists, failing to impede their entry into Manchuria, and closing Manchurian ports to the Nationalists.[138] Stalin intended Manchuria to be under Chinese Communist, not Nationalist sovereignty. Yet he failed to make available military supplies to the Communists until late 1945 and supplied little heavy equipment until the fall of 1947, when the Nationalists were poised to defeat them. Meanwhile, Russia was simultaneously disassembling the portable parts of Manchuria's industrial base and shipping them home, further impoverishing an impoverished land.[139]

Full-scale civil war resumed within the month in July 1946, starting in the Central Plains and Jiangsu followed by Shanxi, Chahar, and Hebei, but not until November in Manchuria, where the Communists had gained a five-month breathing space to regroup and rethink their unsuccessful strategy to take and hold cities. Truman also did some rethinking and began curtailing military aid to the Nationalists. He considered Chiang Kai-shek and his Soong and Kong inlaws as "thieves" who had squandered $750 million in U.S. aid. In retaliation for Chiang's rupture of both U.S.-brokered cease-fires, Truman cut off military aid for eight months from the fall of 1946 until the spring of 1947, when U.S. policy makers blinked at the looming prospect of a unified Communist China. Zhou Enlai and Edgar Snow in separate ways convinced U.S. representatives in China unwittingly to interpret the escalating civil war through a Communist lens.[140] The U.S. cuts were felt by the spring of 1947 with equipment inoperative for lack of parts. Upon the resumption of aid, supplies did not start reaching China until November 1948, as the Nationalists were losing their grip on Manchuria.[141] Thus, just as the Communists received and trained with Russian-supplied equipment, the Nationalists lost their foreign benefactor.

Initially Chiang Kai-shek's decision to deploy north had seemed wise. Nationalist forces under the command of Du Yuming had conducted an operationally and strategically successful general offensive through the end of 1946. The offensive had pushed Communist forces out of the south; divided and isolated their base areas in the north; eliminated the Communist Central Plains and Central China Military districts as well as the Liaodong and Hebei-Rehe-Liaoning subdistricts; and put the Nationalists in possession of southern Manchuria. Communist troops had retreated to the Korean border. Zhou Enlai estimated that the Nationalists had deployed 90 percent of their forces (216 divisions) and taken 170,000 square kilometers of territory and 165 cities, while the Communists had annihilated 40 to 50 Nationalist brigades (at two brigades to a division).[142]

Chiang Kai-shek apparently believed that his general offensive of 1946 had secured Suiyuan, Chahar, Rehe, Shanxi, Anhui, the Central Plains, and most of Jiangsu, Hebei, and Manchuria. As his armies verged on victory, he transferred most of his elite forces to Shaanxi and Shandong for a strong-point offensive conceived as two pincers. The western pincer would decapitate the Communist government at Yan'an, while the eastern pincer targeted the Communists' East China Military District in Shandong. The Communists responded with a highly successful counterstrategy of attacking "secured" areas to overextend the Nationalists. The heaviest fighting took place in Shandong.[143]

Suddenly, the Nationalists, instead of dividing up Communist forces in North China, found the railways connecting their scattered troops besieged, pinning Nationalist armies and preventing the movement of reinforcements. As Sunzi advises, the Communists made "it impossible for the enemy to concentrate." The master explains, "And if I concentrate while he divides, I can use my entire strength to attack a fraction of his. There, I will be numerically superior. Then, if I am able to use many to strike few at the selected point, those I deal with will be in dire straits." Key: "The enemy must not know where I intend to give battle. For if he does not know ... he must prepare in a great many places.... And when he prepares everywhere he will be weak everywhere."[144]

Worse still, the Communists anticipated the western pincer's drive on Yan'an in March 1947, which they sacrificed in a trade of space for time.[145] Like the United States, which benefited greatly from advance knowledge of Japanese plans, in its case from decryptions of their communications, it turns out that the Communists benefited greatly from an extensive spy network that provided them with equally timely information.[146] Sunzi emphasizes espionage. He identifies five types of spies – native, inside, doubled, expendable, and living – which refer, respectively, to enemy nationals, enemy officials, turned enemy spies, spies to spread disinformation, and spies returning with information. He concludes, "Secret operations are essential in war; upon them the army relies to make its every move."[147] Apparently the Communists took the advice to heart.

One of Chiang's bodyguards and a favorite of his wife, the German Walther Stennes, was a Russian spy.[148] In 1947 the personal secretary to Hu Zongnan, the Nationalist general who took Yan'an, reported to Mao daily on the general's plans. Mao had not intended to evacuate Yan'an because of its symbolic importance, but in early March, when the spy furnished him with the Nationalists' complete battle plans, Mao and most of Yan'an decamped for safer ground.[149] Without the spy, the Nationalists might have captured the Great Helmsman himself.

For the duration of World War II until the end of the Chinese Civil War, General Liu Fei, a key assistant to the Nationalist Army chief of staff, reported all major military plans to the Communists. He appointed another spy, Guo Rugui, to the War Planning Board. Although Guo fell under suspicion during the Huai-Hai Campaign over the winter of 1948–9, when the Communists seemed to anticipate every Nationalist move, nothing came of it. Guo represented the Nationalists during final negotiations with the Communists in the spring of 1949.[150]

Cryptography was another area where the Russians aided the Communists. They trained the Chinese Communists to break the Nationalist codes, which the Japanese and the Americans had also broken.[151] So both the Communists and the Japanese had advance warning of Nationalist plans, another factor explaining the poor Nationalist military performance. It is unclear whether Chiang Kai-shek, like the Japanese, was remarkably blind to the possibility that his codes had been compromised and his organization penetrated by spies, or whether he simply lacked the resources to do anything about it.

During the Shandong Campaign, which ran from March 1947 to September 1948, ending with the fall of Jinan on 24 September, a Communist field army for the first time defeated an elite Nationalist force, the Reorganized 74th Division, in the Battle of Menglianggu in southern Shandong fought between 13 and 16 May 1947. This caused a two-month pause in Nationalist operations in Shandong. Nevertheless, during 1947, the Nationalists' eastern pincer took territory in northern Jiangsu and southern Shandong, driving a wider wedge between Communists forces. When the Nationalist pincers in Shandong and Yan'an failed to annihilate the Communist forces or pacify the countryside, the Nationalists faced overextension, particularly since they were conducting simultaneous operations in Manchuria.[152]

The Shandong Campaign fixed Nationalist troops, preventing their deployment elsewhere and opening an opportunity for the Communists to win in Manchuria.[153] Beginning on 6 January 1947, Lin Biao launched a series of probes across the Sungari River that culminated in a major offensive beginning in May, isolating Changchun, Jilin City, and Siping. Lin Biao conducted the offensive from 8 to 28 May in order to cut the Jilin-Shenyang railway line, encircle the Nationalists' 184th Division, reestablish contact with the Liaodong Military Sub-District, eject Nationalist forces from the countryside, and crowd them into the cities and railways in between. For a time, Lin Biao's forces besieged the crucial railway junction at Siping. This separated Du Yuming's main garrisons at Changchun and Shenyang, but the Nationalists successfully relieved Siping in the Second Battle of Siping and at great cost pushed Lin Biao's troops back across the Sungari.[154] The successful defense of Siping was the last important Nationalist victory in the post–World War II phase of the long Chinese civil war.[155] During the Communists' Summer Offensive, they linked their scattered base areas in eastern, western, and southern Manchuria. Simultaneously they launched the Central Plains Counteroffensive in summer of 1947 deep behind Nationalist lines south of the Yellow River in Henan, western Shandong, Hebei, and Shaanxi. General Nie Rongzhen won the Zhengtai Campaign to take the Shijiazhuang (Zhengding)-Taiyuan Railway in May 1947 almost to the junction at Shijiazhuang, Hebei.[156]

The Nationalists' two-pronged offensive and ensuing strong-point offensive maximized their territory – but also maximized their burdens. Nowhere was fully pacified. They failed to wipe out the Communists' armies. The pincers on Shaanxi and Shandong removed pressure from northeast China and Hebei, but the defeats in the Zhengtai Campaign and the Communists' Summer Offensive left the Nationalists with no strategic reserves. Like the Japanese before them, the Nationalists controlled the coastline, the cities, and the railways from Shaanxi to Shandong, but this forced them to garrison it all, leaving few troops to fight.[157] As the United States uneasily observed events from afar, it resumed military aid, but the U.S. Export-Import Bank refused to release loans authorized in 1946. At home, the Nationalists replaced the 1936 draft constitution by promulgating a new one on Christmas 1946 and putting it into effect on Christmas 1947 after holding elections for a National Assembly in November 1947.[158] In theory the period of political tutelage had ended. In practice, war intervened again and the economy imploded.

Liu Shaoqi responded to the Communist defeat at Siping in the spring of 1947 with land reform paired with recruitments. On 9 July 1947 the Communists implemented their Land Reform Law to redistribute all land from rich peasants.[159] Under Lin Biao, they reverted to phase-two guerrilla tactics in Manchuria, attacking the Nationalists' rear as the latter moved northward. The Communists, who had not had the time to collect let alone train with Japanese equipment, had to cede the transportation arteries. But they employed Liu Shaoqi's strategy of "Ceding the Highways, but Taking Both Sides."[160] They focused on positioning themselves to attrite Nationalist armies and to leverage their interior lines of communication to attack the Nationalists' exterior lines – that long and vulnerable supply route by a single railway line to the south via Shanhaiguan.[161]

The Shandong Campaign was vital to the Communist success in Manchuria. The Communists estimated that during the winter of 1947–8, of the 160 potential frontline Nationalist brigades, the Central Plains Field Army under Liu Shaoqi and Deng Xiaoping tied down 90, leaving insufficient numbers to save Manchuria.[162] In the fall of 1947, Lin Biao changed from costly attacks on cities and attempts to take full control of railway lines to just cutting the railway lines supplying the cities, a much simpler proposition.[163] This was the war-winning strategy of encircling the cities from the countryside.[164] In September, the Communists launched an Autumn Offensive to probe the vital transportation link between Shanhaiguan and Shenyang, at its origin at Shanhaiguan and at its midpoint at Jinzhou. Chiang sent reinforcements. To the south on 12 November, forces under Nie Rongzhen finally took the railway junction at Shijiazhuang in southern Hebei separating Nationalist forces in Beijing, Xuzhou, Henan, and Shanxi. Nie's forces also annihilated important Nationalist units on the railway line farther north at Qingfengdian, Hebei.[165] The Communist victory at Shijiazhuang also permitted the unification of the Shanxi-Chahar-Hebei and Shanxi-Hebei-Shandong-Henan base areas and the end of autonomous zones in North China.[166]

These successes allowed Nie to transfer troops back to Manchuria, where Lin Biao was conducting his Winter Offensive. Mao feared that Chiang might withdraw forces from Manchuria to take the Central Plains (the advice of Chiang's U.S. advisers and the plan recommended by General Du Yuming, whom he relieved from command instead). Mao hoped to isolate and destroy the Nationalist army in Manchuria. Chiang's static defense of cities played into this strategy. Lin Biao attacked Siping on 25 February 1948. The fall of Siping on 15 March ended the Winter Offensive. Chiang again reinforced. The Nationalists had lost Jilin City in October 1947 and Yingkou in February 1948 and retained only Changchun – now isolated with the loss of Siping – and Shenyang plus the railway south through the narrow corridor to Shanhaiguan.[167]

The Communists probably had Chiang's battle plan for 1947 defense of Manchuria from spies in the headquarters of General Chen Cheng, the joint chief of staff and Chiang's most trusted adviser. So they cut off the Nationalist supply lines from the south. If the Nationalists had attacked first to the south as Du had recommended, the Communist plan of isolating the Nationalist units and then defeating them sequentially would not have worked.[168] The Communists reduced the Nationalist presence, as the Japanese before them had, to the cities and the railway lines connecting them. The Nationalists then failed to abandon the cities when the Communists cut the railway lines.

By mid-1948, in the preceding two years of warfare, the Communists had suffered 800,000 casualties, recruited 1.1 million, and added 800,000 Nationalist defectors, and 450,000 injured had rejoined. Communist forces expanded from 1.2 to 2.8 million, including 1.49 million regular troops. Meanwhile, the Nationalists had lost 1.52 million, although their forces still numbered 3.65 million including 1.98 million regulars, with 1.74 million engaged in fighting the Communists.[169] Whereas Chiang had a reputation for using the armies of his warlord associates for frontline duty and for summarily executing Communists, the Communists welcomed defectors – at least until they won the war. Housecleaning occurred in a succession of postwar rectification campaigns. While the civil war raged, the Communists treated defectors comparatively well and integrated them into the People's Liberation Army, following Sunzi's strategy of "winning a battle and becoming stronger" through the incorporation of turncoat enemy troops.[170]

In the Liaoning-Shenyang Campaign from 12 September to 2 November 1948, the Nationalists lost their best troops trained by U.S. advisers in Burma along with the best Lend-Lease equipment. Lin Biao had opposed the campaign but he led and won it. Major General David G. Barr, Wedemeyer's successor as lead U.S. military adviser in China, recommended against trying to hold major cities and unsuccessfully pushed Chiang to evacuate Shenyang prior to its encirclement. In 1948 the United States repeatedly advised Chiang to cut his losses and withdraw from Manchuria, but he, like the Japanese, refused to write off his sunk costs and ended up losing everything.[171] His strategy to seek field battles had failed. Manchuria fell in its entirety to the Communists. This Communist victory followed close on the heels of their victory in the Shandong Campaign in September 1948.

THE MANDATE OF HEAVEN

Chiang had survived more than two decades of continuous civil war, coup attempts, and a protracted foreign invasion. His U.S. military aid dwarfed the Russian aid to the Communists. He had never controlled North China, let alone Manchuria, and when he lost in Manchuria, he retained two-thirds of China including his power base.[172] Yet his government fell within a year. After holding out so long – the tumultuous Nanjing decade, the fifteen-year Second Sino-Japanese War, and four more years of civil war – why did he succumb so rapidly in 1949?

Conversely, the Communists had nearly been obliterated in the Long March. Thereafter they had suffered a decade of Japanese and Nationalist persecution. Their base area at Yan'an was situated in one of the most inhospitable parts of China, lacking the industrial capacity to equip a large conventional army. Indeed, they had never had large well-equipped armies until they started winning in Manchuria. How did they so suddenly move up from behind to defeat the Nationalists, who seemed poised for victory when Japan capitulated to the United States? Russian equipment explains why the Communists did not lose, but it does not explain why they won.

The Communist victory in Manchuria produced many fears but no solutions in Washington. A strategy of hope and the domestic political imperative for damage limitation for the impending "loss" of China to communism drove deliveries of additional U.S. military and economic aid. Perhaps more assistance would prove that Chiang's defeat was not the fault of the United States. How to explain to U.S. voters that despite more than $2 billion in aid from the capitulation of Japan to the end of fiscal 1948 China still fell to the Communists?[173] To put this sum in perspective, the entire 1950 defense budget for the United States was $15 billion.[174]

Since General Stilwell's time, U.S. military advisers had been pressuring the Nationalists to integrate their military forces under a unified command. In 1947, General Chen Cheng had belatedly followed this advice to eliminate warlord remnants and personal armies. The reform produced unanticipated results: Thousands of decommissioned officers defected with their troops to the Communists rather than become marginalized by the reforms. In Manchuria, the reforms meant that the Nationalists did not use the nearly 500,000 troops of the Manchukuo puppet army. Instead these troops and their equipment eventually went over to the Communists. The Manchurian Campaign was a close call – these troops might have tipped the balance.[175] On 19 August 1948, as the Nationalist situation was disintegrating, they belatedly decided to follow another piece of U.S. advice: currency reform, which just added to the confusion.[176] Major reforms are difficult enough in peacetime let alone in the midst of an imploding military situation.

From November 1948 to January 1949, the Nationalists lost three major campaigns in rapid succession, the Liaoning-Shenyang Campaign marking the loss of Manchuria, followed by the Huai-hai Campaign in Anhui, and the Beijing-Tianjin Campaign, when the Communists sought and got battles of annihilation, wiping out entire Nationalist armies.[177] These campaigns eliminated more than 1.5 million Nationalist forces through death, injury, or defection.[178]

The Huai-Hai Campaign occurred between the Huai River and Longhai Railway, and focused on taking the critical and much fought over railway junction at Xuzhou.[179] It was the largest campaign of the long Chinese civil war, engaging 1.8 million men along a two-hundred-kilometer front from 6 November 1948 to 10 January 1949. The campaign takes its name from an amalgamation of the names of the Huai River plus the city of Haizhou, the latter located near the eastern terminus of the Longhai Railway that ran westward to Xi'an. The Communists destroyed three Nationalist armies and cleared the way to the Yangzi River.[180] John Melby, a political officer at the U.S. Embassy who flew over the unfolding battle in mid-December, left his impression: "You could see exactly what Lin Biao was doing. This huge enveloping movement was broken up into literally hundreds, maybe thousands of smaller pincer movements. Each one moving in, pinching off one group of Nationalist troops after another. It was magnificent! It was fascinating. As the same time, it was horrible.... And when it was over ... there was no Nationalist Army left."[181]

Again, the Communists greatly benefited from advance warning from spies concerning Nationalist plans.[182] In the Beijing-Tianjin Campaign, General Fu Zuoyi, one of the most talented Nationalist generals, gave up Beijing without a fight, in part through the urging of his daughter, Fu Dong, who was a Communist agent. Tianjin had fallen on 15 January. Beijing was cut off. On 22 January 1949, the day after Chiang Kai-shek resigned as president, General Fu Zuoyi turned over the traditional seat of government to the Communists, his forces intact.[183] From 1 June 1946 to 31 January 1949, the Nationalists lost nearly 5 million soldiers, three-quarters of whom defected to the Communists. These defections concentrated in the final six months of this period, when the

Nationalists suffered 2.6 million losses and the Communists acquired arsenals of U.S. equipment.[184]

With an unrelenting succession of debacles, Chiang Kai-shek resigned as president on 21 January 1949 but retained his post as Nationalist Party leader, effectively hamstringing any successor. As in his previous two resignations, in 1927 and 1931, respectively, Chiang stepped down not in order to relinquish power but to undermine his detractors. His replacement as acting president was his longtime rival Li Zongren of the Guangxi group, whom Chiang had no intention of helping to win the civil war, undoubtedly recalling the Guangxi group coup attempt during the Ichigō Campaign.[185] On 31 January the People's Liberation Army made a triumphal march into Beijing showcasing captured U.S. equipment. Li turned to Ambassador Roshchin, in what the Communists perceived as a Russian attempt to divide China. In 1948, Roshchin had already tried to mediate a peace with the Nationalists and the Communists.[186] In January 1949, he and Li negotiated two agreements, one authorizing Russia to mediate the end of the civil war and the other promoting Nationalist-Russian cooperation.[187]

According to the memoirs of the Yugoslav Communist Vladimir Dedijer, Stalin had recounted in 1948 that he had recommended in 1945 that the Communists negotiate a settlement with the Nationalists.[188] This worked about as well as Marshall's mediation efforts. Stalin allegedly sent a representative in 1948 to advise the Communists to halt their offensive at the Yangzi River and repeated the advice in 1949.[189] Chinese Communist sources accuse the Soviet Politburo member Anastas Mikoyan, in his January 1949 trip to China, of recommending a halt at the Yangzi in order to produce a divided China.[190] In January 1949 Stalin sent Mao a telegram expressing an interest in taking up the Nationalist request for great-power meditation. Given Mao's meteoric military progress, such mediation could only have worked in Chiang's favor.[191] In the spring of 1949 and again in 1957, Mao alluded to this Russian advice. Zhou Enlai stated flatly that Russia had ordered the Communists to stop at the Yangzi.[192]

Li Zongren was determined to defend at the Yangzi River but needed the army, fuel, and ammunition under the control of General Tang Enbo, the commander in chief of the Nanjing-Shanghai-Hangzhou area. Tang refused, focusing instead on the evacuation of troops, supplies, and funds to Taiwan. Back in 1938, during the Battle of Taierzhuang, Li had forced Tang to cooperate with his strategy under threat of court-martial and execution. Chiang rejected the military plan developed by his Guangxi group rivals Li Zongren and General Bai Chongxi to defend at the Yangzi. He apparently preferred to delay the fall of Shanghai, so that he could remove resources and his praetorian guard to Taiwan, rather than to save a South China rump state under the leadership of his rivals. So Chiang interfered with supplies for Bai's defense of Hunan and continually shifted troops nominally under Bai's command to other theaters, producing a succession of defeats.[193]

The Yangzi is one of the world's greatest rivers, running all the way from Tibet to Shanghai. It is navigable by ocean liners six hundred miles inland, while smaller craft can go as far as fifteen hundred miles.[194] The Nationalists' power base lay to the south of the Yangzi, while the Communists' power base lay to the north. According to General Wedemeyer, the Nationalists "could have defended the Yangtze River with broomsticks if they had the will to do so."[195] Instead, the Nationalists did not bother to pay their navy, so the flagship mutinied on 25 February 1949, followed by much of the rest of the navy on 20 April, when the Communists crossed unopposed in three areas, where the river width ranged from eight hundred meters to two kilometers. The Communists gained thirty ships and 1,271 sailors.[196] Formerly they had had no navy.

At the very end, Chiang scrambled to negotiate. He pressed the Chinese Communists, the United States, and Russia, but over the years he had alienated all of them. Like the Japanese before him, he had offended each great power in turn. Apparently neither Japan's wartime leaders nor Chiang considered the world from the point of view of those whose cooperation they sought. To the Communists he gave no quarter. From the Americans he demanded fabulous sums of aid. For 1949 alone he "required" the astronomical sum of $1 billion (which he did not get).[197] One wonders whether those in the know in Washington also saw Chiang's hand in American politics, with the purge of his critics in the State Department and the removals of General Stilwell and Ambassador Gauss.

For sure, the State Department was aware of and reported on an unsettling evolution of Chiang's thinking. In 1947 his new victory plan banked on the outbreak of a third world war. He intended to sit it out while the United States defeated Russia and eliminated the key benefactor of the Chinese Communists so that he could then win the civil war.[198] By 1948 as the cold war escalated in Europe and the United States was taking a careful inventory of its allies, some Nationalists even favored rapprochement with Russia in preparation for Chinese neutrality during the anticipated U.S.-Russian showdown. The Nationalists assumed that the United States would support them no matter what since the alternative was communism.[199] One can imagine the reaction in Washington to this strategy. One might ask, with friends like these, who needs enemies?

When Chiang tried to arrange for an eleventh-hour cease-fire, the Communists kept up the military pressure – in contrast to Chiang's on-again off-again pursuit of them from the 1930s through the mid-1940s.[200] In this, the Communists followed the principle of continuity, emphasized by Clausewitz. Once the enemy is on the run, pursue, pursue, pursue, but with the caveat (missed by Japan) not to the point of overextension.[201] In 1935 and in 1946, Chiang Kai-shek had the Communists on the run and failed to pursue. Perhaps he had reached the geographic limits of the Nationalist warlord coalition, or perhaps he committed fatal errors of strategy.

After the Communists crossed the Yangzi River, negotiations continued between Li and Roshchin in May over Russian rights in Xinjiang, where the Nationalists, much less Li, had no control. The Russians sought a restoration of the privileges they had lost after their warlord protégé, Sheng Shicai, had fallen from power when the Nazi invasion had distracted Russian attention. Roshchin was the only foreign ambassador to accompany the Nationalists on their flight to Guangzhou.[202]

The Communist victory in Manchuria, however, was strategic and decisive. Within five months, the Communists crossed the Yangzi River. Nanjing, Wuhan, and Shanghai then all fell within a month and with them the most industrialized areas outside Manchuria. Chongqing fell in November and Chiang decamped for Taiwan on 9 December 1949. In early 1950, Peng Dehuai took Xinjiang.[203] When Russia made the flight arrangements for the top officials of the breakaway East Turkestan Republic to fly to Beijing for negotiations in August 1949, the plane crashed, killing all on board, ending this chapter in Xinjiang separatism.[204] One wonders whether this was Stalin's way of disposing of a superfluous puppet government. In the spring of 1950 the Communists took Hainan Island in the far south, and in December

1951 they took Tibet, which had been nominally independent since the fall of the Qing dynasty in 1911. Once the Communists had retaken the empire, they set their sights on the peasantry, who lost in the postwar collectivization campaigns the land they treasured and for whose ownership they had fought.

Many would argue that the Communists won because the overwhelming majority of the Chinese population supported their program of social equality, government-sponsored economic development, and party leadership and admired their heroic struggle against Nationalist injustice and Japanese cruelty. This line of reasoning highlights the prescient leadership of Mao Zedong, emphasizing guerrilla warfare, rural base areas, and the conquest of cities from the countryside, and the military skills and upright leadership of his generals.

By 1947, the Communists had developed an effective dual civil-military strategy based on cultivating local support through land reform and political indoctrination at the local level to take the countryside, and then surrounding Nationalist forces trapped in the cities. They had learned how to capitalize on Nationalist blunders such as the public relations disaster of officials' flaunting their wealth, their military blunder of contesting Manchuria in the first place, and then declining to send relief to troops encircled in cities on the mistaken assumption that the encircled troops would have to fight to the death.

The Communists played a deft public relations game, leveraging the long-standing Chinese resentment against Western imperialism to play off the Nationalists' ties with the United States, with no mention of their own significant ties with Russia, which had just deindustrialized Manchuria. They blamed the incumbent government for the failure to defend China against Japan, even though their own troops had not defended China either, and their preferred strategy would have escalated the war with Japan starting in 1931 instead of waiting until 1937 for an additional six years of misery. There is a strong a positive case to be made for the Communist victory.

Others would make a negative case against the Nationalists to argue that the Communists did not so much win as the Nationalists lost. This conventional tale highlights the hyperinflation, starvation, conscription, requisitions at gunpoint and indiscriminate retaliation afflicting the poor, in combination with the corruption, conspicuous consumption, callousness, and administrative ineptitude of the Nationalist elite.

The China hands at the State Department made this case starting in 1945, and since then many others have found it compelling.

U.S. military advisers in China considered Nationalist field commanders to be incompetent and criticized them for routinely abusing conscripts. The State Department China hands made even less flattering assessments of the Nationalist civil leadership, whom they believed the populace increasingly loathed for very compelling reasons. According to the State Department, the Nationalists tolerated a suffocating level of corruption that included unchecked inflation, hoarding, and profiteering; confiscatory rural rents and interest rates; excessive and arbitrary taxation; and conscription of the poor but exemption of the elite. The Nationalists made appointments through connections. As their power base lay in South and Central China, when they reached North China, they appointed southerners to all key positions, alienating the local population.[205]

The State Department also criticized Chiang for his police-state tactics, arrest of dissenters, government by intimidation and assassination, consistent refusal to create democratic institutions, and highly unpopular tolerance of Japanese sympathizers. As early as 1945, the State Department considered the popular dissatisfaction with the Nationalist government and military to be widespread and growing.[206] In the final days of 1948, as the Nationalist situation imploded, the U.S. consul general at Shanghai reported: "The tragedy of China is not that Communism is about to take the country over, evil though we know Communism to be. The tragedy is that China had such a rotten government, which clung stubbornly to power even after it had obviously forfeited the people's confidence. Thereby those who wanted a change had but one place to go."[207]

Particularly unpopular Nationalist actions included the assassination in Kunming, Yunnan, of leaders of the Democratic League on 16 July 1946. During the Second Sino-Japanese War, the Nationalists alienated Mongols with the slogan "Resistance of Japan must be preceded by extinction of the Mongols."[208] Likewise, they alienated those who had suffered under the Japanese occupation, treating them as collaborators.[209] They called the long-suffering Manchurians "slaves who have no country of your own."[210]

The conventional tale places great emphasis on inflation. Even by the standards for hyperinflation, the numbers astound. Taking the first six months of 1937 before the Japanese escalation as the base period to construct a price index and setting these years as 100, over the course of the Second Sino-Japanese War, prices rose to 264,180 in 1946. During the endgame of the civil war, the index entered the stratosphere at 2,803,609 in January 1948 and reached 47,070,539 by August 1948 on the eve of the loss of Manchuria. The closer to the seat of the Nationalist government, the worse the inflation became.[211] It far outstripped Chiang Kai-shek's ability to print money.[212]

The economic implosion produced rampant hoarding, speculation, smuggling, and tax evasion that exacerbated economic problems. The Nationalist government repeatedly tried to mandate price controls once in 1939, then from January 1940 to December 1942, and again in January 1943. Its attempt in January 1941 to create a government monopoly for daily necessities produced increased prices, reduced profits, and decreased production.[213] No juggling of the bookkeeping could make up for the enormous goods shortage caused by the war or the insatiable demand for food, clothing, and equipment from the millions of people under arms. Upon retreating to Taiwan, the Nationalists made a comprehensive after-action report to analyze why they had lost. Their conclusions align with the negative case: Their failure to control corruption and to conduct land reform cost them the war.[214]

The Renaissance adviser to Italian city-states and founding father of political science, Niccolò Machiavelli, argued that political loyalties are based on three factors: love, fear, and hate. He advised rulers not to seek the love of their subjects because love is fickle and the deserving are not necessarily loved. Instead, he recommended that rulers rely on fear, because they can induce fear and people tend to respond in predictable ways. Fear, he believed, was a reliable basis for power. But at all costs, he warned, avoid becoming hated, because hatred hardens the enemy and transforms loyalists into enemies.[215]

While there is much dispute concerning the degree to which the Communists were loved by their compatriots, there is little dispute concerning the situation that by the end of the civil war many Chinese hated the Nationalist government of Chiang Kai-shek. They blamed him, as the incumbent leader, for all that they had endured since 1928. Not only had he been unable to fix the obvious ills of his country – its poverty, its subjection to rapacious foreign powers, and the ceaseless warfare – but he and his loyalists were perceived to be the source of

China's escalating problems. Nationalist officials lived in comparative splendor, populated the dance halls, and profited from black market rackets, while their compatriots starved in the countryside and cities or died on the battlefield.[216] At the end, Chiang was unwilling to do the noble thing, to fall on his sword, take responsibility for these failures, and then allow others in the Nationalist Party to take over and support their effort to defend at the Yangzi River. There is a strong case to be made that the Communists won not primarily because they were loved, but because the Nationalists were reviled.

It also turns out that Sunzi, the revered Classical Chinese military theorist, offers much bad advice that Chiang Kai-shek carefully followed. Sunzi recommends putting one's own troops on death ground, so that they fight to the death, while leaving enemy troops an escape route so they flee.[217] According to the ancient master: "Throw the troops into a position from which there is no escape and even when faced with death they will not flee ... [but will] "stand firm." "To assemble the army and throw it into a desperate position is the business of the general. He leads the army deep into hostile territory and there releases the trigger."[218] Chiang followed Sunzi's advice to "throw" soldiers "into a desperate position" over and over again. He deployed his armies and particularly those of his more iffy generals deep into Manchuria, where, rather than fight to the death, they defected to the Communists en masse. Mao reversed Sunzi to lure the enemy (not his own troops) deep into hostile territory, where he put the enemy (not his own troops) on death ground until the enemy defected to his side and he welcomed the defectors. This was part of his strategy to foster "the disintegration of the enemy."[219] The welcome wore out during the Korean War, when he sent the defectors to the front lines for disposal, just as Chiang Kai-shek had eliminated unreliable warlord armies.

Sunzi insists that on the battlefield, the military leader not the civil leader decides what to do. Over the course of the Second Sino-Japanese War, Chiang neutered the Nationalist civil leadership, put officers in senior civil positions, subsumed both the civil and military sides of governance within his own person, and focused on military matters without adequate consideration of civil issues.[220] In 1935 the last strong civil leader, Wang Jingwei, suffered the fate of Japan's last strong civil leaders, a nearly successful assassination attempt. Like the Japanese, Chiang focused exclusively on operational success and, in his case, failed to address the poverty overwhelming the peasants whom he expected to fight in his armies.[221] The Communists reversed Sunzi to insist that the civil leadership through the party must control the military.[222] Communist civil leaders in consultation with their military commanders and with Russian civil and military leaders set grand strategy, which had equally important economic and military components: land reform and military operations. Sunzi offers more bad advice: When deep in enemy territory, say Manchuria, Sunzi advises, "plunder." He recommends that troops live off the enemy land. Chiang's troops did so by treating the areas formerly occupied by Japan as enemy territory, alienating local loyalties and presumably aiding Communist recruitments.[223]

Mao apparently found meaning in other chapters, particularly the last one on spies.[224] He repeatedly quoted Sunzi's chestnut "Know the enemy and know yourself; in a hundred battles you will not be in peril" and spent much time analyzing the nature of the war and his, Chiang's, Japan's, and U.S. strengths and weaknesses.[225] Most notably he followed Sunzi's hierarchy of strategies. Sunzi recommends attacking first an enemy's strategy (Mao used spies to acquire Chiang's battle plans), then if necessary his alliances (Zhou Enlai did a number on the U.S.-Nationalist alliance), then his armies (Lin Biao annihilated Chiang's armies), and, only if unavoidable, his cities (Liu Shaoqi strangled the urban economy to corrode Nationalist loyalties).[226] Together these caused the disintegration of the Nationalists.

In *On Protracted War*, Mao had written in May 1938, "Our three major principles for the army's political work are, first, unity between officers and men; second, unity between the army and the people; and third, the disintegration of the enemy forces."[227] Note the choice of words, "disintegration" not "annihilation." Chiang had fought annihilation campaigns against the Communists, whereas the latter induced the Nationalist armies to disintegrate and annihilated only later during the many postvictory political campaigns. I suppose the lesson is: Do not treat the classics as religious texts of faith; although they have spoken to many generations, they still require a critical reading and an adaptation to changed circumstances.

Mao also derived insights from board games. Like chess, the Chinese game of *weiqi*, often known in the West by its Japanese Romanization of *go*, emphasizes the elimination of enemy pieces, but unlike chess also focuses on envelopment and the domination of the board. Mao likened battles to the capture of enemy pieces and base areas to the domination of the board.[228] While Chiang strove to eliminate Mao's pieces, he failed to understand that the board was not China's cities and narrow transportation routes but its rural vastness.

The Communists took a page from the Japanese playbook. Japan had destroyed China's economy, but the Nationalist government had reaped the blame. In the fall of 1947, the Communists implemented a war-winning strategy of pushing Nationalist troops back to the cities, where the infrastructure and provisions were insufficient to feed incoming armies. Then they cut off the railways linking the cities with food from the countryside and waited as the urban economy imploded and the Nationalist government again reaped the blame, not the Communists, whose military strategy had caused the implosion. This undermined any allegiance to the Nationalist government, which left cities at the mercy of desperate and lawless troops.[229] As Nationalist authorities looked worse and worse during an economic meltdown caused by the Communist military strategy, disaffected Nationalists switched sides until a critical mass had been reached and the war rapidly wound down in the final year.

So there is a strong positive case to be made for Communist leadership and an at least equally strong negative case to be made concerning Nationalist errors. But neither argument explains the suddenness of the shift in loyalties in 1949 after four years of bitter fighting. Whereas the Germans fought with grim determination all the way back to Berlin in World War II, the Nationalists gave up territory at a breathtaking pace once they had lost Manchuria.[230] They scarcely defended the areas where they had always been the strongest.

An explanation requires an examination of culture. Different civilizations portray time differently. Westerners typically envision time as a linear progression forward or from left to right along a timeline. Chinese historically have envisioned time as cyclical. Just as seasons run in cycles, so do the lives of human beings, as well as the passage of dynasties. New life is born in the spring, reaches maturity in the summer, bears fruit in the fall, and dies in the winter, only to yield new life in the spring. Such views can become self-fulfilling prophesies when those who hold them, by acting in keeping with their views, transform belief into reality through human agency.

During the great rebellions of the mid-nineteenth century, many Chinese believed the Qing dynasty had entered the declining phase of the dynastic cycle. Its swift collapse in 1911 surprised few. The armies of the Qing rapidly shifted their loyalties from the dynasty often to their mutinous commanding officers, who became the key warlords of North China. During the ensuing warlord period of ruined civil institutions, the primary loyalties of troops were to their commanding officers. When commanding officers changed sides in the multilateral phase of the civil war, their men generally followed. In a political environment without strong institutions, such personal ties of loyalty are the social glue holding people together.

Unlike in the West, where defections of entire armies are rare, they are common in Chinese history. The Ming dynasty army became the Green Standard Army of the Qing dynasty. During the fall of a dynasty, numerous armies change sides to work in the service of the rising new dynasty. The desertion of the old order for the new reflects a belief in the dynastic cycle and the immutable force of nature. Loyalties change in a tidal wave when it becomes clear to the many that the mandate of heaven has shifted from the collapsing old order to the ascendant new one.

During the long Chinese civil war, more than two decades elapsed before the chaos settled into a bilateral Communist-Nationalist civil war, followed by three years of bitter fighting in Manchuria before the masses of Chinese concluded that the Communists, not the Nationalists, held the mandate of heaven and that China's thirty-eight-year war-blighted interregnum would soon end. When this happened, loyalties shifted at a bewildering rate. Beliefs in dynastic cycles, the mandate of heaven, and in-group loyalties account for the rapidity of the Nationalist collapse after the loss of Manchuria. So the conventional tale also misses the differences between civilizations. Culture and beliefs differ, and the differences matter.

Americans do not believe in the dynastic cycle. Yet by 1947 the U.S. Embassy concluded that "China for the foreseeable future can not be a positive asset to the United States; the range of American choice is confined to whether it will be a minor or major liability."[231] By early 1948 members of State Department and Central Intelligence Agency wanted Chiang out, but as the U.S. ambassador to China, John Leighton Stuart, pointed out, there were no alternatives. Chiang's career-long strategy to retain power relied on making sure that no obvious alternatives ever survived his dragnet. The United States had tried coalition governments, truces, generous aid, and the termination of aid. As in the case of many civil wars, assassinations, purges, and rectification campaigns carried out by both sides had eliminated the political middle ground required by U.S. schemes for democracy.[232]

Chiang had an astute understanding of the warlord politics of China and a deep understanding of Japan, where he had lived for several years. In the 1930s, he had believed that sooner or later the United States or Western Europe would return to Asia, the United States the more likely candidate, and would tip the balance in China's favor in the Second Sino-Japanese War. The Axis Alliance of 1940 confirmed his expectations. After Pearl Harbor, he anticipated generous U.S. military aid. Again his estimation of the situation proved correct.[233] After Japan's capitulation, Chiang expected the United States to support him to the finish line, when he defeated the Communists.

But he failed to perceive that the United States attached different values to the defeat of the Japanese versus the defeat of the Chinese Communists. Whereas he had always focused on the civil war, the United States had always focused on the global war – formerly World War II and thereafter the cold war. While American leaders were determined to impose unconditional surrender on Japan for its attack on Pearl Harbor and its combined attempt with Germany to bring down the global order, they had no equivalent grudge against the Chinese Communist Party. The Stilwell-Chiang relationship poisoned U.S.-Nationalist relations. After Chiang's retreat to Taiwan, the State Department predicted that the Communists would invade and occupy Taiwan between mid-June and the end of July of 1950. There was no talk of doing anything to stop them.[234] The unexpected outbreak of the Korean War in June, however, changed these calculations, and the United States has been protecting Taiwan ever since.

U.S. mediation of the Chinese civil war angered the Communists and the Nationalists alike. The Communists saw the United States as a double-dealer, which provided massive aid to one side, instead of serving as an honest broker.[235] The Russian daily, *Pravda*, equated the U.S. decision to extend Lend-Lease aid to the Nationalists on 28 June 1946 as the removal of its "neutrality mask." Thereafter, Russian publications ramped up the anti-Nationalist, anti–United States, and antiimperialist content of their articles.[236] The cold war was off and running.

The Nationalists believed that U.S. interference impeded their ability to win the civil war and resented the gratuitous economic and political advice along the way.[237] U.S. policy recommendations were predicated on a unified Nationalist government and army. This key assumption was false. Chiang presided over a fraying coalition, where buy-offs of key generals were the glue holding their allegiance. His rule through connections was not mere corruption but the only way he had ever exercised power in the institutional vacuum left by the fall of the Qing dynasty. However desirable, he could not implement land reform under wartime conditions when he required the loyalties of those whose land would be expropriated.

In the end, U.S. policy makers decided to cut U.S. losses and leave Chiang to his fate. They concluded that checkbook intervention had failed and effective intervention would entail large U.S. troop deployments that, given China's vast size and proximity to Russia, were not affordable economically, strategically, or politically back at home.[238] Chiang could not believe that the United States would ever abandon him, since this would result in a unified, hostile Communist China. He guessed wrong. China was not the center of the universe after all.

9

CONCLUSION

Civil War as the Prologue and Epilogue to Regional and Global Wars

轉戰千里
Revolving wars for 1,000 miles.
(Incessant warfare.)

Japan, the United States, and Russia all intervened in the long Chinese civil war but none achieved their desired long-term goals. Japan sought a productive extension of its empire. The United States envisioned a unified, democratic, and capitalistic China. Russia planned for a dependent and dependable client state. Instead, Japanese military strategy produced the very outcome it was designed to prevent. By destroying the Nationalists' conventional forces while the Chinese Communists cultivated rural support behind Japanese lines, the strategy positioned the Communists to win the final chapter of the long Chinese civil war to produce a unified, Communist, and viscerally anti-Japanese China. U.S. diplomacy in the 1930s instead of deterring, accelerated Japanese expansion to transform a regional war in China into a two-front global war for the United States. Likewise, Japanese attempts to deter the United States from intervening in Asia produced U.S. intervention on an unprecedented scale. Meanwhile, U.S. aid to the Nationalists caused long-term Chinese Communist antipathy without any compensating Nationalist loyalty. In the short term, Russia alone achieved its intermediary goal to set up China in 1936 to fight Japan in 1937 so that Japan and Germany would not combine against Russia in a fatal two-front war. Brokering the Communist-Nationalist Second United Front was Stalin's greatest diplomatic achievement because it saved communism in Russia. In the long term, however, Chinese animosity toward Russia built as Chinese leaders slowly realized that Russia's China policy was designed to meet Russian not Chinese goals and that these goals, despite their shared faith in communism, often sharply diverged.

FEAR, AMBITION, DILEMMAS, NESTED WARS, AND PIVOTAL DECISIONS

Leaders in Japan, China, and Russia were all motivated by powerful ambitions and deep-seated fears, which produced intractable dilemmas. Within living memory Japanese leaders had transformed a traditional society into a great power. They were intent upon retaining Japan's place among the powers and carving out a role in international relations commensurate with its economic and political achievements at home. With the Great Depression they feared for Japan's economic well-being in a world of escalating tariffs and spreading communism among the world's unemployed. In particular, they feared Russian expansion in China and attempts to take advantage of the debilitating civil war that had broken out upon the fall of the Qing dynasty. Japanese leaders had compelling reasons to intervene in China. Capitalism was down for the count. Communism was anathema. Diplomacy was ineffective. Playing by the rules established by the Western powers promised economic disaster, while disregarding the rules risked war and isolation. Uninvited, the Imperial Japanese Army stepped in to the rescue.

The Nationalist leaders of China also nursed powerful ambitions and deep-seated fears. Chiang Kai-shek had just achieved the impossible by reunifying China through military force and astute coalition building during the Northern Expedition. His generation of Nationalist leaders dreamed of creating the modern institutions to restore China to its traditional place of greatness in all fields of human endeavor. Yet lethal dilemmas dogged their steps: Essential land and tax reforms threatened to return outraged warlords to the field of battle; the restoration of Chinese sovereignty threatened foreign interests – particularly those of Japan, which had repeatedly shown a willingness to intervene militarily; unified military command risked defections. Chiang played the careful balancer of competing factions, dividing in order to rule. Consistent policy would have been antithetical to the requirements for political survival in an environment lacking strong institutions. The Nationalists needed foreign aid, but only the Germans and the Russians were forthcoming, and the latter exacted a dangerous price: protection of the Chinese Communist Party, whose ultimate objective was the overthrow of the Nationalist Party and of the social structure of China.

To become strong enough to withstand these many threats, the Nationalists required decades of peace to create, build, and reform, but the tone-deaf Japanese orchestration of events stirred public demands in China for retaliation. Retaliation, however self-satisfying in the mind's eye, led to a war that derailed any hopes of reform. Yet unrelenting Japanese territorial expansion finally left Chiang little choice – the government was dead either way, so better to go down fighting. As he said, "It is better to fight to the death than surrender to death."[1]

The Chinese Communists also faced lethal dilemmas. They aimed high at regime change but had few resources at their disposal. At the beginning they openly worked within Nationalist civil and military organizations during the First United Front as they slowly acquired administrative and military expertise, but with the White Terror they barely survived their early education. They then applied their learning in scattered base areas, where they put their governmental skills into practice. Again they barely survived their continuing education after a succession of Nationalist annihilation campaigns culminated in the Long March. They sought protection from Nationalist predations through a Second United Front, in the hope that Nationalist attentions would turn from them to the Japanese and that, when Japan intervened, Japanese attentions would focus on the Nationalists not the Communists. The Communists required foreign aid to fight conventionally, but the powers capable of providing the aid demanded a high price: Manchuria's industrial base (for Russia) or democracy (for the United States).

Russia's leaders had also aspired to the impossible. They had reunited the tsarist empire and implemented a political, social, and economic revolution, wiping out entire social classes to become the world's first communist nation and to live the dream of Karl Marx. They envisioned world revolution and communism for all, but external events were not encouraging. Communist revolutions failed in Europe, leaving the least industrialized and therefore least likely environments for proletarian revolution. The great powers reacted viscerally to Russia's social and economic revolution, which promised to overturn their own social and economic structures as well. They united to isolate Russia diplomatically. Russia also needed peace to rebuild after a world war and a civil war but feared foreign invasion. For many years, its leaders did not believe their system could survive without sister revolutions abroad. So they sought friends where they could and found many in China, where intellectuals saw Russia's recent experience as a model to restore their own shattered land. Russian ideological expansion then threatened the great powers, particularly Japan, which paid the most careful attention to events in China.

The Western powers get underserved credit for their supposed influence over the course of modern Chinese history. They operated in highly visible treaty ports, where the Western historians of China congregated. Chinese leaders, like many politicians, often solidified their political base by heaping blame for their country's ills on an external enemy in order to deflect attention from the domestic causes for which they might bear responsibility. Blaming others obviated the need to take positive actions themselves. In the tragic story of the long Chinese civil war, China, Japan, and Russia were the main protagonists. Only at the very end did the United States play a very visible but highly ineffective role. The other Western powers played even smaller supporting roles. They simply tried to ride out the civil war, whichever way it went, and focused on the treaty ports, where they hoped to maintain commerce as usual.

China's civil war was not a simple war, but rather a complex nested war. It was a multigeneration civil war within a protracted regional war with Japan, within a multiyear global war involving all the great powers. The intervening powers each focused on their layer of the conflict, the regional war for Japan and then the global war after it attacked U.S., British, and Dutch interests across the Pacific. The United States focused exclusively on the global war and never understood why the civil war had to remain the focus for the Chinese. The Chinese knew full well that once the global war ended and the United States left, the civil war would resume full throttle, so they fought the global war always with an eye to its impact on the civil war and expected the global war to determine the outcome of the regional war. The Russians also focused on the global war and played China to their best advantage in the territorial results of that war. Unlike the Americans, the Russians also paid careful attention to both the regional and civil wars because these events took place on their borders. The outcome of all three layers of conflict had direct national security implications for Russia, whereas wide oceans insulated the Western powers.

The long Chinese civil war was a two-generation national calamity. For thirty-eight years there was no unitary state. In Max Weber's measure for effective governance, the state did not have a monopoly on the legitimate use of violence.[2] Those in command of armies used violence against whomever they pleased. Chiang had more armies owing him personal loyalty than anyone else plus a lethal secret police, which together kept him at the top of China's seething political rivalries. The command structure of the Nationalist military reflected the coalitional nature of the army and government. Warlords joined the Nationalists and defected from the Nationalists, taking their armies with them, in a yin-and-yang pattern. When Chiang's star was rising during the Northern Expedition and Nanjing decade, they joined. When they saw his star falling in Manchuria, they defected en masse.

China's problems multiplied with the outbreak of regional war when Japanese leaders could no longer tolerate the escalating chaos in their most important neighbor. The Japanese military envisioned a quick decisive victory in China that would yield stability and then prosperity in both countries. Events did not play out as anticipated. When the Nationalists refused to recognize Japanese dominance of Manchuria, the Japanese ratcheted up the military pressure and the area of military operations in order to bring China to terms. This escalated the costs for Japan and, before long, threatened military overextension. Regardless, the political survival of Japan's civil and military leaders depended on success in China, but the military strategy chosen to achieve success produced economic exhaustion instead, requiring ever greater winnings to justify the escalating costs. But greater demands and escalating cruelty made the Chinese less, not more likely to reach an accommodation.

Desperation among Japanese leaders took a suicidal turn with the decision to expand the war across the Pacific to cut U.S. and British supplies to the Nationalist government and to seize Dutch oil interests to overcome the Western oil embargo. On 7–8 December 1941, Japan expanded its list of active adversaries from one (China) to five with the addition of the United States, Britain, Australia, and New Zealand. Japanese overseas resource dependence in combination with U.S. maritime dominance spelled disaster for the Japanese empire. The United States intervened massively but influenced events primarily on the littoral, not in China. It forced the Japanese back to the home islands by cutting their sea lines of communication, so they could supply neither their expeditionary forces nor the home front. Russian influence over China, as the bordering land power, was far more significant than that of the distant maritime powers. In the final weeks of the war, Russia deployed 1.5 million men to occupy Manchuria and influence the unfolding final chapter to the long Chinese civil war.

The global war in combination with the regional war altered the outcome of the long Chinese civil war. Japan uprooted the social structure, binding people to the land in rural China. The gentry lost its hold and many fled, opening the way to Communist guerrilla forces. The Japanese gutted the Nationalists' armies and discredited Chiang's military and economic leadership, while inadvertently allowing the Communists to cultivate a mass following in North China. Together Japan and the United States removed the most effective bastions against the spread of communism in Asia: Japan gravely weakened the Nationalists in the regional war, while the United States overthrew Japan in the global war. Russian leaders took swift steps to help the Chinese Communist Party fill the political vacuum.

Foreign intervention in other people's civil war has unpredictable results. Although the Russians successfully set up the Chinese to fight Japan in World War II, the Chinese Communists subsequently ignored repeated admonitions to halt their offensive at the Yangzi River. Stalin wanted a divided China, like the reconfigured Poland, Germany, Azerbaijan, and Korea, whose division kept these neighbors weak. Mao ignored the advice and pressed on. Instead of a weak China, Russia faced a resurgent and increasingly hostile great power, whose rise portended long-term foreign-policy complications.

Japanese intervention in the Chinese civil war produced the opposite of the intended outcome. The Japanese failed to perceive the strategic consequences of their military operations. They did not adequately examine their own rationale for going to war against the United States, let alone their tragically misguided military strategy in China, which strengthened rather than weakened their foes. They then botched their diplomacy inside and outside China: They could have settled with the Nationalists to keep Manchuria de facto if not de jure. Under anything but the most extreme circumstances, the United States was not positioned to intervene aggressively in Asian affairs, let alone in Japanese domestic affairs. Japanese attacks throughout the Pacific produced the extreme circumstances. In the 1920s, Japan and the United States still shared an interest in a stable, non-Communist China. Going to war with each other had disastrous implications for the future of China, opened the way to communism, and took the lives of a generation of young men, lives that could have been more productively spent in virtually any other pursuit than in killing each other.

Japan mastered the economic aspects of economic development as demonstrated by Manchukuo, by Japan's own rapid postwar resurrection, and by the postwar economic miracles of its primary former colonies of Taiwan and Korea, but its military strategy of overextension and increasingly cruel treatment of its subject peoples and its diplomatic strategy deaf to the interests of others alienated every great power sequentially and alienated for generations those countries it had occupied. Its preferred war plan aimed to relieve Russia of Siberia; it signed a meaningless alliance with the Nazis – meaningless because it betrayed them within the year with a neutrality pact with Russia; and it attacked every available Western interest across the Pacific. In the end Japanese national strategy created a world of enemies, bereft of friends. To this day, the Japanese army, whatever its name, remains haunted by its past. The ends could not justify the means because the chosen means precluded the desired ends and were so heinous that they remain emblematic for the most baneful aspects of human nature.

Likewise, the Nationalist Party engaged in revolving abuse of its allies, first Russia then the United States, and of its domestic coalition partners, undercutting their political power and making them the cannon fodder for Nationalist ambitions. Nationalist government actions presumed incredible stupidity in others. Perhaps it could shape events in China, but not in Russia or the United States. How could Russia miss Chiang's dragnet anti-Communism in the White Terror or the United States miss his evolving plans for a U.S.-Russian nuclear Armageddon? The Japanese and then the Nationalists botched their diplomacy by betraying all the great powers in sequence, so that in the end, all were alienated not in sequence but together. Neither tried to develop win-win strategies as the basis for diplomacy; both stuck to a dead-end zero-sum approach.

Russia was able to play the game of serial betrayal much longer than Japan or China. Its Communist government signed nonaggression, mutual assistance, or neutrality pacts with its neighbors early and often: with Turkey in 1925, Germany in 1926, Belgium in 1927, Persia in 1927, Afghanistan in 1931, Finland in 1932, Latvia in 1932, Estonia in 1932, Poland in 1932, France in 1933, Italy in 1933, Lithuania in 1933, Romania in 1933, Czechoslovakia in 1935, and Mongolia in 1936. Yet by war's end, Russia had taken territory from virtually all of them and kept it at least until 1991.[3] As long as Russia was willing to deploy the Red Army to occupy its conquests, it kept them. Eastern Europeans, however, slipped the leash at the earliest possible moment – a moment long in coming – and, as insurance against future Russian army deployments in their direction, immediately lined up to join the North Atlantic Treaty Organization (NATO), the cold war era Western alliance that long contained Russia.

Prior to the attack on Pearl Harbor, U.S. attempts to influence events on the Asian mainland were also counterproductive. The debuts of U.S. deterrence through economic embargoes and Japan's through alliance with Germany and Italy both appalled rather than persuaded their intended audiences. They precipitated the expansion of the war that they were designed to forestall. Both sides calculated the costs imposed on the other without also tabulating the value the other attached to its goals. In fact, the international order was at issue, making the stakes second only to immediate national survival.[4] So escalating embargoes and diplomatic threats precipitated rather than prevented further Japanese expansion and additional Western aid to China.

The United States then wasted billions of dollars to influence the course of the long Chinese civil war. It provided the Nationalists with $781 million in post–World War II Lend-Lease supplies alone, ranging from ordnance to aircraft.[5] The Communists won anyway. As the United States had no intention of deploying large forces to China, its influence was marginal if highly annoying to both the Nationalists and the Communists. As Russian history illustrates, troops on the ground tend to influence events decisively although not necessarily in intended directions. Postwar U.S. policies in Japan, enforced by boots on the ground, succeeded beyond expectations, transforming a bitter foe into America's strongest ally in Asia.

While Western foreign policy receives undue credit for its supposed influence over Chinese history, the United States does not get the credit it deserves for the unintended contribution of its domestic economic policies to the outbreak of war in Asia. Although protectionism resounded with American voters in 1930, it helped tank the international economy and made less wealthy countries desperate. It is no coincidence that Japan invaded Manchuria the year after the United States passed the Hawley-Smoot tariff closing its markets to Japan. America leaders did not adequately consider the consequences of a piece of domestic legislation for the foreign countries most deeply affected but vainly attempted to export U.S. problems.

The United States was not alone in failing fully to apprehend the nexus between domestic economic policy and foreign policy. The Japanese prosecuted a military strategy in order to promote national security, but the strategy destroyed the economy of both China, the object of Japanese imperialism, and Japan, taking down Japanese national security in the process. Russia peddled ill-founded ideas about state planning and social revolution, highly effective to take power in a shattered state, but incapable of delivering prosperity thereafter, so that in the long run, time was not on the side of communist states.

Given Mao's successful use of the Soviet method for wresting power from within, many countries decolonized after World War II followed in his footsteps to apply a little Trotsky and a lot of Lenin to seize power and, like Mao, to employ the nonperforming Stalinist economic model thereafter. The economic model delivered poverty not prosperity, while the political model yielded dictatorship not democracy, and together the economic and political models caused the violent deaths of millions of Chinese. The Soviet model had equally pernicious effects throughout the Soviet empire and among its allies in Africa and Asia. That mess has yet to be cleaned up. Today Russia is a much reduced power, itself belatedly decolonized in 1991, and few clamor to follow in its footsteps anymore. As much as its leaders deceived others, they also deceived themselves, with tragic consequences for their country, their people, their neighbors, and their allies. The Russians did not intend this result, but their actions predisposed it. For three generations, they genuinely believed in the accuracy of the Marxist prophecy.

A failure to understand the implications of events produced a tragedy on multiple levels. Japanese military strategy destroyed the considerable progress at state building being made by the Nationalists and set the conditions for a Communist victory instead. Sixty years on, we are still dealing with the aftermath of Japanese foreign policy blunders. In addition to missing more promising opportunities, the sheer human carnage is a measure of the tragedy. The violence did not end in 1949 but continued unabated as the Chinese Communists forced a social revolution on their country, wiping out entire social classes in unrelenting political campaigns lasting until the Great Helmsman's death in 1976. The Chinese have yet to discover a graceful exit from communism, a system whose record for human carnage is unparalled.

For the last generation, military history has fallen into disfavor among professional historians. Yet in East Asia the pivotal events occurring from 1931 to 1949 were overwhelmingly military. A pivotal event changes the course of history. It constitutes a divide between what came before and what came after so that there is no going back to the status quo ante. The fall of the Qing dynasty, the Northern Expedition, the Japanese invasion of Manchuria, the escalation at the Marco Polo Bridge, the Japanese attacks on Western interests throughout the Pacific, the Nationalist decision to contest the Manchurian theater after 1945, and the Communist victory in 1949 were all pivotal events. They altered the course of Chinese history by deflecting it in new directions.

After the Qing dynasty collapsed in 1911, there was no putting Humpty Dumpty back together again. Strong central institutions became meaningless without the military power to enforce their writ, and they vanished. Two thousand years of imperial history ended with frightening swiftness. The central power, once smashed, proved incredibly difficult to reconstitute. The Qing dynasty was done; no Han Chinese were clamoring to restore it. Decades of fighting then ruined the Chinese economy, undermined its social structure, and left its people to live in a Hobbesian state of nature, where life was "poor, nasty, brutish, and short" and all lived in a state of "continual fear" and in "danger of violent death."[6]

The Nationalists repeatedly tried to form a national government in Guangzhou but failed until they built a military force with the help of Russia to impose their will. Russian military aid made possible the Northern Expedition, which transformed Chiang Kai-shek into a national leader above all others and in command of the preponderance of armies in China. Singleton warlords found survival alone increasingly perilous, and over time, non-Communist warlords found nowhere to go but into the Nationalist fold. The Northern Expedition and the Great War of the Central Plains, in combination with the Japanese intervention in Manchuria, solidified the Nationalist coalition around an anti-Japanese platform and strengthened Chiang as the supreme leader. All remaining warlords had regional followings at best.

In 1936 when the Communists and Nationalists decided to form a Second United Front to go to war against Japan and the Japanese decided to accept the challenge in 1937, again there was no going back. The costs of the war were so high that neither side could reach an accommodation with the other. What was barely enough for one was politically untenable for the other. By the end of the desperate struggle against Japan, the Chinese civil war had narrowed into a bilateral Communist-Nationalist fight to the finish. There were no other well-armed independent military forces left. Chiang had militarily neutralized his warlord opposition in large measure by deploying them to the front to have Japanese forces eliminate them.

Japan's desperate Pearl Harbor–and-beyond strategy passed through another point of no return, and Chiang Kai-shek's decision to contest the Manchurian theater passed yet another. Had he ceded Manchuria without a fight in 1945, blaming his withdrawal on the Russian occupation, his armies could never have been surrounded and annihilated in any other theater because no other theater was surrounded by the Soviet empire on three sides, and in every other theater, the Communists were weaker than the Nationalists. Chiang would have retained both South and Central China at least as far north as the Yellow River and probably all the way to the Great Wall. Finally, the Communist victory and the upending of land tenure and social status throughout China produced another point of no return. By the time Mao had finished his many political campaigns, whole social groups were dead. Again, there was no going back.

Thus, the fall of the Qing dynasty, the Northern Expedition, the Second United Front, the outbreak of the war of the Pacific, the decision to contest Manchuria, and the Communist victory in the Chinese civil war were all pivotal events altering the course of Asian history.

Pivotal events often occur in pairs because events usually occur not by the decision of one side but in combination with the reaction of the other. Western protectionism in combination with strident Japanese nationalism precipitated the Japanese invasion of Manchuria. Russian brokering of the Second United Front at Xi'an in combination with the Japanese knee-jerk reaction to the Nationalists' alliance with the Communists produced the lethal escalation of the Second Sino-Japanese

War in 1937. The Japanese decision to expand the war throughout the Pacific and the visceral U.S. reaction to the attack on Pearl Harbor produced the march on Japan. The combined decisions of the Nationalists and Communists to focus on the Manchurian theater shaped the outcome of the Chinese civil war. The Guangxi group's desire to defend at the Yangzi was insufficient without Chiang's support, so no pivotal event emerged. Major miscalculations on both sides yield catastrophe. It takes two bad drivers or one stupendously reckless driver to produce a collision. Asia in the mid-twentieth century had both.

Yet history remains highly contingent. Play the game of takeaway. Remove any of the following factors and the outcome of the Chinese civil war changes: Japan's invasion of Manchuria, its reliance on brutality and military operations to achieve its political goals in China, its unwillingness to offer generous peace terms, Russia's military aid to the Communists, its repairs of the Manchurian railway system, the decision to contest Manchuria by both sides, the Nationalist failure to follow General Du Yumin's strategy to attack south from Manchuria to avoid entrapment, the Communist spy system supplying advance notice of Chiang's campaign plans, Mao's escape prior to the fall of Yan'an, and so on. Together these factors delivered a Communist victory with Mao as the kingpin. Take away any one factor, let alone several, and the outcome would not necessarily have been a Nationalist victory, but perhaps a fractured Qing empire or a divided China or a greater role for the Guangxi group or a Nationalist China without Chiang Kai-shek. If the Nationalists had won the long Chinese civil war, it is unlikely that the wars in Korea and Vietnam would have turned out as they did, since the North Korean and North Vietnamese war efforts depended on the supply lines from a Communist China. This does not mean that there would have been a happy ending for either Korea or Vietnam, just a different one.

THE REST OF THE STORY

Individuals made the decisions leading to these pivotal events. We often make heroes of wartime leaders – or at least of the leaders on the winning side. Those who lead in peacetime and perhaps deftly dodge war receive no credit, while those who fall into deep holes receive accolades for the heroic climb out, instead of assuming culpability for the fall.

The cast of characters in China's long civil war seems to be largely a rogue's gallery of artless diplomats, myopic political leaders, narrow-minded officers, and mass murderers. Yet the rogues in many ways were remarkably unremarkable people, caught in the floodtide of national ambitions and fears well beyond their powers of creation or resolution. Rather ordinary people made decisions with extraordinary implications, which they generally did not perceive at the time. Regardless, the pivotal decision, once made, irrevocably set the tide of events on a new course.

In Japan, on 24 November 1940, ninety-one-year-old Saionji Kinmochi, the last surviving *genrō* of the brilliant Meiji generation of leaders, from his deathbed asked his secretary, Harada Kumao, "Things are in a terrible state. I pity [Prime Minister] Konoe. I don't want to make a big issue of it, but what exactly is his political objective? How does he intend to resolve the China Incident? And does he really think Japan's foreign policy can go on like this? Ask Konoe these three things for me." Saionji died too soon to receive an answer. Characteristically for his generation, he asked about the political objective and the strategy to reach it, not about the operational level of warfare that consumed the next generation of leaders, who brought disaster to Japan.[7] It turns out that Prime Minister Konoe Fumimaro did not have an answer to Japan's narrowing options and was out of office within a year. In 1945 this descendant of one of the five great clans that had provided imperial consorts for centuries poisoned himself on the eve of being taken into custody, rather than suffer the indignity of death by hanging as a war criminal. When Japan had celebrated the success at Pearl Harbor back on 8 December 1941 he had said: "It is a terrible thing that has happened. I know that a tragic defeat awaits us at the end. I can feel it. Our luck will not last more than two or three months at best." He died four years later at age fifty-four. His eldest son died in a Russian prisoner of war camp.[8]

The former foreign and prime minister Hirota Kōki, who had insisted on punitive peace terms for China from the start, overseen Japan's accession to the Anti-Comintern Pact, and then in 1945 tried to turn on a dime to negotiate a separate peace with Russia was the only civilian hanged as a class-A war criminal in 1948. He was seventy. His wife had already committed suicide in 1946. The former foreign minister Shidehara Kijūrō played a wiser game by retiring from high political position soon after the Japanese invasion of Manchuria in 1931. He served as prime minister during the postwar U.S. occupation and died in 1951 at age seventy-nine.[9]

Baron and Lieutenant General Honjō Shigeru and Lieutenant General Ishiwara Kanji, the architects of Japan's invasion of Manchuria, did not adequately consider China's or the Western powers' likely response. Perhaps, Japan could have weathered Chinese resistance or Western reprisals, but not both in a precarious economy. General Honjō resigned from the military in 1936 after his son-in-law became implicated in the famous officers' uprising that year.[10] Not long after Honjō had ritually disemboweled himself rather than suffer prosecution as a class-A war criminal in 1945, the first hot wars of the cold war erupted in Asia. Russian and Chinese involvement in the Korean and Vietnam Wars made these conflicts intractable. Back in 1932, General Honjō had warned the Lytton Commission of the dire threat posed by communist expansion. Had he lived until the cold war, he undoubtedly would have said, "I told you so."

General Ishiwara left behind a string of quotations documenting his thinking concerning Japan's escalating war in Asia. When his emulators expanded the war in 1937 to encompass coastal China, he believed the area too large for Japan to digest: "Those who excite the public by claims of victory, just because the army has captured some out-of-the-way little area, do so only to conceal their own incompetence as they squander the nation's power in an unjustifiable war." After Japan escalated the war in 1941 to encompass the Pacific, he accurately predicted, "Inevitably we will lose this war. It will be a struggle in which Japan, even though it has only a thousand yen in its pocket, plans to spend ten thousand, while the United Sates has a hundred thousand yen, but only needs to spend ten thousand.... We simply cannot last.... Japan started this war without considering its resources beforehand."[11] He had wished to stop with Manchuria.[12]

At the post–World War II International Military Tribunal, Ishiwara told off an Allied prosecutor:[13]

> Haven't you ever heard of Perry [the American commodore, who forcibly opened Japan to international trade in 1854]? Don't you know anything about our country's history?... Tokugawa Japan believed in isolation; it didn't want to have anything to do with other countries, and had its doors locked tightly. Then along came Perry from your country in his black ships to open

> those doors; he aimed his big guns at Japan and warned "If you don't deal with us, look out for these; open your doors, and negotiate with other countries too." And then when Japan did open its doors and tried dealing with other countries, it learned that all those countries were a fearfully aggressive lot. And so for its own defense it took your own country as its teacher and set about learning how to be aggressive. You might say we became your disciples. Why don't you subpoena Perry from the other world and try *him* as a war criminal?

Ishiwara escaped imprisonment but was diagnosed with bladder cancer in 1946 and died in 1949 at age sixty.[14]

In 1946, the mastermind of the strategy of alliance with Germany, the former foreign minister Matsuoko Yōsuke, became clinically insane – some might argue that his insanity had developed much earlier. In his few appearances at the war crimes tribunal, he made incoherent remarks before dying in a hospital in 1946 at age sixty-six.[15] Like Britain's Prime Minister Neville Chamberlain, he lived to understand the ruinous consequences of his diplomacy and died shortly after this realization. Chamberlain passed away within two years of his Munich agreement and just months after the fall of France, when the Nazi armies' sweep through Europe made clear to all that his strategy of appeasement had left his country in dire straits.

Admiral Yamamoto Isoroku, the author of the Pearl Harbor war plan, had died years before at age fifty-nine. Until his death, he had remained steeped in the samurai tradition of avenging of perceived wrongs, loyal service to the emperor, and self-sacrifice. He penned a poem, "Mikado's shield I always strive to be, / Never caring for my fame or life."[16] In the end, he did not shield the emperor but became famous in death when American gunners got their man, strafing his plane over the Solomons sixteen months after Pearl Harbor. The Japanese still did not draw the conclusion that the ability of the United States to hit such a specific and high-value target meant that someone had broken their code. They looked into the matter but concluded that as they had changed the code key register on 1 April 1943, and as Admiral Yamamoto had died on 18 April, the Allies could not have decrypted the messages so rapidly.[17] Wrong. Even in death, Yamamoto failed to save his beloved country.

Around that time, in a speech delivered to the graduating class at Tokyo Imperial University, General Tōjō Hideki, whose service as prime minister included the decision to attack Pearl Harbor, opined that many considered mediocre at graduation through perseverance could go on to become great leaders. "One good example is this man you see before you.... When I was younger I was mediocre among the mediocre, but," and he ended on a proud and pregnant pause.[18] By the fall of his cabinet in July 1944, he might have concluded that the early assessment of his mediocrity turned out to be a gross exaggeration of his abilities. In addition to promoting the ruin of his country, he even bungled his own suicide attempt with a loaded pistol. Apart from his failure to kill a stationary target at point-blank range, his contemporaries were disgusted by this army officer's unwillingness to commit a samurai's ritual suicide, which requires swords not guns. On 22 December 1948 the war crimes tribunal hangman succeeded where Tōjō had failed. He was sixty-four.[19]

Emperor Hirohito dodged the hangman because he proved useful to the U.S. occupation force. He signed virtually any paper put before him in return for the survival of the imperial line. His failure to resign and take symbolic responsibility for the war saddled future generations of Japanese with a baneful legacy. Apparently he offered to take personal responsibility, but MacArthur declined to accept. Although he did not fall on his sword, many Japanese fell on theirs for him – a very unprepossessing man, whose most intense interest concerned his fish specimens. Emperor Hirohito embodied the reasons why so many countries have dispensed with royalty. He died at age eighty-eight in 1989 just as the Japanese economic bubble burst.[20]

Many of Emperor Hirohito's samurai remained devoted to him to the very end. Admiral Yonai Mitsumasa fell on his sword to serve as navy minister from July 1944 to October 1945. He had opposed the army's expansion into Southeast Asia as well as the Axis alliance and supported accepting the Potsdam Declaration for unconditional surrender. He gave evidence at the war crimes tribunals but was not indicted. His peers considered him one of Japan's three greatest admirals. He died of pneumonia in 1948 at age sixty-eight.[21]

On 15 August, the day of Japan's surrender, Minister of War Anami Korechika committed ritual suicide, having bowed to Emperor Hirohito's wishes to bear the unbearable. He was fifty-eight. That same day, General Sugiyama Gen, who had served as war minister at the time of 1937 escalation, committed suicide with his wife. He was sixty-five.[22] General Tanaka Shizuichi, a graduate in English literature of Oxford

University, who had stopped the eleventh-hour coup attempt just days before, shot himself to death on 24 August 1945. He was fifty-eight.[23]

Admiral Toyoda Soemu, navy chief of staff, refused to show up on USS *Missouri* to sign the surrender documents, ordering to go in his stead his operations officer, Baron and Rear Admiral Tomioka Sadatoshi, who had opposed the operations for both Pearl Harbor and Midway, saying, "You lost the war ... so you go." The war crimes tribunal acquitted Toyoda and he died of a heart attack in 1957 at age seventy-two. High points of his career included the Battle of the Philippine Sea, known to U.S. pilots as the Great Marianas Turkey Shoot of June 1944 in reference to the ease of shooting down green Japanese pilots, and the Battle of Leyte Gulf in October 1944, where most of the Imperial Japanese Navy went to the bottom. He finished his days in active service ordering suicide missions when he lacked the assets to do otherwise.[24]

Likewise, the career of Admiral Nagumo Chūichi, the operational commander for the attack on Pearl Harbor, went rapidly downhill. After he served as operational commander at the disastrous Battle of Midway, his life took a turn for the catastrophic as commander of the Central Pacific Area Fleet headquartered in Saipan, where he remained until the United States invaded. By that time the Japanese fleet was mostly under water and Nagumo, his chief of staff, and two generals had their aides shoot them to death in caves at sunrise on 8 July 1944, the day after the seventh anniversary of the Marco Polo Bridge escalation. He was fifty-seven.[25]

General Doihara Kenji, known as Lawrence of Manchuria in the Western press, and General Matsui Iwane, known less flatteringly as the Butcher of Nanjing, both received death sentences from the war crimes tribunal and were hanged at Sugamo prison in 1948. Doihara was sixty-five and Matsui was seventy. General Minami Jirō, who had served as war minister at the time of the invasion of Manchuria and subsequently the commander in chief of the Kantō Army, was sentenced to life imprisonment but was released for ill health and died in 1955 at age eighty-one.[26] The army chief of staff, Umezu Yoshijirō, whose armies had run roughshod through North China in the early 1930s, signed the surrender documents on USS *Missouri*. The war crimes tribunal sentenced him in 1947 to prison, where he converted to Christianity and died of cancer in 1949 at age sixty-seven.[27] General Tada Hayao, the commander of Japanese forces in China in the mid-1930s, was also arrested as a war criminal but died in prison in 1948 at age sixty-six just before his scheduled release. Lieutenant General Hata Hikosaburō, the Kantō Army chief of staff, had the misfortune of surrendering to the Russians, who kept him as a prisoner of war from 1945 to 1956. He died in 1959 at age sixty-nine. The garrulous ambassador and lieutenant general Ōshima Hiroshi, whose many and detailed communications from Berlin proved so useful to the Allies, received a life sentence but was released in 1955 and died in 1975 at age eighty-nine.[28] Similarly long-lived, Admiral, Baron, and Prime Minister Suzuki Kantarō, who had requested Emperor Hirohito's tie-breaking vote essential to war termination in August 1945, died in 1948 at age eighty-one.[29] His fellow officer, Admiral Hasegawa Kiyoshi, who expanded the war up and down the Chinese coast in 1937, helped establish Japan's postwar Maritime Self-Defense Force and died in 1970 at age eighty-seven.

Defection to the Nationalists proved a better course of action than trial by the Allies. General Okamura Yasuji's Three Alls Campaign, which had decimated the Communists, earned him the lasting friendship of Chiang Kai-shek. Okamura served as Chiang's military adviser during the final chapter of the long Chinese civil war. Chiang gave him a pass on war crimes, saving him from class A war criminal status and perhaps a trip to the gallows. After the loss of his third war – the Second Sino-Japanese War, World War II Pacific, and the long Chinese civil war – Okamura returned home, where he helped establish the Japanese Self-Defense Forces. He died in 1966 at age eighty-two.[30]

Chiang Kai-shek, the mastermind of the Northern Expedition, ended his days at the head of a police state in Taiwan, bankrolled by U.S. aid. The United States resumed the aid, not because he was an astute diplomat, but because the outbreak of the Korean War made the island of Taiwan useful to contain China. Indeed, Chiang became the primary beneficiary of the Korean War. Without joining the fight, his country was placed under the U.S. nuclear umbrella. To his credit, he and his generation of leaders spent the U.S. money well, positioning Taiwan for economic takeoff under his son. Chiang senior died at age eighty-eight in 1975, the year before his nemesis, Mao Zedong. His son, appropriately named Chiang "Ching-kuo," or "manage the country," took over the family business and, in response to intense public pressure, set Taiwan on the path to democracy. Chiang junior's legitimate sons all died within a few years of his own death, ending the short-lived Chiang dynasty. Meanwhile, Madame Chiang (Soong Mayling) left Taiwan after the Generalissimo's death for the Upper East Side of New York City, where she died in 2003 at the ripe old age of 105.[31] Her sister, the widow of Sun Yat-sen, preceded her, dying in 1981 at age 88 on the opposite side of the Taiwan Strait.

From the Xi'an Incident onward, Zhang Xueliang remained a ward of the Chiang family and under house arrest in Taipei until 1988, the year Chiang Ching-kuo died. Zhang spent his final years in exile, dying in Hawaii in 2001 at an even 100.[32] His coconspirator at Xi'an, Yang Hucheng, was not so lucky. He and his immediate family were all imprisoned and eventually shot in 1949 as the Nationalists fled to Taiwan. Yang was sixty-six. Yan Xishan, whose rule in Shanxi began in 1912, by 1949 could hold out no longer and fled to Taiwan, where he held a variety of high political positions until his death at age seventy-seven in 1960.[33] Sheng Shicai, the Xinjiang warlord, who had vacillated between Soviet and Nationalist loyalities before being removed by Chiang, served in various sinecures before retiring to Taiwan, where he died in 1970 at age seventy-five.[34]

The leaders of the Guangxi group wound up on opposite sides of the Taiwan Strait. In December 1949, General Li Zongren fled to the United States with his family. He returned to China in 1965, where he died in 1969 at age seventy-nine.[35] Meanwhile General Bai Chongxi died of a heart attack in Taiwan in 1966 as age seventy-four. General Tang Enbo, the man who had refused to cooperate with their defense at the Yangzi, fled to Taiwan in 1949 via Jinmen, known in the West as Quemoy, which he successfully defended against the Communists. He had numerous Japanese friends, in part for his kindness shown to surrendering Japanese soldiers and civilians, and he died at age fifty-five in a Tokyo hospital in 1954.[36]

General Song Zheyuan, whose 29th Army had kicked off the 1937 escalation at the Marco Polo Bridge, died at age fifty-five of declining health just two years after he lost his army covering the Nationalist retreat after the Battle of Taierzhuang.[37] Someone may have taken care of Dai Li, Chiang's hated secret police chief, who died in a plane crash in 1946 at age forty-nine. One of the Chen brothers of the CC Group, Chen Lifu, lived out his life in Taiwan, where he tried chicken farming (unsuccessfully), and New Jersey, where he retired. He died in in 2001 at age 101. The other brother, Chen Guofu, died after a long fight with tuberculosis in Taipei at age fifty-nine in 1951.[38]

Included among those who fled to Taiwan were Chiang Kai-shek's war minister, He Yingqin, and his second in command in the party and government, Chen Cheng. He Yingqin ended on a high note, becoming active in the World Moral Rearmament movement, and died in 1987 at age ninety-seven. The favored, Chen Cheng, who had led the Fourth and Fifth Encirclement Campaigns as well as the disastrous defense against the Communist Winter Offensive of 1947–8 resulting in the complete annihilation of his troops, oversaw highly successful land reform in Taiwan that became the model for other countries. Less successfully, he headed the Planning Committee for the Recovery of the Mainland. He died of liver cancer in 1965 at age 68. General Xue Yue, who blew the Yellow River dikes in 1938, killing nearly a million, retired to Taiwan as its senior Guangzhou general. He died in 1998 at age 102.[39]

General Du Yuming, whose plan to avoid entrapment in Manchuria was ignored, was not so lucky. The Communists captured him during the Huai-Hai Campaign, where he had been leading the Nationalist rearguard out of Xuzhou. His attempt to flee disguised as a common soldier failed, and he was imprisoned for a decade. He became one of thirty-three former Nationalist leaders pardoned by Mao for good behavior in December 1959. He died in 1981 at age seventy-eight.[40]

Heads of puppet governments fared even less well. The leader of the main puppet government in China, Wang Jingwei, did not survive the war but died at age sixty-one in a Japanese hospital on 10 October 1944 at the height of the Ichigō Campaign on the thirty-third anniversary of the 1911 Revolution. He is considered a traitor in both China and Taiwan. Chiang detested Wang enough to blow up his tomb.[41] Neither Wang Kemin nor Liang Hongzhi, whose separate puppet governments were amalgamated under Wang Jingwei's super puppet government in 1940, survived the war. The Nationalists arrested Wang Kemin in 1945 and he died at age seventy-two in a Beijing prison on 26 December 1945. After Liang's retirement as head of state, he spent the balance of the war collecting rare art from people desperate to raise funds, acquiring numerous Song dynasty paintings. The Nationalists captured him in 1945 and executed him the following year. He was sixty-three.[42] The invading Russian army captured Puyi and incarcerated him for five years in Khabarovsk before returning him to China for nine years of thought-reform prison. Upon his release, Mao forced upon him a Han Chinese bride (his fifth wife), officially killing the imperial line by sullying Manchu bloodlines. The last emperor finished his days as a gardener in the botanical gardens of the capital he once ruled and working on his autobiography. In 1967 he died at age sixty-one at the beginning of the Cultural Revolution, allegedly tortured to death by Red Guards.[43]

Defectors to the Communist side did better, at least initially. Mao awarded the Liberation Medal to Fu Zuoyi, the Nationalist general who had turned over Beijing to the Communists. He spent the rest of his working years as the minister of water conservancy and electric power and died at age seventy-nine in 1974.[44] Zhang Zhizhong, the general who torched Changsha, represented the Nationalists in negotiations with the Communists until 1949, when in the final round he defected. He subsequently helped the Communists subdue Xinjiang, where he had served as governor from 1946 to 1947. He died in 1969 at age seventy-eight. Posthumously, he has been accused of being a long-term Communist spy instrumental in pushing Chiang to open hostilities against Japan in Shanghai in 1937.[45]

Of the Seven Gentlemen against Japan of the National Salvation Association arrested by Chiang in 1936, the lawyers Shen Junru, Sha Qianli, and Shi Liang (the only woman among the "gentlemen") went on to hold high administrative positions in the People's Republic of China; the banker Zhang Naiqi and the political scientist Wang Zaoshi became victims of the Anti-Rightist Campaign of 1957 and 1958; the journalist Zou Taofen became a Communist sympathizer but died of cancer in 1944; and the educator Li Gongpu was assassinated in 1946 in Kunming, while his more famous colleague in the Democratic League, the acclaimed poet Wen Yiduo, was assassinated on the way back from Li's funeral. Both assassinations were attributed to the Nationalists.[46]

Mao Zedong built the most amazing resume of all. The junior librarian of Beijing University rose to the emperor of China and, with Stalin's death, the senior leader of the international Communist movement. In the 1970s, he congratulated the visiting Japanese prime minister Tanaka Kakuei for Japan's decisive contribution to the Communist victory in China.[47] In the United States, Mao's achievements dazzled a generation of Sinologists until the live coverage of the 1989 massacre at Tiananmen Square by his successors put a damper on his legacy by giving a human face to the anonymous millions who had died violent deaths under his stewardship. The collapse of the Soviet Union and revelations concerning the low standard of living produced by communism then put the lie to communism as the antidote to capitalism, so that Mao's whole enterprise and the many sacrifices endured by the Chinese people suddenly seemed extravagantly costly in human lives.

Senior cadres and generals did not often fare as well as the Great Helmsman, who lived to the ripe old age of eighty-three, although he was virtually blind and could hardly express himself at the end.[48] Peng Zhen, who had prepared the political ground for the Manchurian Campaign, became the first Politburo-level victim of the Cultural Revolution. He was lucky in that he survived to be rehabilitated after Mao's death and died in 1997 at age ninety-eight.[49] Liu Shaoqi and Marshal Peng Dehuai were not so fortunate. Both came to grief as a result of their criticism of the Great Leap Forward of 1958, which caused the nationwide famine from 1959 to 1961 that killed more than 30 million Chinese. In 1969 Liu was tortured to death at age sixty-nine for the temerity to replace Mao as chairman of the republic and start undoing the damage of the Great Famine. In 1974 Marshal Peng, who led Chinese troops to victory in the Korean War, preserving the North Korean government against the wishes of a coalition of all the Western great powers, was tortured to death at age seventy-six. Marshal Lin Biao, who led Communist forces to victory in the decisive Manchurian Campaign, became Mao's designated successor during the Cultural Revolution but, after a falling out, died at age sixty-four allegedly in a plane crash fleeing to Mongolia in 1971. Zhou Enlai remained China's quasi–foreign minister and economic rationalist until his death at age seventy-eight of cancer in 1976. Marshal Zhu De, who with Mao had served, respectively, as the military and political commissars in the Jiangxi Soviet, wisely retired in the early 1960s and died at age ninety, six months after Zhou Enlai and two months before Mao Zedong.[50] In 1992, Nie Rongzhen, the last survivor of the ten marshals of the People's Republic of China, died at age ninety-three.[51] Some spies were equally long-lived. The lieutenant generals Liu Fei and Guo Rugui, who kept the Communists well informed of Chiang's plans, died, respectively, in 1983 at age eighty-five and in 1997 at age ninety.

Lev Mikhailovich Karakhan, whose manifesto so enchanted Chinese intellectuals, died during Stalin's purges in 1937 at age forty-eight after a show trial for being on the wrong side of the Stalin-Trotsky divide. Shortly before his arrest and death, he married the prima ballerina of the Bolshoi Ballet, a woman twenty years his junior, who apparently had a stronger grasp of ballet than politics. Many of Russia's original China hands suffered similar fates minus the ballerina. Adolf Joffe, who had signed the pact with Sun Yat-sen providing the original Russian aid establishing the Whampoa Military Academy and making the Northern Expedition possible, committed suicide at age forty-four in 1927 before the secret police came for him. Joffe knew his number was up when his mentor, Lev Trotsky, lost to Stalin. Dmitrii Vasil'evich Bogomolov, who served as ambassador to China from 1933 to 1937, was recalled to Moscow that year, arrested, tried, and shot at age forty-seven. Ambassador Nikolai V. Roshchin made the critical benchmark of outliving Stalin. He remained in China until 1952 and thereafter served in the Foreign Ministry and the Defense Ministry, dying in 1960 at age fifty-nine.[52] Petr Parfenovich Vladimirov left Yan'an in late 1945, served as the general consul for Shanghai from 1948 to 1951, and was slated for a diplomatic post in Burma but died in 1953 at age forty-eight. Railway engineering seems to have been a far safer profession. Ivan Vladimirovich Kovalev, the man who restored Manchuria's railways, lived until 1993, when he died at age ninety-two.

Marshal of the Soviet Union Georgii K. Zhukov, the hero of Nomonhan, went on to defend Moscow in 1941, turn the German advance at Stalingrad in 1942, relieve Leningrad (St. Petersburg) in 1943, continue the advance toward Germany (1943–4), and receive Germany's surrender in Berlin in 1945.[53] He somehow escaped Stalin's dragnet, dying at age seventy-eight in 1974. Initially, Stalin ignored the lessons of Nomonhan concerning the efficacy of mechanized warfare and the utility of tanks. Instead he immediately disbanded his mechanized units on the basis of flawed lessons drawn from the Spanish Civil War, where these units had failed to prevent a fascist victory. In the fall of 1941, immediately after the German invasion of Russia in June, Stalin executed Colonel General Grigorii Mikhailovich Shtern, the commander of the Soviet Far East at the time of Nomonhan, and Lieutenant General Iakov Vladimirovich Smushkevich, who had been promoted to the head of the Russian Air Force on the basis of his achievements.[54] Presumably their personal experiences at Nomonhan made clear that Stalin's military decisions thereafter for a static forward defense on a broad front had greatly facilitated the rapid German advance through Russia.[55]

Joseph Stalin kept relations with China in order until his death in 1953. As in the Second Sino-Japanese War, he ensured that Chinese, not Russian soldiers fought in the Korean War. This time around, Chinese leaders began to discern a pattern but could do little for many years until China developed the atomic bomb in 1964 and the thermonuclear bomb in 1967. In quick succession Mao then threatened war against Russia on the Amur River in 1969 and played the America card in 1971. He began the process of restoring Sino-U.S. relations in order to bring down the Soviet Union by forcing an economically unsustainable militarization on Soviet borders in East and West. Mao's foreign policy had come full circle, back to cultivating ties with the United States as he had in the early 1940s, when Russia was incapable of providing aid.

Stalin spent his final hours sprawled out on the floor of his bedroom because no one dared or desired to force open the locked door when he did not turn up at the usual time. No one hurried to call a doctor when they found him conscious but unable to speak. He died three days after the initial stroke from the slow and tortured asphyxiation it caused at age seventy-four.[56] Four years later, his successors began the process of de-Stalinization and publicized some of his worst atrocities against Russians.

Those Americans who had made life difficult for Chiang Kai-shek did not do well. In 1942, the recently defeated Republican candidate for president, Wendell Willkie, is alleged to have had an affair with Madame Chiang. The Generalissimo apparently found out. The Generalissimo and the Madame allegedly had high hopes for Willkie in the 1944 elections, but he failed to win the Republican nomination and suddenly died in October, allegedly of heart failure at the unripe age of fifty-two. If he had been a Chinese politician, there would have been one explanation for his demise – retribution by Chiang. Under enormous pressure from Chiang, President Roosevelt recalled General Joseph W. Stilwell on 19 October 1944. Stilwell died at age sixty-three almost two years later to the day on 12 October 1946 of stomach cancer that had spread to his liver.[57]

Roosevelt's wartime aide to Chiang Kai-shek, Owen Lattimore, and John S. Service of the State Department, along with virtually all of the department's other primary China hands, came to grief during the McCarthy era witch hunts for communists. They were fired from their jobs and deprived of their pensions, despite numerous investigations proving they were not communists, but exonerated in court cases much later, Lattimore in 1955 and Service in 1956. In the meantime, they were blamed for America's "loss" of China, the version of events pushed by Chiang Kai-shek and the ten lobbying firms he employed in Washington, despite the dubiousness of the concept. China had never been America's to lose.[58] The lobbying firms trumped the State Department's attempt at damage limitation, its so-called White Paper issued on 7 August 1949.[59] The witch hunters, instead of examining the document trail produced by the U.S. government, bought the story peddled by the dictator who actually did lose China, Chiang Kai-shek, who, if nothing else, knew how to destroy his personal enemies. It turns out that Russia was not alone in persecuting its China hands. Even General George C. Marshall, the protector of Stilwell, came under attack from the notorious Republican senator from Wisconsin Joseph R. McCarthy, who was not censured by the Senate until 1954 for his ruinous slander of others. By then the damage was done. The purge of the Asianists positioned the United States poorly to understand the nature of the wars that soon consumed its energies in Korea and Vietnam. Three years after his censure, McCarthy died at age forty-nine of severe alcoholism that had rotted his liver.[60] Service and Lattimore long survived him, the former living to ninety and the latter to eighty-nine.

Edgar Snow, the journalist who made Mao Zedong and the "Yan'an way" famous in the English-speaking world, also became an entry on McCarthy's black list. He emigrated to Switzerland. Mao invited him back to China in 1960, 1964–5, and, most importantly, 1970 to carry an invitation to the former witch hunter President Richard Nixon to visit China. Snow had planned to cover Nixon's visit for *Life* magazine but fell ill. Mao, who had also planned to have Snow cover the visit, sent doctors. Snow died of pancreatic cancer at age sixty-seven in 1972, the week Nixon arrived in China, and his ashes were divided between his two homes, the one on the Hudson River and the other at Beijing University.[61]

Major General Patrick J. Hurley greatly contributed to setting the conditions for the purge of the China hands with his parting shots in late 1945 over his own failed mission in China. He ended his long career in three unsuccessful campaigns to represent New Mexico as senator in 1946, 1948, and 1952. He died in 1963 at age eighty.[62] General Douglas MacArthur also made a bid for public office after his dismissal in 1951 in the middle of the Korean War for attempting to usurp the constitutional power of the president as commander in chief. He tried to solve the problem by becoming the commander in chief but failed to win presidential nomination in 1952 and died in 1964 at age eighty-four.[63] Admiral of the Fleet Chester W. Nimitz much more modestly refused to write his own autobiography and died at age eighty-one in 1966.[64] Lieutenant General Claire L. Chennault, after his own removal, founded an air cargo service company to supply the Nationalists in the unfolding final phase of the civil war. He retired in 1955 and died of cancer in 1958 at age sixty-eight. General Albert Wedemeyer, another ardent anticommunist with no sympathy for the State Department China hands, retained a great faith in America's capacity to fix all ills. He blamed the defeat of the Nationalists on the U.S. arms embargo against Chiang and inadequate U.S. military support. He died in 1989 at age ninety-two.[65]

Lieutenant Colonel James H. Doolittle, who commanded the first U.S. bombing run over the Japanese home islands in 1942, by the end of the war rose to the rank of lieutenant general, the highest rank of any reserve officer, before resuming work at Shell Oil. He died in 1993 at age ninety-seven. Cordell Hull, America's longest-serving secretary of state, whose note had so incensed the Japanese, won the 1945 Nobel Prize in peace for his work establishing the United Nations. He died in 1955 at age eighty-four. And last, but certainly not least, General George C. Marshall received the Nobel Prize in peace in 1953, becoming the only general to do so. His name lives on in the Marshall Plan, which helped restore Western European economies to prosperity and ranks among America's greatest foreign policy successes. He died in 1959 at age seventy-nine.[66] These are some of the cast of characters, who helped shape the pivotal events of their time.

The conventional tale would omit many of these colorful personalities to leave us with one infamous day at Pearl Harbor to explain to Americans the outbreak of World War II in a grand monocausal monologue and wrap up the single-stranded story in 1945 without looking into the implications. In fact, the outbreak of what Americans call World War II reflected a complicated interaction among three revanchist powers, the status quo powers, and a failed state. The leaders of the revanchist powers, all in their own separate ways, intended to take down the prevailing global order and cared not a whit for any human life that stood in their way. The status quo powers jumped in to save the status quo on which their economic health and survival depended only at the eleventh hour, when the threat of imminent attack left them no choice. A very large failed state, with no one at the helm, became the battlefield for many intervening powers in frustrated attempts to control events well beyond their capacity to shape in desired directions.

The revanchist powers were Russia, Germany, and Japan. The United States dealt with them sequentially; it allied with Russia and the British Commonwealth to defeat the other two. But this strategy left a long cold war against Russia. In the 1930s, the status quo powers – Britain, France, and the United States – ignored Germany's remilitarization and Japan's anticommunist litany until German and Japanese pivotal choices posed lethal threats and a generation of young men and the civilians caught on the battlefield suffered the consequences. Before these military events spiraled out of control, the Western powers failed to deal adequately with the Great Depression, which created hothouse conditions for revanchist powers and extremists. It turns out that we live in an interconnected world, in which our economic problems cannot be wished away for others to bear the costs – the rationale for the protectionism that gripped the West in the 1930s.

Those who formulated foreign policy exclusively on the basis of domestic concerns without reference to the vital interests of the affected foreign states conjured forces beyond the control of any power. They thought they were cultivating home turf but reaped the whirlwind. Using China as a domestic political football was a risky game, played at various times in Japan, Russia, and the United States. Japan never ever should have plunged so deeply into China. Contrary to Japanese perceptions, Manchuria was not Japan's lifeline, but the quicksand that swallowed a nation. However useful Stalin found China as a piece to be played against Trotsky and others, as well as to insulate himself from wars against Japan and in Korea, the Chinese eventually figured out that they had been played, leaving Russia with a very angry neighbor and soon-to-be rising power on its least defensible frontier. The Democratic-Republican spitting contest of the 1940s and 1950s produced a witch hunt antithetical to the American ideals of life, liberty, and the pursuit of happiness. Those who did the spitting remain among the most despised politicians in American history – in particular, one Joseph R. McCarthy, whose smear tactics mimicked those of the Soviet Union, which he so reviled.

Chinese politicians played political football with Japan at even greater cost. In the 1920s and 1930s, they expressed outrage at Japan's infrastructure investments, which their country desperately needed to develop a functioning economy. They singled out Japan among the colonial powers for special scorn. The price tag was a regional war. Decades later, the Chinese have yet to make a full psychological recovery from that war and continue to craft their Japan policy with an eye to shifting domestic anger at the Chinese Communist Party to Japanese atrocities of three generations ago. As it turns out, foreign policy is serious business. Those who play it with an overly domestic focus without considering the likely countermeasures by others do so at their own and their people's peril.

Three nested wars decisively shaped what China became. The most fundamental war of the three was the civil war, which was a Chinese show. Without the civil war there would have been no Second Sino-Japanese War. Without the Second Sino-Japanese War there would have been no Pearl Harbor attack. Together these wars produced intense Chinese fears of internal chaos, deep suspicions of the United States, smoldering anger against Russia, and an even deeper hatred of Japan. In the early twenty-first century, China is the angry rising power, terribly aggrieved over past wrongs and blind to the possibility of its own complicity or culpability in the horror show that is modern Chinese history.

Shattered societies cannot be reconstituted rapidly. Russia and China, the shattered powers of the twentieth century, are still trying to overcome the lethal hand dealt to them by history. Both have deep suspicions about the world order favored by the Western maritime powers based on international law, free trade, and open seas. Communism is out, but what is in? The question of which "ism" for New China and New Russia, at the root of so much of the bloodshed, remains unanswered. The maritime powers can influence these events only on the margins, on the littoral, where they can project their economic, diplomatic, and military influence and where their favored global system has its deepest roots. Whither China? The choice will not be made in the West, but in Beijing or perhaps in the vast Chinese hinterland, where the much abused peasantry lives. Whatever the decision, it will affect us all.

Why has modern Chinese history been so violent? Why have so many Chinese died unnatural deaths, often at the hands of their own countrymen? Why have military leaders figured so prominently in their history? Do warlords come out of nowhere? Surely there is a social basis for the many to follow the few and for the masses of peasant youth to trade plowshares for swords. What if by the 1920s, the Chinese had followed rather than resisted Japanese recommendations for economic development – Japan's strong suit? Alternatively, what if Japan had stopped with Manchuria? Might the outcome have been win-win instead of the lose-lose that played out? What if in the 1930s, the Communists and Nationalists had been wise to Stalin's plans to use them to fight Japan? Could they have set up Japan to fight Russia instead? If so, would Hitler have won, or would he, like the Japanese, have choked on his conquests? What if in the 1940s, Chiang Kai-shek had focused on helping Li Zongren defend at the Yangzi, rather than transporting troops, art treasures, and bullion to Taiwan? What if Mao had honored the sacrifices made by the peasantry and let them keep their land? What if the key personalities had made different choices at the pivotal events? Long ago Confucius observed, "When Heaven sends down calamities, / There is hope of weathering them; / When man brings them upon himself, / There is no hope of escape."[67] Wars are acts of man, not nature.

CHRONOLOGY

Date	Civil War	Regional War	Global War	Miscellaneous
10 Oct 1911	Wuchang Uprising			
10 Oct 1911–12 Feb 1912	**Xinhai Revolution**			
12 Feb 1912	Abdication of Manchu dynasty			
Jul–Sep 1913	Second Revolution			
Dec 1915–Jun 1916	Third Revolution			
1917				Russian Revolution
14–24 Jul 1920	Zhili-Anhui War			
12 Nov 1921–6 Feb 1922				Washington Naval Conference
9 Apr–18 Jun 1922	First Zhili-Fengtian War			
1923–1927	First United Front			
15 Sep–3 Nov 1924	Second Zhili-Fengtian War			
Dec 1924–Jan 1925	Fengtian-Zhejiang War			
Nov 1925–Mar 1926	Fengtian-Feng Yuxiang War			
1 Jul 1926–Jun 1928	**Northern Expedition (Part I)**			
12 Jul 1926	KMT takes Changsha			
10 Oct 1926 (10/10/26)	KMT takes Wuchang			
5 Nov 1926	KMT takes Jiujiang			
8 Nov 1926	KMT takes Nanchang			

(continued)

Date	Civil War	Regional War	Global War	Miscellaneous
18 Dec 1926	KMT takes Fuzhou			
18 Feb 1927	KMT takes Hangzhou			
1927–1930				Famine in northwest China
22 Mar 1927	KMT takes Shanghai			
24 Mar 1927	KMT takes Nanjing			
12 Apr 1927	White Terror begins. End of First United Front			
1–5 Aug 1927	Nanchang Uprising			
9–29 Sep 1927	Autumn Harvest Uprising			
11–13 Dec 1927	Canton Commune			
Apr–29 Dec 1928	Northern Expedition (Part II)			
3 May 1928		Jinan Incident		
4 Jun 1928		Zhang Zuolin killed		
8 Jun 1928	KMT takes Beijing			
12 Jun 1928	KMT takes Tianjin			
Aug 1928	Barga Uprising			
Mar–Jun 1929	Guangxi group uprising			
May 1929	Feng Yuxiang First Henan Uprising			
17 July–22 Dec 1929		Railway War, ending with Khabarovsk Protocol		
Oct 1929				U.S. Stock market crash
Oct–Nov 1929	Feng Yuxiang Second Henan Uprising			
Dec 1929–Jan 1930	Zhengzhou Mutiny			
11 May–4 Nov 1930	**Great War of the Central Plains**			
Nov 1930–Jan 1931	First Encirclement Campaign			

(continued)

CHRONOLOGY

Date	Civil War	Regional War	Global War	Miscellaneous
1931				Famine in Jiangsu, Anhui
Mar–May 1931	Second Encirclement Campaign			
Jul–Sep 1931	Third Encirclement Campaign			
Sep 1931	Guangdong-Guangxi group invasion of Hunan			
18 Sep 1931		**Manchurian Incident**		
19 Sep 1931		Japan takes Shenyang		
20 Sep 1931		Japan takes Changchun		
21 Sep 1931				KMT appeals to League of Nations
22 Sep 1931		Japan takes Jinlin City		
8 Oct 1931		Japan bombs Jinzhou		
17 Oct 1931		October Incident (arrests for Manchurian Incident)		
10 Nov 1931		First Tianjin Incident		
19 Nov 1931		Japan takes Qiqihaer		
13 Dec 1931				Japanese cabinet falls
15 Dec 1931				Chiang steps down
26 Dec 1931		Second Tianjin Incident		
3 Jan 1932		Japan takes Jinzhou		
7 Jan 1932			Stimson Note	
28 Jan–5 May 1932		First Shanghai Incident (28 January Incident)		
5 Feb 1932		Japan takes Harbin		

(*continued*)

Date	Civil War	Regional War	Global War	Miscellaneous
9 Mar 1932		Establishment of Manchukuo monarchy		
Apr–Aug 1932	KMT eliminates Hubei-Henan-Anhui Soviet			
15 May 1932				May 15 Incident (Japan's prime minister killed)
Jun 1932–Mar 1933	Fourth Encirclement Campaign			
1 Jan 1933		Japan takes Shanhaiguan		
30 Jan 1933			Hitler becomes chancellor of Germany	
17 Feb–3 Mar 1933		Rehe Campaign		
24 Feb 1933				League of Nations denounces Japan
5 Mar–31 May 1933		Great Wall Campaign ending with Tanggu Truce		
27 Mar 1933				Japan leaves League of Nations
1933–1936		North China Campaign		
May–Aug 1933	Feng Yuxiang Chahar Uprising			
Sep 1933–Oct 1934	**Fifth Encirclement Campaign (beginning of Long March)**			
1934				Famine in China
1934–1936	Three-Year War in South China			
First half 1935		Chahar Campaign		
23 Mar 1935				Russian sale of Chinese Eastern Railway
10 Jun 1935		Umezu-He Agreement		
27 Jun 1935		Doihara-Qin Agreement		
3 Oct 1935–9 May 1936			Italian-Ethiopian War	

(*continued*)

Date	Civil War	Regional War	Global War	Miscellaneous
20 Feb–5 May 1936	CCP Eastern Expedition			
26 Feb 1936				Young Officers' Revolt (February 26 Incident)
7 Mar 1936			German remilitarization of Rhineland	
Jun–Jul 1936	Guangdong-Guangxi group invasion of Hunan			
18 Jul 1936–28 Mar 1939				Spanish Civil War
Nov–Dec 1936		Suiyuan Campaign		
25 Nov 1936			Anti-Comintern Pact	
Dec 1936	**Xi'an Incident; start of Second United Front**			
7 Jul 1937		**Marco Polo Bridge Incident, major escalation of war**		
27 Jul 1937		Japan takes Beijing		
30 Jul 1937		Japan takes Tianjin		
12 Aug–24 Sep 1937		Chahar Campaign		
13 Aug–9 Dec 1937		**Shanghai Campaign, Second Shanghai Incident**		
1937–1945		Japan air campaign over China		
1937				Famine in Henan, Shaanxi, Sichuan
21 Aug 1937		Sino-Russian Non-Aggression Pact		
Sep–Nov 1937		Taiyuan Campaign		
13 Sep 1937		Japan takes Datong		
24 Sep 1937		Japan takes Baoding		
25 Sep 1937		CCP victory at Pingxingguan		

(*continued*)

Date	Civil War	Regional War	Global War	Miscellaneous
10 Oct 1937		Japan takes Shijiazhuang		
13 Oct 1937		Japan takes Xinkou		
9 Nov 1937		Japan takes Taiyuan		
1–13 Dec 1937		Nanjing Campaign		
24 Dec 1937		Japan takes Hangzhou		
26 Dec 1937		Japan takes Jinan		
Dec 1937–19 May 1938		**Xuzhou Campaign**		
12 Mar 1938			Germany annexes Austria	
22 Mar–7 Apr 1938		KMT defeats Japan at Taierzhuang		
5 + 7 June 1938		KMT blows up Yellow River dikes		
12 Jun 1938		Japan takes Anqing		
12 Jun–25 Oct 1938		**Wuhan Campaign**		
11 Jul–10 Aug 1938		Russo-Japanese Battle of Zhanggufeng		
26 Jul 1938		Japan takes Jiujiang		
29 Sep 1938			Munich Agreement	
21 Oct 1938		Japan takes Guangzhou		
12 Nov 1938		KMT burns Changsha		
10 Feb 1939		Japan takes Hainan Island		
Mar 1939		Burma Road completed		
17–27 Mar 1939		Nanchang Campaign		
1–20 May 1939		Suixian-Zaoyang Campaign		
11–31 May 1939		First Nomonhan Incident		

(*continued*)

Date	Civil War	Regional War	Global War	Miscellaneous
19 Jun–16 Sep 1939		Battle of Nomonhan (Second Nomonhan Incident)		
26 Jul 1939			U.S. renounces commercial treaty with Japan	
23 Aug 1939			Nazi-Soviet Pact	
1 Sep 1939			German invasion of Poland	
3 Sep 1939			**World War II in Europe begins**	
14 Sep–6 Oct 1939		First Battle of Changsha		
19–24 Nov 1939		Nanning Campaign		
30 Nov 1939–12 Mar 1940			Finnish War	
winter 1939–1940		KMT Winter Offensive		
Dec 1939–Feb 1940		Battle of Kunlun Pass		
1 May–12 Jun 1940		Zaoyang-Yichang Campaign		
22 Jun 1940			**Fall of France**	
17 Jul 1940		Britain closes Burma Road		
19 Jul 1940			U.S. passes Two-Ocean Navy Act	
20 Aug–5 Dec 1940		CCP Hundred Regiments Campaign		
16 Sep 1940			First peacetime conscription in U.S. history	
22 Sep 1940			Japan occupies northern Indochina	
27 Sep 1940			**Tripartite (Axis) Alliance**	
17 Oct 1940		Britain reopens Burma Road		
4–14 Jan 1941	New Fourth Route Army Incident			
25 Jan–7 Feb 1941		Battle of Southern Henan		

(*continued*)

CHRONOLOGY

Date	Civil War	Regional War	Global War	Miscellaneous
11 Mar 1941			U.S. passes Lend-Lease Act	
15 Mar–9 Apr 1941		Battle of Shanggao		
13 Apr 1941			Soviet-Japanese Neutrality Pact	
7–27 May 1941		Battle of Southern Shanxi		
22 Jun 1941			**German invasion of Russia (BARBAROSSA)**	
24–27 Jul 1941			Japan occupies southern Indochina	
26 Jul 1941			U.S. freezes Japanese assets	
1 Aug 1941			U.S. oil embargo	
7 Sep–9 Oct 1941		Second Battle of Changsha		
26 Nov 1941			Hull Note	
7–8 Dec 1941			**World War II Pacific begins**	
11 Dec 1941			Germany declares war on U.S.	
24 Dec 1941–15 Jan 1942		Third Battle of Changsha		
Jan–May 1942			Burma Campaign	
8 Mar 1942			Burma Road closed	
18 Apr 1942			Doolittle Raid	
May–Sep 1942		Battle of Zhejiang and Jiangxi		
4 Jun 1942			Battle of Midway	
7 Aug 1942–Feb 1943			Guadalcanal Campaign	
13 Sep 1942–2 Feb 1943			**Stalingrad Campaign**	
fall 1942–1943				Famine in Henan
8 Nov 1942–13 May 1943			U.S. invasion of North Africa	
10 Dec 1942		Gogō Campaign called off		
May–Jun 1943		Battle of Western Hubei		

(*continued*)

Date	Civil War	Regional War	Global War	Miscellaneous
5 Jul–23 Aug 1943			Battle of Kursk	
9–10 Jul–17 Aug 1943			Allied invasion of Sicily	
3 Sep 1943–2 May 1945			Allied invasion of Continental Italy	
22–26 Nov 1943			Cairo Conference	
Nov–Dec 1943		Battle of Changde		
23 Nov 1943			U.S. takes Makin and Tarawa (Gilbert Islands)	
1944				Famine in Henan
4 Feb 1944			U.S. takes Kwajelien Atoll (Marshall Islands)	
8 Mar–Jul 1944			Imphal Campaign	
17 Apr 1944–Feb 1945		**Ichigō Campaign**		
Apr–Jun 1944		Battle of Central Henan		
May–Aug 1944		Battle of Changsha and Hengyang		
6 June 1944			**D-Day Normandy Invasion**	
15 Jun–8 Aug 1944			Marianas Campaign	
15 Jun 1944–9 Aug 1945			**U.S. air campaign over Japan**	
18 Jun 1944		Japan takes Changsha		
8 Aug 1944		Japan takes Hengyang		
Sep–Dec 1944		Battle of Guilin-Liuzhou		
23–26 Oct 1944			Battle of Leyte Gulf	
11 Nov 1944		Japan takes Guilin and Liuzhou		
24 Nov 1944		Japan takes Nanning		
24 Nov 1944			U.S. starts bombing Japan from Marianas	
9 Jan–15 Aug 1945			Battle of Luzon	

(*continued*)

CHRONOLOGY

Date	Civil War	Regional War	Global War	Miscellaneous
28 Jan 1945		Burma Road reopened		
4–11 Feb 1945			Yalta Conference	
19 Feb–26 Mar 1945			Battle of Iwo Jima	
10 Mar 1945			U.S. firebombs Tokyo; 16 sq. mi. incinerated	
1 Apr–22 Jun 1945			Battle of Okinawa	
7 May 1945			**Surrender of Germany**	
26 Jul 1945			Potsdam Declaration	
6 Aug 1945			U.S. atomic bombing of Hiroshima	
8 Aug 1945			Russian declaration of war on Japan	
9 Aug 1945			U.S. atomic bombing of Nagasaki	
9 Aug–5 Sep 1945			**Russian invasion of Manchuria (AUGUST STORM)**	
14 Aug 1945			KMT-Russian Friendship Treaty	
15 Aug 1945			**Surrender of Japan**	
2 Sep 1945			**Official surrender ceremony on USS *Missouri***	
Oct 1945	**Resumption of civil war**			
15–16 Nov 1945	Battle of Shanhaiguan			
1946				nationwide famine
10 Jan 1946	Marshall's first cease-fire in Manchuria			
13 Mar–23 May 1946	civil war resumes; KMT takes southern Manchuria			
13 Mar 1946	KMT takes Shenyang from CCP			

(*continued*)

Date	Civil War	Regional War	Global War	Miscellaneous
4 Apr–19 May 1946	KMT takes Siping First Battle of Siping			
14 Apr–23 May 1946	Battle of Changchun			
23 May 1946	Russia completes evacuation of Manchuria, retaining naval base at Lüshun			
6 Jun 1946	Marshall's second cease-fire			
Jul 1946	full-scale civil war resumes			
fall 1946–spring 1947	U.S. halts military aid to KMT			
19 Mar 1947	KMT takes Yan'an			
Mar 1947–Sep 1948	**Shandong Campaign**			
8 Apr–4 May 1947	Zhengtai Campaign			
13–16 May 1947	Battle of Menglianggu			
May–Jun 1947	Second Battle of Siping			
May–July 1947	CCP Summer Offensive in Manchuria			
summer 1947	CCP Central Plains Counteroffensive			
15 Sep–15 Nov 1947	CCP Autumn Offensive in Manchuria			
12 Nov 1947	CCP takes Shijiazhuang			
15 Dec 1947–15 Mar 1948	CCP Winter Offensive in Manchuria			
15 Mar 1948	CCP takes Siping			
12 Sep–2 Nov 1948	**Liaoning-Shenyang Campaign**			
24 Sep 1948	CCP takes Jinan			
6 Nov 1948–10 Jan 1949	**Huai-Hai Campaign**			

(*continued*)

Date	Civil War	Regional War	Global War	Miscellaneous
Nov 1948–22 Jan 1949	**Beijing-Tianjin Campaign**			
15 Jan 1949	CCP takes Tianjin			
21 Jan 1949	Chiang resigns as president			
22 Jan 1949	Beijing surrenders to CCP			
25 Feb 1949	Mutiny of KMT flagship			
20 Apr 1949	Mutiny of KMT navy			
27 May 1949	CCP takes Shanghai			
1 Oct 1949	**Mao Zedong proclaims the foundation of the People's Republic of China**			
9 Dec 1949	Chiang Kai-shek flees to Taiwan			
5 Mar–1 May 1950	Battle of Hainan Island			
Oct 1949–Apr 1950	CCP takes Xinjiang			
Dec 1951	CCP takes Tibet			

Key: KMT = Nationalists; CCP = Chinese Communists.

NOTES

ACKNOWLEDGMENTS

1 Mao Zedong, *Selected Military Writings of Mao Tse-tung*, 2nd ed. (Beijing: Foreign Languages Press, 1967), 273.

TECHNICAL NOTE

1 Chang Jui-te, "The Nationalist Army on the Eve of the War" in *The Battle for China: Essays on the Military History of the Sino-Japanese War of 1937–1945*, eds., Mark Peattie, Edward J. Drea, and Hans van de Ven (Stanford, CA: Stanford University Press, 2011), 89; Iu. V. Chudodeev, ed., *По дорогам Китая 1937–1945: Воспоминания* (*Along the Roads of China 1937–1945: Memoirs*) (Moscow: Издательство «наука» главная редакция восточной литературы, 1989), 22–3; Boris Grigor'evich Sapozhnikov, *Японо-китайская война и колониальная политика Японии в Китае (1937–1941)* (*The Sino-Japanese War and Japan's Colonial Policy in China [1937–1941]*) (Moscow: Издательсво «наука» Главная редакция восточной литературы, 1970), 36–8; George F. Nafziger, "The Growth and Organization of the Chinese Army (1895–1945)" (Westchester, OH: Nafziger Collection, 1999), 82.

1 INTRODUCTION: THE ASIAN ROOTS OF WORLD WAR II

1 David M. Glantz, *The Soviet Strategic Offensive in Manchuria, 1945 "August Storm"* (London: Frank Cass, 2003), xviii, xxv, 49, 143.
2 Maochun Yu, *The Dragon's War: Allied Operations and the Fate of China 1937–1947* (Annapolis, MD: Naval Institute Press, 2006), 22.
3 Carl Boyd, *Hitler's Japanese Confidant: General Ōshima Hiroshi and MAGIC Intelligence 1941–1945* (Lawrence: University of Kansas Press, 1993), 141.
4 吉田裕 (Yoshida Yutaka) and 纐纈厚 (Kōketsu Atsushi), "日本軍の作戦・戦闘・補給" ("Military Operations, Combat, and the Supply of the

Japanese Military") in 十五年戦争史 (*A History of the Fifteen Year War*), eds. 藤原彰 (Fujiwara Akira) and 今井清一 (Imai Seiichi), Vol. 3 (Tokyo: 青木書店, 1989), 106.

5 Francis Bacon, "Of the True Greatness of Kingdoms and Estates" in *Essays Civil and Moral* cited in Julian S. Corbett, *Some Principles of Maritime Strategy* (New York: Longmans, Green and Co., 1911), 55.

6 Confucius, *The Analects*, trans. Raymond Dawson (Oxford: Oxford University Press, 1993), book 13, paragraph 3.

7 奥村房夫 (Okumura Fusao) and 近藤新治 (Kondō Shinji), eds., 近代日本戦争史 (*Modern Japanese Military History*), Vol. 4, 大東亜戦争 (*The Great East Asian War*) (Tokyo: 同台経済懇話会, 1995); Herbert P. Bix, *Hirohito and the Making of Modern Japan* (New York: HarperCollins, 2000), 443.

8 Takafusa Nakamura, *A History of Shōwa Japan 1926–1989*, trans. Edwin Whenmouth (Tokyo: University of Tokyo Press, 1998), 145.

9 R. J. Rummel, *China's Bloody Century: Genocide and Mass Murder since 1900* (New Brunswick, NJ: Transaction Publishers, 1991), v. The number includes both war and famine deaths, since the two are interrelated.

2 JAPAN 1931–1936: THE CONTAINMENT OF RUSSIA AND NATIONAL RESTORATION

1 外務省外交資料館 (Japan, Foreign Ministry, Diplomatic Records Office) (Hereafter abbreviated as JFM), A.1.1.0–21, 満州事件 (The Manchurian Incident), Vol. 1, 19 September 1931, to Foreign Minister Shidehara from Consul General Hayashi, urgent, top secret, pp. 291, 297; 張學良 (Zhang Xueliang), 張學良口述歷史 (*An Oral History by Zhang Xueliang*), ed. 唐德剛 (Tang Degang). Taipei: 遠流出版社, 2009), 275.

2 石島紀之 (Ishijima Noriyuki), 中国抗日戦争史 (*A History of China's Anti-Japanese War*) (Tokyo: 青木書店, 1984), 11; 江口圭一 (Eguchi Kei-ichi), 十五年戦争小史 (*A Short History of the Fifteen Year War*) (Tokyo: 青木書店, 1996), 43; Mark R. Peattie, *Ishiwara Kanji and Japan's Confrontation with the West* (Princeton, NJ: Princeton University Press, 1975), 128; Henry L. Stimson, *The Far Eastern Crisis: Recollections and Observations* (New York: Harper & Brothers, 1936), 60.

3 防衛庁防衛研究所図書館 (Japan, Defense Agency, Defense Research Center Archives) (Hereafter abbreviated as JDA), 満州全般３９満洲建国秘史の一齣 (An Episode in the History of Nation Building in Manchuria), 8 November 1936, 朝鮮軍参謀三浦忠次郎 (Chōsen Army staff officer), pp. 34–43.

4 George S. Sokolsky, *The Tinder Box of Asia* (Garden City, NY: Doubleday, Doran & Co., 1934), 273.

5 S. C. M. Paine, *Imperial Rivals: China, Russia, and Their Disputed Frontier* (Armonk, NY: M. E. Sharpe, 1996), 307*n*.21.

6 満史会 (Manchurian History Committee), ed., 満州開発四十年史 (*A Forty Year History of Manchurian Development*), Vol. 1 (Tokyo: 謙光社, 1964), 79–80.
7 金安泰 (Jin Antai),"'九一八'事变与美国外交" ("The Manchurian Incident and U.S. Foreign Policy"), 史学集刊 (*Collected Papers of Historical Studies*) 12, no. 3 (1983), 73.
8 林明德 (Lin Mingde), "日本軍國主義的形成—九一八事變的探討—" ("Formation of Japanese Militarism: An Investigation of the Manchurian Incident"), 台灣師範大學歷史學報 (*Taiwan Normal University Bulletin of Historical Research*) 11 (June 1983), 259–60; Yoshihisa Tak Matsusaka, *The Making of Japanese Manchuria, 1904–1932* (Cambridge, MA: Harvard University Press, 2001), 113, 218–19.
9 Louis Frédéric, *Japan Encyclopedia*, trans. Käthe Roth (Cambridge, MA: Harvard University Press, 2002), 282.
10 Keiichiro Komatsu, *Origins of the Pacific War and the Importance of "Magic"* (New York: St. Martin's Press, 1999), 42; Bruce A. Elleman, *Wilson and China: A Revised History of the Shandong Question* (Armonk, NY: M. E. Sharpe, 2002), 175; Sadao Asada, *From Mahan to Pearl Harbor: The Imperial Japanese Navy and the United States* (Annapolis, MD: Naval Institute Press, 2006), 79–90.
11 Akira Iriye, *The Cambridge History of American Foreign Relations*, Vol. 3, *The Globalizing of America, 1913–1945* (Cambridge: Cambridge University Press, 1993), 77–8; 林明德 (Lin Mingde), "Formation of Japanese Militarism: An Investigation of the Manchurian Incident," 259–60; Sadao Asada, *From Mahan to Pearl Harbor*, 126, 153.
12 Jay Taylor, *The Generalissimo: Chiang Kai-shek and the Struggle for Modern China* (Cambridge, MA: Harvard University Press, 2009), 84; Donald A. Jordan, *China's Trial by Fire: The Shanghai War of 1932* (Ann Arbor: University of Michigan Press, 2001), 5.
13 Jonathan Fenby, *Chiang Kai-shek China's Generalissimo and the Nation He Lost* (New York: Carroll & Graf, 2003), 204–6; Howard L. Boorman, ed., *Biographical Dictionary of Republican China*, Vol. 3 (New York: Columbia University Press, 1970), 373; 徐友春 (Xu Youchun), 民國人物大辭典 (*Comprehensive Biographical Dictionary for the Republican Period*), Vol. 2 (Shijiazhuang, Hebei: 河北人民出版社, 2007), 2237.
14 Arnold C. Brackman, *The Last Emperor* (New York: Charles Scribner's Sons, 1975), 215; Takehiko Yoshihashi, *Conspiracy at Mukden: The Rise of the Japanese Military* (New Haven: Yale University Press, 1963), 74–5.
15 Edward J. Drea, *Japan's Imperial Army: Its Rise and Fall, 1853–1945* (Lawrence: University of Kansas Press, 2009), 171; Donald A. Jordan, *Chinese Boycotts versus Japanese Bombs: The Failure of China's*

"Revolutionary Diplomacy," 1931–32 (Ann Arbor: University of Michigan Press, 1991), 277–80.

16 功刀俊洋 (Kunugi Toshihiro), "軍縮から軍拡へ" ("From Arms Limitations to Rearmament") in *History of the Fifteen Year War*, eds. 藤原彰 (Fujiwara Akira) and 今井清一 (Imai Seiichi), 115.

17 Sadako N. Ogata, *Defiance in Manchuria: The Making of Japanese Foreign Policy, 1931–1932* (Berkeley: University of California Press, 1964), 121–8.

18 杨卫敏 (Yang Weimin),"民国政府与一二八淞沪抗战" (The Nationalist Government and the 1932 Shanghai War of Resistance), 近代史研究 (*Modern Chinese History Studies*) 58, no. 4 (July 1990), 228–9.

19 Alvin D. Coox, *Nomonhan: Japan against Russia* (Stanford, CA: Stanford University Press, 1990), 44–54.

20 Ibid., 55.

21 石島紀之 (Ishijima Noriyuki), *History of China's Anti-Japanese War*, 17–19; 外務省外交史料館 (Japan, Foreign Ministry, Diplomatic History Archive), 日本外交史辞典編纂委員会 (The Committee for Compiling a Dictionary on Japanese Diplomatic History), comp. 日本外交史辞典 (*The Japanese Diplomatic History Dictionary*) (Tokyo: 山川出版社, 1992), 388–9. For other figures, see Donald A. Jordan, *China's Trial by Fire*, 187–8, 190–5, 198, 241; 高綱博文 (Takatsuna Hirobumi), "上海事変と日本人居留民—日本人居留民による中国人民衆虐殺背景—" ("The Shanghai Incident and the Japanese Expatriate Community: The Background to the Chinese Carnage According to Japanese Expatriates") in 日中戦争日本・中国・アメリカ (*The Sino-Japanese War: Japan, China, and America*), ed., 中央大学人文科学研究所 (Chūō University Human Sciences Research Center), Research Publication no. 10 (Tokyo: 中央大学出版社, 1993), 25.

22 George S. Sokolsky, *Tinder Box of Asia*, 256.

23 Edward Bing-Shuey Lee, *One Year of the Japan-China Undeclared War* (Shanghai: Mercury Press, 1922), 320; William Henry Chamberlin, *Japan over Asia* (Boston: Little, Brown, 1938), 27; Yûzô Yamamoto, "Japanese Empire and Colonial Management," in *Economic History of Japan 1914–1955: A Dual Structure*, eds., Takafusa Nakamura and Kônosuke Odaka, trans, Noah S. Brannen (Oxford: Oxford University Press, 1999), 224.

24 JDA, 満州全般 7 8 満洲国軍政ノ指導 (The Leadership of the Manchukuo Military Government), 1 August 1934, enclosure 2; Galina Fominichna Zakharova, *Политика Японии в Маньчжурии 1932–1945* (*The Policy of Japan in Manchuria 1932–1945*) (Moscow: «Наука» Главная редакция восточной литературы, 1990), 47–8.

25 Chong-Sik Lee, "Counterinsurgency in Manchuria: the Japanese Experience, 1931–1940," Memorandum RM-5012-ARPA (Santa

Monica: RAND Corp, 1967), 32; Chong-Sik Lee, *Revolutionary Struggle in Manchuria: Chinese Communism and Soviet Interest, 1922–1945* (Berkeley: University of California Press, 1983), 263–4; FMA, A.6.2.0–2–8–1, 満洲国政況関係雑纂治安状況：匪賊動静並討伐状況関係 (Miscellaneous Papers on the Pacification Situation Related to the Manchurian Political Situation: Bandit Activities and Bandit Suppression), Vol. 1, September 1937–September 1938, passim; 加藤豊隆 (Katō Toyotaka), 満洲国警察小史ー満洲国権力の実態について (*A Short History of the Manchukuo Police: The Actual Situation of Manchukuo Sovereignty*) (Tokyo: 第一法規出版株式会社, 1968), 24–5, 108–9; 吉田裕 (Yoshida Yutaka), "軍事支配（１）満州事変期" ("Military Rule [1] during the Manchurian Incident") in 日本帝国主義の満州支配——一五年戦争期を中心に— (*Manchuria under Japanese Imperialism, Focusing on the Fifteen Year War Period*), eds. 小林英夫 (Kobayashi Hideo) and 浅田喬二 (Asada Kyōji) (Tokyo: 時潮社, 1986), 99; 満州国軍刊行委員会 (Manchukuo Army Publication Committee), 満州国軍 (*Manchukuo Army*) (Tokyo: 正光印刷株式会社, 1970), 423.

26 Bruce A. Elleman and S. C. M. Paine, *Modern China Continuity and Change 1644 to the Present* (Boston: Prentice Hall, 2010), 254.

27 塚瀬進 (Tsukase Susumu), 満州国「民族協和」の実像 (*Manchukuo "Racial Harmony" in Reality*) (Tokyo: 吉川弘文館, 1998), 17; 江口圭一 (Eguchi Keiichi), *A Short History of the Fifteen Year War*, 32; Ian Nish, *Japanese Foreign Policy in the Interwar Period* (Westport, CT: Praeger, 2002), 60.

28 Hoover Institution Archives, Stanley K. Hornbeck papers, Box 286, "Manchukuo-Japan Protocol," 22 September 1932, p. 38; John Gunther, *Inside Asia*, 31st ed. (New York: Harper & Brothers, 1939), 225.

29 JDA, 満洲：地誌資料１０満洲事変関係、地図各国新聞 (Maps and Newspapers from Various Countries Concerning the Manchurian Incident), "Outstanding Issues in Manchuria and Mongolia," *Herald of Asia*, Library of Contemporary History, no. 2. (Tokyo: Herald Press, 1931); JDA, 満洲：満洲事変１８満洲事変正統史 (The Correct History of the Manchurian Incident), 1931, pp. 34–6; Japan, Legation, China, "Some Representative Types of Chinese Violations of Japanese Rights and Interests in Manchuria," n.p. ca. 1931; Takeo Itoh, *China's Challenge in Manchuria: Anti-Japanese Activities in Manchuria Prior to the Manchurian Incident* (Dalian?: South Manchuria Railway Co., 1932?); Hoover Institution Archives, Vladimir D. Pastuhov papers, Box 10, Osaka Chamber of Commerce and Industry, "Summary of Political and Economic Relations between Japan and China 1931," p. 2; ibid, Boxes 17, 24, 33; Yoshihisa Tak Matsusaka, *The Making of Japanese Manchuria, 1904–1932*, 115, 321; K. K. Kawakami, *Manchoukuo Child of Conflict* (New York: Macmillan, 1933), 43–5.

30 満史会 (Manchurian History Committee), ed., *A Forty Year History of Manchurian Development*, Vol. 1, 357.
31 Louise Young, *Japan's Total Empire: Manchuria and the Culture of Wartime Imperialism* (Berkeley: University of California Press, 1998), 38.
32 満史会 (Manchurian History Committee), ed., *A Forty Year History of Manchurian Development*, Vol. 2, 778.
33 王良行 (Wang Lianghang), "1929年中国国定税则性质数量分析" ("A Statistical Analysis of the Chinese National Tax Regulation of 1929"), 近代史研究 (*Modern Chinese History Studies*) 88, no. 4 (July 1995), 209–48.
34 张生 (Zhang Sheng), "南京民国政府初期关税改革述评" ("A Discussion of Customs Reform in the Early Nanjing Nationalist Government"), 近代史研究 (*Modern Chinese History Studies*) 74, no. 2 (March 1993), 208–20.
35 Richard J. Smethurst, *From Foot Soldier to Finance Minister: Takahashi Korekiyo Japan's Keynes* (Cambridge, MA: Harvard University Press, 2007), 250.
36 张生 (Zhang Sheng), "A Discussion of Customs Reform in the Early Nanjing Nationalist Government," 208–20.
37 Chih Meng, *China Speaks on the Conflict between China and Japan* (New York: Macmillan, 1932), 61.
38 JDA, 満洲：地誌資料１０満洲事変関係、地図各国新聞 (Maps and Newspapers from Various Countries Concerning the Manchurian Incident), "The Origin and History of the Anti-Japanese Movement in China," *Herald of Asia*, Library of Contemporary History, no. 7 (Tokyo: Herald Press, 1932), p. ii; Sandra Wilson, *The Manchurian Crisis and Japanese Society, 1931–33* (London: Routledge, 2002), 173; Donald A. Jordan, *Chinese Boycotts versus Japanese Bombs*, 32, 259; Henry L. Stimson, *The Far Eastern Crisis*, 111.
39 Thomas W. Burkman, *Japan and the League of Nations: Empire and World Order, 1914–1938* (Honolulu: University of Hawai'i Press, 2008), 10.
40 Herbert P. Bix, *Hirohito*, 206; Takafusa Nakamura, *History of Shōwa Japan*, 21, 40.
41 森武麿 (Mori Takemaro), "恐慌と戦争—１９３０〜１９４５年—" ("The Great Depression and the War, 1930–1945") in 現代日本経済史 (*Modern Japanese Economic History*), eds. 森武麿 (Mori Takemaro) et al. (Tokyo: 有斐閣Sシリーズ, 1993), 1–7; Kerry Smith, *A Time of Crisis: Japan, the Great Depression, and Rural Revitalization* (Cambridge, MA: Harvard University Press, 2001), 52–3; Takehiko Yoshihashi, *Conspiracy at Mukden*, 11–12; 平賀明彦 (Hiraga Akihiko), "日中戦争の拡大と農業政策の転換一１９３２〜１９３９年の農業生産力維持、拡充策を中心

としてー" ("The Expansion of Japan's War in China and the Change in Agricultural Policy, 1932–1939"), 歴史学研究 (*Journal of Historical Studies*) no. 545 (September 1985), 1–17.

42 Roy Hidemichi Akagi, *Japan's Foreign Relations 1542–1936* (Tokyo: Hokuseido Press, 1936), 526; George Brown Tindall and David E. Shi, *America: A Narrative History*, Vol. 2, 4th ed. (New York: W. W. Norton, 1996), 1144.

43 JFM, A.6.1.5–9, 満州事件ニ際スル天津暴動関係一件 (Document Concerning the Unrest in Tianjin during the Manchurian Incident), "Memorandum on the Disturbances in Tientsin of November 1931," submitted by the people of Tientsin, pp. 8–9.

44 This section concerning Honjō's testimony before the Lytton Commission is from JDA, 満洲: 満洲事変40関東軍司令官カ連盟調査委員トノ最後ノ会見ニテ説明セラレタル事項 (Explanatory Items Concerning the Last Meeting of the Commanding Officer of the Kantō Army with the League [of Nations] Investigator), 関東軍参謀部 (Kantō Army General Staff), 2 June 1932?, pp. 1–14.

45 塚瀬進 (Tsukase Susumu), *Manchukuo "Racial Harmony" in Reality*, 18; 江口圭一 (Eguchi Kei-ichi), *A Short History of the Fifteen Year War*, 33, 62; Kikujiro Ishii, *Diplomatic Commentaries*, trans. William R. Langdon (Baltimore: Johns Hopkins University Press, 1936), 129; Hirosi Saito, *Japan's Policies and Purposes* (Boston: Marshall Jones, 1935), 21–22; Yoshihisa Tak Matsusaka, *Making of Japanese Manchuria, 1904–1932*, 380; Galina Fominichna Zakharova, *The Policy of Japan in Manchuria 1932–1945*, 24; Henry L. Stimson, *The Far Eastern Crisis*, 17.

46 金安泰 (Jin Antai), "The Manchurian Incident and U.S. Foreign Policy," 73.

47 林明德 (Lin Mingde), "Formation of Japanese Militarism: An Investigation of the Manchurian Incident," 254–5; 邢丽雅 (Xing Liya), "'九・一八' 事变前后日本对 '满蒙政策' 的演变" ("The Evolution of Japan's Policy regarding Manchuria and Mongolia around the Time of the Manchurian Incident"), 史学集刊 (*Collected Papers of Historical Studies*) no. 3 (1999) 35–6.

48 JDA, 満洲: 満洲事変40関東軍司令官カ連盟調査委員トノ最後ノ会見ニテ説明セラレタル事項 (Explanatory Items Concerning the Last Meeting of the Commanding Officer of the Kantō Army with the League [of Nations] Investigator), 2 June 1932.

49 林明德 (Lin Mingde), "Formation of Japanese Militarism: An Investigation of the Manchurian Incident," 251–2; Japanese Delegation to the League of Nations, "The Manchurian Question: Japan's Case in the Sino-Japanese Dispute as Presented before the League of Nations" (Geneva: Japanese Delegation to the League of Nations, 1933), 7; S. C.

M. Paine, *The Sino-Japanese War of 1894 to 1895: Perceptions, Power, and Primacy* (Cambridge: Cambridge University Press, 2003), 247–332; S. C. M. Paine, *Imperial Rivals*, 234–268.

50 JFM, A.1.1.0–21–12–2, 満州事件（昭６.９.１８）善後措置関係 国際連盟支那調査員関係 (Regarding the Carefully Considered Measures concerning the Manchurian Incident of 18 September 1931 and the League of Nations Investigatory Commission on China), Vol. 6, Evening edition of *Osaka Asahi*, 3 March 1932, p. 1030.

51 JFM, A.1.1.0–21–35, 満州事件 満州事件及上海事件関係公報集 (Manchurian Incident: Collection of Public Announcements on the Manchurian and Shanghai Incidents), Vol. 2, 満州事件関係発表集（二） (Announcements on the Manchurian Incident, part 2), Baron Shidehara interviewed by International News Service, 15 November 1931, p. 41–2.

52 William H. Harris and Judith S. Levey, *The New Columbia Encyclopedia*, 4th ed. (New York: Columbia University Press, 1975), 694, 781, 1175, 1937, 2055; Peter Teed, *Dictionary of 20th Century History 1914–1990* (Oxford: Oxford University Press, 1992), 358.

53 JFM, A.1.1.0–21–35, 満州事件 満州事件及上海事件関係公報集 (Manchurian Incident: Collection of Public Announcements on the Manchurian and Shanghai Incidents), Vol. 2, 満州事件関係発表集（二） (Announcements on the Manchurian Incident, part 2), Address of Yoshizawa at 60th Session of Diet, 21 January 1932, pp. 79–80.

54 Cited in 金安泰 (Jin Antai), "The Manchurian Incident and U.S. Foreign Policy," 73.

55 James Reardon-Anderson, *Reluctant Pioneers: China's Expansion Northward 1644–1937* (Stanford, CA: Stanford University Press, 2005), 98.

56 JFM, A.1.1.0–21–35, 満州事件 満州事件及上海事件関係公報集 (Manchurian Incident: Collection of Public Announcements on the Manchurian and Shanghai Incidents), Vol. 2, 満州事件及上海事件関係発表集（五） (Announcements on the Manchurian and Shanghai Incidents, part 5), Report of the Assembly [of the League of Nations], 31 March 1933; Seki Hiroharu, "The Manchurian Incident, 1931" in *Japan Erupts: The London Naval Conference and the Manchurian Incident, 1928–1932*, ed. James William Morley (New York: Columbia University Press, 1984), 211; JFM, A.1.1.0–21, 満州事件 (The Manchurian Incident), Vol. 2, "Mr. Matsuoka's Conversation with the Members of the League Commission," 24 March 1932, pp. 637–41.

57 Thomas G. Rawski, *Economic Growth in Prewar China* (Berkeley: University of California Press, 1989), 166.

58 S. C. M. Paine, "Japanese Puppet-State Building in Manchukuo," in *Nation Building, State Building, and Economic Development*, ed. S. C. M. Paine (Armonk, NY: M. E. Sharpe, 2010), 67–70.

59 JDA, 満洲：地誌資料２４極東蘓連資料要覽、参謀本部 (Summary of Materials Concerning the Soviet Far East, General Staff Headquarters), 10 October 1935, p. 1; Ann Rasmussen Kinney, *Japanese Investment in Manchurian Manufacturing, Mining, Transportation and Communications 1931–1945* (New York: Garland, 1982), 6; Mark R. Peattie, *Ishiwara Kanji and Japan's Confrontation with the West*, 220, 223; Hirosi Saito, *Japan's Policies and Purposes*, 33, 50; Yoshihisa Tak Matsusaka, *Making of Japanese Manchuria, 1904–1932*, 15, 214–23, 379–80; 居之芬 (Ju Zhifen), "日本对华北经济的统制和掠夺" ("Japanese Economic Control and Plunder of North China"), 历史研究 (H*istorical Research*) no. 2 (1995), 99.

60 西村成雄 (Nishimura Shigeo),"日本政府の中華民国認識と張学良政権—民族主義的凝集性の再評価" ("The Japanese Government's Recognition of the Republic of China and Zhang Xueliang's Sovereignty: A Reappraisal of National Cohesion") in 「満洲国」の研究 (*Research on "Manchukuo"*), ed. 山本有造 (Yamamoto Yūzō), (Tokyo: 緑蔭書房, 1995), 5, 12–14, 19–21.

61 JDA, 満洲満蒙１８４満蒙資源使用摘要、参謀本部 (Summary of Useful Resources in Manchuria and Mongolia, General Staff Headquarters), August 1931, pp. 130–4; 疋田康行 (Hikida Yasuyuki), "財政・金融構造"(Public Finance and Credit Organizations) in *Manchuria under Japanese Imperialism*, eds. 小林英夫 (Kobayashi Hideo) and 浅田喬二 (Asada Kyōji), 828; JFM, E.1.2.0-XI-MAI, Vol. 1, 各国財政経済及金融関係雑件満州国ノ部 (Miscellaneous Papers on Various Countries' Public Finance and Credit, Section on Manchukuo), January 1931–June 1932, 関機高 5233, part 2, 6 May 1932; Ronald Suleski, *Civil Government in Warlord China: Tradition, Modernization and Manchuria* (New York: Peter Lang, 2002), 175.

62 満州国軍刊行委員会 (Manchukuo Army Publication Committee), *Manchukuo Army*, 3.

63 Alvin D. Coox, *Nomonhan*, 27; Takehiko Yoshihashi, *Conspiracy at Mukden*, 183.

64 For an essay on nation building, state building, and economic development in Manchukuo, see S. C. M. Paine, "Japanese Puppet-State Building in Manchukuo," 66–82.

65 西村成雄 (Nishimura Shigeo), "The Japanese Government's Recognition of the Republic of China and Zhang Xueliang's Sovereignty: A Reappraisal of National Cohesion," 23.

66 佐藤和夫 (Satō Kazuo), "戦間期日本のマクロ経済とミクロ経済"(The Microeconomics and Macroeconomics of Interwar Japan) in 戦間期の日本経済分析 (*An Analysis of the Interwar Japanese Economy*), ed., 中村隆英 (Nakamura, Takafusa) (Tokyo: 山川出版社, 1981), 9; Tuvia Blumenthal, "戦間期の日本経済" ("The Interwar Japanese Economy")

in ibid., 43–5; 江口圭一 (Eguchi Kei-ichi), *A Short History of the Fifteen Year War*, 63; Kerry Smith, *A Time of Crisis*, 42.

67 李国平 (Li Guoping), "战前东北地区工矿业开发与结构变化研究" ("A Study of the Development and Structural Changes of Industry and Mining in Pre-War Northeast China"), 中国经济史研究 (*Research in Chinese Economic History*) no. 4 (1998), 89; 山本有造 (Yamamoto Yūzō), "「満洲国」をめぐる対外経済関係の展開ー国際収支分析を中心としてー" ("Development of Foreign Economic Relations Concerning 'Manchukuo' Focusing on an Analysis of International Receipts and Expenditures") in *Research on "Manchukuo,"* ed. 山本有造 (Yamamoto Yūzō), 195–6, 198, 215–16; Louise Young, *Japan's Total Empire*, 214.

68 Ibid., 219; 西沢泰彦 (Nishizawa Yasuhiko), "「満洲国」の建設事業" ("'Manchukuo's' Construction Industry") in *Research on "Manchukuo,"* ed. 山本有造 (Yamamoto Yūzō), 388–9; 満史会 (Manchurian History Committee), ed., *A Forty Year History of Manchurian Development*, Vol. 1, 357. For a map and table of construction see 高橋泰隆 (Takahashi Yasutaka),"鉄道支配と満鉄" ("Railway Administration and the Manchurian Railway") in *Manchuria under Japanese Imperialism*, eds. 小林英夫 (Kobayashi Hideo) and 浅田喬二 (Asada Kyōji), 690–1.

69 西沢泰彦 (Nishizawa Yasuhiko), "'Manchukuo's' Construction Industry," 392, 390. Another source puts the total mileage at 11,479. 満史会 (Manchurian History Committee), ed., *A Forty Year History of Manchurian Development*, Vol. 1, 333; 荒川憲一 (Arakawa Ken-ichi), 戦時経済体制の構想と展開：日本陸海軍の経済史的分析 (*Plans for and Development of the Wartime Economic System: An Economic Historical Analysis of the Japanese Army and Navy*) (Tokyo: 岩波書店, 2011), 86.

70 西沢泰彦 (Nishizawa Yasuhiko), "'Manchukuo's' Construction Industry," 405, 407.

71 Ibid., 395–6.

72 山本有造 (Yamamoto Yūzō), "Development of Foreign Economic Relations Concerning 'Manchukuo' Focusing on an Analysis of International Receipts and Expenditures," 217; 原朗 (Hara Akira), "一九三〇年代の満州経済統制政策" ("The Manchurian Economic Controls Policy in the 1930s") in 日本帝国主義下の満州 (*Manchuria under Japanese Imperialism*), ed. 満州史研究会 (Manchurian History Research Committee) (Tokyo: 御茶の水書房, 1972), 113; JDA, 満洲全般 1 8 3 満州に関する用兵的観察 (Survey of Military Tactics for Manchuria), Vol. 7, "満洲軍需産業指導要綱策定当時の軍需工場" ("Current Munitions Factories Producing under the General Plan for the Manchurian Munitions Industry"); E. B. Schumpeter, "The Mineral Resources of the Japanese Empire and Manchukuo" in *The Industrialization of Japan and*

Manchukuo 1930–1940: Population, Raw Materials and Industry, ed. E. B. Schumpeter (New York: Macmillan, 1940), 378–9.

73 JFM, E.1.2.0-XI-MAI, Vol. 4, 各国財政経済及金融関係雑件満州国ノ部 (Miscellaneous Papers on Various Countries' Public Finance and Credit, Section on Manchukuo), July–December 1933, Dr. Ben Dorfman, "Japan Gains Little in Her Manchurian Adventure," *San Francisco Chronicle*, 6 August 1933, p. F5.

74 朱绍文 (Zhu Shaowen), "日本帝国主义九· 一八事变后对我国东北的经济掠夺" ("The Economic Plunder of Manchuria by Japanese Imperialism after the Manchurian Incident"), 中国经济史研究 (*Research in Chinese Economic History*), no. 3 (1999), 3–4.

75 JDA, 059/M/205, 満州鉱工年鑑 (*Manchurian Mining and Manufacturing Yearbook*), 1944, pp. 107–67; 東北財経委員会調査統計處 (Northeast Financial Committee, Statistical Survey Department), ed., 旧満州経済統計資料 (*Northeast Financial Data for the Puppet Manchukuo Period*) (1949, reprint; Tokyo: 柏書株式会社, 1991), 164.

76 山室信一 (Yamamuro Shin'ichi), "「満洲国 」統治過程語" ("Discussion of the Evolution of the Rule of 'Manchukuo'") in *Research on "Manchukuo,"* ed. 山本有造 (Yamamoto Yūzō), 114–19.

77 原朗 (Hara Akira), "The Manchurian Economic Controls Policy in the 1930s," 55; 満史会 (Manchurian History Committee), ed., *A Forty Year History of Manchurian Development*, Vol. 2, 646, 722, 876. For an overview of Japanese economic development in Manchukuo, see Kungtu C. Sun and Ralph W. Huenemann, *The Economic Development of Manchuria in the First Half of the Twentieth Century* (Cambridge, MA: Harvard University Press, 1969); 小林英夫 (Kobayashi Hideo), ("The Creation and Collapse of 'Manchukuo'") in *Manchuria under Japanese Imperialism*, eds. 小林英夫 (Kobayashi Hideo) and 浅田喬二 (Asada Kyōji), 87; G. C. Allen, "The Development of Industrial Combinations" in *The Industrialization of Japan and Manchukuo 1930–1940*, ed. E. B. Schumpeter, 719–24.

78 東北財経委員会調査統計處 (Northeast Financial Committee, Statistical Survey Department), ed., *Northeast Financial Data for the Puppet Manchukuo Period*, 5, 36; 朱绍文 (Zhu Shaowen), "The Economic Plunder of Manchuria by Japanese Imperialism after the Manchurian Incident," 4; 董长芝 (Dong Changzhi), "日本帝国主义对东北工矿业的掠夺及其后果" ("The Plunder of Manchuria's Industry and Mining by Japanese Imperialism and the Consequences"), 中国经济史研究 (*Research in Chinese Economic History*) no. 4 (1995), 115; 松本俊郎 (Matsumoto Toshirō), "満洲鉄鋼業開発と「満洲国」経済一１９４０年代を中心に一" ("Development of the Manchurian Iron and Steel Industry and 'Manchukuo's' Economy Focusing on the 1940s") in *Research on "Manchukuo,"* ed. 山本有造 (Yamamoto Yūzō), 317.

79 満史会 (Manchurian History Committee), ed., *A Forty Year History of Manchurian Development*, Vol. 2, 537–9; JDA, 満洲全般 1 4 8 満洲における電力事業に関する調査 (Survey of the Manchurian Electric Power Industry), April 1951, passim.

80 Christopher Howe, *The Origins of Japanese Trade Supremacy* (Chicago: University of Chicago Press, 1996), 403; A. M. Ledovsky, *The USSR, the USA, and the People's Revolution in China*, trans. Nadezhda Burova (Moscow: Progress Publishers, 1982), 102; Lloyd E. Eastman, *Seeds of Destruction: Nationalist China in War and Revolution 1937–1949* (Stanford, CA: Stanford University Press, 1984), 224; O. Borisov, *Советский Союз и маньчжурская революционная база 1945–1949* (*The Soviet Union and the Manchurian Revolutionary Base 1945–1949*) (Moscow: Издательство «Мысль», 1975), 49, 53–4, 56; Thomas R. Gottschang and Diana Lary, *Swallows and Settlers: The Great Migration from North China to Manchuria* (Ann Arbor: University of Michigan, 2000), 45.

81 君島和彦 (Kimishima Kazuhiko), "鉱工業支配の開発" ("Development of the Management of Mining and Manufacturing") in *Manchuria under Japanese Imperialism*, eds. 小林英夫 (Kobayashi Hideo) and 浅田喬二 (Asada Kyōji), 589, 670.

82 山本有造 (Yamamoto Yūzō), "Development of Foreign Economic Relations Concerning 'Manchukuo' Focusing on an Analysis of International Receipts and Expenditures," 210, 230–1.

83 君島和彦 (Kimishima Kazuhiko), "Development of the Management of Mining and Manufacturing," 600.

84 Ibid., 600; 満史会 (Manchurian History Committee), ed., *A Forty Year History of Manchurian Development*, Vol. 1, 751.

85 東北財経委員会調査統計處 (Northeast Financial Committee, Statistical Survey Department), ed., *Northeast Financial Data for the Puppet Manchukuo Period*, 6, 36, 299.

86 塚瀬 進 (Tsukase Susumu), 中国近代東北経済史研究 (*Research on the Modern Economic History of Northeast China*) (Tokyo: 東方書店, 1993), 36.

87 According to Nishimura, there were more than 70 circulating currencies. 西村成雄 (Nishimura Shigeo), "The Japanese Government's Recognition of the Republic of China and Zhang Xueliang's Sovereignty: A Reappraisal of National Cohesion," 21; 安富歩 (Yasutomi Ayumu), "「満洲国」経済開発と国内資金流動" ("Economic Development of 'Manchukuo' and Domestic Capital Flows") in *Research on "Manchukuo,"* ed. 山本有造 (Yamamoto Yūzō), 239, 246–7; JDA, 059/M/6384, 満洲年鑑 (*Manchurian Yearbook*) (Dairen: 満洲文化協会発行, 1933), pp. 152–7; 満史会 (Manchurian History Committee), ed., *A Forty Year History of Manchurian Development*, Vol. 2, 853; 小林英夫 (Kobayashi Hideo), "満州金融構造の再編成過程—一九三〇年代前半期を中心として—" ("The

Course of the Reforms of the Manchurian Financial System, Focusing on the Early 1930s") in *Manchuria under Japanese Imperialism*), ed. 満州史研究会 (Manchurian History Research Committee), 169.

88 JFM, E.2.3.2–12–1, Vol. 2, "The Central Bank of Manchou and Appendix of Laws Pertaining Thereto," Hsinking, the Central Bank of Manchou, 1934, pp. 1–4, 10–11; Manchoukuo Government, Department of Foreign Affairs, *Proclamations, Statements and Communications of the Manchoukuo Government*, series 3 (Hsinking, Manchuria, 1932), 1–26.

89 満州中央銀行史研究会 (Manchurian Central Bank Historical Research Committee), ed., 満州中央銀行史通貨・金融政策の軌跡 (*A History of the Manchurian Central Bank: The Course of Currency and Financial Policy*) (Tokyo: 東洋経済新報社, 1988), 48, 118–20.

90 塚瀬 進 (Tsukase Susumu), *Manchukuo "Racial Harmony" in Reality*, 31; K. K. Kawakami, *Manchoukuo Child of Conflict*, 141; Manchoukuo Government, Department of Foreign Affairs, *Proclamations, Statements and Communications of the Manchoukuo Government*, series 2, 1–45.

91 古屋哲夫 (Furuya Tetsuo), "「満洲国」の創出" ("The Creation of 'Manchukuo'") in *Research on "Manchukuo,"* ed. 山本有造 (Yamamoto Yūzō), 60, 62.

92 副島昭一 (Soejima Shōichi), "「満洲国」統治と治外法権撤廃" ("Abolition of Privileges Concerning Political Control and Extraterritoriality in 'Manchukuo'") in *Research on "Manchukuo,"* ed. 山本有造 (Yamamoto Yūzō), 135, 148.

93 張芳杰 (Zhang Fangjie), ed., 遠東漢英大辭典 (*Far East Chinese-English Dictionary*) (臺北：遠東圖書公司印行, 1996), 271.

94 山室信一 (Yamamuro Shin'ichi), "Discussion of the Evolution of the Rule of 'Manchukuo,'" 94, 111; Prasenjit Duara, *Sovereignty and Authenticity: Manchukuo and the East Asian Modern* (Lanham, MD: Rowman & Littlefield, 2003), 66.

95 臼井勝美 (Usui Katsumi), 日中外交史研究—昭和前期— (*Research on Sino-Japanese Diplomatic History: The Early Hirohito Period*) (Tokyo: 吉川弘文館, 1998, 63.

96 滝川正次郎 (Takikawa Masajirō) and 衛藤瀋吉 (Eifuji Shinyoshi), 満洲建国十年史 (*A Ten Year History of Nation Building in Manchuria*) (1941, reprint; Tokyo: 原書房, 1969), 274.

97 JDA, 満洲：満洲事変１８満洲事変正統史 ("The Correct History of the Manchurian Incident"), 1930–1, p. 8; 江口圭一 (Eguchi Kei-ichi), *A Short History of the Fifteen Year War*, 41.

98 Arnold C. Brackman, *Last Emperor*, 334; 塚瀬進 (Tsukase Susumu), *Manchukuo "Racial Harmony" in Reality*, 31, 34; Yamamuro Shin'ichi, *Manchuria under Japanese Dominion*, trans. Joshua A. Fogel (Philadelphia: University of Pennsylvania Press, 2006), 109.

99 S. C. M. Paine, "Japanese Puppet-State Building in Manchukuo," 71–3.

100 China, Central Archives (中央档案馆), comp., 伪满洲国的统治与内幕 (*The Inside Story and the Rulers of the Puppet State of Manchukuo*) (Beijing: 中华书局, 2000), 793–810; K. K. Kawakami, *Manchoukuo Child of Conflict*, 158; Yamamuro Shin'ichi, *Manchuria Under Japanese Dominion*, 110.

101 古屋哲夫 (Furuya Tetsuo), "The Creation of 'Manchukuo,'" 70; 山室信一 (Yamamuro Shin'ichi), "Discussion of the Evolution of the Rule of 'Manchukuo,'" 113–16; 塚瀬 進 (Tsukase Susumu), *Manchukuo "Racial Harmony" in Reality*, 43, 45; Yamamuro Shin'ichi, *Manchuria under Japanese Dominion*, 118.

102 満州国軍刊行委員会 (Manchukuo Army Publication Committee), *Manchukuo Army*, 216, 927–50.

103 古屋哲夫 (Furuya Tetsuo), "The Creation of 'Manchukuo,'" 74–6; Galina Fominichna Zakharova, *The Policy of Japan in Manchuria 1932–1945*, 120.

104 JFM, D.2.1.2–4-2, 満州国警察機関々係件 保甲制度関係, from Consul at Chifeng, Seino Chōtarō to special plenipotentiary to Manchukuo Minami Jirō, 16 April 1935; Owen Lattimore, *The Mongols of Manchuria* (New York: John Day Co., 1934), 21.

105 風間秀人 (Kazama Hideto),"農村行政支配" ("The Management of Rural Administration") in *Manchuria under Japanese Imperialism*, eds. 小林英夫 (Kobayashi Hideo) and 浅田喬二 (Asada Kyōji), 279.

106 John W. Dower, *War without Mercy: Race and Power in the Pacific War* (New York: Pantheon Books, 1986), 203.

107 松村高夫 (Matsumura Takao), "満州国成立以降における移民,労働政策の形成と展開" ("The Formation and Development of Immigration and Labor Policies after the Creation of Manchukuo") in *Manchuria under Japanese Imperialism*, ed. 満州史研究会 (Manchurian History Research Committee), 301; Yamamuro Shin'ichi, *Manchuria under Japanese Dominion*, 200.

108 江口圭一 (Eguchi Kei-ichi), *A Short History of the Fifteen Year War*, 88–90; Jung Chang, *Wild Swans: Three Daughters of China* (New York: Anchor Books, 1991), 62–70.

109 Galina Fominichna Zakharova, *The Policy of Japan in Manchuria 1932–1945*, 51; Chong-Sik Lee, "Counterinsurgency in Manchuria: The Japanese Experience, 1931–1940," 25–9.

110 Galina Fominichna Zakharova, *The Policy of Japan in Manchuria 1932–1945*, 77; JFM, J.1.2.0-J15, Vol. 3, 業務概要, Manchurian Development Co., secret, December 1944, pp. 1–2; Ibid. Vol. 2, 満州日々新聞社 (Manchuria-Japan Daily Newspaper Co.), Dalian, 1937, pp. 10–12; 高乐才 (Gao Lecai), "日本'百万户移民'国策评析" ("Evaluation and Analysis of the Japanese Policy of 'One Million Households of

Immigrants'"), 历史研究 (*Historical Research*), no. 3, (1999) 114–25; 幕内光雄 (Maku'uchi Mitsuo), 満州国警察外史 (*An Unofficial History of the Manchukuo Police*) (Tokyo: 三一書房, 1996), 202–6, 210, 215–16, 222–3; 江口圭一 (Eguchi Kei-ichi), *A Short History of the Fifteen Year War*, 94–5; Bruce A. Elleman and S. C. M. Paine, "Japanese Immigration to Manchukuo and Its Impact on the USSR," *Working Series in International Studies*, I-95–6, Hoover Institution, Stanford University (June 1995), passim.

111 飯島満 (Iijima Mitsuru), "満洲国における「軍警統合」の成立と崩壊" ("Establishment and Collapse of the 'Combined Army-Police' in Manchukuo"), 駿台史学 (*Sundai Historical Review*) 108 (December 1999), 56.

112 西沢泰彦 (Nishizawa Yasuhiko), "'Manchukuo's' Construction Industry," 407–9; 満史会 (Manchurian History Committee), ed., *A Forty Year History of Manchurian Development*, Vol. 2, 351; 新人物往来社 (Association for Rising Talent), 満洲古写真帖 (*Old Photo Album of Manchuria*) 戦記シリーズ, no. 67 (Tokyo: 新人物往来社, 2004), 12–13, 23, 40–1, 72–3, 104–5.

113 西沢泰彦 (Nishizawa Yasuhiko), "'Manchukuo's' Construction Industry," 437; 満史会 (Manchurian History Committee), ed., *A Forty Year History of Manchurian Development*, supplemental volume, 302–15, 339–62.

114 *Manchoukuo Gives Birth to New Culture* (Hsinking: Manchuria Daily News, 1940), 36–8, 40; 偽滿洲國政府公報 (*The Puppet Manchukuo* Government Gazette), Vol. 120 (Shenyang: 遼瀋書社, 1990), 187.

115 満史会 (Manchurian History Committee), ed., *A Forty Year History of Manchurian Development*), supplemental volume, 101, 122–9; Manchoukuo State Council, Bureau of Information, ed., *An Outline of the Manchoukuo Empire 1939* (Dalian: Manchuria Daily News, 1939), 111–19.

116 Jung Chang, *Wild Swans*, 62–3, 69–70.

117 朱绍文 (Zhu Shaowen), "The Economic Plunder of Manchuria by Japanese Imperialism after the Manchurian Incident," 4; 君島和彦 (Kimishima Kazuhiko), "Development of the Management of Mining and Manufacturing," 586; 李宇平 (Li Yuping), "一九三〇年代中國經濟恐慌的若干現象" ("Some Phenomena during the Chinese Depression in the 1930s"), 台灣師範大學歷史學報 (*Taiwan Normal University Bulletin of Historical Research*). no. 25 (June 1997), 81; 松野周治 (Matsuno Shūji), "関税および関税制度から見た「満州国」—関税改正の経過と語点—" ("'Manshukuo' Seen from Tariffs and the Customs System: The Disputed Course of Tariff Reform") in *Research on "Manchukuo,"* ed. 山本有造 (Yamamoto Yūzō), 332, 334, 339, 367.

118 松野周治 (Matsuno Shūji), "'Manshukuo' Seen from Tariffs and the Customs System: The Disputed Course of Tariff Reform," 332, 334, 339, 367.

119 塚瀬進 (Tsukase Susumu), *Manchukuo "Racial Harmony" in Reality*, 50–1.

120 JFM, E.1.2.0-XI-MAI, Vol. 4, 各国財政経済及金融関係雑件満州国ノ部 (Miscellaneous Papers on Various Countries' Public Finance and Credit, Section on Manchukuo), July–December 1933, Dr. Ben Dorfman, "Japan Gains Little in Her Manchurian Adventure," *San Francisco Chronicle* 6 August 1933, p. F5; Sandra Wilson, *The Manchurian Crisis and Japanese Society, 1931–33*, 173–4; Donald A. Jordan, *Chinese Boycotts versus Japanese Bombs*, 109, 114; Shimada Toshihiko, "The Extension of Hostilities, 1931–1932" in *Japan Erupts*, ed. James William Morley, 305–6.

121 林明德 (Lin Mingde), "Formation of Japanese Militarism: An Investigation of the Manchurian Incident," 263.

122 居之芬 (Ju Zhifen) and 华杰 (Hua Jie), "日本'北支那开发株式会社'的经济活动及略夺" ("The Economic Activities and the Plunder of Japan's 'North China Development Co.'"), 近代史研究 (*Modern Chinese History Studies*) 77 no. 5 (September 1993), 245.

123 Herbert P. Bix, *Hirohito*, 258; Ronald Suleski, *Civil Government in Warlord China*, 143.

124 飯島満 (Iijima Mitsuru), "Establishment and Collapse of the 'Combined Army-Police' in Manchukuo," 47, 51.

125 Parks M. Coble, *Facing Japan: Chinese Politics and Japanese Imperialism, 1931–1937* (Cambridge, MA: Harvard University Press, 1991), 94–5; Herbert P. Bix, *Hirohito*, 260; 江口圭一 (Eguchi Kei-ichi), *A Short History of the Fifteen Year War*, 17; 武月星 (Wu Yuexing), 中国现代史地图集 (*Modern Chinese History Map Collection*) (Beijing: 中国地图出版社, 1997), 70.

126 林明德 (Lin Mingde), "Formation of Japanese Militarism: An Investigation of the Manchurian Incident," 269; 江口圭一 (Eguchi Kei-ichi), *A Short History of the Fifteen Year War*, 71; Alvin D. Coox, *Nomonhan*, 53.

127 Historical Research Center (歴史学研究会), comp., *История войны на Тихом океане* (*History of the Pacific War*), trans. B. V. Pospelova, Vol. 1 (Moscow: Издательство иностранной литературы, 1957), 365.

128 Thomas W. Burkman, *Japan and the League of Nations*, xi, 116, 141.

129 Cited in Westel W. Willoughby, *The Sino-Japanese Controversy and the League of Nations* (Baltimore: Johns Hopkins University Press, 1935), 462.

130 Hans J. van de Ven, *War and Nationalism in China 1925–1945* (London: Routledge, 2003), 151.

131 武月星 (Wu Yuexing), *Modern Chinese History Map Collection*, 71; Herbert P. Bix, *Hirohito*, 271–2.

132 JDA, 満洲：満洲事変 1 8 満洲事変正統史 ("The Correct History of the Manchurian Incident"), 1930–1, pp. 9–13; Zoia Dmitrievna Katkova, *Китай и державы 1927–1937* (*China and the Powers 1927–1937*) (Moscow: «Восточная литература» РАН, 1995), 110.

133 居之芬 (Ju Zhifen), "Japanese Economic Control and Plunder of North China," 95.

134 James E. Sheridan, *Chinese Warlord: The Career of Feng Yü-hsiang* (Stanford, CA: Stanford University Press, 1966), 78–83, 112; Jay Taylor, *The Generalissimo*, 58.

135 Jonathan Fenby, *Chiang Kai-shek*, 155.

136 Marjorie Dryburgh, "Regional Office and the National Interest: Song Zheyuan in North China, 1933–1937" in *Chinese Collaboration with Japan, 1932–1945: The Limits of Accommodation*, eds. David P. Barrett and Larry N. Shyu (Stanford, CA: Stanford University Press, 2001), 43, 45–6.

137 山田朗 (Yamada Akira),"満州支配（２）日中戦争・太洋戦争期" ("Military Rule [2] during the Sino-Japanese War and the War of the Pacific") in *Manchuria under Japanese Imperialism*, eds. 小林英夫 (Kobayashi Hideo) and 浅田喬二 (Asada Kyōji), 204.

138 Richard Fuller, *Shōkan Hirohito's Samurai: Leaders of the Japanese Armed Forces, 1926–1945* (London: Arms and Armour, 1992), 73; Yang Tianshi, "Chiang Kai-shek and the Battles of Shanghai and Nanjing" in *The Battle for China*, eds. Mark Peattie et al., 155; Tobe Ryōichi, "The Japanese Eleventh Army in Central China, 1938-1941" in ibid., 217; Edward J. Drea and Hans van de Ven, "An Overview of Major Military Campaigns during the Sino-Japanese War, 1937–1945" in ibid., 28, 30.

139 芳井研一 (Yoshii Ken'ichi), "華北分離工作と準戦時体制" ("The Partition of North China and the Organizational Structure in the Preparatory Period") in *History of the Fifteen Year War*, eds. 藤原彰 (Fujiwara Akira) and 今井清一 (Imai Seiichi), Vol. 1, 247–50.

140 Ian Nish, *Japanese Foreign Policy 1869–1942 Kasumigaseki to Miyakezaka* (London: Routledge & Kegan Paul, 1977), 211; Richard Fuller, *Shōkan Hirohito's Samurai*, 225–226; Parks M. Coble, *Facing Japan*, 195–8.

141 Thomas E. Ewing, *Between the Hammer and the Anvil? Chinese and Russian Policies in Outer Mongolia, 1911–1921*, Indiana University

Uralic and Altaic Studies, Vol. 138 (Bloomington, IN: Research Institute for Inner Asian Studies, 1980), 67.

142 臼井勝美 (Usui Katsumi), *Research on Sino-Japanese Diplomatic History*, 260; Howard L. Boorman, ed., *Biographical Dictionary*, Vol. 2, 79–84; ibid., Vol. 1, 386–7; 石島紀之 (Ishijima Noriyuki), *History of China's Anti-Japanese War*, 31–8; Michael A. Barnhart, *Japan Prepares for Total War* (Ithaca: Cornell University Press, 1987), 40; B. Winston Kahn, "Doihara Kenji and the North China Autonomy Movement" in *China and Japan: Search for Balance since World War I*, eds. Alvin D. Coox and Hilary Conroy (Santa Barbara, CA: ABC-Clio, 1978), 183–4.

143 Cited in Hugh Ragsdale, *The Soviets, the Munich Crisis, and the Coming of World War II* (Cambridge: Cambridge University Press, 2004), xvii.

144 Owen Lattimore, *The Mongols of Manchuria*, 14, 40; Howard L. Boorman, ed., *Biographical Dictionary*, Vol. 2, 6–10; Sechin Jagchid, *The Last Mongol Prince: The Life and Times of Demchugdongrob, 1902–1966* (Bellingham, WA: Center for East Asian Studies, Western Washington University, 1999), 1, 106; Liu Xiaoyuan, *Reins of Liberation: An Entangled History of Mongolian Independence, Chinese Territoriality, and Great Power Hegemony, 1911–1950* (Stanford, CA: Stanford University Press, 2006), 31; Zoia Dmitrievna Katkova, *China and the Powers 1927–1937*, 122, 189.

145 F. C. Jones, *Japan's New Order in East Asia: Its Rise and Fall 1937–1945* (London: Oxford University Press, 1954), 72.

146 Shimada Toshihiko, "Designs on North China, 1933–1937" in *The North China Quagmire: Japan's Expansion on the Asian Continent 1933–1941*, ed. James William Morley (New York: Columbia University Press, 1983), 216–18.

147 Ian Nish, *Japanese Foreign Policy 1869–1942*, 212–13.

148 Edward J. Drea, *Japan's Imperial Army*, 191; Sechin Jagchid, *The Last Mongol Prince*, 159, 161; Howard L. Boorman, ed., *Biographical Dictionary*, Vol. 2, 8–9; Shimada Toshihiko, "Designs on North China, 1933–1937," 218–24; 武月星 (Wu Yuexing), *Modern Chinese History Map Collection*, 87.

149 石島紀之 (Ishijima Noriyuki), *A History of China's Anti-Japanese War*, 34, 38; Takafusa Nakamura, "Japan's Economic Thrust into North China, 1933–1938" in *The Chinese and the Japanese*, ed. Akira Iriye (Princeton, NJ: Princeton University Press, 1980), 226, 232–3; Ian Nish, *Japanese Foreign Policy 1869–1942*, 212–13; Shimada Toshihiko, "Designs on North China, 1933–1937," 195; 解学诗 (Xie Xueshi) and 宋玉印 (Song Yuyin), "'七・七' 事变后日本掠夺华北资源的总枢纽" ("The Fulcrum of Japan's Plundering of North China's Resources after

1937"), 中国经济史研究 (*Research in Chinese Economic History*) no. 4 (1990), 44–57.

150 Ian Nish, *Japanese Foreign Policy 1869–1942*, 212–13; Sechin Jagchid, *The Last Mongol Prince*, 120, 157; Herbert P. Bix, *Hirohito*, 286, 322; William Henry Chamberlin, *Japan over Asia*, 88, 91; Shimada Toshihiko, "Designs on North China, 1933–1937," 158; George E. Taylor, *The Struggle for North China* (New York: Institute of Pacific Relations, 1940), 20.

151 李宇平 (Li Yuping), "Some Phenomena during the Chinese Depression in the 1930s," 81.

152 Michael A. Barnhart, *Japan Prepares for Total War*, 39; William Henry Chamberlin, *Japan over Asia*, 96; 张利民 (Zhang Limin),"抗战期间日本对华北经济统治方针政策的制定和演变" ("Establishment and Evolution of Japanese Policies for the Economic Control of North China during the Sino-Japanese War"), 中国经济史研究 (*Research in Chinese Economic History*) no. 2 (1999), 38–40; 石島紀之 (Ishijima Noriyuki), *History of China's Anti-Japanese War*, 34, 38; Takafusa Nakamura, "Japan's Economic Thrust into North China, 1933–1938," 226, 232–3; Ian Nish, *Japanese Foreign Policy 1869–1942*, 212–13; 居之芬 (Ju Zhifen), "Japanese Economic Control and Plunder of North China," 95.

153 武月星 (Wu Yuexing),"日本华北驻屯军及侵华行径" ("The Japanese North China Occupation Force and Its Aggressive Behavior"), 近代史研究 (*Modern Chinese History Studies*) 58, no. 4 (July 1990): 206, 209–11; Shimada Toshihiko, "Designs on North China, 1933–1937," 167–8.

154 曾业英 (Zeng Yeying), "日本侵占华北海关及其后果" ("The Japanese Seizure of the North China Customs and Its Consequences"), 近代史研究 (*Modern Chinese History Studies*) 88, no. 4 (July 1995), 48–67.

155 居之芬 (Ju Zhifen) "Japanese Economic Control and Plunder of North China," 96, 98; 张利民 (Zhang Limin), "华北开发株式会社与日本政府和军部" ("The North China Development Company and the Japanese Government and Military"), 历史研究 (*Historical Research*) no. 1 (1995), 156–68; Usui Katsumi, "The Politics of War, 1937–1941" in *The North China Quagmire*, ed. James William Morley, 326.

156 居之芬 (Ju Zhifen) and 华杰 (Hua Jie), "The Economic Activities and the Plunder of Japan's 'North China Development Co.,'" 245–67.

157 中村隆英 (Nakamura Takafusa), "北支那開発株式会社の成立" ("The Formation of the North China Development Joint-Stock Corporation") in 日中戦争と日中関係 (*The Sino-Japanese War and Sino-Japanese Relations*), eds. 井上清 (Inōe Kyoshi) and 衛藤瀋吉 and (Etō Shinkichi) (Tokyo: 原書房, 1988), 359, 362.

158 Ann Rasmussen Kinney, *Japanese Investment in Manchurian Manufacturing, Mining, Transportation and Communications*

1931–1945, 25, 152–5; *The Manchoukuo Year Book 1942* (Hsinking, Manchoukuo: Manchoukuo Year Book Co., 1943), 66, 254–5, 271, 326–30, 425, 492–3, 500, 531–2, 539–40, 490; Kungtu C. Sun and Ralph W. Huenemann, *The Economic Development of Manchuria in the First Half of the Twentieth Century*, 86–7; Kang Chao, *The Economic Development of Manchuria: The Rise of a Frontier Economy*, Michigan Papers in Chinese Studies no. 43 (Ann Arbor: University of Michigan Center for Chinese Studies, 1982), 83; Kerry Smith, *A Time of Crisis*, 242, 251; Mikiso Hane, *Peasants, Rebels, Women, and Outcasts: The Underside of Modern Japan*, 2nd ed. (Lanham, MD: Rowman & Littlefield, 1982), 114–15; Kozo Yamamura, "The Japanese Economy, 1911–1930: Concentration, Conflicts, and Crises" in *Japan in Crisis: Essays on Taishō Democracy*, eds. Bernard Silberman and H. D. Harootunian (Princeton, NJ: Princeton University Press, 1974), 304; Sandra Wilson, *The Manchurian Crisis and Japanese Society, 1931–33*, 219; Takehiko Yoshihashi, *Conspiracy at Mukden*, 113–15.

159 Takafusa Nakamura, "The Age of Turbulence, 1937–54" in *Economic History of Japan 1914–1955*, eds. Takafusa Nakamura et al., 70–1; Nakamura Takafusa, "Depression, Recovery, and War, 1920–1945" in *Shōwa Japan: Political, Economic and Social History 1926–1989*, ed. Stephen S. Large, Vol. 1 (London: Routledge, 1998), 78.

160 Richard J. Smethurst, *From Foot Soldier to Finance Minister*, 2–4, 6, 105–9, 238.

161 Cited in ibid., 290.

162 Cited in ibid., 294; see also 268, 274.

163 Cited in ibid., 296.

164 Takafusa Nakamura, *History of Shōwa Japan*, 128; Herbert P. Bix, *Hirohito*, 297–8, 301.

165 江口圭一 (Eguchi Kei-ichi), *A Short History of the Fifteen Year War*, 106–7; Takafusa Nakamura, *History of Shōwa Japan*, 125.

166 Takafusa Nakamura, *History of Shōwa Japan*, 125.

167 Thomas W. Burkman, *Japan and the League of Nations*, 193; John Gunther, *Inside Asia*, 93; Ben-Ami Shillony, "The February 26 Affair: Politics of a Military Insurrection" in *Shōwa Japan*, ed. Stephen S. Large, Vol. 1, 90.

168 Takafusa Nakamura, *History of Shōwa Japan*, 118–30; Herbert P. Bix, *Hirohito*, 244; Barbara J. Brooks, *Japan's Imperial Diplomacy: Consuls, Treaty Ports, and War in China 1895–1938* (Honolulu: University of Hawai'i Press, 2000), 7.

169 Herbert P. Bix, *Hirohito*, 297–8, 301; Edward J. Drea, *Japan's Imperial Army*, 181; 功刀俊洋 (Kunugi Toshihiro), "From Arms Limitations to Rearmament," 115.

170 Takafusa Nakamura, *History of Shōwa Japan,* 128.
171 Richard J. Smethurst, *From Foot Soldier to Finance Minister*, 3–4, 6, 238, 297.
172 Takafusa Nakamura, *History of Shōwa Japan,* 125; Richard J. Smethurst, *From Foot Soldier to Finance Minister*, 260.
173 William Henry Chamberlin, *Japan over Asia*, 231, 258, 270; Westel W. Willoughby, *The Sino-Japanese Controversy and the League of Nations*, 433.
174 Edward J. Drea, *Japan's Imperial Army*, 181.
175 Mark R. Peattie, *Ishiwara Kanji and Japan's Confrontation with the West*, 120; Alvin D. Coox, *Nomonhan*, 19.
176 神田文人 (Kanda Fuhito),"「天皇制」と戦争" ("'The Emperor System' and the War") in *History of the Fifteen Year War*, eds. 藤原彰 (Fujiwara Akira) and 今井清一 (Imai Seiichi), Vol. 3, 37–9; Herbert P. Bix, *Hirohito*, 150; Takafusa Nakamura, *History of Shōwa Japan,* 3–4.
177 Ienaga Saburō, *The Pacific War, 1931–1945*, trans. Frank Baldwin (New York: Pantheon Books, 1978), 39, 230; Richard J. Smethurst, *From Foot Soldier to Finance Minister*, 204; Takafusa Nakamura, *History of Shōwa Japan,* 3–4.
178 Takehiko Yoshihashi, *Conspiracy at Mukden*, 236–7.
179 Cited in Barbara J. Brooks, *Japan's Imperial Diplomacy*, 1, 8, 42–3, 140, 165.
180 神田文人 (Kanda Fuhito), "'The Emperor System' and the War," 37, 51–2.
181 JFM, A.1.1.0–21 滿洲事変 (Manchurian Incident), Vol. 1, passim.
182 熊沛彪 (Xiong Peibiao),"九一八事变后日本的对华外交及战略意图—兼论南京国民政府的对策" ("Japan's Foreign Policy Regarding China and Its Strategic Intentions after the Manchuria Incident plus a Discussion of the Nanjing Government's Counter-Strategy"), 历史研究 (*Historical Research*) no. 4 (1998), 79.
183 Cited in 王真 (Wang Zhen), "论抗战初期苏联援华政策性质" ("The Nature of the Soviet Policy to Assist China Early in the Anti-Japanese War"), 中共党史研究 (*Research on the History of the Chinese Communist Party*) no. 5, (1993), 50.

3 CHINA 1926–1936: CHAOS AND THE QUEST FOR THE MANDATE OF HEAVEN

1 Bruce A. Elleman and S. C. M. Paine, *Modern China Continuity and Change 1644 to the Present*, 15–18.
2 王光远 (Wang Guangyuan) and 姜中秋 (Jiang Zhongqiu),"汪蒋矛盾与三二〇事件" ("The Contradiction between Wang Jingwei and Chiang Kai-shek and the 20 March Incident"), 中共党史研究 (*Research on the*

History of the Chinese Communist Party) no. 1 (1992), 45; John Gunther, *Inside Asia*, 253, 263.

3 Yang Tianshi, "Perspectives on Chiang Kaishek's Early Thought from His Unpublished Diary" in *The Chinese Revolution in the 1920s: Between Triumph and Disaster*, eds. Mechthild Leutner et al. (London: RoutledgeCurzon, 2002), 86–91; 姚金果 (Yao Jinguo), "对国民党试图加入共产国际问题的初步探讨" ("A Preliminary Investigation into the Nationalists' Attempt to Join the Communist International"), 中共党史研究 (*Research on the History of the Chinese Communist Party*) no. 4 (2000), 48–52.

4 易豪精 (Yi Haojing), "试论中华苏维埃共和国的政权建设" ("A Discussion of the Construction of the Chinese Soviet Republic") 近代史研究 (*Modern Chinese History Studies*) 57, no. 3 (May 1990), 166–80; Donald W. Klein and Anne B. Clark, *Biographic Dictionary of Chinese Communism 1921–1965*, Vol. 2, (Cambridge, MA: Harvard University Press, 1971), 1055; Howard L. Boorman, *Biographical Dictionary*, Vol. 3, 326; ibid., Vol. 1, 41; Maochun Yu, *Dragon's War*, 54.

5 Howard L. Boorman, ed., *Biographical Dictionary*, Vol. 1, 319–25; 蒋永敬 (Jiang Yongjing), "南京国民政府初期实施训政的背景及挫折—军权，党权，民权的较量" ("The Background and Setbacks of the Implementation of Political Tutelage during the Early Period of the Nationalist Government in Nanjing – The Competition among Military, Party, and People's Rights"), 近代史研究 (*Modern Chinese History Studies*) 77, no. 5 (September 1993), 90; Lee Hudson Teslik, "Backgrounder: Iraq, Afghanistan, and the U.S. Economy," *New York Times*, 4 February 2008; Hans J. van de Ven, *War and Nationalism in China 1925–1945*, 132–3.

6 Donald A. Jordan, *The Northern Expedition: China's National Revolution of 1926–1928* (Honolulu: University of Hawai'i Press, 1976), 68.

7 沈予 (Shen Yu),"国民革命与日蒋关系" ("The National Revolution and the Relationship between Japan and Chiang Kai-shek"), 近代史研究 (*Modern Chinese History Studies*) no. 2 (1997), 43.

8 Hans J. van de Ven, *War and Nationalism in China 1925–1945*, 119.

9 Cited in 刘会军 (Liu Huijun), "民国党特务组织" ("The Nationalist Party Spy Organization"), 史学集刊 (*Collected Papers of Historical Studies*) 39, no. 2 (1990), 39–40.

10 沈予 (Shen Yu), "The National Revolution and the Relationship between Japan and Chiang Kai-shek," 44–7.

11 Hans J. van de Ven, *War and Nationalism in China 1925–1945*, 119; 王奇生 (Wang Qisheng), 党员，党权 与党争： 1924〜1949年中国国民党的组织形态 (*Party Members, Party Authority, and Party Infighting: The Organizational Structure of the Chinese Nationalist Party, 1924–1949*) (Shanghai: 上海书店出版社, 2009, 95–6.

12 黄道炫 (Huang Daoxuan), "关于蒋介石第一次下野的几个问题" ("Several Questions Concerning Chiang Kai-shek's First Exit from the Political Arena"), 近代史研究 (*Modern Chinese History Studies*) no. 4 (1999), 138–61.
13 申晓云 (Shen Xiaoyun),"四一二前后的蒋介石与列强" ("Relations between Chiang Kai-shek and the Imperialist Powers around the Time of the 12 April Massacre"), 历史研究 (*Historical Research*) no. 6 (2000), 104–5.
14 沈予 (Shen Yu), "The National Revolution and the Relationship between Japan and Chiang Kai-shek," 51–5.
15 Ibid., 47–9, 56–9.
16 Cited in 申晓云 (Shen Xiaoyun), "Relations between Chiang Kai-shek and the Imperialist Powers around the Time of the 12 April Massacre," 103–4.
17 林明德 (Lin Mingde), "Formation of Japanese Militarism: An Investigation of the Manchurian Incident," 256; 江口圭一 (Eguchi Kei-ichi), *A Short History of the Fifteen Year War*, 32.
18 沈予 (Shen Yu), "The National Revolution and the Relationship between Japan and Chiang Kai-shek," 51–5; Yoshihisa Tak Matsusaka, *Making of Japanese Manchuria, 1904–1932*, 274; Takehiko Yoshihashi, *Conspiracy at Mukden*, 15.
19 Cho Tsun-hung (卓遵宏), "H. H. K'ung and His Monetary Policy for Resistance against the Japanese Invasion (1933–1938)," 台灣師範大學歷史學報 (*Taiwan Normal University Bulletin of Historical Research*) 15 (June 1987), 453, 456; Wesley M. Bagby, *The Eagle-Dragon Alliance: America's Relations with China in World War II* (Newark: University of Delaware Press, 1992), 43; Jay Taylor, *Generalissimo*, 27.
20 申晓云 (Shen Xiaoyun), "Relations between Chiang Kai-shek and the Imperialist Powers around the Time of the 12 April Massacre," 106.
21 Thomas W. Burkman, *Japan and the League of Nations*, 15; 沈予 (Shen Yu), "The National Revolution and the Relationship between Japan and Chiang Kai-shek," 52; Louise Young, *Japan's Total Empire*, 31.
22 沈予 (Shen Yu), "The National Revolution and the Relationship between Japan and Chiang Kai-shek," 47–9, 56–9.
23 Owen Lattimore, *Mongols of Manchuria*, 39.
24 Arthur Waldron, "War and the Rise of Nationalism in Twentieth-Century China" in *Warfare since 1600*, ed. Kenneth Swope (Aldershot, UK: Ashgate, 2005), 308–9.
25 Jasper Becker, *Hungry Ghosts: Mao's Secret Famine* (New York: Free Press, 1996), 13–14.
26 味岡徹 (Ajioka Tōru), "国民党「訓政」と抗日戦争" ("The Nationalist Party's 'Political Tutelage' and the Anti-Japanese War") in *The Sino-*

Japanese War, ed. 中央大学人文科学研究所 (Chūō University Human Sciences Research Center), 368.

27 Ibid., 261–2.

28 味岡徹 (Ajioka Tōru), "The Nationalist Party's 'Political Tutelage' and the Anti-Japanese War," 368, 376–7, 385.

29 陈梅芳 (Chen Meifang), "试论十年内战时期国民党政府的农村经济政策" ("On the Rural Economic Policy of the Nationalist Government, 1927–1937"), 中国经济史研究 (*Research in Chinese Economic History Quarterly*) no. 4 (1991), 63–76; 邱松庆 (Qiu Songqing), "简评南京国民政府初建时期的农业政策" ("Comment on the Agricultural Policy of the Early Nanjing Government"), 中国社会经济史研究 (*Research on Chinese Social and Economic History*) no. 4 (1999), 72–6.

30 金普森 (Jin Pusen) and 王国华 (Wang Guohua), "南京国民政府1933–1937年之内债" ("The Internal Debt of the Nanjing Government 1933–37"), 中国社会经济史研究 (*Research on Chinese Social and Economic History*) no. 2 (1993), 88.

31 董卉 (Dong Hui), "南京政府公务员制度（1930–1937）考析" ("An Examination of the Nanjing Government's Civil Service System [1930–1937]"), 近代史研究 (*Modern Chinese History Studies*) 68 no. 2 (March 1992), 167–85.

32 "枪杆子里面出政权" appears in chapter 5 of Mao's *Little Red Book*, citing his 1938 essay "Problems of War and Strategy."

33 Cited in 蒋永敬 (Jiang Yongjing), "The Background and Setbacks of the Implementation of Political Tutelage," 98–100. See also ibid., 80–7.

34 王光远 (Wang Guangyuan) and 姜中秋 (Jiang Zhongqiu), "The Contradiction between Wang Jingwei and Chiang Kai-shek and the 20 March Incident," 50.

35 Cited in Jonathan Fenby, *Chiang Kai-shek,* 130.

36 Howard L. Boorman, ed., *Biographical Dictionary*, Vol. 3, 373.

37 孙季萍 (Sun Jiping), "抗战以前国民政府法制改革评议"(An Evaluation of the Reforms of the Nationalist Legal System before the Sino-Japanese War), 文史哲 (*Journal of Literature, History, and Philosophy*) 263, no. 2 (2001), 112–18; Hsia Taotai, "Wartime Judicial Reform in China" in *China's Bitter Victory: The War with Japan 1937–1945*, eds. James C. Hsiung and Steven I. Levine (Armonk, NY: M. E. Sharpe, 1992), 276.

38 J. Megan Greene, *The Origins of the Developmental State in Taiwan* (Cambridge, MA: Harvard University Press, 2008), 22–6.

39 石川禎浩 (Ishikawa Yoshihiro), "南京政府時期の技術官僚の形成と発展" ("The Formation and Development of Technocrats in Nationalist China") 史林 (*Journal of History*) 74, no. 2 (March 1991), 1–19.

40 杨天石 (Yang Tianshi), "1935年国民党内的倒汪迎胡暗潮" ("Undercurrents in the Nationalist Party to Replace Wang Jingwei with Hu Hanmin

in 1935"), 近代史研究 (*Modern Chinese History Studies*) no. 4 (1997), 273–85; 秦孝儀 (Qin Xiaoyi), 中國現代史辭典：人物部分 (*Dictionary of Modern Chinese History: Biographic Volume*) (Taipei: 近代中國出版社, 1985), 100; Wang Ke-wen, "Wang Jingwei and the Policy Origins of the 'Peace Movement,' 1932–1937" in *Chinese Collaboration with Japan, 1932–1945*, eds. David P. Barrett and Larry N. Shyu, 27–9; John Hunter Boyle, *China and Japan at War 1937–1945: The Politics of Collaboration* (Stanford, CA: Stanford University Press, 1972), 38.

41 杨天石 (Yang Tianshi), "Undercurrents in the Nationalist Party to Replace Wang Jingwei with Hu Hanmin in 1935," 273–85.

42 Howard L. Boorman, ed., *Biographical Dictionary*, Vol. 1, 407; 王建朗 (Wang Jianlang), "芦沟桥事件后国民政府的战和抉择" ("The Nationalist Government's Decision for War or Peace after the Marco Polo Bridge Incident"), 近代史研究 (*Modern Chinese History Studies*) no. 2 (1999), 166.

43 All quotations cited in Wang Ke-wen, "Wang Jingwei and the Policy Origins of the 'Peace Movement,' 1932–1937," 30–1, 36.

44 Parks M. Coble, *Facing Japan*, 241.

45 唐凌 (Tang Ling), "抗战时期的中国煤矿市场" ("The Chinese Coal Market during the Sino-Japanese War"), 近代史研究 (*Modern Chinese History Studies*) 95, no. 5 (September 1996), 87.

46 徐建生 (Xu Jiansheng), "1927～1937年中国基础化学工业的发展及其特点" ("The Development and Characteristics of China's Basic Chemical Industry from 1927 to 1937"), 中国经济史研究 (*Research in Chinese Economic History*) no. 2 (2000), 57–65; June Grasso, Jay Corrin, and Michael Kort, *Modernization and Revolution in China: From the Opium Wars to World War*, 3rd ed. (Armonk, NY: M. E. Sharpe, 2004), 104.

47 李宇平 (Li Yuping), "Some Phenomena during the Chinese Depression in the 1930s," 71–9.

48 Ibid.; 平野和由 (Hirano Kazuyoshi), "中国の金融構造と幣制改革" ("The Financial Structure of China and the Currency Reform") in 中国の幣制改革と国際関係 (*China's Currency Reform and International Relations*), ed. 野沢豊 (Nozawa Yutaka) (Tokyo: University of Tokyo Press, 1981), 62; Jonathan Fenby, *Chiang Kai-shek*, 236; Arthur N. Young, *China and the Helping Hand 1937–1945* (Cambridge, MA: Harvard University Press, 1963), 6–9.

49 张水良 (Zhang Shuiliang), "二战时期国统区的三次灾荒及其对社会经济的影响" ("The Three Great Famines in the Areas Ruled by the Nationalists during the Second World War and Its Influence upon the Social Economy"), 中国社会经济史研究 (*Journal of Chinese Social and Economic History*) no. 4 (1990), 90–8; 李宇平 (Li Yuping), "Some Phenomena during the Chinese Depression in the 1930s," 109, 116;

李宇平 (Li Yuping), "一九三〇年代世界經濟大恐慌對中國經濟之衝擊（一九三一〜一九三五）" ("The Impact of the Great Depression on China's Economy in the 1930s [1931–1935]"), 台灣師範大學歷史學報 (*Taiwan Normal University Bulletin of Historical Research*) no. 22 (June 1994), 338–9; 刘克祥 (Liu Kexiang),"1927–1937年的地价变动与土地买卖—30年代土地问题研究之一" ("Land Price Changes and Land Sales, 1927–1937: Research on the Land Question of the 1930s"), 中国经济史研究 (*Research in Chinese Economic History*) no. 1 (2000), 21–36.

50 陈梅芳 (Chen Meifang), "On the Rural Economic Policy of the Nationalist Government, 1927–1937," 63–76; 邱松庆 (Qiu Songqing), "Comment on the Agricultural Policy of the Early Nanjing Government," 72–6.

51 Michael A. Barnhart, *Japan Prepares for Total War*, 41; 邱松庆 (Qiu Songqing), "略论南京国民政府的法币政策" ("On the Currency Policy Pursued by the Nationalist Government"), 中国社会经济史研究 (*Research on Chinese Social and Economic History*) no. 4 (1997), 79–80; Cho Tsun-hung (卓遵宏), "H. H. K'ung and His Monetary Policy," 433, 438, 446–8, 454; Arthur N. Young, *China's Wartime Finance and Inflation, 1937–1945* (Cambridge, MA: Harvard University Press, 1965), 5–6, 131.

52 Shimada Toshihiko, "Designs on North China, 1933–1937," 146–7, 149.

53 刘慧宇 (Liu Huiyu), "论南京国民政府时期国地财政划分制度" ("Discussing the Transfer System of Finance during the Nanjing Decade"), 中国经济史研究 (*Research in Chinese Economic History*) no. 4 (2001), 42–8.

54 Wang Ke-wen, "Wang Jingwei and the Policy Origins of the 'Peace Movement,' 1932–1937," 25.

55 臼井勝美 (Usui Katsumi), *Research on Sino-Japanese Diplomatic History*, 267–8.

56 邱松庆 (Qiu Songqing), "南京国民政府初建时期财经政策述评" ("A Review of the Financial Policy of the Nationalist Government during the Early Period in Nanjing"), 中国社会经济史研究 (*Research on Chinese Social and Economic History*) no. 4 (1996), 75.

57 菊池一隆 (Kikuchi Kazutaka), "重慶政府の戦時金融" ("Wartime Finances of the Chongqing Government") in 中国国民政府史の研究 (*Research on the History of the Chinese Republican Government*), ed. 中国現代史研究会 (Committee for Research on Modern Chinese History) (Tokyo: 汲古書院刊, 1986), 400.

58 Donald G. Gillin, "Problems of Centralization in Republican China: the Case of Ch'en Ch'eng and the Kuomintang," *Journal of Asian Studies* 29, no. 4 (August 1970), 837.

59 Eugene William Levich, *The Kwangsi Way in Kuomintang China, 1931–1939* (Armonk, NY: M. E. Sharpe, 1993), 6, 227, passim.

60 Ch'i Hsi-sheng, *Nationalist China at War: Military Defeats and Political Collapse, 1937–45* (Ann Arbor: University of Michigan Press, 1982), 10.

61 土田哲夫 (Tsuchida Akio),"南京政府期の国家統合—張学良東北政権（一九二八〜三一年）との関係の例—" ("National Integration during the Nanjing Period – the Connection with Zhang Xueliang's Sovereignty over Manchuria ([1928–31] as an Example") in *Research on the History of the Chinese Republican Government*, ed. 中国現代史研究会 (Committee for Research on Modern Chinese History), 165; K. K. Kawakami, *Manchoukuo Child of Conflict*, 49–50; Hsi-sheng Ch'i, *Nationalist China at War*, 37.

62 Sergei Leonidovich Tikhvinskii, ed., *Русско-китайские отношения в XX веке* (*Russo-Chinese Relations in the 20th Century*), Vol. 4, part 2, 1937–45 (Moscow: «Памятники исторической мысли», 2000), 529.

63 Tien Hung-mao, *Government and Politics in Kuomintang China 1927–1937* (Stanford, CA: Stanford University Press, 1972), 45–6, 50; Gregor Benton, *New Fourth Army: Communist Resistance along the Yangtze and the Huai 1938–1941* (Berkeley: University of California Press, 1999), 111; 王奇生 (Wang Qisheng), *Party Members, Party Authority, and Party Infighting*, 242.

64 Lionel Max Chassin, *The Communist Conquest of China: A History of the Civil War 1945–1949*, Timothy Osato and Louis Gelas, trans. (Cambridge, MA: Harvard University Press, 1965), 46, 252; Tien Hung-mao, *Government and Politics in Kuomintang China 1927–1937*, 47–53.

65 Robert A. Kapp, *Szechwan and the Chinese Republic: Provincial Militarism and Central Power, 1911–1938* (New Haven: Yale University Press, 1973), 127, 135; Tien Hung-mao, *Government and Politics in Kuomintang China 1927–1937*, 65–7; Lionel Max Chassin, *The Communist Conquest of China*, 26.

66 Tien Hung-mao, *Government and Politics in Kuomintang China 1927–1937*, 52–3, 61, 65–7; Tien Hung-mao, "Factional Politics in Kuomintang China, 1928–1937: An Interpretation" in *China at the Crossroads: Nationalists and Communists, 1927–1949*, ed. F. Gilbert Chan (Boulder, CO: Westview Press, 1980), 28; Lionel Max Chassin, *The Communist Conquest of China*, 26; 張瑞德 (Zhang Ruide), 抗戰時期的國軍人事 (*Personnel Matters of the Nationalist Army during the War of Resistance*) (Taipei: 中央研究院近代史研究所, 1993), 6.

67 Tien Hung-mao, *Government and Politics in Kuomintang China 1927–1937*, 56, 58; Gregor Benton, *New Fourth Army*, 115.

68 Tien Hung-mao "Factional Politics in Kuomintang China, 1928–1937," 29–31; Tien Hung-mao, *Government and Politics in Kuomintang China 1927–1937*, 65, 71–2.

69 Lionel Max Chassin, *The Communist Conquest of China*, v, 45; Howard L. Boorman, ed., *Biographical Dictionary,* Vol. 2, 48–51; ibid., Vol. 3, 55–6.

70 A. Doak Barnett, *China on the Eve of Communist Takeover* (New York: Frederick A. Praeger, 1963), 161, 220, 284; Robert A. Kapp, *Szechwan and the Chinese Republic*, 148; Lloyd E. Eastman, *Seeds of Destruction*, 40; Suzanne Pepper, "The KMT-CCP Conflict 1945–1949" in *The Cambridge History of China*, Vol. 13, eds. John K. Fairbank and Albert Feuerwerker (Cambridge: Cambridge University Press, 1986), 776.

71 Odd Arne Westad, *Decisive Encounters: The Chinese Civil War, 1946–1950* (Stanford, CA: Stanford University Press, 2003), 149; Lloyd E. Eastman, *Seeds of Destruction*, 164–6.

72 Richard J. Smith, *China's Cultural Heritage: The Qing Dynasty 1644–1912* (Boulder, CO: Westview Press, 1994), 18.

73 Robert L. Jarman, ed., *China Political Reports 1911–1960*, Vol. 8 (Chippenham, Wilts: Archive Editions, 2001), 175.

74 王奇生 (Wang Qisheng), "党政关系：国民党党治在地方层级的运作" ("Relations between the Nationalist Party and the Government: Party Rule at the Local Level [1927–1937]"), 中国社会科学 (*Social Studies in China*) no. 3 (2001), 187–203.

75 住筱新 (Zhu Xiaoxin), ed., 历史词典 (*Historical Dictionary*) (Beijing: 学苑出版社, 2005), 295; 李宇平 (Li Yuping), "Some Phenomena during the Chinese Depression in the 1930s," 79.

76 James E. Sheridan, *Chinese Warlord*, 281.

77 Howard L. Boorman, ed., *Biographical Dictionary*, Vol. 4, 49

78 武月星 (Wu Yuexing), *Modern Chinese History Map Collection*, 57, 69; Edward L. Dreyer, *China at War, 1901–1949* (London: Longman, 1995), 168–9.

79 Howard L. Boorman, ed., *Biographical Dictionary,* Vol. 2, 165.

80 Ibid., 339.

81 武月星 (Wu Yuexing), *Modern Chinese History Map Collection*, 61; Edward L. Dreyer, *China at War, 1901–1949*, 168–9.

82 杨卫敏 (Yang Weimin), "The Nationalist Government and Shanghai Incident," 232; Donald A. Jordan, *China's Trial by Fire*, ix, xv, 5, 8, 239; Jay Taylor, *Generalissimo*, 84.

83 臼井勝美 (Usui Katsumi), Research on Sino-Japanese Diplomatic History, 98–106; 石島紀之 (Ishijima Noriyuki), *History of China's Anti-Japanese War*, 10–12, 17, 39–40; Ian Nish, *Japanese Foreign Policy in the Interwar Period*, 73.

84 林明德 (Lin Mingde), "Formation of Japanese Militarism: An Investigation of the Manchurian Incident," 261; 張學良 (Zhang Xueliang), *An Oral History by Zhang Xueliang*, 275.

85 Edward L. Dreyer, *China at War, 1901–1949*, 168–9.
86 Iurii Mikhailovich Ovchinnikov, *Становление и развитие единого национального фронта сопротивления Японии в Китае* (*The Creation and Development of the United National Front to Resist Japan in China*) (Moscow: Издательсво «наука» Главная редакция восточной литературы, 1985), 59–60.
87 Wang Ke-wen, "Wang Jingwei and the Policy Origins of the 'Peace Movement,' 1932–1937," 23; 味岡徹 (Ajioka Tōru), "The Nationalist Party's 'Political Tutelage' and the Anti-Japanese War," 368.
88 武月星 (Wu Yuexing), *Modern Chinese History Map Collection*, 79–80; Edward L. Dreyer, *China at War, 1901–1949*, 186–7.
89 武月星 (Wu Yuexing), *Modern Chinese History Map Collection*, 69, 77; 石島紀之 (Ishijima Noriyuki), *History of China's Anti-Japanese War*, 27.
90 Edward L. Dreyer, *China at War, 1901–1949*, 182–3, 190–4; Gregor Benton, *Mountain Fires: The Red Army's Three-Year War in South China, 1934–1938* (Berkeley: University of California Press, 1992), 4; 武月星 (Wu Yuexing), *Modern Chinese History Map Collection*, 77–9.
91 Donald W. Klein and Anne B. Clark. *Biographic Dictionary of Chinese Communism 1921–1965*, Vol. 1, 247–9; ibid., Vol. 2, 681; June Grasso, Jay Corrin, and Michael Kort, *Modernization and Revolution in China*, 120.
92 Michael Clodfelter, *Warfare and Armed Conflicts: A Statistical Reference to Casualty and Other Figures 1618–1991*, Vol. 2 (Jefferson, NC: McFarland, 1992), 927.
93 Gregor Benton, *New Fourth Army*, 3–4, 14; Gregor Benton, *Mountain Fires*, xxxii, 1, 8, 469.
94 Parks M. Coble, *Facing Japan*, 149.
95 石島紀之 (Ishijima Noriyuki), *History of China's Anti-Japanese War*, 17, 39–40; Sergei Leonidovich Tikhvinskii, *Путь Китая к объединению и независимости 1898–1949* (*China's Path to Unification and Independence 1898–1949*) (Moscow: Издательство фирма «Восточная литература» РАН, 1996), 268–71; Parks M. Coble, *Facing Japan*, 192.
96 Michael A. Barnhart, *Japan Prepares for Total War*, 41.
97 Wang Ke-wen, "Wang Jingwei and the Policy Origins of the 'Peace Movement,' 1932–1937," 32–3.

4 RUSSIA 1917–1936: IMPENDING TWO-FRONT WAR AND WORLD REVOLUTION

1 Japan, Defense Agency, National Defense College, Military History Department (防衛庁防衛研修所戦史部), ed., 関東軍 (*The Kantō Army*), Vol. 1

(Tokyo: 朝雲新聞社, 1969), 49–56; 黒野耐 (Kurono Taeru), 日本を滅ぼした国防方針 (*Japan's Disastrous National Defense Policy*) (Tokyo: 文芸春秋社, 2002), 22–5; 北岡伸一 (Kitaoka Shin'ichi), 日本陸軍と大陸政策１９０６–１９１８年 (*The Japanese Army and Its Strategy for the Asian Mainland 1906–1918*) (Tokyo: 東京大学出版社, 1985), 9; 角田順 (Tsunoda Jun), 満州問題と国防方針—明治期における国防環境の変動— (*The Manchurian Question and National Defense Policy: Changes in the Late-Meiji National Defense Environment*) (Tokyo: 原書房, 1967), 678–700; 大山梓 (Ōyama Azusa), ed., 山県有朋意見書 (*The Written Opinions of Yamagata Aritomo*) (Tokyo: 原書房, 1966), 292, 294–300; David Isaakovich Gol'dberg, *Внешняя политика Японии в 1941–1945 гг.* (*The Foreign Policy of Japan 1941–1945*) (Moscow: Издательство социально-экономической литературы, 1962), 71; Shimada Toshihiko, "Designs on North China, 1933–1937," 198.

2 Nicholas V. Riasanovsky, *A History of Russia*, 5th ed. (New York: Oxford University Press, 1993), 418; Richard Pipes, *The Russian Revolution* (New York: Vintage Books, 1990), 206, 454; W. Bruce Lincoln, *Red Victory: History of the Russian Civil War 1918–1921* (New York: Da Capo Press, 1999), 175–6.

3 Duncan Townson, *The New Penguin Dictionary of Modern History 1789–1945* (London: Penguin Books, 1994), 99.

4 Nicholas V. Riasanovsky, *A History of Russia*, 483.

5 Sun Tzu, *The Art of War*, trans. Samuel B. Griffith (Oxford: Oxford University Press, 1963), 131, 134–5.

6 Nicholas V. Riasanovsky, *A History of Russia*, 488; R. J. Rummel, *Lethal Politics: Soviet Genocide and Mass Murder since 1917* (New Brunswick, NJ: Transaction Publishers, 1990), 6.

7 Quoted in Petr Parfenovich Vladimirov, *Особый район Китая 1942–1945* (*A Special Region in China 1942–1945*) (Moscow: Издательство Агентства печаты Новости, 1977), 512.

8 W. Bruce Lincoln, *Red Victory*, 48–9.

9 Cited in Evan Mawdsley, *The Russian Civil War* (Boston: Unwin Hyman, 1987), 60–2, 69; W. Bruce Lincoln, *Red Victory*, 175; Isaac Deutscher, *The Prophet Armed Trotsky: 1879–1921* (Oxford: Oxford University Press, 1980), 405, 408–9, 414–16, 430, 432; Mark von Hagen, *Soldiers in the Proletarian Dictatorship: The Red Army and the Soviet Socialist State, 1917–1930* (Ithaca: Cornell University Press, 1990), 32–3, 40, 91, 97–8, 100, 126; Peter Kenez, *Civil War in South Russia: The Defeat of the Whites* (Berkeley: University of California Press, 1977), 4, 7, 11–16, 24, 58; Leon Trotsky, *Marxism and Military Affairs, 1921–1924* (Colombo, Ceylon: Young Socialist Publication, 1969), 21, 58.

10 Robert A. Lewis, "The Mixing of Russians and Soviet Nationalities and Its Demographic Impact," in *Soviet Nationality Problems*, ed. Edward Allworth (New York: Columbia University Press, 1971), 125–6, 131.

11 John P. LeDonne, *The Russian Empire and the World 1700–1917: The Geopolitics of Expansion and Containment* (New York: Oxford University Press, 1997), 155–223.

12 S. C. M. Paine, *Imperial Rivals*, passim.

13 Ibid., 234, 246.

14 K. K. Kawakami, *Japan in China: Her Motives and Aims* (London: John Murray, 1938), 8–9, 12.

15 S. C. M. Paine, *Imperial Rivals*, 28–9, 327–9, 341, 352.

16 FMA, A.4.6.1-MA/X-2–2-2–7, 満州国々境地方ニ於ケル紛争雑件 (Miscellaneous Papers on Manchukuo Frontier Disputes), various agreements, 15 October 1941.

17 Cited in S. C. M. Paine, *Imperial Rivals*, 320. Emphasis as in *China Year Book 1924–5*, ed. H. G. W. Woodhead (Tianjin: Simplin, Marshall, Hamilton, Kent, 1926), 869.

18 Bruce A. Elleman, "Soviet Territorial Concessions in China and the May 30th Movement: 1917–1927," *Journal of Oriental Studies* 32, no. 2 (1994), 162–78; Bruce A. Elleman, *Diplomacy and Deception: The Secret History of Sino-Soviet Diplomatic Relations, 1917–192* (Armonk, NY: M. E. Sharpe, 1997), 24–50; 饶良伦 (Rao Lianglun), 张秀兰 (Zhang Xiulan), 段光达 (Duan Guangda),"九一八事变前黑龙江区的中苏关系" ("Sino-Soviet Relations in the Heilongjiang Area Prior to the Manchurian Incident"), 近代史研究 (*Modern Chinese History Studies*) 75, no. 3 (May 1993), 219–26; 杜君 (Du Jun),"1917–1924年苏俄在中东铁路问题上的对华政策再探" ("A Reexamination of Soviet Russia's China Policy Concerning the Chinese Eastern Railway Question from 1917–1924") 史学集刊 (*Collected Papers of History Studies*) no. 4 (November 2000), 36–42.

19 JDA, 満洲全般４１０満洲の工業開発を語る等, "自昭和六年九月八日至昭和八年六月中旬満洲事変経過ノ概要" ("Summary of the Course of the Manchuria Incident from 8 September 1931 to mid-June 1933"), 1933, p. 18.

20 S. C. M. Paine, *Imperial Rivals*, 187.

21 Bruce A. Elleman, *Diplomacy and Deception*, 238–48.

22 Robert L. Jarman, ed., *China Political Reports 1911–1960*, Vol. 4, 283–5, 311–19; Chong-Sik Lee, *Revolutionary Struggle in Manchuria*, 96; Bruce A. Elleman, *Modern Chinese Warfare, 1795–1989* (London: Routledge, 2001), 182–9; 楊奎松 (Yang Kuisong), "难以确定的对手（1917〜1949）" ("The Inscrutable Opponent, 1917–1949") in 中苏关系史纲：1917〜1991年中苏关系若干问题再探讨 (*A Survey of Sino-Soviet Relations: A Reexamination*

of Questions Concerning Sino-Soviet Relations, 1917–1991), rev. ed., ed. 沈志华 (Shen Zhihua) (Beijing: 社会科学文献出版社, 2011), 43; George Alexander Lensen, *The Damned Inheritance: The Soviet Union and the Manchurian Crises 1924–1935* (Tallahassee, FL: Diplomatic Press, 1974), 59–68, 73, 80; Felix Patrikeeff, "Railway as Political Catalyst: The Chinese Eastern Railway and the 1929 Sino-Soviet Conflict" in *Manchurian Railways and the Opening of China*, eds. Bruce A. Elleman and Stephen Kotkin (Armonk, NY: M. E. Sharpe, 2010), 83–6.

23 饶良伦 (Rao Lianglun), 张秀兰 (Zhang Xiulan), 段光达 (Duan Guangda), "Sino-Soviet Relations in the Heilongjiang Area Prior to the Manchurian Incident"), 233; 臼井勝美 (Usui Katsumi), *Research on Sino-Japanese Diplomatic History*, 41; Rana Mitter, *The Manchurian Myth: Nationalism, Resistance, and Collaboration in Modern China* (Berkeley: University of California Press, 2000), 49–50; Stephen Chao Ying Pan, *American Diplomacy Concerning Manchuria* (Washington, DC: Catholic University of America, 1938), 195–225; Peter S. H. Tang, *Russian and Soviet Policy in Manchuria and Outer Mongolia 1911–1931* (Durham: Duke University Press, 1959), 199–200, 218–32, 243.

24 Bruce A. Elleman, *Modern Chinese Warfare, 1795–1989*, 190–1.

25 Bruce Elleman, *Moscow and the Emergence of Communist Power in China, 1925–30: The Nanchang Uprising and the Birth of the Red Army* (London: Routledge, 2009), 72–9, 206–9; Steve Smith, "Moscow and the Second and Third Armed Uprisings in Shanghai, 1927" in *The Chinese Revolution in the 1920s*, eds. Mechthild Leutner et al., 237–8; Isaac Deutscher, *The Prophet Outcast Trotsky: 1929–1940* (Oxford: Oxford University Press, 1963), 504.

26 Bruce Elleman, *Moscow and the Emergence of Communist Power in China, 1925–30*, 206, passim; 石島紀之 (Ishijima Noriyuki), *History of China's Anti-Japanese War*, 31.

27 A. Doak Barnett, *China on the Eve of Communist Takeover*, 27–8, 244–57; Andrew D. W. Forbes, *Warlords and Muslims in Chinese Central Asia: A Political History of Republican Sinkiang 1911–1949* (Cambridge: Cambridge University Press, 1986), 144–8; James E. Sheridan, *Chinese Warlord*, 196–202, 225; Bruce A. Elleman, *Diplomacy and Deception*, 127–31; David J. Dallin, *The Rise of Russia in Asia* (1949, reprint; Hamden, CT: Archon Books, 1971), 196, 225; K. K. Kawakami, *Japan in China*, 12; Sergei Leonidovich Tikhvinskii, ed., *Russo-Chinese Relations in the 20th Century*, Vol. 4, part 1, 1937–45, 307, 569.

28 Ronald Suleski, *Civil Government in Warlord China*, 30–1; James E. Sheridan, *Chinese Warlord*, 281.

29 JDA, 満洲全般４１０満洲の工業開発を語る等, "自昭和六年九月八日至昭和八年六月中旬満洲事変経過ノ概要" ("Summary of the Course of the

Manchuria Incident from 8 September 1931 to Mid-June 1933"), 1933, pp. 30–9; Linda Benson, *The Ili Rebellion: The Moslem Challenge to Chinese Authority in Xinjiang 1944–1949* (Armonk, NY: M. E. Sharpe, 1990), 36; Andrew D. W. Forbes, *Warlords and Muslims in Chinese Central Asia*, 166; Sergei Leonidovich Tikhvinskii, ed., *Russo-Chinese Relations in the 20th Century*, Vol. 4, part 1, 1937–45, 522; Linda Benson and Ingvar Svanberg, *China's Last Nomads: The History and Culture of China's Kazaks* (Armonk, NY: M. E. Sharpe, 1998), 66, 68; 袁同禮 (Yuan Tongli), comp. 中俄西北條約集 (*Russo-Chinese Treaties and Agreements Relating to Sinkiang 1851–1949*) (Hong Kong: 袁同禮, 1963), 95–116; Arthur C. Hasiotis, Jr., *Soviet Political, Economic, and Military Involvement in Sinkiang from 1928 to 1949* (New York: Garland Publishing, 1987), 95–6, 115–16, 188; 中央研究院近代史研究所檔案館 (Academia Sinica. Institute of Modern History Archives [Hereafter abbreviated as ASA]), 197.1/0005, 盛蘇密約譯本 (Sheng Shicai-USSR Secret Treaty Translation), 11-WAA-00145, 26 November 1940, pp. 30–46.

30 JFM, A.2.2.0-C/R1–3, 支那蘇連邦外交関係雑纂 蘇支蒙彊関係 (MiscellaneousPapersonSino-SovietDiplomacy:Soviet-Chinese-Mongol-Xinjiang Relations), to Foreign Minister Hirota from the Tianjin consul-general 川越, 3 February 1936, top secret, p. 380–1; Arthur C. Hasiotis, Jr., *Soviet Political, Economic, and Military Involvement in Sinkiang*, 100.

31 任骏 (Ren Jun),"蒋廷黻与七七事变前后的中苏关系" ("Jiang Tingfu and Sino-Soviet Relations before and after the Marco Polo Bridge Incident"), 近代史研究 (*Modern Chinese History Studies*) no. 1, (1991), 184; A. Doak Barnett, *China on the Eve of Communist Takeover*, 244–5; Linda Benson, *The Ili Rebellion*, 27–8; Andrew D. W. Forbes, *Warlords and Muslims in Chinese Central Asia*, 144–6, 148, 232; 香島明雄 (Kashima Akio), 中ソ外交史研究１９３７－１９４６ (*Research on Sino-Soviet Diplomatic History, 1937–1946*) (Tokyo: 世界思想社, 1990), 33; F. C. Jones, *Japan's New Order in East Asia*, 173–7.

32 Linda Benson, *Ili Rebellion*, 36; Andrew D. W. Forbes, *Warlords and Muslims in Chinese Central Asia*, 166.

33 Andrew D. W. Forbes, *Warlords and Muslims in Chinese Central Asia*, 166; Linda Benson, *Ili Rebellion*, 36–9; A. Doak Barnett, *China on the Eve of Communist Takeover*, 247.

34 Howard L. Boorman, ed., *Biographical Dictionary*, Vol. 3, 1–2, 123; 秦孝儀 (Qin Xiaoyi), *Dictionary of Modern Chinese History*, 328; Arthur C. Hasiotis, Jr., *Soviet Political, Economic, and Military Involvement in Sinkiang*, 129–36.

35 Linda Benson, *Ili Rebellion*, 5–7, 21, 39; A. Doak Barnett, *China on the Eve of Communist Takeover*, 247; David D. Wang, *Under the Soviet Shadow: The Yining Incident* (Hong Kong: Chinese University Press, 1999), 61,

120, 149; Arthur C. Hasiotis, Jr., *Soviet Political, Economic, and Military Involvement in Sinkiang*, 142, 155–6; Andrew D. W. Forbes, *Warlords and Muslims in Chinese Central Asia*, 195, 201, 215; K. K. Kawakami, *Manchoukuo Child of Conflict*, 193–5; 楊奎松 (Yang Kuisong), "The Inscrutable Opponent, 1917–1949," 79

36 JDA, 満洲全般２２５満洲に関する用兵的観察, Vol. 13, part 5, 極東ソ軍の戦略的特性に関する調査 (Survey of the Strategy of the Far Eastern Soviet Military), March 1953, 復員局資料整理課元陸軍大佐林三郎 (Demobilization Bureau, Documents Section, Former Army Colonel Hayashi Saburō?), pp. 27–8; Alvin D. Coox, *Nomonhan*, 75; Herbert P. Bix, *Hirohito*, 248–9; Harriet L. Moore, *Soviet Far Eastern Policy 1931–1945* (Princeton, NJ: Princeton University Press, 1945), 10–11; Stephen Chao Ying Pan, *American Diplomacy Concerning Manchuria*, 223–4; Sergei Leonidovich Tikhvinskii, ed., *Russo-Chinese Relations in the 20th Century*, Vol. 3, September 1931–September 1937, 6, 10–11; Boris Slavinsky, *Japanese-Soviet Neutrality Pact: A Diplomatic History, 1941–1945*, trans. Geoffrey Jukes (London: Routledge, 2004), 14

37 K. K. Kawakami, *Manchoukuo Child of Conflict*, 193.

38 Galina Fominichna Zakharova, *The Policy of Japan in Manchuria 1932–1945*, 85; Sergei Leonidovich Tikhvinskii, ed., *Russo-Chinese Relations in the 20th Century*, Vol. 3, September 1931–September 1937, 206; Harriet L. Moore, *Soviet Far Eastern Policy 1931–1945*, 31–2, 44; JFM, 条約MA4, 北満鉄道（東支鉄道）譲渡協定 (Northern Manchurian Railway [Chinese Eastern Railway] Transfer Agreement), 23 March 1935, Tokyo.

39 香島明雄 (Kashima Akio), *Research on Sino-Soviet Diplomatic History, 1937–1946*, 62; Sergei Leonidovich Tikhvinskii, ed., *Russo-Chinese Relations in the 20th Century*, Vol. 3, September 1931–September 1937, 13–14; JFM, A.2.2.0-C/R1–3, 支那蘇連邦外交関係雑纂 蘇支蒙彊関係 (Miscellaneous Papers on Sino-Soviet Diplomacy: Soviet-Chinese-Mongol-Xinjiang Relations), 28 April 1936, p. 221; ASA, 112.6/0012, 中蘇條約集 (Sino-Soviet Treaty Collection), 11-WAA-0089, 8 April 1936, p. 117.

40 Adolf Hitler, *Mein Kampf*, trans. Ralph Manheim (1925, reprint; Boston: Houghton Mifflin, 1971), 641–64, 654; JFM, A.2.2.0-C/R1–3, 支那蘇連邦外交関係雑纂 蘇支蒙彊関係 (Miscellaneous Papers on Sino-Soviet Diplomacy: Soviet-Chinese-Mongol-Xinjiang Relations), Agence Hanas, 8 April 1936, USSR, "Le protocole d'assistance mutuelle entre l'U.R.S.S. et la Mongolie," Tass, pp. 224–7.

41 Sadao Asada, *From Mahan to Pearl Harbor*, 168.

42 扬奎松 (Yang Kuisong), 国民党的"联共"与、"反共" (*Kuomintang: Unity with Communists and Anti-communism*) (Beijing: 社会科学文献出版社, 2008), 332–6.

43 臼井勝美 (Usui Katsumi), *Research on Sino-Japanese Diplomatic History*, 183; Historical Research Center (歴史学研究会), comp., *History of the Pacific War*, Vol. 2, 343–6; JFM, B.1.1.0-J/X2, 日独伊防共協定関係一件 (Item Concerning the Japanese-German-Italian Anti-Comintern Pact), *Anti-Comintern Pact* and associated supplementary agreements, 25 November 1936; JFM, B.1.1.0-J/X3, 日独伊同盟条約関係一件 (Item Concerning the Japanese-German-Italian Alliance), Vol. 1, *Anti-Comintern Pact* and associated supplementary agreements, 25 November 1936; Tajima Nobuo, "The Berlin-Tokyo Axis Reconsidered: From the Anti-Comintern Pact to the Plot to Assassinate Stalin" in *Japanese-German Relations, 1895–1945*, eds. Christian W. Spang and Rolf-Harald Wippich (London: Routledge, 2006), 165–9, Gerhard L. Weinberg, *The Foreign Policy of Hitler's Germany* (Chicago: University of Chicago Press, 1970), 342–3.

44 Leon Trotsky, *Marxism and Military Affairs*, 20–1, 58; Iu. V. Chudodeev, ed., *Along the Roads of China 1937–1945: Memoirs*, 25; Hsi-sheng Ch'i, *Nationalist China at War*, 94; 王奇生 (Wang Qisheng), *Party Members, Party Authority, and Party Infighting*, 14, 24, 26.

45 宋金寿 (Song Jinshou),"陕甘宁边区在抗战中的地位和作用" ("The Position and Role of the Shaan-Gan-Ning; Gerhard L. Weinberg, *The Foreign Policy of Hitler's Germany: Diplomatic Revolution in Europe 1933–36* (Chicago: University of Chicago Press, 1970), 342–3. Border Area in the War of Resistance") 中共党史研究 (*Research on the History of the Chinese Communist Party*) no. 5 (1995), 41.

46 Wesley M. Bagby, *The Eagle-Dragon Alliance*, 104–5, 114–21; Petr Parfenovich Vladimirov, *Special Region in China 1942–1945*, 362.

47 Edgar Snow, *Red Star over China*, rev. ed. (New York: Grove, 1968); Michael M. Sheng, *Battling Western Imperialism: Mao, Stalin, and the United States* (Princeton, NJ: Princeton University Press, 1997), 29; Jay Taylor, *Generalissimo*, 96, 122, 135; Hans J. van de Ven, *War and Nationalism in China 1925–1945*, 181; Jung Chang and Jon Halliday, *Mao the Unknown Story* (New York: Alfred A. Knopf, 2005), 191–2.

48 Petr Parfenovich Vladimirov, *Special Region in China 1942–1945*, 5, 183.

49 林明德 (Lin Mingde), "Formation of Japanese Militarism: An Investigation of the Manchurian Incident," 264.

50 刘喜发 (Liu Xifa) and 王彦堂 (Wang Yantang), "试论国内外舆论对西安事变和平解决的作用" ("The Role of Domestic and International Public Opinion on the Peaceful Solution of the Xi'an Incident"), 史学集刊 (*Collected Papers of Historical Studies*) 71, no. 2 (1998), 37–8; 林祥庚 (Lin Xianggeng), "民主党派与中国共产党的'逼将抗日'方针" ("The Democratic Parties' and the CCP's Guiding Principle of 'Compelling Chiang to Resist Japan'"), 中共党史研究 (*Research on the History of the Chinese Communist Party*) no.

3 (1996), 29–30; 金冲及 (Jin Chongji),"华北事变和抗日救亡高潮的兴起" ("The North China Incident and the High Tide of the Resist Japan–Save the Nation Movement"), 历史研究 (*Historical Research*) no. 4 (1995), 3–22; Parks M. Coble, "The National Salvation Association as a Political Party" in *Roads Not Taken: The Struggle of Opposition Parties in Twentieth-Century China*, ed. Roger B. Jeans (Boulder, CO: Westview Press, 1992), 135; 田中仁 (Tanaka Hitoshi), １９３０年代中国政治史研究：中国共産党の危機と再生 (*Research on Chinese Political History in the 1930s: The Crisis and Rebirth of the Chinese Communist Party*) (Tokyo: 勁草書房, 2002), 87, 89.

51 Howard L. Boorman, ed., *Biographical Dictionary*, Vol. 1, 88; ibid., Vol. 3, 88, 100, 320–1, 397.

52 林祥庚 (Lin Xianggeng), "The Democratic Parties' and the CCP's Guiding Principle of 'Compelling Chiang to Resist Japan,'" 33–4; Sergei Leonidovich Tikhvinskii, *China's Path to Unification and Independence 1898–1949*, 271.

53 Howard L. Boorman, ed., *Biographical Dictionary*, Vol. 1, 160–3; ibid., Vol. 2, 340; ibid., Vol. 3, 54–5; Gregor Benton, *New Fourth Army*, 103–4.

54 Eugene William Levich, *The Kwangsi Way in Kuomintang China, 1931–1939*, 6, 227, passim.

55 王锦侠 (Wang Jinxia) and 张奇 (Zhang Qi),"两广事变与中国共产党'逼蒋抗日'方针的形成" ("The Guangdong-Guangxi Incident and the Chinese Communist Party's Policy Formulation of 'Compelling Chiang and Resisting Japan'"), 中共党史研究 (*Research on the History of the Chinese Communist Party*) no. 2 (1990), 37–41.

56 Howard L. Boorman, ed., *Biographical Dictionary*, Vol. 1, 66.

57 石島紀之 (Ishijima Noriyuki), *History of China's Anti-Japanese War*, 43; Jonathan Haslam, *The Soviet Union and the Threat from the East, 1933–1941* (Pittsburgh: University of Pittsburgh Press, 1992), 70–2.

58 杨奎松 (Yang Kuisong), "关于共产国际与中国共产党'联蒋抗日'方针的关系问题" ("An Investigation of Zhang Xueliang's Activities against Chiang Kai-shek"), 历史研究 (*Historical Research*) no. 6 (1997), 161, 177; Iurii Mikhailovich Ovchinnikov, *Creation and Development of the United National Front*, 52; 扬奎松 (Yang Kuisong), *Kuomintang: Unity with Communists and Anti-communism*, 326.

59 吴天威 (Wu Tianwei),"张学良与西安事变再研究［续］"("A Reconsideration of Zhang Xueliang and the Xi'an Incident [Sequel]"), 中共党史研究 (*Research on the History of the Chinese Communist Party*) no. 2 (1997), 52–9.

60 蒋永敬 (Jiang Yongjing),"西安事变前张学良所谓'一二月内定有变动'何指？" ("What Did Zhang Xueliang Mean in His Pre-Xi'an Incident So-called 'Required Changes in One or Two Months'?"), 近代史研究 (*Modern Chinese History Studies*) no. 1 (1997), 268.

61 任振河 (Ren Zhenhe), "张学良五访阎锡山" ("Zhang Xueliang's Five Visits to Yan Xishan"), 近代史研究 (*Modern Chinese History Studies*)

80, no. 2 (March 1994), 313–18; 秦孝儀 (Qin Xiaoyi), *Dictionary of Modern Chinese History*, 562.

62 江口圭一 (Eguchi Kei-ichi), *A Short History of the Fifteen Year War*, 105; Michael M. Sheng, *Battling Western Imperialism*, 26; David S. G. Goodman, *Social and Political Change in Revolutionary China: The Taihang Base Area in the War of Resistance to Japan, 1937–1945* (Lanham, MD: Rowman & Littlefield, 2000), 47; Shum Kui-kwong, *The Chinese Communists' Road to Power: The Anti-Japanese National United Front, 1935–1945* (Hong Kong: Oxford University Press, 1988), 61, 68; Hans J. van de Ven, *War and Nationalism in China 1925–1945*, 183–5; Shimada Toshihiko, "Designs on North China, 1933–1937," 197; 武月星 (Wu Yuexing), *Modern Chinese History Map Collection*, 82, 88.

63 蔣永敬 (Jiang Yongjing), "What Did Zhang Xueliang Mean in His Pre-Xi'an Incident So-called 'Required Changes in One or Two Months'?" 269; Howard L. Boorman, ed., *Biographical Dictionary*, Vol. 4, 49; Sechin Jagchid, *Last Mongol Prince*, 162; Edward J. Drea, *Japan's Imperial Army*, 191.

64 任振河 (Ren Zhenhe), "Zhang Xueliang's Five Visits to Yan Xishan," 313–18.

65 Feng Chongyi, "The Making of the Jin Sui Base Area," in *North China at War: The Social Ecology of Revolution, 1937–1945*, eds. Feng Chongyi and David S. F. Goodman (Lanham, MD: Rowman & Littlefield, 2000), 157–8, 161.

66 Cited in Jonathan Fenby, *Chiang Kai-shek*, 280.

67 杨奎松 (Yang Kuisong), "An Investigation of Zhang Xueliang's Activities against Chiang Kai-shek," 161, 177; Iurii Mikhailovich Ovchinnikov, *Creation and Development of the United National Front*, 51.

68 Jonathan Haslam, *Soviet Union and the Threat from the East, 1933–1941*, 70–2.

69 Ibid., 70–2; 塚瀨進 (Tsukase Susumu), *Manchukuo "Racial Harmony" in Reality*, 228–9; Iurii Mikhailovich Ovchinnikov, *Creation and Development of the United National Front*, 54–6.

70 Michael M. Sheng, *Battling Western Imperialism*, 21.

71 石島紀之 (Ishijima Noriyuki), *History of China's Anti-Japanese War*, 43.

72 杨奎松 (Yang Kuisong), "关于共产国际与中国共产党'联蒋抗日'方针的关系问题" ("The Relationship between the Comintern and the Chinese Communist Party's Policy of 'Alliance with Chiang to Resist Japan'"), 中共党史研究 (*Research on the History of the Chinese Communist Party*) no. 4 (1989), 51–9; Howard L. Boorman, ed., *Biographical Dictionary*, Vol. 1, 232; Jonathan Haslam, *Soviet Union and the Threat from the East, 1933–1941*, 60.

73 杨奎松 (Yang Kuisong), "张学良与西安事变之解决" ("Zhang Xueliang and the Solution for the Xi'an Incident"), 中国社会科学 (*Social Studies*

in China) no. 4 (September 1996), 190–1; Michael A. Barnhart, *Japan Prepares for Total War*, 79; 杨奎松 (Yang Kuisong), 张学良与中共关系之谜 (*The Riddle of Zhang Xueliang's Relations with the Chinese Communists*) (Nanjing: 江苏人民出版社, 2006), passim.

74 Michael M. Sheng, *Battling Western Imperialism*, 32–3.

75 鄧元忠 (Deng Yuanzhong),"國共第二次合作前的第一次秘密商談接觸：從一份俄文資料談起" ("The First Secret Negotiations and Contacts before the Second Nationalist-Communist United Front: Discussion Based on Russian Documents"), 台灣師範大學歷史學報 (*Taiwan Normal University Bulletin of Historical Research*) 23 (June 1995), 289–310.

76 杨奎松 (Yang Kuisong), "西安事变期间'三位一体'的军事协商与部署" ("The Military Negotiations and Deployments of the 'Trinity' during the Xi'an Incident"), 近代史研究 (*Modern Chinese History Studies*) 96, no. 6 (November 1996), 81–96; 林祥庚 (Lin Xianggeng), "The Democratic Parties' and the CCP's Guiding Principle of 'Compelling Chiang to Resist Japan,'" 31.

77 任振河 (Ren Zhenhe), "Zhang Xueliang's Five Visits to Yan Xishan," 313–18.

78 金光耀 (Jin Guangyao),"1932年中苏复交谈判中的何士渠道" ("The Mediation of Hussey during the 1932 Negotiations to Restore Sino-Soviet Diplomatic Relations"), 近代史研究 (*Modern Chinese History Studies*) no. 2 (1999), 305–14.

79 O. Edmund Clubb, *China & Russia: The "Great Game"* (New York: Columbia University Press, 1971), 272.

80 熊沛彪 (Xiong Peibiao), "Japan's Foreign Policy Regarding China and Its Strategic Intentions after the Manchuria Incident," 76.

81 鄧元忠 (Deng Yuanzhong), "The First Secret Negotiations and Contacts before the Second Nationalist-Communist United Front," 289–310; Michael M. Sheng, *Battling Western Imperialism*, 32–3; Zoia Dmitrievna Katkova, *China and the Powers 1927–1937*, 165–6; Iurii Mikhailovich Ovchinnikov, *Creation and Development of the United National Front*, 44–8; Hans J. van de Ven, *War and Nationalism in China 1925–1945*, 180–1; Sergei Leonidovich Tikhvinskii, *China's Path to Unification and Independence 1898–1949*, 286–7; 楊奎松 (Yang Kuisong), "The Inscrutable Opponent, 1917–1949," 58–60; Ch'en Li-fu, *The Storm Clouds Clear over China: The Memoir of Ch'en Li-fu*, eds. and comps., Sidney H. Chang and Ramon H. Myers (Stanford, CA: Hoover Institution Press, 1994), 119, 123.

82 JFM, A.2.2.0-C/R1–3, 支那蘇連邦外交関係雑纂 蘇支蒙彊関係 (Miscellaneous Papers on Sino-Soviet Diplomacy: Soviet-Chinese-Mongol-Xinjiang Relations), to Foreign Minister Hirota from the Japanese

plenipotentiary in Manchukuo, Minami Jirō, 24 October 1935, p. 308.

83 鄧元忠 (Deng Yuanzhong), "The First Secret Negotiations and Contacts before the Second Nationalist-Communist United Front," 289–310; Michael M. Sheng, *Battling Western Imperialism*, 32–3; Sergei Leonidovich Tikhvinskii, ed., *Russo-Chinese Relations in the 20th Century*, Vol. 3, September 1931–September 1937, 21–2; 扬奎松 (Yang Kuisong), *Kuomintang: Unity with Communists and Anti-communism*, 321.

84 JFM, A.2.2.0-C/R1–3, 支那蘇連邦外交関係雑纂 蘇支蒙彊関係 (Miscellaneous Papers on Sino-Soviet Diplomacy: Soviet-Chinese-Mongol-Xinjiang Relations), to Foreign Minister Hirota from the acting envoy Inōe, 28 January 1936, pp. 12–13.

85 扬奎松 (Yang Kuisong), *Kuomintang: Unity with Communists and Anti-communism*, 336, 338.

86 Jonathan Haslam, *Soviet Union and the Threat from the East, 1933–1941*, 78–9; 蒋永敬 (Jiang Yongjing), "What Did Zhang Xueliang Mean in His Pre-Xi'an Incident So-called 'Required Changes in One or Two Months'?" 269; Howard L. Boorman, ed., *Biographical Dictionary*, Vol. 2, 176; Colin Mackerras, *Modern China: A Chronology from 1842 to the Present* (San Francisco: W. H. Freeman, 1982), 360; Iurii Mikhailovich Ovchinnikov, *Creation and Development of the United National Front*, 58; 扬奎松 (Yang Kuisong), *Kuomintang: Unity with Communists and Anti-communism*, 329, 344.

87 Michael A. Barnhart, *Japan Prepares for Total War*, 79.

88 Jonathan Fenby, *Chiang Kai-shek*, 282–3.

89 Howard L. Boorman, ed., *Biographical Dictionary*, Vol. 1, 67, 353.

90 Jonathan Haslam, *Soviet Union and the Threat from the East, 1933–1941*, 78–9; 蒋永敬 (Jiang Yongjing), "What Did Zhang Xueliang Mean in His Pre-Xi'an Incident So-called 'Required Changes in One or Two Months'?" 269.

91 Jonathan Haslam, *Soviet Union and the Threat from the East, 1933–1941*, 80–1.

92 F. C. Jones, *Japan's New Order in East Asia*, 406.

93 Sergei Leonidovich Tikhvinskii, ed., *Russo-Chinese Relations in the 20th Century*, Vol. 4, part 1, 1937–45, 152, 386.

94 功刀俊洋 (Kunugi Toshihiro), "From Arms Limitations to Rearmament," 115.

95 石島紀之 (Ishijima Noriyuki), *History of China's Anti-Japanese War*, 49.

96 Jonathan Haslam, *Soviet Union and the Threat from the East, 1933–1941*, 53, 80–1.

97 张魁堂 (Zhang Kuitang), "中共中央和平解决西安事变方针的制定" ("The Central Committee of the Chinese Communist Party's Decision to Settle the Xi'an Incident Peacefully"), 近代史研究 (*Modern Chinese History Studies*) 62, no. 2 (March 1991), 252.

98 Jonathan Haslam, *Soviet Union and the Threat from the East, 1933–1941*, 83; Sergei Leonidovich Tikhvinskii, ed., *Russo-Chinese Relations in the 20th Century*, Vol. 4, part 1, 1937–45, 701; Michael M. Sheng, *Battling Western Imperialism*, 36; Jay Taylor, *Generalissimo*, 129; Shum Kui-kwong, *Chinese Communists' Road to Power*, 89–90.

99 任骏 (Ren Jun), "Jiang Tingfu and Sino-Soviet Relations before and after the Marco Polo Bridge Incident," 185; 杨奎松 (Yang Kuisong), "Zhang Xueliang and the Solution for the Xi'an Incident," 192; 吴天威 (Wu Tianwei), "Reconsideration of Zhang Xueliang and the Xi'an Incident [Sequel]," 52–9; 郑德荣 (Zheng Derong),"西安事变若干问题的新思考" ("New Reflections on Some Questions about the Xi'an Incident"), 中共党史研究 (*Research on the History of the Chinese Communist Party*) no. 1 (1997), 20; Harriet L. Moore, *Soviet Far Eastern Policy 1931–1945*, 77; Jay Taylor, *Generalissimo*, 130–1; Iurii Mikhailovich Ovchinnikov, *Creation and Development of the United National Front*, 71.

100 张魁堂 (Zhang Kuitang), "The Central Committee of the Chinese Communist Party's Decision to Settle the Xi'an Incident Peacefully," 255; 石島紀之 (Ishijima Noriyuki), *History of China's Anti-Japanese War*, 49–51.

101 刘喜发 (Liu Xifa) and 王彦堂 (Wang Yantang), "The Role of Domestic and International Public Opinion on the Peaceful Solution of the Xi'an Incident," 39.

102 杨奎松 (Yang Kuisong), "Investigation of Zhang Xueliang's Activities against Chiang Kai-shek," 86; John Gunther, *Inside Asia*, 226; Iurii Mikhailovich Ovchinnikov, *Creation and Development of the United National Front*, 74.

103 王真 (Wang Zhen), "孙科与战时国民政府的对苏关系" ("The Relations with the Soviet Union of Sun Ke and the Wartime Nationalist Government"), 近代史研究 (*Modern Chinese History Studies*) 77, no. 5 (September 1993), 102–3; Liu Xiaoyuan, *Reins of Liberation*, 106; 香島明雄 (Kashima Akio), *Research on Sino-Soviet Diplomatic History, 1937–1946*, 16, 27, 29–30; 王真 (Wang Zhen), "抗战初期中苏在苏联参战问题上的分歧" ("Divergent Views between China and the Soviet Union on Soviet Participation in the Early Period of the War of Resistance"), 历史研究 (*Historical Research*) no. 6 (1994), 112.

104 陈英吴 (Chen Yingwu) and 胡充寒 (Hu Chonghan), "抗战初期苏联援华政策的几个问题" ("Some Questions Concerning the Soviet Aid Policy to China in the Early War of Resistance") 文史哲 (*Journal of Literature,*

History, and Philosophy) no. 5 (1991), 31–5; 任骏 (Ren Jun), "Jiang Tingfu and Sino-Soviet Relations before and after the Marco Polo Bridge Incident," 187–97; 香島明雄 (Kashima Akio), *Research on Sino-Soviet Diplomatic History, 1937–1946*, 16, 27, 29–30; Sergei Leonidovich Tikhvinskii, ed., *Russo-Chinese Relations in the 20th Century*, Vol. 4, part 1, 1937–45, 262, 311–12; Yang Tianshi, "Chiang Kai-shek and the Battles of Shanghai and Nanjing," 157; John W. Garver, "Chiang Kai-shek's Quest for Soviet Entry into the Sino-Japanese War," *Political Science Quarterly* 102, no. 2 (Summer 1987), 306, 315.

105 Sergei Leonidovich Tikhvinskii, ed., *Russo-Chinese Relations in the 20th Century*, Vol. 4, part 1, 1937–45, 155, 156; Zhang Baijia, "China's Quest for Military Aid" in *Battle for China*, eds. Mark Peattie et al., 292.

106 Dieter Heinzig, *The Soviet Union and Communist China 1945–1950* (Armonk, NY: M. E. Sharpe, 2004), 27; 江口圭一 (Eguchi Kei-ichi), *A Short History of the Fifteen Year War*, 140; Sergei Leonidovich Tikhvinskii, ed., *Russo-Chinese Relations in the 20th Century*, Vol. 4, part 1, 1937–45, 88–90; JDA, 満洲全般２２５満洲に関する用兵的観察, Vol. 13, part 5, 極東ソ軍の戦略的特性に関する調査 (Survey of the Strategy of the Far Eastern Soviet Military), March 1953, 復員局資料整理課元陸軍大佐林三郎 (Demobilization Bureau, Documents Section, Former Army Colonel Hayashi Saburō?), pp. 33–4; Yin Ching Chen, *Treaties and Agreements between the Republic of China and Other Powers, 1929–1954* (Washington, DC: Sino-American Publishing Service, 1957), 113–14; ASA, 112.6/0003, 中蘇互不侵犯條約 (Sino-Soviet Non-Aggression Treaty), 11-WAA-00080, 21 August 1936, pp. 167–70, 176.

107 John W. Garver, *Chinese-Soviet Relations 1937–1945* (New York: Oxford University Press, 1988), 20–1; S. C. M. Paine, *Imperial Rivals*, 274–6; Hans J. van de Ven, *War and Nationalism in China 1925–1945*, 172.

108 Jay Taylor, *The Generalissimo's Son: Chiang Ching-kuo and the Revolutions in China and Taiwan* (Cambridge, MA: Harvard University Press, 2000), 53; Jay Taylor, *Generalissimo*, 34.

109 任骏 (Ren Jun), "Jiang Tingfu and Sino-Soviet Relations before and after the Marco Polo Bridge Incident," 187–97; K. P. Ageenko, P. N. Bobylev, T. S. Manaenkov, R. A. Sabyshkin, and I. F. Iakushin, *Военная помощь СССР в освободительной борбье китайского народа* (*Soviet Military Aid in the Liberation Struggle of the Chinese People*) (Moscow: Military Press of the Ministry of Defence, 1975), 49.

110 Raisa A. Mirovitskaia, *Китайская государственность и советская политика в Китае* (*Chinese Statehood and Soviet Policy in China*)

(Moscow: «Памятники исторической мысли», 1999), 43; 香島明雄 (Kashima Akio), *Research on Sino-Soviet Diplomatic History, 1937–1946*, 33–5; F. C. Jones, *Japan's New Order in East Asia*, 173–7; Dieter Heinzig, *The Soviet Union and Communist China 1945–1950*, 27; K. P. Ageenko et al., *Soviet Military Aid in the Liberation Struggle of the Chinese People*, 49, 56; Jonathan Haslam, *Soviet Union and the Threat from the East, 1933–1941*, 123.

111 Jonathan Haslam, *Soviet Union and the Threat from the East, 1933–1941*, 111.

5 FLASHBACK TO 1911 AND THE BEGINNING OF THE LONG CHINESE CIVIL WAR

1 Translation based on Moss Roberts in Luo Guanzhong, *Three Kingdoms*, trans. Moss Roberts (Beijing: Foreign Languages Press, 1995), 5; 羅貫中 (Luo Guanzhong), 三國演義 (*Romance of the Three Kingdoms*) (Taipei: 三民書局, 1985), 1)

2 S. C. M. Paine, *Imperial Rivals*, 129*n*.41.

3 John W. Dower, *War without Mercy*, 295–9. The total is derived from 39 million deaths in Europe, 10 million Chinese, 2.7 million Japanese, 4 million Indonesian, and 1.5 million other southeast Asian and Australasian deaths.

4 The discussion in this section relies on Bruce A. Elleman and S. C. M. Paine, *Modern China Continuity and Change 1644 to the Present*, 222–99.

5 章有义 (Zhang Youyi), 中国近代农业史资料 (*Materials on Modern Chinese Agricultural History*), Vol. 2 (Beijing: 三联书店, 1957), 609; Edward L. Dreyer, *China at War, 1901–1949*, 86, 101, 108, 110, 374–5; Arthur Waldron, "War and the Rise of Nationalism in Twentieth-Century China," 308–9.

6 Arthur Waldron, *From War to Nationalism: China's Turning Point, 1924–1925* (Cambridge: Cambridge University Press, 1995), 177; Bruce A. Elleman, *Diplomacy and Deception*, 55–76.

7 Carl von Clausewitz, *On War*, eds. and trans., Michael Howard and Peter Paret (Princeton, NJ: Princeton University Press, 1976), 80.

8 石島紀之 (Ishijima Noriyuki), *History of China's Anti-Japanese War*, 7.

9 Edgar Snow, *Red Star over China*, 190–206.

10 Donald W. Klein and Anne B. Clark, *Biographic Dictionary of Chinese Communism 1921–1965*, Vol. 1, 247–9; ibid., Vol. 2, 681; June Grasso, Jay Corrin, and Michael Kort, *Modernization and Revolution in China*, 120.

11 Michael M. Sheng, *Battling Western Imperialism*, 19–25.

12 Mao Zedong, *Selected Military Writings*, 77–286; Jung Chang and Jon Halliday, *Mao the Unknown Story*, 281; 楊奎松 (Yang Kuisong), 走向破裂：恩恩怨怨 (*Heading for Rupture: Gratitude and Grudges between Mao Zedong and Stalin*) (Hong Kong: 三聯書店, 1999), 491–2.

13 Both works cited in John W. Garver, *Chinese-Soviet Relations 1937–1945*, 73, 127–8. See also Mao Zedong, *Selected Military Writings*, 241, 262.

14 Cited in 金冲及 (Jin Chongji), "North China Incident and the High Tide of the Resist Japan–Save the Nation Movement," 20.

15 JDA, 満洲全般 1 8 6 満洲に関する用兵的観察, Vol. 11, part 4, 満洲に於ける各種作戦の史的観察 (Historical Survey of All Types of Military Operations in Manchuria), chapter 7, 国境問題 (Border Questions), chapter 8, 国境築城 (Border Fortifications), October 1952, 復員局資料整理課 (Demobilization Bureau, Documents Section), pp. 11–22; 熊沛彪 (Xiong Peibiao), "Japan's Foreign Policy Regarding China and Its Strategic Intentions after the Manchuria Incident," 83; P. I. Zyriakov, ed., *Пограничные войска СССР 1929–1938: Сборник документов и материалов* (*Border Forces of the USSR 1929–1938: Collection of Documents and Materials*) (Moscow: Издательство «наука», 1972), 577, 694.

16 Cited by 金冲及 (Jin Chongji), "North China Incident and the High Tide of the Resist Japan–Save the Nation Movement," 21.

17 Cited by 沈予 (Shen Yu),"论日本近卫文麿内阁的对华政策" ("Discussion of the Konoe Fumimaro Cabinet's China Policy"), 近代史研究 (*Modern Chinese History Studies*) no. 1 (1998), 38. I have removed the underlining added to the original for emphasis by Shen Yu.

18 Ian Nish, *Japanese Foreign Policy 1869–1942*, 212–13; Alvin D. Coox, *Nomonhan*, 70–3; Howard L., Boorman, ed., *Biographical Dictionary*, Vol. 2, 9; Sechin Jagchid, *Last Mongol Prince*, 162.

19 Donald A. Jordan, *China's Trial by Fire*, 191, 193–5, 198.

20 Takafusa Nakamura, *History of Shōwa Japan*, 92.

21 Galina Fominichna Zakharova, *Policy of Japan in Manchuria 1932–1945*, 233*n*8; 塚瀬 進 (Tsukase Susumu), *Manchukuo "Racial Harmony" in Reality*, 152.

22 Jonathan Haslam, *Soviet Union and the Threat from the East, 1933–1941*, 28; Tsuyoshi Hasegawa, *Racing the Enemy: Stalin, Truman, and the Surrender of Japan* (Cambridge, MA: Harvard University Press, 2005), 12.

23 Mark R. Peattie, *Ishiwara Kanji and Japan's Confrontation with the West*, 198. For a table comparing Russian and Japanese troop strength on the Asian mainland, see Alvin D. Coox, *Nomonhan*, 84; Hata Ikuhiko, "The Japanese Soviet Confrontation, 1935–1939" in *Deterrent Diplomacy:*

Japan, Germany, and the USSR 1935–1940, ed. James William Morley (New York: Columbia University Press, 1976), 131.

24 JDA, 満洲全般２２３満洲に関する用兵的観察, Vol. 1, part 1, 満洲に於ける日本軍の対ソ作戦計画 (Soviet War Plans against the Japanese Army in Manchuria), May 1952, 復員局資料整理課元陸軍大佐股部四郎 (Demobilization Bureau, Documents Section), p.77; JDA, 満洲全般２２５満洲に関する用兵的観察, Vol. 13, part 5, 極東ソ軍の戦略的特性に関する調査 (Survey of the Strategy of the Far Eastern Soviet Military), March 1953, 復員局資料整理課元陸軍大佐林三郎 (Demobilization Bureau, Documents Section, Former Army Colonel Hayashi Saburō?), p. 62.

6 REGIONAL WAR: THE SECOND SINO-JAPANESE WAR

1 藤原彰 (Fujiwara Akira) and 今井清一 (Imai Seiichi), eds., *History of the Fifteen Year War*, 3 vols.

2 Confucius, *The Analects*, 49.

3 Cited in Thomas W. Burkman, *Japan and the League of Nations*, 2008), 194.

4 刘庭华 (Liu Tinghua) and 岳思平 (Yue Siping), "抗日与统一和安内攘外 ("Unified Resistance against Japan and the Policy of Internal Pacification, External Resistance"), 中共党史研究 (*Research on the History of the Chinese Communist Party*) no. 6 (1994), 76; 刘培平 (Liu Peiping), " '安内攘外' 与 '反将抗日' " ("'Internal Pacification, External Resistance' versus 'Opposing Chiang, Resisting Japan'"), 文史哲 (*Journal of Literature, History, and Philosophy*) 230, no. 5 (1995), 23; 王维礼 (Wang Weili) and 程舒伟 (Cheng Shuwei), "关于南京国民政府 '安内攘外' 政策的评价" ("An Evaluation of the Nanjing Government's Policy of 'Internal Pacification, External Resistance'"), 中共党史研究 (*Research on the History of the Chinese Communist Party*) 32, no. 2 (1993), 43.

5 Cited in 王维礼 (Wang Weili) and 程舒伟 (Cheng Shuwei), "An Evaluation of the Nanjing Government's Policy of 'Internal Pacification, External Resistance,'" 38.

6 刘培平 (Liu Peiping), "'Internal Pacification, External Resistance' versus 'Opposing Chiang, Resisting Japan,'"), 22–7; 刘庭华 (Liu Tinghua) and 岳思平 (Yue Siping), "Unified Resistance against Japan and the Policy of Internal Pacification, External Resistance," 74–8.

7 和田春樹 (Wada Haruki), 金日成と満州抗日戦争 (*Kim Il-sung and the Manchurian War of Resistance against Japan*) (Tokyo: 平凡社, 1992), 40–1, 75–89, 93–5; 幕内光雄 (Maku'uchi Mitsuo), *An Unofficial History of the Manchukuo Police*, 119; 塚瀬進 (Tsukase Susumu), *Manchukuo "Racial Harmony" in Reality*, 226–7, 235–6, 239–40. For a table summarizing the decline of local resistance, the communist insurgency, and

banditry from 1931 to 1940, see 小林英夫 (Kobayashi Hideo), "日本の「満州」支配と抗日運動" ("Japanese Rule in 'Manchukuo' and the Anti-Japanese Movement") in 講座中国近現代史 (*Series of Studies in Modern and Contemporary Chinese History*), Vol. 6, 抗日戦争 *(The Anti-Japanese War)*, eds. 野沢豊 (Nozawa Yutaka) et al. (Tokyo: University of Tokyo Press, 1978), 226; Galina Fominichna Zakharova, *The Policy of Japan in Manchuria 1932–1945*, 48; FMA, A.6.2.0–2-8–1, 満洲国政況関係雑纂治安状況：匪賊動静並討伐状況関係 (Miscellaneous Papers on the Pacification Situation Related to the Manchurian Political Situation: Bandit Activities and Bandit Suppression), Vol. 1, September 1937–September 1938, maps.

8 Odoric Y. K. Wou, "Communist Sources for Localizing the Study of the Sino-Japanese War," in *Chinese Collaboration with Japan, 1932–1945*, eds. David P. Barret and Larry N. Shyu, 227.

9 Cited in 杨天石 (Yang Tianshi), "30年代初期国民党内部的反蒋抗日潮流—读台湾所藏胡汉民资料之一" ("Anti–Chiang Kai-shek and Anti-Japanese Currents in the Nationalist Party in the Early 1930s Based on Documents Retained in Taiwan Concerning Hu Hanmin"), 历史研究 (*Historical Research*) no. 1 (1998), 64.

10 江口圭一 (Eguchi Kei-ichi), *Short History of the Fifteen Year War*, 117; Takafusa Nakamura, *History of Shōwa Japan*, 141; 太平洋戦争研究会 (Pacific War Research Center), ed., 日中戦争 (*Sino-Japanese War*) (Tokyo: 河出書房新社, 2000), 11.

11 武月星 (Wu Yuexing), "The Japanese North China Occupation Force and Its Aggressive Behavior," 212; William Henry Chamberlin, *Japan Over Asia*, 96; Edward L. Dreyer, *China at War, 1901–1949*, 210–11; Howard L. Boorman, ed., *Biographical Dictionary*, Vol. 3, 190–1; Marjorie Dryburgh, *North China and Japanese Expansion 1933–1937: Regional Power and Nationalist Interest* (Richmond, Surrey: Curzon, 2000), 8–9, 101, 134–5; Zoia Dmitrievna Katkova, *China and the Powers 1927–1937*, 140–1; Meirion Harries and Susie Harries, *Soldiers of the Sun: The Rise and the Fall of the Imperial Japanese Army* (New York: Random House, 1991), 202.

12 王建朗 (Wang Jianlang), "The Nationalist Government's Decision for War or Peace after the Marco Polo Bridge Incident," 154; Shimada Toshihiko, "Designs on North China, 1933–1937," 158; George E. Taylor, *Struggle for North China*, 20.

13 Cited in 王建朗 (Wang Jianlang), "The Nationalist Government's Decision for War or Peace after the Marco Polo Bridge Incident," 153.

14 Joseph Needham, *Science and Civilization in China*, Vol. 2, *History of Scientific Thought* (Cambridge: Cambridge University Press, 1962), 262–6.

15 近藤新治 (Kondō Shinji), "陸軍の開戦準備" ("The Army's Preparations for Opening the War") in *Modern Japanese Military History*, Vol. 4, eds. 奥村房夫 (Okumura Fusao) and 近藤新治 (Kondō Shinji), 317, 322–5; Edward J. Drea, *Japan's Imperial Army*, 197; F. F. Liu, *A Military History of Modern China 1924–1949* (1956; reprint, Port Washington, NY: Kennikat Press, 1972), 205.

16 Cited in 王建朗 (Wang Jianlang), "The Nationalist Government's Decision for War or Peace after the Marco Polo Bridge Incident," 159.

17 Cited in ibid., 166, 161.

18 Cited by 沈予 (Shen Yu), "Discussion of the Konoe Fumimaro Cabinet's China Policy," 39; Takafusa Nakamura, *History of Shōwa Japan,* 142.

19 Michael A. Barnhart, *Japan Prepares for Total War*, 91, 95; Edward J. Drea, *Nomonhan: Japanese Soviet Tactical Combat* (Honolulu: University Press of the Pacific, 1981), 13.

20 F. F. Liu, *Military History,* 205; Meirion Harries and Susie Harries, *Soldiers of the Sun*, 260.

21 吉田裕 (Yoshida Yutaka) and 纐纈厚 (Kōketsu Atsushi), "Military Operations, Combat, and the Supply of the Japanese Military," 82–4; Sadao Asada, *From Mahan to Pearl Harbor*, 266, 286; Haruko Taya Cook and Theodore F. Cook, *Japan at War: An Oral History* (New York: New Press, 1992), 303.

22 Edward J. Drea, *Japan's Imperial Army*, 195–7; Hsu Long-hsuen and Chang Ming-kai, *History of the Sino-Japanese War (1937–1945)*, trans. Wen Ha-hsiung, 2nd ed. (Taipei: Chung Wu Publishing, 1972), map 1, map 6; 武月星 (Wu Yuexing), *Modern Chinese History Map Collection*, 108, 129–31; Mark Peattie et al., *Battle for China*, 8, 26–7; 太平洋戦争研究会 (Pacific War Research Center), ed., *Sino-Japanese War*, 56–7; George E. Taylor, *Struggle for North China*, 34–5, 105, 171–2.

23 程晓 (Cheng Xiao),"抗日战争初期中国和日本的战略淞沪会战" ("The Chinese and Japanese Strategy in the Shanghai Campaign of the Early War of Resistance against Japan"), 中共党史研究 (*Research on the History of the Chinese Communist Party*) no. 6 (1995), 17–21; Frederic Wakeman, Jr., *Policing Shanghai 1927–1937* (Berkeley: University of California Press, 1995), 278.

24 Diana Lary, *The Chinese People at War: Human Suffering and Social Transformation, 1937–1945* (Cambridge: Cambridge University Press, 2010), 22–3; Bradford A. Lee, *Britain and the Sino-Japanese War 1937–1939* (Stanford, CA: Stanford University Press, 1973), 36; K. K. Kawakami, *Japan in China*, 172–3; Frederic Wakeman, Jr., *Policing Shanghai 1927–1937*, 280–1.

25 Herbert P. Bix, *Hirohito*, 323–5.

26 石島紀之 (Ishijima Noriyuki), *A History of China's Anti-Japanese War*, 74; Shuhsi Hsu, *The War Conduct of the Japanese* (Shanghai: Kelly and Walsh, 1938), 70–1; Diana Lary, *The Chinese People at War*, 23; Mark R. Peattie, *Sunburst: The Rise of Japanese Naval Air Power, 1909–1941* (Annapolis, MD: Naval Institute Press, 2001), 103–4, 117; Arakawa Ken-ichi, "Japanese Naval Blockade of China in the Second Sino-Japanese War, 1937–41" in *Naval Blockades and Seapower: Strategies and Counter-strategies, 1805–2005*, eds. Bruce A. Elleman and S. C. M. Paine (London: Routledge, 2006), 106, 108–11; Herbert P. Bix, *Hirohito*, 323–5; Michael A. Barnhart, *Japan Prepares for Total War*, 99; Edward J. Drea, *Japan's Imperial Army*, 195–6; Edward J. Drea and Hans van de Ven, "Overview of Major Military Campaigns during the Sino-Japanese War, 1937–1945," 29–30; Yang Tianshi, "Chiang Kai-shek and the Battles of Shanghai and Nanjing," 150–1; John W. Garver, "China's Wartime Diplomacy" in *China's Bitter Victory*, eds. James C. Hsiung and Steven I. Levine, 7–8; 武月星 (Wu Yuexing), *Modern Chinese History Map Collection*, 121–2.

27 Michael A. Barnhart, *Japan Prepares for Total War*, 99.

28 Takafusa Nakamura, *History of Shōwa Japan*, 144.

29 Edward J. Drea, *Japan's Imperial Army*, 195–6; Yang Tianshi, "Chiang Kai-shek and the Battles of Shanghai and Nanjing," 143.

30 斎藤道彦 (Saitō Michihiko), "日本軍毒ガス作戦日誌初稿— 一九三七、三八年を中心に—" ("A First Attempt at a Journal of the Poison Gas Operation of the Japanese Army Focusing on 1937 and 1938") in *The Sino-Japanese War*, ed. 中央大学人文科学研究所 (Chūō University Human Sciences Research Center), 164; Herbert P. Bix, *Hirohito*, 361.

31 Yang Tianshi, "Chiang Kai-shek and the Battles of Shanghai and Nanjing," 153–4; Stephen R. MacKinnon, *Wuhan 1938: War, Refugees, and the Making of Modern China* (Berkeley: University of California Press, 2008), 23.

32 Stephen R. MacKinnon, *Wuhan 1938*, 20; Chang Jui-te, "The Nationalist Army on the Eve of the War," 85; Gregor Benton, *New Fourth Army*, xxi; Hans J. van de Ven, *War and Nationalism in China 1925–1945*, 159–60; 武月星 (Wu Yuexing), *Modern Chinese History Map Collection*, 133; Hsu Long-hsuen and Chang Ming-kai, *History of the Sino-Japanese War (1937–1945)*, map 8.

33 臼井勝美 (Usui Katsumi), *Research on Sino-Japanese Diplomatic History*, 317, 328, 332.

34 单冠初 (Shan Guanchu), "日本侵华的 '以战养战' 政策" ("The Japanese Policy of 'Providing for the War with War' during the Invasion of China"), 历史研究 (*Historical Research*) no. 4 (1991), 77–91.

35 S. C. M. Paine, *The Sino-Japanese War of 1894 to 1895*, 122, 172.

36 江口圭一 (Eguchi Kei-ichi), 日中アヘン戦争 (*The Japanese-Chinese Opium War*) (Tokyo: 岩波新書, 1988), 44, 92, 98, 104, 118, 161; 江口圭一 (Eguchi Kei-ichi), 証言日中アヘン戦争 (*Testimony for the Japanese-Chinese Opium War*) (Tokyo: 岩波新書, 1991), 18, 32, 45; Frederic Wakeman, Jr., *Policing Shanghai 1927–1937*, 273.

37 斎藤道彦 (Saitō Michihiko), "A First Attempt at a Journal of the Poison Gas Operation of the Japanese Army Focusing on 1937 and 1938," 157–274; 石島紀之 (Ishijima Noriyuki), *A History of China's Anti-Japanese War*, 171; 江口圭一 (Eguchi Kei-ichi), "中国戦線の日本軍" ("The Japanese Army on the China Front") in *History of the Fifteen Year War*, eds. 藤原彰 (Fujiwara Akira) and 今井清一 (Imai Seiichi), Vol. 2, 60–2.

38 Peter Williams and David Wallace, *Unit 731: Japan's Secret Biological Warfare in World War II* (New York: Free Press, 1989), passim.

39 武月星 (Wu Yuexing), *Modern Chinese History Map Collection*, 112–16.

40 斎藤道彦 (Saitō Michihiko), "A First Attempt at a Journal of the Poison Gas Operation of the Japanese Army Focusing on 1937 and 1938," 177.

41 Jonathan Fenby, *Chiang Kai-shek,* 359

42 斎藤道彦 (Saitō Michihiko), "A First Attempt at a Journal of the Poison Gas Operation of the Japanese Army Focusing on 1937 and 1938," 217, 225, 242, 257, 264–5, 267, 269.

43 Carl von Clausewitz, *On War*, 485–6, 595–6.

44 George E. Taylor, *Struggle for North China*, 178.

45 石島紀之 (Ishijima Noriyuki),"日中全面戦争の衝撃—中国の国民統合と社会構造" ("The Impact of the Total War between Japan and China: China's National Integration and Social Structure") in 太平洋戦争 (*The Pacific War*), eds. 細谷千博 (Hosoya Chihiro) et al. (Tokyo: University of Tokyo Press, 1993), 469–71; 黄立人 (Huang Liren), "抗日战争时期公厂内迁的考察" ("A Study of Moving Factories into the Chinese Hinterland during the War of Resistance against Japan"), 历史研究 (*Historical Research*) no. 4 (1994), 120–36; 石島紀之 (Ishijima Noriyuki), "国民党政権の対日抗戦力" ("The Military Strength against Japan of the Nationalist Regime") in *Series of Studies in Modern and Contemporary Chinese History*, Vol. 6, eds., 野沢豊 (Nozawa Yutaka) et al., 50.

46 菊池貴晴 (Kikuchi Takaharu), "中国革命における第三勢力の成立と展開" ("The Formation and Development of a Third Power in the Chinese Revolution") in *Series of Studies in Modern and Contemporary Chinese History*, Vol. 7, eds. 野沢豊 (Nozawa Yutaka) et al., 119.

47 菊池一隆 (Kikuchi Kazutaka), "抗日戦争時期の中国工業工作運動" ("The Chinese Industrial Cooperative Movement during the Anti-Japanese War"), 歴史学研究 (*Journal of Historical Studies*) no. 486 (November 1980), 29–45.

48 吉沢南 (Yoshizawa Minami), "総語" ("General Discussion") in 講座中国近現代史 (*Series of Studies in Modern and Contemporary Chinese History*), Vol. 7, eds. 野沢豊 (Nozawa Yutaka) et al., 11.

49 谢放 (Xie Fang), "抗战前中国城市局的初步考察" ("Distribution of Chinese Urban Industry before 1937"), 中国经济史研究 (*Research in Chinese Economic History*) no. 3 (1998), 96–105.

50 吉沢南 (Yoshizawa Minami), "General Discussion," 11.

51 姚会元 (Yao Huiyuan), "1933年－1936年日本在华北的走私活动" ("On the Japanese Smuggling Activities in North China, 1933–1936"), 中国社会经济史研究 (*Research on Chinese Social and Economic History*) no. 1 (1986), 118–20; 连心豪 (Lian Xinhao), "南京国民政府建立初期海关缉私工作述评" ("Commentary on the Nationalist Government's Early Anti-Smuggling Work"), 中国社会经济史研究 (*Research on Chinese Social and Economic History*) no. 4 (1989), 77–83.

52 姚会元 (Yao Huiyuan), "On the Japanese Smuggling Activities in North China, 1933–1936," 118–20; 江口圭一 (Eguchi Kei-ichi), *A Short History of the Fifteen Year War*, 103–4; 臼井勝美 (Usui Katsumi), *Research on Sino-Japanese Diplomatic History*, 289.

53 張瑞德 (Zhang Ruide), "抗戰時期大後方工商業者的心態與行動" ("Businessmen of Nationalist China in the Great Rear during the Sino-Japanese War, 1937–1945"), 台灣師範大學歷史學報 (*Taiwan Normal University Bulletin of Historical Research*) no. 27 (June 1999), 131.

54 干于黎 (Gan Yuli), "抗战前期国民党地方财政收入状况述略" ("A Brief Narrative of the Nationalist Government's Local Finance and Income in the Early Period of the War of Resistance"), 中国社会经济史研究 (*Research on Chinese Social and Economic History*) no. 3 (1989), 86–91; Jonathan Fenby, *Chiang Kai-shek*, 338.

55 董廷之 (Dong Tingzhi), "抗日战争时期国民党统治区的通货膨胀" ("Inflation in Nationalist-ruled Territory during the Anti-Japanese War"), 中共党史研究 (*Research on the History of the Chinese Communist Party*) no. 2 (1989), 36–8.

56 Jonathan Fenby, *Chiang Kai-shek*, 348.

57 金普森 (Jin Pusen) and 王国华 (Wang Guohua), "南京国民政府1927–1931年之内债" ("The Internal Debt of the Nanjing Government, 1927–1937"), 中国社会经济史研究 (*Research on Chinese Social and Economic History*) no. 4 (1991), 96–103.

58 吴景平 (Wu Jingping),"美国和抗战时期中国的平准基金" ("On the U.S. Stabilization Fund for the Chinese Currency during the War of Resistance"), 近代史研究 (*Modern Chinese History Studies*) no. 5 (1997), 94.

59 張瑞德 (Zhang Ruide), *Personnel Matters of the Nationalist Army during the War of Resistance*, 92; Jonathan Fenby, *Chiang Kai-shek*, 349.

60 孙修福 (Sun Xiufu), "蒋介石与鸦片特税" ("Chiang Kai-shek and the Special Opium Tax"), 近代史研究 (*Modern Chinese History Studies*) no. 2 (1997), 182–201.
61 Herbert P. Bix, *Hirohito*, 333; Hattori Satoshi and Edward J. Drea, "Japanese Operations from July to December 1937" in *The Battle for China*, eds. Mark Peattie et al., 179.
62 Timothy Brook, *Collaboration: Japanese Agents and Local Elites in Wartime China* (Cambridge, MA: Harvard University Press, 2005), 91–4.
63 李恩涵 (Li Enhan), "日本軍南京大屠殺的屠殺數目問題" ("A Reappraisal of the Massacre Figures for the Japanese Army's Rape of Nanjing"), 台灣師範大學歷史學報 (*Taiwan Normal University Bulletin of Historical Research*) 18 (June 1990), 475–6; Jonathan Fenby, *Chiang Kai-shek*, 305; Herbert P. Bix, *Hirohito*, 333–4, 336; Ben-Ami Shillony, "February 26 Affair," 91.
64 Diana Lary, "A Ravaged Place: The Devastation of the Xuzhou Region, 1938," in *Scars of War: The Impact of Warfare on Modern China*, eds. Diana Lary and Stephen R. MacKinnon (Vancouver: UBC Press, 2001), 106–8.
65 Stephen R. MacKinnon, "Refugee Flight at the Outset of the Anti-Japanese War," in ibid., 121–2.
66 Diana Lary, *The Chinese People at War*, 120.
67 Dagfinn Gatu, *Village China at War: The Impact of Resistance to Japan 1937–1945* (Vancouver: UBC Press, 2008), 50–1.
68 Ugaki Matome, *Fading Victory: The Diary of Admiral Matome Ugaki 1941–1945*, trans. Masataka Chihaya, eds. Donald M. Goldstein and Katherine V. Dillon (Pittsburgh: University of Pittsburgh Press, 1991), 21.
69 鹿锡俊 (Lu Xijun), "中日战争时期日本对蒋政策的演变" ("The Evolution of Japan's Policy Regarding Chiang Kai-shek during the Sino-Japanese War"), 近代史研究 (*Modern Chinese History Studies*) 64, no. 4 (July 1991), 215; Hattori Satoshi and Edward J. Drea, "Japanese Operations from July to December 1937," 161.
70 Takafusa Nakamura, *History of Shōwa Japan*, 153; Edward J. Drea, *Japan's Imperial Army*, 195; Stephen R. MacKinnon, *Wuhan 1938*, 31–2; 武月星 (Wu Yuexing), *Modern Chinese History Map Collection*, 135.
71 Edward L. Dreyer, *China at War, 1901–1949*, 215; Hattori Satoshi and Edward J. Drea, "Japanese Operations from July to December 1937," 165; 武月星 (Wu Yuexing), *Modern Chinese History Map Collection*, 129.
72 John W. Garver, *Chinese-Soviet Relations 1937–1945*, 39; Edward J. Drea and Hans van de Ven, "Overview of Major Military Campaigns during the Sino-Japanese War, 1937–1945," 29; Hattori Satoshi and Edward J. Drea, "Japanese Operations from July to December 1937," 167.

73 Takafusa Nakamura, *History of Shōwa Japan,* 153; K. P. Ageenko et al. *Soviet Military Aid in the Liberation Struggle of the Chinese People*, 51, 53–4.
74 Diana Lary, "Defending China: The Battles of the Xuzhou Campaign," in *Warfare in Chinese History*, ed. Hans J. van de Ven (Leiden: Brill Academic Publishers, 2000), 398–427.
75 Stephen R. MacKinnon, *Wuhan 1938*, 32.
76 Edward J. Drea, *Japan's Imperial Army*, 201; Stephen R. MacKinnon, *Wuhan 1938*, 36–7.
77 Diana Lary, *The Chinese People at War*, 61; Jonathan Fenby, *Chiang Kai-shek,* 320.
78 Diana Lary and Stephen R. MacKinnon, eds., *Scars of War*, 3, 112; Edward J. Drea, *Japan's Imperial Army*, 201.
79 Diana Lary, "A Ravaged Place," 112; Odoric Y. K. Wou, "Food Shortage and Japanese Grain Extraction in Henan" in *China at War*, eds. Stephen R. MacKinnon et al., 177.
80 Bruce A. Elleman and S. C. M. Paine, *Modern China Continuity and Change 1644 to the Present*, 323.
81 Edward L. Dreyer, *China at War 1901–1949,* 207, 228.
82 Jonathan Fenby, *Chiang Kai-shek,* 119.
83 Stephen R. MacKinnon, *Wuhan 1938*, 1.
84 Herbert P. Bix, *Hirohito*, 364; Arakawa Ken-ichi, "Japanese Naval Blockade of China in the Second Sino-Japanese War, 1937–41," 108.
85 Diana Lary, *The Chinese People at War*, 24, 87; 江口圭一 (Eguchi Kei-ichi), *A Short History of the Fifteen Year War*, 127; Hagiwara Mitsuru, "The Japanese Air Campaigns in China, 1937–1945" in *The Battle for China*, eds. Mark Peattie et al., 249; Mark R. Peattie, *Sunburst*, 118; Jay Taylor, *Generalissimo*, 164; Theodore H. White, *In Search of History: A Personal Adventure* (New York: Harper & Row, 1978), 82.
86 Edward J. Drea, *Japan's Imperial Army*, 201; Edward J. Drea and Hans van de Ven, "Overview of Major Military Campaigns during the Sino-Japanese War, 1937–1945," 34; Japan, Defense Agency, National Defense College, Military History Department (防衛庁防衛研修所戦史部), ed., *The Kantō Army*), Vol. 1, 310–11; 山田朗 (Yamada Akira), "Military Rule [2] during the Sino-Japanese War and the War of the Pacific," 224; Edward L. Dreyer, *China at War, 1901–1949,* 233; Alvin D. Coox, *The Anatomy of a Small War: The Soviet-Japanese Struggle for Changkufeng/Khasan, 1938* (Westport, CT: Greenwood Press, 1977), 4, 6, 324; Michael T. Kikuoka, *The Changkufeng Incident: A Study in Soviet-Japanese Conflict, 1938* (Lanham, MD: University Press of America, 1988), 163.
87 Ian Nish, *Japanese Foreign Policy 1869–1942,* 232.
88 Alvin D. Coox, *Nomonhan*, 135, 136.

89 香島明雄 (Kashima Akio), *Research on Sino-Soviet Diplomatic History, 1937–1946*, 32; JDA, 満洲全般２２５満洲に関する用兵的観察, Vol. 13, part 5, 極東ソ軍の戦略的特性に関する調査 (Survey of the Strategy of the Far Eastern Soviet Military), March 1953, 復員局資料整理課元陸軍大佐林三郎 (Demobilization Bureau, Documents Section, Former Army Colonel Hayashi Saburō?), p. 56; Maochun Yu, *The Dragon's War*, 19.

90 K. P. Ageenko et al., *Soviet Military Aid in the Liberation Struggle of the Chinese People*, 77; Iu. V. Chudodeev, ed., *Along the Roads of China 1937–1945: Memoirs*, 67; Stephen R. MacKinnon, *Wuhan 1938*, 25; Edward J. Drea, "The Japanese Army on the Eve of the War" in *The Battle for China*, eds. Mark Peattie et al., 114–15; Boris Grigor'evich Sapozhnikov, *Китайский фронт во Второй мировой войны* (*The Chinese Front in the Second World War*) (Moscow: Издательство «наука» Главная редакция восточной литературы, 1971), 161–2.

91 江口圭一 (Eguchi Kei-ichi), *A Short History of the Fifteen Year War*, 133–4; Stephen R. MacKinnon, *Wuhan 1938*, 41, 53; 武月星 (Wu Yuexing), *Modern Chinese History Map Collection*, 141.

92 Stephen R. MacKinnon, *Wuhan 1938*, 42.

93 武月星 (Wu Yuexing), *Modern Chinese History Map Collection*, 144; Maochun Yu, *Dragon's War*, 15–16.

94 石島紀之 (Ishijima Noriyuki), *History of China's Anti-Japanese War*, 119.

95 Edward L. Dreyer, *China at War, 1901–1949*, 235.

96 Sadao Asada, *From Mahan to Pearl Harbor*, 210; 武月星 (Wu Yuexing), *Modern Chinese History Map Collection*, 143; Arakawa Ken-ichi, "Japanese Naval Blockade of China in the Second Sino-Japanese War, 1937–41," 109; Maochun Yu, *Dragon's War*, 47–8.

97 丁文江 (Ding Wenjiang) et al., eds., 中華民國新地圖 (*New Atlas of the Republic of China*), 申報六十周年紀念 (*Shenbao* newspaper 60th anniversary edition) (Shanghai: 申報館, 1934), map 1 and map 3.

98 小林英夫 (Kobayashi Hideo),"幣制改革をめぐる日本と中国" ("Japan, China, and the Currency Reform") in *China's Currency Reform and International Relations*, ed. 野沢豊 (Nozawa Yutaka), 238.

99 石島紀之 (Ishijima Noriyuki), *A History of China's Anti-Japanese War*, 75.

100 Jay Taylor, *Generalissimo*, 186; Jonathan Fenby, *Chiang Kai-shek*, 229.

101 张北根 (Zhang Beigen), "1933–1941年的中德关系" ("Sino-German Relations, 1933–1941"), 历史研究 (*Historical Research*) no. 2 (1995), 108, 111–12; 易豪精 (Yi Haojing),"从'蜜月'到断交—抗日战争爆发前后中德关系的演变" ("From 'Honeymoon' to Diplomatic Split: The Evolution of Sino-German Relations around the Outbreak

of the Sino-Japanese War"), 中共党史研究 (*Research on the History of the Chinese Communist Party*) no. 5 (1995), 57, 60; 李兰琴 (Li Lanqin),"试论20世纪30年代德国对华政策" ("German Policy Regarding China in the 1930s"), 历史研究 (*Historical Research*) no. 1 (1989), 180–1; 王建朗 (Wang Jianlang), "二战爆发前国民政府外交综论" ("A Comprehensive Review of the Diplomacy of the Nationalist Government on the Eve of World War II"), 历史研究 *(Historical Research*) no. 4 (1995), 40.

102 F. C. Jones, *Japan's New Order in East Asia*, 41; John P. Fox, *Germany and the Far Eastern Crisis 1931–1938: A Study in Diplomacy and Ideology* (Oxford: Clarendon Press, 1982), 246.

103 Sergei Leonidovich Tikhvinskii, ed., *Russo-Chinese Relations in the 20th Century*, Vol. 4, part 1, 1937–45, 11 , 99, 105–6, 567; ibid., part 2, 473; 王建朗 (Wang Jianlang), "A Comprehensive Review of the Diplomacy of the Nationalist Government on the Eve of World War II," 41.

104 江口圭一 (Eguchi Kei-ichi), *A Short History of the Fifteen Year War*, 140; 宓汝成 (Mi Rucheng),"抗战时期的中国外债" ("The Foreign Loans to China during the War of Resistance"), 中国经济史研究 (*Research in Chinese Economic History*) no. 2 (1998), 51–2; Sergei Leonidovich Tikhvinskii, ed., *Russo-Chinese Relations in the 20th Century*, Vol. 4, part 1, 1937–45, 212, 253, 263, 451.

105 Raisa A. Mirovitskaia, *Chinese Statehood and Soviet Policy in China*, 43; 香島明雄 (Kashima Akio), *Research on Sino-Soviet Diplomatic History, 1937–1946*, 33–5; F. C. Jones, *Japan's New Order in East Asia*, 173–7; Dieter Heinzig, *Soviet Union and Communist China 1945–1950*, 27; K. P. Ageenko et al., *Soviet Military Aid in the Liberation Struggle of the Chinese People*, 49, 56; Jonathan Haslam, *Soviet Union and the Threat from the East, 1933–1941*, 123.

106 王真 (Wang Zhen), "The Nature of the Soviet Policy to Assist China Early in the Anti-Japanese War," 53; Sergei Leonidovich Tikhvinskii, ed., *Russo-Chinese Relations in the 20th Century*, Vol. 4, part 1, 1937–45, 11–12; ibid., part 2, 473.

107 杨云若 (Yang Yunruo),"苏德战争和太平洋战争前后中苏美关系的演变" ("The Evolution of Sino-Soviet-American Relations at the Time of the European and Pacific Wars"), 中共党史研究 (*Research on the History of the Chinese Communist Party*) no. 6 (1988), 69; 石島紀之 (Ishijima Noriyuki), *A History of China's Anti-Japanese War*, 95; Aleksandr Ya. Kalyagin, *Along Alien Roads*, trans. Steven I. Levine, *Occasional Papers of the East Asian Institute* (New York: Columbia University, 1983), 9–11; Iu. V. Chudodeev, ed., *Along the Roads of China 1937–1945: Memoirs*, 61, 147; Raisa A. Mirovitskaia, *Chinese Statehood and Soviet*

Policy in China, 43; 香島明雄 (Kashima Akio), *Research on Sino-Soviet Diplomatic History, 1937–1946*, 33–5; F. C. Jones, *Japan's New Order in East Asia*, 173–7; 任骏 (Ren Jun), "Jiang Tingfu and Sino-Soviet Relations before and after the Marco Polo Bridge Incident," 187–97; K. P. Ageenko et al., *Soviet Military Aid in the Liberation Struggle of the Chinese People*, 49; 江口圭一 (Eguchi Kei-ichi), *A Short History of the Fifteen Year War*, 140; 杨云若 (Yang Yunruo), "The Evolution of Sino-Soviet-American Relations at the Time of the European and Pacific Wars," 69.

108 王真 (Wang Zhen), "The Nature of the Soviet Policy to Assist China Early in the Anti-Japanese War," 53.

109 Ian Nish, *Japanese Foreign Policy 1869–1942*, 195–6.

110 宓汝成 (Mi Rucheng), "The Foreign Loans to China during the War of Resistance," 55; Sergei Leonidovich Tikhvinskii, ed., *Russo-Chinese Relations in the 20th Century*, Vol. 4, part 1, 1937–45, 394.

111 楊克林 (Yang Kelin) and 曹紅 (Cao Hong) eds., 中國抗日戰爭圖誌 (*A Cartographic Record of the Chinese War of Resistance against Japan*), Vol. 2 (Hong Kong: 天地圖書, 1992), 648–50, 664–7; 鹿锡俊 (Lu Xijun), "The Evolution of Japan's Policy Regarding Chiang Kai-shek during the Sino-Japanese War," 217; Hsu Long-hsuen and Chang Ming-kai, *History of the Sino-Japanese War (1937–1945)*, maps 13–20; Hans J. van de Ven, *War and Nationalism in China 1925–1945*, 245; 武月星 (Wu Yuexing), *Modern Chinese History Map Collection*, 169–70, 173.

112 Liu Xiaoyuan, *Reins of Liberation*, 69.

113 Alvin D. Coox, *Nomonhan*, 914–16; Maochun Yu, *Dragon's War*, 19.

114 Cited in Jonathan Haslam, *The Soviet Union and the Threat from the East, 1933–1941*, 164.

115 市來俊男 (Ichiki Toshio), "海軍の開戦準備" ("The Navy's Preparations for the Opening of the War"), in *Modern Japanese Military History*, Vol. 4, eds., 奥村房夫 (Okumura Fusao) and 近藤新治 (Kondō Shinji), 337–70.

116 江口圭一 (Eguchi Kei-ichi), *A Short History of the Fifteen Year War*, 109–10.

117 Sergei Leonidovich Tikhvinskii, ed., *Russo-Chinese Relations in the 20th Century*, Vol. 4, part 1, 1937–45, 483; Carl Boyd, *The Extraordinary Envoy: General Hiroshi Ōshima and Diplomacy in the Third Reich, 1934–1939* (Washington, DC: University Press of America, 1980), 149.

118 江口圭一 (Eguchi Kei-ichi), *Short History of the Fifteen Year War*, 141–3; Herbert P. Bix, *Hirohito*, 354.

119 Ian Nish, *Japanese Foreign Policy 1869–1942*, 227; Edward J. Drea and Hans van de Ven, "Overview of Major Military Campaigns during the Sino-Japanese War, 1937–1945," 37, 40–1; Tobe Ryōichi, "The Japanese Eleventh Army in Central China, 1938–1941," 220; Hans J. van de Ven,

War and Nationalism in China 1925–1945, 239–42; Arakawa Ken-ichi, "Japanese Naval Blockade of China in the Second Sino-Japanese War, 1937–41," 109; Hsu Long-hsuen and Chang Ming-kai, *History of the Sino-Japanese War (1937–1945)*, 311–16, 325, map 19; 楊克林 (Yang Kelin) and 曹紅 (Cao Hong), eds., *Cartographic Record of the Chinese War of Resistance*, Vol. 2, 693.

120 Diana Lary, *The Chinese People at War*, 602–3; Howard L. Boorman, ed., *Biographical Dictionary*, Vol. 1, 41–3; Stephen R. MacKinnon, *Wuhan 1938*, 42.

121 Edward L. Dreyer, *China at War, 1901–1949*, 236–7, 243–4, 277.

122 楊克林 (Yang Kelin) and 曹紅 (Cao Hong) eds., *A Cartographic Record of the Chinese War of Resistance against Japan*), Vol. 2, 648–50, 664–7; 鹿锡俊 (Lu Xijun), "The Evolution of Japan's Policy Regarding Chiang Kai-shek during the Sino-Japanese War," 217; Hsu Long-hsuen and Chang Ming-kai, *History of the Sino-Japanese War (1937–1945)*, maps 13–20; Hans J. van de Ven, *War and Nationalism in China 1925–1945*, 245.

123 Ian Nish, *Japanese Foreign Policy 1869–1942*, 227; Edward J. Drea and Hans van de Ven, "Overview of Major Military Campaigns during the Sino-Japanese War, 1937–1945," 37, 40–1; Tobe Ryōichi, "The Japanese Eleventh Army in Central China, 1938–1941," 220; Hans J. van de Ven, *War and Nationalism in China 1925–1945*, 239–42; Arakawa Ken-ichi, "Japanese Naval Blockade of China in the Second Sino-Japanese War, 1937–41," 109.

124 Meizhen Huang and Hanqing Yang, "Nationalist China's Negotiating Position during the Stalemate, 1938–1945," trans. David P. Barrett in *Chinese Collaboration with Japan, 1932–1945*, eds. David P. Barrett and Larry N. Shyu, 65.

125 鹿锡俊 (Lu Xijun), "The Evolution of Japan's Policy regarding Chiang Kai-shek during the Sino-Japanese War," 224; Hans J. van de Ven, *War and Nationalism in China 1925–1945*, 246–7; John Hunter Boyle, *China and Japan at War 1937–1945*, 306; 鈴木 晟 (Suzuki Akira), "日中戦争期におけるアメリカの対日経済制裁と対華援助" ("U.S. Economic Sanctions against Japan and Aid to China during the Sino-Japanese War") アジア研究 (*Asian Studies*) 33, no. 1 (April 1986), 60; Mark Peattie et al., eds., *The Battle for China*, 15.

126 Sergei Leonidovich Tikhvinskii, ed., *Russo-Chinese Relations in the 20th Century*, Vol. 4, part 1, 1937–45, 250, 322–3.

127 Cited in 莫岳云 (Mo Yueyun),"略论国民党敌后抗日游击战之兴衰" ("A Brief Discussion of the Rise and Fall of Nationalist Party's Anti-Japanese Guerrilla War behind Enemy Lines"), 史学集刊 (*Collected Papers of Historical Studies*) 69, no. 4 (1997), 38; Japan, Defense Agency, National

Defense College, Military History Department, (防衛庁防衛研修所戦史部), ed., 北支の治安戦 (*The North China Insurgency*), Vol. 1 (Tokyo: 朝雲新聞社, 1968), 132–4, 143.

128 石島紀之 (Ishijima Noriyuki), *A History of China's Anti-Japanese War*, 100.

129 Edward J. Drea and Hans van de Ven, "Overview of Major Military Campaigns during the Sino-Japanese War, 1937–1945," 35; Chang Jui-te, "Nationalist Army on the Eve of the War," 88; Yang Kuisong, "Nationalist and Communist Guerrilla Warfare in North China" in *The Battle for China*, eds. Mark Peattie et al., 308.

130 莫岳云 (Mo Yueyun), "A Brief Discussion of the Rise and Fall of Nationalist Party's Anti-Japanese Guerrilla War behind Enemy Lines," 36–7.

131 Cited in Jonathan Fenby, *Chiang Kai-shek,* 310, 333.

132 石島紀之 (Ishijima Noriyuki), *History of China's Anti-Japanese War*, 136; 莫岳云 (Mo Yueyun), "Brief Discussion of the Rise and Fall of Nationalist Party's Anti-Japanese Guerrilla War behind Enemy Lines," 40.

133 Cited in Jonathan Fenby, *Chiang Kai-shek,* 321, 326–7; Robert L. Jarman, ed., *China Political Reports 1911–1960*, Vol. 6, 318.

134 石島紀之 (Ishijima Noriyuki), *History of China's Anti-Japanese War*, 100.

135 Theodore H. White and Annalee Jacoby, *Thunder out of China* (1946; reprint, New York: Da Capo Press, 1974), 124; Sergei Leonidovich Tikhvinskii, ed., *Russo-Chinese Relations in the 20th Century*, Vol. 4, part 2, 1937–45, 528.

136 Cited in Stephen R. MacKinnon, *Wuhan 1938*, 18–19, 28; Howard L. Boorman, ed., *Biographical Dictionary,* Vol. 2, 53–4.

137 石島紀之 (Ishijima Noriyuki), *History of China's Anti-Japanese War*, 101.

138 Cited in Diana Lary, *Chinese People at War*, 60–1; Howard L. Boorman, ed., *Biographical Dictionary,* Vol. 2, 155.

139 See the following Sinocentric article, which overlooks the roles played by the Nationalists, the United States, Britain, and the Soviet Union in the defeat of Japan: 李蓉 (Li Rong), "一个大的战略决策：向沦陷区发展" ("A Great Strategic Decision: Whether to Expand into Enemy-occupied Areas"), 中共党史研究 (*Research on the History of the Chinese Communist Party*) no. 3 (2000), 68–74.

140 Mao Zedong, *Selected Military Writings*, 54, 66, 174, 182, 226–7, 260–1.

141 李海文 (Li Haiwen), "关于中央军委与中革军委之间的关系" ("The Relationship between the Central Military Affairs Commission and the

Chinese Revolutionary Military Committee"), 中共党史研究 (*Research on the History of the Chinese Communist Party*) no. 6 (1990), 88–9.

142 Donald W. Klein and Anne B. Clark, *Biographic Dictionary of Chinese Communism 1921–1965*, Vol. 2, 1064, 1114–15.

143 Japan, Defense Agency, National Defense College, Military History Department (防衛庁防衛研修所戦史部), ed., *The North China Insurgency*, Vol. 1, 517; Gregor Benton, *New Fourth Army*, 33.

144 Hsu Long-hsuen and Chang Ming-kai, *History of the Sino-Japanese War (1937–1945)*, 587.

145 杨小池 (Yang Xiaochi) and 王乃德 (Wang Naide), "毛泽东关于把山西作为敌后抗战战略支点的构想与实践" ("Mao Zedong's Theories and Practice Concerning Making Shanxi the Strategic Strongpoint behind Enemy Lines in the War of Resistance against Japan"), 中共党史研究 (*Research on the History of the Chinese Communist Party*) no. 1 (1994), 25–30; 石島紀之 (Ishijima Noriyuki), *History of China's Anti-Japanese War*, 62, 110; Jonathan Haslam, *Soviet Union and the Threat from the East, 1933–1941*, 104; 王辅一 (Wang Fuyi),"毛泽东与新四军的创建" ("Mao Zedong and the Founding of the New Fourth Army"), 中共党史研究 (*Research on the History of the Chinese Communist Party*) no. 6 (1993), 35–9.

146 Gregor Benton, *New Fourth Army*, 14, 49, 54, 77, 574, 576–7, 601; Howard L. Boorman, ed., *Biographical Dictionary*, Vol. 4, 39.

147 The term "disposal force" is from Julian S. Corbett, *Some Principles of Maritime Strategy*, 58

148 Tian Youru, "Social and Political Change in the Villages of the Taihang Anti-Japanese Base Area," in *North China at War*, eds. Feng Chongyi and David S. F. Goodman, 117; Edgar Snow, *Red Star over China*, 176.

149 This estimate is based on the study of a North China county. The Communists were prevalent in North China, the Nationalists were not, so the generalization applies to the Communists. Peter J. Seybolt, "The War within a War: A Case Study of a County on the North China Plain," in *Chinese Collaboration with Japan, 1932–1945*, eds. David P. Barret and Larry N. Shyu, 223–4.

150 Dieter Heinzig, *Soviet Union and Communist China 1945–1950*, 29. For a map showing the expanding Japanese line of conquest in tandem with the expanding guerrilla movements in the Japanese rear, see 西 順蔵 (Nishi Junzō), ed., 原典中国近代思想史国共分裂から解放戦争まで (*Modern Chinese Intellectual History in Documents from the Nationalist-Communist Split to the War of National Liberation*), Vol. 6 (Tokyo: 岩波書店, 1976), 543; Dagfinn Gatu, *Village China at War*, 24.

151 Stephen R. MacKinnon, *Wuhan 1938*, 23.
152 王家福 (Wang Jiafu), "二战时期远东中苏美关系的战略演化" ("The Strategic Evolution of the Relations among China, the Soviet Union, and the United States in the Far East during the Second World War"), 史学集刊 (*Collected Papers of Historical Studies*) 59, no. 2 (1995), 6.
153 Cited in Jonathan Fenby, *Chiang Kai-shek*, 441.
154 Jay Taylor, *Generalissimo*, 169, 298.
155 Gregor Benton, "Comparative Perspectives: North China and Central China in the Anti-Japanese Resistance," in *North China at War*, eds. Feng Chongyi and David S. F. Goodman, 192–3; Boris Grigor'evich Sapozhnikov, *Китай в огне войны 1931–1950* (*China in the Fire of War 1931–1950*) (Moscow: Издательство «наука» Главная редакция восточной литературы, 1977), 180; T'ien-wei Wu, "The Chinese Communist Movement" in *China's Bitter Victory*, eds. James C. Hsiung and Steven I. Levine, 79.
156 Hans J. van de Ven, *War and Nationalism in China 1925–1945*, 17, 255–7.
157 西岡虎之助 (Nishioka Toranosuke) et al., eds., 日本歴史地図 (*Historical Maps of Japan*) (Tokyo: 株式会社全教図, 1978), 297.
158 石島紀之 (Ishijima Noriyuki), *A History of China's Anti-Japanese War*, 131.
159 黄正林 (Huang Zhenglin), "边钞与抗战时期陕甘宁边区的金融事业" ("Research on the Currency of the Shaanxi-Gansu-Ningxia Border Region and the Region's Financial Enterprises in the War of Resistance"), 近代史研究 (*Modern Chinese History Studies*) no. 2 (1999), 192–4; Gregor Benton, *New Fourth Army*, 84.
160 石島紀之 (Ishijima Noriyuki), *A History of China's Anti-Japanese War*, 102.
161 Ibid., 171; 江口圭一 (Eguchi Kei-ichi), "The Japanese Army on the China Front," 60–2; Edward L. Dreyer, *China at War, 1901–1949*, 253–4; Dagfinn Gatu, *Village China at War*, 357–60.
162 石島紀之 (Ishijima Noriyuki), *A History of China's Anti-Japanese War*, 161–4, 171; 姫田光義 (Himata Mitsuyoshi), "三光政策· 三光作戦をめぐって" ("The Three Alls Policy and Three Alls Military Strategy") in *The Sino-Japanese War*, 中央大学人文科学研究所 (Chūō University Human Sciences Research Center, ed., 120; Richard Fuller, *Shōkan Hirohito's Samurai*, 179–80; 居之芬 (Ju Zhifen) and 华杰 (Hua Jie), "The Economic Activities and the Plunder of Japan's 'North China Development Co.,'" 252–3; Chen Yung-fa, *Making Revolution: The Communist Movement in Eastern and Central China, 1937–1945* (Berkeley: University of California Press, 1986), 79–80.

163 Edward J. Drea and Hans van de Ven, "Overview of Major Military Campaigns during the Sino-Japanese War, 1937–1945," 39.
164 Herbert P. Bix, *Hirohito*, 367.
165 石島紀之 (Ishijima Noriyuki), *History of China's Anti-Japanese War*, 63.
166 黄正林 (Huang Zhenglin), "Research on the Currency of the Shaanxi-Gansu-Ningxia Border Region," 192–4.
167 Gregor Benton, *New Fourth Army*, 296, 425, 465, 511–12; David S. G. Goodman, *Social and Political Change in Revolutionary China*, 51–2.
168 John W. Garver, *Chinese-Soviet Relations 1937–1945*, 129–30, 142–5; 石仲泉 (Shi Zhongquan), "周恩来与新四军" ("Zhou Enlai and the New Fourth Army"), 近代史研究 (*Modern Chinese History Studies*) 77, no. 5 (September 1993), 34–57; 黄正林 (Huang Zhenglin), "Research on the Currency of the Shaanxi-Gansu-Ningxia Border Region," 192–4; Gregor Benton, *New Fourth Army*, 511, 513, 520–1, 572, 600.
169 Zhang Baijia, "China's Quest for Military Aid," 293; Michael M. Sheng, *Battling Western Imperialism*, 49; Gregor Benton, *New Fourth Army*, 594.
170 楊奎松 (Yang Kuisong), *Heading for Rupture*, 493.
171 Sergei N. Goncharov, John W. Lewis, and Xue Litai, *Uncertain Partners: Stalin, Mao, and the Korean War* (Stanford, CA: Stanford University Press, 1993), 8; Jung Chang and Jon Halliday, *Mao the Unknown Story*, 237.
172 Chen Yung-fa, *Making Revolution*, 77.
173 Nancy Bernkopf Tucker, *China Confidential: American Diplomats and Sino-American Relations, 1945–1960* (New York: Columbia University Press, 2001), 6; Gregor Benton, *New Fourth Army*, 519, 591; Jung Chang and Jon Halliday, *Mao the Unknown Story*, 221–2.
174 Cited in 黄正林 (Huang Zhenglin), "Research on the Currency of the Shaanxi-Gansu-Ningxia Border Region," 195–6.
175 许建平 (Xu Jianping), "抗日战争时期陕甘宁边区私营经济的发展" ("The Development of the Private Economy in the Shaanxi-Gansu-Ningxia Border Region during the Anti-Japanese War"), 中国经济史研究 (*Research in Chinese Economic History*) no. 3 (1995), 125; Jay Taylor, *Generalissimo*, 171.
176 Chong-Sik Lee, "Counterinsurgency in Manchuria: the Japanese Experience, 1931–1940," 339.
177 阎庆生 (Yan Qingsheng) and 黄正林 (Huang Zhenglin), "抗战时期陕甘宁边区税收问题研究" ("Research concerning Tax Receipts in the Shaanxi-Gansu-Ningxi Border Area during the Sino-Japanese War") 中国经济史研究 (*Research in Chinese Economic History*) no. 4 (2001), 49–56.

178 Chong-Sik Lee, "Counterinsurgency in Manchuria: the Japanese Experience, 1931–1940," 339.
179 Edward R. Slack, *Opium, State, and Society: China's Narco-Economy and the Guomindang, 1924–1937* (Honolulu: University of Hawai'i Press, 2001), 154; Sechin Jagchid, *Last Mongol Prince*, 113.
180 江口圭一 (Eguchi Kei-ichi), *Short History of the Fifteen Year War*, 104.
181 Jonathan Fenby, *Chiang Kai-shek,* 442; Jung Chang and Jon Halliday, *Mao the Unknown Story*, 277.
182 黄正林 (Huang Zhenglin), "Research on the Currency of the Shaanxi-Gansu-Ningxia Border Region," 197–210, 220; Jung Chang and Jon Halliday, *Mao the Unknown Story*, 279.
183 Lyman van Slyke, "The Chinese Communist Movement during the Sino-Japanese War 1937–1945" in *The Cambridge History of China*, Vol. 13, eds. Denis Twitchett and John K. Fairbank (Cambridge: Cambridge University Press, 1986), 686.
184 "War can be of two kinds, in the sense that either the objective is to *overthrow the enemy* – to render him politically helpless or militarily impotent, thus forcing him to sign whatever peace we please; or *merely to occupy some of his frontier-districts* so that we can annex them or use them for bargaining at the peace negotiations." Carl von Clausewitz, *On War,* 69. For a thorough guide to Clausewitz's complex thoughts on this subject, see Michael I. Handel, *Masters of War: Classical Strategic Thought,* 3rd ed. (London: Frank Cass, 2001), 432*n*18 and 433*n*19.
185 Herbert P. Bix, *Hirohito*, 325.
186 Cited by Michael A. Barnhart, *Japan Prepares for Total War*, 89.
187 Cited by 沈予 (Shen Yu), "Discussion of the Konoe Fumimaro Cabinet's China Policy," 42–3.
188 Cited in Takafusa Nakamura, *History of Shōwa Japan,* 146.
189 Yoshihisa Tak Matsusaka, *Making of Japanese Manchuria, 1904–1932,* 237–38.
190 Timothy Brook, "The Creation of the Reformed Government in Central China, 1938," in *Chinese Collaboration with Japan, 1932–1945*, eds. David P. Barrett and Larry N. Shyu, 79–80, 84, 86–91, 99–100; 石島紀之 (Ishijima Noriyuki), *A History of China's Anti-Japanese War*, 34, 38; Takafusa Nakamura, "Japan's Economic Thrust into North China, 1933–1938," 226, 232–3; 王建朗 (Wang Jianlang), "失败的外交记录—抗战初期的日本外交综论" ("A Record of Failed Diplomacy: A General Discussion of Japanese Diplomacy Early in the War of Resistance") 近代史研究 (*Modern Chinese History Studies*) 67, no. 1 (January 1992), 230–1.
191 蔡德金 (Cai Dejin) and 李惠贤 (Li Huixian),"关于汪伪政权问题学术讨论会综述" ("A Summary of the Academic Discussion Concerning

the Wang Jingwei Puppet Regime"), 历史研究 (*Historical Research*) no. 5 (1986), 185; 沈予 (Shen Yu), "Discussion of the Konoe Fumimaro Cabinet's China Policy," 48–9.

192 君島和彦 (Kimishima Kazuhiko), "「東亜新秩序」と植民地・占領地" ("'New East Asian Order' and Colonial and Occupied Areas") in *History of the Fifteen Year War*, eds. 藤原彰 (Fujiwara Akira) and 今井清一 (Imai Seiichi), Vol. 2, 94; Lu Minghui, "The Inner Mongolian 'United Autonomous Government'" in *China at War*, eds. Stephen R. MacKinnon et al., 152–61.

193 臼井勝美 (Usui Katsumi), *Research on Sino-Japanese Diplomatic History*, 288.

194 Timothy Brook, "The Creation of the Reformed Government in Central China, 1938," 79–80, 84, 86–91, 99–100.

195 Howard L. Boorman, ed., *Biographical Dictionary*, Vol. 3, 385–6; 君島和彦 (Kimishima Kazuhiko), "'New East Asian Order' and Colonial and Occupied Areas," Vol. 2, 94; Usui Katsumi, "The Politics of War, 1937–1941," 311; George E. Taylor, *Struggle for North China*, 22, 190.

196 Takafusa Nakamura, *History of Shōwa Japan*, 147–8; 君島和彦 (Kimishima Kazuhiko), "'New East Asian Order' and Colonial and Occupied Areas," Vol. 2, 124.

197 George E. Taylor, *Struggle for North China*, 71–5, 182.

198 Timothy Brook, "The Creation of the Reformed Government in Central China, 1938," 79–80, 84, 86–91, 99–100; Bradford A. Lee, *Britain and the Sino-Japanese War 1937–1939*, 180; Takafusa Nakamura, *History of Shōwa Japan*, 147; 君島和彦 (Kimishima Kazuhiko), "'New East Asian Order' and Colonial and Occupied Areas," Vol. 2, 124; 臼井勝美 (Usui Katsumi), *Research on Sino-Japanese Diplomatic History*, 292–3; John Gunther, *Inside Asia*, 282; Diana Lary, *Chinese People at War*, 104.

199 Richard Fuller, *Shōkan Hirohito's Samurai*, 148.

200 Howard L. Boorman, ed., *Biographical Dictionary*, Vol. 2, 351–2.

201 F. C. Jones, *Japan's New Order in East Asia*, 74.

202 Cited in Jonathan Haslam, *Soviet Union and the Threat from the East, 1933–1941*, 121–2.

203 Both cited in Ian Nish, *Japanese Foreign Policy 1869–1942*, 1, 174, 310, 322.

204 汪熙 (Wang Xi), "太平洋戦争と中国" ("The War in the Pacific and China") in *The Pacific War*), ed. 細谷千博 (Hosoya Chihiro) et al., 121.

205 臼井勝美 (Usui Katsumi), *Research on Sino-Japanese Diplomatic History*, 230–1, 237; Boris Grigor'evich Sapozhnikov, *The Sino-Japanese War and Japan's Colonial Policy in China (1937–1941)*, 78–9.

206 臼井勝美 (Usui Katsumi), *Research on Sino-Japanese Diplomatic History*, 280–2; for a table of escalating Japanese peace demands, see

戸部良一 (Tobe Ryūichi), ピース・フィーラー支那事変平和工作の群像 (*Peace-Fire: The Many People Promoting Peace during the Sino-Japanese War*) (Tokyo: 論創社, 1991), 370–2; Iurii Mikhailovich Ovchinnikov, *Creation and Development of the United National Front*, 104–5.

207 沈予 (Shen Yu), "论抗日战争期间日蒋的'和平交涉'" ("'Peace Negotiations' between Japan and Chiang Kai-shek during the Anti-Japanese War"), 历史研究 (*Historical Research*) no. 2 (1993), 108–27.

208 臼井勝美 (Usui Katsumi), *Research on Sino-Japanese Diplomatic History*, 195–6.

209 Boris Grigor'evich Sapozhnikov, *The Sino-Japanese War and Japan's Colonial Policy in China (1937–1941)*, 80–1.

210 臼井勝美 (Usui Katsumi), *Research on Sino-Japanese Diplomatic History*, 302–9.

211 Janet E. Hunter, comp., *Concise Dictionary of Modern Japanese History* (Berkeley: University of California Press, 1984), 284.

212 张北根 (Zhang Beigen), "Sino-German Relations, 1933–1941," 117–18.

213 鹿锡俊 (Lu Xijun), "Evolution of Japan's Policy Regarding Chiang Kai-shek during the Sino-Japanese War," 221.

214 刘建皋 (Liu Jian'gao), "改组派初探" ("Initial Exploration of the Reorganization Faction"), 历史研究 (*Historical Research*) no. 6 (1981), 159–61, 166.

215 Frederic Wakeman, Jr., *Spymaster: Dai Li and the Chinese Secret Service* (Berkeley: University of California Press, 2003), 337–8; Jonathan Fenby, *Chiang Kai-shek*, 343.

216 章绍嗣 (Zhang Shaosi) et al., comps., 中国抗日战争大辞典 (*The Comprehensive Dictionary of the Chinese War of Resistance against Japan*) (Wuhan: 武汉出版社, 1995), 993.

217 沈予 (Shen Yu), "Discussion of the Konoe Fumimaro Cabinet's China Policy," 49.

218 臼井勝美 (Usui Katsumi), *Research on Sino-Japanese Diplomatic History*, 365, 372–7.

219 Takafusa Nakamura, *History of Shōwa Japan*, 160.

220 江口圭一 (Eguchi Kei-ichi), *Short History of the Fifteen Year War*, 152.

221 臼井勝美 (Usui Katsumi), *Research on Sino-Japanese Diplomatic History*, 384–7, 397–404; 江口圭一 (Eguchi Kei-ichi), *A Short History of the Fifteen Year War*, 153.

222 David P. Barrett, "The Wang Jingwei Government, 1940–1945: Continuities and Disjunctures with Nationalist China" in *Chinese Collaboration with Japan, 1932–1945*, eds. David P. Barret and Larry N. Shyu, 105, 108–14.

223 臼井勝美 (Usui Katsumi), *Research on Sino-Japanese Diplomatic History*, 384–7.

224 David P. Barrett, "The Wang Jingwei Government, 1940–1945," 105, 108–14; Colin Mackerras, *Modern China*, 388.

225 古厩忠夫 (Furumaya Tadao), "日本軍占領地域の「清郷」工作と抗戦" ("The War of Resistance and 'Village Purification' Work in Areas under Japanese Military Occupation") in 抗日戦争と中国民衆 (*The War of Japanese Resistance and the Chinese Populace*), ed. 池田誠 (Ikeda Makoto) (Tokyo: 法律文化社, 1987), 181–2.

226 David P. Barrett, "The Wang Jingwei Government, 1940–1945," 105, 108–14.

227 杨天石 (Yang Tianshi), "抗战前期日本'民间人士'和蒋介石集团的秘密谈判" ("Secret Negotiations between the Chiang Kai-shek Clique and 'Unofficial' Japanese Representatives in the Early Stages of the Sino-Japanese War"), 历史研究 (*Historical Research*) no. 1 (1990), 160–75.

228 沈予 (Shen Yu), "Discussion of the Konoe Fumimaro Cabinet's China Policy," 54.

229 臼井勝美 (Usui Katsumi), *Research on Sino-Japanese Diplomatic History*, 384–7; John Hunter Boyle, *China and Japan at War 1937–1945*, 298, 304.

230 石源华 (Shi Yuanhua), "论日本对华新政策下的日汪关系" ("A Discussion of Japan's Relations with Wang Jingwei as an Element of Japan's New China Policy"), 历史研究 (*Historical Research*) no. 2 (1996), 113–14.

231 David P. Barrett, "The Wang Jingwei Government, 1940–1945," 105, 108–14; John W. Garver, *Chinese-Soviet Relations 1937–1945*, 80.

232 Stephen R. MacKinnon, "Refugee Flight at the Outset of the Anti-Japanese War," 121.

233 王磊 (Wang Lei), "抗战时期国民政府内债研究" ("Research on the Internal Debt of the Nationalist Government during the War of Resistance"), 中国经济史研究 (*Research in Chinese Economic History*) no. 4 (1993), 75.

234 贾兴权 (Jia Xingquan), "抗战期间通货膨胀政策对中国社会的影响" ("Influence of Inflationary Policies on Chinese Society during the Sino-Japanese War"), 中国经济史研究 (*Research in Chinese Economic History*) no. 1 (1993); Diana Lary, *Chinese People at War*, 121–2; 張瑞德 (Zhang Ruide), *Personnel Matters of the Nationalist Army during the War of Resistance*, 94.

235 Michael A. Barnhart, *Japan Prepares for Total War*, 94–5; Takafusa Nakamura, "Age of Turbulence, 1937–54," 63–6.

236 Takafusa Nakamura, *History of Shōwa Japan*, 148–50, 159, 193, 196.

237 江口圭一 (Eguchi Kei-ichi), *A Short History of the Fifteen Year War*, 225–6; Boris Grigor'evich Sapozhnikov, *The Sino-Japanese War and Japan's Colonial Policy in China (1937–1941)*, 144; 荒川憲一 (Arakawa

Ken-ichi), *Plans for and Development of the Wartime Economic System*, 285.

238 真保潤一郎 (Shinpo Junichirō), "戦時経済の遺産と経済再建" ("The Wartime Economic Legacy and Economic Reconstruction") in *Modern Japanese Military History*), Vol. 4, eds. 奥村房夫 (Okumura Fusao) and 近藤新治 (Kondō Shinji), 944; 森武麿 (Mori Takemaro), "The Great Depression and the War, 1930–1945," 16.

239 荒川憲一 (Arakawa Ken-ichi), *Plans for and Development of the Wartime Economic System*, 222.

240 江口圭一 (Eguchi Kei-ichi), *Short History of the Fifteen Year War*, 227.

241 森武麿 (Mori Takemaro), "Great Depression and the War, 1930–1945," 9.

242 Cited in John Gunther, *Inside Asia*, 78.

243 江口圭一 (Eguchi Kei-ichi), *Short History of the Fifteen Year War*, 218–20, 223.

244 安部彦太 (Abe Hikota), "大東亜戦争の計数的分析" ("A Statistical Analysis of the Great East Asian War") in *Modern Japanese Military History*, Vol. 4, eds. 奥村房夫 (Okumura Fusao) and 近藤新治 (Kondō Shinji), 825.

245 Michael A. Barnhart, *Japan Prepares for Total War*, 101, 110, 114.

246 近藤新治 (Kondō Shinji), "The Army's Preparations for Opening the War," 328.

247 Diana Lary, *Chinese People at War*, 78.

7 GLOBAL WAR: WORLD WAR II

1 真保潤一郎 (Shinpo Junichirō), "Wartime Economic Legacy and Economic Reconstruction," 937.

2 "Strategic Imports from Southeast Asia," *Far Eastern Survey* 11, no. 1 (12 January 1942), 12; League of Nations, Economic, Financial and Transit Department, *World Economic Survey*, 1942/44 (Geneva: League of Nations, 1945), 71–5; S. Woodburn Kirby, *The War against Japan*, Vol. 1 (London: Her Majesty's Stationery Office, 1957), 477.

3 赵志辉 (Zhao Zhihui), "太平洋战争时期美国的中国大国地位政策的起源" ("The Origin of the U.S. Policy to Regard China as a Great Power during the Pacific War"), 史学集刊 (*Collected Papers of Historical Studies*) no. 3 (August 2000), 64–9.

4 Bruce A. Elleman, *Wilson and China*, passim.

5 David C. Evans and Mark R. Peattie, *Kaigun: Strategy, Tactics, and Technology in the Imperial Japanese Navy 1887–1941* (Annapolis, MD: Naval Institute Press, 1997), 193–201, 235–7, 296–7, 372, 457; Sadao Asada, *From Mahan to Pearl Harbor*, 203–6.

6 Takafusa Nakamura, *History of Shōwa Japan*, 92.

7 Hoover Institution Archives, Vladimir D. Pastuhov papers, Box 18, "The Japanese Invasion of Manchuria" (Shanghai: Publicity Department of the Shanghai Branch of the Central Executive Committee of the Kuomintang, 1932?); ibid., Shuhsi Hsü, *Background of the Manchurian Situation* (Peiping, 1932); ibid., Shuhsi Hsü, *Japan's Fifty-four Cases* (Peiping, 1932); Shuhsi Hsu, *War Conduct of the Japanese*, passim.

8 郑会欣 (Zheng Huixin), "1933年的中美棉麦借款" ("The 1933 U.S. Loan to China for Cotton and Wheat"), 历史研究 (*Historical Research*) no. 5 (1988), 128–37.

9 江口圭一 (Eguchi Kei-ichi), *A Short History of the Fifteen Year War*, 111.

10 David C. Evans and Mark R. Peattie, *Kaigun*, 235, 296; George W. Baer, *One Hundred Years of Sea Power: The U.S. Navy, 1890–1990* (Stanford, CA: Stanford University Press, 1993), 130.

11 任东来 (Ren Donglai), "1934–1936年间中美关系中的白银外交" ("The Sino-U.S. Silver Diplomacy of 1934–1936"), 历史研究 (*Historical Research*) no. 3 (2000), 103–16.

12 吴景平 (Wu Jingping), "On the U.S. Stabilization Fund for the Chinese Currency during the War of Resistance," 76–7.

13 Bradford A. Lee, *Britain and the Sino-Japanese War 1937–1939*, 90–1; George W. Baer, *One Hundred Years of Sea Power*, 130, 134.

14 臼井勝美 (Usui Katsumi), *Research on Sino-Japanese Diplomatic History*, 332, 343; Maochun Yu, *Dragon's War*, 48.

15 Thomas W. Burkman, *Japan and the League of Nations*, 107; Akira Iriye, *Cambridge History of American Foreign Relations*, Vol. 3, 162–4, 166, 180; 江口圭一 (Eguchi Kei-ichi), *Short History of the Fifteen Year War*, 140; Michael A. Barnhart, *Japan Prepares for Total War*, 144.

16 Michael A. Barnhart, *Japan Prepares for Total War*, 45, 156.

17 单冠初 (Shan Guanchu), "The Japanese Policy of 'Providing for the War with War' during the Invasion of China," 90.

18 George W. Baer, *One Hundred Years of Sea Power*, 134–137, 149–151.

19 森茂樹 (Mori Shigeki), "枢軸外交および南進政策と海軍—１９３９〜１９４０年—" ("The Imperial Navy and the Making of Japan's Foreign Policy, 1939–1940"), 歴史学研究 (*Journal of Historical Studies*) no. 727 (September 1999), 3, 9–10.

20 George W. Baer, *One Hundred Years of Sea Power*, 134–7, 149–51; Sadao Asada, *From Mahan to Pearl Harbor*, 240–1; David Isaakovich Gol'dberg, *Внешняя политика Японии (сентябрь 1939 г.-декабрь 1941 г.)* (*The Foreign Policy of Japan [September 1939–December 1941*) (Moscow: Издательство восточной литературы, 1959), 120–1, 282–5.

21 Akira Iriye, *Cambridge History of American Foreign Relations*, Vol. 3, 162–4, 166, 180; 江口圭一 (Eguchi Kei-ichi), *Short History of the Fifteen Year War*, 140.

22 宓汝成 (Mi Rucheng), "The Foreign Loans to China during the War of Resistance," 55.

23 F. C. Jones, *Japan's New Order in East Asia*, 193; Yoshihisa Tak Matsusaka, *Making of Japanese Manchuria, 1904–1932*, 281–2.

24 Cited by Herbert P. Bix, *Hirohito*, 374.

25 Ian Nish, *Japanese Foreign Policy 1869–1942*, 236.

26 F. C. Jones, *Japan's New Order in East Asia*, 119.

27 Alvin D. Coox, *Nomonhan*, 1036; F. C. Jones, *Japan's New Order in East Asia*, 126; Historical Research Center (歴史学研究会), comp., *History of the Pacific War*, Vol. 2, 345–6; ibid., Vol. 3, 372–3.

28 James William Morley, "The Tripartite Pact, 1939–1940, Introduction," in *Deterrent Diplomacy*, ed. James William Morley, 183; Hosoya Chihiro, "Tripartite Pact, 1939–1940," in ibid., 257; Peter A. Berton, "Northern Defense: Introduction" in *The Fateful Choice: Japan's Advance into Southeast Asia, 1939–1941*, ed. James William Morley (New York: Columbia University Press, 1980), 8–9; Hosoya Chihiro, "Japanese-Soviet Neutrality Pact" in ibid., 66, 72; Boris Slavinsky, *Japanese-Soviet Neutrality Pact*, 7.

29 Sadao Asada, *From Mahan to Pearl Harbor*, 221–2, 236.

30 宓汝成 (Mi Rucheng), "Foreign Loans to China during the War of Resistance," 55.

31 Ian Nish, *Japanese Foreign Policy 1869–1942*, 241; 江口圭一 (Eguchi Kei-ichi), *Short History of the Fifteen Year War*, 156; Carl Boyd, *Hitler's Japanese Confidant*, 19, 29–31, 151; Boris Slavinsky, *Japanese-Soviet Neutrality Pact*, 34–56; Gerhard L. Weinberg, *Germany, Hitler, and World War II: Essays in Modern and World History* (Cambridge: Cambridge University Press, 1995), 157, 160, 178.

32 Meirion Harries and Susie Harries, *Soldiers of the Sun*, 310.

33 Boris Slavinsky, *Japanese-Soviet Neutrality Pact*, 52–3.

34 香島明雄 (Kashima Akio), *Research on Sino-Soviet Diplomatic History, 1937–1946*, 38, 56–8; JFM, B.1.0.0-J/RI, 日蘇中立条約関係一件 (Document Concerning the Japanese-Soviet Neutrality Pact), Vol. 3, 日の中立条約の支那への影響と外援問題 (The Influence of Japan's Neutrality Pact over China and the Foreign Aid Question), June 1941, top secret, p. 3.

35 Bruce A. Elleman, "The 1940 Soviet Japanese Secret Agreement and Its Impact on the Soviet-Iranian Supply Route," *Working Papers in International Studies*, I-95-5, Hoover Institution, Stanford University (May 1995), p. 1

36 Carl Boyd, *Hitler's Japanese Confidant*, 21, 117; 江口圭一 (Eguchi Kei-ichi), *Short History of the Fifteen Year War*, 162; Hans-Joachim Krug,

Yōichi Hirama, Berthold J. Sander-Nagashima, and Axel Niestlé, *Reluctant Allies: German-Japanese Naval Relations in World War II* (Annapolis, MD: Naval Institute Press, 2001), 176, 271; Carl Boyd, *Extraordinary Envoy*, 1, 130; David Isaakovich Gol'dberg, *Foreign Policy of Japan (September 1939–December 194)*, 106, 109; Ōhata Tokushirō, "The Anti-Comintern Pact, 1935–1939" in *Deterrent Diplomacy*, ed. James William Morley, 23.

37 Boris Slavinsky, *Japanese-Soviet Neutrality Pact*, 75–6; Louis Frédéric, *Japan Encyclopedia*, 903.

38 JFM, B.1.0.0-J/R1, 日蘇中立条約関係一件, Vol. 2, 「日蘇中立条約ニ関連シ予想セルル質問」("Conjecture Concerning the Japanese-Soviet Neutrality Pact"), 16 April 1941, top secret.

39 JFM, A.7.0.0–9-55, 大東亜戦争関係一件戦争終結ニ関スル日蘇交渉関係 (Concerning the War of the Pacific and Soviet-Japanese War Termination Diplomacy), Vol. 1, to Foreign Minister Shigemitsu from Harbin Consul General Miyagawa, 28 September 1944, top secret; 江口圭一 (Eguchi Kei-ichi), *Short History of the Fifteen Year War*, 159–68, 172.

40 Michael Clodfelter, *Warfare and Armed Conflicts*, Vol. 2, 817–19.

41 江口圭一 (Eguchi Kei-ichi), *Short History of the Fifteen Year War*, 159.

42 Cited in Carl Boyd, *Hitler's Japanese Confidant,* 29.

43 Cited by Alvin D. Coox, *Nomonhan*, 896.

44 Carl Boyd, *Hitler's Japanese Confidant,* 30; 王家福 (Wang Jiafu), "Strategic Evolution of the Relations among China, the Soviet Union, and the United States," 6.

45 Michael A. Barnhart, *Japan Prepares for Total War*, 209.

46 王真 (Wang Zhen), "The Nature of the Soviet Policy to Assist China Early in the Anti-Japanese War," 50–1; JDA, 満洲全般２２３満洲に関する用兵的観察, Vol. 1, part 1, 満洲に於ける日本軍の対ソ作戦計画 (Soviet War Plans against the Japanese Army in Manchuria), May 1952, 復員局資料整理課元陸軍大佐股部四郎 (Demobilization Bureau, Documents Section), p. 77; JDA, 満洲全般２２５満洲に関する用兵的観察, Vol. 13, part 5, 極東ソ軍の戦略的特性に関する調査 (Survey of the Strategy of the Far Eastern Soviet Military), March 1953, 復員局資料整理課元陸軍大佐林三郎 (Demobilization Bureau, Documents Section, Former Army Colonel Hayashi Saburō?), p. 62.

47 Peter A. Berton, "Northern Defense: Introduction," 12.

48 George Brown Tindall and David E. Shi, *America*, Vol. 2, 1227; Meirion Harries and Susie Harries, *Soldiers of the Sun*, 295; JDA, 満洲全般１５２東「ソ」「ソ」軍後方準備調査、大本営陸軍部、軍事極秘 (Survey of Soviet Rear Guard Preparations in the Soviet East), no. 276, March 1945, pp. 111–14, 124.

49 Carl Boyd, *Hitler's Japanese Confidant*, 58, 94–5, 140; 西春彦 (Nishi Haruhiko), ed., 日本外交史 (*A History of Japanese Foreign Relations*), Vol. 15, 日ソ国交問題１９１７－１９４５ (*Questions concerning Japanese-Soviet Diplomatic Relations, 1917–1945*) (Tokyo: 鹿島研究所出版会, 1970), 246.

50 江口圭一 (Eguchi Kei-ichi), *Short History of the Fifteen Year War*, 159.

51 鹿锡俊 (Lu Xijun), "The Evolution of Japan's Policy Regarding Chiang Kai-shek during the Sino-Japanese War," 224–5.

52 Hosoya Chihiro, "Japanese-Soviet Neutrality Pact," 23, 32–3, 35.

53 戸部良一 (Tobe Ryūichi) "米英独ソ等の中国援助" ("U.S., British, German, Soviet, etc. Assistance to China") in 近代日本戦争史 (*Modern Japanese Military History*), Vol. 3, 満州事変・支那事変 (*The Manchurian Incident and the China Incident*), eds., 奥村房夫 (Okumura Fusao) and 河野収 (Kōno Shū) (Tokyo: 同台経済懇話会, 1995), 335, 345–8; 刘卫东 (Liu Weidong), "印支通道的战时功能述论" ("A Narrative of the Wartime Function of the Indochina Passageway"), 近代史研究 (*Modern Chinese History Studies*) no. 2 (May 1999), 173, 185; 江口圭一 (Eguchi Kei-ichi), *Short History of the Fifteen Year War*, 151.

54 F. C. Jones, *Japan's New Order in East Asia*, 230.

55 江口圭一 (Eguchi Kei-ichi), *Short History of the Fifteen Year War*, 154.

56 吴景平 (Wu Jingping), "抗战时期中美租借关系述评" ("Sino-American Lend-Lease Relations during the War against Japan"), 历史研究 (*Historical Research*) no. 4 (1995), 53, 59–60, 64; Arthur N. Young, *China's Wartime Finance and Inflation, 1937–1945*, 114–15; Arthur N. Young, *China and the Helping Hand 1937–1945*, 350; ASA, 431.4/0004, 清理中美戰債 (Settling Accounts for Sino-American Military Debts), 11-NAA-06283, 30 June 1945, pp. 62–81; ASA, 431.4/0007, ibid., 11-NAA-06286, pp. 74–8.

57 Wesley M. Bagby, *Eagle-Dragon Alliance*, 49, 62–3, 65, 67, 103; Jay Taylor, *Generalissimo*, 309; Arthur N. Young, *China's Wartime Finance and Inflation, 1937–1945*, 297.

58 菊池一隆 (Kikuchi Kazutaka), "Wartime Finances of the Chongqing Government," 400.

59 Cited in Carl Boyd, *Hitler's Japanese Confidant*, 57.

60 吴景平 (Wu Jingping), "Sino-American Lend-Lease Relations during the War against Japan," 53, 59–60.

61 宓汝成 (Mi Rucheng), "Foreign Loans to China during the War of Resistance," 55, 59.

62 Herbert P. Bix, *Hirohito*, 400; Mark A. Stoler, *Allies and Adversaries: The Joint Chiefs of Staff, the Grand Alliance, and U.S. Strategy in World War II* (Chapel Hill: University of North Carolina Press, 2000), 59.

63 江口圭一 (Eguchi Kei-ichi), *Short History of the Fifteen Year War*, 162; 近藤新治 (Kondō Shinji), "「物的国力判断」" ("'An Evaluation of National Material Strength'") in *Modern Japanese Military History*, Vol. 4, eds. 奥村房夫 (Okumura Fusao) and 近藤新治 (Kondō Shinji), 212–18.
64 David C. Evans and Mark R. Peattie, *Kaigun*, 475, 537.
65 Ian Nish, *Japanese Foreign Policy 1869–1942*, 232; Herbert P. Bix, *Hirohito*, 368–9; Michael A. Barnhart, *Japan Prepares for Total War*, 168.
66 Cited in Takafusa Nakamura, *History of Shōwa Japan*, 200.
67 Christopher Thorne, *Allies of a Kind: The United States, Britain, and the War against Japan, 1941–1945* (Oxford: Oxford University Press, 1978), 77; Charles A. Beard, *President Roosevelt and the Coming War 1941: A Study in Appearances and Realities* (New Haven: Yale University Press, 1948), 517–18; S. Woodburn Kirby, *The War against Japan*, Vol. 5, 385
68 David C. Evans and Mark R. Peattie, *Kaigun*, 475, 537.
69 David J. Lu, *Japan a Documentary History: The Late Tokugawa Period to the Present*, Vol. 2 (Armonk, NY: M. E. Sharpe, 1997), 433.
70 江口圭一 (Eguchi Kei-ichi), *Short History of the Fifteen Year War*, 182.
71 安部彦太 (Abe Hikota), "Statistical Analysis of the Great East Asian War," 825.
72 Alvin D. Coox, "The Pacific War" in *Cambridge History of Japan*, Vol. 6, *The Twentieth Century*, eds. John W. Hall, Marius B. Jansen, Madoka Kanai, and Denis Twitchett (Cambridge: Cambridge University Press, 1988), 331; David C. Evans and Mark R. Peattie, *Kaigun*, 476.
73 小林道彦 (Kobayashi Michihiko),"世界大戦と大陸政策の変容" ("The Transformation of Japan's Continental Policy during the World War I, 1914–1916") 歴史学研究 (*Journal of Historical Studies*) 657, no. 4 (1994), 2, 14; 江口圭一 (Eguchi Kei-ichi), *Short History of the Fifteen Year War*, 26–7; Hoover Institution Archives, Stanley K. Hornbeck papers, Box 242, "The 'Japanese Monroe Doctrine'," 5 March 1932, p. 1; Parks M. Coble, *Facing Japan*, 153–4; Louise Young, *Japan's Total Empire*, 124, 148.
74 糸永 新 (Itonaga Arata), "開戦前の日米戦争計画" ("Pre-war Japanese and U.S. War Plans") in *Modern Japanese Military History*, Vol. 4, eds. 奥村房夫 (Okumura Fusao) and 近藤新治 (Kondō Shinji), 280–4.
75 Haruko Taya Cook and Theodore F. Cook, *Japan at War*, passim.
76 Edward J. Drea, *In the Service of the Emperor: Essays on the Imperial Japanese Army* (Lincoln: University of Nebraska Press, 1998), 30; David P. Barrett, "Introduction: Occupied China and the Limits of Accommodation" in *Chinese Collaboration with Japan, 1932–1945*, eds. David P. Barrett and Larry N. Shyu, 3–4.

77 David J. Lu, *Japan a Documentary History*, Vol. 2, 427; Meirion Harries and Susie Harries, *Soldiers of the Sun*, 295; Nobutaka Ike, trans. and ed., *Japan's Decision for War: Records of the 1941 Policy Conferences* (Stanford, CA: Stanford University Press, 1967), 223; Alvin D. Coox, "Pacific War," 329..

78 Nobutaka Ike, trans. and ed., *Japan's Decision for War*, 239. Brackets inserted by translator.

79 Cited in Alvin D. Coox, "Pacific War," 329.

80 幕内光雄 (Maku'uchi Mitsuo), *Unofficial History of the Manchukuo Police*, 147.

81 JDA, 満洲全般１９４満蒙計略計画, August 1934, 満蒙問題解決ノ為ノ戦争計画大綱 (General Outline of War Plans to Resolve the Manchuria-Mongolia Problem), pp. 13–23.

82 Nobutaka Ike, *Japan's Decision for War*, 207.

83 池田清 (Ikeda Kiyoshi), ed., 太平洋戦争 (*Great War of the Pacific*) (Tokyo: 河出書房新社, 1995), 163; Robert B. Edgerton, *Warriors of the Rising Sun: A History of the Japanese Military* (New York: W. W. Norton, 1997), 261, 264; Herbert P. Bix, *Hirohito*, 436

84 Cited in Herbert P. Bix, *Hirohito*, 437.

85 David. C. Evans and Mark R. Peattie, *Kaigun*, 488; Ronald H. Spector, *The Eagle against the Sun* (New York: Free Press, 1985), 6; Ken Kotani, "Pearl Harbor Japanese Planning and Command Structure" in *The Pacific War Companion: From Pearl Harbor to Hiroshima,* ed. Daniel Marston (Oxford: Osprey, 2005), 41.

86 Herbert P. Bix, *Hirohito*, 445–7; Ienaga Saburō, *Pacific War 1931–1945*, 143.

87 Robert B. Edgerton, *Warriors of the Rising Sun*, 277; David. C. Evans and Mark R. Peattie, *Kaigun*, 488, 529.

88 Takafusa Nakamura, *History of Shōwa Japan,* 204.

89 Ibid., 201–6.

90 森茂樹 (Mori Shigeki), "Imperial Navy," 8; Robert Edgerton, *Warriors of the Rising Sun*, 260; David C. Evans and Mark R. Peattie, *Kaigun*, 488, 529.

91 Jonathan Fenby, *Chiang Kai-shek,* 368; 鹿锡俊 (Lu Xijun), "The Evolution of Japan's Policy regarding Chiang Kai-shek during the Sino-Japanese War," 225–8.

92 Mark R. Peattie, *Sunburst*, 122.

93 张北根 (Zhang Beigen), "Sino-German Relations, 1933–1941," 119; 易豪精 (Yi Haojing), "From 'Honeymoon' to Diplomatic Split," 63; Gerhard L. Weinberg, *Germany, Hitler, and World War II*, 159–60.

94 Jonathan Fenby, *Chiang Kai-shek,* 369–72.

95 Williamson Murray and Allan R. Millet, *A War to Be Won: Fighting the Second World War* (Cambridge, MA: Harvard University Press, 2000), 87–8.

96 Carl Boyd, *Hitler's Japanese Confidant*, 31; David Isaakovich Gol'dberg, *Foreign Policy of Japan (September 1939–December 1941)*, 111.

97 Richard Overy, *Russia's War: A History of the Soviet War Effort: 1941–1945* (New York: Penguin, 1997), 236.

98 John W. Dower, *War without Mercy*, 273–5.

99 Robert B. Edgerton, *Warriors of the Rising Sun*, 275; Edward J. Drea, *In the Service of the Emperor*, 37.

100 Hagiwara Mitsuru, "Japanese Air Campaigns in China, 1937–1945," 250; Tohmatsu Haruo, "The Strategic Correlation between the Sino-Japanese and Pacific Wars" in *The Battle for China*, eds. Mark Peattie et al., 427; Hsi-sheng Ch'i, "The Military Dimension, 1942–1945" in *China's Bitter Victory*, eds. James C. Hsiung and Steven I. Levine, 160; Wesley M. Bagby, *Eagle-Dragon Alliance*, 74; Jay Taylor, *Generalissimo*, 209; Saburo Hayashi and Alvin D. Coox, *Kōgun: The Japanese Army in the Pacific* (Quantico, VA: Marine Corps Association, 1959), 49; S. Woodburn Kirby, *War against Japan*, Vol. 2, 225.

101 Ugaki Matome, *Fading Victory*, 41; Robert B. Edgerton, *Warriors of the Rising Sun*, 275; Edward J. Drea, *In the Service of the Emperor*, 37; S. Woodburn Kirby, *War against Japan*, Vol. 2, 226.

102 Robert B. Edgerton, *Warriors of the Rising Sun*, 281; David C. Evans and Mark R. Peattie, *Kaigun*, 323; David Stevens, "The New Guinea Campaign during World War II" in *Naval Expeditionary Warfare: Peripheral Campaigns and New Theaters of Naval Warfare*, eds. Bruce A. Elleman and S. C. M. Paine (Abingdon, UK: Routledge, 2011), 104.

103 Robert B. Edgerton, *Warriors of the Rising Sun*, 281; Ienaga Saburō, *Pacific War, 1931–1945*, 39; Takafusa Nakamura, *History of Shōwa Japan*, 206.

104 Herbert P. Bix, *Hirohito*, 449.

105 Diana Lary, *The Chinese People at War*, 89, 112; Edward J. Drea and Hans van de Ven, "An Overview of Major Military Campaigns during the Sino-Japanese War, 1937–1945," 44; 武月星 (Wu Yuexing), *Modern Chinese History Map Collection*, 186, 191, 194; Hsu Long-hsuen and Chang Ming-kai, *History of the Sino-Japanese War (1937–1945)*, maps 29–31, 33–4, 38; Dagfinn Gatu, *Village China at War*, 31.

106 Bradford A. Lee, "A Pivotal Campaign in a Peripheral Theatre: Guadalcanal and World War II" in *Naval Expeditionary Warfare*, eds. Bruce A. Elleman and S. C. M. Paine, 84–98.

107 Saburo Hayashi and Alvin D. Coox, *Kōgun*, 58.

108 Bradford A. Lee, "A Pivotal Campaign in a Peripheral Theatre," 96.

109 安部彦太 (Abe Hikota), "Statistical Analysis of the Great East Asian War," 837; Mark R. Peattie, *Sunburst*, 180.

110 江口圭一 (Eguchi Kei-ichi), *A Short History of the Fifteen Year War*, 209.
111 Michael Clodfelter, *Warfare and Armed Conflicts*, Vol. 2, 823–5.
112 西 春彦 (Nishi Haruhiko), ed., *A History of Japanese Foreign Relations*, Vol. 15, 245.
113 Theodore Gatchel, "The Shortest Road to Tokyo: Nimitz and the Cental Pacific War" in *Pacific War Companion*, ed. Daniel Marston, 164; David Horner, "General MacArthur's War: The South and Southwest Pacific Campaigns 1942–1945" in ibid., 131.
114 Arakawa Ken-ichi, "The Maritime Transport War – Emphasizing a Strategy to Interrupt the Enemy Sea Lines of Communication (SLOCs)" *NIDS Security Reports* no. 3 (March 2002), 114, 119–20.
115 George W. Baer, *One Hundred Years of Sea Power*, 233–4; Williamson Murray and Allan R. Millet, *War to Be Won*, 225; Joel Holwitt, "Unrestricted Submarine Victory: The U.S. Submarine Campaign Against Japan" in *Commerce Raiding and State-sponsored Piracy*, eds. Bruce A. Elleman and S. C. M. Paine (Newport, RI: U.S. Naval War College Press, forthcoming).
116 Michael Clodfelter, *Warfare and Armed Conflicts*, Vol. 2, 948; Richard B. Frank, *Downfall: The End of the Imperial Japanese Empire* (New York: Random House, 1999), 78; S. Woodburn Kirby, *War against Japan*, Vol. 5, 476.
117 Alvin D. Coox, "The Pacific War," 378; Nakamura Takafusa, "Depression, Recovery, and War, 1920–1945," 76; 藤原 彰 (Fujiwara Akira), 日本軍事史 (*Japanese Military History*), Vol. 1 (Tokyo: 日本評論社, 1987), 262–3; S. Woodburn Kirby, *War against Japan*, Vol. 3, 475–6; Tohmatsu Haruo, "Strategic Correlation between the Sino-Japanese and Pacific Wars," 434.
118 荒川憲一 (Arakawa Ken-ichi), *Plans for and Development of the Wartime Economic System*, 132, 147
119 Alfred T. Mahan, *The Influence of Seapower upon History 1660–1783* (1890, reprint; New York: Hill and Wang, 1957), 341–8.
120 Ronald H. Spector, *Eagle against the Sun*, 104–18; Michael D. Pearlman, *Warmaking and American Democracy: The Struggle over Military Strategy, 1700 to the Present* (Lawrence: University of Kansas Press, 1999), 253.
121 O. Edmund Clubb, *Twentieth Century China* (New York: Columbia University Press, 1964), 233; Barbara W. Tuchman, *Stilwell and the American Experience in China, 1911–45* (New York: Macmillan, 1970) 309, 361, 428–9, 458–9, 520; Wesley M. Bagby, *Eagle-Dragon Alliance*, 28, 72–3, 75, 130–1; Jay Taylor, *Generalissimo*, 179, 185–6, 219, 228, 230; Hans J. van de Ven, *War and Nationalism in China 1925–1945*, 25.
122 Jay Taylor, *Generalissimo*, 191; Wesley M. Bagby, *Eagle-Dragon Alliance*, 73, 77. For an entire book highlighting the poisonous U.S.-Chinese relations of this period, see 齊錫生 (Ch'i Hsi-sheng), 劍拔弩張的盟友太平

洋戰爭期間的中美軍事合作關係 (1941–1945) (*Alliance of Unsheathed Swords and Drawn Bows: Sino-American Military Cooperation during the Pacific War [1941–1945]*) (Taipei: 中央研究院聯經出版公司, 2011).

123 Wesley M. Bagby, *Eagle-Dragon Alliance*, 129–30, 134–5, 139; Jonathan Fenby, *Chiang Kai-shek,* 417–21; Hans J. van de Ven, *War and Nationalism in China 1925–1945*, 55.

124 Cited in Jonathan Fenby, *Chiang Kai-shek,* 370.

125 Wesley M. Bagby, *The Eagle-Dragon Alliance*, 89, 138; Jay Taylor, *Generalissimo*, 256–8; Hans J. van de Ven, *War and Nationalism in China 1925–1945*, 44.

126 Hans J. van de Ven, *War and Nationalism in China 1925–1945*, 19–20, 36–7; John Toland, *The Rising Sun: The Decline and Fall of the Japanese Empire, 1936–1945* (New York: Modern Library, 1970), 190, 233.

127 Asano Toyomi, "Japanese Operations in Yunnan and North Burma" in *Battle for China*, eds. Mark Peattie et al., 364.

128 Barbara D. Metcalf and Thomas R. Metcalf, *A Concise History of Modern India*, 2nd ed. (Cambridge: Cambridge University Press, 2006), 205–6; Jay Taylor, *Generalissimo*, 194–6; Maochun Yu, *Dragon's* War, 7.

129 John Toland, *Rising Sun*, 455–6.

130 Note the subtitle of the official British history of the war: S. Woodburn Kirby, *The War against Japan*, Vol. 2, *India's Most Dangerous Hour.*

131 Jonathan Fenby, *Chiang Kai-shek,* 384; John W. Garver, *Chinese-Soviet Relations 1937–1945*, 193.

132 F. C. Jones, *Japan's New Order in East Asia*, 413.

133 鹿锡俊 (Lu Xijun), "The Evolution of Japan's Policy Regarding Chiang Kai-shek during the Sino-Japanese War," 232–4; 王家福 (Wang Jiafu), "Strategic Evolution of the Relations among China, the Soviet Union, and the United States," 9.

134 Wesley M. Bagby, *Eagle-Dragon Alliance*, 36–7; 武月星 (Wu Yuexing), *Modern Chinese History Map Collection*, 190; Hsu Long-hsuen and Chang Ming-kai, *History of the Sino-Japanese War (1937–1945)*, map 32.

135 Robert L. Jarman, ed., *China Political Reports 1911–1960*, Vol. 7, 332.

136 Cited in Hans J. van de Ven, *War and Nationalism in China 1925–1945*, 42; Lianxin Xiang, *Recasting the Imperial Far East: Britain and America in China, 1945–1950* (Armonk, NY: M. E. Sharpe, 1995), 9.

137 Cited in Jonathan Fenby, *Chiang Kai-shek,* 410. Emphasis as in Fenby.

138 Cited in ibid., 410.

139 Edward L. Dreyer, *China at War, 1901–1949,* 284–5; Wesley M. Bagby, *Eagle-Dragon Alliance*, 92; Jay Taylor, *Generalissimo*, 262.

140 鹿锡俊 (Lu Xijun), "Evolution of Japan's Policy regarding Chiang Kai-shek during the Sino-Japanese War," 232–4; 王家福 (Wang Jiafu), "Strategic Evolution of the Relations among China, the Soviet Union, and the United States," 9.

141 Cited in Hans J. van de Ven, *War and Nationalism in China 1925–1945*, 46–7; Wesley M. Bagby, *Eagle-Dragon Alliance*, 100–1, 131; Jay Taylor, *Generalissimo*, 294; Hsu Long-hsuen and Chang Ming-kai, *History of the Sino-Japanese War (1937–1945)*, maps 36–7; 武月星 (Wu Yuexing), *Modern Chinese History Map Collection*, 193; S. Woodburn Kirby, *War against Japan*, Vol. 3, 232.

142 藤原彰 (Fujiwara Akira),"太平洋战争爆发后的日中战争" ("The Sino-Japanese War after the Outbreak of the Pacific War"), trans. 解莉莉 (Xie Lili), 中共党史研究 (*Research on the History of the Chinese Communist Party*) no. 1 (1989), 83; 江口圭一 (Eguchi Kei-ichi), *Short History of the Fifteen Year War*, 209–10; 森松俊夫 (Morimatsu Toshio), "中国大陸の諸作戦" ("Various Military Operations in the Chinese Mainland") in *Modern Japanese Military History*, Vol. 4, eds. 奥村房夫 (Okumura Fusao) and 近藤新治 (Kondō Shinji), 602–3; Edward J. Drea and Hans van de Ven, "An Overview of Major Military Campaigns during the Sino-Japanese War, 1937–1945," 45; Hsi-sheng Ch'i, *Nationalist China at War*, 78–80.

143 石島紀之(Ishijima Noriyuki), *A History of China's Anti-Japanese War*, 181–3; 加藤公一 (Katō Kōichi), "中国共産党の対米認識とソ連の対日参戦問題、１９４４–１９４５年 ―「喪失した機会」と「独立自主」 ―" ("The Chinese Communist Party's Recognition of the United States and the Soviet Entry into the War against Japan, 1944–1945: 'Lost Opportunity' and 'Maintaining Independence and Initiative'"), 歴史学研究 (*Journal of Historical Studies*) 751 (July 2001), 36; Edward J. Drea, *Japan's Imperial Army*, 244–5.

144 Hsu Long-hsuen and Chang Ming-kai, *History of the Sino-Japanese War (1937–1945)*, maps 39–41; 武月星 (Wu Yuexing), *Modern Chinese History Map Collection*, 195–7.

145 Hsi-sheng Ch'i, "The Military Dimension, 1942–1945," 164–5; Tobe Ryōichi, "The Japanese Eleventh Army in Central China, 1938–1941," 224.

146 Wesley M. Bagby, *Eagle-Dragon Alliance*, 129–35, 139; Jonathan Fenby, *Chiang Kai-shek*, 417–21; Hans J. van de Ven, *War and Nationalism in China 1925–1945*, 55; Edward J. Drea, *Japan's Imperial Army*, 244–5; Hsi-sheng Ch'i, *Nationalist China at War*, 77.

147 Diana Lary, *The Chinese People at War*, 147, 153–5.

148 Galina Fominichna Zakharova, *Policy of Japan in Manchuria 1932–1945*, 193; Hara Takeshi, "The Ichigō Offensive" in *Battle for China*, eds. Mark Peattie et al., 394.

149 Hsi-sheng Ch'i, *Nationalist China at War*, 76.
150 石源华 (Shi Yuanhua), "Discussion of Japan's Relations with Wang Jingwei," 116; S. Woodburn Kirby, *War against Japan*, Vol. 3, 393.
151 辻秀雄 (Tsuji Hideo), "本地防空と本土決戦準備" ("Preparations for the Aerial Defenses and the Decisive Battle for Japan") in *Modern Japanese Military History*, Vol. 4, eds. 奥村房夫 (Okumura Fusao) and 近藤新治 (Kondō Shinji), 630, 632, 636; Tohmatsu Haruo, "Strategic Correlation between the Sino-Japanese and Pacific Wars," 437; Richard B. Frank, *Downfall*, 363.
152 Cited in Wesley M. Bagby, *Eagle-Dragon Alliance*, 125; Edward J. Drea, *Japan's Imperial Army*, 244–5; Zhang Baijia, "China's Quest for Military Aid," 303; Tohmatsu Haruo, "The Strategic Correlation between the Sino-Japanese and Pacific Wars," 444; Michael M. Sheng, *Battling Western Imperialism*, 78; 武月星 (Wu Yuexing), *Modern Chinese History Map Collection*, 193.
153 Cited in Wesley M. Bagby, *The Eagle-Dragon Alliance*, 145. See also ibid.,137–8, 146, 154; Hans J. van de Ven, *War and Nationalism in China 1925–1945*, 49, 51.
154 Hagiwara Mitsuru, "Japanese Air Campaigns in China, 1937–1945," 254; Zhang Baijia, "China's Quest for Military Aid," 298–300; Zang Yunhu, "Chinese Operations in Yunnan and Central Burma" in *Battle for China*, eds. Mark Peattie et al., 388; Wesley M. Bagby, *Eagle-Dragon Alliance*, 65; S. Woodburn Kirby, *War against Japan*, Vol. 3, 455; ibid., Vol. 5, 483.
155 Theodore H. White and Annalee Jacoby, *Thunder out of China*, 115; Wesley M. Bagby, *Eagle-Dragon Alliance,* 65–6; Arthur N. Young, *China and the Helping Hand 1937–1945*, 296.
156 Michael M. Sheng, *Battling Western Imperialism*, 77–8; Gregor Benton, *Mountain Fires*, 434; Nancy Bernkopf Tucker, *China Confidential*, 89.
157 Theodore H. White, *In Search of History*, 116.
158 Cited in Petr Parfenovich Vladimirov, *Special Region in China 1942–1945*, 367, 543–4; Michael M. Sheng, *Battling Western Imperialism*, 43–4, 50,78.
159 Michael Clodfelter, *Warfare and Armed Conflicts*, Vol. 2, 951–2; Takafusa Nakamura, *History of Shōwa Japan,* 219, 245; Richard B. Frank, *Downfall*, 77; S. Woodburn Kirby, *The War against Japan*, Vol. 5, 102–5, 162, 484–6.
160 Takafusa Nakamura, *History of Shōwa Japan,* 43; Herbert P. Bix, *Hirohito*, 63, 171, 502–3, 515, 534.
161 Timothy Hoye, *Japanese Politics: Fixed and Floating Worlds* (Upper Saddle River, NJ: Prentice Hall, 1999), xiv; W. G. Beasley "Meiji Political Institutions" in *Cambridge History of Japan*, Vol. 5, Marius Jansen, ed. (Cambridge: Cambridge University Press, 1989), 66; Kenneth B. Pyle,

The New Generation in Meiji Japan: Problems of Cultural Identity, 1885–1895 (Stanford, CA: Stanford University Press, 1969), 11–12.

162 Takafusa Nakamura, *History of Shōwa Japan,* 252.

163 Citing Oka Yoshitake in Ian Nish, *Japanese Foreign Policy 1869–1942,* 222.

164 Term from Masao Maruyama. Tsuyoshi Hasegawa, *Racing the Enemy*, 4; Sadako N. Ogata, *Defiance in Manchuria*, 192; Herbert P. Bix, *Hirohito*, 329, 436.

165 Alvin D. Coox, *Nomonhan*, 103; James William Morley, "Tripartite Pact, 1935–1939 Introduction," 184.

166 Takafusa Nakamura, *History of Shōwa Japan,* 252; Janet E. Hunter, comp., *Concise Dictionary of Modern Japanese History*, 288–9.

167 Herbert P. Bix, *Hirohito*, 420.

168 Robert M. Spaulding, "The Bureaucracy as a Political Force, 1920–1945" in *Dilemmas of Growth in Prewar Japan*, ed. James William Morley (Princeton, NJ: Princeton University Press, 1971), 56, 70, 77.

169 Bradford A. Lee, *Britain and the Sino-Japanese War 1937–1939*, 99.

170 See Herbert P. Bix's Pulitzer Prize–winning *Hirohito*.

171 John W. Dower, *Embracing Defeat: Japan in the Wake of World War II* (New York: W. W. Norton, 1999), 364–73.

172 Cited in Herbert P. Bix, *Hirohito*, 494–5.

173 Haruko Taya Cook and Theodore F. Cook, *Japan at War*, 381.

174 Herbert P. Bix, *Hirohito*, 494–5.

175 Cited in ibid., 498.

176 David Holloway, "Jockeying for Position in the Postwar World: Soviet Entry into the War with Japan in August 1945" in *The End of the Pacific War: Reappraisals*, ed. Tsuyoshi Hasegawa (Stanford, CA: Stanford University Press, 2007), 174; Ronald H. Spector, *In the Ruins of Empire: The Japanese Surrender and the Battle for Postwar Asia* (New York: Random House, 2007), 4; S. Woodburn Kirby, *War against Japan*, Vol. 5, 190; Herbert P. Bix, *Hirohito*, 503–4, 518; Tsuyoshi Hasegawa, *Racing the Enemy*, 221, 227–8, 240.

177 鹿锡俊 (Lu Xijun), "Evolution of Japan's Policy Regarding Chiang Kai-shek during the Sino-Japanese War," 235–6; 臼井勝美 (Usui Katsumi), *Research on Sino-Japanese Diplomatic History*, 183; JFM, A.7.0.0–9-55, 大東亜戦争関係一件戦争終結ニ関スル日蘇交渉関係 (Concerning the War of the Pacific and Soviet-Japanese War Termination Diplomacy), Vol. 1, 箱根会談録 (Hakone Conference), June–July 1945, meetings between former prime minister Hirota Kōki and Russian ambassador to Japan, Iakob Malik, p. 38; JFM, A.7.0.0–9-55, 大東亜戦争関係一件戦争終結ニ関スル日蘇交渉関係 (Concerning the War of the Pacific and Soviet-Japanese War Termination Diplomacy), Vol. 2, 第八十七議

会秘密会ニ於ケル東郷大臣説明要旨 (Summary of Tōgō's Explanation at the Secret Committee of the 87th session of the Diet), 9 June 1945, pp. 5–6, and 最近ノ国際情勢 (The Current Situation), 19 June 1945, Japanese Foreign Minister, top secret, p. 22; JFM, A.7.0.0–9-55, 大東亜戦争関係一件戦争終結ニ関スル日蘇交渉関係 (Concerning the War of the Pacific and Soviet-Japanese War Termination Diplomacy), Vol. 2, Tōjō address to the Privy Council, 15 August 1945.

178 Herbert P. Bix, *Hirohito*, 500–2; Richard Fuller, *Shōkan Hirohito's Samurai*, 289–90; Takafusa Nakamura, *History of Shōwa Japan,* 221.

179 Cited in Haruko Taya Cook and Theodore F. Cook, *Japan at War*, 479.

180 Tsuyoshi Hasegawa, *Racing the Enemy*, 67–8, 180–1.

181 JFM, A.7.0.0–9-55, 大東亜戦争関係一件戦争終結ニ関スル日蘇交渉関係 (Concerning the War of the Pacific and Soviet-Japanese War Termination Diplomacy), Vol. 2, 第八十七議会秘密会ニ於ケル東郷大臣説明要旨 (Summary of Tōgō's Explanation at the Secret Committee of the 87th Session of the Diet), 9 June 1945, p. 5; 塚瀬進 (Tsukase Susumu), *Manchukuo "Racial Harmony" in Reality,* 247.

182 乔宪金 (Qiao Xianjin), "苏联对日本宣战与出兵东北是同一时间" ("The Soviet Declaration of War on Japan and Deployment of Troops in Manchuria Were Simultaneous"), 近代史研究 (*Modern Chinese History Studies*) no. 2 (1995), 283–4.

183 沈志华 (Shen Zhihua), "苏联出兵中国东北：目标和结果" ("The Soviet Troop Deployment into Northeast China: Aims and Consequences"), 历史研究 (*Historical Research*) no. 5 (1994), 102.

184 David Holloway, "Jockeying for Position in the Postwar World," 226.

185 David M. Glantz, *Soviet Strategic Offensive in Manchuria, 1945* 'August Storm,' xviii, xxv–xxvi.

186 Tsuyoshi Hasegawa, *Racing the Enemy*, 251–5; 沈志华 (Shen Zhihua), "Soviet Troop Deployment into Northeast China," 101; David M. Glantz, *Soviet Strategic Offensive in Manchuria, 1945* 'August Storm,' 288, 295, 305.

187 Ronald H. Spector, *In the Ruins of Empire*, 32–5.

188 Tsuyoshi Hasegawa, *Racing the Enemy*, 271; David M. Glantz, *Soviet Strategic Offensive in Manchuria, 1945* 'August Storm,' 288, 295, 305.

189 Tsuyoshi Hasegawa, *Racing the Enemy*, 258, 277, 285, 287, 289.

190 Barton J. Bernstein, "Conclusion" in *End of the Pacific War*, ed. Tsuyoshi Hasegawa, 228; JFM, A.7.0.0–9-55, 大東亜戦争関係一件戦争終結ニ関スル日蘇交渉関係 (Concerning the War of the Pacific and Soviet-Japanese War Termination Diplomacy), Vol. 2, Tōjō address to the Privy Council, 15 August 1945; Edward J. Drea, *In the Service of the Emperor*, 213–15; Tsuyoshi Hasegawa, *Racing the Enemy*, 235.

191 Tsuyoshi Hasegawa, *Racing the Enemy*, 104, 208.

192 Edward J. Drea, *In the Service of the Emperor*, 213–15; Richard B. Frank, "Ketsu Gō: Japanese Political and Military Strategy in 1945" in *End of the Pacific War*, ed. Tsuyoshi Hasegawa, 86–7.
193 江口圭一 (Eguchi Kei-ichi), *Short History of the Fifteen Year War*, 252–7; Richard Fuller, *Shōkan Hirohito's Samurai*, 290; Takafusa Nakamura, *History of Shōwa Japan*, 229–31.
194 Tsuyoshi Hasegawa, *Racing the Enemy*, 231.
195 Robert B. Edgerton, *Warriors of the Rising Sun*, 302.
196 Edward J. Drea, *In the Service of the Emperor*, 213–15; Richard B. Frank, "Ketsu Gō," 86–7.
197 Tsuyoshi Hasegawa, *Racing the Enemy*, 230, 243.
198 江口圭一 (Eguchi Kei-ichi), *Short History of the Fifteen Year War*, 252–7; Takafusa Nakamura, *History of Shōwa Japan*, 231.
199 江口圭一 (Eguchi Kei-ichi), *Short History of the Fifteen Year War*, 252–7; Tsuyoshi Hasegawa, *Racing the Enemy*, 247–9; F. C. Jones, *Japan's New Order in East Asia*, 448–9.
200 Tsuyoshi Hasegawa, *Racing the Enemy*, 241–3.
201 John Toland, *Rising Sun*, 856; Richard Fuller, *Shōkan Hirohito's Samurai*, 290; F. C. Jones, *Japan's New Order in East Asia*, 448–9; Louis Frédéric, *Japan Encyclopedia*, 933–4; S. Woodburn Kirby, *War against Japan*, Vol. 5, 217.
202 Richard B. Frank, "Ketsu Gō," 93.
203 江口圭一 (Eguchi Kei-ichi), *Short History of the Fifteen Year War*, 252–7; Tsuyoshi Hasegawa, *Racing the Enemy*, 247–9; F. C. Jones, *Japan's New Order in East Asia*, 448–9; Ben-Ami Shillony, "February 26 Affair," 90.
204 Tsuyoshi Hasegawa, *Racing the Enemy*, 250.
205 Ibid., 271; David Holloway, "Jockeying for Position in the Postwar World," 180; David M. Glantz, *Soviet Strategic Offensive in Manchuria, 1945* 'August Storm,' 141, 305.
206 Tsuyoshi Hasegawa, *Racing the Enemy*, 237.
207 Hoover Institution Archives, Gilbert Stuart papers, Box 1, "Reel 25 Revolution, OSS Shanghai, Russian Behavior," 27/1, 30/1, 42/1.
208 Richard B. Frank, "Ketsu Gō," 111–12; John Toland, *Rising Sun*, 807, 826; Leon V. Sigal, *Fighting to a Finish: The Politics of War Termination in the United States and Japan, 1945* (Ithaca: Cornell University Press, 1988), 278–9.
209 Werner Gruhl, *Imperial Japan's World War Two 1931–1945* (New Brunswick, NJ: Transaction Publishers, 2007), 203–5; John Toland, *Rising Sun*, 766.
210 Cited in Jonathan Fenby, *Chiang Kai-shek*, 331.
211 Haruko Taya Cook and Theodore F. Cook, *Japan at War*, 263, 269, 278, 357, 459, 475.

212 Cited in Ienaga Saburō, *Pacific War, 1931–1945*, 49.
213 Alvin D. Coox, *Nomonhan*, 979.
214 Ienaga Saburō, *The Pacific War, 1931–1945*, 49.
215 江口圭一 (Eguchi Kei-ichi), *Short History of the Fifteen Year War*, 208–9; 渡辺俊彦 (Watanabe Toshihiko), "七三一部隊と永田鉄山" ("Unit 731 and Nagata Tetsuzan") in *The Sino-Japanese War*, ed. 中央大学人文科学研究所 (Chūō University Human Sciences Research Center), 275–6.
216 江口圭一 (Eguchi Kei-ichi), *Short History of the Fifteen Year War*, 200.
217 Takafusa Nakamura, *History of Shōwa Japan*, 255.
218 真保潤一郎 (Shinpo Junichirō), "Wartime Economic Legacy and Economic Reconstruction," 933.
219 江口圭一 (Eguchi Kei-ichi), *A Short History of the Fifteen Year War*, 172, 226; Takafusa Nakamura, *History of Shōwa Japan*, 253–4.
220 Edward J. Drea and Hans van de Ven, "An Overview of Major Military Campaigns during the Sino-Japanese War, 1937–1945," 46; R. J. Rummel, *China's Bloody Century*, 24–25; Werner Gruhl, *Imperial Japan's World War Two 1931–1945*, 19–20, 59.
221 郭希华 (Guo Xihua), "抗日战争时期中国损失调查及赔偿问题" ("Problems of Assessing China's Losses during the War of Resistance against Japan and the Question of Reparations"), 历史研究 *(Historical Research)* no. 5 (1995), 180.
222 朱玉湘 (Zhu Yuxiang), "抗日战争与中国经济" ("The Anti-Japanese War and the Chinese Economy"), 文史哲 (*Journal of Literature, History, and Philosophy*) 230, no. 5 (1995), 3–9; 居之芬 (Ju Zhifen), "抗战时期日本对华北沦陷区劳工的劫掠和催残" ("Japanese Looting and Humiliation of Workers in Occupied Areas of North China during the Anti-Japanese War"), 中共党史研究 (*Research on the History of the Chinese Communist Party*) no. 4 (1994), 325–8.
223 江口圭一 (Eguchi Kei-ichi), *A Short History of the Fifteen Year War*, 250–1; 幕内光雄 (Maku'uchi Mitsuo), *An Unofficial History of the Manchukuo Police*, 287; Max Beloff, *Soviet Policy in the Far East 1944–1951* (London: Oxford University Press, 1953), 38; 徐焰 (Xu Yan), 一九四五年満州進軍：日ソ戦と毛沢東の戦略 (*The Manchurian Invasion of 1945: The Japanese-Soviet War and Mao Zedong's Strategy*), trans. 朱建榮 (Zhu Jinrong) (Tokyo: 三五館, 1993), 191, 193; Diana Lary, *The Chinese People at War*, 189–190; S. I. Kuznetsov, "The Situation of Japanese Prisoners of War in Soviet Camps (1945–1956)" *The Journal of Slavic Military Studies* 8, no. 3 (September 1995), 620.
224 Herbert P. Bix, *Hirohito*, 360; Edward L. Dreyer, *China at War, 1901–1949*, 215; Ju Zhifen, "Labor Conscription in North China: 1941–1945" " in *China at War*, eds. Stephen R. MacKinnon et al., 218, 222.

225 藤原彰 (Fujiwara Akira), "The Sino-Japanese War after the Outbreak of the Pacific War," 85.
226 Tsuyoshi Hasegawa, *Racing the Enemy*, 263; Richard B. Frank, "Ketsu Gō," 65–67, 71; Richard B. Frank, *Downfall*, 85, 146.
227 Michael Clodfelter, *Warfare and Armed Conflicts*, Vol. 2, 929; Richard B. Frank, *Downfall*, 70.
228 吉田裕 (Yoshida Yutaka) and 纐纈厚 (Kōketsu Atsushi), "Military Operations, Combat, and the Supply of the Japanese Military," 222.
229 Haruko Taya Cook and Theodore F. Cook, *Japan at War*, 458–61, 472–77.
230 Japan, Defense Agency, National Defense College, Military History Department (防衛庁防衛研修所戦史部), ed., *The Kantō Army*, Vol. 2, 296.
231 吉田裕 (Yoshida Yutaka) and 纐纈厚 (Kōketsu Atsushi), "Military Operations, Combat, and the Supply of the Japanese Military," 106.
232 David E. Kaiser, *Economic Diplomacy and the Origins of the Second World War* (Princeton, NJ: Princeton University Press, 1980), 262; Barbara J. Brooks, *Japan's Imperial Diplomacy*, 283.
233 I. C. B. Dear, *The Oxford Companion to World War II* (Oxford: Oxford University Press, 1995), 347; Michael Clodfelter, *Warfare and Armed Conflicts*, Vol. 2, 795.
234 Richard Overy, *Russia's War*, 236, 240.
235 Alvin D. Coox, *Nomonhan*, 1036; 山田朗 (Yamada Akira), "Military Rule [2] during the Sino-Japanese War and the War of the Pacific," 202.
236 Takafusa Nakamura, "Age of Turbulence, 1937–54," 79; 安部彦太 (Abe Hikota), "Statistical Analysis of the Great East Asian War," 827.
237 安部彦太 (Abe Hikota), "Statistical Analysis of the Great East Asian War," 827, 831. See also 荒川憲一 (Arakawa Ken-ichi), *Plans for and Development of the Wartime Economic System*, 184–9; S. Woodburn Kirby, *War against Japan*, Vol. 1, 481–3; ibid, Vol. 5, 466–8.
238 The rough conversion of tons to barrels of oil is 6 to 8 barrels per ton depending on the fuel grade. 真保潤一郎 (Shinpo Junichirō), "Wartime Economic Legacy and Economic Reconstruction," 947; Arakawa Ken-ichi, "The Shipping of Southeast Asian Resources Back to Japan: National Logistics and War Strategy," Tokyo: National Institute for Defense Studies, Military History Department, unpublished paper, ca. 2002.
239 安部彦太 (Abe Hikota), "Statistical Analysis of the Great East Asian War," 830, 832.
240 Peter Teed, *Dictionary of 20th Century History 1914–1990*, 269; William H. Harris and Judith S. Levey, *New Columbia Encyclopedia*, 269; Duncan Townson, *New Penguin Dictionary of Modern History 1789–1945*, 467–8.

241 Takafusa Nakamura, *History of Shōwa Japan*, 236–9.
242 Takafusa Nakamura, "Age of Turbulence, 1937–54," 70–1.
243 安部彦太 (Abe Hikota), "Statistical Analysis of the Great East Asian War," 830, 835.
244 熊谷光久 (Kumagai Teruhisa), "動員・人と物" ("The Mobilization of People and Goods") in *Modern Japanese Military History*, Vol. 4, eds., 奥村房夫 (Okumura Fusao) and 近藤新治 (Kondō Shinji), 815; 安部彦太 (Abe Hikota), "Statistical Analysis of the Great East Asian War," 827.
245 Richard B. Frank, *Downfall*, 163.
246 William C. Kirby, "The Chinese War Economy" in *China's Bitter Victory*, eds. James C. Hsiung and Steven I. Levine, 185.
247 John Toland, *Rising Sun*, 876.
248 森松俊夫 (Morimatsu Toshio), "大東亜戦争の戦争目的" ("The War Goals of the Great East Asian War") in *Modern Japanese Military History*, Vol. 4, eds. 奥村房夫 (Okumura Fusao) and 近藤新治 (Kondō Shinji), 294, 312–15; S. Woodburn Kirby, *War against Japan*, Vol. 5, 435.

8 THE FINAL ACT OF THE LONG CHINESE CIVIL WAR

1 Edgar Snow, *Red Star over China*, 273.
2 Liu Xiaoyuan, *Reins of Liberation*, 103; 張瑞德 (Zhang Ruide), *Personnel Matters of the Nationalist Army during the War of Resistance*, 934.
3 Donald W. Klein and Anne B. Clark. *Biographic Dictionary of Chinese Communism 1921–1965*, Vol. 1, 247–9; ibid., Vol. 2, 681; June Grasso, Jay Corrin, and Michael Kort, *Modernization and Revolution in China*, 120.
4 石島紀之 (Ishijima Noriyuki), *A History of China's Anti-Japanese War*, 114.
5 姫田光義 (Himeta Mitsuyoshi), et al., 中国２０世紀史 (*Twentieth Century Chinese History*) (Tokyo: Tokyo University Press, 2000), 164; R. Keith Schoppa, *The Columbia Guide to Modern Chinese History* (New York: Columbia University Press, 2000), 308–11; Gregor Benton, "Comparative Perspectives," 192–3; Boris Grigor'evich Sapozhnikov, *China in the Fire of War 1931–1950*, 180; T'ien-wei Wu, "Chinese Communist Movement," 79.
6 Lyman van Slyke, "Chinese Communist Movement during the Sino-Japanese War 1937–1945," 685.
7 石島紀之 (Ishijima Noriyuki), "The Impact of the Total War between Japan and China," 474; Diana Lary, *Chinese People at War*, 122, 158–60;

Arthur N. Young, *China's Wartime Finance and Inflation, 1937–1945*, 318–19, 321, 325.

8 Suzanne Pepper, *Civil War in China: The Political Struggle 1945–1949* (Berkeley: University of California Press, 1978), 99

9 Diana Lary, "Defending China," 398–427.

10 For a wonderful read about living through the years of the Nationalist implosion, see Jung Chang, *Wild Swans*, 75–114; Frederic Wakeman, Jr., *Spymaster*, passim.

11 Jonathan Fenby, *Chiang Kai-shek*, 287.

12 石島紀之 (Ishijima Noriyuki), *History of China's Anti-Japanese War*, 160; Jasper Becker, *Hungry Ghosts*, 13–22, 274; Colin Mackerras, *Modern China*, 403; Diana Lary, *Chinese People at War*, 124–6; Robert L. Jarman, ed., *China Political Reports 1911–1960*, Vol. 7, 334; Lyman P. van Slyke, "Chinese Communist Movement during the Sino-Japanese War," 706.

13 Colin Mackerras, *Modern China*, 421; Diana Lary, *Chinese People at War*, 187.

14 Edward L. Dreyer, *China at War, 1901–1949*, 325; Suzanne Pepper, *Civil War in China*, passim.

15 Edgar Snow, *Red Star over China*, 251, 287; Dagfinn Gatu, *Village China at War*, 232.

16 Cited in Theodore H. White, *In Search of History*, 116; Lloyd E. Eastman, "Nationalist China during the Sino-Japanese War, 1937–1945" in *The Nationalist Era in China 1927–1945*, eds. Lloyd E. Eastman et al. (Cambridge: Cambridge University Press, 1991), 33.

17 姜思毅 (Jiang Siyi),"毛泽东军事思想论纲" ("A Sketch of Mao Zedong's Military Thought"), 中共党史研究 (*Research on the History of the Chinese Communist Party*) no. 1 (1994), 19–24.

18 徐晓林 (Xu Xiaolin),"朱德抗日游击战术思想初探" ("Zhu De's Thoughts on Anti-Japanese Guerrilla Tactics"), 中共党史研究 (*Research on the History of the Chinese Communist Party*) no. 4 (1995), 70–3.

19 田玄 (Tian Xuan), "为彭德怀'运动游击战'问题历史公案一辩" ("A Verification of Peng Dehuai's Stand on 'Mobile Guerrilla Warfare'"), 中共党史研究 (*Research on the History of the Chinese Communist Party*) no. 6 (1998), 91–6; Edgar Snow, *Red Star over China*, 272–4.

20 王永君 (Wang Yongjun),"抗战胜利后中共中央对东北的战略方针其形成过程" ("The CCP Central Committee's Military Strategies and Policy for Manchuria after Victory in the Sino-Japanese War"), 中共党史研究 (*Research on the History of the Chinese Communist Party*) no. 4 (2001), 86–90.

21 李蓉 (Li Rong), "刘少奇对抗战时期党的沦陷区工作的贡献" ("Liu Shaoqi's Contributions to the Work in Enemy-Occupied Areas during

the War of Resistance"), 中共党史研究 (*Research on the History of the Chinese Communist Party*) no. 6 (1999), 73–6; 张飞虹 (Zhang Feihong), "中共第一代领导集体在抗战时期形成过程的刘少奇" ("Liu Shaoqi and the Development of the First-Generation Collective Leadership of the Communist Party of China during the War of Resistance"), 中共党史研究 (*Research on the History of the Chinese Communist Party*) no. 4 (1995), 64–9.

22 Nancy Bernkopf Tucker, *China Confidential*, 33.

23 See Chapter 4 for a discussion of the two alleged agreements. 宋金寿 (Song Jinshou), "Position and Role of the Shaan-Gan-Ning Border Area in the War of Resistance," 39; Bruce A. Elleman, *Modern Chinese Warfare, 1795–1989*, 208.

24 李蓉 (Li Rong),"试论抗战时期中共在沦陷区的工作" (" Activities of the Chinese Communist Party in Enemy-Occupied Areas during the War of Resistance"), 中共党史研究 (*Research on the History of the Chinese Communist Party*) no. 4 (1995), 38–42; Sergei Leonidovich Tikhvinskii, ed., *Russo-Chinese Relations in the 20th Century*, Vol. 5, part 1, 1946–February 1950, 15.

25 Chang Chi-yun (張其昀), *National Atlas of China*, Vol. 5, *General Maps of China* (Taipei: National War College, 1962), A9.

26 Chang Chi-yun (張其昀), *National Atlas of China*, Vol. 5, *General Maps of China*, A17–A18; 张水良 (Zhang Shuiliang),"抗日战争时期陕甘宁边区的公营工业" ("Government-Run Industry in the Shaanxi-Gansu-Ningxia Border Area during the Sino-Japanese War"), 中国社会经济史研究 (*Research on Chinese Social and Economic History*), no. 4 (1988), 90–6; Edgar Snow, *Red Star over China*, 205; Dagfinn Gatu, *Village China at War*, 205–6.

27 宋金寿 (Song Jinshou), "毛泽东指导陕甘宁边区经济工作的几个重大思想转折" ("Important Ideological Changes Concerning Economic Work in the Shaanxi-Gansu-Ningxia Border Area under the Leadership of Mao Zedong"), 中共党史研究 (*Research on the History of the Chinese Communist Party*) no. 6 (1998), 24–30.

28 Albert Feuerwerker, "Economic Trends, 1912–49" in *The Cambridge History of China,* Vol. 12, ed. John K. Fairbank (Cambridge: Cambridge University Press, 1983), 82.

29 孔永松 (Kong Yongsong),"试论抗日陕甘宁区的特殊土地问题" ("Discussion of Specific Land Issues during the Sino-Japanese War Period in the Shaanxi-Gansu-Ningxia Base Area"), 中国社会经济史研究 (*Research on Chinese Social and Economic History*) no. 4 (1984), 99, 102, 106.

30 苏小平 (Su Xiaoping) and 贾海维 (Gu Haiwei),"论抗日根据地的统一累进税" ("Unified Progressive Taxation in the Anti-Japanese Base Area"), 中共党史研究 (*Research on the History of the Chinese Communist*

Party) no. 4 (2000), 53–7; 巨文辉 (Ju Wenhui). "晋察冀边区实施的统一累进税述略" ("A Brief Account of Unified Progressive Taxation in the Shanxi-Chahar-Hebei Border Area"), 中共党史研究 (*Research on the History of the Chinese Communist Party*) no. 2 (1996), 37–41; 朱玉湘 (Zhu Yuxiang), "山东抗日根据地的减租减息" ("The Rent and Interest Reduction in the Shandong Base Area during the Sino-Japanese War"), 文史哲 (*Journal of Literature, History, and Philosophy*) 230, no. 3 (1981), 72–7; David S. G. Goodman, *Social and Political Change in Revolutionary China*, 111, 163, 209.

31 孔永松 (Kong Yongsong), "Discussion of Specific Land Issues," 106.

32 宋金寿 (Song Jinshou), "Position and Role of the Shaan-Gan-Ning Border Area in the War of Resistance," 43–5; 章绍嗣 (Zhang Shaosi) et al., comps., *Comprehensive Dictionary of the Chinese War of Resistance against Japan*, 543.

33 塚瀬進 (Tsukase Susumu), *Manchukuo "Racial Harmony" in Reality*, 250.

34 刘一皋 (Liu Yigao), "Land Reform and Rural Political Power," 73–8.

35 Cited in Christopher R. Lew, *The Third Chinese Revolutionary Civil War, 1945–49: An Analysis of Communist Strategy and Leadership* (London: Routledge, 2009), 41.

36 Joseph W. Esherick, "Revolution in a 'Feudal Fortress': Yangjiagou, Mizhi County, Shaanxi, 1937–1948" in *North China at War*, eds. Feng Chongyi and David S. F. Goodman, 78–9.

37 Chen Yung-fa, *Making Revolution*, 134–44, 184, 187; Dagfinn Gatu, *Village China at War*, 320.

38 刘一皋 (Liu Yigao), "解放战争时期华北解放区的土地改革与农村政权" ("Land Reform and Rural Political Power in the Liberated Areas of North China during the War for National Liberation"), 中共党史研究 (*Research on the History of the Chinese Communist Party*) no. 1 (1989), 73–8; Dagfinn Gatu, *Village China at War*, 226, 298.

39 张晓辉 (Zhang Xiaohui), "简论抗战时期中国共产党政权理论的认识和发展" ("A Short Discussion of the Development of the Communist Party's Theory of Political Power during the War of Resistance against Japan"), 中共党史研究 (*Research on the History of the Chinese Communist Party*) no. 6 (1998), 66–71.

40 Hsi-sheng Ch'i, *Nationalist China at War*, 129; 楊奎松 (Yang Kuisong), *Heading for Rupture*, 111–63, 493–4.

41 张晓辉 (Zhang Xiaohui), "A Short Discussion of the Development of the Communist Party's Theory of Political Power," 69; 章绍嗣 (Zhang Shaosi) et al., comps., *Comprehensive Dictionary of the Chinese War of Resistance against Japan*, 543; 宋金寿 (Song Jinshou), "Position and Role of the Shaan-Gan-Ning Border Area in the War of Resistance," 43–5;

石島紀之 (Ishijima Noriyuki), *History of China's Anti-Japanese War*, 82; Mark Selden, *The Yenan Way in Revolutionary China* (Cambridge, MA: Harvard University Press, 1971), 161–2; David S. G. Goodman, *Social and Political Change in Revolutionary China*, 61.

42 Cited in Wesley M. Bagby, *Eagle-Dragon Alliance*, 49. See also ibid., 111.

43 Edgar Snow, *Red Star over China*, 274; Dagfinn Gatu, *Village China at War*, 56.

44 宋金寿 (Song Jinshou), "毛泽东指导陕甘宁边区经济工作的几个重大思想转折" ("Important Ideological Changes Concerning Economic Work in the Shaanxi-Gansu-Ningxia Border Area under the Leadership of Mao Zedong"), 中共党史研究 (*Research on the History of the Chinese Communist Party*) no. 6 (1998), 24–30; Dagfinn Gatu, *Village China at War*, 77.

45 Robert L. Jarman, ed., *China Political Reports 1911–1960*, Vol. 8, 176.

46 Cited in Wang Qisheng, "The Battle of Hunan and the Chinese Military's Response to Operation Ichigō" in *Battle for China*, eds. Mark Peattie et al., 417.

47 Wesley M. Bagby, *Eagle-Dragon Alliance*, 200; Christopher R. Lew, *Third Chinese Revolutionary Civil War, 1945–49*, 39.

48 汪朝光 (Wang Chaoguang), "战后国民党对共政策的重要转折—国民党六届二中全会再研究" ("A Key Turning Point in the Nationalist Policy toward the Communist Party after the War against Japanese Aggression – a Reconsideration of the Second Plenum of the Sixth Central Committee of the Nationalist Party"), 历史研究 (*Historical Research*) no. 4 (2001), 72–87.

49 章百家(Zhang Baijia),"抗日战争时期国共两党的对美政策"("Nationalist and Communist Policies Regarding the United States, 1937–1945"), 历史研究 *(Historical Research)* no. 3 (1987), 14.

50 章百家 (Zhang Baijia), "抗日战争结束前后中国共产党对美国政策的演变" ("The Evolution of the Chinese Communist Party's Policy toward the United States around the end of the War of Resistance against Japan"), 中共党史研究 (*Research on the History of the Chinese Communist Party*) no. 1 (1991), 40.

51 Cited in Jonathan Fenby, *Chiang Kai-shek,* 418–19.

52 Cited in Wesley M. Bagby, *Eagle-Dragon Alliance*, 153–4; Jay Taylor, *Generalissimo*, 298; Odd Arne Westad, *Decisive Encounters*, 358*n*28.

53 Cited in Petr Parfenovich Vladimirov, *Special Region in China 1942–1945*, 354–5, 421–2; Jonathan Fenby, *Chiang Kai-shek,* 438; United States Department of State, *Foreign Relations of the United States Diplomatic Papers 1945*, Vol. 7, *The Far East: China* (Washington, DC: Government Printing Office, 1969), 112, 205–206 (Hereafter abbreviated as FRUS); Michael M. Sheng, *Battling Western Imperialism*, 86, 88, 135.

54 Cited in Michael M. Sheng, *Battling Western Imperialism,* 77. The original spells Chiang as "Jiang."
55 Cited in Suzanne Pepper, "The Student Movement and the Chinese Civil War, 1945–49," *China Quarterly* no. 48 (October-December 1971), 698–700.
56 Ronald H. Spector, *In the Ruins of Empire*, 43; Jonathan Fenby, *Chiang Kai-shek,* 438; Wesley M. Bagby, *Eagle-Dragon Alliance*, 167, 174; Jay Taylor, *Generalissimo*, 298; Petr Parfenovich Vladimirov, *Special Region in China 1942–1945*, 374.
57 FRUS, 1945, Vol. 7, *Far East: China*, 216, 450, 1375.
58 Dean Acheson, *Present at the Creation: My Years in the State Department* (New York: W. W. Norton, 1969), 140.
59 FRUS, 1945, Vol. 7, *Far East: China*, 724, 726, 728–45. Quotation from p. 737.
60 Ibid., 450, 1375; ibid., 1946, Vol. 10, *Far East: China* (Washington, DC: Government Printing Office, 1972), 151, 547.
61 Brian Joseph Murray, "Western versus Chinese Realism: Soviet American Diplomacy and the Chinese Civil War, 1945–1950" (Ph.D. diss., Columbia University, 1995), 308–10.
62 Christopher R. Lew, *Third Chinese Revolutionary Civil War, 1945–49*, 3.
63 Mao Zedong, "On Protracted War (May 1938)" in *Selected Military Writings*, 210–19.
64 I am grateful to CDR Patrick Hansen, once a student of mine at the Naval War College, who made this observation years ago in a seminar.
65 王永君 (Wang Yongjun), "The CCP Central Committee's Military Strategies and Policy for Manchuria," 86–90; Donald W. Klein and Anne B. Clark, *Biographic Dictionary of Chinese Communism 1921–1965*, Vol. 2, 714–15; 徐焰 (Xu Yan), *Manchurian Invasion of 1945*, 128–9, 153–4; 武月星 (Wu Yuexing), *Modern Chinese History Map Collection*, 213.
66 徐焰 (Xu Yan), *Manchurian Invasion of 1945*, 169–70; Michael M. Sheng, *Battling Western Imperialism*, 109–10.
67 Chen Yung-fa, *Making Revolution*, 279.
68 杨奎松 (Yang Kuisong),"美苏冷战的起源及对中国革命的影响" ("The Origins of the U.S.-Soviet Cold War and Its Impact on the Chinese Revolution") 历史研究 (*Historical Research*) no. 5 (July 1999), 5–22; 楊奎松 (Yang Kuisong), "Inscrutable Opponent, 1917–1949," 101.
69 王永君 (Wang Yongjun), "The CCP Central Committee's Military Strategies and Policy for Manchuria," 86–90; Donald W. Klein and Anne B. Clark, *Biographic Dictionary of Chinese Communism 1921–1965*, Vol. 2, 714–15.

70 温瑞茂 (Wen Ruimao), "毛泽东战略构想的演进与大决战" ("The Evolution of Mao Zedong's Thinking on Military Strategy and the Great Decisive Battle"), 中共党史研究 (*Research on the History of the Chinese Communist Party*) no. 4 (1997), 21.
71 Cited in 加藤公一 (Katō Kōichi), "The Chinese Communist Party's Recognition of the United States and the Soviet Entry into the War against Japan, 1944–1945," 38; Yukiko Koshiro, "Eurasian Eclipse: Japan's End Game in World War II," *American Historical Review* 109, no. 2 (April 2004), 438.
72 Brian Joseph Murray, "Western versus Chinese Realism," 380–1; 楊奎松 (Yang Kuisong), "Inscrutable Opponent, 1917–1949," 101. For Roshchin's biographical details, I am grateful to Yu Miin-ling.
73 Xinjun Hu, "The Road to the Post-Yalta System: China's Challenge to the United States in the New World Order, 1945–1949" (Ph.D. diss., Southern Illinois University at Carbondale, 1996), 67–8; Michael M. Sheng, *Battling Western Imperialism*, 107–9.
74 Christopher R. Lew, *Third Chinese Revolutionary Civil War, 1945–49*, 20–1; Sergei N. Goncharov, et al., *Uncertain Partners*, 10–11.
75 王永君 (Wang Yongjun), "The CCP Central Committee's Military Strategies and Policy for Manchuria," 86–90; 加藤公一 (Katō Kōichi), "The Chinese Communist Party's Recognition of the United States and the Soviet Entry into the War against Japan, 1944–1945," 32–51.
76 Chen Jian, *Mao's China and the Cold War* (Chapel Hill: University of North Carolina Press, 2001), 31.
77 Sun Tzu, *Art of War*, 67.
78 Edward L. Dreyer, *China at War, 1901–1949*, 313–14; Xiaoyuan Liu, *A Partnership for Disorder: China, the United States, and Their Policies for the Postwar Disposition of the Japanese Empire, 1941–1945* (Cambridge: Cambridge University Press, 1996), 280; 武月星 (Wu Yuexing), *Modern Chinese History Map Collection*, 209.
79 Lloyd E. Eastman, *Seeds of Destruction*, 210.
80 FRUS 1945, Vol. 7, *Far East: China*, 655.
81 温瑞茂 (Wen Ruimao), "Evolution of Mao Zedong's Thinking on Military Strategy and the Great Decisive Battle," 23.
82 汪朝光 (Wang Chaoguang), "抗战胜利后国民党东北决策研究" ("The Nationalist Policy toward Manchuria after the Victory in the War against Japan"), 历史研究 (*Historical Research*) no. 6 (1995), 123–5.
83 邓野 (Deng Ye), "国民党六届二中全会研究" ("A Study of the Second Plenary Conference of the Sixth Central Committee of the Nationalist Party"), 历史研究 (*Historical Research*) 2000 no 1, 5; 満州中央銀行史研究会 (Manchurian Central Bank Historical Research Committee), ed.,

A History of the Manchurian Central Bank, 227–30. FRUS, 1945, Vol. 7, *Far East: China*, 1050.

84 滿州中央銀行史研究会 (Manchurian Central Bank Historical Research Committee), ed., *History of the Manchurian Central Bank*, 227–30.

85 F. C. Jones, *Manchuria since 1931* (London: Royal Institute of International Affairs, 1949), 229; アジア経済研究所 (Asia Economic Research Bureau), 中国東北地方経済に関する調査研究報告書 (*Research Report on the Survey Concerning the Economy of Manchuria, China*) (Tokyo: 産業研究所, 1986), 53.

86 Ramon Myers, *Japanese Economic Development in Manchuria, 1932 to 1945* (New York: Garland, 1982), 5.

87 香島明雄 (Kashima Akio), *Research on Sino-Soviet Diplomatic History, 1937–1946*, 221–2.

88 The Japanese estimated that the 895 million figure should have been revised upward to 1.2 billion. 滿州中央銀行史研究会 (Manchurian Central Bank Historical Research Committee), ed., *History of the Manchurian Central Bank*, 340–1; アジア経済研究所 (Asia Economic Research Bureau), *Research Report on the Survey Concerning the Economy of Manchuria, China*, 26; Calvin Suey Keu Chin, *A Study of Chinese Dependence upon the Soviet Union for Economic Development as a Factor in Communist China's Foreign Policy* (Hong Kong: Union Research Institute, 1959), 32–3.

89 沈志华 (Shen Zhihua), "Soviet Troop Deployment into Northeast China," 102–3.

90 Hoover Institution Archives, Ray Lyman Wilbur papers, Box 047, materials from Norman Cleaveland, 20 December 1946, pp. 64–5.

91 Suzanne Pepper, "KMT-CCP Conflict 1945–1949," 726; 丁晓春 (Ding Xiaochun), "关于建设东北根据地方针的认识" ("On the Policy of Reconstruction in the Northeast Base Area"), 中共党史研究 (*Research on the History of the Chinese Communist Party*) no. 2 (1990), 51–2.

92 O. B. Borisov, *Soviet Union and the Manchurian Revolutionary Base 1945–1949*, 136.

93 I. F. Kurdiukov, V. N. Nikiforov, and A. S. Perevertailo, comps., *Советско-Китайские отношения 1917–1957 сборник документов* (*Soviet-Chinese Relations 1917–1957, Collection of Documents*) (Moscow: Издательство восточной литературы, 1959), 197, 205, 206; Bruce A. Elleman, "The Final Consolidation of the USSR's Sphere of Influence in Outer Mongolia" in *Mongolia in the Twentieth Century: Landlocked Cosmopolitan*, eds. Stephen Kotkin and Bruce A. Elleman (Armonk, NY: M. E. Sharpe, 1999), 130–1; Sergei Leonidovich Tikhvinskii, ed., *Russo-Chinese Relations in the 20th Century*, Vol. 4, part 2, 1937–45, 152–6, 187–95; Xiaoyuan Liu, *A Partnership for Disorder*, 264–5, 282; Historical Research Center (歴史学研究会), comp., *History of the Pacific*

War, Vol. 4, 277–80; Sergei N. Goncharov et al., *Uncertain Partners*, 3–6; ASA, 112.6/0006 中蘇友好同盟條約之有關文件 (Documents Related to the Sino-Soviet Friendship Treaty), 11-WAA-00083, 14 August 1945, pp. 87–111.

94 Bruce A. Elleman, *Diplomacy and Deception*, 232.

95 林明德 (Lin Mingde), "Formation of Japanese Militarism: An Investigation of the Manchurian Incident," 253; Prasenjit Duara, *Sovereignty and Authenticity*, 68.

96 Yoshihisa Tak Matsusaka, *Making of Japanese Manchuria, 1904–1932*, 298; Galina Fominichna Zakharova, *Policy of Japan in Manchuria 1932–1945*, 82–3.

97 Xinjun Hu, "Road to the Post-Yalta System," 71, 73.

98 塚瀬進 (Tsukase Susumu), *Manchukuo "Racial Harmony" in Reality*, 242–4.

99 Thomas R. Gottschang and Diana Lary, *Swallows and Settlers*, 129; 加藤公一 (Katō Kōichi), "The Chinese Communist Party's Recognition of the United States and the Soviet Entry into the War against Japan, 1944–1945," 32–51.

100 Loren Brandt and Barbara Sands, "Land Concentration and Income Distribution in Republican China" in *Chinese History in Economic Perspective*, eds. Thomas G. Rawski and Lillian M. Li (Berkeley: University of California Press, 1992), 182; Albert Feuerwerker, "Economic Trends, 1912–49," 82; Steven I. Levine, *Anvil of Victory: The Communist Revolution in Manchuria, 1945–1948* (New York: Columbia University Press, 1987), 201.

101 Dieter Heinzig, *Soviet Union and Communist China 1945–1950*, 101; Xinjun Hu, "Road to the Post-Yalta System," 143–4.

102 Xinjun Hu, "Road to the Post-Yalta System," 166; O. B. Borisov and B. T. Koloskov, eds. *Soviet-Chinese Relations, 1945–1970* (Bloomington: Indiana University Press, 1975), 55–8; O. Borisov, *Soviet Union and the Manchurian Revolutionary Base 1945–1949*, 189–97; Sergei Leonidovich Tikhvinskii, ed., *Russo-Chinese Relations in the 20th Century*, Vol. 5, part 1, 1946–February 1950, 118; Sergei N. Goncharov et al., *Uncertain Partners*, 17, 31–2, picture 72–3; 楊奎松 (Yang Kuisong), "Inscrutable Opponent, 1917–1949," 101; Harold M. Tanner, "Railways in Communist Strategy and Operations in Manchuria, 1945–48" in *Manchurian Railways and the Opening of China*, eds. Bruce A. Elleman and Stephen Kotkin, 157–61.

103 アジア経済研究所 (Asia Economic Research Bureau), *Research Report on the Survey Concerning the Economy of Manchuria, China*, 35–6.

104 K. P. Ageenko et al., *Soviet Military Aid in the Liberation Struggle of the Chinese People*, 100; 张盛发 (Zhang Shengfa), "战后初期斯大

林对中国革命的态度和立场” (“Stalin’s Attitude and Position toward the Chinese Revolution in the Early Post-war Period”), 中共党史研究 (*Research on the History of the Chinese Communist Party*) no. 1 (2000), 61; Michael M. Sheng, *Battling Western Imperialism*, 110; David M. Glantz, *Soviet Strategic Offensive in Manchuria, 1945 ‘August Storm,’* 186, 226; Boris Grigor’evich Sapozhnikov, *Народно-освободительная война в Китае (1946–1950 гг.)* (*The People’s Liberation War in China [1946–1950]*) (Moscow: Военное издательство, 1984), 33–4, 40–2, 54, 80, 90.

105 香島明雄 (Kashima Akio), *Research on Sino-Soviet Diplomatic History, 1937–1946*, 158.

106 Dieter Heinzig, *Soviet Union and Communist China 1945–1950*, 101; Xinjun Hu, “The Road to the Post-Yalta System,” 143–4.

107 Xinjun Hu, “Road to the Post-Yalta System,” 143; Jay Taylor, *Generalissimo*, 318, 654*n*82; Sergei N. Goncharov et al., *Uncertain Partners*, 14.

108 西村成雄 (Nishimura Shigeo), “Japanese Government’s Recognition of the Republic of China and Zhang Xueliang’s Sovereignty: A Reappraisal of National Cohesion,” 31.

109 Odd Arne Westad, *Decisive Encounters*, 120, 175, 196.

110 John W. Garver, *Chinese-Soviet Relations 1937–1945*, 73, 127–8.

111 Xinjun Hu, “Road to the Post-Yalta System,” 144; 香島明雄 (Kashima Akio), *Research on Sino-Soviet Diplomatic History, 1937–1946*, 164; ASA, 412.6/0042, 中美新約：各項換文及協定 (New Sino-American Treaties: Various Diplomatic Notes and Agreements), 11-NAA-04756, 8 December 1947, pp. 197–203.

112 Christopher R. Lew, *Third Chinese Revolutionary Civil War, 1945–49*, 29–30; Suzanne Pepper, “KMT-CCP Conflict 1945–1949,” 726; 丁晓春 (Ding Xiaochun), “On the Policy of Reconstruction in the Northeast Base Area,” 51–2; Michael M. Sheng, *Battling Western Imperialism*, 113–14.

113 邓野 (Deng Ye), “A Study of the Second Plenary Conference of the Sixth Central Committee of the Nationalist Party,” 5; Suzanne Pepper, “KMT-CCP Conflict 1945–1949,” 726; 丁晓春 (Ding Xiaochun), “On the Policy of Reconstruction in the Northeast Base Area,” 51–2.

114 満州中央銀行史研究会 (Manchurian Central Bank Historical Research Committee), ed., *History of the Manchurian Central Bank*, 227–30.

115 沈志华 (Shen Zhihua), “Soviet Troop Deployment into Northeast China,” 102–3.

116 Jay Taylor, *Generalissimo*, 327.

117 Andrei Mefod’evich Ledovskii, *СССР и Сталин в судьбах Китая: Документы и свидетальства участника событий 1937–1952* (*The

USSR and Stalin in the Fate of China: Documents and the Testimony of Participants in the Events of 1937–1952) (Moscow: «Памятники исторической мысли», 1999), 25.

118 Dieter Heinzig, *Soviet Union and Communist China 1945–1950*, 101; Xinjun Hu, "Road to the Post-Yalta System," 143–4.

119 ASA,426.1/0084,處理在華美軍事人員刑事案件；美軍駐華(Resolution of Criminal Cases against Military Personnel in China; U.S. Troops Stationed in China), 25 November 1946, pp. 99–100.

120 O. Edmund Clubb, *China & Russia*, 262, 265.

121 Sergei N. Goncharov et al., *Uncertain Partners*, 12; Jay Taylor, *Generalissimo*, 326.

122 汪朝光 (Wang Chaoguang), "The Nationalist Policy toward Manchuria," 128–30.

123 William L. Tung, *The Political Institutions of Modern China* (The Hague: Martinus Nijhoff, 1968), 179; 章百家 (Zhang Baijia), 周恩来与马歇尔使命" ("Zhou Enlai and Marshall's Mission to China"), 近代史研究 (*Modern Chinese History Studies*) no. 4 (1997), 198.

124 滿州中央銀行史研究会 (Manchurian Central Bank Historical Research Committee), ed., *History of the Manchurian Central Bank*, 232; Tony Saich and Hans van de Ven, eds., *The Rise to Power of the Chinese Communist Party: Documents and Analysis* (Armonk, NY: M. E. Sharpe, 1996), xxxv–xxxvi.

125 滿州中央銀行史研究会 (Manchurian Central Bank Historical Research Committee), ed., *History of the Manchurian Central Bank*, 339–40; 汪朝光 (Wang Chaoguang), "Nationalist Policy toward Manchuria," 128–30; 何迪 (He Di), "1945–1949年中国共产党对美国政策的演变" ("The Evolution of the Chinese Communist Party's Policy Regarding the United States, 1945–1949"), 历史研究 *(Historical Research)* no. 3 (1987), 15, 17.

126 Michael M. Sheng, *Battling Western Imperialism*, 130.

127 滿州中央銀行史研究会 (Manchurian Central Bank Historical Research Committee), ed., *History of the Manchurian Central Bank*, 232.

128 汪朝光 (Wang Chaoguang), "Nationalist Policy toward Manchuria," no. 6, 128–30; Ronald H. Spector, *In the Ruins of Empire*, 243–4; 武月星 (Wu Yuexing), *Modern Chinese History Map Collection*, 223.

129 滿州中央銀行史研究会 (Manchurian Central Bank Historical Research Committee), ed., *History of the Manchurian Central Bank*, 232.

130 汪朝光 (Wang Chaoguang), "The Nationalist Policy toward Manchuria," 128–30.

131 滿州中央銀行史研究会 (Manchurian Central Bank Historical Research Committee), ed., *History of the Manchurian Central Bank*, 232, 339–40.

132 徐焰 (Xu Yan), *Manchurian Invasion of 1945*, 170–1.

133 Cited in Edward L. Dreyer, *China at War, 1901–1949*, 324.

134 Andrei Mefod'evich Ledovskii, *USSR and Stalin in the Fate of China*, 333; Sergei Leonidovich Tikhvinskii, ed., *Russo-Chinese Relations in the 20th Century*, Vol. 4, part 2, 1937–45, 673.

135 Odd Arne Westad, *Decisive Encounters*, 44; Tony Saich and Hans van de Ven, eds., *Rise to Power of the Chinese Communist Party*, xxxv; Robert L. Jarman, ed., *China Political Reports 1911–1960*, Vol. 8, 369.

136 ASA, 119.17/0001, 東北共產黨之發展 (The Development of the Communist Party in Manchuria), 11-WAA-00112, p. 12.

137 Raymond L. Garthoff, "Sino-Soviet Military Relations, 1945–66" in *Sino-Soviet Military Relations*, ed. Raymond L. Garthoff (New York: Frederick A. Praeger, 1966), 84.

138 I. F. Kurdiukov et al., comps., *Soviet-Chinese Relations 1917–1957*, 197, 205, 206; Bruce A. Elleman, "The Final Consolidation of the USSR's Sphere of Influence in Outer Mongolia," 130–1; 香島明雄 (Kashima Akio), *Research on Sino-Soviet Diplomatic History, 1937–1946*, 156–7.

139 Odd Arne Westad, *Decisive Encounters*, 31, 112, 352; Raymond L. Garthoff, "Sino-Soviet Military Relations, 1945–66," 83; Suzanne Pepper, "KMT-CCP Conflict 1945–1949," 727; Xinjun Hu, "Road to the Post-Yalta System," 143; Jay Taylor, *Generalissimo*, 318, 654*n*82; Sergei N. Goncharov et al., *Uncertain Partners*, 14.

140 Cited in Wesley M. Bagby, *Eagle-Dragon Alliance*, 52; Odd Arne Westad, *Decisive Encounters*, 49, 112; Michael M. Sheng, *Battling Western Imperialism*, 142–3; 武月星 (Wu Yuexing), *Modern Chinese History Map Collection*, 225.

141 F. F. Liu, *Military History*, 246–7; Jay Taylor, *Generalissimo*, 383.

142 Christopher R. Lew, *Third Chinese Revolutionary Civil War, 1945–49*, 55, 66; Chang Jui-te, "Nationalist Army on the Eve of the War," 89.

143 Christopher R. Lew, *Third Chinese Revolutionary Civil War, 1945–49*, 56.

144 Sun Tzu, *Art of War*, 98, 138.

145 Christopher R. Lew, *Third Chinese Revolutionary Civil War, 1945–49*, 62–6.

146 Ronald H. Spector, *In the Ruins of Empire*, 246, 255.

147 Sun Tzu, *Art of War*, 145–6, 149.

148 Jay Taylor, *Generalissimo*, 156.

149 Odd Arne Westad, *Decisive Encounters*, 152; Ronald H. Spector, *In the Ruins of Empire*, 254–5.

150 Lloyd E. Eastman, *Seeds of Destruction*, 167; Ch'en Li-fu, *Storm Clouds Clear over China*, xxii.

151 Jonathan Fenby, *Chiang Kai-shek*, 261–2, 381; Edward J. Drea, "Japanese Army on the Eve of the War," 132; Richard B. Frank, *Downfall*, 105;

Jay Taylor, *Generalissimo*, 342; Jung Chang and Jon Halliday, *Mao the Unknown Story*, 96.

152 Christopher R. Lew, *Third Chinese Revolutionary Civil War, 1945–49*, 61, 77–86, 137–8; 武月星 (Wu Yuexing), *Modern Chinese History Map Collection*, 237.

153 Robert L. Jarman, ed., *China Political Reports 1911–1960*, Vol. 8, 364, 366.

154 Christopher R. Lew, *Third Chinese Revolutionary Civil War, 1945–49*, 69–70.

155 Edward L. Dreyer, *China at War, 1901–1949*, 330–1.

156 Christopher R. Lew, *Third Chinese Revolutionary Civil War, 1945–49*, 61, 71–2, 77–86, 137–8; 中国人民革命军事博物馆 (Museum of the Chinese People's Revolutionary Military Affairs), ed., 中国战争史地图集 (*Map Collection of Chinese Military History*) (Beijing: 星球地图出版社, 2007), 326.

157 Stephen I. Levine, *Anvil of Victory*, 130; Christopher R. Lew, *Third Chinese Revolutionary Civil War, 1945–49*, 72–5.

158 Robert L. Jarman, ed., *China Political Reports 1911–1960*, Vol. 8, 358, 361, 395.

159 Edward L. Dreyer, *China at War, 1901–1949*, 331; Christopher R. Lew, *Third Chinese Revolutionary Civil War, 1945–49*, 40; Stephen I. Levine, *Anvil of Victory*, 165, 222.

160 丁晓春 (Ding Xiaochun), "On the Policy of Reconstruction in the Northeast Base Area," 51–2.

161 毕健忠 (Bi Jianzhong), "全国解放战争略指导新探" ("A Reexamination of the Guiding Strategy during the War for National Liberation"), 中共党史研究 (*Research on the History of the Chinese Communist Party*) no. 4 (1990), 25–30; 沙友林 (Sha Youlin), "刘少奇对完善抗日游击战争战略方针的贡献 ("Liu Shaoqi's Contribution to the Perfection of the Guerrilla Strategy during the War of Resistance"), 中共党史研究 (*Research on the History of the Chinese Communist Party*) no. 2 (1998), 35–8.

162 Christopher R. Lew, *Third Chinese Revolutionary Civil War, 1945–49*, 97.

163 Edward L. Dreyer, *China at War, 1901–1949*, 331.

164 佟玉民 (Tong Yumin), "关于'农村包围城市'道路的理论形成过程" ("Exploring the Formulation of the Strategy of 'Encircling Cities from the Countryside'"), 历史研究 *(Historical Research)* no. 4 (1981), 25–38.

165 Christopher R. Lew, *Third Chinese Revolutionary Civil War, 1945–49*, 87–93.

166 刘一皋 (Liu Yigao), "Land Reform and Rural Political Power," 77.

167 Christopher R. Lew, *Third Chinese Revolutionary Civil War, 1945–49*, 94–7; Stephen I. Levine, *Anvil of Victory*, 132; Odd Arne Westad, *Decisive Encounters*, 177.

168 Odd Arne Westad, *Decisive Encounters*, 173, 203; Donald G. Gillin, "Problems of Centralization in Republican China," 835, 844, 847–8.

169 Xinjun Hu, "Road to the Post-Yalta System," 155–65.

170 Sun Tzu, *Art of War*, 76.

171 The Liaoning-Shenyang Campaign is also known as the Liaoshen Campaign and the Western Liaoning-Shenyang Campaign. Christopher R. Lew, *Third Chinese Revolutionary Civil War, 1945–49*, 113–14, 139; Brian Joseph Murray, "Western versus Chinese Realism," 361; United States Department of State, *United States Relations with China with Special Reference to the Period 1944–1949* (Washington, DC: Office of Public Affairs, 1949), 323–4; Suzanne Pepper, "KMT-CCP Conflict 1945–1949," 774–5.

172 王奇生 (Wang Qisheng), *Party Members, Party Authority, and Party Infighting*, 295.

173 FRUS, 1948, Vol. 7, *Far East: China*, 409–10, 613, 617, 710; ibid., Vol. 8, 45, 48–50.

174 Glenn D. Paige, *The Korean Decision [June 24–30, 1950]* (New York: Free Press, 1968), 59.

175 Donald G. Gillin, "Problems of Centralization in Republican China," 848–9; F. F. Liu, *Military History*, 235–6; Jay Taylor, *Generalissimo*, 323; Howard L. Boorman, ed., *Biographical Dictionary*, Vol. 1, 152–3.

176 Suzanne Pepper, "KMT-CCP Conflict 1945–1949," 774.

177 Jonathan Fenby, *Chiang Kai-shek*, 478.

178 Xinjun Hu, "Road to the Post-Yalta System," 175.

179 F. F. Liu, *Military History*, 261; Jonathan Fenby, *Chiang Kai-shek*, 483.

180 Christopher R. Lew, *Third Chinese Revolutionary Civil War, 1945–49*, 122; Boris Grigor'evich Sapozhnikov, *People's Liberation War in China (1946–1950)*, 105; Odd Arne Westad, *Decisive Encounters*, 199.

181 Cited in Nancy Bernkopf Tucker, *China Confidential*, 48.

182 Lloyd E. Eastman, *Seeds of Destruction*, 167.

183 Lionel Max Chassin, *Communist Conquest of China*, v, 45; Christopher R. Lew, *Third Chinese Revolutionary Civil War, 1945–49*, 127–8; Odd Arne Westad, *Decisive Encounters*, 224–5; Howard L. Boorman, ed., *Biographical Dictionary*, Vol. 2, 50–1.

184 Boris Grigor'evich Sapozhnikov, *People's Liberation War in China (1946–1950)*, 112.

185 F. F. Liu, *Military History*, 247–8; Edward L. Dreyer, *China at War, 1901–1949*, 315.

186 Dieter Heinzig, *Soviet Union and Communist China 1945–1950*, 171–2; Xinjun Hu, "Road to the Post-Yalta System," 176–80; Brian Murray, "Stalin, the Cold War, and the Division of China: A Multi-Archival Mystery," *Cold War International History Project*, working paper no. 12 (June 1995), 6–10.

187 马风书 (Ma Fengshu), "战后初期苏联对华政策剖析" ("An Analysis of Soviet Policies toward China in the Early Post-war Years"), 文史哲 (*Journal of Literature, History, and Philosophy*) 250, no. 1 (1999), 55.

188 Brian Murray, "Stalin, the Cold War, and the Division of China," 2. Citing Vladimir Dedijer, *Tito Speaks* (London: Weidenfield and Nicolson, 1953), 331.

189 Jonathan Fenby, *Chiang Kai-shek*, 491; Ross Terrill, *Mao a Biography*, rev. ed. (Stanford, CA: Stanford University Press, 1995), 216.

190 Murray, Brian, "Stalin, the Cold War, and the Division of China," 5–6.

191 楊奎松 (Yang Kuisong), "Inscrutable Opponent, 1917–1949," 103.

192 Dieter Heinzig, *Soviet Union and Communist China 1945–1950*, 171–2; Xinjun Hu, "Road to the Post-Yalta System," 176–80; Brian Joseph Murray, "Western versus Chinese Realism," 313–14, 321, 325, 329, 376–7, 380–5.

193 Jonathan Fenby, *Chiang Kai-shek*, 490; Suzanne Pepper, "KMT-CCP Conflict 1945–1949," 784; Howard L. Boorman, ed., *Biographical Dictionary*, Vol. 3, 55–6, 227; Jonathan Fenby, *Chiang Kai-shek*, 492; Stephen R. MacKinnon, *Wuhan 1938*, 34; Jay Taylor, *The Generalissimo*, 403; F. F. Liu, *Military History*, 266–7.

194 Albert Herrmann, *An Historical Atlas of China* (1935 reprint; Chicago: Aldine Publishing, 1966), 62–3.

195 Cited in Lloyd E. Eastman, *Seeds of Destruction*, 168.

196 Bruce A. Elleman, "The *Chongqing* Mutiny and the Chinese Civil War, 1949" in *Naval Mutinies of the Twentieth Century: An International Perspective*, eds. Christopher M. Bell and Bruce A. Elleman (London: Frank Cass, 2003), 232–45; Odd Arne Westad, *Decisive Encounters*, 242–3; F. F. Liu, *Military History*, 266–7; Boris Grigor'evich Sapozhnikov, *People's Liberation War in China (1946–1950)*, 121; Nancy Bernkopf Tucker, *China Confidential*, 48.

197 ASA, 423.1/0005, 民國 3 8 年 4 - 6 月份陸海空軍過渡時期緊急軍品補充計畫 (April–June 1949 Army, Navy, Air Force Transitional Period Urgent Supplementary Military Supply Plan), 11-NAA-05550, pp. 144–50.

198 FRUS, 1947, Vol. 7, *Far East: China*, 264, 700; ibid., Vol. 8, 94; FRUS, 1950, Vol. 7, *Korea*, 152.

199 FRUS, 1948, Vol. 7, *Far East: China*, 56, 623.

200 王真 (Wang Zhen), "斯大林与毛泽东1949年1月往来电文评析" ("An Analysis of the Telegrams between Stalin and Mao Zedong in January

1949"), 近代史研究 (*Modern Chinese History Studies*) no. 2 (1998), 117–29.

201 Carl von Clausewitz, *On War*, 599–600, 570.

202 马风书 (Ma Fengshu), "Analysis of Soviet Policies toward China in the Early Post-war Years," 55; Brian Joseph Murray, "Western versus Chinese Realism," 380–3.

203 Christopher R. Lew, *Third Chinese Revolutionary Civil War, 1945–49*, 146; Odd Arne Westad, *Decisive Encounters*, 289.

204 Linda Benson, *Ili Rebellion*, 175.

205 FRUS 1945, Vol. 7, *Far East: China*, 2, 10, 12, 20, 586, 652, 1372.

206 Ibid., 1371; FRUS 1946, Vol. 9, *Far East: China*, 1395.

207 FRUS, 1948, Vol. 7, *Far East: China*, 717.

208 Cited in Xiaoyuan Liu, *Frontier Passages: Ethnopolitics and the Rise of Chinese Communism, 1921–1945* (Stanford, CA: Stanford University Press, 2004), 136.

209 Ronald H. Spector, *In the Ruins of Empire*, 59–60.

210 Jung Chang, *Wild Swans*, 80.

211 吴宏伟 (Wu Hongwei), "解放前夕南京的物价飞涨状况" ("Inflation on the Eve of Liberation in Nanjing"), 中国经济史研究 (*Research in Chinese Economic History*) no. 1 (1992), 153; 菊池一隆 (Kikuchi Kazutaka), "Wartime Finances of the Chongqing Government," 394.

212 鈴木岩行 (Suzuki Iwayuki), "馬寅初の重慶国民政府批判に関する一試論" ("A Preliminary Essay Concerning Ma Yinchu's Critique of the Nationalist Government in Chongqing") in *Research on the History of the Chinese Republican Government*, ed. 中国現代史研究会 (Committee for Research on Modern Chinese History), 465; 董廷之 (Dong Tingzhi), "Inflation in Nationalist-ruled Territory during the Anti-Japanese War," 36–8; 張瑞德 (Zhang Ruide), "Businessmen of Nationalist China in the Great Rear during the Sino-Japanese War, 1937–1945," 133.

213 張瑞德 (Zhang Ruide), "Businessmen of Nationalist China in the Great Rear during the Sino-Japanese War, 1937–1945," 127–8, 142–4; Robert L. Jarman, ed., *China Political Reports 1911–1960*, Vol. 7, 340.

214 Ezra F. Vogel, *The Four Little Dragons: The Spread of Industrialization in East Asia* (Cambridge, MA: Harvard University Press, 1991), 18.

215 Niccolò Machiavelli, *Machiavelli's The Prince: A Bilingual Edition*, trans. and ed. Mark Musa (New York: St. Martin's Press, 1964), 137–43.

216 For an entire book on the reasons why Chiang Kai-shek was hated, see Suzanne Pepper, *Civil War in China*, passim.

217 Sun Tzu, *Art of War*, 79; Wesley M. Bagby, *Eagle-Dragon Alliance*, 57, 109, 131, 133, 134–5, 139.

218 Sun Tzu, *Art of War*, 134, 137.

219 Mao Zedong, *Selected Military Writings*, 111, 113, 260–1.

220 王奇生 (Wang Qisheng), *Party Members, Party Authority, and Party Infighting*, 172–3; Chang Rui-te, "Chiang Kai-shek's Coordination of Personal Directives" in *China at War: Regions of China, 1937–1945*, eds. Stephen R. MacKinnon, Diana Lary, and Ezra F. Vogel (Stanford, CA: Stanford University Press, 2007), 69.
221 Wesley M. Bagby, *Eagle-Dragon Alliance*, 41, 248.
222 Sun Tzu, *The Art of War*, 83, 112, 128.
223 Ibid., 74, 131, 134
224 Ibid., 144–9.
225 Ibid., 84; Mao Zedong, *Selected Military Writings*, 88, 238.
226 Sun Tzu, *Art of War*, 77–8.
227 Mao Zedong, *Selected Military Writings*, 260.
228 Ibid., 221.
229 佟玉民 (Tong Yumin), "Exploring the Formulation of the Strategy of 'Encircling Cities from the Countryside,'" 25–38; Jay Taylor, *Generalissimo*, 379; Robert L. Jarman, ed., *China Political Reports 1911–1960*, Vol. 8, 364; Mao Zedong, *Selected Military Writings*, 180.
230 张芝连 (Zhang Zhilian) and 刘学荣 (Liu Xuerong), 世界历史地图集 (*World History Map Collection*) (Beijing: 中国地图出版社, 2001), 162–3.
231 FRUS, 1947, Vol. 7, *Far East: China*, 224.
232 Odd Arne Westad, *Decisive Encounters*, 49–50, 185.
233 章百家 (Zhang Baijia), "Nationalist and Communist Policies Regarding the United States, 1937–1945," 3–5.
234 FRUS, 1950, Vol. 6, *East Asia and the Pacific*, 6, 340; John W. Garver, "China's Wartime Diplomacy," 24.
235 Odd Arne Westad, *Decisive Encounters*, 51.
236 Cited in Max Beloff, *Soviet Policy in the Far East 1944–1951*, 51–3.
237 Suzanne Pepper, "KMT-CCP Conflict 1945–1949," 735.
238 FRUS, 1948, Vol. 7, *Far East: China*, 47; ibid, Vol. 8, 47; FRUS, 1947, Vol. 7, *Far East: China*, 223; Harry S. Truman, *Memoirs*, Vol. 2 (Garden City, NY: Doubleday, 1956), 91; John W. Garver, *The Sino-American Alliance: Nationalist China and American Cold War Strategy in Asia* (Armonk, NY: M. E. Sharpe, 1997), 11–13.

9 CONCLUSION: CIVIL WAR AS THE PROLOGUE AND EPILOGUE TO REGIONAL AND GLOBAL WARS

1 Cited in Jay Taylor, *Generalissimo*, 153.
2 Max Weber, "The Profession and Vocation of Politics," in *Weber Political Writings*, eds. Peter Lassman and Ronald Speirs (Cambridge: Cambridge University Press, 1994), 310–11.

3 JFM, B.0.0.0–17, 条約ノ認印、批准、実施其他ノ先例雑件（条約局より引継文書）(Miscellaneous documents on the signing, ratification, and enforcement of treaties and other precedents [records inherited from the Treaty Office]), Vol. 4, 太平洋ノ平和保障ニ関スル諸条約 (*Various Treaties Concerning Guaranteeing Peace in the Pacific Ocean*), July 1937; Boris Slavinsky, *Japanese-Soviet Neutrality Pact*, 13. Slavinsky argues that the nonaggression and neutrality pacts were in place by 1931 (ibid.).
4 Ike Nobutaka, trans. and ed., *Japan's Decision for War*, xxii, 198, 229; Herbert P. Bix, *Hirohito*, 374.
5 United States Department of State, *United States Relations with China with Special Reference to the Period 1944–1949*, 970.
6 Thomas Hobbes, *Leviathan* (1651, reprint; Cleveland: Meridian Books, 1963), 143.
7 Cited in Takafusa Nakamura, *History of Shōwa Japan*, 137, 170.
8 Cited in Yoshitake Oka, *Konoe Fumimaro A Political Biography*, trans. Shumpei Okamoto and Patricia Murray (Lanham, MD: Madison Books, 1992), xii, 193, 234, 237; John Toland, *Rising Sun*, 874.
9 Seiichi Iwao, ed., *Biographical Dictionary of Japanese History*, trans. Burton Watson (Tokyo: Kodansha International, 1978), 344, 466.
10 Louis Frédéric, *Japan Encyclopedia*, 350.
11 Both cited in Mark R. Peattie, *Ishiwara Kanji and Japan's Confrontation with the West*, 307, 340.
12 John Hunter Boyle, *China and Japan at War 1937–1945*, 1–2, 45, 47–8.
13 Cited in Seki Hiroharu, "Manchurian Incident, 1931," 143.
14 Richard Fuller, *Shōkan Hirohito's Samurai*, 115.
15 Ian Nish, *Japanese Foreign Policy 1869–1942*, 235–6, 249.
16 Ugaki Matome, *Fading Victory*, 365.
17 Edward J. Drea, *MacArthur's ULTRA Codebreaking and the War against Japan, 1942–1945* (Lawrence: University of Kansas Press, 1992), 73; Hiroyuki Agawa, *The Reluctant Admiral: Yamamoto and the Imperial Navy*, trans. John Bester (Tokyo: Kodansha International, 1979), 351–8, 362.
18 Cited in Takafusa Nakamura, *History of Shōwa Japan*, 216.
19 Seiichi Iwao, ed., *Biographical Dictionary of Japanese History*, 496; John Toland, *Rising Sun*, 873.
20 John Toland, *Rising Sun*, 875; Arnold C. Brackman, *Last Emperor*, 272.
21 Richard Fuller, *Shōkan Hirohito's Samurai*, 306.
22 John Toland, *Rising Sun*, 847; Richard Fuller, *Shōkan Hirohito's Samurai*, 200.
23 Richard Fuller, *Shōkan Hirohito's Samurai*, 200, 213.
24 Cited in John Toland, *Rising Sun*, 159, 304, 867; Richard Fuller, *Shōkan Hirohito's Samurai*, 296–297.

25 Richard Fuller, *Shōkan Hirohito's Samurai*, 274.

26 Saburo Hayashi and Alvin D. Coox, *Kōgun*, 222–3; Richard Fuller, *Shōkan Hirohito's Samurai*, 89, 149, 153.

27 Saburo Hayashi and Alvin D. Coox, *Kōgun*, 239; Louis Frédéric, *Japan Encyclopedia*, 1014.

28 Carl Boyd, *Extraordinary Envoy*, 136.

29 Richard Fuller, *Shōkan Hirohito's Samurai*, 96, 182, 204, 289–90.

30 Ibid., 180.

31 http://www.danwei.org/internet/song_meiling_dies_at_105.php; Edwin Pak-wah Leung, ed., *Political Leaders of Modern China: A Biographical Dictionary* (Westport, CT: Greenwood Press, 2002), 143; Jay Taylor, *Generalissimo*, 19.

32 Jonathan Fenby, "Zhang Xueliang," *The Independent*, 16 October 2001.

33 Howard L. Boorman, ed., *Biographical Dictionary,* Vol. 4, 49–50.

34 秦孝儀 (Qin Xiaoyi), *Dictionary of Modern Chinese History*, 328.

35 Edwin Pak-wah Leung, ed., *Political Leaders of Modern China*, 97.

36 Howard L., Boorman, ed., *Biographical Dictionary*, Vol. 3, 56, 228.

37 Ibid., 189–92.

38 Ch'en Li-fu, *Storm Clouds Clear over China*, xii.

39 Edwin Pak-wah Leung, ed., *Historical Dictionary of Revolutionary China, 1839–1976* (New York: Greenwood Press, 1992), 43–4, 148; ibid, *Political Leaders of Modern China*, 14; Howard L., Boorman ed., *Biographical Dictionary*, Vol. 1, 152–3; ibid., Vol. 2, 155; Donald G. Gillin, "Problems of Centralization in Republican China," 837; Odd Arne Westad, *Decisive Encounters*, 177.

40 秦孝儀 (Qin Xiaoyi), *Dictionary of Modern Chinese History*, 117; Howard L. Boorman, ed., *Biographical Dictionary*, Vol. 3, 328; Jay Taylor, *Generalissimo*, 399–400.

41 Gerald E. Bunker, *The Peace Conspiracy: Wang Ching-wei and the China War, 1937–1941* (Cambridge, MA: Harvard University Press, 1972), 280, 285; Jonathan Fenby, *Chiang Kai-shek,* 448; John Hunter Boyle, *China and Japan at War 1937–1945*, 323.

42 Howard L., Boorman, ed., *Biographical Dictionary*, Vol. 3, 388; ibid, Vol. 2, 353.

43 Arnold C. Brackman, *Last Emperor*, 325, 330–5, 339; Henry Pu Yi, *The Last Manchu: The Autobiography of Henry Pu Yi Last Emperor of China*, ed. Paul Kramer, trans. Kuo Ying Paul Tsai (London: Arthur Barker, 1967), 224, 258, 270, 299, 306.

44 Edwin Pak-wah Leung, ed., *Historical Dictionary of Revolutionary China*, 133.

45 Howard L. Boorman, ed., *Biographical Dictionary*, Vol. 1, 44–6; Jung Chang and Jon Halliday, *Mao the Unknown Story*, 201–3.

46 Donald W. Klein and Anne B. Clark, *Biographic Dictionary of Chinese Communism 1921–1965*, Vol. 2, 751–2; 秦孝儀 (Qin Xiaoyi), *Dictionary of Modern Chinese History*, 125; 徐友春 (Xu Youchun), *Comprehensive Biographical Dictionary for the Republican Period*, Vol. 1, 276; Howard L. Boorman, ed., *Biographical Dictionary*, Vol. 3, 408–11.

47 Li Zhisui, *The Private Life of Chairman Mao*, trans. Tai Hung-chao (New York: Random House, 1994), 567–8.

48 Ibid., 580–1.

49 Donald W. Klein and Anne B. Clark, *Biographic Dictionary of Chinese Communism 1921–1965*, Vol. 2, 718.

50 Edwin Pak-wah Leung, ed., *Historical Dictionary of the Chinese Civil War* (Lanham, MD: Scarecrow Press, 2002), 37.

51 Colin Mackerras, *The New Cambridge Handbook of Contemporary China* (Cambridge: Cambridge University Press, 2001), 47.

52 C. Martin Wilbur and Julie Lien-ying How, *Missionaries of Revolution: Soviet Advisers and Nationalist China, 1920–1927* (Cambridge, MA: Harvard University Press, 1989), 426, 428; Dan M. Jacobs, *Borodin: Stalin's Man in China* (Cambridge, MA: Harvard University Press, 1981), 313, 326. For the biographical details concerning Bogomolov and Roshchin, I am grateful to Yu Miin-ling.

53 John Paxton, *Companion to Russian History* (New York: Facts On File Publications, 1983), 449.

54 Alvin D. Coox, *Nomonhan*, 188, 629n5, 992, 995; A. M. Prokhorov, ed., *Советский энциклопедический словарь* (*Soviet Encyclopedic Dictionary*), 2nd ed. (Moscow: «Советсткая энциклопедия», 1983), 1223, 1517.

55 Richard Overy, *Russia's War*, 76–8, 87–99.

56 Robert Conquest, *Stalin Breaker of Nations* (New York: Penguin Books, 1991), 311–12; Dmitri Volkogonov, *Stalin Triumph & Tragedy*, trans. Harold Shukman (New York: Grove Weidenfeld, 1988), 571–4.

57 Jonathan Fenby, *Chiang Kai-shek*, 390–2, 423, 430; Jay Taylor, *Generalissimo*, 216–20, 362; Frank Dorn, *Walkout with Stilwell in Burma* (New York: Thomas Y. Crowell, 1971), 35.

58 John Kifner, "John Serice, a Purged 'China Hand,' Dies at 89," *New York Times*, 4 February 1999, B11; Jay Taylor, *Generalissimo*, 333–4, 425, 457; John Toland, *Rising Sun*, 68; Nancy Bernkopf Tucker, *China Confidential*, 67; 金光耀 (Jin Guangyao, "国民党在美国的游说活动—以顾维钧为中心的讨论" ("Nationalist Lobbying in the United States: A Case Study on Wellington Koo"), 历史研究 (*Historical Research*) no. 4 (2000), 61–72.

59 United States Department of State, *United States Relations with China with Special Reference to the Period 1944–1949*; Conrad Brandt,

Benjamin Schwartz, and John K. Fairbank, *A Documentary History of Chinese Communism* (Cambridge, MA: Harvard University Press, 1952), 45.

60 Robert P. Newman, *Owen Lattimore and the "Loss" of China* (Berkeley: University of California Press, 1992), 212, 221, 250, 300; E. J. Kahn, Jr., *The China Hands: America's Foreign Service Officers and What Befell Them* (New York: Viking Press, 1972), 1–3, 7–13, 26–7; Thomas C. Reeves, *The Life and Times of Joe McCarthy: A Biography* (New York: Stein and Day, 1982), 666, 669, 671.

61 Edwin Pak-wah Leung, ed., *Historical Dictionary of Revolutionary China*, 380; Shum Kui-kwong, *Chinese Communists' Road to Power*, 233.

62 Wesley M. Bagby, *Eagle-Dragon Alliance*, 175–7.

63 Peter Teed, *Dictionary of 20th Century History 1914–1990*, 282.

64 United Press International, "Adm. Nimitz Dead; Built Pacific Fleet That Fought Japan," *New York Times*, 21 February 1966.

65 Jay Taylor, *Generalissimo*, 297, 377, 380, 390; Edwin Pak-wah Leung, ed., *Historical Dictionary of Revolutionary China*, 56, 459.

66 Peter Teed, *Dictionary of 20th Century History 1914–1990*, 296.

67 Mencius citing Confucius in *Mencius*, trans. D. C. Lau (London: Penguin, 1970), 121.

BIBLIOGRAPHY

Note: The works are alphabetized by English translation.

ASA. Academia Sinica. Institute of Modern History Archives.

FRUS. United States Department of State. *Foreign Relations of the United States Diplomatic Papers.*

JDA. Japan. Defense Agency. Defense Research Center Archives.

JFM. Japan. Foreign Ministry. Diplomatic Records Office.

安部彦太 (Abe Hikota). "大東亜戦争の計数的分析" ("A Statistical Analysis of the Great East Asian War"). In 近代日本戦争史 *(Modern Japanese Military History),* vol. 4 大東亜戦争 (*The Great East Asian War*), edited by 奥村房夫 (Okumura Fusao) and 近藤新治 (Kondō Shinji), 823–59. Tokyo: 同台経済懇話会, 1995.

中央研究院近代史研究所檔案館 (Academia Sinica. Institute of Modern History Archives). Abbreviated as ASA.

Acheson, Dean. *Present at the Creation: My Years in the State Department.* New York: W. W. Norton, 1969.

Agawa, Hiroyuki. *The Reluctant Admiral: Yamamoto and the Imperial Navy.* Translated by John Bester. Tokyo: Kodansha International, 1979.

Ageenko, K. P., P. N. Bobylev, T. S. Manaenkov, R. A. Sabyshkin, and I. F. Iakushin, *Военная помощь СССР в освободительной борбье китайского народа (Soviet Military Aid in the Liberation Struggle of the Chinese People*). Moscow: Military Press of the Ministry of Defence, 1975.

味岡 徹 (Ajioka Tōru). "国民党「訓政」と抗日戦争" ("The Nationalist Party's 'Political Tutelage' and the Anti-Japanese War"). In 日中戦争 日本・中国・アメリカ *(The Sino-Japanese War: Japan, China, and America),* edited by 中央大学人文科学研究所 (Chūō University Human Sciences Research Center), 361–90. Research publication no. 10. Tokyo: 中央大学出版社, 1993.

BIBLIOGRAPHY

Akagi, Roy Hidemichi. *Japan's Foreign Relations 1542–1936*. Tokyo: Hokuseido Press, 1936.

Allen, G. C. "The Development of Industrial Combinations." In *The Industrialization of Japan and Manchukuo 1930–1940: Population, Raw Materials and Industry*, edited by E. B. Schumpeter, 680–727. New York: Macmillan, 1940.

荒川憲一 (Arakawa Ken-ichi). "Japanese Naval Blockade of China in the Second Sino-Japanese War, 1937–41." In *Naval Blockades and Seapower: Strategies and Counter-strategies, 1805–2005*, edited by Bruce A. Elleman and S. C. M. Paine, 105–16. London: Routledge, 2006.

"The Maritime Transport War – Emphasizing a Strategy to Interrupt the Enemy Sea Lines of Communication (SLOCs)." *NIDS Security Reports* no. 3 (March 2002): 97–120.

戦時経済体制の構想と展開：日本陸海軍の経済史的分析 *(Plans for and Development of the Wartime Economic System: An Economic Historical Analysis of the Japanese Army and Navy)*. Tokyo: 岩波書店, 2011.

"The Shipping of Southeast Asian Resources Back to Japan: National Logistics and War Strategy." Tokyo: National Institute for Defense Studies, Military History Department, unpublished paper, ca. 2002.

Asada, Sadao. *From Mahan to Pearl Harbor: The Imperial Japanese Navy and the United States*. Annapolis, MD: Naval Institute Press, 2006.

Asano, Toyomi. "Japanese Operations in Yunnan and North Burma." In *The Battle for China: Essays on the Military History of the Sino-Japanese War of 1937–1945*, edited by Mark Peattie, Edward J. Drea, and Hans van de Ven, 361–85. Stanford: Stanford University Press, 2011.

アジア経済研究所 (Asia Economic Research Bureau). 中国東北地方経済に関する調査研究報告書 *(Research Report on the Survey Concerning the Economy of Manchuria, China)*. Tokyo: 産業研究所, 1986.

新人物往来社 (Association for Rising Talent). 満洲古写真帖 *(Old Photo Album of Manchuria)*. 戦記シリーズ no. 67. Tokyo: 新人物往来社, 2004.

Baer, George W. *One Hundred Years of Sea Power: The U.S. Navy, 1890–1990*. Stanford: Stanford University Press, 1993.

Bagby, Wesley M. *The Eagle-Dragon Alliance: America's Relations with China in World War II*. Newark: University of Delaware Press, 1992.

Barnett, A. Doak. *China on the Eve of Communist Takeover*. New York: Frederick A. Praeger, 1963.

Barnhart, Michael A. *Japan Prepares for Total War*. Ithaca: Cornell, 1987.

Barrett, David P. "Introduction: Occupied China and the Limits of Accommodation." In *Chinese Collaboration with Japan, 1932–1945: The Limits of Accommodation*, edited by David P. Barrett and Larry N. Shyu, 1–20. Stanford: Stanford University Press, 2001.

"The Wang Jingwei Government, 1940–1945: Continuities and Disjunctures with Nationalist China." In *Chinese Collaboration with Japan, 1932–1945: The Limits of Accommodation*, edited by David P. Barrett and Larry N. Shyu, 102–15. Stanford: Stanford University Press, 2001.

Barrett, David P. and Larry N. Shyu, eds. *Chinese Collaboration with Japan, 1932–1945: The Limits of Accommodation*. Stanford: Stanford University Press, 2001.

Beard, Charles A. *President Roosevelt and the Coming War 1941: A Study in Appearances and Realities*. New Haven: Yale University Press, 1948.

Beasley, W. G. "Meiji Political Institutions." In *The Cambridge History of Japan*, vol. 5, edited by Marius Jansen, 618–73. Cambridge: Cambridge University Press, 1989.

Becker, Jasper. *Hungry Ghosts: Mao's Secret Famine*. New York: Free Press, 1996. "Naval Mutinies of the Twentieth Century: An International Perspective"

Bell, Christopher M. and Bruce A. Elleman, eds. *Naval Mutinies of the Twentieth Century: An International Perspective*. London: Frank Cass, 2003.

Beloff, Max. *Soviet Policy in the Far East 1944–1951*. London: Oxford University Press, 1953.

Benson, Linda. *The Ili Rebellion: The Moslem Challenge to Chinese Authority in Xinjiang 1944–1949*. Armonk, NY: M. E. Sharpe, 1990.

Benson, Linda and Ingvar Svanberg. *China's Last Nomads: The History and Culture of China's Kazaks*. Armonk, NY: M. E. Sharpe, 1998.

Benton, Gregor. "Comparative Perspectives: North China and Central China in the Anti-Japanese Resistance." In *North China at War: The Social Ecology of Revolution, 1937–1945*, edited by Feng Chongyi and David S. F. Goodman, 189–224. Lanham, MD: Rowman & Littlefield, 2000.

Mountain Fires: The Red Army's Three-Year War in South China, 1934–1938. Berkeley: University of California Press, 1992.

New Fourth Army: Communist Resistance along the Yangtze and the Huai 1938–1941. Berkeley: University of California Press, 1999.

Bernstein, Barton J. "Conclusion." In *The End of the Pacific War: Reappraisals*, edited by Tsuyoshi Hasegawa, 228–42. Stanford: Stanford University Press, 2007.

Berton, Peter A. "Northern Defense: Introduction." In *The Fateful Choice: Japan's Advance into Southeast Asia, 1939–1941*, edited by James William Morley, 3–12. New York: Columbia University Press, 1980.

毕健忠 (Bi Jianzhong). "全国解放战争略指导新探" ("A Reexamination of the Guiding Strategy during the War for National Liberation"). 中共党史研究 *(Research on the History of the Chinese Communist Party)*. 1990 no. 4: 25–30.

Bix, Herbert P. *Hirohito and the Making of Modern Japan*. New York: HarperCollins, 2000.

Blumenthal, Tuvia. "戦間期の日本経済" ("The Interwar Japanese Economy"). In 戦間期の日本経済分析 *(An Analysis of the Interwar Japanese Economy)*, 31–52, edited by 中村隆英 (Nakamura Takafusa). Tokyo: 山川出版社, 1981.

Boorman, Howard L., ed. *Biographical Dictionary of Republican China*. 4 vols. New York: Columbia University Press, 1967–71.

Borisov, O. B. *Советский Союз и маньчжурская революционная база 1945–1949 (The Soviet Union and the Manchurian Revolutionary Base 1945–1949)*. Moscow: Издательство «Мысль», 1975.

Borisov, O. B. and B. T. Koloskov, eds. *Soviet-Chinese Relations, 1945–1970*. Bloomington: Indiana University Press, 1975.

Boyd, Carl. *The Extraordinary Envoy: General Hiroshi Ōshima and Diplomacy in the Third Reich, 1934–1939*. Washington, DC: University Press of America, 1980.

Hitler's Japanese Confidant: General Oshima Hiroshi and MAGIC Intelligence, 1941–1945. Lawrence: University Press of Kansas, 1993.

Boyle, John Hunter. *China and Japan at War 1937–1945: The Politics of Collaboration*. Stanford: Stanford University Press, 1972.

Brackman, Arnold C. *The Last Emperor*. New York: Charles Scribner's Sons, 1975.

Brandt, Conrad, Benjamin Schwartz, and John K. Fairbank. *A Documentary History of Chinese Communism*. Cambridge, MA: Harvard University Press, 1952.

Brandt, Loren and Barbara Sands. "Land Concentration and Income Distribution in Republican China." In *Chinese History in Economic Perspective*, edited by Thomas G. Rawski and Lillian M. Li, 179–206. Berkeley: University of California Press, 1992.

Brook, Timothy. *Collaboration: Japanese Agents and Local Elites in Wartime China*. Cambridge, MA: Harvard University Press, 2005.

"The Creation of the Reformed Government in Central China, 1938." In *Chinese Collaboration with Japan, 1932–1945: The Limits of Accommodation*, edited by David P. Barrett and Larry N. Shyu, 79–101. Stanford: Stanford University Press, 2001.

Brooks, Barbara J. *Japan's Imperial Diplomacy: Consuls, Treaty Ports, and War in China 1895–1938*. Honolulu: University of Hawai'i Press, 2000.

Bunker, Gerald E. *The Peace Conspiracy: Wang Ching-wei and the China War, 1937–1941*. Cambridge, MA: Harvard University Press, 1972.

Burkman, Thomas W. *Japan and the League of Nations: Empire and World Order, 1914–1938*. Honolulu: University of Hawai'i Press, 2008.

蔡德金 (Cai Dejin) and 李惠贤 (Li Huixian). "关于汪伪政权问题学术讨论会综述" ("A Summary of the Academic Discussion Concerning the Wang

Jingwei Puppet Regime"). 历史研究 *(Historical Research)* no. 5 (1986): 185–90.

Chamberlin, William Henry. *Japan over Asia*. Boston: Little, Brown, 1938.

Chang, Chi-yun (張其昀). *National Atlas of China*. 5 vols. Taipei: National War College, 1962.

Chang, Jui-te. "抗戰時期大後方工商業者的心態與行動" ("Businessmen of Nationalist China in the Great Rear during the Sino-Japanese War, 1937–1945"). 台灣師範大學歷史學報 (*Taiwan Normal University Bulletin of Historical Research*) no. 27 (June 1999): 121–46.

"Chiang Kai-shek's Coordination of Personal Directives." In *China at War: Regions of China, 1937–1945*, edited by Stephen R. MacKinnon, Diana Lary, and Ezra F. Vogel, 65–87. Stanford: Stanford University Press, 2007.

"The Nationalist Army on the Eve of the War." In *The Battle for China: Essays on the Military History of the Sino-Japanese War of 1937–1945*, edited by Mark Peattie, Edward J. Drea, and Hans van de Ven, 83–104. Stanford: Stanford University Press, 2011.

抗戰時期的國軍人事 *(Personnel Matters of the Nationalist Army during the War of Resistance)*. Taipei: 中央研究院近代史研究所, 1993.

Chang, Jung. *Wild Swans: Three Daughters of China*. New York: Anchor Books, 1991.

Chang, Jung and Jon Halliday. *Mao the Unknown Story*. New York: Alfred A. Knopf, 2005.

Chao, Kang. *The Economic Development of Manchuria: The Rise of a Frontier Economy*. Michigan Papers in Chinese Studies no. 43. Ann Arbor: University of Michigan Center for Chinese Studies, 1982.

Chassin, Lionel Max. *The Communist Conquest of China: A History of the Civil War 1945–1949*. Translated by Timothy Osato and Louis Gelas. Cambridge, MA: Harvard University Press, 1965.

Chen, Jian. *Mao's China and the Cold War*. Chapel Hill: University of North Carolina Press, 2001.

Ch'en, Li-fu. *The Storm Clouds Clear over China: The Memoir of Ch'en Li-fu*. Edited and compiled by Sidney H. Chang and Ramon H. Myers. Stanford: Hoover Institution Press, 1994.

陈梅芳 (Chen Meifang). "试论十年内战时期国民党政府的农村经济政策" ("On the Rural Economic Policy of the Nationalist Government, 1927–1937"). 中国经济史研究 *(Research in Chinese Economic History Quarterly)* 1991 no. 4: 63–76.

Chen, Yin Ching. *Treaties and Agreements between the Republic of China and Other Powers, 1929–1954*. Washington, DC: Sino-American Publishing Service, 1957.

陈英吴 (Chen Yingwu) and 胡充寒 (Hu Chonghan). "抗战初期苏联援华政策的几个问题" ("Some Questions Concerning the Soviet Aid Policy to

China in the Early War of Resistance"). 文史哲 *(Journal of Literature, History, and Philosophy)* 1991 no. 5: 31–5.

Chen, Yung-fa. *Making Revolution: The Communist Movement in Eastern and Central China, 1937–1945*. Berkeley: University of California Press, 1986.

程晓 (Cheng Xiao). "抗日战争初期中国和日本的战略淞沪会战" ("The Chinese and Japanese Strategy in the Shanghai Campaign of the Early War of Resistance against Japan"). 中共党史研究 *(Research on the History of the Chinese Communist Party)* 1995 no. 6: 17–21.

齊錫生 (Ch'i Hsi-sheng). 劍拔弩張的盟友太平洋戰爭期間的中美軍事合作關係 (1941–1945) *(Alliance of Unsheathed Swords and Drawn Bows: Sino-American Military Cooperation during the Pacific War [1941–1945])*. Taipei: 中央研究院聯經出版公司, 2011.

"The Military Dimension, 1942–1945." In *China's Bitter Victory: The War with Japan 1937–1945*, edited by James C. Hsiung and Steven I. Levine, 157–84. Armonk, NY: M. E. Sharpe, 1992.

Nationalist China at War: Military Defeats and Political Collapse, 1937–45. Ann Arbor: University of Michigan Press, 1982.

Chin, Calvin Suey Keu. *A Study of Chinese Dependence upon the Soviet Union for Economic Development as a Factor in Communist China's Foreign Policy*. Hong Kong: Union Research Institute, 1959.

China. Central Archives (中央档案馆), comp. 伪满洲国的统治与内幕 *(The Inside Story and the Rulers of the Puppet State of Manchukuo)*. Beijing: 中华书局, 2000.

Cho Tsun-hung (卓遵宏). "H. H. K'ung and His Monetary Policy for Resistance against the Japanese Invasion (1933–1938)." 台灣師範大學歷史學報 *(Taiwan Normal University Bulletin of Historical Research)* 15 (June 1987): 429–56.

Chudodeev, Iu. V., ed., *По дорогам Китая 1937–1945: Воспоминания (Along the Roads of China 1937–1945: Memoirs)*. Moscow: Издательство «наука» главная редакция восточной литературы, 1989.

中央大学人文科学研究所 (Chūō University Human Sciences Research Center), ed. 日中戦争日本・中国・アメリカ *(The Sino-Japanese War: Japan, China, and America)*. Research publication no. 10. Tokyo: 中央大学出版社, 1993.

Clausewitz, Carl von. *On War*, edited and translated by Michael Howard and Peter Paret. Princeton: Princeton University Press, 1976.

Clodfelter, Michael. *Warfare and Armed Conflicts: A Statistical Reference to Casualty and Other Figures 1618–1991*. Vol. 2. Jefferson, NC: McFarland, 1992.

Clubb, O. Edmund. *China & Russia: The "Great Game."* New York: Columbia University Press, 1971.

Twentieth Century China. New York: Columbia University Press, 1964.

Coble, Parks M. *Facing Japan: Chinese Politics and Japanese Imperialism, 1931–1937*. Cambridge, MA: Harvard University Press, 1991.

"The National Salvation Association as a Political Party." In *Roads Not Taken: The Struggle of Opposition Parties in Twentieth-Century China*, edited by Roger B. Jeans. Boulder, CO: Westview Press, 1992.

中国現代史研究会 (Committee for Research on Modern Chinese History), ed. 中国国民政府史の研究 (Research on the History of the Chinese Republican Government). Tokyo: 汲古書院刊, 1986.

Confucius. *The Analects*. Translated by Raymond Dawson. Oxford: Oxford University Press, 1993.

Conquest, Robert. *Stalin Breaker of Nations*. New York: Penguin Books, 1991.

Cook, Haruko Taya and Theodore F. Cook. *Japan at War: An Oral History*. New York: New Press, 1992.

Coox, Alvin D. *The Anatomy of a Small War: The Soviet-Japanese Struggle for Changkufeng/Khasan, 1938*. Westport, CT: Greenwood Press, 1977.

Nomonhan: Japan against Russia. Stanford: Stanford University Press, 1990.

"The Pacific War." In *The Cambridge History of Japan: The Twentieth Century*, vol. 6, edited by John W. Hall, Marius B. Jansen, Madoka Kanai, and Denis Twitchett, 315–84. Cambridge: Cambridge University Press, 1988.

Corbett, Julian S. *Some Principles of Maritime Strategy*. New York: Longmans, Green and Co., 1911.

Dallin, David J. *The Rise of Russia in Asia*. 1949, reprint; Hamden, CT: Archon Books, 1971.

Dear, I. C. B. *The Oxford Companion to World War II*. Oxford: Oxford University Press, 1995.

邓野 (Deng Ye). "国民党六届二中全会研究" ("A Study of the Second Plenary Conference of the Sixth Central Committee of the Nationalist Party"). 历史研究 *(Historical Research)* 2000 no 1: 3–20.

鄧元忠 (Deng Yuanzhong). "國共第二次合作前的第一次秘密商談接觸：從一份俄文資料談起" ("The First Secret Negotiations and Contacts before the Second Nationalist-Communist United Front: Discussion Based on Russian Documents"). 台灣師範大學歷史學報 *(Taiwan Normal University Bulletin of Historical Research)* 23 (June 1995): 289–310.

Deutscher, Isaac. *The Prophet Armed Trotsky: 1879–1921*. Oxford: Oxford University Press, 1980.

The Prophet Outcast Trotsky: 1929–1940. Oxford: Oxford University Press, 1963.

丁文江 (Ding Wenjiang) et al. eds. 中華民國新地圖 *(New Atlas of the Republic of China)*. 申報六十周年紀念 (Shenbao 60th anniversary edition). Shanghai: 申報館, 1934.

丁晓春 (Ding Xiaochun). "关于建设东北根据地方针的认识" ("On the Policy of Reconstruction in the Northeast Base Area"). 中共党史研究 *(Research on the History of the Chinese Communist Party)* 1990 no. 2: 50–7.

董长芝 (Dong Changzhi). "日本帝国主义对东北工矿业的掠夺及其后果" ("The Plunder of Manchuria's Industry and Mining by Japanese Imperialism and the Consequences"). 中国经济史研究 *(Research in Chinese Economic History)* 1995 no. 4: 106–16.

董卉 (Dong Hui). "南京政府公务员制度1930–1937考析" ("An Examination of the Nanjing Government's Civil Service System [1930–1937]"). 近代史研究 *(Modern Chinese History Studies)* 68 no. 2 (March 1992): 167–85.

董廷之 (Dong Tingzhi). "抗日战争时期国民党统治区的通货膨胀" ("Inflation in Nationalist-ruled Territory during the Anti-Japanese War"). 中共党史研究 *(Research on the History of the Chinese Communist Party)* 1989 no. 2: 36–41.

Dorn, Frank. *Walkout with Stilwell in Burma*. New York: Thomas Y. Crowell, 1971.

Dower, John W. *Embracing Defeat: Japan in the Wake of World War II*. New York: W. W. Norton, 1999.

War without Mercy: Race & Power in the Pacific War. New York: Pantheon Books, 1986.

Drea, Edward J. *In the Service of the Emperor: Essays on the Imperial Japanese Army.* Lincoln: University of Nebraska Press, 1998.

Japan's Imperial Army: Its Rise and Fall, 1853–1945. Lawrence: University Press of Kansas, 2009.

"The Japanese Army on the Eve of the War." In *The Battle for China: Essays on the Military History of the Sino-Japanese War of 1937–1945*, edited by Mark Peattie, Edward J. Drea, and Hans van de Ven, 105–38. Stanford: Stanford University Press, 2011.

MacArthur's ULTRA Codebreaking and the War against Japan, 1942–1945. Lawrence: University Press of Kansas, 1992.

Nomonhan: Japanese Soviet Tactical Combat. Honolulu: University Press of the Pacific, 1981.

Drea, Edward J. and Hans van de Ven, "An Overview of Major Military Campaigns during the Sino-Japanese War, 1937–1945." In *The Battle for China: Essays on the Military History of the Sino-Japanese War of 1937–1945*, edited by Mark Peattie, Edward J. Drea, and Hans van de Ven, 27–47. Stanford: Stanford University Press, 2011.

Dreyer, Edward L. *China at War, 1901–1949*. London: Longman, 1995.

Dryburgh, Marjorie. *North China and Japanese Expansion 1933–1937: Regional Power and Nationalist Interest.* Richmond, Surrey: Curzon, 2000.

"Regional Office and the National Interest: Song Zheyuan in North China, 1933–1937." In *Chinese Collaboration with Japan, 1932–1945: The Limits of Accommodation*, edited by David P. Barrett and Larry N. Shyu, 38–55. Stanford: Stanford University Press, 2001.

杜君 (Du Jun). "1917–1924年苏俄在中东铁路问题上的对华政策再探" ("A Reexamination of Soviet Russia's China Policy Concerning the Chinese Eastern Railway Question from 1917–1924"). 史学集刊 *(Collected Papers of Historical Studies)* (Nov. 2000) no. 4: 36–42.

Duara, Prasenjit. *Sovereignty and Authenticity: Manchukuo and the East Asian Modern.* Lanham, MD: Rowman & Littlefield, 2003.

Eastman, Lloyd E. "Nationalist China during the Sino-Japanese War, 1937–1945." In *The Nationalist Era in China 1927–1945*, edited by Lloyd E. Eastman, Jerome Ch'en, Suzanne Pepper, and Lyman P. van Slyke, 1–52. Cambridge: Cambridge University Press, 1991.

Seeds of Destruction: Nationalist China in War and Revolution 1937–1949. Stanford: Stanford University Press, 1984.

Edgerton, Robert B. *Warriors of the Rising Sun: A History of the Japanese Military.* New York: W. W. Norton, 1997.

江口圭一 (Eguchi Kei-ichi). "中国戦線の日本軍" ("The Japanese Army on the China Front"). In 十五年戦争史 *(A History of the Fifteen Year War)*, vol. 2, edited by 藤原 彰 (Fujiwara Akira) and 今井清一 (Imai Seiichi), 47–86. Tokyo: 青木書店, 1989.

日中アヘン戦争 *(The Japanese-Chinese Opium War)*. Tokyo: 岩波新書, 1988.

十五年戦争小史 *(A Short History of the Fifteen Year War)*. Tokyo: 青木書店, 1996.

証言日中アヘン戦争 *(Testimony for the Japanese-Chinese Opium War)*. Tokyo: 岩波新書, 1991.

Elleman, Bruce A. "The *Chongqing* Mutiny and the Chinese Civil War, 1949." In *Naval Mutinies of the Twentieth Century: An International Perspective*, edited by Christopher M. Bell and Bruce A. Elleman, 232–45. London: Frank Cass, 2003.

Diplomacy and Deception: The Secret History of Sino-Soviet Diplomatic Relations, 1917–1927. Armonk, NY: M. E. Sharpe, 1997.

"The Final Consolidation of the USSR's Sphere of Influence in Outer Mongolia." In *Mongolia in the Twentieth Century: Landlocked Cosmopolitan*, edited by Stephen Kotkin and Bruce A. Elleman, 123–36. Armonk, NY: M. E. Sharpe, 1999.

Modern Chinese Warfare, 1795–1989. London: Routledge, 2001.

Moscow and the Emergence of Communist Power in China, 1925–30: The Nanchang Uprising and the Birth of the Red Army. London: Routledge, 2009.

"The 1940 Soviet Japanese Secret Agreement and Its Impact on the Soviet-Iranian Supply Route." *Working Papers in International Studies*, I-95-5. Hoover Institution, Stanford University (May 1995).

"Soviet Territorial Concessions in China and the May 30th Movement: 1917–1927." *Journal of Oriental Studies* 32 no. 2 (1994): 162–81.

Wilson and China: A Revised History of the Shandong Question. Armonk, NY: M. E. Sharpe, 2002.

Elleman, Bruce A. and Stephen Kotkin, eds. *Manchurian Railways and the Opening of China: An International History*. Armonk, NY: M. E. Sharpe, 2010.

Elleman, Bruce A. and S. C. M. Paine. "Japanese Immigration to Manchukuo and Its Impact on the USSR." *Working Series in International Studies*, I-95-6. Hoover Institution, Stanford University (June 1995).

Modern China Continuity and Change 1644 to the Present. Boston: Prentice Hall, 2010.

eds. *Naval Blockades and Seapower: Strategies and Counter-strategies, 1805–2005*. London: Routledge, 2006.

eds. *Naval Expeditionary Warfare: Peripheral Campaigns and New Theaters of Naval Warfare*. Abingdon, UK: Routledge, 2011.

Esherick, Joseph W. "Revolution in a 'Feudal Fortress': Yangjiagou, Mizhi County, Shaanxi, 1937–1948." In *North China at War: The Social Ecology of Revolution, 1937–1945*, edited by Feng Chongyi and David S. F. Goodman, 59–92. Lanham, MD: Rowman & Littlefield, 2000.

Evans, David C. and Mark R. Peattie. *Kaigun: Strategy, Tactics, and Technology in the Imperial Japanese Navy 1887–1941*. Annapolis, MD: Naval Institute Press, 1997.

Ewing, Thomas E. *Between the Hammer and the Anvil? Chinese and Russian Policies in Outer Mongolia, 1911–1921*. Indiana University Uralic and Altaic Studies. Vol. 138. Bloomington, IN: Research Institute for Inner Asian Studies, 1980.

Fairbank, John King, ed. *The Cambridge History of China*. Vol. 12. Cambridge: Cambridge University Press, 1983.

Fenby, Jonathan. *Chiang Kai-shek China's Generalissimo and the Nation He Lost*. New York: Carroll & Graf Publishers, 2003.

"Zhang Xueliang." *Independent*, 16 October 2001.

Feng, Chongyi. "The Making of the Jin Sui Base Area." In *North China at War: The Social Ecology of Revolution, 1937–1945*, edited by Feng Chongyi and David S. F. Goodman, 155–72. Lanham, MD: Rowman & Littlefield, 2000.

Feuerwerker, Albert, "Economic Trends, 1912–49." In *The Cambridge History of China*, vol. 12, edited by John K. Fairbank, 28–127. Cambridge: Cambridge University Press, 1983.

Forbes, Andrew D. W. *Warlords and Muslims in Chinese Central Asia: A Political History of Republican Sinkiang 1911–1949*. Cambridge: Cambridge University Press, 1986.

Fox, John P. *Germany and the Far Eastern Crisis 1931–1938: A Study in Diplomacy and Ideology.* Oxford: Clarendon Press, 1982.

Frank, Richard B. *Downfall: The End of the Imperial Japanese Empire.* New York: Random House, 1999.

"Ketsu Gō: Japanese Political and Military Strategy in 1945." In *The End of the Pacific War: Reappraisals*, edited by Tsuyoshi Hasegawa, 65–94. Stanford: Stanford University Press, 2007.

Frédéric, Louis. *Japan Encyclopedia.* Translated by Käthe Roth. Cambridge, MA: Harvard University Press, 2002.

藤原 彰 (Fujiwara Akira). 日本軍事史 *(Japanese Military History).* Vol. 1. Tokyo: 日本評論社, 1987.

"太平洋战争爆发后的日中战争" ("The Sino-Japanese War after the Outbreak of the Pacific War"), translated by 解莉莉 (Xie Lili). 中共党史研究 *(Research on the History of the Chinese Communist Party)* 1989 no. 1: 79–85.

藤原 彰 (Fujiwara Akira) and 今井清一 (Imai Seiichi), eds. 十五年戦争史 *(A History of the Fifteen Year War).* 3 vols. Tokyo: 青木書店, 1989.

Fuller, Richard. *Shōkan Hirohito's Samurai: Leaders of the Japanese Armed Forces, 1926–1945.* London: Arms and Armour, 1992.

古厩忠夫 (Furumaya Tadao). "日本軍占領地域の「清郷」工作と抗戦" ("The War of Resistance and 'Village Purification' Work in Areas under Japanese Military Occupation"). In 抗日戦争と中国民衆 *(The War of Japanese Resistance and the Chinese Populace),* edited by 池田誠 (Ikeda Makoto), 178–99. Tokyo: 法律文化社, 1987.

古屋哲夫 (Furuya Tetsuo). "「満洲国」の創出" ("Creation of 'Manchukuo'"). In 「満洲国」の研究 *(Research on "Manchukuo"),* edited by 山本有造 (Yamamoto Yūzō), 39–82. Tokyo: 緑蔭書房, 1995.

干于黎 (Gan Yuli). "抗战前期国民党地方财政收入状况述略" ("A Brief Narrative of the Nationalist Government's Local Finance and Income in the Early Period of the War of Resistance"). 中国社会经济史研究 *(Research on Chinese Social and Economic History)* 1989 no. 3: 86–91.

高乐才 (Gao Lecai). "日本'百万户移民'国策评析" ("Evaluation and Analysis of the Japanese Policy of 'One Million Households of Immigrants'"). 历史研究 *(Historical Research)* 1999 no. 3: 114–25.

Garthoff, Raymond L. "Sino-Soviet Military Relations, 1945–66." In *Sino-Soviet Military Relations*, ed. Raymond L. Garthoff, 82–99. New York: Frederick A. Praeger, 1966.

Garver, John W. "Chiang Kai-shek's Quest for Soviet Entry into the Sino-Japanese War." *Political Science Quarterly* 102 no. 2 (Summer 1987): 295–316.

"China's Wartime Diplomacy." In *China's Bitter Victory: The War with Japan 1937–1945*, edited by James C. Hsiung and Steven I. Levine, 3–32. Armonk, NY: M. E. Sharpe, 1992.

Chinese-Soviet Relations 1937–1945: The Diplomacy of Chinese Nationalism. New York: Oxford University Press, 1988.

The Sino-American Alliance: Nationalist China and American Cold War Strategy in Asia. Armonk, NY: M. E. Sharpe, 1997.

Gatchel, Theodore. "The Shortest Road to Tokyo: Nimitz and the Central Pacific War." In *The Pacific War Companion from Pearl Harbor to Hiroshima*, edited by Daniel Marston, 159–78. Oxford: Osprey, 2000.

Gatu, Dagfinn. *Village China at War: The Impact of Resistance to Japan 1937–1945*. Vancouver: UBC Press, 2008.

Gillin, Donald G. "Problems of Centralization in Republican China: The Case of Ch'en Ch'eng and the Kuomintang." *Journal of Asian Studies* 29 no. 4 (Aug. 1970): 835–50.

Glantz, David M. *The Soviet Strategic Offensive in Manchuria, 1945* 'August Storm'. London: Frank Cass, 2003.

Gol'dberg, David Isaakovich. *Внешняя политика Японии в 1941–1945 гг. (The Foreign Policy of Japan 1941–1945)*. Moscow: Издательство социально-экономической литературы, 1962.

Внешняя политика Японии (сентябрь 1939 г. –декабрь 1941 г.) (The Foreign Policy of Japan [September 1939–December 1941]). Moscow: Издательство восточной литературы, 1959.

Goncharov, Sergei N., John W. Lewis, and Xue Litai. *Uncertain Partners: Stalin, Mao, and the Korean War*. Stanford: Stanford University Press, 1993.

Goodman, David S. G. *Social and Political Change in Revolutionary China: The Taihang Base Area in the War of Resistance to Japan, 1937–1945*. Lanham, MD: Rowman & Littlefield, 2000.

Gottschang, Thomas R. and Diana Lary. *Swallows and Settlers: The Great Migration from North China to Manchuria*. Ann Arbor: University of Michigan Press, 2000.

Grasso, June, Jay Corrin, and Michael Kort. *Modernization and Revolution in China: From the Opium Wars to World War*. 3rd ed. Armonk, NY: M. E. Sharpe, 2004.

Greene, J. Megan. *The Origins of the Developmental State in Taiwan*. Cambridge, MA: Harvard University Press, 2008.

Gruhl, Werner. *Imperial Japan's World War Two 1931–1945*. New Brunswick, NJ: Transaction Publishers, 2007.

Gunther, John. *Inside Asia*, 31st ed. New York: Harper & Brothers, 1939.

郭希华 (Guo Xihua). "抗日战争时期中国损失调查及赔偿问题" ("Problems of Assessing China's Losses during the War of Resistance against Japan and the Question of Reparations"). 历史研究 *(Historical Research)* 1995 no. 5: 177–81.

Hagiwara, Mitsuru. "The Japanese Air Campaigns in China, 1937–1945." In *The Battle for China: Essays on the Military History of the Sino-Japanese War of 1937–1945*, edited by Mark Peattie, Edward J. Drea, and Hans van de Ven, 237–55. Stanford: Stanford University Press, 2011.

Handel, Michael I. *Masters of War: Classical Strategic Thought*. 3rd ed. London: Frank Cass, 2001.

Hane, Mikiso. *Peasants, Rebels, Women, and Outcasts: The Underside of Modern Japan*. 2nd ed. Lanham, MD: Rowman & Littlefield, 1982.

原朗 (Hara Akira). "一九三〇年代の満州経済統制政策" ("The Manchurian Economic Controls Policy in the 1930s"). In 日本帝国主義下の満州 *(Manchuria under Japanese Imperialism)*, edited by 満州史研究会 (Manchurian History Research Committee), 1–114. Tokyo: 御茶の水書房, 1972.

Hara, Takeshi. "The Ichigō Offensive." In *The Battle for China: Essays on the Military History of the Sino-Japanese War of 1937–1945*, edited by Mark Peattie, Edward J. Drea, and Hans van de Ven, 392–402. Stanford: Stanford University Press, 2011.

Harries, Meirion and Susie Harries. *Soldiers of the Sun: The Rise and the Fall of the Imperial Japanese Army*. New York: Random House, 1991.

Harris, William H. and Judith S. Levey. *The New Columbia Encyclopedia*. 4th ed. New York: Columbia University Press, 1975.

Hasegawa, Tsuyoshi, ed. *The End of the Pacific War: Reappraisals*. Stanford: Stanford University Press, 2007.

Racing the Enemy: Stalin, Truman, and the Surrender of Japan. Cambridge, MA: Harvard University Press, 2005.

Hasiotis, Jr., Arthur C. *Soviet Political, Economic, and Military Involvement in Sinkiang from 1928 to 1949*. New York: Garland Publishing, 1987.

Haslam, Jonathan. *The Soviet Union and the Threat from the East, 1933–1941*. Pittsburgh: University of Pittsburgh Press, 1992.

Hata, Ikuhiko. "The Japanese Soviet Confrontation, 1935–1939." In *Deterrent Diplomacy: Japan, Germany, and the USSR 1935–1940*, edited by James William Morley, 129–78. New York: Columbia University Press, 1976.

Hattori, Satoshi and Edward J. Drea. "Japanese Operations from July to December 1937." In *The Battle for China: Essays on the Military History of the Sino-Japanese War of 1937–1945*, edited by Mark Peattie, Edward J. Drea, and Hans van de Ven, 159–80. Stanford: Stanford University Press, 2011.

Hayashi, Saburo and Alvin D. Coox. *Kōgun: The Japanese Army in the Pacific*. Quantico, VA: Marine Corps Association, 1959.

何迪 (He Di). "1945–1949年中国共产党对美国政策的演变" ("The Evolution of the Chinese Communist Party's Policy Regarding the United States, 1945–1949"). 历史研究 *(Historical Research)* 1987 no. 3: 15–23.

Heinzig, Dieter. *The Soviet Union and Communist China 1945–1950*. Armonk, NY: M. E. Sharpe, 2004.

Herrmann, Albert. *An Historical Atlas of China*. 1935 reprint; Chicago: Aldine Publishing, 1966.

疋田康行 (Hikida Yasuyuki). "財政・金融構造" ("Public Finance and Credit Organizations"). In 日本帝国主義の満州支配—一五年戦争期を中心に— *(Manchuria under Japanese Imperialism, Focusing on the Fifteen Year War Period)*, edited by 小林英夫 (Kobayashi Hideo) and 浅田喬二 (Asada Kyōji), 819–926. Tokyo: 時潮社, 1986.

姫田光義 (Himeta Mitsuyoshi). "三光政策・三光作戦をめぐって" ("The Three Alls Policy and Three Alls Military Strategy"). In 日中戦争日本・中国・アメリカ *(The Sino-Japanese War: Japan, China, and America)*, edited by 中央大学人文科学研究所 (Chūō University Human Sciences Research Center), 107–56. Research publication no. 10. Tokyo: 中央大学出版社, 1993.

姫田光義 (Himeta Mitsuyoshi), et al. 中国２０世紀史 *(Twentieth Century Chinese History)*. Tokyo: Tokyo University Press, 2000.

平賀明彦 (Hiraga Akihiko). "日中戦争の拡大と農業政策の転換一１９３２ー１９３９年の農業生産力維持、拡充策を中心として一" ("The Expansion of Japan's War in China and the Change in Agricultural Policy, 1932–1939"). 歴史学研究 (*Journal of Historical Studies*) no. 545 (September 1985): 1–17.

平野和由 (Hirano Kazuyoshi). "中国の金融構造と幣制改革" ("The Financial Structure of China and the Currency Reform"). In 中国の幣制改革と国際関係 *(China's Currency Reform and International Relations)*, edited by 野沢豊 (Nozawa Yutaka), 55–86. Tokyo: University of Tokyo Press, 1981.

歴史学研究会 (Historical Research Center), comp. *История войны на Тихом океане (History of the Pacific War)*. Translated by B. V. Pospelova. 5 vols. Moscow: Издательство иностранной литературы, 1957–8.

Hitler, Adolf. *Mein Kampf*. Translated by Ralph Manheim. 1925, reprint; Boston: Houghton Mifflin, 1971.

Hobbes, Thomas. *Leviathan*. 1651, reprint; Cleveland: Meridian Books, 1963.

Holloway, David. "Jockeying for Position in the Postwar World: Soviet Entry into the War with Japan in August 1945." In *The End of the Pacific War: Reappraisals*, edited by Tsuyoshi Hasegawa, 145–88. Stanford: Stanford University Press, 2007.

Holwitt, Joel. "Unrestricted Submarine Victory: The U.S. Submarine Campaign Against Japan." In *Commerce Raiding and State-sponsored Piracy*, edited by Bruce A. Elleman and S. C. M. Paine. Newport, RI: U.S. Naval War College Press, forthcoming.

Hoover Institution Archives. Stanford University. Papers of Stanley K. Hornbeck, Vladimir D. Pastuhov, Gilbert Stuart, Ray Lyman Wilbur.

Horner, David. "General MacArthur's War: The South and Southwest Pacific Campaigns 1942–1945." In *The Pacific War Companion from Pearl Harbor to Hiroshima*, edited by Daniel Marston, 119–42. Oxford: Osprey, 2000.

細谷千博 (Hosoya Chihiro). "The Japanese-Soviet Neutrality Pact." In *The Fateful Choice: Japan's Advance into Southeast Asia, 1939–1941*, edited by James William Morley, 13–114. New York: Columbia University Press, 1980.

"The Tripartite Pact, 1939–1940." In *Deterrent Diplomacy: Japan, Germany, and the USSR 1935–1940*, edited by James William Morley, 191–258. New York: Columbia University Press, 1976.

本間長世 (Homma Nagayo), 入江昭 (Iriye Akira) and 波多野澄雄 (Hatano Sumio), eds. 太平洋戦争 *(The Pacific War)*. Tokyo: University of Tokyo Press, 1993.

Howe, Christopher. *The Origins of Japanese Trade Supremacy*. Chicago: University of Chicago Press, 1996.

Hoye, Timothy. *Japanese Politics: Fixed and Floating Worlds*. Upper Saddle River, NJ: Prentice Hall, 1999.

Hsia, Taotai. "Wartime Judicial Reform in China." In *China's Bitter Victory: The War with Japan 1937–1945*, edited by James C. Hsiung and Steven I. Levine, 275–94. Armonk, NY: M. E. Sharpe, 1992.

Hsiung, James C. and Steven I. Levine, eds. *China's Bitter Victory: The War with Japan 1937–1945*. Armonk, NY: M. E. Sharpe, 1992.

Hsu, Long-hsuen and Chang Ming-kai. *History of the Sino-Japanese War (1937–1945)*. Translated by Wen Ha-hsiung, 2nd ed. Taipei: Chung Wu Publishing, 1972.

Hsu, Shuhsi. *The War Conduct of the Japanese*. Shanghai: Kelly and Walsh, 1938.

Hu, Xinjun. "The Road to the Post-Yalta System: China's Challenge to the United States in the New World Order, 1945–1949." Ph.D diss., Southern Illinois University at Carbondale, 1996.

黄道炫 (Huang Daoxuan). "关于蒋介石第一次下野的几个问题" ("Several Questions Concerning Chiang Kai-shek's First Exit from the Political Arena"). 近代史研究 *(Modern Chinese History Studies)* 1999 no. 4: 138–61.

黄立人 (Huang Liren). "抗日战争时期公厂内迁的考察" ("A Study of Moving Factories into the Chinese Hinterland during the War of

Resistance against Japan"). 历史研究 *(Historical Research)* 1994 no. 4: 120–36.

Huang, Meizhen and Hanqing Yang. "Nationalist China's Negotiating Position during the Stalemate, 1938–1945." Translated by David P. Barrett. In *Chinese Collaboration with Japan, 1932–1945: The Limits of Accommodation*, edited by David P. Barrett and Larry N. Shyu, 56–78. Stanford: Stanford University Press, 2001.

黄正林 (Huang Zhenglin). "边钞与抗战时期陕甘宁边区的金融事业" ("Research on the Currency of the Shaanxi-Gansu-Ningxia Border Region and the Region's Financial Enterprises in the War of Resistance"). 近代史研究 *(Modern Chinese History Studies)* 1999 no. 2: 192–223.

Hunter, Janet E., comp. *Concise Dictionary of Modern Japanese History.* Berkeley: University of California Press, 1984.

市來俊男 (Ichiki Toshio). "海軍の開戦準備" ("The Navy's Preparations for the Opening of the War"). In 近代日本戦争史 *(Modern Japanese Military History)*, vol. 4 大東亜戦争 (*The Great East Asian War*), edited by 奥村房夫 (Okumura Fusao) and 近藤新治 (Kondō Shinji), 337–70. Tokyo: 同台経済懇話会, 1995.

Ienaga, Saburō. *The Pacific War 1931–1945*. Translated by Frank Baldwin. New York: Pantheon Books, 1978.

飯島満 (Iijima Mitsuru). "満洲国における「軍警統合」の成立と崩壊" ("Establishment and Collapse of the 'Combined Army-Police' in Manchukuo"). 駿台史学 *(Sundai Historical Review)* 108 (Dec. 1999): 45–66.

Ike, Nobutaka, trans. and ed. *Japan's Decision for War: Records of the 1941 Policy Conferences*. Stanford: Stanford University Press, 1967.

池田 誠 (Ikeda Makoto), ed. 抗日戦争と中国民衆 *(The War of Japanese Resistance and the Chinese Populace)*. Tokyo: 法律文化社, 1987.

井上 清 (Inōe Kyoshi) and 衛藤瀋吉 (Etō Shinkichi), eds. 日中戦争と日中関係 (*The Sino-Japanese War and Sino-Japanese Relations*). Tokyo: 原書房, 1988.

Iriye, Akira. *The Cambridge History of American Foreign Relations*. Vol. 3, *The Globalizing of America, 1913–1945*. Cambridge: Cambridge University Press, 1993.

Ishii, Kikujiro. *Diplomatic Commentaries*. Translated by William R. Langdon. Baltimore: Johns Hopkins Press, 1936.

石島紀之 (Ishijima Noriyuki). 中国抗日戦争史 *(A History of China's Anti-Japanese War)*. Tokyo: 青木書店, 1984.

日中全面戦争の衝撃—中国の国民統合と社会構造" ("The Impact of the Total War between Japan and China: China's National Integration and Social Structure"). In 太平洋戦争 *(The Pacific War)*, edited by 細谷千博 (Hosoya Chihiro) et al., 463–82. Tokyo: University of Tokyo Press, 1993.

"国民党政権の対日抗戦力" ("The Military Strength against Japan of the Nationalist Regime"). In 講座中国近現代史 *(Series of Studies in*

Modern and Contemporary Chinese History), vol. 6, 抗日戦争 *(The Anti-Japanese War)*, edited by 野沢豊 (Nozawa Yutaka), et al., 31–63. Tokyo: University of Tokyo Press, 1978.

石川禎浩 (Ishikawa Yoshihiro). "南京政府時期の技術官僚の形成と発展" ("The Formation and Development of Technocrats in Nationalist China"). 史林 *(Journal of History)* 74 no. 2 (March 1991): 1–33.

Itoh, Takeo. *China's Challenge in Manchuria: Anti-Japanese Activities in Manchuria Prior to the Manchurian Incident*. Dalian?: South Manchuria Railway Co., 1932?

糸永 新 (Itonaga Arata). "開戦前の日米戦争計画" ("Pre-war Japanese and U.S. War Plans"). In 近代日本戦争史 *(Modern Japanese Military History)*, vol. 4 大東亜戦争 (*The Great East Asian War*), edited by 奥村房夫 (Okumura Fusao) and 近藤新治 (Kondō Shinji), 279–93. Tokyo: 同台経済懇話会, 1995.

Iwao, Seiichi, ed. *Biographical Dictionary of Japanese History*. Translated by Burton Watson. Tokyo: Kodansha International, 1978.

Jacobs, Dan M. *Borodin: Stalin's Man in China*. Cambridge, MA: Harvard University Press, 1981.

Jagchid, Sechin. *The Last Mongol Prince: The Life and Times of Demchugdongrob, 1902–1966*. Bellingham, WA: Center for East Asian Studies, Western Washington University, 1999.

防衛庁防衛研究所図書館 (Japan. Defense Agency. Defense Research Center Archives). (Abbreviated as JDA.)

防衛庁防衛研修所戦史部 (Japan. Defense Agency. National Defense College. Military History Department), ed. 関東軍 *(The Kantō Army)*. Vols. 1–2. Tokyo: 朝雲新聞社, 1969, 1974.

ed. 北支の治安戦 *(The North China Insurgency)*. Vols. 1–2. Tokyo: 朝雲新聞社, 1968.

外務省外交史料館 (Japan. Foreign Ministry. Diplomatic History Archive). 日本外交史辞典編纂委員会 (The Committee for Compiling a Dictionary on Japanese Diplomatic History), comp. 日本外交史辞典 *(The Japanese Diplomatic History Dictionary)*. Tokyo: 山川出版社, 1992.

外務省外交資料館 (Japan. Foreign Ministry. Diplomatic Records Office). (Abbreviated as JFM.)

Japanese Delegation to the League of Nations. *The Manchurian Question: Japan's Case in the Sino-Japanese Dispute as Presented before the League of Nations*. Geneva: Japanese Delegation to the League of Nations, 1933.

Jarman, Robert L. ed. *China Political Reports 1911–1960*. Vols. 4–9. Chippenham, Wilts: Archive Editions, 2001.

贾兴权 (Jia Xingquan). "抗战期间通货膨胀政策对中国社会的影响" ("Influence of Inflationary Policies on Chinese Society during the Sino-

Japanese War"). 中国经济史研究 *(Research in Chinese Economic History)* 1993 no. 1.

姜思毅 (Jiang Siyi). "毛泽东军事思想论纲" ("A Sketch of Mao Zedong's Military Thought"). 中共党史研究 *(Research on the History of the Chinese Communist Party)* 1994 no. 1: 19–24.

蒋永敬 (Jiang Yongjing). "南京国民政府初期实施训政的背景及挫折—军权，党权，民权的较量" ("The Background and Setbacks of the Implementation of Political Tutelage during the Early Period of the Nationalist Government in Nanjing – the Competition among Military, Party, and People's Rights"). 近代史研究 *(Modern Chinese History Studies)*, 77 no. 5 (September 1993): 80–101.

"西安事变前张学良所谓'一二月内定有变动'何指?" ("What Did Zhang Xueliang Mean in His Pre-Xi'an Incident So-called 'Required Changes in One or Two Months'?"). 近代史研究 *(Modern Chinese History Studies)* 1997 no. 1: 266–72.

金安泰 (Jin Antai). "'九一八'事变与美国外交" ("The Manchurian Incident and U.S. Foreign Policy"). 史学集刊 *(Collected Papers of Historical Studies)* (1983), 12 no. 3: 73–80.

金冲及 (Jin Chongji)."华北事变和抗日救亡高潮的兴起" ("The North China Incident and the High Tide of the Resist Japan-Save the Nation Movement"). 历史研究 *(Historical Research)* no. 4 (1995): 3–22.

金光耀 (Jin Guangyao). "1932年中苏复交谈判中的何士渠道" ("The Mediation of Hussey during the 1932 Negotiations to Restore Sino-Soviet Diplomatic Relations"). 近代史研究 *(Modern Chinese History Studies)* 1999 no. 2: 305–14.

国民党在美国的游说活动—以顾维钧为中心的讨论" ("Nationalist Lobbying in the United States: A Case Study on Wellington Koo"). 历史研究 *(Historical Research)* 2000 no. 4: 61–72.

金普森 (Jin Pusen) and 王国华 (Wang Guohua). "南京国民政府1933–1937年之内债" ("The Internal Debt of the Nanjing Government 1933–37"). 中国社会经济史研究 *(Research on Chinese Social and Economic History)* 1993 no. 2: 81–8.

"南京国民政府1927–1931年之内债" ("The Internal Debt of the Nanjing Government, 1927–1937"). 中国社会经济史研究 *(Research on Chinese Social and Economic History)*. 1991 no. 4: 96–103.

Jones, F. C. *Japan's New Order in East Asia: Its Rise and Fall 1937–1945*. London: Oxford University Press, 1954.

Manchuria Since 1931. London: Royal Institute of International Affairs, 1949.

Jordan, Donald A. *China's Trial by Fire: The Shanghai War of 1932*. Ann Arbor: University of Michigan Press, 2001.

Chinese Boycotts versus Japanese Bombs: The Failure of China's "Revolutionary Diplomacy," 1931–32. Ann Arbor: University of Michigan Press, 1991.

The Northern Expedition: China's National Revolution of 1926–1928. Honolulu: University of Hawai'i Press, 1976.

巨文辉 (Ju Wenhui). "晋察冀边区实施的统一累进税述略" ("A Brief Account of Unified Progressive Taxation in the Shanxi-Chahar-Hebei Border Area"). 中共党史研究 *(Research on the History of the Chinese Communist Party)*. 1996 no. 2: 37–41.

居之芬 (Ju Zhifen). "日本对华北经济的统制和掠夺" ("Japanese Economic Control and Plunder of North China"). 历史研究 *(Historical Research)*. 1995 no. 2: 95–106.

"抗战时期日本对华北沦陷区劳工的劫掠和催残" ("Japanese Looting and Humiliation of Workers in Occupied Areas of North China during the Anti-Japanese War"). 中共党史研究 *(Research on the History of the Chinese Communist Party)*. 1994 no. 4: 325–8.

"Labor Conscription in North China: 1941–1945." In *China at War: Regions of China, 1937–1945*, edited by Stephen R. MacKinnon, Diana Lary, and Ezra F. Vogel, 207–26. Stanford: Stanford University Press, 2007.

居之芬 (Ju Zhifen) and 华杰 (Hua Jie). "日本'北支那开发株式会社'的经济活动及略夺" ("The Economic Activities and the Plunder of Japan's 'North China Development Co.'"). 近代史研究 *(Modern Chinese History Studies)*. 77 no. 5 (September 1993): 245–67.

Kahn, Jr., E.J. *The China Hands: America's Foreign Service Officers and What Befell Them*. New York: Viking Press, 1972.

Kahn, Winston. "Doihara Kenji and the North China Autonomy Movement." In *China and Japan: Search for Balance since World War I*, edited by Alvin D. Coox and Hilary Conroy, 177–210. Santa Barbara, CA: ABC-Clio, 1978.

Kaiser, David E. *Economic Diplomacy and the Origins of the Second World War*. Princeton: Princeton University Press, 1980.

Kalyagin, Aleksandr Ya. *Along Alien Roads*. Translated by Steven I. Levine. *Occasional Papers of the East Asian Institute*. New York: Columbia University, 1983.

神田文人 (Kanda Fuhito). "「天皇制」と戦争" ("'The Emperor System' and the War"). In 十五年戦争史 *(A History of the Fifteen Year War)*, vol. 3, edited by 藤原 彰 (Fujiwara Akira) and 今井清一 (Imai Seiichi), 37–80. Tokyo: 青木書店, 1989.

Kapp, Robert A. *Szechwan and the Chinese Republic: Provincial Militarism and Central Power, 1911–1938*. New Haven: Yale University Press, 1973.

香島明雄 (Kashima Akio). 中ソ外交史研究１９３７－１９４６ *(Research on Sino-Soviet Diplomatic History, 1937–1946)*. Tokyo: 世界思想社, 1990.

Katkova, Zoia Dmitrievna. *Китай и державы 1927–1937 (China and the Powers 1927–1937)*. Moscow: «Восточная литература» РАН, 1995.

加藤公一 (Katō Kōichi). "中国共産党の対米認識とソ連の対日参戦問題、１９４４－１９４５年 一「喪失した機会」と「独立自主」一" ("The Chinese Communist Party's Recognition of the United States and the Soviet Entry into the War against Japan, 1944–1945 : 'A Lost Opportunity' and "Maintaining Independence and Initiative'"). 歴史学研究 *(Journal of Historical Studies)* 751 (July 2001): 32–51.

加藤豊隆 (Katō Toyotaka). 満洲国警察小史一満洲国権力の実態について *(A Short History of the Manchukuo Police: The Actual Situation of Manchukuo Sovereignty)*. Tokyo: 第一法規出版株式会社, 1968.

Kawakami, K. K. *Japan in China: Her Motives and Aims*. London: John Murray, 1938.

Manchoukuo Child of Conflict. New York: Macmillan, 1933.

風間秀人 (Kazama Hideto). "農村行政支配" ("The Management of Rural Administration"). In 日本帝国主義の満州支配一一五年戦争期を中心に一 *(Manchuria under Japanese Imperialism, Focusing on the Fifteen Year War Period)*, edited by 小林英夫 (Kobayashi Hideo) and 浅田喬二 (Asada Kyōji), 255–326. Tokyo: 時潮社, 1986.

Kenez, Peter. *Civil War in South Russia: The Defeat of the Whites*. Berkeley: University of California Press, 1977.

Kifner, John. "John Serice, a Purged 'China Hand,' Dies at 89." *New York Times* (4 Feb. 1999): B11.

菊池一隆 (Kikuchi Kazutaka). "抗日戦争時期の中国工業工作運動" ("The Chinese Industrial Cooperative Movement during the Anti-Japanese War"). 歴史学研究 *(Journal of Historical Studies)* no. 486 (November 1980): 29–45.

"重慶政府の戦時金融"("Wartime Finances of the Chongqing Government"). In 中国国民政府史の研究 *(Research on the History of the Chinese Republican Government)*, edited by 中国現代史研究会 (Committee for Research on Modern Chinese History), 373–410. Tokyo: 汲古書院刊, 1986.

菊池貴晴 (Kikuchi Takaharu). "中国革命における第三勢力の成立と展開" ("The Formation and Development of a Third Power in the Chinese Revolution"). In 講座中国近現代史 *(Series of Studies in Modern and Contemporary Chinese History)*, vol. 7, 中国革命の勝利 (*Victory in the Chinese Revolution*), edited by 野沢豊 (Nozawa Yutaka), et al., 87–136. Tokyo: University of Tokyo Press, 1978.

Kikuoka, Michael T. *The Changkufeng Incident: A Study in Soviet-Japanese Conflict, 1938*. Lanham, MD: University Press of America, 1988.

君島和彦 (Kimishima Kazuhiko). "鉱工業支配の開発" ("Development of the Management of Mining and Manufacturing"). In 日本帝国主義の満州支配—一五年戦争期を中心に— *(Manchuria under Japanese Imperialism, Focusing on the Fifteen Year War Period)*, edited by 小林英夫 (Kobayashi Hideo) and 浅田喬二 (Asada Kyōji), 547–673. Tokyo: 時潮社, 1986.

"「東亜新秩序」と植民地・占領地" ("'New East Asian Order' and Colonial and Occupied Areas"). In 十五年戦争史 *(A History of the Fifteen Year War)*, vol. 2, edited by 藤原 彰 (Fujiwara Akira) and 今井清一 (Imai Seiichi), 87–140. Tokyo: 青木書店, 1989.

Kinney, Ann Rasmussen. *Japanese Investment in Manchurian Manufacturing, Mining, Transportation and Communications 1931–1945*. New York: Garland, 1982.

Kirby, S. Woodburn. *The War against Japan*. 5 vols. London: Her Majesty's Stationery Office, 1957–1969.

Kirby, William C. "The Chinese War Economy." In *China's Bitter Victory: The War with Japan 1937–1945*, edited by James C. Hsiung and Steven I. Levine, 185–212. Armonk, NY: M.E. Sharpe, 1992.

北岡伸一 (Kitaoka Shin'ichi). 日本陸軍と大陸政策１９０６–１９１８年 *(The Japanese Army and Its Strategy for the Asian Mainland 1906–1918)*. Tokyo: 東京大学出版社, 1985.

Klein, Donald W. and Anne B. Clark. *Biographic Dictionary of Chinese Communism 1921–1965*. 2 vols. Cambridge, MA: Harvard University Press, 1971.

小林英夫 (Kobayashi Hideo). "満州金融構造の再編成過程—一九三〇年代前半期を中心として—" ("The Course of the Reforms of the Manchurian Financial System, Focusing on the Early 1930s"). In 日本帝国主義下の満州 *(Manchuria under Japanese Imperialism)*, edited by 満州史研究会 (Manchurian History Research Committee), 115–212. Tokyo: 御茶の水書房, 1972.

「満州国」の形成と崩壊 ("The Creation and Collapse of 'Manchukuo'"). In 日本帝国主義の満州支配—一五年戦争期を中心に— *(Manchuria under Japanese Imperialism, Focusing on the Fifteen Year War Period)*, edited by 小林英夫 (Kobayashi Hideo) and 浅田喬二 (Asada Kyōji), 17–92. Tokyo: 時潮社, 1986.

"幣制改革をめぐる日本と中国" ("Japan, China, and the Currency Reform"). In 中国の幣制改革と国際関係 *(China's Currency Reform and International Relations)*, edited by 野沢豊 (Nozawa Yutaka), 233–64. Tokyo: University of Tokyo Press, 1981.

"日本の「満州」支配と抗日運動" ("Japanese Rule in 'Manchukuo' and the Anti-Japanese Movement"). In 講座中国近現代史 *(Series of Studies in Modern and Contemporary Chinese History)*, vol. 6, 抗日戦争 *(The Anti-Japanese War)*, edited by 野沢豊 (Nozawa Yutaka), et al., 219–54. Tokyo: University of Tokyo Press, 1978.

小林英夫 (Kobayashi Hideo) and 浅田喬二 (Asada Kyōji), eds. 日本帝国主義の満州支配——五年戦争期を中心に— *(Manchuria under Japanese Imperialism, Focusing on the Fifteen Year War Period)*. Tokyo: 時潮社, 1986.

小林道彦 (Kobayashi Michihiko). "世界大戦と大陸政策の変容" ("The Transformation of Japan's Continental Policy during the World War I, 1914–1916"). 歴史学研究 *(Journal of Historical Studies)* 657 no. 4 (1994): 1–15.

Komatsu, Keiichiro. *Origins of the Pacific War and the Importance of 'Magic'*. New York: St. Martin's Press, 1999.

近藤新治 (Kondō Shinji). "陸軍の開戦準備" ("The Army's Preparations for Opening the War"). In 近代日本戦争史 *(Modern Japanese Military History)*, vol. 4 大東亜戦争 *(The Great East Asian War)*, edited by 奥村房夫 (Okumura Fusao) and 近藤新治 (Kondō Shinji), 317–36. Tokyo: 同台経済懇話会, 1995.

"「物的国力判断」" ("'An Evaluation of National Material Strength.'" In 近代日本戦争史 *(Modern Japanese Military History)*, vol. 4 大東亜戦争 *(The Great East Asian War)*, edited by 奥村房夫 (Okumura Fusao) and 近藤新治 (Kondō Shinji), 201–26. Tokyo: 同台経済懇話会, 1995.

孔永松 (Kong Yongsong). "试论抗日陕甘宁区的特殊土地问题" ("A Discussion of Specific Land Issues during the Sino-Japanese War Period in the Shaanxi-Gansu-Ningxia Base Area"). 中国社会经济史研究 *(Research on Chinese Social and Economic History)* 1984 no. 4: 99–109.

Koshiro, Yukiko. "Eurasian Eclipse: Japan's End Game in World War II." *The American Historical Review* 109 no. 2 (April 2004): 417–444.

Kotani, Ken. "Pearl Harbor Japanese Planning and Command Structure." In *The Pacific War Companion: From Pearl Harbor to Hiroshima*, edited by Daniel Marston, 31–46. Oxford: Osprey, 2005.

Krug, Hans-Joachim, Yōichi Hirama, Berthold J. Sander-Nagashima, and Axel Niestlé. *Reluctant Allies: German-Japanese Naval Relations in World War II*. Annapolis, MD: Naval Institute Press, 2001.

熊谷光久 (Kumagai Teruhisa). "動員・人と物" ("The Mobilization of People and Goods"). In 近代日本戦争史 *(Modern Japanese Military History)*, vol. 4, 大東亜戦争 *(The Great East Asian War)*, edited by 奥村房夫 (Okumura Fusao) and 近藤新治 (Kondō Shinji), 806–22. Tokyo: 同台経済懇話会, 1995.

功刀俊洋 (Kunugi Toshihiro). "軍縮から軍拡へ" ("From Arms Limitations to Rearmament"). In 十五年戦争史 *(A History of the Fifteen Year War)*, vol. 1, edited by 藤原 彰 (Fujiwara Akira) and 今井清一 (Imai Seiichi), 83–124. Tokyo: 青木書店, 1989.

Kurdiukov, I. F., V. N. Nikiforov, and A. S. Perevertailo, comps. *Советско-Китайские отношения 1917–1957 сборник документов* (*Soviet-Chinese Relations 1917–1957, Collection of Documents*). Moscow: Издательство восточной литературы, 1959.

黒野耐 (Kurono Taeru). 日本を滅ぼした国防方針 *(Japan's Disastrous National Defense Policy)*. Tokyo: 文芸春秋社, 2002.

Kuznetsov, S. I. "The Situation of Japanese Prisoners of War in Soviet Camps (1945–1956)." *The Journal of Slavic Military Studies* 8 no. 3 (September 1995): 612–29.

Large, Stephen S., ed. *Shōwa Japan: Political, Economic and Social History 1926–1989*. Vol. 1. London: Routledge, 1998.

Lary, Diana. *The Chinese People at War: Human Suffering and Social Transformation, 1937–1945*. Cambridge: Cambridge University Press, 2010.

"Defending China: The Battles of the Xuzhou Campaign." In *Warfare in Chinese History*, edited by Hans J. van de Ven, 398–427. Leiden: Brill Academic Publishers, 2000.

"A Ravaged Place: The Devastation of the Xuzhou Region, 1938." In *Scars of War: The Impact of Warfare on Modern China*, edited by Diana Lary and Stephen R. MacKinnon, 98–117. Vancouver: UBC Press, 2001.

Lary, Diana and Stephen MacKinnon, eds. *Scars of War: The Impact of Warfare on Modern China*. Vancouver: UBC Press, 2001.

Lattimore, Owen. *The Mongols of Manchuria*. New York: John Day Co., 1934.

League of Nations. Economic, Financial and Transit Department. *World Economic Survey*. (1942/44) Geneva: League of Nations, 1945.

LeDonne, John P. *The Russian Empire and the World 1700–1917: The Geopolitics of Expansion and Containment*. New York: Oxford University Press, 1997.

Ledovskii (Ledovsky), Andrei Mefod'evich. *СССР и Сталин в судьбах Китая: Документы и свидетальства участника событий 1937–1952 (The USSR and Stalin in the Fate of China: Documents and the Testimony of Participants in the Events of 1937–1952)*. Moscow: «Памятники исторической мысли», 1999.

The USSR, the USA, and the People's Revolution in China. Translated by Nadezhda Burova. Moscow: Progress Publishers, 1982.

Lee, Bradford A. *Britain and the Sino-Japanese War 1937–1939*. Stanford: Stanford University Press, 1973.

"A Pivotal Campaign in a Peripheral Theatre: Guadalcanal and World War II." In *Naval Expeditionary Warfare: Peripheral Campaigns and New Theaters of Naval Warfare*, edited by Bruce A. Elleman and S.C.M. Paine, 84–98. Abingdon, UK: Routledge, 2011.

Lee, Chong-Sik. "*Counterinsurgency in Manchuria: the Japanese Experience, 1931–1940.*" Memorandum RM-5012-ARPA. Santa Monica: RAND Corp, 1967.

Revolutionary Struggle in Manchuria: Chinese Communism and Soviet Interest, 1922–1945. Berkeley: University of California Press, 1983.

Lee, Edward Bing-Shuey. *One Year of the Japan-China Undeclared War*. Shanghai: Mercury Press, 1922.

Lensen, George Alexander. *The Damned Inheritance: The Soviet Union and the Manchurian Crises 1924–1935*. Tallahassee, FL: Diplomatic Press, 1974.

Leung, Edwin Pak-wah, ed. *Historical Dictionary of Revolutionary China, 1839–1976*. New York: Greenwood Press, 1992.

ed. *Historical Dictionary of the Chinese Civil War*. Lanham, MD: Scarecrow Press, 2002.

ed. *Political Leaders of Modern China: A Biographical Dictionary*. Westport, CT: Greenwood Press, 2002.

Leutner, Mechthild , Roland Felber, M. L. Titarenko, and A. M. Grigoriev, eds. *The Chinese Revolution in the 1920s: Between Triumph and Disaster*. London: RoutledgeCurzon, 2002.

Levich, Eugene William. *The Kwangsi Way in Kuomintang China, 1931–1939*. Armonk, NY: M. E. Sharpe, 1993.

Levine, Steven I. *Anvil of Victory: The Communist Revolution in Manchuria, 1945–1948*. New York: Columbia University Press, 1987.

Lew, Christopher R. *The Third Chinese Revolutionary Civil War, 1945–49: An Analysis of Communist Strategy and Leadership*. London: Routledge, 2009.

Lewis, Robert A. "The Mixing of Russians and Soviet Nationalities and its Demographic Impact." In *Soviet Nationality Problems*, edited by Edward Allworth, 117–167. New York: Columbia University Press, 1971.

李恩涵 (Li Enhan). "日本軍南京大屠殺的屠殺數目問題"("A Reappraisal of the Massacre Figures for the Japanese Army's Rape of Nanjing"). 台灣師範大學歷史學報 *(Taiwan Normal University Bulletin of Historical Research)* 18 (June 1990): 449–89.

李国平 (Li Guoping). "战前东北地区工矿业开发与结构变化研究" ("A Study of the Development and Structural Changes of Industry and Mining in Pre-War Northeast China"). 中国经济史研究 *(Research in Chinese Economic History)*, 1998 no. 4: 84–93.

李海文 (Li Haiwen). "关于中央军委与中革军委之间的关系" ("The Relationship between the Central Military Affairs Commission and the

Chinese Revolutionary Military Committee"). 中共党史研究 *(Research on the History of the Chinese Communist Party)*. 1990 no. 6: 88–9.

李兰琴 (Li Lanqin). "试论20世纪30年代德国对华政策"("German Policy regarding China in the 1930s"). 历史研究 *(Historical Research)* no. 1 (1989): 179–91.

李蓉 (Li Rong). "试论抗战时期中共在沦陷区的工作"("The Activities of the Chinese Communist Party in Enemy-Occupied Areas during the War of Resistance"). 中共党史研究 *(Research on the History of the Chinese Communist Party)* 1995 no. 4: 38–42.

"一个大的战略决策：向沦陷区发展" ("A Great Strategic Decision: Whether to Expand into Enemy-occupied Areas"). 中共党史研究 *(Research on the History of the Chinese Communist Party)*, 2000 no. 3: 68–74.

"刘少奇对抗战时期党的沦陷区工作的贡献"("Liu Shaoqi's Contributions to the Work in Enemy-Occupied Areas during the War of Resistance"). 中共党史研究 *(Research on the History of the Chinese Communist Party)* 1999 no. 6: 73–6.

李宇平 (Li Yuping)."一九三〇年代世界經濟大恐慌對中國經濟之衝擊（一九三一〜一九三五）" ("The Impact of the Great Depression on China's Economy in the 1930s [1931–1935]"). 台灣師範大學歷史學報 *(Taiwan Normal University Bulletin of Historical Research)* no. 22 (June 1994): 315–47.

"一九三〇年代中國經濟恐慌的若干現象" ("Some Phenomena during the Chinese Depression in the 1930s"). 台灣師範大學歷史學報 *(Taiwan Normal University Bulletin of Historical Research)* no. 25 (June 1997): 71–118.

Li, Zhisui. *The Private Life of Chairman Mao*. Translated by Tai Hung-chao. New York: Random House, 1994.

连心豪 (Lian Xinhao)."南京国民政府建立初期海关缉私工作述评" ("Commentary on the Nationalist Government's Early Anti-Smuggling Work"). 中国社会经济史研究 *(Research on Chinese Social and Economic History)* 1989 no. 4: 77–83.

林明德 (Lin Mingde). "日本軍國主義的形成—九一八事變的探討— " ("Formation of Japanese Militarism: An Investigation of the Manchurian Incident"). 台灣師範大學歷史學報 *(Taiwan Normal University Bulletin of Historical Research)* 11 (June 1983): 245–79.

林祥庚 (Lin Xianggeng). "民主党派与中国共产党的'逼将抗日'方针"("The Democratic Parties' and the CCP's Guiding Principle of 'Compelling Chiang to Resist Japan'"). 中共党史研究 *(Research on the History of the Chinese Communist Party)* 1996 no. 3: 29–34.

Lincoln, W. Bruce. *Red Victory: A History of the Russian Civil War 1918–1921*. New York: Da Capo Press, 1999.

Liu, F. F. *A Military History of Modern China 1924–1949*. 1956; reprint, Port Washington, NY: Kennikat Press, 1972.

刘会军 (Liu Huijun). "民国党特务组织" ("The Nationalist Party Spy Organization"). 史学集刊 *(Collected Papers of Historical Studies)* 39 no. 2 (1990): 39–44.

刘慧宇 (Liu Huiyu). "论南京国民政府时期国地财政划分制度"("Discussing the Transfer System of Finance during the Nanjing Decade"). 中国经济史研究 *(Research in Chinese Economic History)* 2001 no. 4: 42–8.

刘建皋 (Liu Jian'gao). "改组派初探"("Initial Exploration of the Reorganization Faction"). 历史研究 *(Historical Research)* no. 6 (1981): 153–70.

刘克祥 (Liu Kexiang). "1927–1937年的地价变动与土地买卖一30年代土地问题研究之一" ("Land Price Changes and Land Sales, 1927–1937: Research on the Land Question of the 1930s"). 中国经济史研究 *(Research in Chinese Economic History)*. 2000 no. 1: 21–36.

刘培平 (Liu Peiping). "'安内攘外' 与 '反将抗日' " ("'Internal Pacification, External Resistance' versus 'Oppose Chiang, Resist Japan'"). 文史哲 *(Journal of Literature, History, and Philosophy)* 230 no. 5 (1995): 22–7.

刘庭华 (Liu Tinghua) and 岳思平 (Yue Siping). "抗日与统一和安内攘外" ("Unified Resistance against Japan and the Policy of Internal Pacification, External Resistance"). 中共党史研究 *(Research on the History of the Chinese Communist Party)* 1994 no. 6: 74–8.

刘卫东 (Liu Weidong). "印支通道的战时功能述论"("A Narrative of the Wartime Function of the Indochina Passageway"). 近代史研究 *(Modern Chinese History Studies)* no. 2 (May 1999): 173–91.

Liu, Xiaoyuan. *Frontier Passages: Ethnopolitics and the Rise of Chinese Communism, 1921–1945*. Stanford: Stanford University Press, 2004.

A Partnership for Disorder: China, the United States, and Their Policies for the Postwar Disposition of the Japanese Empire, 1941–1945. Cambridge: Cambridge University Press, 1996.

Reins of Liberation: An Entangled History of Mongolian Independence, Chinese Territoriality, and Great Power Hegemony, 1911–1950. Stanford: Stanford University Press, 2006.

刘喜发 (Liu Xifa) and 王彦堂 (Wang Yantang). "试论国内外舆论对西安事变和平解决的作用" ("The Role of Domestic and International Public Opinion on the Peaceful Solution of the Xi'an Incident"). 史学集刊 *(Collected Papers of Historical Studies)* 71 no. 2 (1998): 37–40.

刘一皋 (Liu Yigao). "解放战争时期华北解放区的土地改革与农村政权" ("Land Reform and Rural Political Power in the Liberated Areas of North China during the War for National Liberation"). 中共党史研究

(Research on the History of the Chinese Communist Party) 1989 no. 1: 73–8.

Lu, David J. *Japan a Documentary History: The Late Tokugawa Period to the Present.* 2 vols. Armonk, NY: M. E. Sharpe, 1997.

Lu, Minghui. "The Inner Mongolian 'United Autonomous Government.'" In *China at War: Regions of China, 1937–1945*, edited by Stephen R. MacKinnon, Diana Lary, and Ezra F. Vogel, 148–71. Stanford: Stanford University Press, 2007.

鹿锡俊 (Lu Xijun). "中日战争时期日本对蒋政策的演变" ("The Evolution of Japan's Policy regarding Chiang Kai-shek during the Sino-Japanese War"). 近代史研究 *(Modern Chinese History Studies)* 64 no. 4 (July 1991): 210–37.

羅貫中 (Luo Guanzhong). 三國演義 *(Romance of the Three Kingdoms).* Taipei: 三民書局, 1985.

Three Kingdoms. Translated by Moss Roberts. Beijing: Foreign Languages Press, 1995.

马风书 (Ma Fengshu). "战后初期苏联对华政策剖析" ("An Analysis of Soviet Policies toward China in the Early Post-war Years"). 文史哲 *(Journal of Literature, History, and Philosophy)* 250 no. 1 (1999): 52–7.

Machiavelli, Niccolò. *Machiavelli's The Prince: A Bilingual Edition.* Translated and edited by Mark Musa. New York: St. Martin's Press, 1964.

Mackerras, Colin. *Modern China: A Chronology from 1842 to the Present.* San Francisco: W.H. Freeman, 1982.

The New Cambridge Handbook of Contemporary China. Cambridge: Cambridge University Press, 2001.

MacKinnon, Stephen R. "Refugee Flight at the Outset of the Anti-Japanese War." In *Scars of War: The Impact of Warfare on Modern China*, edited by Diana Lary and Stephen MacKinnon, 118–35. Vancouver: UBC Press, 2001.

Wuhan 1938: War, Refugees, and the Making of Modern China. Berkeley: University of California Press, 2008.

MacKinnon, Stephen R., Diana Lary, and Ezra F. Vogel, eds. *China at War: Regions of China, 1937–1945.* Stanford: Stanford University Press, 2007.

Mahan, Alfred T. *The Influence of Seapower upon History 1660–1783.* 1890, reprint; New York: Hill and Wang, 1957.

幕内光雄 (Maku'uchi Mitsuo). 満州国警察外史 *(An Unofficial History of the Manchukuo Police).* Tokyo: 三一書房, 1996.

Manchoukuo Gives Birth to New Culture. Hsinking: Manchuria Daily News, 1940.

Manchoukuo Government. Department of Foreign Affairs. *Proclamations, Statements and Communications of the Manchoukuo Government*. Series 2–3. Hsinking, Manchuria, 1932.

Manchoukuo State Council. Bureau of Information. ed., *An Outline of the Manchoukuo Empire 1939*. Dalian: Manchuria Daily News, 1939.

The Manchoukuo Year Book 1942. Hsinking, Manchoukuo: Manchoukuo Year Book Co., 1943.

満州国軍刊行委員会 (Manchukuo Army Publication Committee). 満州国軍 *(Manchukuo Army)*. Tokyo: 正光印刷株式会社, 1970.

満州中央銀行史研究会 (Manchurian Central Bank Historical Research Committee), ed. 満州中央銀行史通貨・金融政策の軌跡 *(A History of the Manchurian Central Bank: The Course of Currency and Financial Policy)*. Tokyo: 東洋経済新報社, 1988.

満史会 (Manchurian History Committee), ed. 満州開発四十年史 *(A Forty Year History of Manchurian Development)*, 2 vols. and supplement. Tokyo: 謙光社, 1964–5.

満州史研究会 (Manchurian History Research Committee), ed. 日本帝国主義下の満州 *(Manchuria under Japanese Imperialism)*. Tokyo: 御茶の水書房, 1972.

Mao, Zedong, *Selected Military Writings of Mao Tse-tung*. 2nd ed. Beijing: Foreign Languages Press, 1967.

Marston, Daniel, ed., *The Pacific War Companion From Pearl Harbor to Hiroshima*. Oxford: Osprey, 2000.

松本俊郎 (Matsumoto Toshirō). "満洲鉄鋼業開発と「満洲国」経済一１９４０年代を中心に一" ("Development of the Manchurian Iron and Steel Industry and 'Manchukuo's' Economy Focusing on the 1940s"). In「満洲国」の研究 *(Research on "Manchukuo")*, edited by 山本有造 (Yamamoto Yūzō), 289–328. Tokyo: 緑蔭書房, 1995.

松村高夫 (Matsumura Takao). "満州国成立以降における移民, 労働政策の形成と展開" ("The Formation and Development of Immigration and Labor Policies after the Creation of Manchukuo"). In 日本帝国主義下の満州 *(Manchuria under Japanese Imperialism)*, edited by 満州史研究会 (Manchurian History Research Committee), 213–314. Tokyo: 御茶の水書房, 1972.

松野周治 (Matsuno Shūji). "関税および関税制度から見た「満州国」—関税改正の経過と論点—" ("'Manchukuo' Seen from the Tariff and the Customs System: The Disputed Course of Tariff Reform"). In「満洲国」の研究 *(Research on "Manchukuo")*, edited by 山本有造 (Yamamoto Yūzō), 329–75. Tokyo: 緑蔭書房, 1995.

Matsusaka, Yoshihisa Tak. *The Making of Japanese Manchuria, 1904–1932*. Cambridge, MA: Harvard University Press, 2001.

Mawdsley, Evan. *The Russian Civil War*. Boston: Unwin Hyman, 1987.

Mencius. *Mencius*. Translated by D.C. Lau. London: Penguin, 1970.

Meng, Chih. *China Speaks on the Conflict between China and Japan*. New York: Macmillan, 1932.

Metcalf, Barbara D. and Thomas R. Metcalf. *A Concise History of Modern India*. 2nd ed. Cambridge: Cambridge University Press, 2006.

宓汝成 (Mi Rucheng). "抗战时期的中国外债" ("The Foreign Loans to China during the War of Resistance"). 中国经济史研究 *(Research in Chinese Economic History)*. 1998 no. 2: 50–62.

Mirovitskaia, Raisa A. *Китайская государственность и советская политика в Китае (Chinese Statehood and Soviet Policy in China)*. Moscow: «Памятники исторической мысли», 1999.

Mitter, Rana. *The Manchurian Myth: Nationalism, Resistance, and Collaboration in Modern China*. Berkeley: University of California Press, 2000.

莫岳云 (Mo Yueyun). "略论国民党敌后抗日游击战之兴衰" ("A Brief Discussion of the Rise and Fall of Nationalist Party's Anti-Japanese Guerrilla War behind Enemy Lines"). 史学集刊 *(Collected Papers of Historical Studies)* 69 no. 4 (1997): 36–41.

Moore, Harriet L. *Soviet Far Eastern Policy 1931–1945*. Princeton: Princeton University Press, 1945.

森茂樹 (Mori Shigeki). "枢軸外交および南進政策と海軍―１９３９～１９４０年―" ("The Imperial Navy and the Making of Japan's Foreign Policy, 1939–1940"). 歴史学研究 *(Journal of Historical Studies)* no. 727 (September 1999): 1–18.

森武麿 (Mori Takemaro). "恐慌と戦争―１９３０－１９４５年―" ("The Great Depression and the War, 1930–1945"). In 現代日本経済史 *(Modern Japanese Economic History)*, edited by 森武麿 (Mori Takemaro) et al., 1–62. Tokyo: 有斐閣Sシリーズ, 1993.

森武麿 (Mori Takemaro). et al., eds. 現代日本経済史 *(Modern Japanese Economic History)* Tokyo: 有斐閣Sシリーズ, 1993.

森松俊夫 (Morimatsu Toshio). "中国大陸の諸作戦" ("Various Military Operations in the Chinese Mainland"). In 近代日本戦争史 *(Modern Japanese Military History)*, vol. 4 大東亜戦争 (*The Great East Asian War*), edited by 奥村房夫 (Okumura Fusao) and 近藤新治 (Kondō Shinji), 596–618. Tokyo: 同台経済懇話会, 1995.

"大東亜戦争の戦争目的" ("The War Goals of the Great East Asian War"). In 近代日本戦争史 *(Modern Japanese Military History)*, vol. 4 大東亜戦争 (*The Great East Asian War*), edited by 奥村房夫 (Okumura Fusao) and 近藤新治 (Kondō Shinji), 294–17. Tokyo: 同台経済懇話会, 1995.

Morley, James William, ed. *Deterrent Diplomacy: Japan, Germany, and the USSR 1935–1940*. New York: Columbia University Press, 1976.

ed. *Dilemmas of Growth in Prewar Japan*. Princeton: Princeton University Press, 1971.

ed. *The Fateful Choice: Japan's Advance into Southeast Asia, 1939–1941*. New York: Columbia, 1980.

ed. *Japan Erupts: The London Naval Conference and the Manchurian Incident, 1928–1932*. New York: Columbia University Press, 1984.

ed. *The North China Quagmire: Japan's Expansion on the Asian Continent 1933–1941*. New York: Columbia University Press, 1983.

"The Tripartite Pact, 1939–1940, Introduction." In *Deterrent Diplomacy: Japan, Germany, and the USSR 1935–1940*, edited by James William Morley, 181–90. New York: Columbia University Press, 1976.

Murray, Brian Joseph. "Stalin, the Cold War, and the Division of China: A Multi-Archival Mystery." *Cold War International History Project*, working paper no. 12, June 1995, 2.

"Western versus Chinese Realism: Soviet American Diplomacy and the Chinese Civil War, 1945–1950." Ph.D. diss., Columbia University, 1995.

Murray, Williamson and Allan R. Millet. *A War to Be Won: Fighting the Second World War*. Cambridge, MA: Harvard University Press, 2000.

中国人民革命军事博物馆, (Museum of the Chinese People's Revolutionary Military Affairs), ed. 中国战争史地图集 *(Map Collection of Chinese Military History*. Beijing: 星球地图出版社, 2007.

Myers, Ramon. *Japanese Economic Development in Manchuria, 1932 to 1945*. New York: Garland, 1982.

Nafziger, George F. "The Growth and Organization of the Chinese Army (1895–1945)." Westchester, OH: Nafziger Collection, 1999.

中村隆英 (Nakamura Takafusa). "The Age of Turbulence, 1937–54." In *Economic History of Japan 1914–1955: A Dual Structure*, edited by Takafusa Nakamura and Kônosuke Odaka. Translated by Noah S. Brannen, 55–110. Oxford: Oxford University Press, 1999.

ed. 戦間期の日本経済分析 *(An Analysis of the Interwar Japanese Economy)*. Tokyo: 山川出版社, 1981.

"Depression, Recovery, and War, 1920–1945." In *Shōwa Japan: Political, Economic and Social History 1926–1989*, vol. 1, edited by Stephen S. Large, 47–83. London: Routledge, 1998.

"北支那開発株式会社の成立" ("The Formation of the North China Development Joint-Stock Corporation"). In 日中戦争と日中関係 *(The Sino-Japanese War and Sino-Japanese Relations)*, edited by 井上清 (Inōe Kyoshi) and 衛藤瀋吉 (Etō Shinkichi), 349–66. Tokyo: 原書房, 1988.

A History of Shōwa Japan 1926–1989. Translated by Edwin Whenmouth. Tokyo: University of Tokyo Press, 1998.

"Japan's Economic Thrust into North China, 1933–1938." In *The Chinese and the Japanese*, edited by Akira Iriye, 220–53. Princeton: Princeton University Press, 1980.

Needham, Joseph. *Science and Civilization in China*. Vol. 2. *History of Scientific Thought*. Cambridge: Cambridge University Press, 1962.

Newman, Robert P. *Owen Lattimore and the "Loss" of China*. Berkeley: University of California Press, 1992.

Nish, Ian. *Japanese Foreign Policy 1869–1942 Kasumigaseki to Miyakezaka*. London: Routledge & Kegan Paul, 1977.

Japanese Foreign Policy in the Interwar Period. Westport, CT: Praeger, 2002.

西 春彦 (Nishi Haruhiko), ed. 日本外交史 *(A History of Japanese Foreign Relations)*. Vol. 15. 日ソ国交問題１９１７−１９４５ (*Questions Concerning Japanese-Soviet Diplomatic Relations, 1917–1945*) Tokyo: 鹿島研究所出版会, 1970.

西 順蔵 (Nishi Junzō), ed. 原典中国近代思想史国共分裂から解放戦争まで *(Modern Chinese Intellectual History in Documents from the Nationalist-Communist Split to the War of National Liberation)*. Vol. 6. Tokyo: 岩波書店, 1976.

西村成雄 (Nishimura Shigeo). "日本政府の中華民国認識と張学良政権—民族主義的凝集性の再評価" ("The Japanese Government's Recognition of the Republic of China and Zhang Xueliang's Sovereignty: A Reappraisal of National Cohesion"). In 「満洲国」の研究 *(Research on "Manchukuo")*, edited by 山本有造 (Yamamoto Yūzō), 1–37. Tokyo: 緑蔭書房, 1995.

西岡虎之助 (Nishioka Toranosuke), et al. eds. 日本歴史地図 *(Historical Maps of Japan)*. Tokyo: 株式会社全教図, 1978.

西沢泰彦 (Nishizawa Yasuhiko). "「満洲国」の建設事業" ("'Manchukuo's' Construction Industry"). In 「満洲国」の研究 *(Research on "Manchukuo")*, edited by 山本有造 (Yamamoto Yūzō), 377–460. Tokyo: 緑蔭書房, 1995.

東北財経委員会調査統計處 (Northeast Financial Committee. Statistical Survey Department), ed. 旧満州経済統計資料 *(Northeast Financial Data for the Puppet Manchukuo Period)*. 1949, reprint; Tokyo: 柏書株式会社, 1991.

野沢豊 (Nozawa Yutaka), ed. 中国の幣制改革と国際関係 *(China's Currency Reform and International Relations)*. Tokyo: University of Tokyo Press, 1981.

野沢豊 (Nozawa Yutaka), et al. eds. 講座中国近現代史 *(Series of Studies in Modern and Contemporary Chinese History)*. Vol. 7, 中国革命の勝利 (*Victory in the Chinese Revolution*). Tokyo: University of Tokyo Press, 1978.

野沢豊 (Nozawa Yutaka), et al. eds. 講座中国近現代史 *(Series of Studies in Modern and Contemporary Chinese History)*. Vol. 6, 抗日戦争 (*War of Japanese Resistance*). Tokyo: University of Tokyo Press, 1978.

Ogata, Sadako N. *Defiance in Manchuria: The Making of Japanese Foreign Policy, 1931–1932*. Berkeley: University of California Press, 1964.

Ōhata, Tokushirō. "The Anti-Comintern Pact, 1935–1939." In *Deterrent Diplomacy: Japan, Germany, and the USSR 1935–1940,* edited by James William Morley, 9–112. New York: Columbia University Press, 1976.

Oka, Yoshitake. *Konoe Fumimaro A Political Biography*. Translated by Shumpei Okamoto and Patricia Murray. Lanham, MD: Madison Books, 1992.

奥村房夫 (Okumura Fusao) and 河野 収 (Kōno Shū), eds. 近代日本戦争史 *(Modern Japanese Military History)*. Vol. 3, 滿州事変· 支那事変 (*The Manchurian Incident and the China Incident*). Tokyo: 同台経済懇話会, 1995.

奥村房夫 (Okumura Fusao) and 近藤新治 (Kondō Shinji) eds. 近代日本戦争史 *(Modern Japanese Military History)*. Vol. 4, 大東亜戦争 (*The Great East Asian War*). Tokyo: 同台経済懇話会, 1995.

Ovchinnikov, Iurii Mikhailovich. *Становление и развитие единого национального фронта сопротивления Японии в Китае (The Creation and Development of the United National Front to Resist Japan in China)*. Moscow: Издательсво «наука» Главная редакция восточной литературы, 1985.

Overy, Richard. *Russia's War: A History of the Soviet War Effort: 1941–1945*. New York: Penguin, 1997.

大山梓 (Ōyama Azusa), ed. 山県有朋意見書 *(The Written Opinions of Yamagata Aritomo)*. Tokyo: 原書房, 1966.

太平洋戦争研究会 (Pacific War Research Center), ed. 日中戦争 *(Sino-Japanese War)*. Tokyo: 河出書房新社, 2000.

Paige, Glenn D. *The Korean Decision [June 24–30, 1950]*. New York: Free Press, 1968.

Paine, S. C. M. *Imperial Rivals: China, Russia, and Their Disputed Frontier*. Armonk, NY: M. E. Sharpe, 1996.

"Japanese Puppet-State Building in Manchukuo." In *Nation Building, State Building, and Economic Development*, edited by S.C.M. Paine, 66–82. Armonk, NY: M. E. Sharpe, 2010.

The Sino-Japanese War of 1894 to 1895: Perceptions, Power, and Primacy. Cambridge: Cambridge University Press, 2003.

Pan, Stephen Chao Ying. *American Diplomacy Concerning Manchuria*. Washington, Catholic University of America, 1938.

Patrikeeff, Felix, "Railway as Political Catalyst: The Chinese Eastern Railway and the 1929 Sino-Soviet Conflict." In *Manchurian Railways and the Opening of China: An International History*, edited by Bruce A. Elleman and Stephen Kotkin, 81–102. Armonk, NY: M. E. Sharpe, 2010.

Paxton, John. *Companion to Russian History*. New York: Facts On File Publications, 1983.

Pearlman, Michael D. *Warmaking and American Democracy: The Struggle over Military Strategy, 1700 to the Present*. Lawrence: University of Kansas Press, 1999.

Peattie, Mark R. *Ishiwara Kanji and Japan's Confrontation with the West*. Princeton: Princeton University Press, 1975.

Sunburst: The Rise of Japanese Naval Air Power, 1909–1941. Annapolis, MD: Naval Institute Press, 2001.

Peattie, Mark R, Edward J. Drea, and Hans van de Ven, eds. *The Battle for China: Essays on the Military History of the Sino-Japanese War of 1937–1945*. Stanford: Stanford University Press, 2011.

Pepper, Suzanne. *Civil War in China: The Political Struggle 1945–1949*. Berkeley, CA: University of California Press, 1978.

"The KMT-CCP Conflict 1945–1949." In *The Cambridge History of China*, vol. 13, edited by John K, Fairbank and Albert Feuerwerker, 723–88. Cambridge: Cambridge University Press, 1986.

"The Student Movement and the Chinese Civil War, 1945–49." *China Quarterly* no. 48 (Oct.–Dec. 1971): 698–735.

Pipes, Richard. *The Russian Revolution*. New York: Vintage Books, 1990.

Prokhorov, A. M. ed. *Советский энциклопедический словарь (Soviet Encyclopedic Dictionary)*. 2nd ed. Moscow: «Советская энциклопедия», 1983.

Pu Yi, Henry. *The Last Manchu: The Autobiography of Henry Pu Yi Last Emperor of China*, edited by Paul Kramer, translated by Kuo Ying Paul Tsai. London: Arthur Barker, 1967.

偽滿洲國政府公報. *(The Puppet Manchukuo* Government Gazette*)*. Vol. 120. Shenyang: 遼瀋書社, 1990.

Pyle, Kenneth B. *The New Generation in Meiji Japan: Problems of Cultural Identity, 1885–1895*. Stanford: Stanford University Press, 1969.

Qi Xisheng (齊錫生), see Ch'i Hsi-sheng.

乔宪金 (Qiao Xianjin). "苏联对日本宣战与出兵东北是同一时间" ("The Soviet Declaration of War on Japan and Deployment of Troops in Manchuria Were Simultaneous"). 近代史研究 *(Modern Chinese History Studies*. 1995 no. 2: 283–4

秦孝儀 (Qin Xiaoyi). 中國現代史辭典：人物部分 *(Dictionary of Modern Chinese History: Biographic Volume)*. Taipei: 近代中國出版社, 1985.

邱松庆 (Qiu Songqing). "简评南京国民政府初建时期的农业政策" ("Comment on the Agricultural Policy of the Early Nanjing Government"). 中国社会经济史研究 *(Research on Chinese Social and Economic History)* 1999 no. 4: 72–6.

"略论南京国民政府的法币政策"("On the Currency Policy Pursued by the Nationalist Government"). 中国社会经济史研究 *(Research on Chinese Social and Economic History)* 1997 no. 4: 79–84.

南京国民政府初建时期财经政策述评" ("A Review of the Financial Policy of the Nationalist Government during the Early Period in Nanjing"). 中国社会经济史研究 *(Research on Chinese Social and Economic History)* 1996 no. 4.

Ragsdale, Hugh. *The Soviets, the Munich Crisis, and the Coming of World War II*. Cambridge: Cambridge University Press, 2004.

饶良伦 (Rao Lianglun), 张秀兰 (Zhang Xiulan), 段光达 (Duan Guangda). "九一八事变前黑龙江区的中苏关系" ("Sino-Soviet Relations in the Heilongjiang Area Prior to the Manchurian Incident"). 近代史研究 *(Modern Chinese History Studies)* 75 no. 3 (May 1993): 219–34.

Rawski, Thomas G. *Economic Growth in Prewar China*. Berkeley: University of California Press, 1989.

Reardon-Anderson, James. *Reluctant Pioneers: China's Expansion Northward 1644–1937*. Stanford: Stanford University Press, 2005.

Reeves, Thomas C. *The Life and Times of Joe McCarthy: A Biography*. New York: Stein and Day, 1982.

任东来 (Ren Donglai). "1934–1936年间中美关系中的白银外交" ("The Sino-U.S. Silver Diplomacy of 1934–1936"). 历史研究 *(Historical Research)* no. 3 (2000): 103–16.

任骏 (Ren Jun). "蒋廷黻与七七事变前后的中苏关系" ("Jiang Tingfu and Sino-Soviet Relations before and after the Marco Polo Bridge Incident"). 近代史研究 *(Modern Chinese History Studies)* no. 1 (1991): 181–200.

任振河 (Ren Zhenhe). "张学良五访阎锡山" ("Zhang Xueliang's Five Visits to Yan Xishan"). 近代史研究 *(Modern Chinese History Studies)* 80 no. 2 (March 1994): 313–18.

Riasanovsky, Nicholas V. *A History of Russia*. 5th ed. New York: Oxford University Press, 1993.

Rummel, R. J. *China's Bloody Century: Genocide and Mass Murder since 1900*. New Brunswick, NJ: Transaction Publishers, 1991.

Lethal Politics: Soviet Genocide and Mass Murder since 1917. New Brunswick, NJ: Transaction Publishers, 1990.

Saich, Tony and Hans van de Ven, eds. *The Rise to Power of the Chinese Communist Party: Documents and Analysis*. Armonk, NY: M. E. Sharpe, 1996.

Saito, Hirosi. *Japan's Policies and Purposes*. Boston: Marshall Jones, 1935.

斎藤道彦 (Saitō Michihiko). "日本軍毒ガス作戦日誌初稿一一九三七、三八年を中心に一" ("A First Attempt at a Journal of the Poison Gas Operation of the Japanese Army Focusing on 1937 and 1938"). In 日中戦争日本・中国・アメリカ *(The Sino-Japanese War: Japan, China, and America)*, edited by 中央大学人文科学研究所 (Chūō University Human Sciences Research Center), 157–274. Research publication no. 10. Tokyo: 中央大学出版社, 1993.

Sapozhnikov, Boris Grigor'evich. *Китай в огне войны 1931–1950* (*China in the Fire of War 1931–1950*). Moscow: Издательство «наука» Главная редакция восточной литературы, 1977.

Китайский фронт во Второй мировой войны (*The Chinese Front in the Second World War*). Moscow: Издательство «наука» Главная редакция восточной литературы, 1971.

Народно-освободительная война в Китае (1946–1950 гг.) (*The People's Liberation War in China [1946–1950]*). Moscow: Военное издательство, 1984.

Японо-китайская война и колониальная политика Японии в Китае (1937–1941) (The Sino-Japanese War and Japan's Colonial Policy in China [1937–1941]. (Moscow: Издательсво «наука» Главная редакция восточной литературы, 1970.

佐藤和夫 (Satō Kazuo). "戦間期日本のマクロ経済とミクロ経済" ("The Microeconomics and Macroeconomics of Interwar Japan"). In 戦間期の日本経済分析 *(An Analysis of the Interwar Japanese Economy), 3–30,* edited by 中村隆英 (Nakamura Takafusa). Tokyo: 山川出版社, 1981.

Schoppa, R. Keith. *The Columbia Guide to Modern Chinese History*. New York: Columbia University Press, 2000.

Schumpeter, E. B. ed. *The Industrialization of Japan and Manchukuo 1930–1940: Population, Raw Materials and Industry*. New York: Macmillan, 1940.

"The Mineral Resources of the Japanese Empire and Manchukuo." In *The Industrialization of Japan and Manchukuo 1930–1940: Population, Raw Materials and Industry*, edited by E. B. Schumpeter, 362–476. New York: Macmillan, 1940.

Seki, Hiroharu. "The Manchurian Incident, 1931." In *Japan Erupts: The London Naval Conference and the Manchurian Incident, 1928–1932*, edited by James William Morley, 139–230. New York: Columbia University Press, 1984.

Selden, Mark. *The Yenan Way in Revolutionary China*. Cambridge, MA: Harvard University Press, 1971.

Seybolt, Peter J. "The War within a War: A Case Study of a County on the North China Plain." In *Chinese Collaboration with Japan, 1932–1945: The Limits of Accommodation*, edited by David P. Barret and Larry N. Shyu, 201–25. Stanford: Stanford University Press, 2001.

沙友林 (Sha Youlin). "刘少奇对完善抗日游击战争战略方针的贡献" ("Liu Shaoqi's Contribution to the Perfection of the Guerrilla Strategy during the War of Resistance"). 中共党史研究 *(Research on the History of the Chinese Communist Party)* no. 2 (1998): 35–8.

单冠初 (Shan Guanchu). "日本侵华的'以战养战'政策" ("The Japanese Policy of 'Providing for the War with War' during the Invasion of China"). 历史研究 *(Historical Research)* 1991 no. 4: 77–91.

申晓云 (Shen Xiaoyun). "四一二前后的蒋介石与列强" ("Relations between Chiang Kai-shek and the Imperialist Powers around the Time of the 12 April Massacre"). 历史研究 *(Historical Research)* no. 6 (2000): 96–106.

沈予 (Shen Yu). "论日本近卫文麿内阁的对华政策" ("Discussion of the Konoe Fumimaro Cabinet's China Policy"). 近代史研究 *(Modern Chinese History Studies)* no. 1 1998: 37–61.

"国民革命与日蒋关系" ("The National Revolution and the Relationship between Japan and Chiang Kai-shek"). 近代史研究 *(Modern Chinese History Studies)* no. 2 1997: 41–61.

"论抗日战争期间日蒋的'和平交涉'" ("'Peace Negotiations' between Japan and Chiang Kai-shek during the Anti-Japanese War"). 历史研究 *(Historical Research)* 1993 no. 2: 108–27.

沈志华 (Shen Zhihua) "苏联出兵中国东北：目标和结果" ("The Soviet Troop Deployment into Northeast China: Aims and Consequences"). 历史研究 *(Historical Research)* 1994 no. 5: 88–103.

ed. 中苏关系史纲：*1917〜1991*年中苏关系若干问题再探讨 *(A Survey of Sino-Soviet Relations: A Reexamination of Questions Concerning Sino-Soviet Relations, 1917–1991)*. Rev. ed. Beijing: 社会科学文献出版社, 2011.

Sheng, Michael M. *Battling Western Imperialism: Mao, Stalin, and the United States*. Princeton: Princeton University Press, 1997.

Sheridan, James E. *Chinese Warlord: The Career of Feng Yü-hsiang*. Stanford: Stanford University Press, 1966.

石源华 (Shi Yuanhua). "论日本对华新政策下的日汪关系" ("A Discussion of Japan's Relations with Wang Jingwei as an Element of Japan's New China Policy"). 历史研究 *(Historical Research)* no. 2 (1996): 103–17.

石仲泉 (Shi Zhongquan). "周恩来与新四军" ("Zhou Enlai and the New Fourth Army"). 近代史研究 *(Modern Chinese History Studies)* 77 no. 5 (September 1993): 34–57.

Shillony, Ben-Ami. "The February 26 Affair: Politics of a Military Insurrection." In *Shōwa Japan: Political, Economic and Social History 1926–1989*, Vol. 1, edited by Stephen S. Large, 84–104. London: Routledge, 1998.

Shimada, Toshihiko. "Designs on North China, 1933–1937." In *The North China Quagmire: Japan's Expansion on the Asian Continent 1933–1941*, edited by James William Morley, 11–231. New York: Columbia University Press, 1983.

"The Extension of Hostilities, 1931–1932." In *Japan Erupts: The London Naval Conference and the Manchurian Incident, 1928–1932*, edited by James William Morley, 241–336. New York: Columbia University Press, 1984.

真保潤一郎 (Shinpo Junichirō). "戦時経済の遺産と経済再建" ("The Wartime Economic Legacy and Economic Reconstruction"). In 近代日本戦争史 *(Modern Japanese Military History)*. Vol. 4 大東亜戦争 (*The Great East Asian War*), edited by 奥村房夫 (Okumura Fusao) and 近藤新治 (Kondō Shinji), 931–52. Tokyo: 同台経済懇話会, 1995.

Shum, Kui-kwong. *The Chinese Communists' Road to Power: The Anti-Japanese National United Front, 1935–1945*. Hong Kong: Oxford University Press, 1988.

Sigal, Leon V. *Fighting to a Finish: The Politics of War Termination in the United States and Japan, 1945*. Ithaca: Cornell University Press, 1988.

Slack, Edward R. *Opium, State, and Society: China's Narco-Economy and the Guomindang, 1924–1937*. Honolulu: University of Hawai'i Press, 2001.

Slavinsky, Boris. *The Japanese-Soviet Neutrality Pact: A Diplomatic History, 1941–1945*. Translated by Geoffrey Jukes. London: Routledge, 2004.

Smethurst, Richard J. *From Foot Soldier to Finance Minister: Takahashi Korekiyo Japan's Keynes*. Cambridge, MA: Harvard University Press, 2007.

Smith, Kerry. *A Time of Crisis: Japan, the Great Depression, and Rural Revitalization*. Cambridge, MA: Harvard University Press, 2001.

Smith, Richard J. *China's Cultural Heritage: The Qing Dynasty 1644–1912*. Boulder, CO: Westview Press, 1994.

Smith, Steve. "Moscow and the Second and Third Armed Uprisings in Shanghai, 1927." In *The Chinese Revolution in the 1920s: Between Triumph and Disaster*, edited by Mechthild Leutner et al., 222–43. London: RoutledgeCurzon, 2002.

Snow, Edgar. *Red Star over China*. Rev. ed. New York: Grove, 1968.

副島昭一 (Soejima Shōichi). "「満洲国」統治と治外法権撤廃" ("Abolition of Privileges Concerning Political Control and Extraterritoriality in 'Manchukuo'"). In 「満洲国」の研究 *(Research on "Manchukuo")*, edited by 山本有造 (Yamamoto Yūzō), 131–55. Tokyo: 緑蔭書房, 1995.

Sokolsky, George S. *The Tinder Box of Asia*. Garden City, NY: Doubleday, Doran & Co., 1934.

宋金寿 (Song Jinshou). "毛泽东指导陕甘宁边区经济工作的几个重大思想转折" ("Important Ideological Changes Concerning Economic Work in the Shaanxi-Gansu-Ningxia Border Area under the Leadership of Mao Zedong"). 中共党史研究 *(Research on the History of the Chinese Communist Party)* 1998 no. 6: 24–30.

"陕甘宁边区在抗战中的地位和作用" ("The Position and Role of the Shaan-Gan-Ning Border Area in the War of Resistance"). 中共党史研究 *(Research on the History of the Chinese Communist Party)* 1995 no. 5: 39–45.

Spaulding, Robert M. "The Bureaucracy as a Political Force, 1920–1945." In *Dilemmas of Growth in Prewar Japan*, edited by James William Morley, 33–80. Princeton: Princeton University Press, 1971.

Spector, Ronald H. *Eagle against the Sun: The American War with Japan*. New York: Free Press, 1985.

In the Ruins of Empire: The Japanese Surrender and the Battle for Postwar Asia. New York: Random House, 2007.

Stevens, David. "The New Guinea Campaign during World War II." In *Naval Expeditionary Warfare: Peripheral Campaigns and New Theaters of Naval Warfare*, edited by Bruce A. Elleman and S. C. M. Paine, 99–112. Abingdon, UK: Routledge, 2011.

Stimson, Henry L. *The Far Eastern Crisis: Recollections and Observations*. New York: Harper & Brothers, 1936.

Stoler, Mark A. *Allies and Adversaries: The Joint Chiefs of Staff, the Grand Alliance, and U.S. Strategy in World War II*. Chapel Hill: University of North Carolina Press, 2000.

"Strategic Imports from Southeast Asia." *Far Eastern Survey* 11 no. 1 (12 January 1942): 12–16.

苏小平 (Su Xiaoping) and 贾海维 (Gu Haiwei). "论抗日根据地的统一累进税" ("Unified Progressive Taxation in the Anti-Japanese Base Area"). 中共党史研究 *(Research on the History of the Chinese Communist Party)* 2000 no. 4: 53–7.

Suleski, Ronald. *Civil Government in Warlord China: Tradition, Modernization and Manchuria*. New York: Peter Lang, 2002.

孙季萍 (Sun Jiping). "抗战以前国民政府法制改革评议" ("An Evaluation of the Reforms of the Nationalist Legal System before the Sino-Japanese War"). 文史哲 *(Journal of Literature, History, and Philosophy)* 263 no. 2 (2001): 112–18.

Sun, Kungtu C. and Ralph W. Huenemann. *The Economic Development of Manchuria in the First Half of the Twentieth Century*. Harvard East Asian Monographs no. 28. East Asian Research Center. Cambridge, MA: Harvard University Press, 1969.

Sun Tzu *The Art of War*. Translated by Samuel B. Griffith. Oxford: Oxford University Press, 1963.

孙修福 (Sun Xiufu). "蒋介石与鸦片特税" ("Chiang Kai-shek and the Special Opium Tax"). 近代史研究 *(Modern Chinese History Studies)* 1997 no. 2: 182–201.

鈴木 晟 (Suzuki Akira), "日中戦争期におけるアメリカの対日経済制裁と対華援助" ("U.S. Economic Sanctions against Japan and Aid to China during the Sino-Japanese War"). アジア研究 *(Asian Studies)* 33 no. 1 (April 1986): 41–74.

鈴木岩行 (Suzuki Iwayuki), "馬寅初の重慶国民政府批判に関する一試論" ("A Preliminary Essay Concerning Ma Yinchu's Critique of the Nationalist Government in Chongqing"). In 中国国民政府史の研究 *(Research on the History of the Chinese Republican Government)*, edited by 中国現代史研究会 (Committee for Research on Modern Chinese History), 447–66. Tokyo: 汲古書院刊, 1986.

Tajima, Nobuo. "The Berlin-Tokyo Axis Reconsidered: From the Anti-Comintern Pact to the Plot to Assassinate Stalin." In *Japanese-German Relations, 1895–1945*, edited by Christian W. Spang and Rolf-Harald Wippich, 161–79. London: Routledge, 2006.

高橋泰隆 (Takahashi Yasutaka). "鉄道支配と満鉄" ("Railway Administration and the Manchurian Railway"). In 日本帝国主義の満州支配——五年戦争期を中心に— *(Manchuria under Japanese Imperialism, Focusing on the Fifteen Year War Period)*, edited by 小林英夫 (Kobayashi Hideo) and 浅田喬二 (Asada Kyōji), 675–818. Tokyo: 時潮社, 1986.

高綱博文 (Takatsuna Hirobumi). "上海事変と日本人居留民—日本人居留民による中国人民衆虐殺背景—" ("The Shanghai Incident and the Japanese Expatriate Community: The Background to the Chinese Carnage According to Japanese Expatriates"). In 日中戦争日本・中国・アメリカ *(The Sino-Japanese War: Japan, China, and America)*, edited by 中央大学人文科学研究所 (Chūō University Human Sciences Research Center), 23–106. Research publication no. 10. Tokyo: 中央大学出版社, 1993.

滝川政次郎 (Takikawa Masajirō) and 衛藤瀋吉 (Eifuji Shinyoshi). 満洲建国十年史 (*A Ten Year History of Nation Building in Manchuria*). 1941 reprint; Tokyo: 原書房, 1969.

田中 仁 (Tanaka Hitoshi). １９３０年代中国政治史研究：中国共産党の危機と再生 (*Research on Chinese Political History in the 1930s: The Crisis and Rebirth of the Chinese Communist Party*). Tokyo: 勁草書房, 2002.

唐凌 (Tang Ling). "抗战时期的中国煤矿市场" ("The Chinese Coal Market during the Sino-Japanese War"). 近代史研究 *(Modern Chinese History Studies)* 95 no. 5 (Sept. 1996): 84–109.

Tang, Peter S. H. *Russian and Soviet Policy in Manchuria and Outer Mongolia 1911–1931*. Durham, NC: Duke University Press, 1959.

Tanner, Harold M. "Railways in Communist Strategy and Operations in Manchuria, 1945–48." In *Manchurian Railways and the Opening of China: An International History*, edited by Bruce A. Elleman and Stephen Kotkin, 149–70. Armonk, NY: M. E. Sharpe, 2010.

Taylor, George E. *The Struggle for North China*. New York: Institute of Pacific Relations, 1940.

Taylor, Jay. *The Generalissimo: Chiang Kai-shek and the Struggle for Modern China*. Cambridge, MA: Harvard University Press, 2009.

The Generalissimo's Son: Chiang Ching-kuo and the Revolutions in China and Taiwan. Cambridge, MA: Harvard University Press, 2000.

Teed, Peter. *Dictionary of 20th Century History 1914–1990*. Oxford: Oxford University Press, 1992.

Terrill, Ross. *Mao a Biography*. Rev. ed. Stanford: Stanford University Press, 1995.

Thorne, Christopher. *Allies of a Kind: The United States, Britain, and the War against Japan, 1941–1945*. Oxford: Oxford University Press, 1978.

田玄 (Tian Xuan). "为彭德怀'运动游击战'问题历史公案一辩" ("A Verification of Peng Dehuai's Stand on 'Mobile Guerrilla Warfare'"). 中共党史研究 *(Research on the History of the Chinese Communist Party)* 1998 no. 6: 91–6.

Tian, Youru. "Social and Political Change in the Villages of the Taihang Anti-Japanese Base Area." In *North China at War: The Social Ecology of Revolution, 1937–1945*, edited by Feng Chongyi and David S. F. Goodman, 115–30. Lanham, MD: Rowman & Littlefield, 2000.

Tien, Hung-mao. "Factional Politics in Kuomintang China, 1928–1937: An Interpretation." In *China at the Crossroads: Nationalists and Communists, 1927–1949*, edited by F. Gilbert Chan, 19–36. Boulder, CO: Westview Press, 1980.

Government and Politics in Kuomintang China 1927–1937. Stanford: Stanford University Press, 1972.

Tikhvinskii, Sergei Leonidovich. *Путь Китая к объединению и независимости 1898–1949* (*China's Path to Unification and Independence 1898–1949*). Moscow: Издательство фирма «Восточная литература» РАН, 1996.

ed. *Русско-китайские отношения в XX веке (Russo-Chinese Relations in the 20th Century)*. Vols. 3–5. Moscow: «Памятники исторической мысли», 2000–10.

Tindall, George Brown and David E. Shi. *America: A Narrative History*. 4th ed. 2 vols. New York: W.W. Norton, 1996.

戸部良一 (Tobe Ryūichi). "The Japanese Eleventh Army in Central China, 1938–1941." In *The Battle for China: Essays on the Military History of the Sino-Japanese War of 1937–1945*, edited by Mark Peattie, Edward J. Drea, and Hans van de Ven, 207–32. Stanford: Stanford University Press, 2011.

ピース・フィーラー支那事変平和工作の群像 *(Peace-Fire: The Many People Promoting Peace during the Sino-Japanese War)*. Tokyo: 論創社, 1991.

"米英独ソ等の中国援助" ("U.S., British, German, Soviet, etc. Assistance to China"). In 近代日本戦争史 *(Modern Japanese Military History)*. Vol. 3, 満州事変· 支那事変 (*The Manchurian Incident and the China*

Incident), edited by 奥村房夫 (Okumura Fusao) and 河野収 (Kōno Shū). Tokyo: 同台経済懇話会, 1995.

Tohmatsu, Haruo. "The Strategic Correlation between the Sino-Japanese and Pacific Wars." In *The Battle for China: Essays on the Military History of the Sino-Japanese War of 1937–1945*, edited by Mark Peattie, Edward J. Drea, and Hans van de Ven, 423–445. Stanford: Stanford University Press, 2011.

Toland, John. *The Rising Sun: The Decline and Fall of the Japanese Empire, 1936–1945*. New York: Modern Library, 1970.

佟玉民 (Tong Yumin). "关于'农村包围城市'道路的理论形成过程" ("Exploring the Formulation of the Strategy of 'Encircling Cities from the Countryside'"). 历史研究 *(Historical Research)* no. 4 (1981): 25–38.

Townson, Duncan. *The New Penguin Dictionary of Modern History 1789–1945*. London: Penguin Books, 1994.

Trotsky, Leon. *Marxism and Military Affairs, 1921–1924*. Colombo, Ceylon: Young Socialist Publication, 1969.

Truman, Harry S. *Memoirs*. Vol. 2. Garden City, NY: Doubleday, 1956.

土田哲夫 (Tsuchida Akio). "南京政府期の国家統合—張学良東北政権（一九二八〜三一年）との関係の例—" ("National Integration during the Nanjing Period – the Connection with Zhang Xueliang's Sovereignty over Manchuria ([1928–31] as an Example"). In 中国国民政府史の研究 *(Research on the History of the Chinese Republican Government)*, edited by 中国現代史研究会 (Committee for Research on Modern Chinese History), 159–92. Tokyo: 汲古書院刊, 1986.

辻 秀雄 (Tsuji Hideo). "本地防空と本土決戦準備" ("Preparations for the Aerial Defenses and the Decisive Battle for Japan"). In 近代日本戦争史 *(Modern Japanese Military History)*. Vol. 4 大東亜戦争 (*The Great East Asian War*), edited by 奥村房夫 (Okumura Fusao) and 近藤新治 (Kondō Shinji), 619–43. Tokyo: 同台経済懇話会, 1995.

塚瀬 進 (Tsukase Susumu). 満州国「民族協和」の実像 *(Manchukuo "Racial Harmony" in Reality)*. Tokyo: 吉川弘文館, 1998.

中国近代東北経済史研究 *(Research on the Modern Economic History of Northeast China)*. Tokyo: 東方書店, 1993.

角田 順 (Tsunoda Jun). 満州問題と国防方針—明治期における国防環境の変動— *(The Manchurian Question and National Defense Policy: Changes in the Late-Meiji National Defense Environment)*. Tokyo: 原書房, 1967.

Tuchman, Barbara W. *Stilwell and the American Experience in China, 1911–45*. New York: Macmillan, 1970.

Tucker, Nancy Bernkopf. *China Confidential: American Diplomats and Sino-American Relations, 1945–1960*. New York: Columbia University Press, 2001.

Tung, William L. *The Political Institutions of Modern China*. The Hague: Martinus Nijhoff, 1968.

Twitchett, Denis and John K. Fairbank, eds. *The Cambridge History of China*. Vol. 13. Cambridge: Cambridge University Press, 1986.

Ugaki, Matome. *Fading Victory: The Diary of Admiral Matome Ugaki 1941–1945*. Translated by Masataka Chihaya, edited by Donald M. Goldstein and Katherine V. Dillon. Pittsburgh: University of Pittsburgh Press, 1991.

United States Department of State. *Foreign Relations of the United States Diplomatic Papers 1945*. Vol. 7, *The Far East: China*. Washington, DC: Government Printing Office, 1969. (Series abbreviated as FRUS.)

Foreign Relations of the United States Diplomatic Papers 1946. Vols. 9–10, *The Far East: China*. Washington, DC: Government Printing Office, 1972.

Foreign Relations of the United States Diplomatic Papers 1947. Vol. 7, *The Far East: China*. Washington, DC: Government Printing Office, 1972.

Foreign Relations of the United States Diplomatic Papers 1948. Vols. 7–8, *The Far East: China*. Washington, DC: Government Printing Office, 1973.

Foreign Relations of the United States Diplomatic Papers 1950. Vol. 6, *East Asia and the Pacific*. Washington, DC: Government Printing Office, 1976.

Foreign Relations of the United States Diplomatic Papers 1950. Vol. 7, *Korea*. Washington, DC: Government Printing Office, 1976.

United States Relations with China with Special Reference to the Period 1944–1949. Washington, D.C.: Office of Public Affairs, 1949.

臼井勝美 (Usui Katsumi). "The Politics of War, 1937–1941." In *The North China Quagmire: Japan's Expansion on the Asian Continent 1933–1941*, edited by James William Morley, 309–436. New York: Columbia University Press, 1983.

日中外交史研究—昭和前期— *(Research on Sino-Japanese Diplomatic History: The Early Hirohito Period)*. Tokyo: 吉川弘文館, 1998.

van de Ven, Hans J. *War and Nationalism in China 1925–1945*. London: Routledge, 2003.

van Slyke, Lyman. "The Chinese Communist Movement during the Sino-Japanese War 1937–1945." In *The Cambridge History of China*, vol. 13, edited by Denis Twitchett and John K. Fairbank, 609–722. Cambridge: Cambridge University Press, 1986.

Vladimirov, Petr Parfenovich. *Особый район Китая 1942–1945 (A Special Region in China 1942–1945)*. Moscow: Издательство Агентства печаты Новости, 1977.

Vogel, Ezra F. *The Four Little Dragons: The Spread of Industrialization in East Asia*. Cambridge, MA: Harvard University Press, 1991.

Volkogonov, Dmitri. *Stalin Triumph & Tragedy*. Translated by Harold Shukman. New York: Grove Weidenfeld, 1988.

von Hagen, Mark. *Soldiers in the Proletarian Dictatorship: The Red Army and the Soviet Socialist State, 1917–1930*. Ithaca: Cornell University Press, 1990.

和田春樹 (Wada Haruki). 金日成と満州抗日戦争 *(Kim Il-sung and the Manchurian War of Resistance against Japan)*. Tokyo: 平凡社, 1992.

Wakeman, Jr., Frederic. *Policing Shanghai 1927–1937*. Berkeley: University of California Press, 1995.

Spymaster: Dai Li and the Chinese Secret Service. Berkeley: University of California Press, 2003.

Waldron, Arthur. *From War to Nationalism: China's Turning Point, 1924–1925*. Cambridge: Cambridge University Press, 1995.

"War and the Rise of Nationalism in Twentieth-Century China." In *Warfare in China since 1600*, edited by Kenneth Swope, 295–314. Aldershot, UK: Ashgate, 2005.

汪朝光 (Wang Chaoguang). "战后国民党对共政策的重要转折—国民党六届二中全会再研究" ("A Key Turning Point in the Nationalist Policy toward the Communist Party after the War against Japanese Aggression – a Reconsideration of the Second Plenum of the Sixth Central Committee of the Nationalist Party"). 历史研究 *(Historical Research)* no. 4 2001: 72–87.

"抗战胜利后国民党东北决策研究" ("The Nationalist Policy toward Manchuria after the Victory in the War against Japan"). 历史研究 *(Historical Research)* 1995 no. 6: 120–33.

Wang, David D. *Under the Soviet Shadow: The Yining Incident*. Hong Kong: Chinese University Press, 1999.

王辅一 (Wang Fuyi). "毛泽东与新四军的创建" ("Mao Zedong and the Founding of the New Fourth Army"). 中共党史研究 *(Research on the History of the Chinese Communist Party)* 1993 no. 6: 35–9.

王光远 (Wang Guangyuan) and 姜中秋 (Jiang Zhongqiu). "汪蒋矛盾与三二〇事件" ("The Contradiction between Wang Jingwei and Chiang Kai-shek and the 20 March Incident"). 中共党史研究 *(Research on the History of the Chinese Communist Party)* 1992 no. 1: 45–51.

王家福 (Wang Jiafu). "二战时期远东中苏美关系的战略演化" ("The Strategic Evolution of the Relations among China, the Soviet Union, and the United States in the Far East during the Second World War"). 史学集刊 *(Collected Papers of Historical Studies)*. 59 no. 2 (1995): 5–15.

王建朗 (Wang Jianlang). "二战爆发前国民政府外交综论" ("A Comprehensive Review of the Diplomacy of the Nationalist Government on the Eve of World War II"). 历史研究 *(Historical Research)* 1995 no. 4: 36–45.

"芦沟桥事件后国民政府的战和抉择" ("The Nationalist Government's Decision for War or Peace after the Marco Polo Bridge Incident"). 近代史研究 *(Modern Chinese History Studies)* no. 2 (1999): 149–68.

"失败的外交记录—抗战初期的日本外交综论" ("A Record of Failed Diplomacy: A General Discussion of Japanese Diplomacy Early in the War of Resistance"). 近代史研究 *(Modern Chinese History Studies)* 67 no. 1 (January 1992): 230–52.

王锦侠 (Wang Jinxia) and 张奇 (Zhang Qi)."两广事变与中国共产党'逼蒋抗日'方针的形成" ("The Guangdong-Guangxi Incident and the Chinese Communist Party's Policy Formulation of 'Compelling Chiang and Resisting Japan'"). 中共党史研究 *(Research on the History of the Chinese Communist Party)* 1990 no. 2: 37–41.

Wang, Ke-wen, "Wang Jingwei and the Policy Origins of the 'Peace Movement,' 1932–1937." In *Chinese Collaboration with Japan, 1932–1945: The Limits of Accommodation*, edited by David P. Barrett and Larry N. Shyu, 21–37. Stanford: Stanford University Press, 2001.

王磊 (Wang Lei). "抗战时期国民政府内债研究" ("Research on the Internal Debt of the Nationalist Government during the War of Resistance"). 中国经济史研究 *(Research in Chinese Economic History)* 1993 no. 4: 74–87.

王良行 (Wang Lianghang). "1929年中国国定税则性质数量分析" ("A Statistical Analysis of the Chinese National Tax Regulation of 1929"). 近代史研究 *(Modern Chinese History Studies)* 88 no. 4 (July 1995): 209–48.

王奇生 (Wang Qisheng). "The Battle of Hunan and the Chinese Military's Response to Operation Ichigō." In *The Battle for China: Essays on the Military History of the Sino-Japanese War of 1937–1945*, edited by Mark Peattie, Edward J. Drea, and Hans van de Ven, 403–20. Stanford: Stanford University Press, 2011.

党员，党权 与党争： *1924～1949* 年中国国民党的组织形态 *(Party Members, Party Authority, and Party Infighting: The Organizational Structure of the Chinese Nationalist Party, 1924–1949)*. Shanghai: 上海书店出版社, 2009.

"党政关系：国民党党治在地方层级的运作" ("Relations between the Nationalist Party and the Government: Party Rule at the Local Level [1927–1937]"). 中国社会科学 *(Social Studies in China)* 2001 no. 3: 187–203.

王维礼 (Wang Weili) and 程舒伟 (Cheng Shuwei). "关于南京国民政府'安内攘外'政策的评价" ("An Evaluation of the Nanjing Government's Policy of 'Internal Pacification, External Resistance'"). 中共党史研究

(Research on the History of the Chinese Communist Party) 32 no. 2 (1993): 38–44.

汪熙 (Wang Xi). "太平洋戦争と中国" ("The War in the Pacific and China"). In 太平洋戦争 *(The Pacific War)*, edited by 細谷千博 (Hosoya Chihiro) et al., 87–132. Tokyo: University of Tokyo Press, 1993.

王永君 (Wang Yongjun). "抗战胜利后中共中央对东北的战略方针其形成过程" ("The CCP Central Committee's Military Strategies and Policy for Manchuria after Victory in the Sino-Japanese War"). 中共党史研究 *(Research on the History of the Chinese Communist Party)* 2001 no. 4: 86–90.

王真 (Wang Zhen). "斯大林与毛泽东1949年1月往来电文评析" ("An Analysis of the Telegrams between Stalin and Mao Zedong in January 1949"). 近代史研究 *(Modern Chinese History Studies)* 1998 no. 2: 117–29.

"抗战初期中苏在苏联参战问题上的分歧" ("Divergent Views between China and the Soviet Union on Soviet Participation the Early Period of the War of Resistance"). 历史研究 *(Historical Research)* 1994 no. 6: 112–25.

"论抗战初期苏联援华政策性质" ("The Nature of the Soviet Policy to Assist China Early in the Anti-Japanese War"). 中共党史研究 *(Research on the History of the Chinese Communist Party)* 1993 no. 5: 48–54.

"孙科与战时国民政府的对苏关系" ("The Relations with the Soviet Union of Sun Ke and the Wartime Nationalist Government"). 近代史研究 *(Modern Chinese History Studies)* 77 no. 5 (September 1993): 102–23.

渡辺俊彦 (Watanabe Toshihiko). "七三一部隊と永田鉄山" ("Unit 731 and Nagata Tetsuzan"). In 日中戦争日本・中国・アメリカ *(The Sino-Japanese War: Japan, China, and America)*, edited by 中央大学人文科学研究所 (Chūō University Human Sciences Research Center), 275–302. Research Publication no. 10. Tokyo: 中央大学出版社, 1993.

Weber, Max. "The Profession and Vocation of Politics." In *Weber Political Writings*, edited by Peter Lassman and Ronald Speirs. Cambridge: Cambridge University Press, 1994.

Weinberg, Gerhard L. *The Foreign Policy of Hitler's Germany: Diplomatic Revolution in Europe 1933–36*. Chicago: University of Chicago Press, 1970.

Germany, Hitler, and World War II: Essays in Modern and World History. Cambridge: Cambridge University Press, 1995.

温瑞茂 (Wen Ruimao). "毛泽东战略构想的演进与大决战" ("The Evolution of Mao Zedong's Thinking on Military Strategy and the Great Decisive Battle"). 中共党史研究 *(Research on the History of the Chinese Communist Party)* 1997 no. 4: 20–7.

Westad, Odd Arne. *Decisive Encounters: The Chinese Civil War, 1946–1950*. Stanford: Stanford University Press, 2003.

White, Theodore H. *In Search of History: A Personal Adventure*. New York: Harper & Row, 1978.

White, Theodore H and Annalee Jacoby. *Thunder out of China*. 1946; reprint, New York: Da Capo Press, 1974.

Wilbur, C. Martin and Julie Lien-ying How. *Missionaries of Revolution: Soviet Advisers and Nationalist China, 1920–1927*. Cambridge, MA: Harvard University Press, 1989.

Williams, Peter and David Wallace. *Unit 731: Japan's Secret Biological Warfare in World War II*. New York: Free Press, 1989.

Willoughby, Westel W. *The Sino-Japanese Controversy and the League of Nations*. Baltimore: Johns Hopkins University Press, 1935.

Wilson, Sandra. *The Manchurian Crisis and Japanese Society, 1931–33*. London: Routledge, 2002.

Wou, Odoric Y. K. "Communist Sources for Localizing the Study of the Sino-Japanese War." In *Chinese Collaboration with Japan, 1932–1945: The Limits of Accommodation*, edited by David P. Barret and Larry N. Shyu, 226–35. Stanford: Stanford University Press, 2001.

"Food Shortage and Japanese Grain Extraction in Henan." In *China at War: Regions of China, 1937–1945*, edited by Stephen R. MacKinnon, Diana Lary, and Ezra F. Vogel, 75–206. Stanford: Stanford University Press, 2007.

吴宏伟 (Wu Hongwei). "解放前夕南京的物价飞涨状况" ("Inflation on the Eve of Liberation in Nanjing"). 中国经济史研究 *(Research in Chinese Economic History)* 1992 no. 1: 152–4.

吴景平 (Wu Jingping). "美国和抗战时期中国的平准基金" ("On the U.S. Stabilization Fund for the Chinese Currency during the War of Resistance"). 近代史研究 *(Modern Chinese History Studies)* no. 5 (1997): 76–106.

"抗战时期中美租借关系述评" ("Sino-American Lend-Lease Relations during the War against Japan"). 历史研究 *(Historical Research)* 1995 no. 4: 48–62.

吴天威 (Wu T'ien-wei). "The Chinese Communist Movement." In *China's Bitter Victory: The War with Japan 1937–1945*, edited by James C. Hsiung and Steven I. Levine, 79–106. Armonk, NY: M. E. Sharpe, 1992.

(Wu Tianwei). "张学良与西安事变再研究［续］" ("A Reconsideration of Zhang Xueliang and the Xi'an Incident [sequel]"). 中共党史研究 *(Research on the History of the Chinese Communist Party)* 1997 no. 2: 52–9.

武月星 (Wu Yuexing). "日本华北驻屯军及侵华行径" ("The Japanese North China Occupation Force and Its Aggressive Behavior"). 近代史研究 *(Modern Chinese History Studies)* 58 no. 4 (July 1990): 201–15.

中国现代史地图集 *(Modern Chinese History Map Collection)*. Beijing: 中国地图出版社, 1997.

Xiang, Lianxin. *Recasting the Imperial Far East: Britain and America in China, 1945–1950*. Armonk, NY: M. E. Sharpe, 1995.

谢放 (Xie Fang). "抗战前中国城市局的初步考察" ("Distribution of Chinese Urban Industry before 1937"). 中国经济史研究 *(Research in Chinese Economic History)* 1998 no. 3: 96–105.

解学诗 (Xie Xueshi) and 宋玉印 (Song Yuyin). "'七・七'事变后日本掠夺华北资源的总枢纽" ("The Fulcrum of Japan's Plundering of North China's Resources after 1937"). 中国经济史研究 *(Research in Chinese Economic History)* 1990 no. 4: 44–57.

邢丽雅 (Xing Liya). "'九・一八'事变前后日本对'满蒙政策'的演变" ("The Evolution of Japan's Policy Regarding Manchuria and Mongolia around the Time of the Manchurian Incident"). 史学集刊 *(Collected Papers of Historical Studies)* (1999) no. 3: 33–8.

熊沛彪 (Xiong Peibiao). "九一八事变后日本的对华外交及战略意图—兼论南京国民政府的对策" ("Japan's Foreign Policy Regarding China and Its Strategic Intentions after the Manchuria Incident plus a Discussion of the Nanjing Government's Counter-strategy"). 历史研究 *(Historical Research)* no. 4 (1998): 71–88.

许建平 (Xu Jianping). "抗日战争时期陕甘宁边区私营经济的发展" ("The Development of the Private Economy in the Shaanxi-Gansu-Ningxia Border Region during the Anti-Japanese War"). 中国经济史研究 *(Research in Chinese Economic History)* 1995 no. 3: 125–34.

徐建生 (Xu Jiansheng). "1927～1937年中国基础化学工业的发展及其特点" ("The Development and Characteristics of the China's Basic Chemical Industry from 1927 to 1937"). 中国经济史研究 *(Research in Chinese Economic History)* 2000 no. 2: 57–65.

徐晓林 (Xu Xiaolin). "朱德抗日游击战术思想初探" ("Zhu De's Thoughts on Anti-Japanese Guerrilla Tactics"). 中共党史研究 *(Research on the History of the Chinese Communist Party)* 1995 no. 4: 70–3.

徐焰 (Xu Yan). 一九四五年満州進軍：日ソ戦と毛沢東の戦略 *(The Manchurian Invasion of 1945: The Japanese-Soviet War and Mao Zedong's Strategy)*. Translated by 朱建榮 (Zhu Jinrong). Tokyo: 三五館, 1993.

徐友春 (Xu Youchun). 民國人物大辭典 *(Comprehensive Biographical Dictionary for the Republican Period)*. 2 vols. Shijiazhuang, Hebei: 河北人民出版社, 2007.

山田朗 (Yamada Akira). "満州支配（２）日中戦争・太洋戦争期" ("Military Rule [2] during the Sino-Japanese War and the War of the Pacific"). In 日本帝国主義の満州支配—一五年戦争期を中心に— *(Manchuria under Japanese Imperialism, Focusing on the Fifteen Year War Period)*, edited by 小林英夫 (Kobayashi Hideo) and 浅田喬二 (Asada Kyōji), 163–254. Tokyo: 時潮社, 1986.

山本有造 (Yamamoto Yūzō). "「満洲国」をめぐる対外経済関係の展開一国際収支分析を中心として一" ("Development of Foreign Economic Relations Concerning 'Manchukuo' Focusing on an Analysis of International Receipts and Expenditures"). In 「満洲国」の研究 *(Research on "Manchukuo")*, edited by 山本有造 (Yamamoto Yūzō), 191–236. Tokyo: 緑蔭書房, 1995.

"Japanese Empire and Colonial Management." In *Economic History of Japan 1914–1955: A Dual Structure*, edited by Takafusa Nakamura and Kônosuke Odaka. Translated by Noah S. Brannen. Oxford: Oxford University Press, 1999.

ed. 「満洲国」の研究 *(Research on "Manchukuo")*. Tokyo: 緑蔭書房, 1995.

Yamamura, Kozo. "The Japanese Economy, 1911–1930: Concentration, Conflicts, and Crises." In *Japan in Crisis: Essays on Taishō Democracy*, edited by Bernard Silberman and H. D. Harootunian, 299–328. Princeton: Princeton University Press, 1974.

山室信一 (Yamamuro Shin'ichi). "「満洲国 」統治過程論" ("Discussion of the Evolution of the Rule of 'Manchukuo'"). In 「満洲国」の研究 *(Research on "Manchukuo")*, edited by 山本有造 (Yamamoto Yūzō), 83–129. Tokyo: 緑蔭書房, 1995.

Manchuria under Japanese Dominion. Translated by Joshua A. Fogel. Philadelphia: University of Pennsylvania Press, 2006.

阎庆生 (Yan Qingsheng) and 黄正林 (Huang Zhenglin). "抗战时期陕甘宁边区税收问题研究" ("Research Concerning Tax Receipts in the Shaanxi-Gansu-Ningxi Border Area during the Sino-Japanese War"). 中国经济史研究 *(Research in Chinese Economic History)* 2001 no. 4: 49–56.

楊克林 (Yang Kelin) and 曹紅 (Cao Hong) eds. 中國抗日戰爭圖誌 *(A Cartographic Record of the Chinese War of Resistance against Japan)*. 3 vols. Hong Kong: 天地圖書, 1992.

楊奎松 (Yang Kuisong). 走向破裂：恩恩怨怨 *(Heading for Rupture: Gratitude and Grudges between Mao Zedong and Stalin)*. Hong Kong: 三聯書店, 1999.

"难以确定的对手（1917〜1949）" ("The Inscrutable Opponent, 1917–1949"). In 中苏关系史纲：*1917〜1991* 年中苏关系若干问题再探讨 *(A Survey of Sino-Soviet Relations: A Reexamination of Questions Concerning Sino-Soviet Relations, 1917–1991)*, rev. ed, edited by 沈志华 (Shen Zhihua), 3–110. Beijing: 社会科学文献出版社, 2011.

"关于共产国际与中国共产党'联蒋抗日'方针的关系问题" ("An Investigation of Zhang Xueliang's Activities against Chiang Kai-shek"). 历史研究 *(Historical Research)* 88 no. 4 (July 1997): 85–96.

国民党的"联共"与、"反共" *(Kuomintang: Unity with Communists and Anti-communism)*. Beijing: 社会科学文献出版社, 2008.

"西安事变期间'三位一体'的军事协商与部署"("The Military Negotiations and Deployments of the 'Trinity' during the Xi'an Incident"). 近代史研究 *(Modern Chinese History Studies)* 96 no. 6 (November 1996): 81–96.

"Nationalist and Communist Guerrilla Warfare in North China." In *The Battle for China: Essays on the Military History of the Sino-Japanese War of 1937–1945*, edited by Mark Peattie, Edward J. Drea, and Hans van de Ven, 308–27. Stanford: Stanford University Press, 2011.

"美苏冷战的起源及对中国革命的影响" ("The Origins of the U.S.-Soviet Cold War and Its Impact on the Chinese Revolution"). 历史研究 *(Historical Research)* no. 5 (July 1999): 5–22.

"关于共产国际与中国共产党'联蒋抗日'方针的关系问题" ("The Relationship between the Comintern and the Chinese Communist Party's Policy of 'Alliance with Chiang to Resist Japan'"). 中共党史研究 *(Research on the History of the Chinese Communist Party)* 1989 no. 4: 51–9.

张学良与中共关系之谜 *(The Riddle of Zhang Xueliang's Relations with the Chinese Communists)*. Nanjing: 江苏人民出版社, 2006.

"张学良与西安事变之解决" ("Zhang Xueliang and the Solution for the Xi'an Incident"). 中国社会科学 *(Social Studies in China)* (September 1996) no. 4: 189–99.

杨天石 (Yang Tianshi). "30年代初期国民党内部的反蒋抗日潮流—读台湾所藏胡汉民资料之一" ("Anti-Chiang Kai-shek and Anti-Japanese Currents in the Nationalist Party in the Early 1930s Based on Documents Retained in Taiwan Concerning Hu Hanmin"). 历史研究 *(Historical Research)* no. 1 (1998): 53–64.

"Chiang Kai-shek and the Battles of Shanghai and Nanjing." In *The Battle for China: Essays on the Military History of the Sino-Japanese War of 1937–1945*, edited by Mark Peattie, Edward J. Drea, and Hans van de Ven, 143–58. Stanford: Stanford University Press, 2011.

"Perspectives on Chiang Kaishek's Early Thought from His Unpublished Diary." In *The Chinese Revolution in the 1920s: Between Triumph and Disaster*, edited by Mechthild Leutner, et al., 77–97. London: RoutledgeCurzon, 2002.

"抗战前期日本'民间人士'和蒋介石集团的秘密谈判"("Secret Negotiations between the Chiang Kai-shek Clique and 'Unofficial' Japanese Representatives in the Early Stages of the Sino-Japanese War"). 历史研究 *(Historical Research)* no. 1 (1990): 160–75.

"1935年国民党内的倒汪迎胡暗潮" ("Undercurrents in the Nationalist Party to Replace Wang Jingwei with Hu Hanmin in 1935"). 近代史研究 *(Modern Chinese History Studies)* no. 4 (1997): 273–85.

杨卫敏 (Yang Weimin). "民国政府与一二八淞沪抗战" ("The Nationalist Government and the Shanghai Incident"). 近代史研究 *(Modern Chinese History Studies)* 58 no. 4 (July 1990): 216–33.

杨小池 (Yang Xiaochi) and 王乃德 (Wang Naide). "毛泽东关于把山西作为敌后抗战战略支点的构想与实践" ("Mao Zedong's Theories and Practice Concerning Making Shanxi the Strategic Strongpoint behind Enemy Lines in the War of Resistance against Japan"). 中共党史研究 *(Research on the History of the Chinese Communist Party)* 1994 no. 1: 25–30.

杨云若 (Yang Yunruo). "苏德战争和太平洋战争前后中苏美关系的演变" ("The Evolution of Sino-Soviet-American Relations at the Time of the European and Pacific Wars"). 中共党史研究 *(Research on the History of the Chinese Communist Party)* 1988 no. 6: 68–75.

姚会元 (Yao Huiyuan). "1933年–1936年日本在华北的走私活动" ("On the Japanese Smuggling Activities in North China, 1933–1936"). 中国社会经济史研究 *(Research on Chinese Social and Economic History)* 1986 no. 1: 118–20.

姚金果 (Yao Jinguo). "对国民党试图加入共产国际问题的初步探讨" ("A Preliminary Investigation into the Nationalists' Attempt to Join the Communist International"). 中共党史研究 *(Research on the History of the Chinese Communist Party)* 2000 no. 4: 48–52.

安富步 (Yasutomi Ayumu). "「満洲国」経済開発と国内資金流動" ("Economic Development of 'Manchukuo' and Domestic Capital Flows"). In 「満洲国」の研究 *(Research on "Manchukuo")*, edited by 山本有造 (Yamamoto Yūzō), 237–88. Tokyo: 緑蔭書房, 1995.

易豪精 (Yi Haojing). "试论中华苏维埃共和国的政权建设" ("A Discussion of the Construction of the Chinese Soviet Republic"). 近代史研究 *(Modern Chinese History Studies)* 57 no. 3 (May 1990): 166–80.

"从'蜜月'到断交—抗日战争爆发前后中德关系的演变" ("From 'Honeymoon' to Diplomatic Split: The Evolution of Sino-German Relations around the Outbreak of the Sino-Japanese War"). 中共党史研究 *(Research on the History of the Chinese Communist Party)* 1995 no. 5: 57–63.

吉田裕 (Yoshida Yutaka). "軍事支配（１）満州事変期" ("Military Rule [1] during the Manchurian Incident"). In 日本帝国主義の満州支配——五年戦争期を中心に— *(Manchuria under Japanese Imperialism, Focusing on the Fifteen Year War Period)*, edited by 小林英夫 (Kobayashi Hideo) and 浅田喬二 (Asada Kyōji), 93–162. Tokyo: 時潮社, 1986.

吉田裕 (Yoshida Yutaka) and 纐纈厚 (Kōketsu Atsushi). "日本軍の作戦・戦闘・補給" ("Military Operations, Combat, and the Supply of the Japanese Military"). In 十五年戦争史 *(A History of the Fifteen Year War)*. Vol. 3, edited by 藤原 彰 (Fujiwara Akira) and 今井清一 (Imai Seiichi), 81–112. Tokyo: 青木書店, 1989.

Yoshihashi, Takehiko. *Conspiracy at Mukden: The Rise of the Japanese Military*. New Haven: Yale University Press, 1963.

芳井研一 (Yoshii Ken'ichi). "華北分離工作と準戦時体制" ("The Partition of North China and the Organizational Structure in the Preparatory Period"). In 十五年戦争史 *(A History of the Fifteen Year War)*. Vol. 1, edited by 藤原 彰 (Fujiwara Akira) and 今井清一 (Imai Seiichi), 247–84. Tokyo: 青木書店, 1989.

吉沢南 (Yoshizawa Minami). "総論" ("General Discussion"). In 講座中国近現代史 *(Series of Studies in Modern and Contemporary Chinese History)*. Vol. 7, 中国革命の勝利 (*Victory in the Chinese Revolution*), edited by 野沢豊 (Nozawa Yutaka), 1–28. Tokyo: University of Tokyo Press, 1978.

Young, Arthur N. *China and the Helping Hand 1937–1945*. Cambridge, MA: Harvard University Press, 1963.

China's Wartime Finance and Inflation, 1937–1945. Cambridge, MA: Harvard University Press, 1965.

Young, Louise. *Japan's Total Empire: Manchuria and the Culture of Wartime Imperialism*. Berkeley: University of California Press, 1998.

Yu, Maochun. *The Dragon's War: Allied Operations and the Fate of China 1937–1947*. Annapolis, MD: Naval Institute Press, 2006.

袁同禮 (Yuan Tongli), comp. 中俄西北條約集 *(Russo-Chinese Treaties and Agreements Relating to Sinkiang 1851–1949)*. Hong Kong: 袁同禮, 1963.

Zakharova, Galina Fominichna. *Политика Японии в Маньчжурии 1932–1945 (The Policy of Japan in Manchuria 1932–1945)*. Moscow: «Наука» Главная редакция восточной литературы, 1990.

Zang, Yunhu. "Chinese Operations in Yunnan and Central Burma." In *The Battle for China: Essays on the Military History of the Sino-Japanese War of 1937–1945*, edited by Mark Peattie, Edward J. Drea, and Hans van de Ven, 386–91. Stanford: Stanford University Press, 2011.

曾业英 (Zeng Yeying). "日本侵占华北海关及其后果" ("The Japanese Seizure of the North China Customs and Its Consequences"). 近代史研究 *(Modern Chinese History Studies)* 88 no. 4 (July 1995): 48–67.

章百家 (Zhang Baijia). "China's Quest for Military Aid." In *The Battle for China: Essays on the Military History of the Sino-Japanese War of 1937–1945*, edited by Mark Peattie, Edward J. Drea, and Hans van de Ven, 283–307. Stanford: Stanford University Press, 2011.

"抗日战争结束前后中国共产党对美国政策的演变" ("The Evolution of the Chinese Communist Party's Policy toward the United States around the End of the War of Resistance against Japan"). 中共党史研究 *(Research on the History of the Chinese Communist Party)* 1991 no. 1: 40–8.

"抗日战争时期国共两党的对美政策" ("Nationalist and Communist Policies Regarding the United States, 1937–1945"). 历史研究 *(Historical Research)* no. 3 (1987): 3–14.

"周恩来与马歇尔使命" ("Zhou Enlai and Marshall's Mission to China"). 近代史研究 *(Modern Chinese History Studies)* 1997 no. 4: 184–213.

张北根 (Zhang Beigen). "1933一1941年的中德关系" ("Sino-German Relations, 1933–1941"). 历史研究 *(Historical Research)* no. 2 (1995): 107–19.

張芳杰 (Zhang Fangjie), ed. 遠東漢英大辭典 *(Far East Chinese-English Dictionary)*. Taipei: 遠東圖書公司印行, 1996.

张飞虹 (Zhang Feihong). "中共第一代领导集体在抗战时期形成过程的刘少奇" ("Liu Shaoqi and the Development of the First-Generation Collective Leadership of the Communist Party of China during the War of Resistance"). 中共党史研究 *(Research on the History of the Chinese Communist Party)* 1995 no. 4: 64–9.

张魁堂 (Zhang Kuitang). "中共中央和平解决西安事变方针的制定" ("The Central Committee of the Chinese Communist Party's Decision to Settle the Xi'an Incident Peacefully"). 近代史研究 *(Modern Chinese History Studies)* 62 no. 2 (March 1991): 243–55.

张利民 (Zhang Limin). "抗战期间日本对华北经济统治方针政策的制定和演变" ("Establishment and Evolution of Japanese Policies for the Economic Control of North China during the Sino-Japanese War"). 中国经济史研究 *(Research in Chinese Economic History)* 1999 no. 2: 38–48.

"华北开发株式会社与日本政府和军部" ("The North China Development Company and the Japanese Government and Military"). 历史研究 *(Historical Research)* 1995 no. 1: 156–68.

張瑞德 (Zhang Ruide). See Chang Jui-te.

章绍嗣 (Zhang Shaosi) et al., comps. 中国抗日战争大辞典 *(The Comprehensive Dictionary of the Chinese War of Resistance against Japan)*. Wuhan: 武汉出版社, 1995.

张生 (Zhang Sheng). "南京民国政府初期关税改革述评" ("A Discussion of Customs Reform in the Early Nanjing Nationalist Government"). 近代史研究 *(Modern Chinese History Studies)* 74 no. 2 (March 1993): 208–20.

张盛发 (Zhang Shengfa). "战后初期斯大林对中国革命的态度和立场" ("Stalin's Attitude and Position toward the Chinese Revolution in the Early Post-war Period"). 中共党史研究 *(Research on the History of the Chinese Communist Party)* 2000 no. 1: 57–62.

张水良 (Zhang Shuiliang). "抗日战争时期陕甘宁边区的公营工业" ("Government-Run Industry in the Shaanxi-Gansu-Ningxia Border Area during the Sino-Japanese War"). 中国社会经济史研究 *(Research on Chinese Social and Economic History)* 1988 no. 4: 90–6.

"二战时期国统区的三次灾荒及其对社会经济的影响" ("The Three Great Famines in the Areas Ruled by the Nationalists during the Second World War and Its Influence upon the Social Economy"). 中国社会经济史研究 *(Research on Chinese Social and Economic History)* 1990 no. 4: 90–8.

张晓辉 (Zhang Xiaohui). "简论抗战时期中国共产党政权理论的认识和发展" ("A Short Discussion of the Development of the Communist Party's Theory of Political Power during the War of Resistance against Japan"). 中共党史研究 *(Research on the History of the Chinese Communist Party)* no. 6 (1998): 66–71.

張學良 (Zhang Xueliang). 張學良口述歷史 *(An Oral History by Zhang Xueliang)*. Edited by 唐德剛 (Tang Degang). Taipei: 遠流出版社, 2009.

章有义 (Zhang Youyi). 中国近代农业史资料 *(Materials on Modern Chinese Agricultural History)*. Vol. 2. Beijing: 三联书店, 1957.

赵志辉 (Zhao Zhihui). "太平洋战争时期美国的中国大国地位政策的起源" ("The Origin of the U.S. Policy to Regard China as a Great Power during the Pacific War"). 史学集刊 *(Collected Papers of Historical Studies)* (Aug. 2000) no. 3: 64–9.

张芝连 (Zhang Zhilian) and 刘学荣 (Liu Xuerong). 世界历史地图集 *(World History Map Collection)*. Beijing: 中国地图出版社, 2001.

郑德荣 (Zheng Derong). "西安事变若干问题的新思考" (New Reflections on Some Questions about the Xi'an Incident). 中共党史研究 *(Research on the History of the Chinese Communist Party)* 1997 no. 1: 19–23.

郑会欣 (Zheng Huixin). "1933年的中美棉麦借款" ("The 1933 U.S. Loan to China for Cotton and Wheat"). 历史研究 *(Historical Research)* no. 5 (1988): 128–37.

Zhou Zunhong, see Cho Tsun-hung.

朱绍文 (Zhu Shaowen). "日本帝国主义九・一八事变后对我国东北的经济掠夺" ("The Economic Plunder of Manchuria by Japanese Imperialism after the Manchurian Incident"). 中国经济史研究 *(Research in Chinese Economic History)* 1999 no. 3: 3–16.

住筱新 (Zhu Xiaoxin), ed. 历史词典 (Historical Dictionary). Beijing: 学苑出版社, 2005.

朱玉湘 (Zhu Yuxiang). "抗日战争与中国经济" ("The Anti-Japanese War and the Chinese Economy"). 文史哲 *(Journal of Literature, History, and Philosophy)* 230 no. 5 (1995): 3–9.

"山东抗日根据地的减租减息" ("The Rent and Interest Reduction in the Shandong Base Area during the Sino-Japanese War"). 文史哲 *(Journal of Literature, History, and Philosophy)* 230 no. 3 (1981): 72–7.

Zyriakov, P. I. ed. *Пограничные войска СССР 1929–1938: Сборник документов и материалов (Border Forces of the USSR 1929–1938: Collection of Documents and Materials)*. Moscow: Издательство «наука», 1972.

INDEX

Bold page numbers indicate maps.

INDEX

For EU product safety concerns, contact us at Calle de José Abascal, 56–1°, 28003 Madrid, Spain or eugpsr@cambridge.org.

www.ingramcontent.com/pod-product-compliance
Ingram Content Group UK Ltd.
Pitfield, Milton Keynes, MK11 3LW, UK
UKHW042137130625
459647UK00011B/1076

* 9 7 8 1 1 0 7 6 9 7 4 7 8 *